Psychological Assessment in Medical Rehabilitation

Psychological Assessment

in

Medical Rehabilitation

edited by

Laura A. Cushman

&

Marcia J. Scherer

Published by the
American Psychological Association
750 First Street, NE
Washington, DC 20002

Copies may be ordered from
APA Order Department
P.O. Box 2710
Hyattsville, MD 20784

In the UK and Europe, copies may be ordered from
American Psychological Association
3 Henrietta Street
Covent Garden, London
WC2E 8LU England

This book was typeset in Futura and New Baskerville by Easton Publishing Services, Inc., Easton, MD

Printer: Braun-Brumfield, Inc., Ann Arbor, MI
Cover designer: Barbieri & Green, Inc., Washington, DC
Technical/production editor: Edward B. Meidenbauer

Library of Congress Cataloging-in-Publication Data
Psychological assessment in medical rehabilitation / edited by Laura A. Cushman and
  Marcia J. Scherer.
      p.   cm.—(Measurement and instrumentation in psychology)
    Includes bibliographical references and index.
    ISBN 1-55798-299-6 (hardcover : alk. paper).—ISBN 1-55798-309-7 (softcover : alk.
  paper)
    1. Medical rehabilitation.   2. Psychological tests.   I. Cushman, Laura A.   II. Scherer,
  Marcia J. (Marcia Joslyn), 1948–   .   III. Series.
    [DNLM: 1. Psychological Tests.   2. Rehabilitation—psychology.   3. Disabled—psy-
  chology.   WM 145 P9738 1995]
  RM930.P78   1995
  617'.03'019—dc20
  DNLM/DLC
  for Library of Congress   95-11109
                                                                                  CIP

British Library Cataloguing-in-Publication Data
A CIP record is available from the British Library.

Printed in the United States of America
First Edition

To those who have nurtured and developed rehabilitation psychology, and to those who will.

Contents

Contributors

Jeffrey R. Campodonico, John Hopkins University School of Medicine
Bruce Caplan, Thomas Jefferson University, Philadelphia
Nancy M. Crewe, Michigan State University
Ellen L. Cronk, University of Rochester
Laura A. Cushman, University of Rochester Medical Center
Marcel Dijkers, Rehabilitation Institute Hospital, Detroit
Leonard Diller, Rusk Institute of Rehabilitation Medicine
Timothy R. Elliott, University of Alabama
Christine Fink, Medical University of South Carolina
Randal J. Gage, University of Alabama
Allen W. Heinemann, Rehabilitation Institute of Chicago
Michael J. Leahy, Michigan State University
Carolyn Lemsky, Mayo Clinic
James Malec, Mayo Clinic
Susan McGlynn, McLean Hospital, Belmont, Massachusetts
Richard Millard, University of Rochester Medical Center
Madhabika Nayak, Medical University of South Carolina
Thomas A. Novack, University of Alabama
Marcia J. Scherer, Rochester Institute of Technology
Judith Shechter, Lanken AU Hospital, Philadelphia
Robert L. Umlauf, National Rehabilitation Hospital
Mark T. Wagner, Medical University of South Carolina

Foreword

Leonard Diller

Is psychological assessment in medical rehabilitation worthwhile? Readers of this volume can come away with a definitive affirmative answer.

When I used to read books about the psychological assessment of people with disabilities in rehabilitation, I would often leave off with a feeling of not having learned anything new. In the 1950s, when psychologists in medical rehabilitation settings began looking for ways to identify, evaluate, and use information from assessment instruments, there were only fragments of technique and theory. Assessment methods were extrapolated from conventional approaches taught in clinical psychology curricula. Hard facts were derived from isolated, scattered psychometric studies that applied tests developed with other population groups to people with disabilities. Anyone teaching a course on psychological assessment in medical rehabilitation would have trouble. A clinically oriented text for a practitioner performing assessments would have to rely on collections of readings in which psychological assessment could be found as a subtopic in chapters devoted to individual categories of impairment such as cerebral palsy or poliomyelitis. The main parts of the chapters were devoted to descriptions of the demographics, etiology, and sequelae of the condition.

A major issue at that time was whether people with disabilities were different from so-called normal people, or people without disabilities. There was discussion about the fairness of psychological assessments when administered to people with impairments. The somatopsychologists (Barker, Meyerson, Gonick, & Kerr), whose conclusions were based on studies often conducted in nonmedical settings, suggested that people with disabilities were not distinguishable from other people by psychological tests. Psychodynamic theories of personality, which dominated assessment, failed to fit the mainstream of activities in medical rehabilitation. Relevant data based on clinical judgment, which might contribute to a therapeutic situation, was a matter of guesswork. Picture the logic in trying to demonstrate the connection between a response to a Rorschach card and why someone does not want to cooperate in physical therapy. Whereas social personality theories put forward by Wright, Dembo et al. were useful in pointing to the person in the situation as a framework for understanding psychological questions, the paradigms did not fit immediate clinical demands. Neither conventional practice in clinical psychology or theory in rehabilitation psychology could do justice to the demands on the practitioner. Most psychologists in this field were self-taught, in the sense that they had to extrapolate from their training and bootstrap solutions to their immediate problems. The APA published a volume on psychological research and rehabilitation, based on a conference in 1960. But the immediate needs of the clinician were not addressed by these efforts.

During this time, medical rehabilitation was growing at an explosive rate, moving in the direction of creating an industry with sets of standards and normative data bases to examine its products. Along with this growth was the creation of a subculture with a vocabulary (impairment, functional limitation, disability, handicap), articulation of roles of team members who deliver actual services, and definition of the needs of emerging populations, such as traumatic brain damage and chronic pain, in psychological terms. For psychology to survive and contribute in an environment where practice is continuously moving ahead of validated knowledge required the assiduous, persistent, and cumulative application of experience in settings that are continuously responding to diverse demands for accountability.

Fortunately, an emerging body of knowledge to reflect the dynamic and creative efforts of psychologists has been identified by the editors. The work is broad in the number of issues it touches and deep in the concern with rigor and sensitivity to the principles and the intent of clinical measurement. The student and the experienced professional can find a stimulating array of instruments and ideas to build on, rather than starting from scratch. The contents can serve as a reference as well as a compilation of contemporary writings. Having them in one place makes me aware of how far the field has developed.

The materials in the book can help both clinicians, who are concerned with the welfare of individual patients, and researchers, who are concerned with data to contribute to public interest and service delivery issues. For clinicians, this volume provides useful advances not only in specific methods (Wagner, Nayak, & Fink; Malec & Lemsky) but in newer emerging areas of clinical interest (functional assessment; family functioning and social support), as well as developments in classical issues in the field (e.g., psychometric tests; personality; vocational interests). Individual chapters reflect specific populations currently associated with medical rehabilitation, serving people with neurologically and physically handicapping conditions. Certain generic psychological issues come to notice more in these populations but have relevance to other populations: pain, unawareness, coping, and adaptation. For the researcher, the topics considered, the instruments used, and the approaches taken lend themselves to applications associated with system issues such as functional assessment. Psychopathology is covered, but does not dominate the picture.

Rehabilitation psychologists have been at the cutting edge of health care. Their tools and concepts have much to offer to the larger psychological community. This volume is very useful as a reference work for these psychologists and for other professionals in the field of medical rehabilitation. It is also useful to psychologists working in settings with overlapping interests including behavioral medicine, neuropsychology, and clinical psychology. At all times the reader is aware of the context in which psychological assessment takes place while maintaining the focus on ideas and techniques of such assessments.

Acknowledgments

We would like to acknowledge the assistance, support, and hard work of several people who helped bring this book into being: Jeanette Hassett, Alan Stetler, and John Scherer.

We would also like to acknowledge those who inspired the book; namely, those individuals who have challenged us to ask more questions and seek more answers in an effort to provide optimal care.

Part One

Introduction

A Model of Rehabilitation Assessment

Marcia J. Scherer

During the 100th American Psychological Association Annual Meeting, Anne Anastasi presented a Master Lecture on psychological testing (Anastasi, 1993) and provided three definitions of assessment: (a) testing as a whole, (b) any information-gathering technique regarding individual behavior, and (c) the clinical and intensive study of an individual in which test scores are considered together with all other relevant data and information. Anastasi said she preferred the third definition. So do the contributors to this volume.

In a recent *Rehab Brief*, the National Institute on Disability and Rehabilitation Research (NIDRR, 1992) summarized the fundamental role of measurement, assessment, and evaluation in rehabilitation as follows: "Consumers are measured to establish their eligibility for benefits or services, to determine which services are appropriate, to assess their needs, to ascertain their current level of functioning, and to estimate their potential" (p. 1).

The philosophy of this book is in keeping with the NIDRR conceptualization and similarly emphasizes the importance of consumer-focused assessment. As noted by Crewe and Dijkers in chapter 4, "The broad domain of assessment includes varied approaches to understanding *individual* [emphasis added] characteristics and capacities" (p. 101). Psychologists working in rehabilitation settings have always focused on the individual rehabilitation consumer, but they have varied over time in the predominance given to capacities versus limitations or deficits.

A Conceptualization of the Targets of Rehabilitation Assessment

The rehabilitation psychologist delivering the highest quality services today needs to have an interdisciplinary, multidimensional, and comprehensive view of the individual. The psychologist must consider the person's presenting and core capacities and rehabilitation needs and concentrate efforts at the outset on the person's capabilities for independent living in the home and community. This perspective is summarized in Figure 1.1. At the center of the concentric circles in Figure 1.1 are the individual's core capacities. These are what the person brings to rehabilitation. They include the individual's cognitive abilities, functional status, and life history. Many of these core capacities are physiologically or biologically driven, but they can themselves be outcomes of such influences as family of origin, socialization, and education. This core corresponds to the World Health Organization's (WHO, 1980) definition of *impairment*, to which we have added an analysis of psychological influences. Examples of measures of core capacities are the patient history, the Functional Independence Measure, and the Mini-Mental Status Examination. Assessment instruments discussed by Crewe and Dijkers in chapter 4 ("Functional Assessment") and by Wagner, Nayak, and Fink in chapter 5 ("Bedside Screening of Neurocognitive Function") are primarily directed at core capacities.

Building on information regarding the individual's core capacities, the book's focus turns to the minimization of "disability," enhancement of capacities and capabilities, and optimization of the individual's functioning. This is the area that has traditionally been most closely associated with the work done in medical rehabilitation settings, and it is represented by the middle circle in Figure 1.1. This is where psychologists are called upon to assess behavior, personality characteristics and psychopathology, pain behavior, awareness of deficits, and coping skills. Measures discussed in the following chapters relate to the middle circle: chapter 3, "Measures of Coping and Reaction to Disability" by Heinemann; chapter 12, "Assessing Awareness of Deficits" by Campodonico and McGlynn; chapter 6, "Traditional and Consensual Approaches to Behavioral Assessment" by Malec and Lemsky; chapter 10, "Measurement of Personality and Psychopathology Following Acquired Disability" by Elliott and Umlauf; and chapter 7, "Assessment of Pain and Pain Behavior" by Millard.

The outer circle represents the aspect of rehabilitation that focuses on the individual's social options and resources (the area of "handicap" in the WHO classification). Efforts here concentrate on the preparation

Figure 1.1

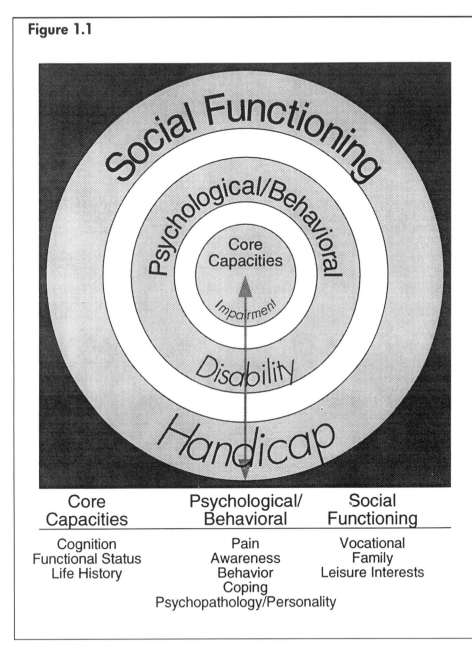

Core Capacities	Psychological/ Behavioral	Social Functioning
Cognition Functional Status Life History	Pain Awareness Behavior Coping Psychopathology/Personality	Vocational Family Leisure Interests

Dynamic, nondiscrete targets of psychological assessment and intervention.

of the individual for employment and a participatory life in the community with family and friends. This aspect is traditionally associated with vocational and outpatient rehabilitation. Psychologists administer aptitude and vocational interest inventories as well as indices of family and social functioning. Two chapters relate to assessment and measures in this area: chapter 8, "Assessment of Family Functioning and Social Support" by Novack and Gage, and chapter 9, "Assessment of Vocational Interests and Aptitude" by Leahy.

Ideally, the individual who has reached this level has moved from the rehabilitation setting into the community and has learned through rehabilitation how to manage both capacities and limitations in order to lead a life that is personally meaningful and rewarding. The individual has learned how to navigate architectural, bureaucratic, sociocultural, and other obstacles and is well on the way to achieving a high quality of life. Unfortunately, ideal scenarios are not necessarily the most frequently occurring ones, and many individuals return to acute and rehabilitation facilities with complications or sequelae related to the disability or with entirely new health problems.

The concentric circles in Figure 1.1 are not discrete and they are not static. In addition to the dynamic nature of rehabilitation and the way focuses can overlap, individuals can vary widely in their needs for assessment within each circle. For example, a 70-year old widower who is retired from work and who is recovering from a moderate stroke will have a much different focus in all the circles than the 18-year old man who received a C-4 spinal cord injury during his freshman year of college. Just as these two individuals vary in their coping, adaptation, and adjustment to disability (see chapter 3 by Heinemann; chapter 12 by Campodonico and McGlynn) and pain experience (chapter 7 by Millard), so do their significant others (chapter 8 by Novack and Gage). The responsibility of the psychologist is to focus on such individual differences, not similarities; to tailor rehabilitation services to the person, not vice versa; and to view the person as an individual interacting within multiple contexts and environments.

Theoretical support for Figure 1.1 comes from a schema developed by Livneh and Male (1993) in which the authors conceptualized three life domains (physical, cognitive, and social) and the static or structural and dynamic or interactive characteristics of each as listed below:

1. a. Physical–structural (missing body parts)
   b. Physical–dynamic (impaired neurological transmission)

2. a. Cognitive–structural (deficits in processing, brain dysfunction, diminished memory and intelligence)

   b. Cognitive–affective (deficits in judgment, decision making, motivation, concentration)

3. a. Social–structural (cosmetic disabilities, impairment in communication)

   b. Social–affective (anger, anxiety, criminality, mental illness)

A related perspective also comes from Rychlak (1993), who sees four discrete "grounds" in psychology that can be found singly or in combination in any given theory. Our ground guides how we view the person and frame theoretical and research questions. Rychlak's four grounds are

1. Physikos—physical principles of phenomena seen in individuals (e.g., how we respond to gravity)
2. Bios—the person as an organic system
3. Socius—the person in groups and cultures
4. Logos–how we come to know and find meaning

These models typify a movement in psychology away from linear to interactive models and, most recently, to chaos theory; that is, by a move beyond sequential analysis to a concept of simultaneity where any given psychological event can be described at multiple levels. Caldwell (1994) provided an example of such simultaneity, choosing sexual arousal to illustrate the point. Sexual arousal can be described at the physiological level, at the subjective level of desire, and at the behavioral level of approach toward a desirable other. Analogies can be made for many disabilities; for example, the loss of a limb may be associated both with depression over one's "disabled experience" (Scherer, 1993) and with lack of motivation to participate in rehabilitation. These levels are not independent of one another and occur simultaneously. Not only have interactive views been applied to clinical problems, but they have also contributed to the development of new models, called "critical paths" (see, e.g., Metcalf, 1991), which facilities have used to provide a map or a set of guidelines for service delivery. Research applications of simultaneity may lead to interventions in areas previously viewed as complicated, random, and full of error.

The psychologist in the medical rehabilitation setting has a key role in assessing the interactions among capacities and limitations at multiple interactive levels so as to ensure that realistic rehabilitation goals are established, that the most appropriate interventions are selected, and that the individual makes progress toward multiple goals simultaneously. Assessment instruments are important resources in the psychologist's tool box, but they themselves have limitations as well as capacities (e.g., Glueck-auf, 1993). Additionally, developments in areas such as testing modifications and adaptations, computerized test administration and scoring, and investigations into the cultural fairness of tests have important practical and ethical implications for their use.

A Model of the Assessment Process in Rehabilitation

In chapter 5, "Bedside Screening of Neurocognitive Function," Wagner, Nayak, and Fink emphasize the *art* of testing and assessment. Tests inform and are guides to treatment planning and clinical judgment but should not be used to determine treatment interventions nor to replace clinical decision making. The authors note that treatment decisions are too often based primarily on test results.

Many considerations need to be applied to psychological testing and assessment in medical rehabilitation settings. I developed the model in Figure 1.2 to organize a discussion of these considerations according to one typical view of the assessment process. It addresses both the art and the science of testing and assessment and is equally applicable to all three aspects of rehabilitation depicted in Figure 1.1.

Determine the Information Needed and Desired

As noted by Wagner, Nayak, and Fink in chapter 5, the delivery of the highest quality rehabilitation care requires that one obtain a comprehensive view of the consumer's personality, preferences, and behaviors as well as those of family members and significant others. A noncomprehensive assessment may save time and money in the short term, but it may have costly results for both the individual and rehabilitation providers over the longer term. Examples of key questions to consider are

- What is known about this person's family, educational, vocational, avocational, psychological, and medical background?
- Who can best provide this data?
- Whose perspective is it important to obtain?
- What is important to find out now in these areas to best help the individual and guide the rehabilitation team?
- What will be important to know later in the rehabilitation process?

Figure 1.2

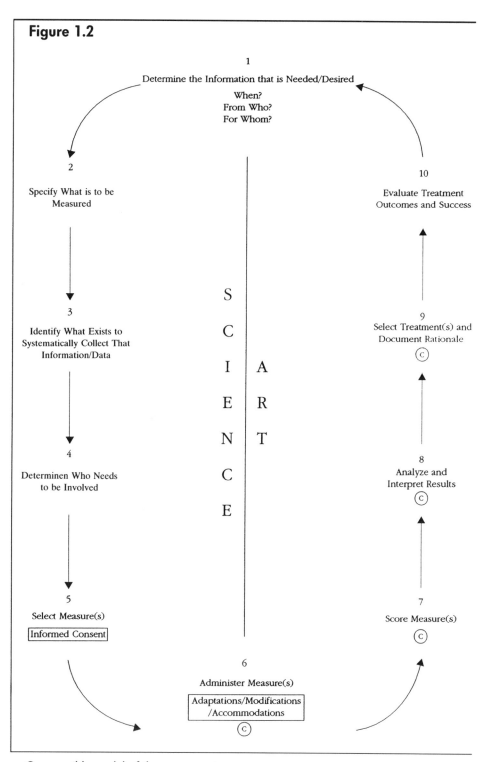

One possible model of the assessment process.

Specify What Is To Be Measured

The assessment of core capacities, functioning, performance, and outcome require different measures, as revealed in the titles of the chapters in this volume. Depending on the focus at a particular point in time (see Figure 1.1) and the type and severity of the disability, it may be less important to measure, for example, neurocognitive function than the absence or presence of psychopathology. Examples of key questions to consider are

- Given the information needed and desired, which chapter or chapters in this volume address the areas in need of assessment?
- Is the desired information specific or general?
- Can the desired information be measured accurately and with precision?
- Will measurement yield better information than clinical judgment?

Identify What Means Exist for Systematically Collecting the Desired Information

Once the assessment goal is established, the practitioner must determine the most appropriate measure. Each chapter in this volume discusses a variety of measures addressing a major area of assessment. Some of the measures are very specific, some global; some are unidimensional, others multidimensional. Some require considerable time to administer, others are brief and can be completed in a few minutes. Some require paper and pencil, others a computer. Knowing what information is desired and weighing that against the available time and resources to obtain it will help narrow the possibilities.

It is becoming increasingly common for psychologists to turn to brief, abbreviated tests in order to save time and costs. Abbreviated, global indices may yield data that is as useful and precise for a particular individual as longer versions with subscales (e.g., Marshall, Hays, Sherbourne, & Wells, 1993). Yet the longer version will be more useful when looking at specific aspects of the domain of interest.

Wagner, Nayak, and Fink note in chapter 5 that the use of brief tests for the assessment of complex problems and for reaching complex treatment and rehabilitation decisions has frequently left important information gaps. The results may not reflect the consumer's background; ethnic, cultural, and gender differences; hearing and vision status, and so on, and these things can affect psychometric properties and the validity or meaningfulness of the results for that individual. Some tests, however, such as the Functional Independence Measure (FIM), have gone through extensive development and refinement. Although the FIM does not measure all key activities, it measures enough to be effective. In fact, a longer and more complex version of the FIM might diminish its advantages in the following areas: (a) It can be administered in any setting. (b) It is appropriate throughout the lifespan. (c) It can be appropriately used by a variety of rehabilitation professionals. Thus, there are trade-offs between abbreviated and long versions of tests. Examples of key questions to consider are

- Is a test instrument the best way to obtain the information needed or desired?
- Do you want or need to construct your own test? If so, the procedures and ethics of test development need to be consulted.
- Which assessment described in the appropriate chapter in this volume seems the most applicable to this individual and this rehabilitation setting?
- Is a global form most appropriate, or one with subscales?
- Is there an abbreviated version? What information is sacrificed by using it?
- What resources are required to use this test (cost of materials, time to administer and score, computer use, etc.)?

Determine Who Needs To Be Involved

It may be useful to assess family members and significant others as well as the consumer because they may be the ones the consumer relies on to maintain rehabilitation outcomes (see chapter 8 by Novack and Gage). It is important when assessing the perspectives of one person not to surround him or her with significant others, lest they interfere with open and honest assessment.

As noted by Caplan and Shechter in chapter 11, people with disabilities often require help in completing measures. They may need to have questions read to them and/or have someone fill in the answer sheet. There may need to be a sign language interpreter or other language translator present. The selection of an assistant needs to be made carefully in order to obtain honest answers on the measure. Examples of key questions to consider are

- Who can best provide the information needed or desired?
- Does the respondent need another person to assist him or her?

- Will the assistant interfere in any way with the collection of accurate information?

Select Measures and Obtain Informed Consent

The selection of an assessment instrument requires attention to its psychometric properties and a weighing of the risks and benefits to the consumer. *Informed consent* is defined in the 1985 *Standards for Educational and Psychological Testing* (presently under revision) co-authored by representatives of the American Educational Research Association, American Psychological Association, and National Council on Measurement in Education. It is important to realize that the broader the domain assessed (from eye contact in conversation to ratings of social behavior), the greater the loss of clarity and specificity. Acceptable levels of subjectivity should be considered.

There are many considerations for judging the quality and usefulness of a test instrument that are beyond the scope of this brief introduction. Fortunately, there are excellent resources available that thoroughly cover such considerations (e.g., Anastasi, 1988; Fuhrer, 1987; Granger & Gresham, 1984; Johnston, Keith, & Hinderer, 1992). Examples of key questions to consider are

- Does the instrument describe, screen, predict, or evaluate?
- What are the populations to which this measure applies?
- Is the reported psychometric evidence adequate?
- Will it give useful information regarding this individual and for this rehabilitation setting?
- What are its limitations?
- Does it have utility in an outcome-based health care system?
- Does it meet the standards of the *Code of Fair Testing Practices*?
- Are the methods and means of obtaining scores and profiles worth the time and expense to get them?
- What are the risks and benefits to the individual?

Administer the Measures and Consider Adaptations, Modifications, and Accommodations

Tests and testing situations must often be modified to accommodate individuals in rehabilitation settings. Limitations in attention span, memory, and other cognitive functions as well as the capabilities to hold a pencil, use a keyboard, or see print require that the rehabilitation psychologist be prepared to adjust the assessment process without sacrificing the integrity of the measure. Examples of test accommodations for individuals with hearing loss are the use of sign language interpreters and the use of graphic assessment measures. Individuals with vision loss can benefit from large print, Braille, or audiocassette versions of instruments. Individuals with motor impairments may require such accommodations as computerized testing or the recording of responses by an assistant. The subject of accommodations in testing and assessment is so important that Caplan and Shechter have contributed a chapter ("The Role of Nonstandard Neuropsychological Assessment in Rehabilitation: History, Rationale, and Examples") to it in this volume. Suffice it to say here that rehabilitation must be a model for all other professions in accommodating the specialized needs of individuals with disabilities in all testing situations. Rehabilitation also needs to be a role model for the involvement of consumers in the assessment process and in the monitoring and comparison of clinician and consumer perspectives (Wax, 1993). In vocational rehabilitation, it has been experimentally demonstrated that consumer involvement in vocational assessment enhances vocational planning and vocational choice (Farley, Bolton, & Parkerson, 1992).

Nearly all assessment today occurs in a multicultural context, necessitating adaptations in tests and testing. Yet cultural loadings (the effects of cultural experience) can be desirable as well as undesirable, depending on the construct being assessed, the context, and the inferences to be drawn. The relationship between culture and test performance is multifaceted and complex, and adequate control is very difficult at best. As Anastasi has stated, "Tests cannot be culture free because human behavior is not culture free" (1993, p. 16).

The assessment of individuals from culturally diverse populations should include, as much as possible, only measures that are culturally and racially bias free and that attend to such cultural differences as variations in definitions of terms, differing views of confidentiality, and different attitudes toward self-disclosure and the role relationship between the test administrator and test taker. The language used in the instrument should be understandable to the individual, and it should contain no culturally offensive or controversial material. If the test selected is not available in the language of the particular consumer, another measure will need to be administered or the results are apt to be meaningless or, worse, misleading when either false positive or false negative results are obtained. Many psychological instruments are available in languages other than English. Other issues regarding the assessment of persons from diverse cultural populations are discussed in *Guidelines for Providers of Psychological Services to Ethnic, Linguistic, and Culturally Diverse Populations* (American Psychological Association Office of Ethnic Minority Affairs, 1993). Examples of key questions to consider are

- Will the individual understand all the words and phrases in the measure's items and not be offended by any of them?
- Do accommodations need to be made in the measure or assessment process to get accurate, unbiased, and meaningful results?
- Will the individual interpret items in the way intended by the test developers and clinicians?

Score Measures

Test scoring can be time-consuming and expensive. If hand scored with templates, the process can be slow; computer scoring requires access to appropriate equipment or the requisite funds to pay to have the test scored. It is often more efficient to train clerical personnel to score the more straightforward tests, but a complex instrument may need to be mailed to the testing service. Scoring by the testing service is advisable if the profile of results is also complicated and choices are available in the means of presenting the data. Examples of key questions to consider are

- Do the necessary resources exist to properly score the instrument?
- Who will get the results?
- Which is the best way of presenting the results for those who will see them?

Analyze and Interpret Results

While Caplan and Shechter present ways to most fairly assess individuals with disabilities in chapter 11, the consequences of not making accommodations and adaptations are also discussed by Elliott and Umlauf in chapter 10:

> Although psychometric assessment is considered a hallmark of psychology, inappropriate and insensitive use of psychological instruments with clientele limited in physical capacity can produce erroneous and misleading results and imprecise observations about the respondent. This is a particular concern in rehabilitation, as test interpretations are usually translated into treatment recommendations, disability determinations, and eligibility for federal and state rehabilitation services.

The purpose of most tests is to focus on and uncover problems. Elliott and Umlauf caution against interpreting scores against the norms of persons without disabilities (for example, a person with a new disability may be appropriately preoccupied with physical sensations and somaticize; norms established on individuals without disabilities may indicate psychopathology). Examples of key questions to consider are

- Are there undue factors that may have influenced the results (e.g., the medication the individual was on at the time the test was administered)?
- Is the norm group appropriate and relevant?
- Do the results make intuitive sense and fit with your clinical judgment and assessment?
- Have all the steps been taken to ensure that the most valid inferences can be drawn?

Select Treatment and Document Rationale

The broad purpose of assessment in rehabilitation is to assist in the derivation of interventions to enhance a person's functioning and ultimate quality of life. The assessment process should reveal obstacles to improved functioning and point the way to areas in need of further exploration. It is important to monitor individuals' progress and repeat tests and assessments during treatment. When this is done, then it is possible to document outcome attainment. Examples of key questions to consider are

- Have assessment data been balanced with good clinical judgment and interpretation and has unfounded personal opinion been minimized?
- Have the data been used to guide the decision making of all the appropriate individuals on the rehabilitation team, including the consumer?

Evaluate Treatment Outcomes and Success

It is becoming increasingly important to demonstrate how much the individual has benefited from the interventions received during rehabilitation as treatments need to be justified for reimbursement. *Outcome assessment* has been defined as follows: "What rehabilitation services ought to achieve for persons receiving them and how achievement can be identified and measured" (Fuhrer, 1987, p. 1). It has also been defined as a systematic procedure for determining the effectiveness, efficiency, and satisfaction with results achieved by persons served following program completion (Commission on the Accreditation of Rehabilitation Facilities, 1995, p. 6).

Outcome assessment is the measure of the difference over time in capability and performance. That is why many functional assessment measures (with their focus on employability, performance of activities of daily living, etc.) are being viewed as means of demonstrating outcome achievement. Without the use of functional assessment measures, the determination of rehabilitation outcome can be affected by incongruence in views held by consumers and therapists regarding the definitions of "disability," "rehabilitation success," and other concepts (Scherer, 1993; Scherer & Galvin, 1994). For example, professionals tend to define independence in terms of physical functioning, whereas consumers more often equate independence with social and psychological freedoms. Confounding may occur if a therapist rates capability during rehabilitation and asks the person about performance at follow up.

The fact that rehabilitation consumers do not typically recover function completely means they need to learn to live with what they have and tolerate some degree of disability. Thus, to many people the acid test of outcome achievement is the subjective sense of well-being and comfort the person has when in the community. Quality of life has come to mean global happiness and satisfaction as well as satisfaction with specific areas of life such as work, social relationships, and finances.

A quality-of-life perspective on outcome achievement reveals that success on one outcome measure may have an associated negative effect on another. For example, improved independence may result in fewer family contacts, which may in turn lead to anxiety.

One means of assessing a person's quality of life is to have the individual prioritize his or her desired outcomes and then rate progress in achieving them over time. This is the system used in the Matching Person and Technology Model (Scherer, 1991). In this way, outcomes are measured in terms of changes in, for example, the person's satisfaction in being able to get to various places, whether by walking or some other means, rather than just by the functional capability to do so. Functional capability, however, is an important means to quality-of-life achievement. Examples of key questions to consider are

- Who wants to know information on outcome achievement?
- What is expected and acceptable as evidence of outcome achievement? From whose perspective?

The Role of Computers in Assessment

Figure 1.2 can be divided in roughly two equal halves: the left side being more scientific in orientation and the right requiring substantial clinical judgment—the art of useful and appropriate assessment. It is somewhat ironic that computerization has affected primarily the right half of the diagram (see the circled *c*'s for "computerized" in Figure 1.2).

Computer-based test interpretations have been available for more than a quarter century. More recently, interactive computer test administration has become popular. The term computer-based assessment refers to computerized (a) test administration, (b) scoring, (c) reporting (commercially prepared profiles), and (d) data and practice management.

In reporting on the equivalence of a new computer-administered form of the Hamilton Anxiety Scale with the clinician-administered form, Kobak, Reynolds, and Greist (1993) noted the following advantages of computer-administered testing: standardization of administration, branching capabilities where a person is cycled up to more difficult questions based on previous responses, enhanced consumer willingness to disclose sensitive information, a freeing of the clinician's time, and reduction of errors due to scoring or data entry. Disadvantages they mentioned include the need for access to one or more computers and a person's reluctance to being interviewed by a computer (most of their subjects reported a preference for being interviewed by a clinician). Other possible pitfalls to computerized assessment include concerns over the equivalence of computerized and paper-and-pencil forms and the fact that computerization can lend an air of precision that does not exist. (A computerized test is only as good as what is programmed into it). Partial computerization—administering paper-and-pencil tests and computer scoring them—can help overcome these pitfalls.

Structured software programs may facilitate cognitive rehabilitation for many individuals, but human memory can be stressed for some people when using them, and slow feedback can be frustrating for others. Interactive computerized testing may not result in a positive experience for the individuals being assessed. Individuals with test anxiety and little or no exposure to computers may experience compounded anxiety. All persons being given an interactive computerized test should first be prepared for and trained in its use.

On the positive side, computerized scoring enables fast processing of all possible score combinations. Graphic computer-generated score reports and profiles have been shown to facilitate visual appreciation and understanding of the results (Straham & Kelly, 1994).

A complete discussion of computer-based assessment is beyond the scope of this book. The interested reader is referred to such specialized resources as the guide published by Division 42 of the American Psychological Association, *Taming Technology: Issues, Strategies and Resources for the Mental Health Practitioner* (Schlosser & Moreland, 1993).

Caplan and Shechter noted in chapter 11 that computerized testing works best for tests that are highly structured and do not require accommodation. The single most important goal of any assessment is to get meaningful and useful information regarding ways to help persons in their rehabilitation. For rehabilitation professionals to make the most informed clinical decisions, the best information needs to obtained from the consumer, and this may or may not be achieved through computer-based assessment.

Ethical Considerations Regarding Psychological Assessment in the Context of Physical Rehabilitation

Increasingly, tests and instruments are being considered only one facet of assessment, because it has become evident that they inadequately measure many of the most important influences on a person's rehabilitation and quality of life. Individualized assessment was always emphasized in rehabilitation, and with the Americans with Disabilities Act and other legislation that empowers consumers, the assessment process is broadening to include observation and interviewing in order to identify the need for such accommodations as changes in the language level of measures and the desirability of computerized testing. Where assessment in the past may have involved the administration of a personality inventory, it now includes testing first for language proficiency.

As the chapters in this book demonstrate, psychologists have available a wide variety of assessment instruments from which to select. The psychologist needs to be familiar with a broad range of assessment instruments in order to gain a full and more accurate picture of a consumer's personality, preferences, and capabilities. Additionally, the psychologist needs to be available to assess individuals throughout the rehabilitation process, and this includes the assessment of outcomes (which require ongoing or repeated assessment).

More and more, rehabilitation professionals must exercise clinical judgment—the art of assessment—in using measures to assess performance as well as capability (and discrepancies between the two). This requires special attention to both the reliability of the measures and their content validity. Raters of capability and performance need training in assessment in order to provide accurate results; performance and content samples need to be representative of the content domain.

A wider range of professionals will require familiarity with testing issues, and the psychologist will be called upon to provide staff development opportunities and other expertise. The psychologist will be providing guidance and education to consumers and parents, who will come from culturally diverse backgrounds. In short, the psychologist working in rehabilitation settings needs to be thoroughly informed of the ethical concerns regarding the full array of assessment from selection, to administration, to the interpretation of data from test instruments.

Guidance regarding the newer assessment issues faced by psychologists is well on its way. Acknowledging developments in psychological assessment since the publication of the 1985 *Standards for Educational and Psychological Testing*, the Joint Committee on the Standards for Educational and Psychological Testing (American Educational Research Association, American Psychological Association, National Council on Measurement in Education) held an open conference on revising the standards in October 1994, and revised standards should be available in the near future.

Organization of This Volume

In most studies and books involving psychological aspects of physical disability, instruments have been discussed in the context of a single (i.e., diagnostic) group of individuals with disabilities for whom they were used or developed. In fact, much of the literature not only on assessment, but also on intervention, theory, and so forth has been similarly developed. In this book, material is instead organized according to the type of assessment or assessment situation required. It is our belief that most salient issues (e.g., social functioning, vocational adaptation, and psychopathology) cross disability group-based boundaries. For example, personality testing, cognitive screening, and family functioning are each treated separately but across diagnostic groups.

The chapters in this volume describe types of assessment that can be seen as situated at various points along a time line (Table 1.1) and

Table 1.1

Chapter and topic areas in relation to the timeline of potential rehabilitation assessment

Timeline → →

Chapter Topic	Onset	Acute medical care	Acute rehabilitation	Post-discharge rehabilitation	Vocational readiness and training	Community living and life changes
Screening assessment	+	+	+			
Coping and adjustment	+	+	+	+	+	+
Assessment of unawareness		+	+	+		
Behavioral assessment		+	+	+	+	+
Personality assessment			+	+	+	
Functional assessment			+	+	+	+
Assessment of pain		+	+	+		+
Family functioning		+	+			+
Vocational assessment			+	+	+	+
Adapting commonly used tests					+	

may involve assessment at any or all of these points. Types of assessment that have traditionally been associated, at least in part, with early- to mid-stage rehabilitation phases, include screening assessment (Wagner, Nayak & Fink), coping and adjustment (Heinemann), personality assessment (Elliott & Umlauf), functional assessment (Crewe & Dijkers), and vocational assessment (Leahy). Types of assessment that have been developed later in the context of rehabilitation, or are often utilized at later points in time, include behavioral assessment (Malec & Lemsky), assessment of family functioning (Novack & Gage), assessment of pain (Millard), assessment of unawareness (Campodonico & McGlynn), and, summarizing across many areas, nonstandard adaptations of tests (Caplan & Shechter).

Within each chapter that follows, a brief overview of the area is followed by a discussion of specific tests chosen by the authors; typically, those that have most often been used, that best serve particular assessment goals, and that have demonstrated psychometric advantages. Factors affecting administration, as well as conclusions regarding use, are specified whenever feasible. Next, comparisons among various test measures and practical considerations for implementation are presented, together with an overall summary. The chapters also address essential next steps in research and clinical application. In this way, the clinician or researcher can gain an appreciation of the functional domains in which given tests may be useful and apply this knowledge to the situation at hand. This structure is also meant, wherever appropriate, to stimulate the potential use of particular tools across as many situations or types of disability as possible. The clinicians who learn more about and use the test measures described in this book will then be those who assist the evolution of measures designed for and used with individuals with disabilities.

I began this introduction with a quote from Anne Anastasi, and it seems fitting that it should end with some of her words of wisdom. During her 1992 Master Lecture, Anastasi stated that the test user is in a continuous cycle of hypothesis formulation, confirmation, and revision and that the goal of testing is to have a rich harvest of leads for further exploration. The bottom line is the preservation of individual variability in context. To do this, Anastasi said, "one needs a backward and forward view of the person," where the antecedents are considered along with the desired outcomes. Numerical scores and quantitative data "can only give the illusion of objectivity" and cannot ensure accuracy of interpretation for any given individual (Anastasi, 1993) . They can tell us how people perform at the time of testing, not why they perform that way. They require corroborative data.

References

American Educational Research Association, American Psychological Association, National Council on Measurement in Education. (1988). *Code of fair testing practices in education.* Washington, DC: American Psychological Association.

American Psychological Association. (1986). *Guidelines for computer-based tests and interpretations.* Washington, DC: Author.

American Psychological Association Office of Ethnic Minority Affairs. (1993). Guidelines for providers of psychological services to ethnic, linguistic, and culturally diverse populations. *American Psychologist, 48,* 45–48.

American Psychological Association Science Directorate. (1991). *Finding information on psychological tests.* Washington, DC: Author.

American Psychological Association Science Directorate. (1991). *Finding unpublished psychological tests and measures.* Washington, DC: Author.

Anastasi, A. (1988). *Psychological testing* (6th ed.). New York: Collier.

Anastasi, A. (1993). A century of psychological testing: Origins, problems, and progress. In T. K. Fagan & G. R. VandenBos (Eds.), *Exploring applied psychology: Origins and critical analysis* (pp. 13–36). Washington, DC: American Psychological Association.

Caldwell, A. B. (1994). Simultaneous multilevel analysis [Comment]. *American Psychologist, 49*(2), 144–145.

Commission on the Accreditation of Rehabilitation Faculties. (1995). *1995 Standards manual and interpretive guidelines for behavioral health.* Tucson, AZ: Author.

Farley, R. C., Bolton, B., & Parkerson, S. (1992). Effects of client involvement in assessment on vocational development. *Rehabilitation Counseling Bulletin, 35*(3), 146–153.

Fuhrer, M. J. (1987). *Rehabilitation outcomes: Analysis and measurement.* Baltimore: Paul H. Brookes.

Glueckauf, R. L. (1993). Use and misuse of assessment in rehabilitation: Getting back to the basics. In R. L. Glueckauf, L. B. Sechrest, G. R. Bond, & E. C. McDonel (Eds.), *Improving assessment in rehabilitation and health* (pp. 135–155). Newbury Park, CA: Sage.

Granger, C. V., & Gresham, G. (Eds.). (1984). *Functional assessment in rehabilitation medicine.* Baltimore: Williams & Wilkins.

Heinemann, A. W., Linacre, J. M., Wright, B. D., Hamilton, B. B., & Granger, C. V. (1994). Prediction of rehabilitation outcomes with disability measures. *Archives of Physical Medicine and Rehabilitation, 75*(2), 133–143.

Johnston, M. V., Keith, R. A., & Hinderer, S. R. (1992). Measurement standards for interdisciplinary medical rehabilitation. *Archives of Physical Medicine and Rehabilitation, 73*(12-S).

Joint Committee on the Standards for Educational and Psychological Testing. (1994, October 7–9). Open Conference on the Revision of the Standards: Oral testimony summaries; summary of panel discussions. Crystal City, VA: Author.

Kobak, K. A., Reynolds, W. M., & Greist, J. H. (1993). Development and validation of a computer-administered version of the Hamilton Anxiety Scale. *Psychological Assessment, 5*(4), 487–492.

Linacre, J. M., Heinemann, A. W., Wright, B. D., Granger, C. V., & Hamilton, B. B. (1994). The structure and stability of the Functional Independence Measure. *Archives of Physical Medicine and Rehabilitation, 75*(2), 127–132.

Livneh, H., & Male, R. (1993, Oct/Nov/Dec). Functional limitations: A review of their characteristics and vocational impact. *Journal of Rehabilitation, 59*(4), 44–50.

Marshall, G. N., Hays, R. D., Sherbourne, C. D., & Wells, K. B. (1993). The structure of patient satisfaction with outpatient medical care. *Psychological Assessment*, 5(4), 477–483.

Metcalf, E. M. (1991). The orthopaedic critical path. *Orthopaedic Nursing*, 10(6), 25–35.

National Institute on Disability and Rehabilitation Research. (1992). Human measurement in rehabilitation. *Rehab Brief*. Washington, DC: Author

Rychlak, J. F. (1993). A suggested principle for complementarity for psychology: In theory, not method. *American Psychologist*, 48(9), 933–942.

Scherer, M. J. (1993). *Living in the state of stuck: How technology impacts the lives of people with disabilities*. Cambridge, MA: Brookline Books.

Scherer, M. J. (1991). *Matching person and technology model (and assessment instruments)*. Rochester, NY: Author.

Scherer, M. J., & Galvin, J. C. (1994). Matching people with technology. *Rehab Management*, 7(2), 128–130.

Schlosser, B., & Moreland, K. L. (Eds.). (1993). *Taming technology: Issues, strategies and resources for the mental health practitioner*. Phoenix, AZ: Division of Independent Practice, American Psychological Association.

Standards for educational and psychological testing. (1985). Washington, DC: American Psychological Association.

Straham, R. F., & Kelly, A. E. (1994). Showing clients what their profiles mean. *Journal of Counseling, & Development*, 72, 329–331.

Wax, T. M. (1993). Matchmaking among cultures: Disability culture and the larger marketplace. In Glueckauf, R. L., Sechrest, L. B., Bond, G. R., & McDonel, E. C. (Eds.), *Improving assessment in rehabilitation and health* (pp. 156–175). Newbury Park, CA: Sage.

World Health Organization. (1980). *International classification of impairments, disabilities, and handicaps: A manual of classification relating to the consequences of disease*. Geneva: Author.

History and Context of Psychological Assessment in Rehabilitation Psychology

Laura A. Cushman

Assessment is arguably the cornerstone of clinical psychology; its principles, refinement, and applications have always been a focus of study. Disability and rehabilitation are primary areas where exceptions to rules, practices, applications, and interpretations frequently occur. One reason is that the majority of assessment tools were developed for and normed with nondisabled individuals. This has resulted in the establishment of a large body of instruments for which intact physical, sensory, and cognitive functioning is presumed and necessary for interpretation. Thus, in trying to bring the resources of psychological assessment to individuals with a disability, a particular challenge exists across virtually all traditional domains of assessment.

The challenge, for each type of assessment, can be summarized by several basic questions. First, what instruments are appropriate for a given disability? What research exists to inform the choice? What considerations are there in applying and interpreting a particular type of assessment for individuals with a disability? Finally, what might be some appropriate modifications if a given measure is not strictly suited to an individual with a disability? The need for answers to these questions is the underlying rationale for this book.

Historical Overview

Psychological assessment is the foundation from which clinical psychology developed. In the field of medical rehabilitation, the growth of psychology has followed much the same path. In the past 40 to 50 years, clinical psychologists have gradually found themselves working in a growing number of hospital departments and human service agencies outside of traditional mental health settings. Beginning in the 1950s, as the new field of physical medicine and rehabilitation took shape and began to serve new clinical populations, psychologists began to be rehabilitation team members. At first, most psychologists interested in rehabilitation were academicians in social, not clinical, psychology, and they were not chiefly interested in assessment per se (Larson, 1993). Much of the scholarly work of that time focused on the issue of adjustment to disability; this issue has remained a focus up to the present.

Since new subgroups of the general population were being served, it was an open question as to whether psychological tests developed and used in psychiatric settings would prove useful with rehabilitation patients as well. The questions to be asked fell into several categories. Initially this involved the "translation" of tests to new populations. The question was whether the normative group for the original population was now appropriate, and whether interpretive guidelines would need to change (e.g., Wachs, 1966). Also, it was not known whether test factor structures would change when applied to patients in rehabilitation programs. There later came an impetus to develop scales for needs and characteristics unique to rehabilitation settings, such as instruments measuring attitude toward disability and levels of functional outcome. Additionally, changes in test administration were often developed in response to the needs of clients with sensory or motor deficits (Raskin, 1962). The research and methodological issues described above are still relevant and timely today, over 40 years later. Early researchers were asking key questions, but answering them proved to be a large task. The scope and practice of rehabilitation psychology grew tremendously in ensuing years and, unfortunately, some basic psychometric needs, such as those for certain disability-specific norms, have gone unmet.

Growth of Rehabilitation-Based Psychological Assessment

As in other disciplines involved in rehabilitation, psychological assessment first took shape in relation to the assessment and treatment of children with disabilities, typically, those with cerebral palsy. Bice (1948) advocated the use of various tests according to the age and handicap of the child, though noting that the Stanford Binet was "less influenced by handicaps of speech, motor control . . . and training" (p. 164) than other intelligence tests. Bice (1949) further wrote to caution those psychologists who would seek to test children with cerebral palsy without any appreciation of their neurological deficits and the effect of these on testing; he additionally forewarned that no universally applicable test existed. He also sought to temper the clinician's desire for a number score at all costs and stressed the importance of ecologically valid data that can help "interpret the child's condition to his parents" (p. 189).

Sensitivity to variance caused by factors other than illness was also recognized in an early study by Wendland, Urmer, and Safford (1960), who cautioned that an apparent decrement in the intellectual functioning of individuals after poliomyelitis might not be a result of the disease, but "due to hospitalization per se" (p. 181). In terms of assessing children with developmental disabilities, Cruickshank and Qualtere (1950, p. 371) wrote that the "usual procedure works to the disadvantage of the child" and stressed that alternate approaches may better serve children with disabilities. Satter (1955) noted increased psychometric scatter among children with mental retardation relative to other children, with the most scatter found among children with an acquired brain injury. He further demonstrated that this variance was due to at least four factors. In these and similar studies, the incremental process of adjusting assessment procedures to meet the needs of individuals with disabilities began.

As some psychologists raised awareness of circumstances hampering the translation of standard psychological tests to individuals with disabilities, others began the task of developing alternate norms and determining the validity of particular instruments or administration procedures for a given group. Each type of disability can render certain psychological measures invalid. Also, individuals with sensory and motoric disability, as well as those with brain injury, can potentially benefit from disability-specific norms. Such norms provide the opportunity for comparison with peers who have had similar life-altering experiences and can be used in comparison with findings based on demographically similar but nondisabled individuals. Because of the complexity of the task, this work has continued to the present day. For example, Needham, Ehmer, Marchesseault, and De l'Aune (1986) investigated the clinical utility of the Mini-Mult with individuals who are blind; Henschen and Horvat (1985) studied the use of the State–Trait Anxiety Inventory with individuals having visual impairments. Braden (1990) used a meta-analysis to discuss the issue of Wechsler Performance Scale (the performance subscales of the Wechsler Adult Intelligence Scale–Revised [WAIS-R]) profiles characteristic of people who are deaf. This last-mentioned study found not only a characteristic psychometric profile, but also evidence that such profiles are affected by administration procedures and by the use of norms that are based on people who were deaf (versus the standardization sample). In a review of personality assessment tools used with children and adolescents who are deaf, Cates and Lapham (1991) emphasized not only the lack of instruments developed for such applications, but also the lack of reliability and validity studies.

Adults with acquired brain injury have been the focus of much attention in terms of both psychological and neuropsychological assessment. In one study, Atkinson, Cyr, Doxey, and Vigna (1989) explored the robustness of WAIS-R factor structures in a large sample of men with head injuries and found no significant discrepancies from other clinical samples reported in the literature. Similarly, the robustness of the WAIS-R factor structure for vocational rehabilitation service recipients was demonstrated by Ryan, Rosenberg, and DeWolfe (1983). Moss and Dowd (1991) used a case report to examine the stability of the New Adult Reading Test after brain injury. Tuokko, Vernon-Wilkinson, and Robinson (1991) looked at the use of the Millon Clinical Multiaxial Inventory with a sample of individuals with head injuries and found that two head injury factors—severity of injury and time since injury—did not predict the number of elevated scales. However, it was also clear that more work is needed in order to determine what scale elevations reflect premorbid versus post-injury phenomena.

Another area of research has focused on the influence of physical disabilities on measures of psychological phenomena. This is especially true regarding assessment of depression in individuals with physical disabilities. For example, in one study, Pardini-Coyle (1991) found the factor structure of the Center for Epidemiological Study—Depression scale to be highly similar for adults with disabilities and nondisabled adults. She also presented evidence that scores were not artificially elevated by somatic issues related to disability. Another instrument, the Personal Orientation Inventory (Sherrill, Gilstrap, Richir, Gench, & Hinson, 1988), purported to measure self-actualization, was shown to be appropriate for both college athletes with disabilities and nondisabled athletes and was not affected by oral versus written administration. Similarly, Mastro, French, Henschen, and Horvat (1985) found that the State–Trait Anxiety Inventory could provide valid results if read to female athletes whether blind or nondisabled. However, using a different clinical instrument, Taylor (1970) was able to show that problems in interpretation of the Minnesota Multiphasic

Personality Inventory (MMPI) scales could occur as a function of physical disability (here, spinal cord injury); items related to somatic concern were shown to affect profile elevation across sexes and among other disability groups (see also chapters 10 and 11 for further discussion of the MMPI). Taylor also presented two methods of scale correction and suggested that other instruments be examined in a similar way. Because not only test items, but also administration and scoring can differentially affect individuals with motor or speech deficits, Berninger, Gans, St. James, and Connors (1988) proceeded to modify all three in a feasibility and comparison study of the WAIS-R. They found that even with substantial modifications, their samples of adults with and without disabilities performed equivalently on both versions; that is, the same abilities were tapped, despite different response requirements.

Administration procedures that involve time limits have often been thought to differentially penalize those with physical disabilities. Centra (1986) studied the effect of extending time limits on Scholastic Aptitude Test performance in groups of students with disabilities and nondisabled students. He showed that scores of students with disabilities did improve when they were given more time, suggesting that increased time may reduce the effect of their disability. However, the relative standing of all students remained stable under both timed and untimed conditions.

Questions of validity have often been raised in connection with testing of individuals with sensory deficits. In testing deaf children, problems of validity have been particularly cited. Most instruments, standardized on hearing subjects, can be invalidated because of violation of the assumption of a normative range of experience and level of language comprehension on the part of the child who is deaf. Many items on common instruments assume a life history that may well not be a part of the life experience of a client with a hearing impairment. Alternatively, with individuals who are blind, changes resulting in oral or Braille administrations have generally been found to be adequate substitutes (e.g., Raskin, 1962). Yet a hypothesized lack of social experience (or applicability of test problems, or both) is cited when addressing the much lower Comprehension scale scores on the Wechsler Intelligence Scale for Children–Revised (WISC-R) typically obtained by children who are blind (Raskin, 1962).

It has been understood from the outset that tests which are affected by, for example, a motoric disability can yield misleading results; however, even if modifications are used, the usefulness of the original norms "becomes at best ambiguous" (Newland, 1955, p. 68). The pattern across several disability groups has often been to first use existing test instruments, then omit or modify parts of these, and finally to create new measures or alternate administration procedures and norms. An example of the latter is the Nebraska Test of Learning Aptitude, which was standardized on and for children who are deaf. It is a smorgasbord of tasks that were added according to psychometric criteria to increase the utility of the test.

The development of various tests has also been guided by the role of psychologists as rehabilitation team members; this role alone has been a reason for the redesign or reinterpretation of certain tools. Sometimes, renewed scrutiny of a given test for a group of people results in no modifications, such as with individuals with amputations (Fishman, 1962). Others have focused on the ability to transfer measures designed for one group or disability to another (e.g., Lamarre & Patten, 1991).

Testing in Rehabilitation: Philosophy and Clinical Practice

Even in the earliest years of psychological testing in rehabilitation settings, it was recognized that particular knowledge and abilities on the part of the examiner were essential: "exceptional skill, tact, and patience are required, as well as . . . special knowledge of neurologically handicapped subjects" (Bice, 1948, p. 166). Special attention has been given to the timeliness of psychologists' test reports, since "one of the primary rights of rehabilitation clients is . . . prompt provision of services" (Cull & Levinson, 1977). Much of the work initiated in the development of disability-based norms and considerations in interpretation and use of test scores came out of the clinical needs of psychologists working in a given area. There have been many efforts to bridge the differences between clinically devised typologies and assessments and those that were more empirically based (e.g., Bolton, 1972). Underlying these efforts have been several assumptions about the nature of assessment for individuals with disabilities. Assessing disability and handicap requires a knowledge of deficits or differences. However, psychological assessment in rehabilitation is not focused primarily on describing the deleterious effects of disability. Its essence is in portraying the true strengths or weaknesses of an individual, moving beyond the (possibly) biased picture portrayed by standardized tests and other appearances. A key contribution of rehabilitation psychologists is often identifying the "silent strengths" of the individual with a disability—those that may not be able to be inferred from traditional measures. There has also been an emphasis on the utility of psychological assessments in furthering client goals. Testing has been viewed as essential in understanding and assessing the disability, identifying counseling needs, setting vocational objectives, and determining aspects of rehabilitation potential. In neuropsychological testing, as in more general aptitude testing, most clinicians emphasize the ability of the individual under optimal conditions; that is, capacity versus performance. What optimal conditions consist of varies with the nature of the individual's disability. For example, in brain injury, maximum freedom from distraction is a key modification; for people with visual impairment, auditory presentation or large print stimuli are the chief modifications. Unfortunately, the clinician is often unable to avail himself or herself of alternative tests and norms or of the research necessary to make needed modifications. This results in the uncomfortable situation in which a clinician must interpret test results without adequate backup by research or use a second-choice measure because the preferred one does not even exist.

Rehabilitation Psychologists

A detailed description of the many psychologists working in medical rehabilitation settings is difficult to compile comprehensively. An overview of psychologists working with a single disability group (individuals who are deaf) was provided by a national survey undertaken by Levine (1974). The top three most frequent majors of those surveyed ($n = 178$) were in educational psychology, special education, and counseling psychology (respectively). Clinical psychology, speech and hearing, and other areas were also represented. The three most commonly administered types of tests were individual intelligence tests, achievement tests, and personality tests. Difficulties in testing individuals who are deaf were reported by 96% of those surveyed. Roughly half of the reported problems involved the tests themselves. Lack of norms, problems in selection and administration, and problems in interpretation were cited. This pattern could no doubt be seen for most of the psychologists providing assessment services to rehabilitation clients.

Parker and Chan (1990) surveyed the directors of psychology departments at 219 CARF (Commission on Accreditation of Rehabilitation Facilities) accredited facilities (from a pool of 316 facilities contacted) to characterize their training and experience. The study was a response to perceived confusion and disagreement regarding the roles, knowledge base, and training of rehabilitation psychologists. Clinical and counseling psychology degrees were held by the majority of directors surveyed (81%). However, only 8% had completed internships in a rehabilitation facility, and only 7% completed postdoctoral training in such a setting. Over half (52%) of those surveyed did not indicate they considered themselves "rehabilitation psychologists." The fact that some respondents cited questions about the definition of the latter was seen as evidence of lack of knowledge about the criteria developed by the Rehabilitation Psychology Division of the American Psychological Association (APA Division 22), and of the apparent mismatch between the low frequency of rehabilitation specialty training and what currently constitutes employer-based criteria. One of the recommendations made by Parker and Chan, namely development of credentialing and specialty criteria, is being pursued as of this writing.

The current membership of APA's Division 22 included 1,318 members in 1993. Women made up 28.9% of the total membership. Eighty-four percent held PhD (80%) or PsyD (4%) degrees and 5% held EdD degrees; the remainder held master's degrees and other doctorate and "unspecified" degrees. The type of program and field of training for rehabilitation psychologists was clinical (39.2%) or rehabilitation psychology (14.9%) for the majority, followed by counseling (11.3%), health psychology (3%), counseling (other; 2.2%), and educational psychology (2.0%); numerous other fields make up the remainder. The five most common employment settings for rehabilitation psychologists are independent practice (27.39%), hospital practice (22.4%), human service agencies (13.6%), universities (11.6%), and medical schools (10.3%). Finally, the vast majority (81.4%) of rehabilitation psychologists are active members of other APA divisions; 35.2% are members of the Division of Neuropsychology (Division 40). In addition, another large proportion also belong to the American Congress of Rehabilitation Medicine.

Medical Rehabilitation Settings

Today, psychologists who identify their primary APA division as Division 22 work in general rehabilitation units (both acute inpatient and outpatient), specialized spinal cord injury centers, traumatic brain injury and neurologic rehabilitation centers, community reentry and transitional living programs, vocational rehabilitation, cardiac and cancer rehabilitation, long-term care and geriatric day programs, and other settings. As the scope and levels of care offered in medical rehabilitation settings increase, the settings and programs in which psychologists are involved become more varied. Even outside of a formal medical rehabilitation setting, psychologists practicing independently (as well as in other hospital or community settings) increasingly see patients with an acquired disability of some kind. The impairments and diagnoses seen are many; a partial list includes sensory impairment (e.g., deafness, blindness), spinal cord injury, neuromuscular and other neurologic disorders (e.g., multiple sclerosis), traumatic brain injury, dementia, stroke, amputation, chronic pain, orthopaedic trauma or joint replacement, and epilepsy. The referral questions and assessment needs of individuals served in medical rehabilitation settings are varied, but they encompass two general themes. The first involves the impact of a given illness or traumatic injury on (a) general cognitive functioning (including competency); (b) psychological and adaptive functioning, including affective and anxiety disorders; (c) functional status and social interaction; and (d) potential for educational and vocational pursuits.

A second area in which rehabilitation psychologists provide input is in tracking current and potential functioning over time and following the course of illness or disability in terms of (a) progression, (b) the effect of various treatments, and (c) long-term outcome. Additionally, psychologists are asked to assess the readiness of clients to live independently, to assume or resume a job or education, or to receive specific technological assistance.

Timing of Assessment

Assessment in rehabilitation is anything but static; it is relevant throughout the journey of the individual with a disability from onset to reintegration into the workforce and community. Traditionally, however, assessment has been fixed at two discrete points in the continuum of disability adaptation (Figure 2.1). The expansion of assessment to more points along the continuum would allow assessment at naturally optimal points in time and would emphasize the point that rehabilitation assessment should correspond to needs of the individual at a given point in time.

Summary

Perhaps the most general summary statement that can be made is that across heterogeneous groups with disabilities in the population, stan-

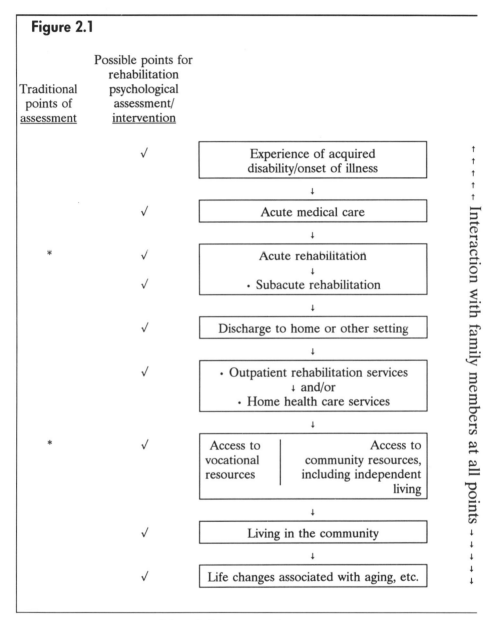

Figure 2.1

Assessment seen as part of the rehabilitation timeline.

dardized test batteries too often do not work. Instead, the psychologist is left to use considerable ingenuity, followed by cautious interpretation. Shontz advises the psychologist in a rehabilitation setting to also note carefully the observations of other team members as "grist for the mill" (Shontz, 1962, p. 436). He states further that, for those psychologists called to assess the capacities of individuals with severe chronic illness, the demand for "acumen, breadth of knowledge, and sensitivity" (p. 436) is at its highest.

Not even the best test can overcome a clinician's deficiencies in clinical judgment or experience. Yet measures that are designed, normed, or used for individuals with disabilities and that have some evidence of psychometric soundness can achieve a degree of utility far beyond that of observation and interview alone.

References

Atkinson, L., Cyr, J., & Doxey, N. C. S. (1989). Generalizability of WAIS-R factor structure within and between populations. *Journal of Clinical Psychology*, *45*, 124–129.

Berninger, V. W., Gans, B. M., St. James, P., & Connors, T. (1988). Modified WAIS-R for patients with speech and/or hand dysfunction. *Archives of Physical Medicine and Rehabilitation*, *69*, 250–255.

Bice, H. V. (1948). Psychological examination of the cerebral palsied. *Journal of Exceptional Children*, *14*, 163–168.

Bice, H. V. (1949). Psychological services for the cerebral palsied. *Nervous Child*, *8*, 183–192.

Bolton, B. (1972). Psychometric validation of a clinically derived typology of deaf rehabilitation clients. *Journal of Clinical Psychology*, *28*, 22–25.

Braden, J. P. (1990). Do deaf persons have a characteristic psychometric profile on the Wechsler performance scales? *Journal of Psychoeducational Assessment*, *8*, 518–526.

Cates, J. A., & Lapham, R. F. (1991). Personality assessment of the prelingual, profoundly deaf child or adolescent. *Journal of Personality Assessment*, *56*(1), 118–129.

Centra, J. A. (1986). Handicapped student performance on the Scholastic Aptitude Test. *Journal of Learning Disabilities*, *19*, 324–327.

Cruickshank, W. M., & Qualtere, T. J. (1950). The use of intelligence tests with children of retarded mental development II. Clinical considerations. *American Journal of Mental Deficiency*, *54*, 370–381.

Cull, J. G., & Levinson, K. F. (1977). State rehabilitation administrators' views on psychological evaluation: A five-year follow-up study. *Rehabilitation Literature*, *38*, 203–204.

Fishman, S. (1962). Amputation. In J. F. Garrett, & E. Levine (Eds.), *Psychological practices with the physically disabled* (pp. 1–50). New York: Columbia University Press.

Henschen, K., & Horvat, M. (1985). Use of the State-Trait Anxiety Inventory for visually impaired athletes. *Perceptual and Motor Skills*, *61*, 775–778.

Lamarre, C. J., & Patten, S. B. (1991). Evaluation of the modified Mini-Mental State Examination in the general psychiatric population. *Canadian Journal of Psychiatry*, *36*, 507–511.

Larson, P. (1993). Personal Communication.

Levine, E. S. (1974). Psychological tests and practices with the deaf: A survey of the state of the art. *The Volta Review, 76*, 298–319.

Mastro, J., French, R., Henschen, K., & Horvat, M. (1985). Use of the State-Trait Anxiety Inventory for visually impaired athletes. *Perceptual and Motor Skills*, *61*, 775–778.

Moss, A. R., & Dowd, T. (1991). Does the NART hold after head injury? A case report. *British Journal of Clinical Psychology*, *30*, 179–180.

Needham, W. E., Ehmer, M. N., Marchesseault, L., & De l'Aune, W. R. (1986). Effectiveness of the Mini-Mult in detecting MMPI pathology in the blind. *Journal of Clinical Psychology*, *42*, 887–890.

Newland, T. (1955). Exceptional children: Psychological assessment. In W. Cruickshank (Ed.), *Psychology of exceptional children in youth* (pp. 61–119). Englewood Cliffs, NJ: Prentice Hall.

Pardini-Coyle, C. V. (1991). Evaluating the psychometric properties of the Center for Epidemiological Studies—Depression Scale for use with adults with physical disabilities. *Dissertation Abstracts International*, *52*, 1119B.

Parker, H. J., & Chan, F. (1990). Psychologists in rehabilitation: Preparation and experience. *Rehabilitation Psychologist*, *35*, 239–248.

Raskin, N. J. (1962). Visual Disability. In J. F. Garrett & E. Levine (Eds.), *Psychological Practices with the Physically Disabled* (pp. 341–375). New York: Columbia University Press.

Ryan, J. J., Rosenberg, S. J., & DeWolfe, A. S. (1983). Generalization of the WAIS-R factor structure with a vocational rehabilitation sample. *Journal of Consulting and Clinical Psychology*, *52*, 311–312.

Satter, G. (1955). Psychometric scatter among mentally retarded and normal children. *The Training School Bulletin*, *52*, 63–68.

Sherrill, C., Gilstrap, T., Richir, K., Gench, B., & Hinson, M. (1988). Use of the Personal Orientation Inventory with disabled athletes. *Perceptual and Motor Skills*, *67*, 263–266.

Shontz, F. C. (1962). Severe chronic illness. In J. F. Garrett & E. Levine (Eds.), *Psychological practices with the physically disabled* (pp. 410–445). New York: Columbia University Press.

Taylor, G. M. (1970). Moderator-variable effect on personality-test-item endorsements of physically disabled patients. *Journal of Consulting and Clinical Psychology*, *35*(2), 183–188.

Tuokko, H., Vernon-Wilkinson, R., & Robinson, E. (1991). The use of the MCMI in the personality assessment of head-injured adults. *Brain Injury*, *5*, 287–293.

Wachs, T. D. (1966). Personality testing of the handicapped: A review. *Journal of Projective Techniques and Personality Assessment*, *30*, 339–355.

Wendland, L. V., Urmer, A. H., & Safford, H. W. (1960). The intellectual functioning of postpoliomyelitic patients. *Journal of Clinical Psychology*, *16*, 179–181.

Part Two

Measures and Instruments

3 Measures of Coping and Reaction to Disability

Allen W. Heinemann

This chapter presents eight measures of coping and reaction to disability. They are only a sample of the diverse indicators of adjustment that are available. Other sources provide broader overviews of assessment techniques: Moos (1974) provides a comprehensive list of interview and naturalistic observations, Q sorts, family interaction tasks, projective methods, problem-solving techniques, and self-report instruments; Kahana, Fairchild, and Kahana (1982) evaluate measures of adaptation that are valuable in gerontology; and McDowell and Newell (1987) evaluate rating scale measures of health. The instruments presented here represent specific assessment methods and foci that would be helpful to graduate students, clinicians, and researchers seeking to address clinical issues in medical rehabilitation settings.

A variety of definitions of coping, adaptation, and adjustment have been proposed by theorists. Haan (1977) described six properties of coping mechanisms. These include behavior that is flexible and purposive, is present and future oriented, is differentiated in response, "meters" disturbing affect, and is tempered. She distinguished 10 ego mechanisms that may have a defending or coping function. The mechanism of sensitivity, for example, defined as apprehension of unexpressed feelings or thoughts of others, could be manifest in projection or empathy. As an example of her model's utility, she factor analyzed lengthy interviewer ratings on a variety of dimensions. In an adult sample, she found two coping factors (controlled coping and expressive coping) and two defense mechanisms (structured defense and primitive, anticognitive defense). Haan reported that adults who used coping efforts had larger increases in intelligence over 20 years, whereas people who used defense mechanisms had smaller increases.

Haan's perspective is complemented by that of Moos and Tsu (1977), who listed seven adaptive tasks related to physical illness. Three are illness-related (dealing with pain and incapacity; dealing with treatment; developing relationships with staff) and four are more global (preserving emotional balance, self-image, and relationships with close others and preparing for uncertainty). They also defined seven coping skills: Minimizing the seriousness of a crisis, seeking information, seeking support, learning illness-related procedures, setting specific goals, anticipating a variety of outcomes, and finding meaning. This definition is easy to operationalize for measurement purposes.

Lazarus and Folkman extend the definition of coping within the context of their cognitive–phenomenological model of stress and coping. They emphasize process rather than trait aspects, coping rather than automatic responses, efforts rather than outcomes of coping efforts, and management of stress rather than mastery. The revised Ways of Coping Questionnaire, one of the instruments reviewed here, evolved from this model.

One of the most influential theories of adaptation related to physical disability and chronic illness was outlined by Dembo, Leviton, and Wright (1956) and expanded by Wright (1960, 1983). They considered issues related to dealing with disability and illness and described the concepts of *spread* (a stereotyping tendency to ascribe negative characteristics to a person based on knowledge of disability), *value loss* (generalizing negative self-evaluations due to loss of physical attractiveness and physique), *expectancy discrepancy* (a tendency to depreciate achievements of persons with disabilities because of their disability), *new and overlapping situations* (situations that may be ambiguous and in which an able-bodied or disabled role may be appropriate), and *as-if behavior* (acting in a manner that denies the presence of a disability), among others. They provided a theoretical context that guided the development of the Acceptance of Disability scale.

Shontz (1982) took exception to the commonly used phrase *adaptation to chronic illness and disability*, because it places these experiences external to the person's body image and adopts an outsider's perspective (Dembo, 1969). It presents a normative perspective that views the task of dealing with disability in terms of the individual coming to terms with personal limitations rather than in terms of societal adaptation to individual needs. He emphasizes that adaptation is not to a condition but instead to the world in which we all live, regardless of disability. He defines the task of adaptation as coming to satisfactory and satisfying terms with the larger world. Several of the idiographic measures reviewed here incorporate the insider's perspective by assessing motivational structure (Motivational Structure Questionnaire), perceptions of adaptation (Q sort), and constructs used to define one's social and psychological world (Role Repertory Technique).

To narrow the long list of tests that could be reviewed I selected those that represent specific theoretical approaches, methods of assessment, and specific behavioral, motivational or belief domains. Two of the measures were selected because they represent important theoretical perspectives. The revised Ways of Coping Checklist (Folkman & Lazarus, 1988) represents a cognitive–phenomenological theory of stress and coping, and the Acceptance of Disability scale is derived from the school of somatopsychology (Barker, Wright, & Gonick, 1946; Dembo et al., 1956; Myerson, 1955; Wright 1960, 1983). Both idiographic (Q sort, Role Repertory Technique, and the Motivational Structure Questionnaire) and normative approaches to measurement are represented by this set of measures. Although many of the instruments are self-report, family reports are incorporated in the Katz Adjustment Scale. One instrument, the Activity Pattern Indicators, focuses on daily activities as a behavioral indicator of adaptation. Substance abuse as an indicator of adjustment is the focus of two measures (the Adaptive Skills Battery and the Motivational Structure Questionnaire). They are examples of a methodology for assessing behavioral competence in a variety of settings and the context within which substance use is related to individuals' goals.

Area of Assessment: Measures of Coping and Reaction to Disability

Acceptance of Disability Scale

The construct of disability acceptance is related to the somatopsychology school of Barker et al. (1946), Dembo et al. (1956), Myerson (1955), and Wright (1960, 1983). The construct emerged, in part, from work that examined the psychological and social adjustment of soldiers who sustained amputations and adults with congenital and acquired hearing loss. The Acceptance of Disability Scale (AD; Linkowski, 1971) is a 50-item self-report measure with a Likert response format that assesses values theorized by Dembo et al. (1956) to be associated with disability acceptance.

Beliefs about disability and the extent to which persons devalue themselves because of physical characteristics is a critical theoretical construct in understanding how people adapt psychologically to an acquired disability. Wright (1960, 1983) defines disability acceptance as a process by which a person comes to view his or her disability as nondevaluating: one's scope of values is enlarged, physique is subordinated relative to other values, disability effects are contained realistically, and one focuses on personal valuable attributes. Enlarging one's scope of values refers to the process by which individuals with disabilities come to appreciate that values apparently lost as a result of disability are only part of a person's larger value system. Such an enlargement allows a person to experience his or her life meaningfully in spite of disability-related limitations.

Wright distinguishes between comparative values and asset values, and views the latter as being crucial to disability acceptance. Developing a personal framework in which one's assets are valued rather than using socially defined, and hence comparative, values to define self-worth also accompanies disability acceptance. In time, people with disabilities recognize that they do have specific abilities, although these may have little, as such, to do with determining personal worth. Linkowski's Acceptance of Disability (AD) scale functions as a measure of self-esteem in persons with disabilities.

This instrument can be used with adults with acquired and congenital disabilities. Adolescents with at least a sixth-grade reading level are also an appropriate population. The AD scale is a self-report paper-and-pencil instrument. A 6-point Likert scale is used to indicate congruence between self-perception and each statement. Several items are scored in a reverse direction to minimize response bias. A total score is obtained by summing responses to each of the 50 items.

Psychometric Properties

Internal consistency was estimated with a split-half reliability coefficient of .86, and a full-scale reliability estimate of .96 was obtained using the Spearman-Brown Prophecy formula. Linkowski (1971) reported that a single component derived from factor analysis of all 50 items accounted for 48% to 69% of the variance of the scale. Keany and Glueckauf (1993) noted that the sample size for this analysis was relatively small (the number of cases was roughly equivalent to the number of items) and that orthogonal rotation of factors was used even though AD scale items were written so that there is not a one-to-one correspondence with value changes. Evidence for content validity was determined through expert opinion.

Construct validity was supported with a concurrent correlation of .81 with the Attitudes Toward Disabled Persons Scale (Yuker, Block, & Younng, 1970). Strong correlations with self-esteem measures were reported for teenagers (Starr & Heiserman, 1977) and college students (Linkowski & Dunn, 1974). The extent to which social desirability may influence self-ratings has not been explored.

Special Considerations, Cautions, and Applications

This scale requires about a sixth-grade level reading ability. As with all paper-and-pencil measures, the test taker must have sufficient manual dexterity to mark responses with pencil. Physical assistance in marking responses or computer administration could minimize these limitations. At 50 items, the scale requires a considerable time period for the single score that is derived. It requires about 15 minutes for most people to complete.

The theoretical foundation of this instrument makes it particularly attractive in clinical settings with a somatopsychological perspective. The use of norms allows clinicians to compare ratings across persons and across occasions. Repeated assessment over time allows the determination of adaptive changes associated with rehabilitation therapies or developmental processes. Clinicians can discuss standard scores with clients in terms of the extent to which they view their condition as nondisabling compared with similar samples. Clinicians can also explore client responses to individual items that evoke a particularly strong response as the beginning point of a discussion about disability acceptance.

The AD scale is a useful instrument for researching adaptive processes within a somatopsychology perspective. Over 62 studies have used the AD scale (cf. Boone, Roessler, & Cooper, 1978; Kaiser, Wingate, Freeman, & Chandler, 1987; Morgan & Leung, 1980). It may be less useful to researchers with other perspectives and interests; in these cases, specific measures of self-esteem, body image, or coping, for example, may be more appropriate. Although individual items assess specific value changes, the total AD score does not distinguish each of the four value changes. Further work on the value structure underlying the instrument would help extend our understanding of the instrument and value change processes more generally.

Studies Reporting Use

Disability acceptance is a central construct in many psychosocial studies. Thomas, Davis, and Hochman (1976) explored disability and demographic correlates of disability acceptance in state rehabilitation agency clients with amputations. They found that women, rehabilitants with more years of formal education, and persons with less severe disabilities reported higher levels of disability acceptance. Occupational and religious differences were also observed. Individuals with clerical and sales occupations had lower levels of disability acceptance than did people with processing occupations. Catholics, followed by Protestants and those with no religious preference, reported higher levels of disability acceptance.

Correlates of disability acceptance in adolescents attending the Kansas State School for the Deaf were explored by Heinemann and Shontz (1982). They reported that a measure of self-esteem was strongly correlated with disability acceptance; reading ability, need achievement, and a sex role measure of masculinity (but not femininity) accounted for a statistically significant proportion of variance in disability acceptance. The results are congruent with observations (Levine & Wagner, 1974) that individuals who are hearing impaired with good reading comprehension and communication skills are characterized by greater emotional maturity.

Ways of Coping Questionnaire

Research interest in coping has blossomed in recent years as evidence has mounted that how people cope with stress is important to their psychological and physical health (Cohen, 1979; Cohen & Lazarus, 1979; Lazarus & Folkman, 1984). Measures of coping have also grown, though the evidence to support their psychometric properties has lagged (Cohen, 1987). One of the most widely used measures of coping is the revised Ways of Coping Checklist (Folkman & Lazarus, 1988). It was developed from Folkman and Lazarus' cognitive–phenomenological theory of stress and coping and has been used primarily for research on coping process rather than on coping dispositions or styles. The developers selected items for the questionnaire on the basis of their ability to identify the thoughts and actions people use to cope with specific stressful situations. Folkman and Lazarus define coping as "the cognitive and behavioral efforts to manage specific external and/or internal demands appraised as taxing or exceeding the resources of the individual" (p. 2). Their definition is similar to that used by Cohen and Lazarus (1979): "efforts, both action-oriented and intrapsychic, to manage (that is, master, tolerate, reduce, minimize) environmental and internal demands, and conflicts among them, which tax or exceed a person's resource" (p. 219). The central features of these definitions emphasize coping as a process, emphasize management of stress rather than mastery, make no judgment about the quality of the coping efforts, and distinguish effortful from automatic responses.

The Ways of Coping Questionnaire evolved from the Ways of Coping Checklist, a product of the Berkeley Stress and Coping project. The original list of 67 strategies included defense efforts, such as avoidance, wishful thinking, intellectualization, isolation, and suppression, and problem-solving efforts such as seeking information, inhibiting action, and taking direct action. Respondents simply marked whether they did or did not use each strategy. The 66-item questionnaire uses a 4-point Likert scale to indicate frequency of using each strategy. Response choices are *does not apply and/or not used* (0), *used somewhat* (1), *used quite a bit* (2), and *used a great deal* (3). Some items were reworded or deleted because of redundancy or ambiguity; other items were added to assure that both problem- and emotion-focused strategies were surveyed. Researchers abandoned an early attempt to develop rationally derived scales from the questionnaire when it became clear that some strategies can serve more than one function. Several factor analyses were conducted on data from different samples; the factors derived from 75 married couples (Folkman, Lazarus, Dunkel-Schetter, DeLongis, & Gruen, 1986) were ultimately retained because they provided the largest array of individual and situational differences.

Eight coping scales are derived from the Ways of Coping Questionnaire: confrontive coping, distancing, self-controlling, seeking social support, accepting responsibility, escape–avoidance, planful problem solving, and positive reappraisal. From 4 to 8 items are summed to compute individual scales; only 50 of the 66 items are used to compute the scales. The questionnaire's manual lists the items that make up each scale along with their means, standard deviations, skewness, and factor loadings.

Studies reporting use of the questionnaire have selected adolescents and adults from a variety of cultures and nations. Individuals in a variety of health care settings have participated, including those undergoing surgery, those in rehabilitation following spinal cord injury, and individuals with cancer, coronary heart disease, and panic disorder, to name only five. No children's version is available.

The Ways of Coping Questionnaire is typically completed in a self-report format; 10 minutes is the average estimated time to complete the items. Respondents are asked to provide responses while considering one specific situation, selected for relevance to researchers' interests. An interviewer can help respondents focus on the situation and recall its details, rather than provide generalized coping strategies. The manual provides directions on how to help individuals focus on a specific situation and to provide descriptions so that coping responses are interpretable. Events during the past week or month are preferred because there is less opportunity for distortion or forgetting. Scoring is provided by computer service from the questionnaire's publisher or by written permission of the publisher for hand-scoring. Two kinds of scores are reported: relative scores and raw sums of the items that constitute each of the eight factors. Relative scores (Vitaliano, Maiuro, Russo, & Becker, 1987) are the average item score for each scale divided by the average item score across all eight scales. Relative scores reveal the extent to which individuals report strategies within each domain, considering the extent to which they use all other coping strategies. They reveal the proportion of effort within each domain. This procedure corrects for the unequal number of items across the scales.

Psychometric Properties

The internal consistency (Cronbach's alpha) of the eight coping scales ranges from .61 (six items related to distancing) to .79 (seven items related to positive reappraisal). The authors do not report test–retest reliability, arguing that these estimates are inappropriate given the process-oriented focus of the questionnaire. The stability of the questionnaire's factor structure reflects the nature of the sample reporting coping strategies. Samples of psychiatric outpatients, spouses of patients with Alzheimer's disease, medical students, and middle class residents generate factors that vary somewhat. This probably reflects their different characteristics, the situations with which they are coping, and differences in test administration. The range of item difficulty, which helps describe the useful range of a set of scores, was not found.

The consistency between theory-based predictions and research findings supports the construct validity of the Ways of Coping Questionnaire. Situations in which problem-focused coping is more likely, that is, situations perceived as more changeable, are in fact the ones in which problem-focused coping strategies are used more often. The different strategies people use as a stressful event unfolds reveal the process of coping. Folkman and Lazarus (1985) reported that college students were more likely to use problem-solving strategies before an exam, distancing after the exam, and wishful thinking, seeking social support, and self-blame after grades were received.

Special Considerations, Cautions, and Applications

Publication of the manual for the Ways of Coping Questionnaire should reduce confusion resulting from the plethora of reports based on the

Ways of Coping Checklist, variable scoring rules based on results of various factor analytic studies, and different administration procedures. Previously, the number of factors and items constituting each factor varied from study to study and resulted in inconsistent reporting of findings. Some investigators administered the items in a way that tended to pull for trait-like predispositions. Users should regard the questionnaire as one of the most useful measures of coping, but should recognize that it is still incompletely developed. The variety and number of samples for which data are available is increasing, though no widely accepted norms are available for cross-study comparisons. The authors also note the need for further test development. Specifically, they note that interpersonal items focused on action tend to be aggressive rather than assertive. The process-oriented nature of coping is not revealed within a single administration of the questionnaire; instead, sequential administration is required to identify the order of strategies.

The questionnaire was developed primarily for clinical research. However, clinicians could use the questionnaire as the basis for discussion with individuals about the strategies they have used to cope with specific situations, the outcome of these efforts, and changes in strategies they might wish to make. Sequential administrations might reveal the extent to which coping efforts change as clients progress through a stressful encounter, enhance their awareness of their changing efforts, and increase their appreciation of the consequences of their efforts. Feedback regarding the nature and consequences of their efforts could empower clients as they face similar and novel situations in the future. Further development is needed before its clinical value is established.

The Ways of Coping Questionnaire is one of the most widely used measures in research on coping. It has been used both as a measure of disposition (trait) and process. Researchers have developed a number of subscales based on factor analyses of various samples. The publication of a manual by its developers allows greater consistency in reporting of results across studies. The diverse applications of the measure reflect its utility and value. A variety of studies have examined gender and age-related differences in coping, situational and personality correlates of coping, and the relationship between psychological adjustment and coping. It has gained increased popularity in medical and rehabilitation settings as a means of understanding how to help people cope with both the acute and the enduring aspects of health problems.

Studies Reporting Use and Results

Jalowiec (1993) reviewed 57 articles published between 1980 and 1990 on stress and coping in the nursing literature, many of which used the

Ways of Coping Checklist or Questionnaire. The recurrent finding was that patients and families most often use a combination of problem- and emotion-focused strategies to deal with illness-related stress. However, the most often used strategies were not necessarily the most effective. Specific strategies—escape/avoidance, wishful thinking, and blaming others—were often associated with negative outcomes, including higher emotional distress, poor psychosocial function, and worse adjustment. Jalowiec noted a multitude of methodological problems across the studies, including small and nonrandom samples, low power to minimize Type II errors, and unmeasured confounding factors that limit the interpretability of the results.

Frank et al. (1987) examined the coping responses and psychological distress of 53 consecutive individuals admitted to a spinal cord injury rehabilitation program. The mean age of the sample was 31 years; 83% were men; and mean time since injury was 44 months, with a range from 1 month to nearly 24 years. Patients completed the Ways of Coping Questionnaire along with the Multidimensional Health Locus of Control scale, Beck's Depression Inventory, the Life Experience Survey, and the Symptom Checklist. Cluster analysis yielded two groups of patients, one of which endorsed all coping strategies more strongly, had a higher external health locus of control, and reported greater depression and subjective distress than did the second group, which reported fewer coping efforts and less depression and distress. This second group indicated a stronger feeling of responsibility for their own health and appeared to be better adjusted than people in the first, externally oriented group. Although this study did not examine the differences among problem-focused and emotionally focused coping strategies, it suggests that situational and dispositional factors may be related to coping efforts. Heinemann, Schmidt, and Semik (1994) sought to extend our understanding of postinjury coping strategies by examining relationships between preinjury drinking patterns and postinjury coping strategies and alcohol expectancies in a sample of individuals in medical rehabilitation. They interviewed a sample of 143 people with recent spinal cord injuries on three occasions: during rehabilitation hospitalization and 6 and 12 months after injury. The rate of heavy drinking decreased from 55% during the 6 months before injury to 20% 1 year after injury. Heavy drinkers before injury were more likely to be heavy drinkers after injury. Twelve months after injury, the preinjury problem drinkers were characterized by less frequent use of positive reappraisal, problem solving, and support seeking, and by greater expectancies that alcohol would reduce tension and enhance social assertiveness, mood, and sleep than were nonsymptomatic drinkers and abstainers. The strong relationships between preinjury drinking patterns and coping strategies suggest that psychologists should explore with patients the relationship between these factors so as to maximize their adaptation.

Motivational Structure Questionnaire

The Motivational Structure Questionnaire (MSQ) was designed to describe the relationships between people's pursuit of nonchemical incentives and their motivation to use drugs (Cox, Klinger, & Blount, 1993). The MSQ asks respondents to name and describe their current concerns and rate their concerns along various dimensions intended to reveal the structure of their motivation. The technique is idiographic in that respondents list their current concerns, which may be unique, and it is nomothetic in that it characterizes goals on a number of dimensions that allow comparisons across individuals. These ratings are intended to reveal the enduring stylistic aspects of drug abusers' motivational structure.

The MSQ is an integral part of a treatment model called Systematic Motivational Counseling (SMC) developed by Cox and Klinger (1988, 1990). The motivational model addresses the major issues that affect drug use. In SMC, the counselor helps patients to reevaluate inappropriate and unrealistic goals and their roles and commitments in relation to them; identify patterns of facilitation and interference among goals; resolve conflicts among interfering goals and disengage themselves from inappropriate goals; identify nonchemical sources of emotional satisfaction; find new sources of self-esteem and eliminate sources of self-condemnation; shift from a negative motivational lifestyle to a positive motivational lifestyle; develop skills for reaching realistic long-range goals and identify subgoals underlying their achievement; and formulate and practice homework assignments for reaching long-range goals and immediately gratifying activities.

The MSQ has been used primarily with adults undergoing chemical dependence treatment (Cox, Klinger, & Blount, 1991). It is applicable to adults with and without physical disabilities who have substance abuse problems. It has been used with clients receiving vocational rehabilitation services and who are in supported employment settings following moderate to severe traumatic brain injury.

The MSQ can be administered individually or in a group setting. After listing their concerns in major life areas, respondents describe each of their concerns with a verb drawn from one of 12 verb classes. The verbs are classified by their valence and goal striving (e.g., appetitive, aversive, agonistic, or epistemic) and indicate the relative strength of respondents' positive and negative motivation.

Respondents next rate each concern on 10 dimensions that include their own role in relation to the goal (i.e. the degree to which they actively participate in goal striving) and commitment. Value ratings indicate the amount of joy that they imagine experiencing if the goal was attained and the amount of sorrow that they imagine feeling if the goal could not be attained. Ambivalence is the amount of unhappiness respondents imagine feeling upon attaining each goal. Also rated are the expected probability of success in attaining each goal, the probability of success if no action is taken, time available before action must be taken on each goal, and nearness to goal attainment. Finally, respondents rate the consequences of drug use on each goal.

The clinician uses indices from these ratings to construct a profile of motivational structure. The indices pertain to the value, perceived accessibility, and imminence of the goals, as well as to commitment to the goals and the nature of desires and roles in regard to them. Psychologists have used these indices clinically to help patients change their motivational structures.

Psychometric Properties

A modified test of stability was reported by Church, Klinger, and Langenberg (1984) on a predecessor version of the MSQ. Nondrug-abusing subjects kept a daily log of their activities for a month and then took the test again. More than 80% of the concerns listed on the first MSQ were either listed the second time or omitted for obvious reasons, indicating a reasonable degree of reliability. Since some concerns changed with time, the indices should fluctuate as well. Klinger and Cox (1986) assessed the stability of the MSQ indices in 42 inpatients undergoing treatment for alcoholism by administering the MSQ during the first week of intake and again 1 month later. Treatment effects were seen not only in changed behaviors but also in current concerns. Some indices from the first administration were unrelated to second administration indices, whereas indices reflecting stylistic features of patients' goal striving were evident on both administrations.

Validity evidence for motivational patterns includes daily activities. Church et al. (1984) asked subjects to judge whether activities recorded in a diary were related to their initial MSQ concerns. During the week following MSQ administration, 81% of the activities were related to MSQ concerns, and 1 month later only 60% of the activities were related to the earlier MSQ concerns. Independent raters corroborated subjects' reports by matching descriptions of daily activities with descriptions of concerns. In another study, Roberson (1989, 1990) used a modified MSQ in an industrial setting and found that the indices predicted both work-activity patterns and work satisfaction. Other studies have demonstrated that current concerns elicited by predecessor versions of the MSQ are related to thought content (Klinger, 1978; Klinger, Barta, & Maxeiner, 1981; Klinger & Cox, 1987–1988), dream content (Hoelscher, Klinger, & Barta, 1981), and skin-conductance responses (Nikula, Klinger, & Larson-Gutman, 1993).

The predictive validity of the MSQ in a sample of patients undergoing chemical dependence treatment (Klinger & Cox; 1986) was assessed by comparing indices obtained at intake with treatment outcome. Successful outcomes were consistently related to goals and concerns favorable to treatment and with goals and concerns avoidant of alcohol. Successful patients also expected to reach their goals sooner than did unsuccessful patients. Patients who successfully completed treatment had more positive and accessible goals to pursue in contrast to unsuccessful patients, who were more ambivalent about their goals and felt that they had less to lose by drinking.

Finally, Cox, Klinger, Blount, Thaler, and Thurmond (1989) evaluated relationships among MSQ indices, Minnesota Multiphasic Personality Inventory scores, and Alcohol Use Inventory scores (Wanberg & Horn, 1987) in order to establish the indices' concurrent validity. The results supported the MSQ indices by the pattern of correlations obtained. In summary, good reliability and validity have been established for samples of adults undergoing chemical dependence treatment.

Special Considerations, Cautions, and Applications
The MSQ is designed to be used during chemical dependence treatment and to predict treatment outcome. The MSQ technique is comprehensive, leading some potential users to suspect that a substance abusing population might have difficulty completing the questionnaire. Experience has not shown this to be a problem. Although a test administrator is usually present, most patients without cognitive impairment are able to understand the instructions readily and to complete the questionnaire in the intended manner. Some patients are able to complete the questionnaire at home or on a hospital ward in their spare time. A considerable time

investment may be required to use the MSQ with persons who have cognitive impairments. Individual administration may be required to assure
that a sufficient number of nonredundant goals are identified and that
the rating structure is understood and applied correctly. Indices are being
modified as additional clinical data are collected. Clinical norms are based
on men undergoing chemical dependence treatment at Veterans Administration facilities; reference norms are based on college student samples.

An application of Systematic Motivational Counseling to a sample
of adults who sustained moderate to severe traumatic brain injury and
who are receiving vocational rehabilitation services is underway at several
midwestern sites (Cox, Heinemann, Miranti, Langley, & Ridgely, 1991).
They complete the MSQ as a prelude to their participation in a 12-week
SMC program and again after program completion; a comparison group
receiving no treatment also completes the MSQ and neuropsychological
measures. Preliminary results suggest that the procedure is effective in
eliciting concerns and in rating goals. Clients with memory, attentional,
and other cognitive impairments usually require additional time to complete the procedure. Clinicians in a variety of rehabilitation settings may
find the MSQ useful in identifying clients' goals and conflicts among goals,
which in turn could allow clients to disengage from inappropriate goals,
identify nonchemical sources of emotional satisfaction, and find new sources
of self-esteem. The interventions provided to clients who have difficulty
identifying nonchemical goals, appear ambivalent about goal attainment,
or report relatively long times to goal attainment could be targeted to
address these specific issues.

The MSQ was designed as a clinical tool; to date, its primary application has been in clinical research. Its utility in treatment outcome research is apparent given its clinical relevance.

Studies Reporting Use and Results

Klinger and Cox (1986) evaluated the motivational structure of 60 men
undergoing inpatient treatment for alcohol dependence at a state hospital.
They were evaluated on three occasions: at the beginning of treatment,
1 month later, and at discharge. The median age was 35 years, the mean
level of education was high school graduation, 93% were white, 40% were
divorced, and 37% were single. Program goals included abstinence and
successful completion of therapies. Treatment outcome was scored using
staff judgments of program success. A total of 29 indices based on MSQ
responses were computed; they included number of concerns, treatment
appetition, commitment, joy, sorrow, and time available for goal attain-

ment. Staff ratings of successful treatment completion correlated significantly with several indices; successful patients were less likely to express
concerns about avoiding alcohol, used more appetitive verbs (e.g., *to get, to
obtain, to accomplish*), and anticipated more immediate attainment of goals.
Relationships among alcohol concerns and treatment concern variables were
also examined. Patients who were concerned about approaching alcohol
were more ambivalent in their goals, whereas those who were concerned
about avoiding alcohol expected goal attainment to be less immediate. One
half of the 52 cases were regarded as having successful treatment outcome.
They were distinguished by more concerns appetitive to treatment and fewer
concerns about avoiding alcohol compared with unsuccessful patients. Successful patients also expected to reach their goals sooner than did the unsuccessful patients. These results support the importance of patients' motivational structure in treatment participation and outcome, and the MSQ as
a useful means of assessing motivational structure.

Adaptive Skills Battery

The modified Adaptive Skills Battery (ASB) is a 12-item instrument based
on a predecessor version published by Jones, Kanfer, and Lanyon (1982).
The instrument was revised by Langley (Langley & Ridgely, 1994) to
evaluate coping skillfulness in various situational categories that involve
negative emotional states; anger, frustration, and conflict; social pressure
to use; and cue-exposure to alcohol or other drugs. Langley simplified
language and presentation for use by clients with neurological impairments. Scoring criteria have been expanded to provide additional examples of responses. However, the essential structure, content, and scoring process of the original items have been retained.

The ASB is a verbal role-playing test designed for use in a skill-based
substance abuse prevention counseling model (Langley & Ridgely, 1994).
This model uses a skill acquisition sequence in which clients are first taught
to recognize specific high-risk situations related to their pre-injury lifestyle. This is followed by strategies to improve problem solving and response flexibility in each high-risk situation. The client is taught to monitor and use feedback and to apply skills automatically, with little disruption
by external influences, in a variety of contexts. Family and support group
members are taught to understand specific high-risk situations, anticipate
problems, and reinforce effective responses. This model views brain impairment and substance abuse as being closely related; each may exacerbate problems with the other. Accordingly, rehabilitation is designed

to structure an alternative lifestyle in which drinking is less central. Four stages of treatment are described in this model: Comprehensive evaluation, motivational enhancement, coping skill training, and structured generalization. In each stage, a multidisciplinary approach is adopted and behavioral techniques are taught and rehearsed, taking into account clients' neuropsychological strengths and weaknesses. Each item on the ASB describes a situation that requires a solution to a problem or some decision for appropriate action (Appendix 1). Behavior-analytic methodology (Goldfriend & D'Zurilla, 1969) was used to identify ecologically relevant problem situations for substance abusers. These situations were chosen because effective responses have a low likelihood of occurring, automatic responses are unlikely to be effective, and new learning and problem solving are required. Clients respond to each situation by anticipating and describing their real-life response. Effectiveness of responses is evaluated using scoring criteria developed with behavior analytic methods. Skillfulness in each of the four situational categories is evaluated by three items. Six situations are intrapersonal and six are interpersonal; six situations are alcohol specific and six are not alcohol specific. Specific situations are feeling worthless, being alone and feeling bored on a Saturday afternoon, being unjustly criticized by a supervisor, dealing with an insistent friend who wants to drink, dealing with unemployment, craving alcohol, and passing a familiar liquor store.

The original ASB was designed for use by adults who are alcohol dependent and do not have cognitive impairments; the revision was adapted for clients with neurological impairments, including traumatic brain injury and stroke. The instrument uses the kinds of predisability situations they are likely to have encountered. Most of the situations are likely to be relevant after injury.

The ASB manual contains detailed instructions and a practice situation. The evaluator reads each situation aloud and the clients describe their usual responses in detail. In the case of interpersonal situations, role-played responses may be elicited. Clients are encouraged to describe their thoughts, feelings, and actions. Responses are transcribed verbatim, although they can be audio taped for scoring and reliability checks. Administration time is approximately 20 minutes.

Responses are scored as *competent* (2 points), *incompetent* (0 points), or *intermediate* (1 point). General and item-specific criteria are used to determine competence. Item-specific criteria are listed to provide parameters of competence; a variety of examples of potential responses are listed. In general, a competent response is defined as one that maximizes possible positive gains in the situation for the individual while minimizing possible negative consequences. Intermediate responses may entail constructive action but fail to maximize positive gains. Incompetent responses are those that are likely to minimize potential positive gains and maximize negative consequences. "I don't know" and substance use are always scored zero.

Psychometric Properties

A high level of interrater reliability can be attained with relatively brief periods of training. Jones and Lanyon (1981) report interrater reliability of .92 on their version of the ASB. Raters achieved an agreement rate greater than 95% in a study of vocational rehabilitation clients with traumatic brain injury (Cox, Heinemann, et al., 1991). Published psychometric data are limited regarding the internal consistency of the items. Rating Scale Analysis (Wright & Stone, 1979; Wright & Masters, 1982) was used with data provided by a sample of 125 vocational rehabilitation clients to evaluate the measurement properties of the ASB using BIGSTEPS software (Wright, Linacre, & Schultz, 1989). Analysis of all 12 items revealed that although the item separation reliability was high (.93), one item, feeling bored on a weekend afternoon, fit poorly. Deletion of this item enhanced the fit of the remaining items without reducing the internal consistency of the instrument. The range of item difficulties distinguished levels of client skill level effectively. In summary, the 11 items provide an internally consistent measure of client skill, the derived measure spans a useful range of client ability levels, and the summed score can be converted to a linear measure.

Special Considerations, Cautions, and Applications

Patients with severe impairments may have trouble responding reliably to the instruments. Based on the sample of responses from clients with traumatic brain injury reported above, it appears to be valuable in distinguishing levels of skill in clients with neurologic impairment.

The ASB is intended for use in a treatment setting and in conjunction with skill-based substance abuse counseling. It may be useful in other kinds of treatment programs where behavior change is a goal. Feedback to clients about the competence of their responses and the possible consequences of incompetent responses could serve as the starting point for a discussion about risky situations and the skills needed to deal with these situations. Use of the ASB could identify specific situations in which clients are likely to have difficulty maintaining abstinence. The ASB scoring criteria could be used with additional scenarios devised for clients who have difficulty with situations not included as part of the ASB.

An application of skill-based substance abuse counseling to a rehabilitation sample is underway in a collaborative project, funded by the National Institute on Disability and Rehabilitation Research, and involving Employment Resources, Inc., and Vocational Consulting Services of Madison, Wisconsin, Advocap, Inc., of Oshkosh, Wisconsin, Curative Rehabilitation Center of Green Bay, Wisconsin, and the Rehabilitation Institute of Chicago (Cox, Heinemann, et al., 1991). Adults who have sustained moderate to severe traumatic brain injury and who are receiving supported employment services are invited to participate in a 12-week skill-based program. They complete the ASB as a prelude to their participation and again after program completion. A comparison group receiving no treatment also completes the ASB and neuropsychological measures. Preliminary results suggest that the procedure is effective in assessing skill level. Clients with memory, attentional, and other cognitive impairments usually require additional time to complete the procedure.

The ASB was designed as a clinical tool; to date, its primary application has been in clinical research. Its utility in treatment outcome research is apparent given its clinical relevance.

Studies Reporting Use and Results

Jones and Lanyon (1981) administered their ASB to 38 of 66 adults who underwent a 28-day inpatient alcohol treatment program and were available for a 1-year follow-up interview. Men composed 82% of the sample; the mean age was 46 years (range 27 to 61); 68% were married; 76% were employed. The demographic characteristics of patients who were not found for follow-up were similar. The duration and severity of alcoholism symptoms, as measured by the Alcohol Use Inventory, was similar to those of patients in other inpatient programs. The follow-up interview was modeled on Marlatt's Drinking Profile (Marlatt, 1976). At follow-up, 53% of the sample had been abstinent, 18% had binges or drinking leading to legal action, 18% demonstrated controlled drinking or a limited number of binges, and the remaining 11% had uncontrolled drinking. The proportion of variance in treatment outcome explained by usual responses to ASB situations was 30%. Best responses shared only 14% variance with treatment outcome. Of note was the observation that symptom severity at admission was unrelated to ASB responses 1 year later, suggesting that adaptive skills were acquired during or following treatment.

Jones et al. (1982) used the ASB as part of an assessment battery to compare the outcomes of patients assigned to one of three conditions: skill training, a discussion control group, and a standard alcoholism treatment program. The skill training group's focus was on dealing with potential relapse-precipitating events, tactics for specific situations, and in-group rehearsal of behaviors under the supervision of group leaders. In contrast, the discussion control group focused on the emotional aspects of problems and emotional issues that limited effective responses. The groups were comparable on demographics, symptom severity, and skill level at admission. Skill level increased significantly from admission to discharge, though skill level increased an equivalent amount in each group. Although only 46% of the sample was available at a 1-year follow-up, the skill training and discussion groups had consumed less alcohol and had fewer days intoxicated compared with the standard treatment group. The authors speculate that this sample may have required less concrete training procedures because of their relatively higher socioeconomic status. In contrast, patients from lower socioeconomic backgrounds may require and benefit from more structured skills training.

Katz Adjustment Scale

The Katz Adjustment Scale (KAS) was developed to objectively assess the adjustment and social behavior of psychiatric patients in hospital and community settings (Katz & Lyerly, 1963). Although it was originally developed to assess community adjustment of psychiatric rehabilitation clients, many of the items are relevant to the social and behavioral adaptation of persons who have sustained traumatic brain injury (TBI). Accordingly, it has gained increasing interest as a tool to evaluate the adjustment of persons sustaining TBI, particularly in light of the few standardized measures that have been developed to assess adjustment and social behavior following TBI (Prigatano, 1986; Lezak, 1987). People with TBI often have difficulty with self- and social awareness as well as impaired capacity for self-monitoring and memory deficits. These deficits impair the individual's ability to adapt to social environments following TBI and draw into question the accuracy of self-report measures of adjustment and social behavior. Therefore, observer reports are valuable in supplementing these measures. The KAS provides a combination of self- and observer reports of social adaptation that are clinically valuable.

The definition of adjustment used by the KAS developers considers mental health generally and the absence of gross signs of psychopathology specifically. The five domains considered in their definition include clinical adjustment, adequacy of social functioning, social adjustment, personal adjustment, and social behavior. The items relate closely to concepts of well-being. Reports from a close family member and from the patient are incorporated in five scores.

The KAS is intended for use by adults residing in community settings. It has gained recent interest for use with patients who have sustained traumatic brain injury.

The KAS provides separate scales for the client and for a relative's report. Written directions to be read aloud by an interviewer provide specific directions and specify the time period of interest. The directions could also be printed for relatives' use. Form R1 includes 127 items that are titled Relative's Ratings of Patient Symptoms and Social Behavior. The respondent rates each item on a 4-point scale ranging from *almost never* (1) to *almost always* (4). Form R2, Level of Performance of Socially Expected Activities, includes 16 activities related to social responsibilities, social activities, self-care, home adjustment, and community activities. The family member uses a 3-point scale that ranges from *is not doing* (1), to *is doing some* (2), to *is doing regularly* (3). Form R3, Level of Expectations, asks the family member to rate the same 16 items on a 3-point scale that ranges from *did not expect him to be doing* (1), to *expected him to be doing some* (2), to *expected him to be doing regularly* (3). The discrepancy between the sum of R2 and R3 measures satisfaction with the patient's social activities.

Form RS4, Level of Free-Time Activities, includes 23 items related to social, community, and self-improvement activities along with hobbies. A family member rates these items on a 3-point scale with points labeled *frequently* (1), *sometimes* (2), and *practically never* (3). Form R5, Level of Satisfaction with Free-Time Activities, uses the same 23 items with a 3-point scale labeled *satisfied with what he does here* (1), *would like to see him do more of this* (2), and *would like to see him do less* (3). The second and third categories define dissatisfaction; the total score reflects the sum of items with which the family member is satisfied.

For clients, Symptom Discomfort (Form S1) includes 55 items related to physical, affective, and neurotic symptoms. The client rates the items on a 4-point scale that ranges from *not at all* (1) to *always* (4). The total score is the sum of the individual items. The client also completes the following forms: Level of Performance of Socially Expected Activities (S2, identical to R2), Level of Expectations (Form S9, identical to R3), Level of Free-Time Activities (Form RS4, also completed by a relative), and

Level of Satisfaction with Free-Time Activities (S5, identical to R5). Scoring follows the same rules used for the corresponding relative scales.

Psychometric Properties

Katz and Lyerly reported estimates of internal consistency in two samples of psychiatric patients' relatives ranging from .41 to .87, with a median of .71, across 11 factor-analytically derived scores. Discriminative validity was evaluated by comparing patients judged to have good or poor community adjustment based on extensive clinical interviews. The two groups differed significantly on relative ratings in the expected manner on sums of items assessing minor and major psychiatric symptoms and interpersonal disturbance from Forms R1, R2, R3, RS4, R5, and the discrepancy between R2 and R3. Family members described better functioning patients as engaging in more socially expected and leisure activities. Patient self-reports also differed significantly on these measures.

Factor analysis of 100 family member responses for recently admitted psychiatric patients on the 127 Form R1 items resulted in 12 factors ranging in length from 3 to 24 items. A larger study of 404 relatives of patients admitted to nine hospitals with a diagnosis of schizophrenia corroborated the factor structure. Second-order factor analysis of this sample resulted in three factors: Social Obstreperousness, Acute Psychoticism, and Withdrawal Depression.

Fabiano and Goran (1992) completed a principal components analysis of Form R1 in a brain injury rehabilitation sample. Relatives of 88 clients with severe brain injury who were enrolled in a postacute rehabilitation program completed the KAS an average of 20 months after injury. Fabiano and Goran derived 10 factors with internal consistency estimates ranging from .78 to .94. Their factors reflected belligerence, apathy, social irresponsibility, and other behaviors. Neither duration of coma nor time since injury were correlated with the 10 scores.

Special Considerations, Cautions, and Applications

Respondents must be able to read at about a sixth-grade level in order to comprehend and respond reliably to the scales. McDowell and Newell (1987) criticize the age of the KAS and the lack of evidence for its reliability and validity.

The KAS has obvious clinical utility in describing client or patient functioning at admission to and discharge from a rehabilitation or treatment program. Use at follow-up could measure change in client functioning since discharge. Clinicians can identify specific areas of difficulty by the subscores. Use of KAS scores could allow rehabilitation staff to evaluate the social and behavioral adjustment of clients as reported by family members and to target interventions at behavior distressing to family members or treatment program staff.

Clinical research on patient outcomes has been a primary use of the KAS. The scores provided by this instrument can enhance studies of program effectiveness and outcome.

Studies Reporting Use and Results

Goran and Fabiano (1993) conducted an item analysis of Form R1 items and identified 79 items that contributed to the internal consistency of 10 subscales. After they removed items that detracted from scale consistency, their estimates of internal consistency ranged from .75 to .93. Correlations among these revised 10 factors were found to be moderate. Second-order factor analysis revealed two components that accounted for 62% of the variance in the first order factors. The components, Emotional Sensitivity and Physical/Intellectual Functioning, were correlated .49. These factor analyses of Form R1 suggest a number of useful behavioral dimensions; however, the measurement properties of potential subscales have not been described thoroughly. Heinemann, Baker, Schmidt, Langley, and Miranti (1994) examined the psychometric properties of Form R1 in a sample of 129 family members of individuals who had sustained TBI. The average age of the TBI sample was 34 years, and an average of 4 years had elapsed since injury. The patient sample was composed primarily of men (74%) and Caucasians (65%). All had sustained loss of consciousness of varying durations, and the mean Galveston Orientation and Amnesia Test score was 90. In the first set of analyses, the 10 subscales reported by Fabiano and Goran were subjected to Rating Scale Analysis (Wright & Masters, 1982; Wright & Stone, 1979) using BIGSTEPS software (Wright et al., 1989). Item difficulty, item separation reliability, and fit statistics were examined for each of the 10 subscales to determine the extent to which each set of items was internally consistent. Reliability estimates varied from .83 (for 7 items relating to antisocial behavior) to .96 (for 10 items relating to belligerence), with the exception of 5 items relating to apathy (reliability estimate of .52). Poorly fitting items were identified in several subscales; improved fit was obtained in the longer subscales after poorly fitting items were removed. The range of item difficulty was adequate for several of the subscales, suggesting that a useful range of behavior was being rated; however, the apathy, antisocial behavior, and paranoid ideation subscales evaluated only a narrow range of behavior.

The goal in the second set of analyses was to incorporate as many of the 75 items from Part I of Form R1, relating to interpersonal behavior, and the 52 items from Part II, pertaining to behavioral problems, as was statistically feasible into two measures. A reliability estimate of .93 was obtained from all 75 items of Part I; fit statistics revealed only 7 items that provoked idiosyncratic responses. These items assessed legal problems, intoxication, responsiveness to questions, shyness, tearfulness, and social withdrawal. Reanalysis of the remaining items after these 7 were removed still resulted in a reliability estimate of .93, but with much improved fit. The reliability estimate obtained for the 52 Part II items was .91; 5 items fit poorly, revealing idiosyncratic responses (speaks softly, speaks clearly, moves about hurriedly, moves about slowly, remembers names). Removal of these items resulted in considerable improvement in the fit statistics and an adequate measure. In summary, good measurement properties of several factor analytically derived KAS subscores were found. However, KAS users may prefer the more parsimonious index of social and behavioral adjustment provided by the two measures derived from Parts I and II of Form R1. This two-subscale version of the KAS possesses good psychometric properties and incorporates all but 15 items; in contrast, the 10-subscale version omits 45 items. The linear measures derived from KAS raw scores allow rehabilitation staff to evaluate the social and behavioral adjustment of adults with TBI as reported by family members. Construct validity of Form R1 of the KAS was explored by Baker, Schmidt, Heinemann, Ridgely, and Miranti (1994). Although several studies have reported on the utility of the KAS among people with TBI (Fordyce, Roueche, & Prigatano, 1983; Jackson, Hopewell, Glass, Ghadliali, & Warburg, 1991; Klonoff, Costa, & Snow 1986; Prigatano, 1986), no studies have specifically examined the validity of its use in this population. The factors identified by Fabiano and Goran (1992) were labeled Belligerence, Apathy, Social Irresponsibility, Orientation, Antisocial Behavior, Speech/Cognitive Dysfunction, Bizarreness, Paranoid Ideation, Verbal Expansiveness, and Emotional Sensitivity. Correlations were examined between KAS scores provided by 129 family members (mostly spouses or parents) and Symptom Checklist-90—Revised scores (SCL-90-R; Derogatis, 1983) provided by persons with TBI. The SCL-90-R is a self-report symptom checklist designed to reflect the psychological symptom patterns of psychiatric and medical patients. Scores derived from the SCL-90-R include Somatization, Obsessive–Compulsive, Interpersonal Sensitivity, Depression, Anxiety, Hostility, Phobic Anxiety, Paranoid Ideation, and Psychoticism. Seven of the nine symptom clusters on the SCL-90-R correlated significantly with the KAS factor labeled Paranoid Ideation. This KAS component includes behaviors such as ideas of reference, dread, expressed fears, and tangential thought processes. The SCL-90-R Obsessive–Compulsive score correlated significantly with a number of KAS Form R1 factors. Individuals with high Obsessive–Compulsive scores are characterized by slowness in initiating and processing information, trouble concentrating, and overly cautious behaviors. Correlated KAS Form R1 factors were Apathy (amotivational behaviors), Orientation (memory and orientation problems), Bizarreness (talks to self, lability, and strange beliefs), Emotional Sensitivity (self-critical, worries, frets), and Paranoid Ideation. In general, observable symptoms as measured by the KAS corresponded well with self-report on the SCL-90-R, whereas symptoms more difficult for people with cognitive impairments to recognize, such as interpersonal sensitivity and depression, were not correlated with KAS scores. That is, items endorsed by observers on the KAS appear to reflect common behaviors for people with TBI that were not endorsed on self-report measures because of limited self-awareness in social settings. These deficits are likely to account for the absence of a correlation among self-report and the KAS R1 dimensions of Belligerence, Antisocial Behavior, and Emotional Sensitivity.

The results of this study support the validity of the KAS and the use of both self-report and observer ratings to assess psychological adjustment and social behavior following TBI. Each source contributes valuable information that can guide treatment and enhance adaptive functioning. Observer ratings provide information on social functioning beyond an individual's awareness, whereas self-report measures provide important data on subjective psychological distress.

Activity Pattern Indicators

The Activity Pattern Indicators (APIs; Diller, Fordyce, Jacobs, & Brown, 1981) assess participation in various classes of activities, typically over a weekday and a weekend day. APIs provide a method to describe systematically an individual's pattern of daily activity in terms of the duration and location of activities, degree of functional assistance received, and degree of concurrent social interaction. Client needs as well as progress toward goals can be gleaned from a behavioral description of activities, assistance, and social interaction. The API Timeline format provides a self-report diary and an interview format. Evaluators can use software written by the instrument developers (Orazem, Brown, & Gordon, 1985) to derive the duration of each category of activities as well as summary indicators of overall frequency of activity or tempo (that is, how often a person shifts from one activity to another) and diversity of activities (the number of different activities). What the person *does do* is the focus of APIs rather than what the person is capable of doing. Estimates of social integration and physical independence are provided as well. Interviewer training materials are available from the Rehabilitation Indicators Project staff (Brown, 1985a, 1985b; Diller et al., 1981).

APIs are part of a family of tools called Rehabilitation Indicators (Diller, Fordyce, Jacobs, & Brown, 1982). The tools were developed from the efforts of a task force composed of Division 22 (Rehabilitation) members of the American Psychological Association (Brown et al., 1977). Other Rehabilitation Indicators include the Skill Indicators, which measure behavior competence, or what a person is capable of doing. Users select from over 700 specific skills within vocational, educational, recreational, family role, self-care, and other areas depending on their needs. Status Indicators provide a common language for describing employment status, transportation access, and progress toward various goals in rehabilitation. Part of the API family of instruments is an inventory of activities that can be used to catalog activities people engage in. A Delegatable Activities form is available to describe who is responsible for household and related tasks. A Special Events form is used to describe infrequent events, such as voting and opening a bank account, that serve as benchmarks in community integration. Self-report or interviews may be used to collect this information.

APIs are intended for use by rehabilitation recipients for the purpose of describing their activities, which reflect extent of independent functioning or community participation. They describe functional elements of the whole person rather than traits or part processes. Adults can provide information via self-report or through interview, and information from children can be obtained through observation or interview of caretaker. Interviewer training is accomplished by detailed printed guides and an audiotape of a standard interview. Clinical researchers use a BASIC or executable DOS program file to reduce data of individual activities to summary statistics. Interviews with working adults typically take 10 to 30 minutes per day of activities; data entry and reduction takes an equivalent amount of time. The computer program produces an ASCII text file that lists the frequency and duration of several classes of activities along with total number of activities, diversity of activities, a social interaction index, and location of activities. Appendix 2 reproduces the Timeline Diary Instructions and an example of a client's activities for a single day.

Psychometric Properties

Adequately trained interviewers can easily attain interrater reliability in coding activities, locations, social interaction, and physical assistance that exceed .95. The content validity of APIs is obvious, because they are behavior descriptions of what people actually do. Construct validity is evident in changes in activity patterns from the beginning to end of rehabilitation, and between adults (Brown, Gordon, & Ragnarsson, 1987) and children (Brown & Gordon, 1987) with and without disabilities.

Evidence for construct validity was reported by Fordyce (1978) in the correlations between API indices from 52 patients with chronic pain who were beginning an operant treatment program and their spouses. Validity evidence included a negative correlation between patient and spouse housecleaning (the more the spouse did, the less the patient did), and positive correlations between patient housecleaning and spouse household repair (evidence for sex role-related tasks), between spouse assistance of patient and number of agency home visits (reflecting severity of disability in the home), and between patient napping and spouse playing solitary games. Comparison of pre-rehabilitation APIs with 6-month follow-up APIs of patients with chronic pain revealed significant increases in household maintenance and reductions in resting and television viewing. Comparison of patients with chronic pain or stroke and their spouses also revealed expectable differences between men and women, between patients and spouses, and between the two impairment groups.

Special Considerations, Cautions, and Applications

Respondents' recall of the prior day's events is critical to the validity of APIs. Motivation to distort or minimize some activities, social desirability, and memory lapses can invalidate information. The self-report diary format is helpful when interviewing respondents to assure that they accurately recall activities rather than guess or provide a typical day's activities. It is important to assure the cooperation of respondents. Informing them of the data collection purpose and the extent of data confidentiality should enhance accurate reporting.

APIs are valuable for case management; program evaluation, administration, and planning; and research. They enable the clinician to assess the impact of rehabilitation activities on level of independence, extent of physical assistance received, and participation in social and productive activities. The clinician can also determine clients' or patients' activities at the beginning and end of treatment as well as at follow-up. Age-related developmental differences can be observed, as can differences between

groups with different impairments. Clinicians can present activity information graphically to clients to illustrate time spent in various activities
(i.e., a pie chart) or changes in activities across time (i.e., line graphs with
various lines representing different activities). Clients' awareness of how
they spend their time could allow them to examine the social consequences
of impairment and to make different choices based on their values and
goals.

Because APIs provide valuable information about rehabilitation outcome they are useful in clinical research where behavioral indicators of
time utilization, independence, social interaction, and community participation are sought. They provide a consistent format for reporting activities across respondents and interviewers.

Studies Reporting Use and Results

The impact of handicapping conditions on the activities of adults with
spinal cord injury (SCI) was explored using APIs (Brown, Gordon, & Ragnarsson, 1987). Handicapping conditions were defined as variables that
increase the negative impact of an impairment. Architectural barriers,
lack of accessible transportation, and attitudes are examples of these conditions. A matched sample of 22 men with spinal cord injuries resulting
in paraplegia and 22 men without physical disabilities were compared on
the frequency and duration of time spent in vocational activities, personal
care, household tasks, child care, recreation, socializing, and travel. Time
out of residence, concurrent talking, and activities completed without
physical assistance were also compared. The researchers controlled for
role and demographic variables by matching the cases and minimized
differences in resource adequacy by selecting men who had more than
adequate access to resources such as income and private transportation.
Consequently, any impact of handicapping conditions would be revealed.
The sample's age range was from 20 to 53 years ($M = 39$); the average
household income was about $50,000. All but one participant was mar-
ried; an average of two other persons resided with each participant. The
nondisabled group spent more time in household tasks and active recreation, while the men with SCI engaged in 20% fewer activities, primarily
activities related to personal care, household tasks, active recreation, and
travel. Men with SCI tended to spend greater time within vocational,
personal care, quiet recreation, and social activities. It may be that they
spent more time during each episode of these activities in order to minimize their energy expenditure and to minimize the impact of architectural barriers. The groups did not differ on total time spent in vocational,

inactive, personal care, child care, television, quiet recreation, social, and travel-related activities. These results reveal the complex relationship between impairment and handicap when demographic characteristics and resources are equivalent.

In another study this group of researchers (Brown & Gordon, 1987) compared the activity patterns of 239 children with and 519 without disabilities in order to evaluate developmental and impairment-related effects. All children lived at home, were enrolled in school, and spoke English. They ranged in age from 7 to 19 years. Spina bifida and cerebral palsy were the most common impairments; mental retardation was a diagnosis for one-quarter of the disability group.

Children with disabilities had a slower pace and less diverse activities, engaged in more activities in which they were dependent on someone else, and spent more time in quiet recreation and personal care compared with children without disabilities. In contrast, they spent less time in social activities, active recreation, household chores, and in activities outside their home. With the exception of dependence on others, the magnitude of these differences was minimal to moderate. Age was strongly related to activity patterns, revealing different developmental patterns for children with and without disabilities. With increasing age, children with disabilities spent more time watching television and less time in educational activities. The authors discuss their results in terms of how a "curriculum for socialization" becomes distorted for children with disabilities and how activity limitations are cumulative, resulting in a reduced sense of competence. The results reveal the rich data provided by APIs and how they can be used to examine the social consequences of impairment.

Heinemann, Goranson, Ginsburg, and Schnoll (1989) explored relationships between activity patterns during inpatient rehabilitation and predisability alcohol use in 90 persons with recent-onset spinal cord injury. Study participants reported biographic information, alcohol use, and drinking problems during the 6 months prior to injury; completed the Acceptance of Disability Scale; and were interviewed in order to describe a weekday and a weekend day using the Activity Pattern Indicators. Activities were summed in four categories: productive activities (e.g., rehabilitation, educational, and vocational), quiet time (e.g., sleeping, napping, resting, and thinking), social activities (e.g., socializing, letter writing, and making telephone calls), and quiet recreation (e.g., television viewing, reading, card playing, listening to music, smoking, drinking). In addition, three measures related to quality of life were examined: duration of activities performed without assistance (independence), the number of different kinds of activities (diversity), and the absolute frequency of activities (tempo).

The longest activity was quiet time followed by quiet recreation, social activities and productive activities (4.0 hours over 2 days). Participants spent 89% of their time in activities without physical assistance. Path analysis was used to explore the impact of drinking and drinking patterns on activity patterns. Persons who drank more before injury and who reported more family drinking problems also reported a greater number of drinking problems. Persons with more drinking problems reported spending less time in quiet activities such as sleeping and resting during rehabilitation hospitalization, but spent more time in quiet recreation (e.g., watching television and reading). Furthermore, persons who drank more before injury reported spending less time in productive activities such as rehabilitation therapies. Participants were coded as abstainers both before and during hospitalization ($N = 13$), drinkers who did not drink while hospitalized ($N = 69$), or drinkers who drank while hospitalized ($N = 10$). These groups differed in the number of activities completed independently, such that persons who stopped drinking while hospitalized performed relatively fewer activities independently than did the other two groups.

The API data are valuable in that they reveal differences between people with and without preinjury drinking problems that may affect postdischarge adaptation. People with drinking problems may not benefit as much from rehabilitation and may have a less successful transition from hospital to community. Individuals reporting drinking problems before injury and who do not avail themselves of rehabilitation services during hospitalization may be at a distinct disadvantage in adapting to disability-related and environmental limitations following this transition.

Q Sort

One of the most useful but often overlooked methods of describing personality is with a procedure first described by Stephenson in 1935. Understanding the utility of Q methodology requires that we distinguish purposes of psychological measurement. In contrast to *dimensional* procedures in which groups of people are characterized as having more or less of some attribute, *morphogenic* procedures allow us to examine intraindividual differences. Allport (1962) coined these terms to distinguish variable-centered and person-centered methods. Block (1961) helped psychologists to differentiate methods that use variables to characterize individuals and methods that focus on people to define distinguishing characteristics.

The Q methodology is one of several tools that allow a person-centered assessment approach for the study of personality development in general, and processes of adaptation such as those which may follow traumatic injury or chronic illness in particular. Block (1971) published a now classic study of personality development using the Q methodology.

Psychologists have considerable flexibility in using the Q sort with a broad range of clients because the items can be selected on the basis of relevance to a target population. Most adolescents and adults should possess the cognitive abilities to comprehend the sorting task.

The methodology common to all sets of Q items involves judges ranking items to characterize some target. Items are usually verbal statements, though they may be pictures or photographs. Judges may be the focus of study when they provide self-descriptions. Alternatively, the focus of study may be the target, which is another person or a situation. The intended distribution of the sorted items is usually defined in advance, usually in a quasinormal array. This arrangement requires that all judges make a limited number of distinctions among ties. Block (1961) described the Q-sort method of person description as a means by which judges could report their subjective impressions of a person in an objective and quantitative manner. Averages of several judges' sorts can be used to counter idiosyncratic biases and errors.

Items in Q sets are regarded as samples from a larger population of statements that are relevant in describing persons or situations. Stephenson (1953) advocated that standard item sets not be used as this would violate the purpose of the methodology This position was countered by Block (1961), who noted the pragmatic and methodologic advantages of using a standard set of items. His California Q set grew from this conviction, and is probably the most widely used set of Q items. As with the construction of any measure, item selection for a Q set requires that the domain of interest be specified, that items be written that fit within this domain, and that some means of demonstrating consensus about the categories of items exists. Desirable items are those that judges agree are characteristic and for which adequate variance is demonstrated, redundancy is minimal, and patterns of correlations are intelligible.

Psychometric Properties

Item and person reliability can be evaluated when a fully crossed (or three facet) design of Judge X Person X Item is used. Consistency across short time periods when describing a person, and between judges, when the object of rating is known well, are usually obtained.

Special Considerations, Cautions, and Applications

The shape of the item distribution determines, in part, the psychometric properties of the item set. With unlimited time and tolerance for making fine discriminations, judges could be asked to rank order each item from most to least characteristic. A more practical solution is to specify a number of categories, usually seven to nine. The number of items in a category is specified so that it approaches a quasinormal distribution such that more items are sorted into the middle categories. Such a forced distribution creates ipsative data in which each judge's item means and standard deviations are equal. Some judges may be forced to make what they regard as irrelevant distinctions between items. One consequence of ipsative data is that factor analyses of items are not possible due to singular correlation matrices. Though mathematically possible, principal component factor analysis may account for relatively little of the variance or produce unstable components unless the sample size is large (Guadagnoli & Velicer, 1988).

Clinicians can use Q sorts to describe clients who are beginning, in the process of, and approaching the end of rehabilitation or some other therapy. The clinician can have the client rank specific items, perhaps reflecting optimal adaptation, and review these directly or can compute their correlations with a sorting intended to reflect ideal adjustment. Differences between judges' perceptions can be evaluated, as well as discrepancies between client and clinician perceptions of adaptation. The set of items used can be previously published or tailored specifically to the client. The flexibility of the procedure may seem confusing at first. Users should consider whether they are interested in judges, persons, or items in tailoring the procedure to meet their needs. An interest in congruence among judges, among persons, or among items would determine the specific analysis used. Changes in item ratings across time or situations may also be of interest. The example below provides one rehabilitation-related example.

Clinical research applications parallel the examples listed above. They also include comparisons of clients by computing correlations among various sortings. The similarity among sortings provided by clients who are characterized by some external measure, such as the sort provided by successful clients, could also be of interest.

Studies Reporting Use and Results

Heinemann and Shontz (1984, 1985) developed a 48-item Q sort to describe four theoretical stages of reaction to crises described by Fink (1967).

The stages included shock, defensive retreat, acknowledgment, and adaptation. A list of 64 statements consisting of single words or short phrases was generated to illustrate each stage. Expert opinion was used to select 12 items in each category. Final items were those on which four of five judges, who were familiar with the theoretical model, agreed. Table 3.1 lists the items. As part of a representative case study of adaptation following traumatic injury, two participants, who represented extremes of favorable and unfavorable psychological adaptation, sorted the items in a quasinormal distribution to describe their typical and ideal selves at each of four episodes that characterized their course of adaptation: (a) preinjury, (b) shortly after injury onset, (c) a period of despair, and (d) a period when hope was restored. They also provided sortings to describe their current situation. The degree of congruence between these sortings was assessed by simple correlations calculated among sortings provided by each person separately. These ratings were expected to illustrate the stage of crisis adjustment through time. Sortings of two items, "depressed" and "sad," were expected to peak during the period of despair.

The first participant's sortings were consistent with the hypothesized model of adaptation. Correlations between her typical and ideal selves were most strongly opposed at Episode 3 ($r = -.72$) and were increasingly positively correlated subsequently (.44 and .95 at Episode 4 and her current rating, respectively). By comparing the ranks of the 12 items within each hypothesized stage of adaptation, it became apparent that Episode 2, shortly after injury, was when she most strongly endorsed items related to defensive retreat, Episode 3 was when she most strongly endorsed items related to acknowledgment and when suicide appeared most attractive, and Episode 4 was when she most strongly endorsed items related to adaptation.

The second participant sorted the items to provide fairly consistent correlations between typical and ideal selves across time periods (.62, .49, .75, and .63 at Episodes 2, 3, 4, and at present, respectively). These sortings were not consistent with the hypothesized stage model of adjustment in that he selected acknowledgment items as being most characteristic of himself at all episodes except the fourth; he selected adaptation items as being characteristic of himself at the fourth episode. He consistently rejected items related to shock and defensive retreat. These responses can be understood in the context of extensive interviews during which it became apparent that he had never consciously mourned any loss; instead, he quickly adopted a position of doing the best he could. This resolve was apparently shaken only once when he attempted suicide

Table 3.1

Q-Sort Items Developed to Describe Four Theoretical Stages of Reaction to Crises Described by Fink (1967)

Shock

(1) Threatened by what is happening to me
(2) Wonder if I will survive
(3) More is happening to me than I can absorb
(4) Too much is happening at once
(5) Panicked
(6) Anxious
(7) Helpless
(8) Afraid
(9) Thinking is disorganized
(10) Irrational
(11) In doubt about what's happening to me
(12) Confused about what has happened to me

Defensive Retreat

(13) Feel I am the same as I've always been
(14) Believe my current state is just temporary
(15) I'll soon be just like I was before
(16) Never think about my injury
(17) My paralysis will disappear
(18) Soon be my old self again
(19) Everything in my life is under control
(20) Relieved knowing I'll soon be well and on my feet again
(21) Indifferent to things happening about me
(22) Intend to continue my familiar way of doing things
(23) Plan to keep the goals and values I've had all my life
(24) Determined to keep on living exactly as before

Acknowledgment

(25) Wonder if I am still the same person I was before my accident
(26) No longer the person I was before my accident
(27) Worse than I was before my accident
(28) Feel of little worth
(29) The grim reality of my situation can't be avoided
(30) Often wonder what's the use of doing anything
(31) Feel the world should take care of me now
(32) Depressed
(33) Sad
(34) Bitter about what has happened to me
(35) Often ask myself why this happened to me
(36) My disability is in the forefront of my attention

continued

Table 3.1, cont

Adaptation and Change

(37) Can learn to be of value to the world
(38) A person of worth
(39) Having this disability is a valuable experience
(40) Exploring strengths and resources again
(41) I didn't choose to be disabled; but, I have a choice in what to do about it now that I am
(42) Getting to know own abilities
(43) Satisfied with the new things I'm doing
(44) Learning the satisfaction of a challenge well met
(45) Planning for the future in line with my known strengths and weaknesses
(46) New values and goals will bring satisfaction in the future
(47) Am able to cope with my new situation
(48) Know my handicaps and am learning how to deal with them

during a urinary tract infection. He saw the power to end his life with an overdose of medication as a means of regaining control when he felt hopeless and powerless.

Role Repertory Technique

Kelly's Role Repertory Test (1955) provides a method of identifying the constructs used by people in conceptualizing persons who occupy important roles in their lives. In turn, these constructs can be used to rate people in various roles, including aspects of themselves. One rehabilitation-relevant set of roles was described by Heinemann and Shontz (1984, 1985); they asked individuals who had sustained traumatic injury to define constructs based on 12 comparisons of 16 roles. These roles included one's typical and ideal selves in the present, before injury, and 1 year in the future; a best friend; mother; father; brother; sister; the most intelligent, successful, and interesting individuals known personally; a typical patient encountered while in the hospital; and a person with the same kind of disability. Congruence among the self-related roles across time revealed important information about the psychology of the participants.

This idiographic technique addresses recent concern and criticism that many studies on personality use large groups in experimental designs that span only a single session and involve deception (Carlson, 1971). Such an orthodox methodology precludes an in depth, holistic understanding of individuals, the organization and stability of personality, and the process by which goals are sought. Kelly's technique is consonant with that of Allport (1955, 1960), who advocated the development of idiographic methods so that an increasingly mechanistic view of man could be enriched with constructs that highlight uniqueness, identity, will, and other concepts emerging from a humanistic tradition (Marceil, 1977). Lewin (1935) highlighted the compatibility between general laws and individual cases; Murray (1938) proposed the term *personology* and stated that "personalities constitute the subject matter of psychology, the life history of a single man being a unit with which [psychology] has to deal" (p. 3). Others, including Angyal (1941), Bertlanffy (1975), and Murphy (1947, 1958) supported the development of methods to understand individuals, individuality, and sense of personal identity.

Kelly's technique fits well with Shontz' Representative Case Method (Shontz, 1965, 1976, 1978; Spotts & Shontz, 1980), which combines the holistic approach, characteristics of the case study, and the rigor and generalizability of group studies. The participant is viewed as an "expert consultant" who is in a unique position to understand the processes being investigated. This method is particularly attractive in studying adjustment processes following disability. For example, the extent to which general stages of adjustment are individually experienced or are instead unique processes that defy generalization can be evaluated with this method.

Appropriate populations for the Role Repertory Technique include adults and adolescents who are capable of sufficient abstract reasoning and conceptual skills to comprehend the task. Individuals who have difficulty thinking in psychological terms are likely to generate rather concrete constructs. This information, however, is helpful in characterizing their psychological organization. The set of roles and role comparisons described by Heinemann and Shontz are applicable to adolescents and adults who have sustained permanent disability resulting from traumatic injury. Their research application is described below.

Kelly's Role Repertory Technique is used to determine significant persons in each participant's life and constructs defined by these roles. Kelly's personal construct psychology views persons as "scientists" who build theories that are constantly tested, refined, and revised. This theory-building process results in the elaboration of multiple construct–contrast dimensions that are used to make sense of experience, particularly social relationships. For example, different people may act toward a person in various ways that may be construed as forming an aggressive–affectionate dimension. Similarly, different aspects of one's self can be construed as constituting dimensions through time, such as mature–immature. Dimensions of particular interest to rehabilitation psychologists are those

---

Figure 3.1

Role Comparisons

1	1	2	3
2	1	2	4
3	2	4	6
4	1	3	5
5	7	8	9
6	1	10	11
7	1	13	14
8	5	15	16
9	4	12	16
10	3	13	16
11	6	12	15
12	5	7	14

Note. Twelve constructs were generated by asking the respondent to compare the combination of three roles listed above so as to say how two of the roles are similar in a way that is different from the third role.

---

formed by self-experience through time and discrepancies between one's typical self and ideal self that are associated with impairment, disability, and handicap. Selection of role comparisons can highlight self changes occurring during mourning processes.

Heinemann and Shontz specified 16 roles applicable to persons who have sustained traumatic injury, including six self roles (usual and ideal self before injury, currently, and 1 year in the future); another person with the same disability; best friend; mother; father; brother; sister; intelligent, successful, and interesting persons; and a typical patient met during rehabilitation. Next, each person develops 12 constructs (or dimensions) by examining triads of role designators, telling how two are similar and how the third differs from them. Figure 3.1 shows the combination of roles proposed to the participants in order to generate the constructs. The first comparison was intended to identify constructs related to any self changes that occurred since injury, the second comparison to identify any anticipated self changes, the third comparison to identify changes in ideal self from before to after injury, and the fourth comparison to identify changes in typical self from before to after injury.

Roles and role comparisons were selected for study that were expected to illustrate self changes through time and similarities, or differences, with important persons in each participant's life. For example, one comparison included current typical self, mother, and father, and another comparison included current typical and ideal self and preinjury typical self. Clinicians and researchers should modify these role combinations to highlight other changes or differences.

Constructs can be written on separate cards. This allows clients to rate each role on each construct. A 7-point Likert scale, anchored with *very much like this role* ($+3$) and *not at all like this role* (-3), can facilitate rating of roles on constructs.

Psychometric Properties

Reliability is contingent on the extent to which raters seriously attend to the task and generate constructs that are personally relevant. Validity also reflects the extent to which constructs are psychologically relevant. Test–retest reliability can be computed by examining simple correlations among role ratings across occasions. For example in the study reported below, the typical self ratings provided by one participant across four situations ranged from .65 to .85, whereas those provided by another participant ranged from $-.13$ to .78. However, the negative correlations in the second case reflect the changing perception of the participant over time rather than unreliable self-ratings. Within an idiographic context, construct validity hinges primarily on the cooperation of the participant. In general, the relevance and meaningfulness of the constructs is assured by the person-focused nature of the task.

Special Considerations, Cautions, and Applications

The person-focused nature of this procedure can be regarded as both a strength and a short-coming, depending on one's purposes. The in-depth understanding of a person that the Role Repertory Technique provides may not be appropriate for some group-focused research. The time commitment required may also be a barrier for some users. However, the method's clinical applications are particularly attractive. This procedure may help clinicians quickly identify concerns and issues related to adaptation, provide an objective basis for helping people recognize the manner in which they conceptualize their experience, and suggest alternate ways of understanding their world. Though some participants may find the role rating procedure to be somewhat tedious, those who have an interest in their psychological world may find the set of constructs they generate and associations among the roles to provide an effective means of making their experience more accessible and understandable.

The clinical applications of this procedure are self-evident. It provides a structured technique that allows clients to identify constructs by which they characterize themselves and other relevant people and then to describe the extent to which constructs are relevant to themselves and others. In so doing, the subtleties and nuances of their inner worlds can be revealed, making them amenable to reconsideration and reconstruing. This procedure could serve as an entrée to self-exploration for persons who may be somewhat resistant or at a loss as to how to proceed. Clinicians should select roles that are relevant to the client and consider a variety of role contrasts to generate constructs that are meaningful. The collaborative nature of this task enhances clients' participation in counseling and curiosity about the way in which they construe their worlds.

The set of roles and contrasts specified by Heinemann and Shontz (1984, 1985) for two participants resulted in the constructs and contrasts listed in Tables 3.2 and 3.4. The constructs generated by the first participant, Deirdre, reveal greater psychological sophistication and a concern with nurturance. Her first construct, characteristic of her current typical and ideal selves but in contrast to her preinjury typical self is "interested in internal growth." This contrasts with "interested in outside world and social convention." Deirdre's current typical and ideal selves are alike by seeking integration with the universe (Construct 2) and unlike her preinjury ideal self, which sought an insular world. Her current and future ideal selves are alike in that they are open to the world and giving (Construct 3), whereas her preinjury ideal self was constricted to giving to only a few people. Deirdre decided that the fourth and fifth constructs were identical after generating them. Her typical selves in the present and future are alike in perceiving multiple levels of reality (Construct 4), whereas her best friend and father are alike in acknowledging multiple levels of reality (Construct 5). Unlike her sister, her typical self and younger brother are even-tempered and slow to anger (Construct 6). Deirdre's typical self is similar to an interesting person, a peer in a counseling program, in that they are less involved in professional interests (Construct 7) than is a successful person, a psychology professor at her undergrad-

Table 3.2

Role Repertory Test Constructs and Contrasts Generated by the First Research Participant, Deirdre

Construct	Contrast
(1) Interested in internal growth	(1) Interested in outside world and social convention
(2) Seeks integration with universe	(2) Seeks insular world
(3) Open to world and giving	(3) Constricted, giving to only a few
(4) Perceives multiple levels of reality	(4) Perceives single level of reality
(5) Acknowledges multileveled reality	(5) Acknowledges conventional Christian reality
(6) Even-tempered, slow to anger	(6) Hyper, quick-tempered
(7) Less involved in professional interests	(7) More involved in professional interests
(8) Accepting of one's disability	(8) Attempts to conceal one's disability
(9) Seeks to nurture through parenting	(9) Disinterested in parenting
(10) Feels antipathy towards organizations	(10) Prefers organizations in achieving goals
(11) Achieved integration of professional and personal interests	(11) Emphasizes professional interests
(12) No-holds-barred nurturance	(12) Strings-attached nurturance
(13) Copes well with adversity	
(14) Acknowledges limitations and lives life to the fullest	
(15) Values physical achievement and skill	
(16) Values physique and physical attractiveness	
(17) Compares self with others	
(18) Values self because of intrinsic assets or characteristics	
(19) Experiences emotions intensely	

uate university. Deirdre's typical self in the future and a middle-aged man who broke his neck about 20 years ago are alike in accepting their disabilities (Construct 8), unlike a recently injured, typical patient at the rehabilitation center. Seeking to nurture through parenting (Construct 9) is characteristic of Deirdre's ideal self preinjury and an intelligent person, a psychotherapist, but unlike a man with quadriplegia. Deirdre's typical, preinjury self and a successful person are alike in feeling antipathy toward organizations (Construct 10), unlike the man with quadriplegia. Achieving integration of professional and personal interests (Construct 11) is characteristic of her future ideal self and an intelligent person, but unlike a typical patient. Finally, her typical self in the future and her best friend are characterized by no-holds-barred nurturance, unlike an interesting person (Construct 12).

Table 3.3

Principal Components Factor Analysis of Deirdre's Construct Ratings With Item Loadings of .50 or Greater for the Five Factors With Eigenvalues Greater Than 1.0

Factor	Eigen-value	Roles	Factor Load-ings	Characteristic Constructs
I	5.578	(1) current typical self	.788	Perceives multiple levels of reality
		(2) current ideal self	.952	Even-tempered
		(5) future typical self	.788	Copes well with adversity
		(6) future ideal self	.952	Values self because of intrinsic assets
		(12) intelligent person	.868	
		(13) successful person	.685	
II	3.138	(3) preinjury typical self	.595	Seeks insular world
		(4) preinjury ideal self	.551	Perceives single level of reality
		(10) brother	.864	Values physical achievement
		(15) typical patient	.948	
		(16) person with same disability	.698	
III	2.730	(4) preinjury ideal self	.559	Seeks to nurture through parenting
		(8) mother	.878	Experiences emotion intensely
IV	1.651	(9) father	.694	Compares self with others
		(11) sister	.927	Involved in professional interests
		(14) interesting person	.579	
V	1.014	(7) boyfriend	.844	Nurtures with no-holds-barred
				Open to the world and giving

Principal components factor analysis of Deirdre's construct ratings revealed the structure of correlations among the roles. Table 3.3 shows that five factors with eigenvalues greater than 1.0 emerged. The first factor included her current and future typical and ideal selves along with the intelligent and successful person. These roles were alike in perceiving multiple levels of reality, being even-tempered, coping well with adversity, and valuing self because of intrinsic assets. Her preinjury typical and ideal selves constitute the second factor along with her brother, a typical patient, and a person with quadriplegia in seeking an insular world, perceiving a single level of reality, and valuing physical achievement. This analysis provides a clear distinction between who she is (accepting of disability and coping effectively) and who she was (insular, conventional). The constructs generated by Craig, the second participant, reveal interests in specific persons or activities including children, outdoor recreation, music, and science and a concern with physical function, achievement, and competence (Table 3.4). Notably, physical activity is associated with success and happiness. His first construct, characteristic of his current ideal self and typical preinjury self but which contrasts with his current typical self is "physically capable and successful." His preinjury and current ideal selves are alike by being successful in achieving goals and happy (Construct 2), in contrast with his current typical self. His current and future ideal selves are alike by being happy and interested in work while recognizing physical limitations (Construct 3), in contrast with his ideal self before injury. Being less happy and less physically capable (Construct 4) are characteristic of his current and future typical selves, unlike his typical self preinjury. His parents are alike in that they like children (Construct 5), unlike his best friend and attendant.

Outdoor interests (Construct 6) are shared by his current typical self and his brother, but contrast with his sister's social interests. An interesting person, Craig's former room mate who has a masters degree in music, is like his current typical self by possessing an interest in playing a musical instrument (Construct 7). His department chairman, the successful person, has no such interest. Intellectual interests (Construct 8) are shared by his future typical self and a person with quadriplegia. Having physical interests contrasts with this construct and describes the typical patient, a laborer who is married with children. His ideal self before injury and an intelligent person, the former president of his hang-gliding club, share scientific and engineering interests (Construct 9), unlike the person with quadriplegia who has interests in psychology and the humanities. Having science interests plus physical ability (Construct 10) characterizes Craig's typical self preinjury and the successful person, unlike the person with quadriplegia. Being intelligent and competent (Construct 11) describes Craig's future ideal self and an intelligent person, but is unlike the typical patient. His future typical self and an interesting person perceive humor in many situations, unlike his best friend and attendant (Construct 12).

Table 3.4

Role Repertory Test Constructs and Contrasts Generated by the Second Research Participant, Craig

Construct	Contrast
(1) Physically capable and successful	(1) Less physically capable
(2) Successful in achieving goals and happy	(2) Less successful and less happy
(3) Happy and interested in work while recognizing physical limitations	(3) Less bound by physical limits
(4) Less happy and less physically capable	(4) Happier and more physically capable
(5) Likes children	(5) Not interested in parenting
(6) Outdoor interests	(6) Social interests
(7) Possesses interests in playing musical instrument	(7) No interest in playing musical instruments
(8) Intellectual interests	(8) Physical interests
(9) Scientific/engineering interests	(9) Psychology/humanities interests
(10) Science interests and physical ability	(10) Social science interests and low physical ability
(11) Intelligence and competence	(11) Inactive, not applying self in few situations
(12) Perceives humor in many situations	(12) Perceives humor in few situations
(13) Copes well with adversity	
(14) Acknowledges limitations and lives life to the fullest	
(15) Values physical achievement and skill	
(16) Values physique and physical attractiveness	
(17) Compares self with other	
(18) Values self because of intrinsic assets or characteristics	
(19) Experiences emotion intensely	

Principal components factor analysis of Craig's construct ratings (Table 3.5) shows that four factors with eigenvalues greater than 1.0 emerged. The first factor included his preinjury, current, and future ideal selves along with his mother, sister, and an interesting person. They share characteristics of being happy and interested in work, possessing outdoor and intellectual interests, and competence. His preinjury typical self along with his best friend, brother, and the intelligent and successful persons are alike by being physically able, interested in science, and coping well with adversity. His current and future typical self constitute the third factor—they are alike in sharing interests in outdoor activities, music,

Table 3.5

Principal Components Factor Analysis of Craig's Construct Ratings with Item Loadings of .50 or Greater for the Four Factors Which had Eigenvalues Greater than 1.0

Factor	Eigen-value	Roles	Factor Load-ings	Characteristic Constructs
I	6.106	(2) current ideal self	.831	Happy and interested in work
		(4) preinjury ideal self	.766	Possesses outdoor and intellectual interests
		(6) future ideal self	.831	Intelligent; competent
		(8) mother	.905	
		(11) sister	.593	
		(14) interesting person	.742	
II	2.400	(3) preinjury typical self	.639	Physically able
		(7) best friend	.521	Interested in science
		(10) brother	.757	Copes well with adver-sity
		(12) intelligent person	.963	
		(13) successful person	.586	
III	1.903	(1) current typical self	.940	Interests in outdoors, music performance, science and engi-neering
		(5) future typical self	.896	
IV	1.527	(9) father	.689	Likes children
		(15) typical patient	.707	Perceives humor in many situations

science, and engineering. The consistency in his ideal selves across time is striking: The person he wants to be is unchanged in spite of disability. His interests in nature, music, and science are expected to continue in the future; however, it is a loss of physical ability that defines who he was in the past and is now and will be in the future. This analysis provides a clear distinction between who he wants to be, and who he was, is, and expects to be. It provides a different solution to the imposition of disability than is demonstrated by Deirdre.

Studies Reporting Use and Results

Application of the Role Repertory Technique to understanding the psychological impact of functional neuromuscular stimulation (FNS) on persons with spinal cord injury was reported by Heinemann and associates (Baker, Heinemann, Yarkony, & Jaeger, 1989; Heinemann, 1983; Heinemann, & Baker, 1990; Heinemann, Geist, & Magiera, 1983; Heinemann, Magiera-Planey, Gimenes, & Geist, 1985). Participants in a biomedical engineering project that investigated mechanisms of achieving stance and ambulation underwent psychological testing as part of the research protocol. The Role Repertory Technique was used to generate constructs at recruitment to the study and then at 6-month intervals over several years. Baker and Heinemann reported the results of two psychological assessments, conducted 6 months apart, of persons with spinal cord injuries who were participating in functional neuromuscular stimulation research to achieve stance. The purpose was to assess the effects of FNS on psychological well-being. Case reports were summarized for 6 individuals, three of whom completed psychological assessments before beginning FNS participation. Stimulation did not appear to cause negative effects, per se, though persons who were able to stand successfully appeared to have lower levels of well-being prior to an initial assessment and at follow-up. Successful research participation may have allowed participants to avoid a grieving process, whereas participants with less successful research involvement enhanced their sense of well-being by coming to view their condition in less disabling terms. The impact of electrical stimulation-induced stance and ambulation varied across individuals in ways that reflected the kind of person-specific adaptation that was attained after injury and before research participation.

Comparisons of Tests

Relative Efficacy

The instruments described in this chapter are effective means of evaluating specific domains with a specific method. The tests were not selected because of their relative efficacy, but because of their diversity in procedures, issues, and approaches. Their utility and efficacy for specific purposes must be judged by potential users. Depending on one's purpose, idiographic or normative approaches may be more appropriate. Relevance to one's clinical or research purpose must also be considered. Direct descriptions of behavior, such as those provided by the API; family reports of adjustment, as provided by a family member on the KAS; or self-report measures of coping or disability acceptance may be most suited to a given purpose.

Additional Considerations in Selecting Test Instruments

Clinical researchers should not only consider the domain of adaptation, but also be clear whether it is their intent to focus on the perspective of the person, the family, the environment, or the interaction between person and environment when selecting measures. Dembo's distinction between insider and outsider perspectives is important to consider when selecting measures. The idiographic measures presented here provide an opportunity to describe the insider's perspective in terms that are relevant to clinical activities. Family members' perspectives can be captured with the Katz Adjustment Scale, and they can be compared to the client's report when it is completed as a self-report measure. Feedback regarding the instruments' scores can also provide an opportunity to discuss with patients or clients their strengths and limitations and their perspective on their situation and to explore psychological issues that may serve as barriers to rehabilitation participation.

Pragmatic concerns include the time needed to train users to a sufficient level of reliability and to administer, score, and interpret the instrument. Several of the instruments, such as the MSQ and the API, require a considerable time investment. Although I believe the benefits provided by the information are worth the investment, it is important to anticipate the time needed to train staff, conduct the evaluation, score the protocol, and interpret the information. For normative measures, the availability and relevance of published norms is an important consideration. Although norms for the Ways of Coping Questionnaire, the Acceptance of Disability Scale, and the Motivational Structure Questionnaire are available, their relevance to the user's case or sample must be considered.

The theoretical constructs underlying the instrument are important to consider as well as the context within which measurement results will be used. Rehabilitation programs with a behavioral focus may find the Activity Pattern Indicators to be useful in characterizing tempo and pace of daily activities while being less concerned with a somatopsychological concept such as disability acceptance. Practitioners and researchers who employ a cognitive–phenomenological framework may find the Ways of Coping Questionnaire to be useful, whereas programs that emphasize skill development would find the Adaptive Skills Battery to be valuable. Finally, a treatment context providing substance abuse prevention or treatment services certainly could consider the Motivational Structure Questionnaire and the Adaptive Skills Battery, whereas settings in which longer term adjustment processes are a concern could find the Q sort or Role Repertory Technique to be valuable.

The adequacy of the rating scale measures' psychometric properties is an important consideration. Few of the rating scales described here have been subjected to contemporary Rasch analysis; this analysis provides information about item difficulty and fit and person ability and fit to the measurement model. Examples of rating scale analysis were given for the Adaptive Skills Battery and the Katz Adjustment Scale to illustrate the wealth of information provided by this analytic approach. In general, the limitations of factor analysis as a means of exploring the structure of rating scale items, their applicability to a sample, and of generating subscale scores are insufficiently recognized by measure developers. The absence of suitable and relevant norms may also limit the utility of the measures for some purposes. Future research directions are obvious. Rating scale developers should rely less on factor analysis: this method does not describe the range of ability measured nor the extent to which a set of items form a coherent measure.

Conclusion

Psychologists have a wealth of instruments to consider for clinical and research purposes in medical and rehabilitation settings. The instruments selected for review here are intended to help readers evaluate innovative methods that extend beyond the usual self-report measures. Frequently used normative measures of cognitive function and personality certainly have their place in medical and rehabilitation settings, and clinician familiarity and comfort with instruments are important considerations in their selection. The rarely considered methodological options for assessment described in this chapter can enrich our understanding of clients and the settings in which they live, engage them as active participants in rehabilitation, and enhance the outcomes of our work with them. This chapter will have met its goal if psychologists and other professionals in medical and rehabilitation settings consider and adopt instruments such as these that draw on a diverse and rich tradition of idiographic and normative measures and focus on specific realms of psychological and social functioning. The investment of time and effort needed to develop expertise in the use of these instruments will be rewarded with a more finely honed appreciation for psychological constructs salient to a variety of clients in different clinical and rehabilitation settings.

References

Allport, G. (1955). *Becoming: Basic considerations for a psychology of personality.* New Haven, CT: Yale University Press.

Allport, G. (1960). *Personality and social encounter.* Boston: Beacon Press.

Allport, G. (1962). The general and the unique in psychological science. *Journal of Personality, 30,* 405–442.

Angyal, A. (1941). *Foundations for a science personality.* New York: Oxford University Press.

Baker, K. A., Schmidt, M. F., Heinemann, A. W., Ridgely J., & Miranti, S. V. (1994). *The validity of the Katz Adjustment Scale in a Post-TBI Sample.* Paper submitted for presentation consideration at the 1994 American Psychological Association convention.

Baker, R. C., Heinemann, A. W., Yarkony, G., Jaeger, R. (1989, August). *Psychological effects of functional electrical stimulation for stance and ambulation.* Paper presented at the annual convention of the American Psychological Association, New Orleans.

Barker, R., Wright, B., & Gonick, M. (1946). *Adjustment to physical handicaps and illness: A survey of the social psychology of physique and disability.* New York: Social Science Research Council.

Bertalanffy, L. (1975). *Perspectives on general system theory: Scientific-philosophical studies.* New York: George Braziller.

Block, J. (1961). *The Q-sort method in personality assessment and psychiatric research.* Springfield, IL: Charles C Thomas.

Block, J. (1971). *Lives through time.,* Berkeley, CA: Bancroft Book.

Boone, S. E., Roessler, R. T., & Cooper, P. G. (1978). Hope and manifest anxiety: Motivational dynamics of acceptance of disability. *Journal of Counseling Psychology, 25,* 551–556.

Brown, M. (1985a). *Activity pattern indicators timeline diary coding manual.* New York: New York University Medical Center.

Brown, M. (1985b). *Activity pattern indicators timeline diary reviewing manual.* New York: New York University Medical Center.

Brown, M., & Gordon, W. A. (1987). Impact of impairment on activity patterns of children. *Archives of Physical Medicine and Rehabilitation, 68,* 828–832.

Brown, M., & Gordon, W. A., & Ragnarsson, K. (1987). Unhandicapping the disabled: What is possible? *Archives of Physical Medicine and Rehabilitation, 68,* 206–209.

Brown, M., Diller, L., Fordyce, W., Jacobs, D., Barry, J., Gordon, W., Mayer, J. (1977, October). *Accountability: Definitions, problems and the response of Rehabilitation Indicators.* Paper presented at the annual meeting of the National Rehabilitation Association, Washington, D.C.

Carlson, R. (1971). Where is the person in personality research? *Psychology Bulletin, 75,* 203–291.

Church, A.T., Klinger, E., & Langenberger, C. (1984). Combined idiographic and nomothetic assessment of the current concerns motivational construct: Reliability & validity of the interview questionnaire. Unpublished manuscript cited in Klinger, E. (1987). *Advances in Personality Assessment, 6,* 31–48.

Cohen, F. (1979). Personality, stress and the development of physical illness. In G. C. Stone, F. Cohen, N. E. Adler, and Associates (Eds.), *Health psychology—A handbook: theories, applications, and challenges of a psychological approach to the health care system* (pp. 77–111). San Francisco: Jossey-Bass.

Cohen F. (1987). Measurement of coping. In S. V. Kasl & C. L. Cooper (Eds.), *Stress and health: Issues in research methodology* (pp. 283–305). New York: Wiley.

Cohen, F., & Lazarus, R. S. (1979). Coping with the stresses of illness. In G. C. Stone, F. Cohen, N. E. Adler, and Associates (Eds.), *Health psychology—A handbook: Theories, applications, and challenges of a psychological approach to the health care system* (pp. 217–254). San Francisco: Jossey-Bass.

Cox, W. M., Heinemann, A. W., Miranti, S. V., Langley, M., & Ridgely, M. (1991). *Substance abuse as a barrier to employment following traumatic brain injury.* Demonstration grant funded by the National Institute on Disability and Rehabilitation Research. Rehabilitation Research Foundation.

Cox, W. M., & Klinger, E. (1988). A motivational model of alcohol use. *Journal of Abnormal Psychology, 97,* 168–180.

Cox, W. M., & Klinger, E. (1990). Incentive motivation, affective change and alcohol use: A model. In W. M. Cox (Ed.), *Why people drink: Parameters of alcohol as a reinforcer.* New York: Gardener Press.

Cox, W. M., Klinger, E., & Blount, J. P. (1991). Alcohol use and goal hierarchies: Systematic motivation counseling for alcoholics. In W. R. Miller & S. Rollnick (Eds.), *Motivational interviewing: Preparing people for change* (pp. 260–271). New York: Guilford Press.

Cox, W. M., Klinger, E., & Blount, J. P. (1993). *Systematic motivational counseling: A treatment manual.* (Available from the first author at Psychology Service, 116B, North Chicago Veterans Administration Medical Center, 3001 Green Bay Road, North Chicago, Illinois 60064).

Cox, W. M., Klinger, E., Blount, J. P., Thaler, D., & Thurmond, B. (1989, August). Concurrent validity of the Motivational Structure Questionnaire for Alcoholics. Paper presented at the Annual Convention of the American Psychological Association, New Orleans.

Dembo, T. (1969). Rehabilitation psychology and its immediate future: A problem of utilization of psychological knowledge. *Rehabilitation Psychology, 16,* 63–72.

Dembo, T., Leviton, G., & Wright, B. A. (1956). Adjustment to misfortune—A problem of social psychological rehabilitation. *Artificial Limbs, 3,* 4–62.

Derogatis, L. R. (1983). Symptom Checklist-90—Revised Manual. Towson, MD: Clinical Psychometric Research.

Diller, L., Fordyce, W., Jacobs, D., & Brown, M. (1981). *Activity pattern indicators timeline training manual.* New York: New York University Medical Center.

Diller, L., Fordyce, W., Jacobs, D., & Brown, M. (1982). *Decision-making guidelines for potential users of RI's.* New York: New York University Medical Center.

Fabiano, R. J., & Goran, D. A. (1992). A principal component analysis of the Katz Adjustment Scale in a traumatic brain injury rehabilitation sample. *Rehabilitation Psychology, 37,* 75–85.

Fink, S. L. (1967). Crisis and motivation: A theoretical model. *Archives of Physical Medicine, & Rehabilitation, 48,* 592–597.

Folkman, S., & Lazarus R. S. (1985). If it changes it must be a process: Study of emotion and coping during three stages of a college examination. *Journal of Personality and Social Psychology, 48*(1), 150–170,

Folkman, S., & Lazarus, R. S. (1988). *Manual for the Ways of Coping Questionnaire.* Palo Alto: Consulting Psychologists Press.

Folkman, S., Lazarus, R. S., Dunkel-Schetter, C., DeLongis, A., & Gruen, R. J. (1986). The dynamics of a stressful encounter: Cognitive appraisal, coping, and encounter outcomes. *Journal of Personality and Social Psychology, 50,* 992–1003.

Fordyce, W. E. (1978, August). *Application of RI's to pain and stroke patients and spouses.* Paper presented at the annual meeting of the American Psychological Association, Toronto, Ontario, Canada.

Fordyce, D. J., Roueche, J. R., & Prigatano, G. P. (1983). Enhanced emotional reactions in chronic head trauma patients. *Journal of Neurology, Neurosurgery, and Psychiatry, 46,* 620–624.

Frank, R. G., Umlauf, R. L., Wonderlich, S. A., Askanazi, G. S., Buckelew, S. P., & Elliott, T. R. (1987). Differences in coping styles among persons with spinal cord injury: A cluster analytic approach. *Journal of Consulting and Clinical Psychology, 55,* 727–731.

Goran, D. A., & Fabiano, R. J. (1993). The scaling of the Katz Adjustment Scale in a traumatic brain injury rehabilitation sample. *Brain Injury, 7,* 219–229.

Guadagnoli, E., & Velicer, W. F. (1988). Relation of sample size to the stability of component patterns. *Psychological Bulletin, 103,* 265–275.

Goldfriend, M. R., & D'Zurilla, T. J. (1969). A behavior analytic model for assessing competence. In C. D. Spielberger (Ed.), *Current topics in clinical and community psychology* (Vol. 1, pp. 151–196). New York: Academic Press.

Haan, N. (1977). *Coping and defending: Processes of self-environment organization.* New York: Academic Press.

Heinemann, A. (1983, May). *Psychosocial aspects of functional electrical stimulation research participation.* Paper presented at the Illinois Rehabilitation Association annual meeting, Rockford, Illinois.

Heinemann, A. W., & Baker, R. (1990, April). *Functional electrical stimulation: A model for integrating nomothetic and idiographic data in behavioral medicine research.* Paper presented at the Society of Behavioral Medicine annual meeting, Chicago, Illinois.

Heinemann, A. W., Baker, K. A., Schmidt, M. F., Langley, M., & Miranti, S. V. (1994, August). *Measurement properties of the Katz Adjustment Scale in a Post-TBI Sample.* Paper presented at the American Psychological Association convention, Los Angeles, CA.

Heinemann, A. W., Geist, C., & Magiera, R. (1983, August). *Psychosocial issues in medical engineering: Functional electrical stimulation and paraplegia.* Paper presented at the National Rehabilitation Association annual meeting, Boston.

Heinemann, A. W., Goranson, N., Ginsburg, K., & Schnoll, S. (1989). Alcohol use and activity patterns following spinal cord injury. *Rehabilitation Psychology, 34,* 191–206.

Heinemann, A. W., Magiera-Planey, R., Gimenes, G., & Geist, C. (1985). Evaluating the special needs of functional neuromuscular stimulation research participants. *Journal of Medical Engineering and Technology, 9,* 167–173.

Heinemann, A. W., Schmidt, M. F., & Semik, P. (in press). *Drinking after spinal cord injury: Effect on preinjury drinking expectancies and coping.*

Heinemann, A.W., & Shontz, F. (1982). Acceptance of disability, self-esteem and sex role identity in deaf adolescents. *Rehabilitation Counseling Bulletin, 25,* 197–203.

Heinemann, A. W., & Shontz, F. (1984). Adjustment following disability: Representative cases, *Rehabilitation Counseling Bulletin, 28,* 3–14.

Heinemann, A. W., & Shontz, F. C. (1985). Methods of studying persons. *The Counseling Psychologist, 13*(1), 111–125.

Hoelscher, T. J., Klinger, E., & Barta, S. G. (1981). Incorporation of concern- and non-concern-related verbal stimuli into dream content. *Journal of Abnormal Psychology, 49,* 88–91.

Jackson, H. F., Hopewell, C. A., Glass, C. A., Ghadliali, E., & Warburg, R. (1991, March). *The Katz Adjustment Scale: Modification for use with victims of traumatic brain injury and spinal cord injury.* Paper presented at the International Brain Injury Symposium, New Orleans.

Jalowiec, A. (1993). Coping with illness: Synthesis and critique of the nursing coping literature from 1980–1990. In J. S. Barnfather, & B. L. Lyon (Eds.), *Stress and coping: State of the science and implications for nursing theory, research and practice.* Indianapolis, IN: Center Nursing Press of Sigma Theta Tau International.

Jones, S. L., & Lanyon, R. I. (1981). Relationship between adaptive skills and outcome of alcoholism treatment. *Journal of Studies on Alcohol, 42,* 521–525.

Jones, S. L., Kanfer, R., & Lanyon, R. I. (1982). Skills training with alcoholics: A clinical extension. *Addictive Behaviors, 7,* 285–290.

Kahana, E., Fairchild, T., & Kahana, B. (1982). Adaptation. In D. J. Mangen & W. A. Peterson (Eds.), Research instruments in social gerontology: Clinical and social psychology (Vol. 1, pp. 145–194). Minneapolis: University of Minnesota Press.

Kaiser, S. B., Wingate, S. B., Freeman, C. M., & Chandler, J. L. (1987). Acceptance of physical disability and attitudes toward personal appearance. *Rehabilitation Psychology, 32,* 51–58.

Katz, M. M., & Lyerly, S. B. (1963). Methods for measuring adjustment and social behavior in the community. I: Rationale, description, discriminative validity and scale development. *Psychological Reports, 13,* 503–535.

Keany, C. M-H., & Glueckauf, R. L. (1993). Disability and value change: An overview and reanalysis of acceptance of loss theory. *Rehabilitation Psychology, 38,* 199–210.

Kelly, G. (1955). *A theory of personality: The psychology of personal constructs.* New York: Norton.

Klinger, E. (1978). Dimensions of thought and imagery in normal waking states. *Journal of Altered States of Consciousness, 4,* 97–113.

Klinger, E., Barta, S. G., & Maxeiner, M. E. (1981). Current concerns: Assessing therapeutically relevant motivation. In P. C. Kendall & S. D. Hollon (Eds.), *Assessment strategies for cognitive–behavioral interventions.* New York: Academic Press.

Klinger, E., & Cox, W. M. (1986). Motivational predictors of alcoholics' responses to inpatient treatment. *Advances in Alcohol and Substance Abuse, 6,* 35–44.

Klinger, E., & Cox, W. M. (1987–88). Dimensions of thought flow in everyday life. *Imagination, Cognition and Personality, 7,* 105–128.

Klonoff, P. S., Costa, L. D., & Snow, W. G. (1986). Predictors and indicators of quality of life in patients with closed-head injury. *Journal of Clinical and Experimental Neuropsychology, 8,* 469–485.

Langley, M. J., & Ridgely, M. P. (1994). *Skill-based substance abuse prevention counseling: Behavioral interventions for clients with neurological disabilities.* (Available from the first author at Midwest Neurological Rehabilitation Center, 1710 Sharp Road, Waterford, Wisconsin 53185).

Lazarus, R. S., & Folkman, W. (1984). *Stress, appraisal and coping.* New York: Springer.

Levine, E. S., & Wagner, E. E. (1974). Personality patterns among the deaf. *Perceptual and Motor Skills, 39,* 1167–1236.

Lewin, K. (1935). *A dynamic theory of personality: Selected papers.* New York: McGraw-Hill.

Lezak, M. D. (1987). Relationships between personality disorders, social disturbances, and physical disability following traumatic brain injury. *Journal of Head Trauma Rehabilitation, 2,* 57–69.

Linkowski, D. (1971). A scale to measure acceptance of disability. *Rehabilitation Counseling Bulletin, 14,* 236–244.

Linkowski, D. C., & Dunn, M. A. (1974). Self-concept and acceptance of disability. *Rehabilitation Counseling Bulletin, 18,* 28–32.

Marceil, J. (1977). Implicit dimensions of idiography and nomothesis: A reformulation. *American Psychologist, 32,* 1046–1055.

Marlatt, G. A. (1976). The drinking profile: A questionnaire for the behavioral assessment of alcoholism. In E. J. Mash & L. G. Terdal (Eds.), *Behavior-therapy assessment: Diagnosis, design and evaluation* (pp. 121–137). New York: Springer.

McDowell, I., & Newell, C. (1987). *Measuring health: A guide to rating scales and questionnaires.* New York: Oxford University Press.

Moos, R. H. (1974). Psychological techniques in the assessment of adaptive behavior. In G. V. Coelho, D. A. Hamburg, & J. E. Adams (Eds.), *Coping and adaptation* (pp. 334–399). New York: Basic Books.

Morgan, B., & Leung, P. (1980). Effects of assertion training on acceptance of disability by physically disabled college students. *Journal of Counseling Psychology, 27,* 209–212.

Moos, R. H., & Tsu, V. D. (1977). The crisis of physical illness: An overview. In R. H. Moos (Ed.), *Coping with physical illness* (pp. 1–22). New York: Plenum.

Murphy, G. (1947). *Personality: A biosocial approach to origins and structure.* New York: Basic Books.

Murphy, G. (1958). *Human potentialities.* New York: Basic Books.

Murray, H. (1938). *Explorations in personality.* New York: Oxford University Press.

Myerson, L. (1955). Somatopsychology of physical disability. In W. M. Cruickshank (Ed.), *Psychology of exceptional children and youth* (pp. 1–60). Englewood Cliffs, NJ: Prentice-Hall.

Nikula, R., Klinger, E., & Larson-Gutman, M. K. (1993). Current concerns and electrodermal reactivity: Responses to words and thoughts. *Journal of Personality, 61,* 63–84.

Orazem, J., Brown, M., & Gordon, W. A. (1985). *Activity pattern indicators timeline diary data entry and reduction program.* New York: New York University Medical Center.

Prigatano, G. P. (1986). *Neuropsychological rehabilitation after brain injury.* Baltimore, MD: Johns Hopkins University Press.

Roberson, L. (1989). Assessing personal work goals in the organization setting: Development and evaluation of the Work Concerns Inventory. *Organizational Behavior and Human Decision Processes, 44,* 345–367.

Roberson, L. (1990). Prediction of job satisfaction from characteristics of personal work goals. *Journal of Organizational Behavior, 11,* 29–41.

Shontz, F. (1965). *Research methods in personality.* New York: Appleton-Century-Crofts.

Shontz, F. (1976). Single organism versus conventional research. In P. Bentler, D. Lettier, & G. Austin (Eds.), *Data analysis strategies and designs for substance abuse research.* Washington, DC: National Institute of Drug Abuse.

Shontz, F. (1978). Single organism research and the representative case method. In D. Lettieri (Ed.), *Drugs and suicide: When other strategies fail.* Beverly Hills: Sage Publications.

Shontz, F. (1982). Adaptation to chronic illness and disability. In T. Millon, C. Green, & R. Meagher (Eds.), *Handbook of clinical health psychology* (pp. 153–172). New York: Plenum Press.

Spotts, J., & Shontz, F. (1980). *Cocaine users: A representative case approach.* New York: The Free Press.

Starr, P., & Heiserman, K. (1977). Acceptance of disability by teenagers with oral-facial clefts. *Rehabilitation Counseling Bulletin, 20,* 198–201.

Stephenson, W. (1935). Correlating persons instead of tests. *Character and Personality, 6,* 1724.

Stephenson, W. (1953). *The study of behavior: Q-technique and its methodology.* Chicago: University of Chicago Press.

Thomas, K. R., Davis, R. M., & Hochman, M. E. (1976). Correlates of disability acceptance in amputees. *Rehabilitation Counseling Bulletin, 19,* 509–511

Vitaliano P. P., Maiuro R. D., Russo, J., & Becker, J. (1987). Raw versus relative scores in the assessment of coping strategies. *Journal of Behavioral Medicine, 10*(1), 1–18.

Wanberg, K., & Horn, J. L. (1987). The assessment of multiple conditions in persons with alcohol problems. In W. M. Cox (Ed.), *Treatment and prevention of alcohol problems: A resource manual* (pp. 27–55). Orlando, FL: Academic Press.

Wright, B. A. (1960). *Physical Disability: A psychological approach.* New York: Harper & Row.

Wright, B. (1983). *Physical disability: A psychosocial approach.* New York: Harper & Row.

Wright, B. D., Linacre, J. M., & Schultz, M. (1989). BIGSTEPS: A Rasch program for rating scale analysis. Chicago: MESA Press.

Wright B. D., Masters G. (1982). *Rating scale analysis: Rasch measurement.* Chicago: MESA Press

Wright, B. D., & Stone, M. H. (1979). *Best test design: Rasch measurement.* Chicago, IL: MESA Press.

Yuker, H., Block, J., & Younng, J. (1970). *The measurement of attitudes toward disabled persons.* Albertson, NY: Human Resources Center.

Appendix 1
Adaptive Skills Battery[1]

Negative Emotional States

1. You made a costly mistake at work. It was your fault and you were thoroughly chewed out by your boss. Now you really feel low. One thought keeps running through your head . . . "I'm just no good. I am really worthless." How do you handle this?
2. You find yourself alone on a Saturday afternoon. You've watched TV until you can't stand it anymore, and you are really bored. Everyone you know seems to be busy with other things. You feel that you've had too much time on your hands recently. What do you do?
3. You used to be quite good at meeting people at parties when you had had quite a few drinks. Now that you are not drinking anymore, it really feels awkward. You just tried to meet someone but it didn't go well, and the person excused themselves quickly. You really feel tense, nervous, and down on yourself. How do you handle this situation?

Anger, Frustration, and Conflict

4. At work, one of your supervisors really humiliates you publicly by criticizing your work. You feel his criticism is unjustified and you try to explain, but he won't listen. He closes with, "and you'd better straighten up, or you will be looking for a new job." He turns and storms off. How do you handle it?
5. In the past, you were used to getting drunk after a fight with someone. You've just had a really big fight with a person and they walked out on you. You still feel like you've got a lot of pent-up anger. What do you do?
6. At work you are forced to work with a very depressed person who is always griping about the boss and your co-workers. His continued chatter makes it hard for you to concentrate and your boss has already told you that he noticed a fall in your performance. How do you handle it?

---

[1]Copyright, 1994. By M. J. Langley and M. P. Ridgely. Midwest Neurological Rehabilitation Center, 1710 Sharp Road, Waterford, WI 53185.

Social Pressure

7. You've gone to spend some time with friends socially in the park. Several of your friends are drinking. One shoves a beer in your hand. You say; "no thank you" and set it down, but he says loudly; "Why can't you take a drink; you think you're so much better than the rest of us?" What do you say?

8. You used to drink with a particular friend at a certain bar. One day 30 minutes before work is over this person walks up to you and is very insistent, saying, "Come on, lets have a few for old times sake. It's been a hard day—a couple of cold ones will sure taste good." What do you say?

9. You are unemployed and feel really depressed and tempted to get drunk when you are alone. Every day there is no one around during working hours. The only people you know who are home seem to drink quite heavily all the time. What do you do?

Cue-Exposure

10. You're not sure why, but you really feel like getting drunk. It's really a strong craving. There's nothing to stop you as you have the money and the evening is free. What do you do?

11. Every day coming home you pass the liquor store where you used to buy a lot of the booze you drank. It seems to bother you each time you pass it, and you find yourself having thoughts about how much fun you used to have getting drunk with your buddies. What do you do?

12. It has been one of those days at work. Now on your way home you feel tense, irritable and lonely because there will be no one home when you get there. You hate the thought of how bad the evening is going to be. Just then you remember a place where some alcohol (or other drug) is stashed for just such times. What do you do?

Scoring Criteria

General scoring criteria:

Competent response (2 points)—Maximizes possible positive gains in the situation for the individual while minimizing possible negative consequences.

Intermediate response (1 point)—is neither classified as competent or incompetent. Many entail constructive action but fail to maximize positive gains.

Incompetent response (0 points)—Minimizes potential positive gains and maximizes negative consequences. "I don't know" is always scored zero. Substance use is always scored zero.

Item-specific scoring guidelines:

1. I am really worthless

   2 points—Appropriate strategy likely to lead to rapid restoration of feelings of self-worth. Examines mistake, takes action to correct; tries to resolve conflict with boss; talks to friends to get support and encouragement; reassures self about personal worth, perhaps by thinking about positive achievements.

   1 point—Undefined strategy to examine mistake and correct it. Tries to work harder, not make the same mistake again.

   0 points—Counterproductive strategy. Aggressive response; does nothing; continues as usual; ruminates over negative feelings; quits job.

2. Alone on Saturday afternoon

   2 points—Appropriate short- and long-term actions. Deals with immediate boredom by initiating a reinforcing activity, keeping busy, exercising, etc.; keeps in the company of nondrinkers; problem-solving about new activities/interests to prevent future boredom; makes list of activities and pins it on the refrigerator; joins support group or tries to make new social contacts.

   1 point—Short-term strategy only. Initiates a reinforcing activity; keeps busy; exercises; visits nondrinking friends, etc.

   0 points—Counterproductive strategy. Visits old drinking buddies; goes to bar; does nothing; sleeps; unsure.

3. Meeting people

   2 points—Adaptive strategy for meeting people, and recognizing a need to overcome uneasiness. Tries to join groups/clubs to meet new friends; starts a conversation with a friend; listens to other's opinions; compliments someone; uses humor; spontaneous positive behavior; rehearses conventional skills; asks a friend for advice: Uses relaxation/breathing strategies; self-instructions to stay calm; attributes problem to situational factors rather than personal factors.

   1 point—Undefined strategy to deal with immediate feelings only. Person does not take it personally; avoids self-criticism; tries to enjoy the party; does nothing in particular.

0 points—Counterproductive strategy. Leaves party; is aggressive to the person who gave him the cold shoulder; drinks or uses other drugs.

4. Unjustly critical supervisor

2 points—Assertive strategy to solve problem with supervisor and deal with feelings. Recognition that supervisor may have a personal problem at the time; allows time for things to settle down and then discusses the matter privately with supervisor; tries to unwind, finds ways to let off steam alone or with a close friend; asks friend for advice; thinks through different actions and their consequences; listens carefully to supervisor; tries to compromise.

1 point—Incomplete response, somewhat assertive but without attempt to resolve problem with supervisor. Assertively confronts supervisor immediately; deals with problem indirectly, i.e., writes letter of complaint, goes above the supervisor to complain; ignores the incident and tries to work harder.

0 points—Counterproductive strategy. Aggressively confronts supervisor immediately; quits job; does nothing; blames self; ruminates.

5. Fight

2 points—Appropriate strategy for dealing with anger in place of drinking. Does breathing/relaxation exercises; takes a long shower; takes a long walk; swims, or works out; lets off steam in a safe way; talks the problem out with a friend; thinks through several different solutions; tries to see things from the other person's point of view; thinks calm, relaxing thoughts; tries to resolve the conflict; downplays the value of drinking; thinks about the negative effects of substance use; thinks about the benefits of abstinence.

1 point—Undefined strategy for self-restraint without appropriate anger management. Stays around house without constructive alternative activity; watches TV, stomps around house; isolates self.

0 points—Counterproductive response. Aggression; drinks alcohol; ruminates; goes to hang out with friends at bar.

6. Depressed co-worker

2 points—Assertive response to co-worker. Confronts co-worker tactfully, explaining feelings, and asking for termination of the distracting comments; offers to talk with co-worker during break; strategies to improve own work performance.

1 point—Indirect coping strategy. Goes directly to boss, tries to ignore co-worker, works harder, tries relaxation, stress-management techniques.

0 points—Aggressive response. Aggressive confrontation; refusing to work with co-worker; demanding action against co-worker; blaming co-worker for fall in performance, staying home from work or quitting.

7. Friend in park

2 points—Assertive refusal, providing reasons for abstinence. Gives an appropriate reason for abstinence without insulting person; takes control of the situation; appropriate strategy to avoid drinking, may leave the situation if temptation becomes overpowering.

1 point—Refusal. Provides an unconvincing refusal; fails to provide reason.

0 points—Passive or aggressive response. Aggressively rejects the offer; gives in and accepts drink; makes a false excuse.

8. Insistent friend

2 points—Assertive refusal which allows friendship to continue. Provides an acceptable reason for abstinence; provides positive alternative to the other person: Strategy for dealing with temptation, i.e., recalls previous negative effects of drinking, considers benefits of abstinence.

1 point—Refusal without alternatives for maintaining friendship. Provides reason for abstinence or simply refuses without offering positive alternatives to the other person.

0 points—Counterproductive response. Gives in and drinks with friend; goes along to bar with intention of not drinking; provides a false excuse; simply avoids the person; aggressive responses.

9. Unemployed

2 points—Primary focus on long-range planning. Response shows evidence of problem solving and systematic approach to increasing activities (job, friends, and/or hobbies); instrumental actions to obtain employment, e.g., reads through help wanted ads, writes up a resume; makes list of activities; avoids people who are drinking; short-term strategy for keeping busy and meaningfully occupied, e.g., goes for a walk, cleans the house.

1 point—Appropriate short-term solution. Attends social sup-

port group such as AA; calls friends/family, goes window shopping; avoids people who are drinking.

0 points—No action or counterproductive response. Goes to bar to play pool; spends time with people who are drinking; does nothing, watches TV, sleeps, drinks alcohol, or uses other drugs.

10. Craving

2 points—Immediate cognitive and behavioral prevention response. Seeks out effective social support, calls up someone who understands problem; implements distraction/substitution activities, buys alternative beverages, gets busy with alternative activity; stimulus control activities, keeps away from bars, drinking friends; cognitive cueing, reads through list of reasons to abstain, looks at pictures of self right after accident; problem solving, identifies cause of the craving and tries to deal with; alternative thoughts, puts alcohol thoughts out of mind; negative thoughts about substance use; positive thoughts about abstinence.

1 point—Undefined, incomplete response. Ignores the feeling; gets on with plans for the evening; no concrete behavioral prevention response; inactivity; isolates self; watches TV; denies urge.

0 points—Counterproductive response. Gives in, drinks; spends time with drinking friends or in situations containing alcohol cues; tests ability to face cues without drinking, i.e., goes to restaurant next to bar.

11. Passing old liquor store

2 points—Effective stimulus control or cognitive strategy. Changes route to avoid bar or thinks about negative consequences of drinking to balance out the positive feelings; recognizes urges and discusses them with a friend; avoids drinking friends; implements distraction/substitution activities.

1 point—Undefined, incomplete response. Tries not to think about it; just drives on by; no action to deal with underlying craving; denies urge.

0 points—Counterproductive response. Stops in and buys a non-alcoholic drink to test ability to abstain; drinks; goes in to play pool; spends time with drinking buddies.

12. Remembers alcohol

2 points—Appropriate strategy for dealing with feelings coupled with stimulus control strategy. Efforts to relax and relieve stress; emotion-focused coping, e.g., positive comparisons or

seeking meaning; implements distraction/substitution activities; gets rid of bottle if considered safe to do so or asks someone else to do so; seeks social support; thinks through costs of drinking vs. benefits of abstinence.

1 point—Incomplete response. Gets rid of bottle, but without dealing with feelings; implements alternative activities without getting rid of bottle.

0 points—Counterproductive response. Tries not to feel like that; does nothing; tests ability to keep bottle around; postpones decision about what to do with bottle; spends time in bar, plays pool, or talks with drinking buddies.

Appendix 2

Timeline Diary Instructions[1]

What Is This About?

Knowing how people spend their time is very important for planning a person's rehabilitation program. In this folder are two booklets; in each you will be asked to record what you do on a **typical day—one weekend day** and **one weekday**.

In filling out this diary, you should try to write down all of the activities of your day—from midnight to midnight. The purpose of this is not to be nosy, but instead to get as full a picture of your life as possible.

What Do You Need to To?

- First, **read the sample page** so that you see the types of activities you should be recording. Your activities will be somewhat different; this just gives you examples.
- Second, write the **date of the day recorded**, circle the **day of the week,** and write **your initials** at the top of the page of the first booklet. You can start with either the weekday or weekend day. During the day in question stop every few hours to **make entries in the diary**. For example, soon after getting out of bed, stop to record your hours of sleep and your first activities after rising.

---

[1]Copyright, 1982. By L. Diller, W. Fordyce, D. Jacobs and M. Brown. Rehabilitation Indicators Project, New York University Medical Center, 400 East 34th Street, New York City, NY 10016. All rights reserved. The Timeline Diary version of Activity Pattern Indicators is one of several forms.

Then, later in the day record again. Record each day's activity from **midnight to midnight**.

- Be sure to **fill out one booklet for a weekday and one for a day on the weekend**.
- Please be sure to fill out all your activities, even the small ones like making a phone call, opening the mail or using the toilet.
- In the "**Talk with Anyone**?" column, "Yes" means that you talked during the activity with another person. "No" means you talked with no one.
- The "**Supervised**" and "**Physical Help**" columns refer to someone actively telling you how to do things (supervision) or giving you a hand (physical help)—for example, helping you out at work or carrying groceries at the store.
- If the day turns out to be **very unusual** (for example, you become ill or something else creates a large break in your usual pattern), you should stop recording. **Small** differences do **not** call for stopping (for example, going to see a movie rather than the more usual TV watching).
- Don't worry if you can't complete some of the information requested. Just do the best you can. **If you have questions, they can be answered in the follow-up interview.**

Timeline Diary

What did you do all day starting at midnight?

What did you do?	Time began	Time ended	Where were you?	Talk with anyone?	Were you super- vised?	Any physical help?	Doing anything else?
Sleep	12:00	7:30	home	no	no	no	no
Showered & shampoo	7:30	7:45	home	no	"	no	"
Groomed	7:45	7:55	home	no	"	no	"
Used toilet	7:55	8:00	home	no	"	no	read magazines
Got dressed	8:00	8:30	home	yes	"	yes	no
Ate breakfast	8:30	8:40	home	yes	"	yes	TV
Took bus to work	8:40	9:00	in transit	no	"	no	read book
Worked at desk	9:00	10:30	work	yes	"	no	no
Took break—got coffee	10:30	10:40	"	yes	"	no	"
Toilet	10:40	10:45	"	no	"	no	"
Desk work	10:45	12:30	"	yes	"	yes	sipped coffee
Lunch	12:30	1:00	city park	no	"	no	read paper
Bus to store	1:00	1:45	bus	yes	"	"	no
Shopped—clothes	1:45	3:00	Jones store	yes	"	"	no
Bus to work	3:00	3:40	bus	no	"	"	read novel
Desk work	3:40	6:30	work	yes	yes	yes	no

4 Functional Assessment

Nancy M. Crewe and Marcel Dijkers

Functional assessment is the measurement of purposeful behavior in interaction with the environment, which is interpreted according to the assessment's intended uses. (Halpern & Fuhrer, 1984, p. 3)

The broad domain of assessment includes varied approaches to understanding individual characteristics and capacities, two of which are psychometric testing and functional assessment. These areas cannot always be separated with precision, but they typically differ along major dimensions including the types of items used and the degree of inference that separates the assessment measures and the criterion behavior. In norm-referenced testing, the actual items that constitute the test may have little intrinsic significance, but they may be used because they correlate with a certain outcome or behavior. For example, a particular analogy or vocabulary word on a graduate school admissions examination may not have great importance in and of itself, but it may help to predict success in an academic setting. A specific response to an item on a personality test may be similarly insignificant on its own, but it may help to tap an underlying construct such as depression or anxiety.

In contrast, functional assessment is not so much concerned with measuring underlying traits. Instead, it attempts to directly measure a person's ability to carry out meaningful behavioral tasks or to observe his or her actual performance of these tasks. Functional assessment also tends to occur within a realistic setting that approximates the one in which the actual criterion behavior will occur. Thus, functional assessment could be done repeatedly under varying conditions, revealing how an individual's performance is affected by environmental characteristics such as the behavior of other people, distractors such as noise or heat, and the availability of coaching or assistive devices.

Another common difference between functional assessment and psychometric testing is the degree to which the client may be involved in structuring and interpreting the assessment process. With norm-referenced testing, the conditions of administration are usually carefully standardized, and any deviation from procedures threatens the validity of the test (see chapter 10 in this book). In contrast, functional assessments are often less formal, with the client playing an active role in planning and interpreting the assessment. This process may seem more useful to the client and provide a broader bank of information.

Because functional assessment instruments have been developed specifically for use with persons with disabilities and their administration typically allows for flexibility, modification to accommodate impairment is not needed. Because of the similarity between the tasks involved and the kind of behavior being predicted, content validity is of special importance in functional assessment. Nevertheless, all assessment procedures, even those with great face and content validity, need to be evaluated carefully in terms of reliability and criterion validity.

Developers of functional assessment instruments have been taken to task for treating scores on their instruments as though they represent interval measures, without providing evidence supporting that assumption (Silverstein, Fisher, Kilgore, Harley, & Harvey, 1992). The rating scales used in most functional instruments produce ordinal data, and yet they are often summed to produce total scores and used in statistical operations that require interval data. Increasingly, however, major instruments are being subjected to Rasch analysis (A. G. Fisher, 1993) to test the characteristics of the scales and to determine whether the assumptions underlying addition of scores are justified.

Distinctions between functional and norm-referenced testing involve not only the kinds of tests chosen but the way that the tests are used. Standardized neuropsychological tests, which have traditionally been used for diagnostic purposes (such as localizing areas of brain dysfunction), are frequently used now to identify behavioral strengths and limitations of individuals with brain injuries (McCue 1989). In this capacity, they actually become tools for functional assessment.

The field of rehabilitation has been interested in functional assessment for at least 20 years. Demands for accountability in health care have grown increasingly urgent, and functional measures have been identified as a key to documenting rehabilitation medicine outcomes. With the passage of the Americans with Disabilities Act (ADA), functional assessment also has assumed a role of elevated importance in vocational rehabilitation (Crewe, 1992). Under the ADA, an individual's functional capacities are to be compared with the essential demands of a job, and reasonable accommodations must be provided when they will enable an otherwise qualified person to meet the demands of the job. Clearly, measures of functional assessment are essential to carrying out the ADA's mandate.

Rehabilitation is not the only field to display an interest in this area. Functionally oriented assessment practices have captured the interest of other segments of society as well. For example, in the field of education performance, portfolio and "authentic" assessments have been gaining increasing visibility as an alternative to group-administered achievement testing (Meisels, Liaw, Dorfman, & Fails, 1993). Students demonstrate their skills or knowledge by conducting experiments; writing stories, essays, or journals; producing art work or oral presentations, and assembling a portfolio of their work. These products of actual classroom-based activities become the basis for assessment. Because the portfolio contains many diverse samples of work, produced over an extended period of time, the assessments can be individualized to some degree to fit the needs and goals of a given person.

In many settings, interest in alternative approaches to assessment has grown in part because of questions that have been raised about the fairness of standardized testing to ethnic and racial minorities, to women, and to people with disabilities. For example, the General Aptitude Test Battery (Droege, 1987), which was the product of nearly 40 years of research and development, is no longer being used in its original capacity by the employment services offices of the U.S. Department of Labor. (It is still being used in some offices for counseling purposes, but not as the primary basis for deciding which job seekers should be selected for position referrals.) Yet the need for tools to help with individual and group decision making has not diminished, and functional measures may help to fill the gap.

The purpose of all kinds of functional assessment is to gain an accurate and multifaceted picture of an individual that can help in setting realistic goals, determining what services are appropriate, and documenting progress toward the goals. In general, assessment should help to make services more sensitive to individual needs and preferences. Frey and Nieuwenhuijsen (1990) pointed out that before good assessment tools were available, approaches to vocational rehabilitation were oriented around the disability rather than the whole person. Efforts were made to identify lists of jobs that would be "appropriate" for persons with a particular impairment, and then clients were helped to choose among those alternatives. Needless to say, this method tended to overlook important individual differences on other dimensions such as interests, abilities, and values while it treated disability as the dominant characteristic determining vocational choice. In contrast, assessment concentrates on the individual, thus reorienting service decisions in a more appropriate direction.

Assessment serves a similar purpose in the context of any service or treatment program. It provides a detailed picture of individual abilities and deficits that allows a program to be tailored to the person. Without assessment, everyone is usually put through an identical process and expected to achieve the same goals. This is rarely acceptable to adults who have unique needs.

Functional assessment instruments have been developed to meet the needs of many different populations and programs, including those for persons with pain (Mikail, DuBreuil, & D'Eon, 1993), head injury (Ross, O'Malley, Stein, & Spettell, 1992), Alzheimers's disease (Mahurin, De-Bettignies, & Pirozzolo, 1991; Oakley, Sunderland, Hill, & Phillips, 1991; Oswald & Gunzelmann, 1992), mental retardation (Derby, Wacker, Sasso, & Steege, 1992; Downing & Perino, 1992; Foss, Bullis, & Vilhauer, 1984), psychiatric disability (Anthony & Farkas, 1982; Cohen & Anthony, 1984; Curtin & Klyczek, 1992), deafness (Garner, Becker, Schur, & Hammer, 1991; McCrone & Jacobs, 1990), arthritis (Jacobs, 1993), visual impairment (Graves, 1990), and learning disability (McCue 1989). They also have been developed by practitioners in varied disciplines, including occupational therapy (Bonder, 1993; Velozo, 1993), speech and language pathology (Frattali, 1992), and physical therapy (Wickstrom, 1990).

There is no way to know how many functional assessment tools have been created, but the number is very large. This chapter focuses on a small number of instruments that are meant to be used with diverse patient or client groups and that address the key concerns of rehabilitation: capacity for self-care, work, and independent living. It also emphasizes measures that are often administered by psychologists, alone or as members of a treatment team. Some functional measures, for example the Sickness Impact Profile (Bergner, Bobbitt, Carter, & Gilson, 1981), are featured in other chapters within this book (chapters 6 & 7) and are omitted here.

The first four instruments covered here, the Barthel Index (BI), the Level of Rehabilitation Scale III (LORS), the Patient Evaluation and Conference System (PECS), and the Functional Independence Measure (FIM), are most often used by inpatient medical rehabilitation settings to quantify extent of physical disability and capacity for self-care. The remaining instruments are primarily concerned with psychosocial and vocational dimensions of function and are more likely to be applied in outpatient settings or vocational rehabilitation facilities and agencies.

Measures of Functional Assessment

The Barthel Index and the Modified Barthel Index

The Barthel Index was developed as a measure of disability in people whose impairment interfered with independent use of their limbs. Published in 1965 (Mahoney & Barthel, 1965), the BI was the first disability measure to become available to medical rehabilitation that used a summary score (Granger & Hamilton, 1990). It was widely used in the 1970s and 1980s. As late as 1988, it was proposed as *the* standard index of physical disability (Wade & Collin, 1988). The BI includes the 10 activities of daily living (self-care and mobility) that are commonly included in activities of daily living (ADL) checklists and physical function instruments (see Table 4.1). A number of modifications of the BI have been developed. The Modified Barthel Index (MBI; Table 4.2) is a family of modifications propagated by Granger (1982) and associates (Gresham & Labi, 1984; Granger, Albrecht, & Hamilton, 1979). McGinnis, Sewell, DeJong, and Osberg (1986) developed a self-report questionnaire version of the MBI that has also been referred to as the MBI.

The BI was developed to assess functional independence before and after rehabilitation treatment and to reflect the amount of nursing care necessary (Mahoney, Wood, & Barthel, 1958), and it is administered in a number of ways. Typically, a professional caregiver (nurse, therapist) of the target person scores the inventory on the basis of his or her knowledge of the person's day-to-day performance. Completing the form takes only a few minutes. If administered as a test (with simulated activities, and some asking in regard to bladder and bowel continence items), the BI takes about 10 to 15 minutes (Roy, Togneri, Hay, & Pentland, 1988) to 1 hour (Law & Letts, 1989). All items on the BI are rated on a 2- or 3-point scale in terms of degree of dependence, with weights reflecting burden of care on professional staff or family. The total score, derived by simple addition across items, ranges from zero to 100, in 5-point

Table 4.1

The Barthel Index (*BI*)

Item	Can do alone	Can do with help	Cannot do at all
1. Feeding	10	5	0
2. Dressing	10	5	0
3. Grooming	5	0	0
4. Washing or bathing	5	0	0
5. Bladder control	10	5 (accidents)	0 (incontinent)
6. Bowel control	10	5 (accidents)	0 (incontinent)
7. Chair/bed transfer	15	10ª	0
8. Toilet transfer	10	5	0
9. Walking 50 yards	15	0	0
IF NOT WALKING: Propelling wheelchair	5	5	0
10. Walking up/down one flight	10	5	0

Note. From "Functional evaluation: The Barthel Index" by F. I. Mahoney and D. W. Barthel, 1965, *Maryland Medical Journal, 14*, pp. 61–65.
ªScore 5 if much help is needed.

increments. The MBI is characterized by more sensitive scoring (typically using four rather than three levels of ability) and added items. In all MBI versions, scoring has been adjusted so that the maximum remains at 100 points, and the minimum at zero (or −2, if brace/limb is included). Commonly, two subscores are used: one for self-care (0–53 range), and one for mobility (0–47 range).

Psychometric Properties

Reliability. A number of studies have indicated excellent intra- and interrater reliability for the BI. Loewen and Anderson (1988) had five occupational therapists and physical therapists rate videotapes of seven patients and obtained generalized kappas for interrater agreement on individual BI items of .65 or over. Intrarater reliability was assessed by rerating the tapes after 1 month. Kappa values for the individual BI items for each therapist–patient combination were generally in the .75 to 1.00 range, with none less than .41. Roy et al. (1988) had three people rate 20 patients, with one using patient interview and the other two using testing in a simulated home unit. The two testers came up with very similar total BI ratings ($r = .99$), and their ratings were also similar to those of the interviewer (rs = .88 and .89). Similarly, Collin, Wade, Davies, and Horne (1988) compared interviews of patient or family caregiver

Table 4.2

Modified Barthel Index (*MBI*)

Item	Can do alone	Can do with help	Cannot do at all
Self-care subscore			
1. Drinking from a cup	4	0	0
2. Eating	6	0	0
3. Dressing upper	5	3	0
4. Dressing lower body	7	4	0
5. Donning brace/limb	0	−2	0 (not applicable)
6. Grooming	5	0	0
7. Washing or bathing	6	0	0
8. Bladder control	10	5 (accidents)	0 (incontinent)
9. Bowel control	10	5 (accidents)	0 (incontinent)
Mobility subscore			
10. Chair transfer	15	7	0
11. Toilet transfer	6	3	0
12. Tub/shower transfer	1	0	0
13. Walking 50 yds (level)	15	10	0
14. Walking up/down one flight IF NOT WALKING:	10	5	0
15. Propelling wheelchair	5	0	0 (not applicable)

Note. From "Outcome of comprehensive medical rehabilitation: Measurement by PULSES profile and the Barthel Index," by C. V. Granger, G. L. Albrecht, and B. B. Hamilton, 1979, *Archives of Physical Medicine and Rehabilitation, 60,* p. 154. Copyright 1979 by the American Congress of Rehabilitation Medicine and the American Academy of Physical Medicine and Rehabilitation. Adapted by permission.

(Method A), staff nurse rating (Method B), testing by a trained nurse (Method C) and testing by an occupational therapist (Method D) for 25 patients. Kendall's *W* was .93 over all four methods. Patient/caregiver report agreed least with the other methods. Methods B, C, and D agreed to within 4 points on the total BI score in 23 out of 25 cases (92%). There was no trend for any rating method to systematically result in higher scores.

In the Shinar et al. (1987) study, one of a pair of trained nurses tested 18 patients, with both nurses making MBI ratings independently. Within a day, the patient was retested by a second pair of nurses. Paired *t* tests found no significant differences between testers or between tests. Mean correlation between raters was Pearsons's r = 0.99 for MBI total score, and at least Spearman's rho = 0.80 for individual items. These researchers also administered the MBI by telephone to 72 patients (or their caregivers) living in a community and tested them 5 to 8 days later. Even though this was a high-functioning group (resulting in restriction of range), correlations for total MBI ($r = .99$) and individual items (at least $r_s = .83$) were very good. No systematic differences between testing and interview were found.

High MBI test–retest ($r = .89$) and interrater (intercoder) reliability ($r = .95$) were also reported for a study using descriptive information abstracted from the medical record (Granger et al., 1979).

The internal consistency of the BI has been reported as high, with an alpha value of .95 (Kane & Kane, 1981). A later study reported alpha values of .87 (admission) and .92 (discharge) (Shah, Vanclay, & Cooper, 1988). A factor analysis confirmed that a single domain is measured by the items (Wade & Langton Hewer, 1987).

Validity. The BI has been shown to correlate highly with other well-known measures of function (in the broad meaning of that term). In a study of 148 Framingham cohort survivors of stroke, kappa for agreement of grouped scores on the BI with Katz Index of ADL ratings was .77; for the Kenny Self-Care Evaluation, Spearman's rho was .73 for the same group (Gresham, Philips, & Labi, 1980). High correlations were also reported for a study of 364 day-center patients with a physical disability: rhos were .65 for the correlation with PULSES and .69 for the correlation with the Edinburgh Rehabilitation Status Scale (ERSS; Mattison, Aitken, & Prescott, 1992).

Because the Barthel Index has been used so widely, there is much research demonstrating construct validity. Scores on the BI are associated, for example, with rehabilitation discharge destination (Granger, Dewis, Peters, Sherwood, & Barrett, 1979; Granger, Greer, Liset, Coulombe, & O'Brien, 1975), extent of motor loss in stroke patients (Wade & Langton Hewer, 1987), stroke survival (Granger & Greer, 1976), age, social role activity, and depression (Fortinsky, Granger, & Seltzer, 1981). In persons with multiple sclerosis, actual minutes per day of caregiver help correlated well with BI total score (Granger, Cotter, Hamilton, Fiedler, & Hens, 1990).

Special Considerations, Cautions, and Applications

The BI (or MBI) is easy to learn, simple to administer in a short time, and easy to score. It includes a representative sample of self-care and mobility items, which are measured with sufficient sensitivity to capture the type of changes typically seen in rehabilitation inpatients between admission and discharge.

The BI is useful for evaluating physical disability in patients in nursing homes or inpatient rehabilitation settings. It appears less applicable to most categories of community-living persons with a disability, because it lacks sensitivity to the smaller changes commonly observed after rehabilitation is completed, or differences in high-functioning groups (cf. Granger & Hamilton, 1990). In addition, a ceiling effect because of the lack of differentiation among those who do not require help from others, and a floor effect, or lack of differentiation among those who do not qualify for a rating of "needs (some) help," severely limit clinical, management and research applications among such populations (McDowell & Newell, 1987; Granger et al., 1990).

A major shortcoming of the BI for use in medical rehabilitation programs is the fact that cognition and communication disabilities are not assessed.

Scores on the BI and the MBI have been used as a basis for making decisions on discharge destination of rehabilitation inpatients, nurse staffing needs (Mahoney et al. 1958), and other patient management issues. In spite of the omission of cognition and communication, the BI has been used in research most often with people who have had strokes. Applications in other diagnostic groups, however, have also been published. Both research on clinical interventions and health services research have been performed using the BI and the MBI.

Level of Rehabilitation Scale

The Level of Rehabilitation Scale (LORS) was developed as a simple, reliable, and valid measure of rehabilitation inpatients' functioning for use in program evaluation (Carey & Posavac, 1978, 1982). Aimed to provide a moderate level of detail, it originally consisted of 47 items in five categories: ADL, cognition, home activities (instrumental ADL), outside activities (in public), and social activities (in public and private areas). Thus, LORS captures aspects of disablement wider than disability: some aspects of handicap are covered in the last three scales. The latest editions of the instrument (LORS-III) have not maintained this wide coverage (Formations, 1992). Version III includes 5 ADL items, 2 mobility items, 4 communication items, and 6 cognitive ability items (see Table 4.3).

The highest possible score on each LORS item is defined as *normal*, and all four lower scores are intended (based on extensive rehabilitation staff input) to be at equidistant points of the continuum from *normal* to *unable*, allowing the conversion of scores to *percentage of normal* (Carey & Posavac, 1978, 1982; Carey, Seibert, & Posavac, 1988; Santopoalo, 1989). On the LORS-III, however, the highest rating may be given to someone

---

Table 4.3

Level of Rehabilitation Scale (*LORS-III*)

Item	Description
Activities of daily living	
1. Dressing	Includes upper and lower, dressing and undressing. Rated by nurse and OT.
2. Grooming	Includes hair care, oral care, make-up, shaving and body care. Rated by nurse and OT.
3. Washing/bathing	Includes transfer in/out of tub/shower, washing, drying, or alternative: bed bath, sink bathing. Rated by nurse and OT.
4. Toileting	Includes transfer to/from toilet/commode, toileting and hygiene, or alternative: catheter/colostomy management. Rated by nurse and OT.
5. Feeding	Includes set-up, feeding, swallowing, or alternative: enteral/parenteral feeding management. Rated by nurse and OT.
Mobility	
6. Wheelchair management	Includes propelling on level surfaces and transfer to/from chair/bed. Rated by nurse and PT.
7. Ambulation	Includes ambulation on level surfaces and transfer to/from chair. Rated by nurse and PT.
Communication	
8. Auditory comprehension	Rated by nurse and speech pathologist.
9. Oral expression	Rated by nurse and speech pathologist.
10. Reading comprehension	Rated by speech pathologist.
11. Written expression	Rated by speech pathologist.
12. Alternate communication	(gestural expression or augmentative communication device). Rated by nurse and speech pathologist.
Cognitive ability	
13. Attention	Rated by OT and speech pathologist.
14. Orientation	Rated by OT and speech pathologist.
15. Problem solving	Rated by OT and speech pathologist.
16. Sequencing	(of self-care tasks). Rated by OT.
17. Short-term memory	Rated by any two of nurse, OT, speech pathologist or psychologist.
18. Long-term memory	Rated by any two of nurse, OT, speech pathologist or psychologist.

Note. OT = occupational therapist; PT = physical therapist. Adapted from *Level of Rehabilitation Scale (LORS-III) Reference Manual.* Formations in Health Care, Inc., 1992.

using assistive equipment (see Table 4.4). Short-term and long-term memory are rated on a simple 2-point scale (*impaired* vs. *not impaired*).

The LORS is applicable to all adult rehabilitation inpatients. *Restore* (formerly Rehabilitation Outpatient Program Evaluation System, or ROPES)

Table 4.4

Level of Rehabilitation Scale (*LORS-III*): Description of the Levels of Function

Level	Description
0	Unable to perform any aspect of the activity.
1	Requires *maximum* physical assistance for *all* or *most* aspects of the activity. Contributes some effort, but requires another person to do most of the task. Equivalent to 25% of independence.
2	Requires *moderate* physical assistance for *some* aspects of the activity, but patient contributes significantly to accomplishing the task. Equivalent to 50% of independence.
3	Requires *minimal* to *stand-by* assistance (such as cuing, placing articles within reach) and supervision of standing, etc. for safety. Equivalent to 75% of independence.
4	Performs activity independently, with or without assistance, equipment.
5	Not applicable: no therapy planned or provided.

Note. Adapted from *Level of Rehabilitation Scale (LORS-III) Reference Manual.* Formations in Health Care, Inc., 1992.

---

is the name of an offshoot of LORS that has been designed for outpatients. It involves different scale items and scoring criteria, including endurance and speed.

Specifying ratings of functional status for inpatients is normally done by clinicians. Unique among disability scales, standard use of LORS calls for completion of most items by a pair of staff members (nurse and either occupational therapist [OT], physical therapist [PT], or speech–language pathologist [SLP]; Carey & Posavac, 1982). Only items in an area for which the patient actually receives therapy are rated, so scoring is done by means of averaging all items completed in a particular LORS subscale. Administration takes about 1 minute per item (Gonnella, 1992).

The LORS has become part of a larger entity, the Formations Outcomes System, a computer-based system for recording, aggregating, and reporting descriptive and predictive data at the level of the individual, as well as the program or institution. This test is licensed to rehabilitation units and hospitals for their use. Staff must participate in inservice training before the hospital is allowed to enter its patients' information in the database. Uniquely among the three major data systems (the Formations Outcomes System, the Patient Evaluation and Conference System, and the Uniform Data System), the Formations Outcomes System offers users the opportunity to use the information for case management. Regression equations are used to predict, at admission, a particular patients' length of stay, total charges, and discharge functional level on the basis of demographic data, diagnosis, and admission functional status.

Psychometric Properties

Reliability. High interrater reliability was reported by Carey and Posavac (1978) for the original LORS-I (which was scored on the basis of an interview of informants by program evaluation staff). Correlation for two nurse informants was reported as .95 for ADL and .89 for cognition. In 1988, Carey and Seibert reported interrater reliability (Pearson product–moment correlation) for pairs consisting of nurse and OT, PT, or speech-language pathologist, of .77 at admission and .87 at discharge for ADL; corresponding figures were .65 and .76 for mobility, and .75 and .79 for verbal communication. These data were based on over 12,000 patients in a large number of institutions. It is not clear whether the correlations refer to subscale totals or to averages for individual items in these scales.

Malzer (1988) compared ratings by (LORS-trained) nurses, on the one hand, and OTs and PTs on the other. He found only modest correlations for six individual items at admission, ranging from .34 to .59 ($M = .49$); at discharge, correlations were higher, with a range from .72 to .91 ($M = .78$). On all six admission items, the therapists claimed higher independence than the nurses. These differences were smaller on the parallel discharge items, but still sufficiently large to be significant on four out of six.

In a recent study, Velozo, Magalhaes, Pan, and Weeks (1993) selected five ADL items from the LORS-III, completed by both a nurse and an OT, and submitted them to Rasch analysis. They used a plot of item calibrations for raters of each group to compare systematic differences, and found a consistent tendency for nurses to see less patient independence.

Carey and Posavac (1978) reported an alpha of .94 for LORS ADL, and of .88 for cognition, in the case of inpatients. Alphas for the other three subscales were reported to be between .64 and .65, for outpatients.

Validity. In 1978, Carey and Posavac, relying on the assumption that LORS scores indicate percentage of normal, reported a general improvement of about 20 percentage points between admission and discharge for a sample of 69 stroke patients. On the basis of two follow-up contacts, improvement slowed down postdischarge; the social interaction, home activities, and outside activities subscales showed improvement from the first to the second follow-up. Expected admission-to-discharge and discharge-to-follow-up improvements were also reported by Carey and Posavac (1982) for a larger sample.

The LORS-I was used in a study of 105 persons with stroke living in the community, performed by Schmidt et al. (1986). Data were collected from the patients or their spouses. The researchers found that patients living alone scored higher on the ADL, cognition, and home activities subscales, but lower on the outside activities and social interaction subscales. The latter may have been due to the fact that individuals living alone do not have a partner available (e.g., to play cards with).

Gains scores, differentiated by age, diagnostic group, length of stay, and admission functional level, were reported by Carey et al. (1988). These confirmed standard assumptions (e.g., older persons make less progress) and indicated a ceiling effect.

Special Considerations, Cautions, and Applications

The LORS appears to have somewhat weaker interrater reliability than comparable instruments (BI, FIM, parallel sections of PECS). However, standard completion of items by both nurses and therapists provides information on two different aspects: ability (performance in therapy when challenged to give one's best) and burden of care (usual performance when adequate help is available). The LORS is normally available only to those who subscribe to the Formations Outcomes System.

The LORS has been used extensively for program evaluation and for other administrative purposes (e.g., quality assurance, utilization review). As mentioned earlier, individual case management is now emerging as an application, in addition to simple progress monitoring. The LORS has found very limited research applications, although it could be used for the same purposes as the BI, PEC, and FIM.

Patient Evaluation and Conference System

The Patient Evaluation and Conference System (PECS) was developed by Harvey and Jellinek (1981, 1983) as a sensitive measure of functional performance (in the broad sense), to include medical, physical, psychological, social, and vocational aspects. Its primary use was to set goals, monitor and document progress, and evaluate quality of care for medical rehabilitation inpatients. The PECS has undergone several modifications. Currently, it consists of 97 items divided into 16 categories, which are to be completed by specific members of the interdisciplinary team (see Table 4.5). Each item is measured on a 7-point ordinal scale, ranging from 1

Table 4.5

Patient Evaluation and Conference System (*PECS*): Listing of Items

Category and item	Category and item
I. Rehabilitation Medicine 　1. Motor loss (IS) 　2. Spasticity/involuntary movement (IS) 　3. Joint limitations (IS) 　4. Autonomic disturbance (IS) 　5. Sensory deficiency (IS) 　6. Perceptual and cognitive deficits (CC) 　7. Associated medical problems (IS) 　8. Postural deviations (IS) II. Rehabilitation Nursing 　1. Performance of bowel program (ASC) 　2. Performance of urinary program (ASC) 　3. Performance of skin care program (ASC) 　4. Assumes responsibility for self-care (ASC) 　5. Performs assigned interdisciplinary activities (ASC) 　6. Patient education (ASC) 　7. Safety awareness (ASC) III. Physical Mobility 　1. Performance of transfers (MC) 　2. Performance of ambulation (MC) 　3. Performance of wheelchair mobility (MC) 　4. Ability to handle environmental barriers (e.g., stairs, rugs, elevators (MC) 　5. Performance of car transfers (MC) 　6. Driving mobility 　7. Assumes responsibility for mobility (MC) 　8. Position changes (MC) 　9. Endurance (MC) 　10. Balance (MC) IV. Activities of Daily Living 　1. Performance in feeding (MC) 　2. Performance in hygiene/grooming (MC) 　3. Performance in dressing (MC) 　4. Performance in home management (MC)	5. Performance of mobility in the home environment (including utilization of environmental adaptations for communication) (MC) 　6. Bathroom transfers (MC) V. Communication 　1. Ability to comprehend spoken language (CC) 　2. Ability to produce language (CC) 　3. Ability to read (CC) 　4. Ability to produce written language (CC) 　5. Ability to hear 　6. Ability to comprehend and use gestures 　7. Ability to produce speech 　8. Ability to swallow VI. Medications 　1. Knowledge of medications (ASC) VII. Nutrition 　1. Nutritional status—body weight 　2. Nutritional status—lab values 　3. Knowledge of nutrition and/or modified diet 　4. Skill with nutrition and diet (adherence to nutritional plan) 　5. Utilization of nutrition and diet (nutritional health) VIII. Assistive Devices 　1. Knowledge of assistive mobility devices 　2. Skill with assuming operating position of assistive mobility devices 　3. Utilization of assistive mobility devices IX. Psychology 　1. Distress/comfort 　2. Helplessness/self efficacy (CR) 　3. Self-directed learning skills (CR) 　4. Skill in self-management of behavior and emotions (CR) 　5. Skill in interpersonal relations (CR) 　6. Ability to participate in the rehabilitation program 　7. Acceptance/understanding of disability (CR)

continued

Table 4.5, cont

Category and item	Category and item

X. Neuropsychology
  1. Impairment of short-term memory (CC)
  2. Impairment of long-term memory (CC)
  3. Impairment in attention-concentration skills (CC)
  4. Impairment in verbal-linguistic processing (CC)
  5. Impairment in visual-spatial processing (CC)
  6. Impairment in basic intellectual skills (CC)
  7. Orientation (CC)
  8. Alertness/coma state (CC)
XI. Social Issues
  1. Ability to problem solve and utilize resources (CC)
  2. Family: communication/resources (CR)
  3. Family: understanding of disability (CR)
  4. Economic resources
  5. Ability to live independently (CR)
  6. Living arrangements
XII. Vocational/Education Activity
  1. Active participation in realistic vocational/educational planning (CR)
  2. Realistic perception of work-related activity (CR)
  3. Ability to tolerate planned num-
	ber of hours of vocational/educational activity (CR)
	  4. Vocational/educational placement
	  5. Physical capacity for work (CR)
	XIII. Therapeutic Recreation
	  1. Participation in group activities (CR)
	  2. Participation in community activities (CR)
	  3. Interaction with others (CR)
	  4. Participation and satisfaction with individual leisure activities (CR)
	  5. Active participation in sports (CR)
	XIV. Pain
	  1. Pain behavior
	  2. Physical activity
	  3. Social interaction
	  4. Pacing
	  5. Sitting tolerance
	  6. Standing tolerance
	  7. Walking tolerance
	  8. Use of body mechanics
	  9. Use of relaxation techniques
	  10. Performance of medication program
	XV. Pastoral Care
	  1. Awareness of spiritual dimensions of illness/disability
	  2. Knowledge of spiritual resources
	  3. Skill in self-management of spirituality
	  4. Utilization of spiritual resources

Note: Abbreviations within brackets refer to Rasch analysis-derived subscales, as reported in Kilgore et al., 1993. Meaning of abbreviations: IS: Impairment severity; ASC: Applied self-care; MC: Motoric competence; CC: Cognitive competence; CR: Community reintegration. From *The Rehabilitation Outcome Reporting System with PECS™. Manual for Clinicians.* (Version 3.0 2nd printing). Marianjoy Rehabilitation Hospital and Clinics, 1992. Copyright 1992 by Marianjoy, Inc., and PECS, Inc. Adapted by permission.

(*most dependent/total dysfunction*) to 7 (*independence/normal function*), with 0 allowed for *not rated* or *not applicable*. Although specific descriptions for various codes differ from item to item (see Table 4.6 for an example), the disability items all use codes 1 through 4 for successive levels of dependence and 5 through 7 for various types of independence (Marianjoy, 1992a).

Table 4.6

Patient Evaluation and Conference System (*PECS*): Sample Item Description

Item	Description
Physical mobility 2—Ambulation	
1. Maximal assistance	Patient attempts to participate or provide some physical assistance in carrying out the activity, but requires significant physical and verbal assistance to complete the activity. Patient is able to assist with up to 25% of the activity.
2. Moderate assistance	Patient attempts to participate or provide some physical assistance in carrying out the activity. Patient is able to assist with 25%–75% of the activity.
3. Minimal assistance	Patient is able to participate fully in the activity, but requires intermittent physical assistance and/or contact guard. Patient is able to assist with 75% or more of the activity.
4. Standby assistance	Patient performs the activity without physical/hands on assist. May require verbal cuing, prior demonstration or supervision to complete the activity safely.
5. Limited independent	Patient is independent in the activity but requires an assistive device or environmental modification.
6. Functional independent	Patient is independent in the activity but demonstrates an altered quality of movement or requires beyond a reasonable amount of time.
7. WNL (within normal limits)	Patient is independent in the activity with reaction time and quality of movement appropriate for age.

Note. From *The Rehabilitation Outcome Reporting System With PECS™. Manual for Clinicians* (Version 3.0 2nd printing). Marianjoy Rehabilitation Hospital and Clinics, 1992. Copyright 1992 by Marianjoy, Inc. and PECS, Inc. Adapted by permission.

The PECS was not developed to yield subscores and a total score—its use was to assess initial status, set goals, and monitor progress, with all numerical results displayed primarily graphically in profile format (e.g., Harvey & Jellinek, 1983). Initially, simple summing across categories and across all items in the instrument was sometimes used to calculate subscores or a total score. Of late, the PECS development group has started to use Rasch analysis to isolate unidimensional scales with interval qualities from among the PECS items (e.g., Kilgore, Fisher, Silverstein, Harley, & Harvey, 1993; Silverstein et al., 1992). The PECS manual refers to five such subscales: cognitive ability, motoric ability, applied self-care, impairment severity, and community reintegration; the last incorporates social, emotional, psychological, and vocational components. The PECS was designed for use with adults with a physical disability who are rehabilitation inpatients. Some research has successfully used the measure with other populations with a disability, for example, nursing home patients and rehabilitation outpatients (Harvey et al., 1992). Clydesdale, Fahs, Kilgore, and Splaingard (1990) used a selection of PECS items in a study of pediatric patients, including children under 6 years of age. In the standard administration, clinical staff familiar with the target person's status and typical performance rate his or her performance. Completing the PECS rating for a patient takes 10 to 40 minutes, depending on the number of items scored (Gonella, 1992). The PECS is part of the Rehabilitation Outcome Reporting System with PECS (Marianjoy, 1992a, 1992b, 1992c), a microcomputer-based system for collecting, summarizing, aggregating, and reporting rehabilitation data, and is not separately available. The five Rasch analysis-based subscores are automatically computed by the software, which is also used for production of standard individual and aggregate reports.

Psychometric Properties

Reliability. Harvey and Jellinek (1981) reported interrater reliability rates ranging from .68 to .80 for a sample of 125 patients. Additional intrarater or interrater reliability studies could not be identified in the published literature on the PECS.

Validity. No formal content validity studies have been reported. Items have been added to and deleted from PECS over the years, based on clinician feedback as to the need for new items and the usefulness of existing ones. A substantial number of studies have been performed using PECS data, but most have been published in abstract format only and do not provide enough information on methodology and outcomes for us to judge evidence for or against validity. Sensitivity has been supported by studies demonstrating PECS item change for various diagnostic groups from inpatient rehabilitation admission to discharge (e.g., Clydesdale et al., 1990; Harvey & Jellinek, 1981).

A study by Silverstein et al. (1992) reported on a Rasch analysis of 55 PECS variables and concluded that the items could be combined to create four unidimensional, additive scales. Comparison of difficulty calibration for selected items in the cognitive competence scale and five corresponding items in the FIM (see next section) social cognition scale provided a correlation of .84. A correlation of .93 was found between the calibration difficulty of 7 FIM motor scale items and the difficulty of comparable items in the PECS motoric competence scale. These results under-score the validity of the PECS. Further evidence of the validity of the PECS, based on direct cocalibration of FIM and PECS items, is provided by Fisher, Taylor, Kilgore, Harvey, and Kelly (1993).

Construct validity of the PECS was further demonstrated in a study which showed that the admission PECS subscale scores discriminated be-tween individuals with stroke and those with brain injury ($N = 304$) in inpatient hospital rehabilitation, nursing home rehabilitation, and out-patient day rehabilitation.

Earlier studies supporting construct validity of the PECS either used individual items or constructed subscales using simple addition of items without benefit of Rasch analysis. For instance, Chaudhuri, Harvey, Sul-ton, and Lambert (1988) found an association between computed to-mography brain scan classification in 100 stroke patients and PECS dis-charge scores in the areas of self-care, ambulation, and bowel and bladder function. Earlier, Rao, Jellinek, Harvey, and Flynn (1984) had reported an association between a CAT scan and improvement in rehabilitation for a sample of 30 head trauma patients. For another small sample, Malec and Niemeyer (1983) reported a correlation of .39 between discharge PECS bladder and skin care scores and an admission depression score. Rao and Kilgore (1992) found that in a sample of 57 traumatic brain injury patients, four PECS subscale scores individually and together predicted return to work/school about as well as the Disability Rating Scale and the Levels of Cognitive Functioning ("Rancho") Scale.

Special Considerations, Cautions, and Applications

Existing evidence for inter- and intrarater reliability of the PECS is some-what weak. The degree to which PECS items in all 16 categories can be scored reliably in daily practice of inpatient medical rehabilitation is un-known. No information has been identified regarding utility and relia-bility in other groups (e.g., community-living elderly with a disability). The wide scope of the items included and the option to complete only those categories or items of interest to the clinician/researcher or appli-cable to the patient make the PECS a flexible instrument. Participation in the Rehabilitation Outcomes Reporting System is normally required to have access to PECS.

The primary use of PECS is to assess patients' initial status, set goals, and monitor and report progress. Korner-Bitensky with her associates has published two studies of the utility of PECS information (completed by occupational and physical therapists) for these applications (Korner-

Bitensky, Mayo, Cabot, Becker, & Coopersmith, 1989; Korner-Bitensky, Mayo, & Poznanski, 1990). Aggregated over all patients in a particular program or in an entire institution, PECS scores are also used for administrative applications: quality assurance, utilization review, and program evaluation. Data from PECS have been used for studies of rehabilitation patient characteristics and of clinical interventions with these and other groups. Service delivery and health care services research also can fruitfully use PECS data as input, outcome, or moderator variables.

The Functional Independence Measure

The Functional Independence Measure (FIM) was developed as part of a uniform national data system for rehabilitation as a means of documenting inputs, costs, and outcomes of inpatient medical rehabilitation (Granger, Hamilton, Keith, Zielezny, & Sherwin, 1986; Hamilton, Granger, Sherwin, Zielezny, & Tashman, 1987; Keith, Granger, Hamilton, & Sherwin, 1987). The Uniform Data System (UDS) database, in addition to FIM disability information, also includes information on patients' impairment and disability.

The FIM consists of 18 items (see Table 4.7), which are all measured on a 7-point ordinal scale (State University of New York at Buffalo, 1993). The levels of function distinguished are described in broad outline in Table 4.8. The UDS guide gives specific instructions for scoring each item. There is no code for *no information*: the scoring instructions in the guide specify that items for which information is missing should be coded 1, *total assistance*, as should be tasks that the target person does not do.

The FIM is a "basic indicator of severity of disability." The underlying conceptual basis is "burden of care (type and amount of assistance) required for a disabled individual to perform basic life activities effectively" (Hamilton et al., 1987, p. 141), regardless of nature or severity of the disabling disorder or its resulting impairments. Burden of care "should translate into consumption of social and economic resources" (p. 141).

Although its primary application is in the description of rehabilitation inpatients and their status after discharge, the FIM was designed to be (a) applicable to a variety of settings (including rehabilitation inpatient units, nursing homes, outpatient clinics, and private residences) and (b) germane to all age groups from childhood to old age. The FoneFIM was developed as a version of the FIM that can be used in instances where patients or their caregivers are interviewed in order to develop estimates

Table 4.7

Functional Independence Measure: Listing of Items

Item	Description
A. Eating	Includes the use of suitable utensils to bring food to the mouth, chewing and swallowing once the meal is presented in the customary manner on a table or tray. Performs safely.
B. Grooming	Includes oral care, hair grooming (combing and brushing hair), washing the hands and washing the face, and either shaving the face or applying make-up. If there is no preference for shaving or applying make-up, then disregard. Performs safely.
C. Bathing	Includes bathing (washing, rinsing and drying) the body from the neck down (excluding the back); may be either tub, shower, or sponge/bed bath. Performs safely.
D. Dressing—upper body	Includes dressing and undressing above the waist, as well as applying and removing a prosthesis or orthosis when applicable. Performs safely.
E. Dressing—lower body	Includes dressing and undressing from the waist down, as well as applying and removing a prosthesis or orthosis when applicable. Performs safely.
F. Toileting	Includes maintaining perineal hygiene and adjusting clothing before and after using toilet or bedpan. Performs safely.
G. Bladder management	Includes complete intentional control of urinary bladder and, if necessary, use of equipment or agents for bladder control.
H. Bowel management	Includes complete intentional control of bowel movements and, if necessary, use of equipment or agents for bowel control.
I. Transfer: bed, chair, wheelchair	Includes all aspects of transferring to and from a bed, chair, and wheelchair, or coming to a standing position, if walking is the typical mode of locomotion. Performs safely.
J. Transfers: toilet	Includes getting on and off a toilet. Performs safely.
K. Transfers: tub or shower	Includes getting into and out of a tub or shower stall. Performs safely.
L. Locomotion: walk/wheelchair	Includes walking, once in a standing position, or if using a wheelchair, once in a seated position, on a level surface. Performs safely. The most frequent mode of locomotion (walk or wheelchair) is also reported.
M. Locomotion: stairs	Goes up and down 12 to 14 stairs (one flight) indoors. Performs safely.

continued

Table 4.7, cont

Item	Description
N. Comprehension	Includes understanding of either auditory or visual communication (e.g., writing, sign language, gestures). The usual mode of comprehension (Auditory or Visual) is also reported.
O. Expression	Includes clear vocal or nonvocal expression of language. This item includes either intelligible speech or clear expression of language using writing or a communication device. The usual mode of expression (Vocal or Nonvocal) is also reported.
P. Social interaction	Includes skills related to getting along and participating with others in therapeutic and social situations. It represents how one deals with one's own needs *together with* the needs of others.
Q. Problem solving	Includes skills related to solving problems of daily living. This means making reasonable, safe, and timely decisions regarding financial, social and personal affairs, and initiating, sequencing and self-correcting tasks and activities to solve problems.
R. Memory	Includes skills related to recognizing and remembering while performing daily activities in an institutional or community setting. Memory in this context includes the ability to store and retrieve information, particularly verbal and visual. The functional evidence of memory includes recognizing people frequently encountered, remembering daily routines, and executing requests without being reminded.

Note. From *Guide for the Uniform Data Set for Medical Rehabilitation (Adult FIM)* (Version 4). State University of New York at Buffalo, 1993. Copyright 1993 by Uniform Data System for Medical Rehabilitation, UB Foundation Activities, Inc. Adapted by permission.

of the target person's abilities—which is especially relevant to nonhospitalized groups or to follow-up of former inpatients.

Because even nondisabled children under 6 years of age are not independent in all tasks included in the FIM, a special version was developed for children: the WeeFIM (Granger, Hamilton, & Kayton, 1989; McCabe & Granger, 1990).

The FIM was designed to be suitable for completion by any medical rehabilitation professional. Completion is based on a patient's actual performance, as known to the clinicians who deal with the patient on a regular basis. Many facilities assign parts of the FIM to team members on the basis of expertise. Completion of the FIM has been reported to take an average

---

Table 4.8

Functional Independence Measure: Description of the Levels of Function

Independent: Another person is not required for the activity (No helper)
  7. Complete Independence. All of the tasks described as making up the activity are typically performed safely, without modification, assistive devices, or aids, and within a reasonable amount of time.
  6. Modified Independence. One or more of the following may be true: the activity requires an assistive device; the activity takes more than reasonable time, or there are safety (risk) considerations.
Dependent: Subject requires another person for either supervision or physical assistance in order for the activity to be performed, or it is not performed (Requires helper).
  Modified dependence: The subject expends half (50%) or more of the effort. The levels of assistance required are:
  5. Supervision or Setup. Subject requires no more help than standby, cuing, or coaxing, without physical contact, or, helper sets up needed items or applies orthoses.
  4. Minimal Contact Assistance. Subject requires no more help than touching, and expends 75% or more of the effort.
  3. Moderate Assistance. Subject requires more help than touching, or expends half (50%) or more (up to 75%) of the effort.
  Complete dependence. The subject expends less than half (less than 50%) of the effort. Maximal or total assistance is required, or the activity is not performed. The levels of assistance required are:
  2. Maximal Assistance. Subject expends less than 50% of the effort, but at least 25%.
  1. Total Assistance. Subject expends less than 25% of the effort.

Note. From *Guide for the Uniform Data Set for Medical Rehabilitation (Adult FIM)* (Version 4). State University of New York at Buffalo, 1993. Copyright 1993 by Uniform Data System for Medical Rehabilitation, UB Foundation Activities, Inc. Adapted by permission.

of 32 minutes (Gonella, 1992). A FIM total score is calculated by addition of all item scores. Subscores have been used frequently, either for two domains, motoric ability (Items 1 through 13) and social cognition (Items 14 through 18), or for the six major categories: self-care; bowel/bladder management, locomotion, transfers, communication, and cognition.

Psychometric Properties

Reliability. Published studies of the reliability of the FIM are limited. The best-known research involved 263 medical rehabilitation inpatients in 21 different hospitals who were rated by pairs of clinicians. The intraclass correlation coefficient (ICC) for the FIM total score was .97. The ICCs for six subscales ranged from .93 to .96. Values of kappa for individual items ranged from .61 to .76 (Hamilton, Laughlin, Granger, & Kayton, 1991).

Whiteneck (1988) reported on a study of interrater reliability that involved 127 spinal cord injury patients being treated in 13 model systems. Interrater reliability was .83 at admission and .96 at discharge. Another study of interrater reliability with a spinal cord injured sample (Segal, Ditunno, and Staas, 1992) also reported correlations of .83 for the total FIM score.

In a study reported by Adamovich (1992), 28 stroke patients were rated on the four FIM language items by both nurses and certified speech and language pathologists at both admission and discharge. For both time points, the nurses tended to give higher ratings (i.e., observe less disability) than the therapists; correlations were not reported. In a study by Fricke, Unsworth, and Worrell (1992), therapists also rated higher patterns of disability than did a UDS expert.

Validity. Content validity was addressed to some degree in the FIM's development. During both a pilot and a trial phase, over 100 participating clinicians representing many institutions used the instrument to rate patients and, subsequently, answered specific questions. They were almost unanimous that there were no unnecessary items (99% and 97%, respectively), and generally agreed (59% and 83%, respectively) that there was no need to add items (Hamilton et al., 1987). Whiteneck (1988) asked the same questions of a sample of over 30 spinal cord injury clinicians, and results were similar.

Direct comparisons of the FIM with other disability scales have been limited to the Barthel Index. A study of 41 spinal cord injury patients found correlations between the MBI and total scores for corresponding items of the FIM (rs = .94, .92, and .91 for rehabilitation admission, discharge, and follow-up, respectively; Roth, Davidoff, Haughton, & Ardner, 1990). Changes in BI from admission to discharge and from discharge to follow-up correlated well with changes in FIM.

A factor analysis of FIM data performed for a mixed rehabilitation population indicated that the FIM is not unidimensional, as its developers had assumed (Reid & Bonwich, 1989). This was confirmed by Rasch analysis of the UDS FIM data of almost 15,000 patients representing all major inpatient rehabilitation diagnostic groups (Linacre, Heinemann, Wright, Granger, & Hamilton, 1991). Analysis of all 18 items together suggested separating the five social cognition items from the 13 motoric items. When separate Rasch analyses were performed, fit statistics for both admission and discharge scores improved for both sets, with better calibration of items. Two later reports (Granger, Hamilton, Linacre, Hei-nemann, & Wright, 1993; Heinemann, Linacre, Wright, Hamilton, & Granger, 1993) involving UDS data on over 27,000 patients, confirmed the validity of the two-factor FIM. These authors also demonstrated that the difficulties of items relative to one another were very much the same across 13 diagnostic groups (right and left strokes, spinal cord injury, orthopedic impairment, traumatic brain injury, etc.), especially for the motoric items.

Many studies have offered results indicating construct validity of the FIM. Increases in FIM total scores and subscores from rehabilitation ad-mission to discharge have been reported by several investigators (e.g., Dodds, Martin, Stolov, & Deyo, 1993; Granger & Hamilton, 1992; Gran-ger, Hamilton, & Fiedler, 1992) and for many diagnostic groups. Dodds et al. (1993) also found a predicted relationship in rehabilitation inpatients of FIM scores with (a) age, (b) number of comorbidities, (c) discharge destination, (d) level of injury in spinal injury patients, and (e) side of stroke in cardiovascular accident patients. They failed, however, to find a predicted relationship between FIM score and amputation level among lower-extremity amputees. Granger et al. (1992) demonstrated a rela-tionship between FIM score and age, side of stroke, and discharge desti-nation.

In a sample of 21 stroke patients, Granger, Cotter, Hamilton, and Fiedler (1993) found strong correlations between actual help (in minutes per day) received and total FIM score ($r = .81$), motor FIM score ($r = .79$), and the self-care ($r = .72$), mobility ($r = .79$), and locomotion ($r = .69$) subscores. In a parallel study of 24 persons with multiple sclerosis, the FIM total score had a similar correlation with help in minutes per day ($r = .77$; Granger et al., 1990). In another study focusing on help required, hours of care needed per week was estimated for 72 individuals with disability that was due to chronic neurological conditions. This estimate had a correlation of .76 with the FIM total score (Disler, Roy, & Smith, 1993).

Special Considerations, Cautions, and Applications

The FIM offers a compromise between short instruments, which may lack reliability or sensitivity, and longer ones that offer unnecessary duplica-tion of items or include elements of impairment or handicap in what is supposedly a disability measure.

Several studies have suggested that the FIM, in spite of its 7-point scale, lacks sensitivity (Davidoff, Roth, Haughton, & Ardner, 1990; Marion et al., 1993). It appears this is the case for subjects at the extremes of the range considered in specific areas of ability.

Although extensive information is available on the reliability and validity of the FIM with respect to rehabilitation inpatients, we do not know the utility, reliability, or validity of this measure when used with community-dwelling subjects, whether for service management and evaluation or for research. Ceiling effects have been hinted at in some of the studies of inpatients. Gutierrez and Keith (1993) reported ceiling effects for traumatic brain injury outpatients with respect to self-care and locomotion items, and for stroke outpatients for self-care items.

Although designed primarily as an instrument for documenting effectiveness and efficiency of (inpatient) rehabilitation at the institution level, the FIM has been used for a number of other purposes, including goal setting for individual patients, progress monitoring, and reporting. The American Spinal Injury Association has included the FIM in its *Standards for Neurological and Functional Classification of Spinal Cord Injury* (1992), which provides standards for performing patient testing and recording of neurological and functional information in medical records. At the program or institution level, the scale is also used for utilization review, quality assurance, program evaluation, and marketing.

The FIM has been used extensively for research. The national data bases of the spinal cord injury and traumatic brain injury model systems groups are using it as an outcome measure, as does the National Acute Spinal Cord Injury Study III (NASCIS III) collaborative research group (Ditunno, 1992). In research, FIM scores have been used both as outcome variables in the evaluation of rehabilitation interventions and as correlates of other variables of interest, for example, depression.

Because the FIM was originally developed with federal government funding, the instrument is available royalty free. That presumably is the reason for its frequent use in research. The number of publications reporting its use is too large to cite here (but many have been noted above).

Functional Assessment Inventory

The Functional Assessment Inventory (FAI) was designed to help counselors to collect and to organize vocationally relevant information about clients. It consists of 30 behaviorally anchored rating scales that cover the full range of characteristics thought to influence employability and a checklist of 10 special strengths. The FAI focuses on observable behaviors or traits rather than on attributes that can only be inferred. Each of the rating scales range from zero (representing normal or better

Table 4.9

Functional Assessment Inventory: Listing of Items in Order of Loading on Factor Scales

Category	Item
1.	Adaptive Behavior
	29. Congruence of behavior with rehabilitation goals
	28. Judgment
	27. Effective interaction with employers and co-workers
	24. Work habits
	25. Social support system
	30. Initiative and problem solving ability
2.	Motor Functioning
	10. Hand functioning
	9. Upper extremity functioning
	11. Motor speed
	12. Ambulation or mobility
3.	Cognition
	1. Learning ability
	2. Ability to read and write in English
	3. Memory
	4. Spatial and form perception
4.	Physical Condition
	14. Endurance
	15. Loss of time from work
	13. Capacity for exertion
	16. Stability of condition
	12. Ambulation or mobility
5.	Communication
	7. Speech
	6. Hearing
	8. Language functioning
6.	Vocational Qualifications
	18. Acceptability to employers
	22. Access to job opportunities
	17. Work history
	21. Economic disincentives
	19. Personal attractiveness
	20. Skills
	23. Requirements for special working conditions
7.	Vision
	5. Vision

levels of functioning) to 3, representing substantial degrees of impairment.

Table 4.9 lists the major dimensions of the FAI that have been identified in repeated factor analytic studies (Crewe & Athelstan, 1981, 1984;

Crewe & Turner, 1984), together with the items that load most heavily on each factor.

The Personal Capacities Questionnaire (PCQ) is an item-by-item translation of the FAI into first-person terms. It can be completed by the client, and the scores can be compared with those produced by the counselor on the FAI. The FAI is intended to be used with late adolescents or adults who have any type of disability and who are receiving vocational counseling. It is typically administered and scored using a paper-and-pencil booklet and answer sheet. Information on which counselors may base their FAI ratings can be gathered from diverse sources including interviews, observations, tests, work samples, medical and other reports, and so forth. Once the counselor has done a thorough job of collecting background information about the client, only 5 to 10 additional minutes are needed to respond to the items of the FAI. Scores can be tallied to produce a *total limitations* score and approximate scores on each of the factors. A computer-based version that calculates factor scores and produces graphic profiles of scores was developed by Abt Associates (Cambridge, MA).

Psychometric Properties

Reliability. Interrater reliability was measured by having pairs of counselors view 25 live interviews and rate the client on the FAI. On 75% of the ratings, the counselors assigned the identical score, and on another 22% they differed by only 1 point on the 4-point scale (Crewe & Athelstan, 1984). Another series of interviews produced comparable results, leading the authors to conclude that the interrater reliability of the FAI is satisfactory.

Cronbach's alpha and standardized item alpha analyses were calculated in another study (Turner, 1982) in which 54 counselors read case materials and viewed a videotaped interview. The average reliability coefficient alpha was .80, and the average Cronbach's alpha for each item was .74 for one interview and .79 for the second interview. Turner (1982) concluded that the findings demonstrate "with some certainty that, taken as a whole, the FAI is reliable, and that the individual items were scored reliably as well" (p. 55).

Validity. Several field tests of the FAI are reported in the manual (Crewe & Athelstan, 1984). Summarizing the extensive data presented, the authors documented logical relationships between the functional limitations scales and primary diagnosis. They also found significant correlations between total FAI scores and counselors' judgments of their clients' severity of disability (.60) and prospects for work (−.61).

With respect to predictive validty, Crewe and Athelstan found that 21 of the 30 functional limitations scales and four of the strength items were significantly related to the achievement of competitive work goals. In general, individuals in competitive work were much less likely to have limitations, whereas those in sheltered employment were rated as most limited. People who were not working at all were rated as having a moderate level of limitation.

Turner (1982), using a national sample of vocational rehabilitation clients, identified significant correlations in the predicted directions between FAI scores and diagnostic categories, work status at closure, and earnings at closure.

Special Considerations, Cautions, and Applications

Because the FAI was designed to provide a holistic assessment of capacities with the fewest items and minimum burden, it does not examine any single area in great depth. Furthermore, although satisfactory interrater reliability has been demonstrated under research conditions, the inventory is based on behavioral rating scales. As such, it relies on counselor judgment and objectivity for its accuracy. It is possible that ratings could be skewed if the incentive exists to do so (for example, to demonstrate positive change in functioning as an outcome of services.) Interpretation of the FAI factor scores and total functional limitations score still need to be clarified through the application of a Rasch analysis of the instrument.

The FAI has been used by the state and federal vocational rehabilitation programs in several states (including Wisconsin, Minnesota, and Vermont) to aid in making and documenting decisions regarding eligibility and service provision. Used together, the FAI and the PCQ can provide a global picture of an individual's strengths and limitations as they relate to vocational planning. The PCQ presents the client's view, which may provide new information to the counselor. Discrepancies between ratings on the two instruments may serve as the basis for fruitful discussions in counseling sessions. The FAI can also be used as a measure of severity of disability in vocational rehabilitation studies.

Wallner (1989) studied the FAI with a sample of clients with severe and persistent mental health problems. He found that the Total Functional Limitations score and 5 subgroups of items (including stability of condition, work habits, and judgment) were significantly related to job tenure. Lynch (1981) conducted a study using 270 cases from the Wisconsin Division of Vocational Rehabilitation and found that 45% of the criterion variance (case outcomes) could be accounted for by FAI scores and demographic characteristics. In addition, he demonstrated that client typologies associated with probabilities of success could be constructed, providing a basis for identifying clients in need of special services to avert the probability of failure in rehabilitation.

The Ertomis Assessment Method

The Ertomis Assessment Method (EAM) was developed in Germany in the mid 1970s (Frey & Nieuwenhuijsen, 1990), and in Europe it has been found to be useful in the assessment and placement of injured workers and individuals with other disabilities. It provides for the parallel assessment of a worker and his or her job site, so that congruence between the two can be determined.

The evaluator collects information of various types including educational, environmental, demographic, psychometric, and other work-related data. Eventually this information is used as a basis for completing the Ability Profile that describes the capacities of the worker. The Requirement Profile is developed following observation of correct job performance and consultation with a supervisor. Each Ertomis instrument consists of 65 items that are rated on a 5-point scale. The items span seven work-related categories:

- Upper and lower extremities, coordination of movements
- Basic postures and motions
- Sensory abilities
- Mental abilities
- Speaking and writing as a means of communicating
- Tolerance of work-related environmental conditions
- Leadership abilities

At the same time that data are gathered for the Requirement Profile, risk factors for reinjury are identified. These include repetitiveness, mechanical stress, specific postures, vibrations, and low temperatures (Frey & Nieuwenhuijsen, 1990). As the final step, the two profiles are compared. Areas where the ratings match or where the worker's capacity exceeds the demands of the job (*under demand* areas) are considered satisfactory. *Over demands*, however, point to potential problems unless accommodations can be made.

Psychometric Properties

The ERTOMIS System has been widely used and studied in Europe in vocational, industrial, and rehabilitation settings. According to Frey and Nieuwenhuijsen (1990), the reliability of the EAM has been affirmed in several studies in Germany. The same authors briefly cite multiple validation studies involving the successful placement of injured workers and also the identification of over demand characteristics that resulted in unsatisfactory job performance among workers.

Special Considerations, Cautions, and Applications

Because virtually all of the developmental work on the EAM was done in Europe, literature on this instrument is less readily available to American practitioners. Research is needed to determine the extent to which the EAM is valid and useful in this country. Reports of studies involving this instrument in Europe have been published by Jochhein, Koch, Mittelsten Scheid, Schian, and Weinman (1984) and Mittelsten Scheid (1984). The EAM has the potential to be very useful to vocational rehabilitation practitioners. A special strength of the instrument is that identical profiles are provided to facilitate the evaluation of the individual worker and the job site, thus providing the basis for an informed opinion about the person's capacity for succeeding in the position. Furthermore, the EAM could be used to evaluate satisfactoriness of vocational rehabilitation outcomes.

Matching Person and Technology (MPT) Model

The MPT assessment (Scherer, 1993a, b, c) process is designed to aid in collaborative decision-making about what assistive technology would be most appropriate for a given individual. Several instruments make up the MPT assessment package, with versions of each to be completed by the consumer and by the service provider. They include (a) The Survey of Technology Use (SOTU); (b) The Assistive Technology Device Predisposition Assessment (ATD PA); (c) The Workplace Technology Predisposition Assessment (WP PA); (d) The Health Care Technology Predisposition Assessment (HCT PA); and (e) The Educational Technology Predisposition Assessment (ET PA).

The assumption underlying the MPT model is that personal and environmental factors are just as significant as the characteristics of an assistive device itself in determining whether a particular type of technology will be adopted and used successfully. Potentially negative influences must be identified and counteracted through careful assessment in order to avoid frustration and the wasting of resources. Completion of the inventories leads to the development of written plans for selection and support of assistive devices.

The target population for the MPT is individuals with physical or sensory disabilities. Age is not specified, although the client forms appear to require reading skills and judgment at a level beyond childhood. Two forms of each instrument are provided—one to be filled out by the consumer and one by a teacher, therapist, or employer. Ratings are done on one- or two-page forms. Components include checklists and rating scales, with blank spaces for recording final plans. Each instrument is made up of subscales that separately assess characteristics of the user's temperament, the technology, and the environment in which the person will be using the technology. Instructions are provided in the manual for scoring each of the forms.

Psychometric Properties

Reliability. Thirty rehabilitation students and professionals read case histories and viewed three videotaped interviews with individuals who were considering using an assistive or educational technology (Scherer & McKee, 1992). They then completed the Assistive Technology Device Predisposition Assessment (ATD PA). The percentage of exact agreement ranged from 21.1% to 100%, with higher consistency on items related to technology and its use at work or home and lower consistency on items related to user characteristics and incentives. In a study of interrater reliability of the Educational Technology Predisposition Assessment (ET PA), ratings were generally higher, with most raters agreeing exactly on a majority of items.

Validity. Content validity is assumed, inasmuch as the MPT instruments were based on the actual experiences of individuals who had used or discarded assistive technologies (Scherer, 1991). Criterion-related validity has been examined using contrasted group studies (Scherer & McKee, 1992). Deaf students who participated in a course delivered by electronic mail were interviewed using the ET PA. Those who were least satisfied with the course reported the most negative feelings about computers. In another study that compared the responses of people in a self-help group for the hard-of-hearing with a group of adults in the same age range who had hearing loss but did not use hearing aids, a significant difference was apparent in responses to the ATD PA. Individuals in the self-help group reported a great deal of perceived benefit from hearing aids, whereas those in the other group reported the opposite. For examples of items assessed in the ATD PA, please see Table 4.10.

Table 4.10

The Assistive Technology Device Predisposition Assessment (ATD PA) Consumer Form: Examples of Items Assessed in Each Subscale

Characteristics of the Disability

Rating of current capabilities in the following areas:

vision	hearing
speech	dexterity
mobility	upper extremity control
learning speed	lower extremity control
physical strength/stamina	

Rating of satisfaction with current status in each of the following areas:

activities of daily living	communication skills
physical comfort & well-being	overall health
social & recreational involvement	ability to go where desired
educational attainment	employment status/potential
emotional well-being	

Characteristics of the Person's Temperament and Personality

encouragement from family/friends	patience
curiosity and excitement about new things	cooperativeness
intimidation by technology	self-discipline
preference for a quiet, inactive life	anxiety
desire to go to school or work	motivation
outlook	compliance
self-image/identity	life satisfaction
sociability	independence
anger	depression

Characteristics of the Psychosocial Environments in which the Person will Use the Technology

assistance for use of the technology
comfort using the technology
   around family
   around friends
   at school/work
   out in public

Characteristics of the Assistive Technology

usability
aesthetics
affordability

Note. From Scherer. *Matching Person and Technology Model,* 1991, and *Living in the State of Stuck: How Technology Impacts the Lives of People with Disabilities,* Cambridge, MA: Brookline Books, 1993.

The instruments are still new and have not been widely studied except by the developer. They should be useful in a variety of medical, educational and vocational rehabilitation settings. They should aid consumers and professionals to predict whether an assistive device under consideration would likely be a worthwhile investment or whether it would probably be discarded soon after purchase. Factors likely to result in technology abandonment are identified by consumers themselves. Once they are identified, education and training efforts can be directed to intervening in obstacles to optimal technology use. Increasing numbers of assistive devices are becoming available to rehabilitation consumers. The MPT instruments may be applied in studies of device selection and utilization.

Craig Handicap Assessment and Reporting Technique (CHART)

The CHART is probably unique among functional assessment instruments in that it was designed to measure handicaps rather than disabilities (Whiteneck, Charlifue, Gerhart, Overholser, and Richardson, (1992). Handicaps, as defined by the World Health Organization (WHO; 1980), occur when a person is unable to fulfill usual social roles. Handicaps come into existence through interaction between the disabilities of an individual and the restrictions of the environment. Rehabilitation seeks to reduce handicaps by both alleviating a person's limitations and by eliminating barriers in the community, and CHART is the first comprehensive effort to measure such outcomes.

The CHART measures five of the six dimensions of handicap distinguished by the WHO (physical independence, mobility, occupation, social integration, and economic self-sufficiency), omitting only orientation, which did not lend itself to measurement. Physical independence is assessed in terms of the need for care and assistance. Mobility reflects the number of hours out of bed each day, days per week out of the house, and accessibility of home and transportation. Occupation includes various productive ways to use time: working, schooling, homemaking, maintaining one's home, doing volunteer work, engaging in active recreation, and engaging in self-improvement activities. Social integration is measured by questions involving who shares the individual's household and the frequency and diversity of other social contacts. Economic self-sufficiency reflects adjusted total family income. The CHART utilizes measurable behavioral descriptors to compare target individuals with the norms for able-bodied individuals in society.

The CHART is designed for use with adults with a physical disability who are living in the community. To date, it has been applied primarily with individuals who have spinal cord injuries. It consists of 27 items that measure the extent to which an individual is fulfilling social roles that are normally expected of able-bodied individuals. The items involve behaviors rather than attitudes or perceptions. Each of the five scales was calibrated to produce a score of 100 for most able-bodied individuals. Lower scores reflect a dissonance between what the individual is accomplishing and what independent adults ordinarily accomplish. The total maximum score is 500.

Psychometric Properties

Eight model spinal cord injury centers have cooperated in studies of the psychometric properties of CHART (Dijkers, 1991).

Reliability. Test—retest reliability for 135 subjects over a 1-week period ranged from .80 to .95 for the individual dimensions and reached .93 for the overall score. Another reliability study examined the correlation between responses provided by the subject and those given by a family member or other proxy. The resulting correlations were in the low .80s for all dimensions except for social integration, which was .28 (or .57 when only subjects living with spouses were included in the calculation).

Validity. The 135 subjects were rated by rehabilitation professionals as having either a high or a low level of handicap, and the resulting groups were compared in terms of CHART scores. Significant differences were identified on all dimensions except for economic self-sufficiency. A Rasch analysis showed that the CHART is "a well-calibrated linear scale, with a good fit of both items and persons to its data" (Whiteneck et al., 1992, p. 523).

The CHART was applied during follow-up to 342 former patients of a regional spinal injury system. Scores were calculated separately for six groups divided on the basis of American Spinal Injury Association (ASIA) motor scores. Across all dimensions, more severe levels of impairment were reflected in lower CHART scores.

Special Considerations, Cautions, and Applications

When handicap is used as a measure of program success, it must be recognized that some environmental factors that contribute to handicap may be beyond the reach of a rehabilitation program's influence. The applicability of CHART to populations other than those with spinal cord injury has not been evaluated. The CHART has the potential for being used to assess the status of individuals with disabilities at the time of follow-up to determine needs for further interventions. It also has potential for use in program evaluation.

Comparisons of These Tests and Conclusion

The first four instruments described in this chapter are designed primarily to measure disability within an inpatient medical rehabilitation setting. The BI is the oldest and one of the least burdensome to use. It focuses on physical capacities and does not assess cognition or communication. The FIM is a newer instrument that is also readily available and relatively low in burden. It is part of the Uniform Data System that is being promoted as the method for gathering consistent information about the efficacy of rehabilitation. Users are required to be trained and to pass a proficiency examination. The PECS and the Formations Outcomes System are both more detailed systems that are commercially available and that also require training for implementation.

Medical rehabilitation functional assessment instruments developed from simple Activities of Daily Living checklists. They differ from such lists in terms of measurement precision (up to 7 scale points vs. a simple *yes* or *no*) and nature of items included. As noted, the BI and MBI, which were created first, do not refer to any cognitive or communicative functioning, but the LORS and FIM do, and the PECS includes a large number of such items in the Communication, Psychology, and Neuropsychology sections. These items or sections are not intended to replace standardized tests used by speech and language pathologists or neuropsychologists. Rather, they reflect professional judgment on real-life performance. As such, they are ecologically valid—albeit for a hospital environment. Social functioning, omitted completely from the BI, the MBI, and LORS, is covered minimally in the FIM. The PECS adequately covers this area. According to the World Health Organization conceptual scheme of disablement, social, vocational, and family functioning are components of *handicap* (social role performance deficits) rather than *disability*, and they should be conceptualized and measured separately. The CHART, and another measure that is gaining some distribution, the Community Integration Questionnaire

(Willer, Rosenthal, Kreutzer, Gordon, & Kempel, 1993), were developed specifically to assess functioning in such wider social roles.

Bowling (1991) has noted that function can be measured using a variety of techniques including physical tests, direct observation of behavior, and interviews with the index person or a proxy. The functional assessment instruments developed in medical rehabilitation (including BI, LORS, PECS and FIM) almost without exception use direct observation as the primary technique. This results in a description of what the patient *does* do, rather that what he or she *can* do. In practice, the latter may be reflected because in inpatient facilities, patients are continuously exhorted to do the best they can. For reports on functioning at home (used, e.g., in program evaluation) interview is the primary data collection method; these reports are more likely to reflect what the person does. Very limited information is available on the comparability of observational and self-report data on function.

Self-report methods of functional ability are frequently used by researchers and by professionals in medical and other disciplines that have less opportunity to observe behavior over extended time periods. The functional assessment instruments devised by practitioners in disciplines other than rehabilitation tend to be less widely applicable than the measures discussed above, and they often include aspects of functioning other than those classified under disability. Reviews of these measures may be found for rheumatoid arthritis (Bell, Bombardier, and Tugwell, 1990), traumatic brain injury (Hall 1992), geriatrics (Applegate, Blass, and Williams, 1990), low back pain (Deyo, 1988), orthopedics (Liang, Fossel, and Larson, 1990), and pediatrics (Haley, Coster,and Ludlow, 1991), to mention some of the fields in which functional assessment has found a role.

Keith (1994) has noted that there is much overlap between the concept of *functional status*, as typically used in medical rehabilitation, and *health status*, a term used in health services research. Health status generally is conceptualized more broadly, often including such components as social role functioning, pain, mental health, and health perceptions. Instruments developed to measure health status typically contain various subscales, the totals of which become part of a profile reflecting health status. Such measures, for instance the Short-Form Health Survey (Ware & Sherbourne, 1992), are beginning to be used more widely by clinicians in addition to the health services research applications. Keith (1994) discusses conceptual, application, and method differences between functional assessment instruments and health status measures and describes their converging history.

A very recent trend is toward using a functional assessment instrument (by itself or supplemented with other measures) or a health status profile as a measure of quality of life (see, e.g., Spilker, 1990). However, these instruments lack information on how patients themselves judge their functional or health status, as is done in the Scherer MPT model (with the possible exception of the Health Care Technology Predisposition Assessment). Opinions on the relative importance of the various components of health or functional status, and expressions of satisfaction with each of them, would be expected to be more relevant to quality of life than a rating of proficiency on a series of ADL tasks generated by a professional. The issue of incorporating patient preferences and judgments into functional status measures has been discussed by several authors (e.g., W. P. Fisher, 1993), but no consensus has been reached on either the desirability of such, or on a method.

Two of the instruments described in the chapter, the FAI and the EAM, were developed for use in vocational rehabilitation. Each has some advantages and some drawbacks. The FAI is brief, low in burden, and readily available. Further, a comparable form, the PCQ, is available for the client to fill out. This client-generated data can provide new and important information to the rehabilitation counselor. On the other hand, the EAM is more detailed, and it has the advantage of offering a parallel form to use for evaluation of the workplace. This provides a method for matching individual capacities with job demands to determine the adequacy of fit provided by a potential placement. The other instruments described in this chapter each have unique purposes and cannot reasonably be compared with other functional assessment tools.

The field of functional assessment has progressed significantly in recent years with the development of instruments that are much improved in terms of their psychometric qualities. They represent essential tools for program evaluation, and they also contribute significantly to the assessment of individuals in medical, vocational, and independent living rehabilitation programs.

References

Adamovich, B. L. D. (1992). Pitfalls in functional assessment. A comparison of FIM ratings by speech-language pathologists and nurses. *Neurorehabilitation, 2*, 42–51.

American Spinal Injury Association. (1992). *Standard for neurological and functional classification of spinal cord injury* (Rev. ed.). Chicago: Author.

Anthony, W. A., & Farkas, M. (1982). A client outcome planning model for assessing psychiatric rehabilitation interventions. *Schizophrenia bulletin, 8*, 13–38.

Applegate, W. B., Blass, J. P., & Williams, T. F. (1990). Instruments for the functional assessment of older patients. *The New England Journal of Medicine, 322*, 1207–1213.

Bell, M. J., Bombardier, C., & Tugwell, P. (1990). Measurement of functional status, quality of life, and utility in rheumatoid arthritis. *Arthritis and Rheumatism, 33*, 591–601.

Bergner, M., Bobbitt, R. A., Carter, W. B., & Gilson, B. S. (1981). The Sickness Impact Profile: Development and final revision of a health status measure. *Medical Care, 19*, 787–805.

Bonder, B. R. (1993). Issues in the assessment of psychosocial components of function. *American Journal of Occupational Therapy, 47*, 211–216.

Bowling, A. (1991). *Measuring health: A review of Quality of life measurement scales.* Milton Keynes: Open University Press.

Carey, R. G., & Posavac, E. J. (1978). Program evaluation of a physical medicine and rehabilitation unit: A new approach. *Archives of Physical Medicine and Rehabilitation, 59*, 330–337.

Carey, R. G., & Posavac, E. J. (1982). Rehabilitation program evaluation using a Revised Level of Rehabilitation Scale. *Archives of Physical Medicine and Rehabilitation, 63*, 367–370.

Carey, R. G., & Seibert, J. H. (1988). Integrating program evaluation, quality assurance, and marketing for inpatient rehabilitation. *Rehabilitation Nursing, 13*, 66–70.

Carey, R. G., Seibert, J. H., & Posavac, E. J. (1988). Who makes the most progress in inpatient rehabilitation? An analysis of functional gain measured by the Revised Level of Rehabilitation Scale. *Archives of Physical Medicine and Rehabilitation, 69*, 337–343.

Chaudhuri, G., Harvey, R. F., Sulton, L. D., & Lambert, R. W. (1988). Computerized tomography head scans as predictors of functional outcome of stroke patients. *Archives of Physical Medicine and Rehabilitation, 69*, 496–498.

Clydesdale, T. T., Fahs, I. J., Kilgore, K. M., & Splaingard, M. L. (1990). Social dimensions to functional gain in pediatric patients. *Archives of Physical Medicine and Rehabilitation, 71*, 469–472.

Cohen, B. F., & Anthony, W. A. (1984). Functional assessment in psychiatric rehabilitation. In A. S. Halpern & M. Fuhrer (Eds.), *Functional assessment in rehabilitation* (pp. 79–100). Baltimore: Brookes.

Collin, C., Wade, D. T., Davies, S., & Horne, V. (1988). The Barthel ADL Index: A reliability study. *International Disabilty Studies, 10*, 61–63.

Crewe, N. M. (1992). Functional assessment and the Americans with Disabilities Act. In J. K. O'Brien (Ed.), *ADA train the trainer program.* Carbondale: Southern Illinos University.

Crewe, N. M., & Athelstan, G. T. (1981). Functional assessment in vocational rehabilitation: A systematic approach to diagnosis and goal setting. *Archives of Physical Medicine and Rehabilitation, 62*, 299–305.

Crewe, N. M., & Athelstan, G. T. (1984). *Functional assessment inventory manual.* Menomonie: The Materials Development Center, University of Wisconsin—Stout.

Crewe, N. M., & Turner, R. R. (1984). Functional assessment in vocational rehabilitation. In A. Halpern & M. Fuhrer (Eds.), *Functional assessment in rehabilitation.* (pp. 223–238). Baltimore: Brookes.

Curtin, M., & Klyczek, J. P. (1992). Comparison of Ba FPE–TOA scores for inpatients and outpatients. *Occupational Therapy in Mental Health, 12*, 61–75.

Davidoff, G. N., Roth, E. J. Haughton, J. S., & Ardner, M. S. (1990). Cognitive dysfunction in spinal cord injury patients: Sensitivity of the Functional Independence Measure subscales vs. neuropsychologic assessment. *Archives of Physical Medicine and Rehabilitation, 71,* 326–329.

Derby, K. M., Wacker, D. P., Sasso, G., & Steege, M. (1992). Brief functional assessment techniques to evaluate aberrant behavior in an outpatient setting: A summary of 79 cases. *Journal of Applied Behavior Analysis, 25,* 713–721.

Deyo, R. A. (1988). Measuring the functional status of patients with low back pain. *Archives of Physial Medicine and Rehabilitation, 69,* 1044–1053.

Dijkers, M., with the CHART study group. (1991). Scoring CHART: Survey and sensitivity analysis. *Journal of the American Paraplegia Society, 14,* 85–86.

Disler, P. B., Roy, C. W., & Smith, B. P. (1993). Predicting hours of care needed. *Archives of Physical Medicine and Rehabilitation, 74,* 139–143.

Ditunno, J. F., Jr. (1992). Functional assessment measures in CNS trauma. *Journal of Neurotrauma, 9*(Suppl. 1), S301–S305.

Dodds, T. A., Martin, D. P., Stolov, W. C., & Deyo, R. A. (1993). A validation of the Functional Independence Measure and its performance among rehabilitation inpatients. *Archives of Physical Medicine and Rehabilitation, 74,* 531–536.

Downing, J. E., & Perino, D. M. (1992). Functional vs. standardized assessment procedures: Implications for educational programming. *Mental Retardation, 30,* 289–295.

Droege, R. C. (1987). The USES testing program. In B. Bolton (Ed.), *Handbook of measurement and evaluation in rehabilitation* (pp. 169–182). Baltimore: Brookes.

Fisher, A. G. (1993). The assessment of IADL motor skills: An application of many-faceted Rasch analysis. *American Journal of Occupational Therapy, 47,* 319–329.

Fisher, W. P. (1993). Measurement-related problems in functional assessment. Special issue: Alternative strategies for functional assessment. *American Journal of Occupational Therapy, 47,* 331–338.

Fisher, W. P., Taylor, P., Kilgore, K. M., Harvey, R. F., & Kelly, C. K. (1993). REHABITS: Towards a common language of functional assessment [Abstract]. *Archives of Physical Medicine and Rehabilitation, 74,* 661.

Formations. (1992). *Level of Rehabilitation Scale (LORS-III) Reference Manual.* Chicago: Formations in Health Care.

Fortinsky, R. H., Granger, C. V., & Seltzer, G. B. (1981). The use of functional assessment in understanding home care needs. *Medical Care, 19,* 489–497.

Foss, G., Bullis, M. D., & Vilhauer, D. A. (1984). Assessment and training of job-related social competence for mentally retarded adolescent and adults. In A. S. Halpern & M. Fuhrer (Eds.), *Functional assessment in rehabilitation* (pp. 145–157). Baltimore: Brookes.

Frattali, C. M. (1992). Functional assessment of communication: Merging public policy with clinical views. *Aphasiology, 6,* 63–83.

Frey, W. D., & Nieuwenhuijsen, R. R. (1990). The Ertomis Assessment Method: An innovative job placement strategy. In M. Berkowitz (Ed.), *Forging linkages: Modifying disability benefit programs to encourage employment* (pp. 121–156). New York: Rehabilitation International.

Fricke, J., Unsworth, C., & Worrell, D. (1992). Reliability of the Functional Independence Measure with occupational therapists. *Australian Occupational Therapy Journal, 40,* 7–15.

Garner, D., Becker, H., Schur, S., & Hammer, E. (1991). An innovative program for multihandicapped deaf students using the FSSI. *American Annals of the Deaf, 136,* 265–269.

Gonnella, C. (1992). Program evaluation. In G. F. Fletcher, J. D. Banja, B. B. Jann, &

S. L. Wolf (Eds.), *Rehabilitation medicine: clinical perspectives* (pp. 243–268). Philadelphia: Lea & Febiger.

Granger, C. V. (1982). Health accounting: Functional assessment of the long-term patient. In F. J. Kottke, G. K. Stillwell, & J. F. Lehmann (Eds.), *Krusen's handbook of physical medicine and rehabilitation* (3rd ed., pp. 253–274). Philadelphia: Saunders.

Granger, C. V., Albrecht, G. L., & Hamilton, B. B. (1979). Outcome of comprehensive medical rehabilitation: measurement by PULSES profile and the Barthel Index. *Archives of Physical Medicine and Rehabilitation, 60*, 145–154.

Granger, C. V., Cotter, A. C., Hamilton, B. B. & Fiedler, R. C. (1993). Functional assessment scales: A study of persons after stroke. *Archives of Physical Medicine and Rehabilitation, 74*, 133–138.

Granger, C. V., Cotter, A. C., Hamilton, B. B., Fiedler, R. C., & Hens, M. M. (1990). A study of persons with multiple sclerosis. *Archives of Physical Medicine and Rehabilitation, 71*, 870–875.

Granger, C. V., Dewis, L. S., Peters, N. C., Sherwood, C. S., & Barrett, J. E. (1979). Stroke rehabilitation: Analysis of repeated Barthel Index measures. *Archives of Physical Medicine and Rehabilitation, 60*, 14–17.

Granger, C. V., & Greer, D. S. (1976). Functional status measurement and medical rehabilitation outcomes. *Archives of Physical Medicine and Rehabilitation, 57*, 103–109.

Granger, C. V., Greer, D. S., Liset, E., Coulombe, J., & O'Brien, E. (1975). Measurement of outcomes of care for patients. *Stroke, 6*, 34–41.

Granger, C. V., & Hamilton, B. B. (1990). Measurement of stroke rehabilitation outcome in the 1980s. *Stroke, 21* (Suppl. II), 46–47.

Granger, C. V., & Hamilton, B. B. (1992). UDS report: The Uniform Data System for Medical Rehabilitation report for first admissions for 1990. *American Journal of Physical Medicine and Rehabilitation, 71*, 108–113.

Granger, C. V., Hamilton, B. B., & Fielder, R. C. (1992). Discharge outcome after stroke rehabilitation. *Stroke, 23*, 978–982.

Granger, C. V., Hamilton, B. B., & Kayton, R. (1989). *Guide for the use of the Functional Independence Measure (WeeFIM) of the Uniform Data Set for Medical Rehabilitation*. Buffalo: Research Foundation of the State University of New York.

Granger, C. V., Hamilton, B.B., Keith, R. A., Zielezny, M., & Sherwin, F. S. (1986). Advances in functional assessment for medical rehabilitation. *Topics in Geratric Rehabilitation, 1*, 59–74.

Granger, C. V., Hamilton, B. B., Linacre, J. M., Heinemann, A. W., & Wright, B. D. (1993). Performance profiles of the Functional Independence Measure. *American Journal of Physical Medicine and Rehabilitation, 72*, 84–89.

Graves, W. H. (1990). Vocational capacity with visual impairments. In S. Scheer (Ed.), *Multidisciplinary perspectives in vocational assessment of impaired workers* (pp. 155–166). Rockville, MD: Aspen.

Gresham, G. E., & Labi, M. L. C. (1984). Functional assessment instruments currently available for documenting outcomes in rehabilitation medicine. In C. V. Granger & G. E. Gresham (Eds.), *Functional assessment in rehabilitation medicine* (pp. 65–85). Baltimore: Williams & Wilkins.

Gresham. G. E., Phillips, T. F., & Labi, M. L. C. (1980). ADL status in stroke: Relative merits of three standard indexes. *Archives of Physical Medicine and Rehabilitation, 61*, 355–358.

Gutierrez, P., & Keith, R. A. (1993). The Functional Independence Measure (FIM) with outpatients [Abstract]. *Archives of Physical Medicine and Rehabilitation, 74*, 669.

Haley, S. M., Coster, W. J., & Ludlow, L. H. (1991). Pediatric functional outcome measures. *Physical Medicine and Rehabilitation Clinics of North America, 2*, 689–723.

Hall, K. M. (1992). Overview of functional assessment scales in brain injury rehabilitation. *Neurorehabilitation, 2*, 98–113.

Halpern, A. S., & Fuhrer, M. J. (1984). *Functional assessment in rehabilitation*. Baltimore: Brookes.

Hamilton, B. B., Granger, C. V., Sherwin, F. S., Zielezny, M., & Tashman, J. S. (1987). A uniform national data system for medical rehabilitation. In M. J. Fuhrer (Ed.), *Rehabilitation outcomes. Analysis and measurement* (pp. 137–147). Baltimore: Brookes.

Hamilton, B. B., Laughlin, J. A., Granger, C. V., & Kayton, R. M. (1991). Interrater agreement of the seven level Functional Independence Measure (FIM) [Abstract]. *Archives of Physical Medicine and Rehabilitation, 72*, 790.

Harvey, R. F., & Jellinek, H. M. (1981). Functional performance assessment: A program approach. *Archives of Physical Medicine and Rehabilitation, 62*, 456–461.

Harvey, R. F., & Jellinke, H. M. (1983). Patient profiles: Utilization in functional performance assessment. *Archives of Physical Medicine and Rehabilitation, 64*, 268–271.

Harvey, R. F., Silverstein, B., Venzon, M. A., Kilgore, K. M., Fisher, W. P., Steiner, M., & Harley, J. P. (1992). Applying psychometric criteria to functional assessment in medical rehabilitation: III. Construct validity and predicting level of care. *Archives of Physical Medicine and Rehabilitation, 73*, 887–892.

Heinemann, A. W., Linacre, J. M., Wright, B. D., Hamilton, B.B., & Granger, C. (1993). Relationships between impairment and physical disability as measured by the Functional Independence Measure. *Archives of Physical Medicine and Rehabilitation, 74*, 566–573.

Jacobs, J. W. (1993). Measurement of functional ability and health status in the arthritic patient. *Patient Education and Counseling, 20*, 121–132.

Jochheim, K. A., Koch, M., Mittelsten Scheid, E., Schian, H. M., & Weinman, S. (1984). *ERTOMIS ability and requirement profiles: Aid for the vocational reintegration of the disabled.* Wuppertal, Germany: Gemeinnustsige Stiftung ERTOMIS.

Kane, R. A., & Kane, R. L. (1981). *Assessing the elderly*. Lexington, MA: Heath.

Keith, R. A. (1994). Functional status and health status. *Archives of Physical Medicine and Rehabilitation, 75*, 478–483.

Keith, R. A., Granger, C. V., Hamilton, B. B., & Sherwin, F. S. (1987). The functional Independence Measure: A new tool for rehabilitation. *Advances in Clincial Rehabilitation, 1*, 6–18.

Kilgore, K. M., Fisher, W. P., Silverstein, B., Harley, J. P., & Harvey, R. F. (1993). Application of Rasch analysis to the Patient Evaluation and Conference System. *Physical Medicine and Rehabilitation Clinics of North America, 4*, 493–515.

Korner-Bitensky, N., Mayo, N., Cabot, R., Becker, R., & Coopersmith, H. (1989). Motor and functional recovery after stroke: Accuracy of physical therapists' predictions. *Archives of Physical Medicine and Rehabilitation, 70*, 95–99.

Korner-Bitensky, N., Mayo, N. E., & Poznanski, S. G. (1990). Occupational therapists' accuracy in predicting sensory, perceptual–cognitive and functional recovery post-stroke. *Occupational Therapy Journal of Research, 10*, 237–249.

Law, M., & Letts, L. (1989). A critical review of scales of activities of daily living. *American Journal of Occupational Therapy, 43*, 522–528.

Liang, M. H., Fossel, A. H., & Larson, M. G. (1990). Comparisons of five health status instruments for orthopedic evaluation. *Medical Care, 28*, 632–642.

Linacre, J. M., Heinemann, A. W., Wright, B. D., Granger, C. V., & Hamilton, B. B.

(1991). *The Functional Independence Measure as a measure of disability* (Research Report No. 91–01). Chicago: Rehabilitation Institute of Chicago.

Loewen, S. C., & Anderson, B. A. (1988). Reliability of the Modified Motor Assessment Scale and the Barthel Index. *Physical Therapy, 68*, 1077–1081.

Lynch, R. K. (1981). Functional factors related to vocational rehabilitation outcome: Implications for service providers and researchers. *Journal of Applied Rehabilitation Counseling, 12*, 113–122.

Mahoney, F. I., & Barthel, D. W. (1965). Functional evaluation: The Barthel Index. *Maryland Medical Journal, 14*, 61–65.

Mahoney, F. I., Wood, O. H., & Barthel, D. W. (1958). Rehabilitation of chronically ill patients: The influence of complications on the final goal. *Southern Medical Journal, 51*, 605–609.

Mahurin, R. K., DeBettignies, B. H., & Pirozzolo, F. J. (1991). Structured assessment of independent living skills: Preliminary report of a performance measure of functional abilities in dementia. *Journal of Gerontology, 46*, 58–66.

Malec, J., & Niemeyer, R. (1983). Psychological prediction of duration of inpatient spinal cord injury rehabilitation and performance of self-care. *Achives of Physical Medicine and Rehabilitation, 64*, 359–363.

Malzer, R. L. (1988). Patient performance level during inpatient physical rehabilitation: Therapist, nurse and patient perspectives. *Archives of Physical Medicine and Rehabilitation, 69*, 363–365.

Marianjoy, Inc. (1992a). *The Rehabilitation Outcome Reporting System with PECS: Manual for clinicians* (Version 3.0, 2nd printing). Wheaton, IL: Marianjoy Rehabilitation Hospital and Clinics.

Marianjoy, Inc. (1992b). *The Rehabilitation Outcome Reporting System with PECS. Manual for managers* (Version 3.0). Wheaton, IL: Marianjoy Rehabilitation Hospital and Clinics.

Marianjoy, Inc. (1992c). *The Rehabilitation Outcome Reporting System with PECS: Software manual* (Version 3.1). Wheaton, IL: Marianjoy Rehabilitation Hospital and Clinics.

Marino, R. J., Huang, M., Knight, P., Herbison, G. J., Ditunno, J. F., Jr, & Segal, M. (1993). Assessing selfcare status in quadriplegia: Comparison of the Quadriplegia Index of Function (QIF) and the Functional Independence Measure (FIM). *Paraplegia, 31*, 225–233.

Mattison, P. G., Aitken, R. C. B., & Prescott, R. J. (1991). Rehabilitation status–The relationship between the Edinburgh Rehabilitation Status Scale (ERSS), Barthel Index, and PULSES profile. *International Disability Studies, 13*, 9–11.

McCabe, M. A., & Granger, C. V. (1990). Content validity of a pediatric functional independence measure. *Applied Nursing Research, 3*, 120–122.

McCrone, W. P., & Jacobs, R. (1990). Assessing the vocational capacity of the hearing impaired individual. In S. Scheer (Ed.), *Multidisciplinary perspectives in vocational assessment of impaired workers* (pp. 167–183). Rockville, MD: Aspen.

McCue, M. (1989). The role of assessment in the vocational rehabilitation of adults with specific learning disability. *Rehabilitation Counseling Bulletin, 33*, 18–37.

McDowell, I., & Newell, C. (1987). *Measuring health: A guide to rating scales and questionnaires*. New York: Oxford University Press.

McGinnis, G. E., Seward, M. L., DeJong, G., & Osberg, J. S. (1986). Program evaluation of physical medicine and rehabilitation departments using self-report Barthel. *Archives of Physical Medicine and Rehabilitation, 67*, 123–125.

Meisels, S. J., Liaw, F., Dorfman, A., & Fails, R. (1993, April). *When teachers teach by studying how children learn: The effectiveness of a comprehensive performance assessment for young children*. Paper presented at the meeting of the American Educational Research Association, Atlanta, GA.

Mikail, S. F., DuBreuil, S. C., & D'Eon, J. L. (1993). A comparative analysis of measures used in the assessment of chronic pain patients. *Psychological Assessment, 5*, 117–120.

Mittelsten Scheid, E. (1984). Abilities and requirements profiles: A tool to facilitate reintegration of persons with disabilities into employment. *International Rehabilitation Medicine, 7*, 82–84.

Oakley, F., Sunderland, T., Hill, J. L., & Phillips, S. L. (1991). The Daily Activities Questionnaire: A functional assessment for people with Alzheimer's Disease. *Physical and Occupational Therapy in Geriatrics, 10*, 67–81.

Oswald, W. D., & Gunzelmann, T. (1992). Functional rating scales and psychometric assessment in Alzheimer's Disease. *International Psychogeriatrics, 4*, 79–88.

Rao, N., Jellinek, H. M., Harvey, R. F., & Flynn, M. M. (1984). Computerized tomography head scans as predictors of rehabilitation outcome. *Archives of Physical Medicine and Rehabilitation, 65*, 18–20.

Rao, N., & Kolgore, K. M. (1992). Predicting return to work in traumatic brain injury using assessment scales. *Archives of Physical Medicine and Rehabilitation, 73*, 911–916.

Reid, J. C., & Bonwich, E. B. (1989). An investigation of the factor structure of the National Uniform Data System Functional Independence Measure [Abstract]. *Archives of Physical medicine and Rehabilitation, 70*(Suppl. A), 31.

Ross, S. E., O'Malley, K. F., Stein, S., & Spettell, C. M. (1992). Abbreviated injury scaling of head injury as a prognostic tool for functional outcome. *Accident Analysis and Prevention, 24*, 181–185.

Roth, E., Davidoff, G., Haughton, J., & Ardner, M. (1990). Functional assessment in spinal cord injury: A comparison of the Modified Barthel Index and the "adapted" Functional Independence Measure. *Clinical Rehabilitation, 4*, 277–285.

Roy, C. W., Togneri, J., Hay, E., & Pentland, B. (1988). An inter-rater reliability study of the Barthel Index. *International Journal of Rehabilitation Reserach, 11*, 67–70.

Santopoalo, R. (1989). From a LORS advocate [Letter to the editor]. *Archives of Physical Medicine and Rehabilitation, 70*, 863.

Scherer, M. J. (1991). *Matching person and technology model (and assessment instruments)*. Rochester, NY: Author.

Scherer, M. (1993a). *Living in the state of stuck: How technology impacts the lives of people with disabilities*. Cambridge, MA: Brookline Books.

Scherer, M. (1993b). Assessing the outcomes of AT use. In M. Binion (Ed.), *Proceedings of the RESNA International '93 Conference: Engineering the ADA* (pp. 49–50). Washington, DC: RESNA Press.

Scherer, M. (1993c, June). The Assistive Technology Device Predisposition Assessment: How does it measure up as a measure? [Abstract]. *Archives of Physical Medicine & Rehabilitation, 74*(6), 665.

Scherer, M. J., & McKee, B. G. (1992, April). *Early validity and reliability data for two instruments assessing the predispositions people have toward technology use: Continued integration of quantitative and qualitative methods*. Paper presented at the meeting of the American Educational Research Association, San Francisco, (ERIC Document Reproduction Service No. ED 346124).

Schmidt, S. M., Herman, L. M., Koenig, P., Leuze, M., Monahan, M. K., & Stubbers, R. W. (1986). Status of stroke patients: A community assessment. *Archives of Physical Medicine and Rehabilitation, 67*, 99–102.

Segal, M. E., Ditunno, J. F., & Staas, W. E. (1993). Interinstitutional agreement of individual Functional Independence Measure (FIM) items measured at two sites on one sample of SCI patients. *Paraplegia, 31,* 622–631.

Shah, S., Vanclay, F., & Cooper, B. (1989). Improving the sensitivity of the Barthel Index for stroke rehabilitation. *Journal of Clinical Epidemiology, 42,* 703–709.

Shinar, D., Gross, C. R., Bronstein, K. S., Licata-Gehr, E. E., Eden, D. T., Cabrera, A. R., Fishman, I. G., Roth, A. A., Barwick, J. A., & Kunitz, S. C. (1987). Reliability of the Activities of Daily Living Scale and its use in telephone interview. *Archives of Physical Medicine and Rehabilitation, 68,* 723–728.

Silverstein, B., Fisher, W. P., Kilgore, K. M., Harley, J. P., & Harvey, R. F. (1992). Applying psychometric criteria to functional assessment in medical rehabilitation: II. Defining interval measures. *Archives of Physical Medicine and Rehabilitation, 73,* 507–518.

Spilker, B. (Ed.), (1990). *Quality of life assessments in clinical trials.* New York: Raven Press.

State University of New York at Buffalo. (1993). *Guide for the Uniform Data Set for Medical Rehabilitation (Adult FIM)* (Version 4.0). Buffalo, NY: Author.

Turner, R. R. (1982). *Invitational symposium: Functional assessment. Summary of Proceedings* (Research Report, Contract No. 105-78-4012). Cambridge, MA: Abt Associates.

Velozo, C. A. (1993). Work evaluations: Critique of the state of the art of functional assessment at work. *American Journal of Occupational Therapy, 47,* 203–209.

Velozo, C. A., Magalhaes, L., Pan, A., & Weeks, D. K. (1993). Measurement qualities of the Level of Rehabilitation Scale-III (LORS-III) [Abstract]. *Archives of Physical Medicine and Rehabilitation, 74,* 661.

Wade, D. T., & Collin, C. (1988). The Barthel ADL Index: A standard measure of physical disability? *International Disability Studies, 10,* 64–67.

Wade, D. T., & Langton Hewer, R. (1987). Functional abilities after stroke: Measurement, natural history and prognosis. *Journal of Neurology, Neurosurgery and Psychiatry, 50,* 177–182.

Wallner, R. J. (1989). The Functional Assessment Inventory and job tenure for persons with severe and persistent mental health problems. *Journal of Applied Rehabilitation Counseling, 20,* 13–15.

Ware, J. E., & Sherbourne, C. D. (1992). The MOS 36-item Short-Form Health Survey (SF-36): Conceptual framework and item selection. *Medical Care, 30,* 473–483.

Whiteneck, G. G. (1988). A Functional Independence Measure trial in spinal cord injury model systems [Abstract]. *Proceedings of the American Spinal Injury Association, 14,* 48.

Whiteneck, G. G., Charlifue, S. W., Gerhart, K. A., Overholser, J. D., & Richardson, G. N. (1992). Quantifying handicap: A new measure of long-term rehabilitation outcomes. *Archives of Physical Medicine and Rehabilitation, 73,* 519–526.

Wickstrom, R. J. (1990). Functional capacity testing, In S. Scheer (Ed.), *Multidisciplinary perspectives in vocational assessment of impaired workers* (pp. 73–88). Rockville, MD: Aspen.

Willer, B., Rosenthal, M., Kreutzer, J. S., Gordon, W. A., & Rempel, R. (1993). Assessment of community integration following rehabilitation for traumatic brain injury. *Journal of Head Trauma Rehabilitation, 8,* 75–87.

World Health Organization. (1980). *The international classification of impairments, disabilities and handicaps: A manual of classification relating to the consequences of disease.* Geneva: Author.

Bedside Screening of Neurocognitive Function

Mark T. Wagner, Madhabika Nayak, and Christine Fink

The purpose of this chapter is to review some of the brief bedside mental status instruments and techniques currently in use for screening of suspected central nervous system dysfunction. Several assumptions bias this review. The first is the premise that there is no quick fix. Generally speaking, increased brevity in the mental status examination results in proportionally limited applicability of the obtained findings. This is true for diagnostic considerations and is especially the case for neuro-rehabilitative applications. The clinician who feels a 10-minute mental status examination can substitute for a comprehensive neurocognitive examination does not understand the limitations of the instrument or the diagnostic procedure.

The second bias is toward caution. Appropriate neurobehavioral training and experience of the clinician relates to the validity and usefulness of the obtained results. Defining a standard of care in neuropsychology has been, and continues to be, a very serious problem for the profession. The difficulty in establishing a standard of care is embedded in the fact that virtually anyone can learn to effectively and reliably administer and score a neurobehavioral test, as well as compare the obtained psychometric values with normative data, with as little as several hours of training. The question of what constitutes a neurobehavioral exam, selection of the appropriate psychometric measure to use for what question, the limitations of the psychometric technique in general, and the clinical training and experience needed for appropriate interpretation of the findings are just some of the problematic issues. The situation is analogous to laboratory medicine. For example, with very little technical training, an individual can learn how to draw blood and send the sample for blood chemistry analysis. Most laboratories produce a blood chemistry panel so that obtained values are compared with the normative population. However, the competency to meaningfully interpret obtained findings in conjunction with the clinical presentation is a much more complex matter.

Finally, this review is guided by the fact that the empirical literature does not provide strong consistent evidence supporting one bedside screening measure as the "gold standard." Therefore, to the extent that there is no indisputable standard, mental status screening remains somewhat of an art, dependent on the skill of the clinician. Experience teaches that the various measures have certain strengths and weaknesses that might be useful in one situation, but not in another. Therefore, thoughtful choice, application, interpretation, and awareness of limitations of bedside screening, is today's standard of care.

With recognition of the various cautions, neurocognitive bedside screening is indeed useful in many applications, including clinical assessment, teaching, and research. From a clinical perspective, we believe that accurate diagnosis should always precede treatment. In the case of the patient with possible or known neurologic dysfunction, the use of the bedside mental status examination is the first step in providing an accurate diagnosis of the neuropsychologic syndrome, and this sets the stage for intervention. Depending on the neurorehabilitative needs, a more detailed analysis of neurocognitive function can be implemented for the purpose of individually tailored prognostication, treatment planning, patient and family counseling, and so on.

Mental status quantification is useful not only in cases of known brain dysfunction, but also in monitoring the general neurologic health of nondisabled individuals who are at risk for neurologic disease and in providing secondary rehabilitative care during routine health care visits. This is especially applicable to the geriatric patient population, where repeat examinations can serve to monitor neurologic health and serve as an objective indicator of when further diagnostic work-up may be needed.

The goal of this chapter is to provide a review of bedside mental status screening measures and techniques, including several commonly used bedside instruments as well as several lesser known, but clinically useful measures.

Method of Review

A review of the literature does not reveal any consistent empirical evidence strongly supporting the superiority of one bedside screening measure over another. In fact, most measures are highly correlated. This impression is consistent with a previous review (Nelson, Fogel, & Faust, 1986). Each bedside screening measure of neurocognitive function appears to have its own particular relative strengths and weaknesses in terms of the ease of administration, focus of use, and general scientific recognition (based on frequency of appearance in the empirical literature). As a result, we selected 9 bedside mental status instruments for review. Measures selected for review conformed to the focus of the chapter, that is, to sample both the most popular measures (from frequency of empirical citations in the literature) and newly emerging bedside measures that seem to hold promise. Traditional bedside measures exemplified by the Mini-Mental State Examination to the more esoteric measures exemplified by the draw-a-clock test are reviewed. What follows is a description of each test, a description of the target population, a review of the administration and scoring procedures, a review of the psychometric properties, and a discussion of special considerations for use of the particular measure and a brief comment on the application of these mental status measures.

Bedside Mental Status Screening Measures

Mini-Mental State Examination

Of the numerous neurocognitive measures used for bedside screening, the Mini-Mental State Examination (MMSE; Folstein, Folstein, & McHugh, 1975) was the first to achieve widespread popularity and continues to be the most frequently employed brief, objective measure of cognitive function. With the increasing role of clinical neuropsychology in medical settings, intense interest in dementia, Alzheimer's disease in particular, and the trend toward cost- and time-efficient assessment procedures, the time was ripe for the development of such an instrument. The utility of the MMSE was quick to catch on, particularly within training facilities, and enthusiasm for the instrument has not waned over the past two decades. Since its initial publication in 1975, the instrument has been translated into at least 10 different languages (Bird, Canino, Stipec, & Shrout, 1987; Fratiglioni, Viitanen, Backman, Sandman, & Winblad, 1992; Katzman, Zhang, et al., 1988; Lindal & Stefansson, 1993; Noser, Schonenberger, & Wettstein, 1988; Park & Ha, 1988; Rocca et al., 1990; van der Cammen, van Harskamp, Stronks, Passchier, & Schudel, 1992), and is used extensively for clinical and research purposes throughout the world.

As a clinical instrument, the MMSE has been used to detect impairment following the course of an illness and to monitor response to treatment (Folstein, Anthony, Parhad, Duffy, & Gruenberg, 1985; Folstein et al., 1975; Horton, Slone, & Shapiro, 1987; Teng, Chui, Schneider, & Metzger, 1987; Tune & Folstein, 1986). As a research tool, it has been used to screen for cognitive impairment in epidemiologic studies of institutionalized and community dwelling populations (George, Landerman, Blazer, & Anthony, 1991; Li, Shen, Chen, Zhao, Li, & Lu, 1989; Rovner, Kafonek, Filipp, Lucas, & Folstein, 1986; Steele, Rovner, Chase, & Folstein, 1990) and to follow cognitive change in clinical trials (Balestreri, Fontana, & Astengo, 1987; Devanand, Sackeim, Brown, & Mayeux, 1989; Indaco & Carrieri, 1988; Steele, Lucas, & Tune, 1986).

The MMSE currently is one of the tests recommended by the National Institute of Neurological and Communicative Disorders and Stroke and the Alzheimer's Disease and Related Disorders Association (NINCDS-ADRDA) to document the probable clinical diagnosis of Alzheimer's disease (McKhann et al., 1984). In addition, it is used extensively in the United Kingdom as a result of government requirements to provide annual mental status screening of all individuals over the age of 75 (Department of Health and the Welsh Office, 1989). More recently, the MMSE has been used successfully in the screening of children as young as 4 years of age in pediatric outpatient settings (Ouvrier, Goldsmith, Ouvrier, & Williams, 1993). Given the wealth of cross-cultural and cross-generational uses for the MMSE, our review is limited to information regarding the psychometric properties and utility of the original English version of the MMSE and its application to medical rehabilitation settings.

The MMSE is divided into two sections. The first section consists of verbal-response items designed to address orientation to time (5 points), orientation to place (5 points), registration of three words (3 points), attention and calculation (i.e., serial 7s or *world* spelled backwards; 5 points), and recall of three words (3 points), yielding a maximum score of 21. The second section tests ability to name objects (2 points), repeat a phrase (1 point), follow verbal and written instructions (4 points), spontaneously write a sentence (1 point), and copy a complex polygon figure (1 point). The maximum score is 9 for the second section, yielding a total of 30 possible points.

The materials necessary to administer the MMSE are a blank piece of paper, a watch, a pencil, and preprinted copies of the statement *close your eyes* and a design of two overlapping pentagons. Variations in wording and content of some of the items commonly occur. For example, in the original version of the MMSE the authors routinely administered the serial 7s task as a measure of attention and calculation. Patients had the option to spell *world* backward, however, if they were unable to perform the serial 7s task. Many administrators continue to follow guidelines suggested in the original manuscript (Folstein et al., 1975). Others, however, have routinely used only the serial 7s task (Beatty & Goodkin, 1990; Fillenbaum, Heyman, Wilkinson, & Haynes, 1987; Roth et al., 1986; Zillmer, Fowler, Gutnick, & Becker, 1990), only the spell *world* backward test (Morris, Mohs, Rogers, Fillenbaum, & Heyman, 1988), or both of the tasks (Bird et al., 1987; Galasko et al., 1990; Holzer, Tischler, Leaf, & Myers, 1984; Jorm, Scott, Henderson, & Kay, 1988).

The original MMSE also left the choice of stimuli used to test a person's registration and ability to recall three words up to the discretion of the examiner. When the MMSE was incorporated into the Diagnostic Interview Schedule (National Institute of Mental Health, 1979) as part of the five-site Epidemiological Catchment Area (ECA) study, the words *apple*, *table* and *penny* became fairly conventional standards. Additional words that have been used, however, with some frequency include: *ball*, *brown*, *dog*, *elephant*, *flag*, *honesty*, *ring*, *rose*, and *shirt* (Ashford, Kolm, Colliver, Bekian, & Hsu, 1989; Beatty & Goodkin, 1990; Galasko et al., 1990; Murden, McRae, Kaner, & Bucknam, 1991; Teng & Chiu, 1987). In summary, the MMSE briefly samples a wide spectrum of neurocognitive functions, allowing for objective quantification of patient performance.

The MMSE was developed initially as a brief test to quantify the cognitive status of patients with a psychiatric diagnosis, older adults, and individuals without neuropsychiatric disease along several cognitive dimensions (Folstein et al., 1975). The majority of empirical data has continued to focus on the instrument's utility for discriminating patients with degenerative dementia of the Alzheimer's type from patients without neurologic disease. The literature consistently suggests that the sensitivity of the instrument increases with the degree of cognitive impairment. For older adults, normative data on this measure suggest that it is relatively free of age effects until the 6th or 7th decade and free of educational confounds except at less than the ninth-grade level (Tombaugh & McIntyre, 1992). Caution is especially advised, however, when using this instrument as the sole neurocognitive screening test for cognitive impairment in the poorly educated, elderly population (Crum, Anthony, Bassett, & Folstein, 1993).

The MMSE has been found to be insensitive to the cognitive impairment associated with multiple sclerosis (Beatty & Goodkin, 1990; Swirsky-

Sacchetti et al., 1992). Severe somatic and physical conditions have been found to artificially reduce patient performance on the MMSE (Cavanaugh & Wettstein, 1989). Likewise, low scores on the MMSE have been found to peak 1 to 2 days postcardiotomy (Harrell & Othmer, 1987). A recent review of the literature (Tombaugh & McIntyre, 1992) indicates that the MMSE has low to moderate sensitivity for cognitive impairment for patients with a neurologic or psychiatric diagnosis. This is primarily due to the simplicity of language items included on the MMSE, which limits the instrument's ability to detect mild impairment. The MMSE has also been found to be insensitive to neurocognitive impairment for developmentally disabled patients scoring in the moderately mentally deficient range (i.e., IQ less than 55) and persons with reading disability (i.e., Verbal IQ less than 70; Myers, 1987). In summary, inasmuch as the utility of the MMSE has recently begun to be empirically investigated in diverse populations, its greatest utility continues to reside in the detection of neurocognitive impairment in individuals who have progressed beyond the mild stages of degenerative impairment.

The MMSE is typically administered verbally in an individualized format. Recently, the MMSE has been successfully administered in a written format for persons who are hearing-impaired (Uhlmann, Teri, Rees, Mozlowski, & Larson, 1989) and in a group setting (Rizzolo, Wildman, & Bentz, 1991). Although there is no time limit, the measure takes approximately 5 to 10 minutes to administer. The administrator records the patient's response to each item on the one-page test form. The score on the MMSE is the total number of items answered correctly. Unfortunately, Folstein et al. (1975) provide few guidelines for scoring complex test items (i.e., spell *world* backwards, write a complete sentence, copying task). Lack of response to an item is typically scored as a failure for that item (Fillenbaum, George, & Blazer, 1988). No suggestions are provided for appropriate prompting or coaching of the patient. When both the serial 7s task and spell *world* backwards are administered, the higher of the two items generally is recommended for calculating the total score (Tombaugh & McIntyre, 1992). The total score can range from 0 to 30 points, placing an individual with lower scores on a scale of cognitive functioning associated with diminished performance. A cut-off score of 23 or fewer points generally has been accepted as indicative of the presence of possible cognitive impairment. More recently, however, classification of the severity of cognitive impairment has occurred along a continuum: 24–30 = *no cognitive impairment*; 18–23 = *mild cognitive impairment*; 0–17 = *severe cognitive impairment* (George et al., 1991).

Teng and Chui (1987) presented the initial data for a modified version of the MMSE, which includes four additional test items, specific guidelines for scoring more ambiguous responses, an expanded range of scores (0–100 versus 0–30), and modified scoring criteria that allow for partial credit on some items. Although their initial results appear to be promising, it is unfortunate that the expanded range of scores does not render their guidelines applicable to current cut-off scores for the MMSE.

In a second effort to improve upon the psychometric properties of the MMSE, Molloy, Alemaheyu, and Roberts (1991) expanded the original guidelines for administration and scoring. Unfortunately, the new standardized guidelines were not included in their publication. However, the authors refer to providing partial credit for near misses, setting time-limits for each item, and defining specific guidelines for scoring the copying figure (Molloy et al., 1991). After nearly a quarter of a century, the paucity of research attempting to standardize the administration and scoring of the MMSE is startling.

Psychometric Properties

In the original study, Folstein et al. (1975) demonstrated that the MMSE was capable of high test–retest reliability. Test–retest correlation coefficients were .89 at 24 hours using the same examiner, .83 at 24 hours using two different examiners, and .99 at 28 days. Furthermore, the MMSE was sensitive to change in cases of reversible cognitive impairment due to metabolic delirium, head injury, and depression. Similarly, Anthony, LeResche, Niaz, Von Korff, and Folstein (1982) reported test–retest correlation coefficients of .85 for nondisabled patients and .90 for patients with a diagnosis of dementia at 24 hours.

A recent review of the literature shows that reliability coefficients for individuals with and without a condition producing cognitive decline generally fall between .80 and .96 (Tombaugh & McIntyre, 1992). There is some suggestion that patients may "study" for mental status testing by rehearsing answers given to test items on previous administrations (Keating, 1987). Several studies also report that practice effects can contribute to increased scores upon retesting (Jorm, Scott, Cullen, & MacKinnon, 1991; O'Connor et al., 1989; Pfeffer, Kurosaki, Chance, Filos, & Bates, 1984; Thal, Grundman, & Golden, 1986).

Many of the extant validity studies of the MMSE have focused on the sensitivity (ability to correctly identify individuals with cognitive impairment) and specificity (ability to correctly identify individuals without cognitive impairment) of the MMSE. Anthony et al. (1982) were among the first to observe that an MMSE cut-off score of 23 or lower correctly identified 87% of the patients with a condition producing dementia or delirium on a general medical ward when compared with criterion diagnoses identified with the *Diagnostic and Statistical Manual of Mental Disorders*, third edition (DSM-III; American Psychiatric Association, 1980). In their review of the validity literature, Tombaugh and McIntyre (1992) indicated that 75% of the studies of patients with a diagnosis of dementia report a similar level of sensitivity with the 23-point cut-off score (range 20 to 100% for sensitivity). The level of cognitive impairment in patient samples with a diagnosis of dementia appears to be the primary factor involved in differentiating between high and low MMSE sensitivity. That is, sensitivity increases with the degree of cognitive impairment in study participants. For example, the MMSE has been found to be an insensitive indicator of the subtle impairment present in the very early stages of Alzheimer's disease (Galasko et al., 1990; Huff et al., 1987).

The sensitivity of the MMSE is consistently lower for patients with a psychiatric or neurologic diagnosis, ranging from 21 to 76% (Tombaugh & McIntyre, 1992). A recent study with patients with a psychiatric diagnosis indicated that the MMSE misclassified 20% of patients diagnosed with schizophrenia and 14% of patients diagnosed with dysthymia as having substantial cognitive impairment (Fabrega, Mezzich, Cornelius, & Ahn, 1989). Some investigators have suggested that the heterogeneity of patients with psychiatric or neurologic diagnoses makes it difficult to identify cognitive impairment (Chandler & Gerndt, 1988). Other studies suggest that limitations of the MMSE itself are responsible for the lower sensitivity in these populations. For example, the MMSE's bias toward verbal items results in a relative insensitivity to damage in the right hemisphere, which increases the rate of false negatives (Nelson et al., 1986; Salmon, Thal, Butters, & Heindel, 1990; Schwamm, Van Dyke, Kiernan, Merrin, & Mueller, 1987). The language items of the MMSE have also been criticized for being too simplistic to detect mild impairments (Galasko et al., 1990; Mayeux, Stern, Rosen, & Leventhal, 1981; Schwamm et al., 1987). Despite variable levels of sensitivity, most studies report moderate to high levels of specificity, generally ranging from 60 to 100% (Tombaugh & McIntyre, 1992). The inclusion of patients with a psychiatric diagnosis in the comparison group appears to be the primary factor in lower specificity (Davous, Lamour, Debrand, & Rondot, 1987; Folstein et al., 1985).

A variety of factors have been investigated to assess the construct validity of the MMSE, including the degree to which the MMSE correlates with other measures of cognitive functioning, neuropsychological tests, and ability to function independently in daily living. Folstein et al. (1975) reported statistically significant correlations of .78 and .66 between the MMSE and Wechsler Adult Intelligence Scale (WAIS, Wechsler, 1955) Verbal and Performance IQs, respectively. Likewise, the MMSE has been found to correlate .83 with the WAIS Full Scale IQ ($p < .0001$; Farber, Schmitt, & Logue, 1988). Comparable results have been found in other studies using the revised version of the WAIS (Faustmen, Moses, & Csernansky, 1990; Giordani et al., 1990; Mitrushina & Satz, 1991) and the Wechsler Memory Scales (Giordani et al., 1990; Myers, 1987).

The MMSE has been found to correlate significantly with other cognitive screening measures and behavioral scales, including the Blessed Information–Memory–Concentration test and the abbreviated Blessed Orientation–Memory–Concentration test (rs ranged from $-.66$ to $-.93$; Davous et al., 1987; Fillenbaum et al., 1987; Thal et al., 1986; Zillmer et al., 1990), the cognitive portion of the Alzheimer's Disease Assessment Scale (Burch & Andrews, 1987), the Modified Dementia Rating Scale (Uhlmann, Larson, & Buchner, 1987), the Informant Questionnaire on Cognitive Decline in the Elderly (Jorm et al., 1991), the cognitive section of The Cambridge Examination for Mental Disorders of the Elderly (CAMDEX, Blessed, Black, Butler, & Kay, 1991), the Short Test of Mental Status (Kokmen, Smith, Petersen, Tangalos, & Ivnik, 1991), the Mental Status Questionnaire (Pearson, Cherrier, & Terri, 1989), the Cognitive Capacity Screening Examination, the Blessed Dementia Scale, and the Gottfries-Brane-Steen scale (Villardita & Lomeo, 1992). Research suggests that the MMSE significantly correlates with neuropsychological tests as well, including the Consortium to Establish a Registry for Alzheimer's Disease (CERAD; Morris et al., 1989) and the Luria–Nebraska Neuropsychological Battery (Faustmen et al., 1990). Positive correlations for the MMSE and this representative sample of cognitive screening tests generally have ranged from .70 to .90.

Scores on the MMSE also have been found to be related to various neurologic and neuroradiographic parameters. These include cerebral atrophy as seen on CAT scans of the brain (Colohan, O'Callaghan, Larkin, & Waddington, 1989; Tsai & Tsuang, 1979); cerebral ventricle size (Pearlson & Tune, 1986); the magnitude of periventricular white-matter lesions assessed through magnetic resonance imaging (Bondareff, Raval, Woo, Hauser, & Colletti, 1990); and a negative relationship between MMSE scores and plaque counts postmortem (Martin et al., 1987).

Correlations between the MMSE and scores obtained from Activities of Daily Living (ADL) measures typically range from .40 to .75, suggesting that lower MMSE scores are also related to decreased independence (Ashford et al., 1989; Ashford, Hsu, Becker, Kumar, & Bekian, 1986; Breen, Larson, Reifler, Vitaliano, & Lawrence, 1984; Kafonek et al., 1989; Teri, Larson, & Reifler, 1988; Uhlmann et al., 1987; Warren et al., 1989), particularly for instrumental behaviors that are independent of physical health and mobility (Fillenbaum, Hughes, Heyman, George, & Blazer, 1988; Fisk & Pannill, 1987; Stern, Hesdorffer, Sano, & Mayeux, 1990).

Because the MMSE is organized into discrete, cognitive domains (e.g., Orientation, Recall), there has also been a recent trend to use subsection scores, individual items (Teng et al., 1987), or cognitive profiles (Brandt, Folstein, & Folstein, 1988) as indicators of specific cognitive dysfunction. Although overall performance on the MMSE appears to have moderate to high correlations with other comprehensive neuropsychological assessment instruments, extreme caution must be exercised when interpreting these correlations. For example, the three-word recall task has been found to be a poor index of memory in that a significant portion of individuals without cognitive impairment perform in the impaired range, recalling zero or only one word (Cullum, Thompson, & Smernoff, 1993). Furthermore, although the MMSE is significantly correlated with the Luria–Nebraska Neuropsychological Battery, it explained only a small portion (7%) of the variance and resulted in a high rate of false negative classifications when the Luria–Nebraska was used as the criterion measure (Faustmen et al., 1990).

Factor analysis has suggested that 66% of the scale variance actually can be accounted for by two factors: an Educational factor consisting of the serial 7s task, reading and writing items, and a Recent Memory factor that includes recall and orientation items (Fillenbaum et al., 1987). Results of this factor analysis and others (Tinklenberg et al., 1990; Zillmer et al., 1990) consistently indicate that the number of cognitive domains assessed by the MMSE is fewer than the seven categories into which the MMSE items generally are grouped. Additional research consistently suggests that MMSE items or subsections should not be viewed as highly specific measures of cognitive function (Feher et al., 1992; Giordani et al., 1990; Zillmer et al., 1990). Although the MMSE can be an effective screening instrument, its abbreviated nature does not allow for a comprehensive and detailed diagnostic profile.

Special Considerations, Cautions, and Applications
Numerous reports (Anthony et al., 1982; Escobar et al., 1986; Bird et al., 1987; Folstein et al., 1985; Holzer et al., 1984; Magaziner, Bassett, &

Hebel, 1987; Jorm et al., 1988; O'Connor, Pollitt, Treasure, Brook, & Reiss, 1989) have noted that people with fewer years of educational attainment obtain lower scores on the MMSE. Furthermore, education level has been found to affect the distribution of errors across individual items and cognitive domains assessed with the MMSE (Brayne & Calloway, 1990; Magaziner et al., 1987; Murden et al., 1991; Uhlmann & Larson, 1991). Extensive empirical investigation has suggested that education represents both a psychometric bias of the MMSE and a risk factor for poorer performance on the instrument (see Tombaugh & McIntyre, 1992, for further review of this literature).

In an effort to avoid potential misclassification due to education, several researchers have proposed education-specific norms (Murden et al., 1991; Uhlmann & Larson, 1991). Others have suggested mathematical transformations for adjusting raw MMSE scores for education level (Fillenbaum et al., 1988; Kittner et al., 1986; Magaziner et al., 1987). Results of a longitudinal study (Murden et al., 1991) suggest retaining the standard 23- to 24-point cut-off when screening for dementia in those with at least a ninth-grade education. The authors suggest reducing the cut-off score to 17 to 18 points for those with less than a ninth-grade education, and closely monitoring individuals scoring in the 18- to 23-point range for evidence of functional decline. As noted by Uhlmann and Larson (1991), additional research is needed to determine whether different norms are needed for highly educated individuals.

As with the education confound, extensive research indicates that MMSE scores decline with increasing age (Anthony et al., 1982; Brayne & Calloway, 1990; Bleecker, Bolla-Wilson, Kawas, & Agnew, 1988; Escobar et al., 1986; Fillenbaum et al., 1988; George et al., 1991; Jagger, Clarke, Anderson, & Battcock, 1992; Magaziner et al., 1987). The majority of age-related change begins at about age 55 or 60 and then dramatically accelerates over the age of 75 or 80 (George et al., 1991; Holzer et al., 1984).

Recently, Crum et al. (1993) reported MMSE scores by age and education based on an assessment of individuals surveyed in the five-site National Institute of Mental Health ECA Program. As is consistent with the aforementioned research, these investigators found that age and education were associated with MMSE performance. The MMSE scores were lower for the oldest age groups and for those with fewer years of education. The investigators call for the use of percentile distributions as a more viable means of evaluating the range of scores for specific age and educational categories (Crum et al., 1993).

Gender differences have not been found to account for a substantial portion of variance on MMSE scores (Bleecker et al., 1988; Buckwalter, Sobel, Dunn, Diz, & Henderson, 1993; Cavanaugh & Wettstein, 1983; Fillenbaum et al., 1988; Holzer et al., 1984). However, it is interesting to note that men typically perform better on the MMSE if the serial 7s task of attention is used; whereas women do better if the reverse spelling of *world* is used (Lindal & Stefansson, 1993).

A recent summary report of the five ECA sites indicates that race and ethnicity have a significant effect on MMSE scores (George et al., 1991) as do race and ethnicity in an earlier report of English and Hispanic residents of the Los Angeles catchment site (Escobar et al., 1986). Similar effects have been observed for social class and socioeconomic status (Cavanaugh & Wettstein, 1983; Jagger et al., 1992; Uhlmann & Larson, 1991). In summary, demographic variables of education, age, gender, and race or ethnicity can have a significant impact on MMSE performance. We are unaware of any attempts to develop a culture-fair version of the MMSE.

Because of the limited number of items assessing cognitive abilities, overinterpretation and misinterpretation can easily occur when the MMSE is the only assessment device employed. Although the MMSE has been found to be reasonably sensitive as a screening tool in the detection of cognitive impairment associated with dementia, it is less sensitive in discriminating degrees of cognitive impairment, particularly at the extremes of test performance (Ashford et al., 1989). The risk of false negatives in mild dysfunction probably is greatest among individuals of high premorbid intellect and education, where "normal" results can be obtained even if these patients have experienced a significant decline in cognitive function. Given that items on the MMSE are highly language dependent and that verbal intellectual skills generally are preserved in individuals diagnosed with early-stage Alzheimer's disease (Naugle, Cullum, Bigler, & Massman, 1985), case examples have demonstrated that these individuals are sometimes capable of passing the MMSE despite the presence of neuropsychological deficits (Naugle & Krawczak, 1989). At the other extreme, MMSE scores typically reach 0 at a relatively early stage in the disease, after which a patient may continue to deteriorate for several years. At this phase, there is little left to evaluate with the MMSE in the way of cognitive function (Ashford et al., 1989). Dysphasia presents a similar problem.

Conclusion

Since its publication in 1975, the MMSE has been touted by some as the gold standard of brief cognitive screening. Due to its brevity, ease of administration, and ease of scoring, the MMSE became an integral component in the initial and ongoing assessment of a variety of inpatient populations. Developers suggested that the instrument could be administered by virtually anyone, including "psychiatrist, resident, nurse, or volunteer" (Folstein et al., 1975, p. 189). Since the publication of this measure in 1975, the MMSE has been used in diverse inpatient and outpatient populations, clinical research trials, and epidemiological studies. Unfortunately, the instrument's user friendliness may have outserved its limited neuropsychological utility.

It is grossly unrealistic to expect that the MMSE could substitute for a comprehensive neuropsychological examination. This limitation, however, has prompted investigators to comment that the MMSE's "shortcomings lie less in the test itself than in expectations exceeding those that should be placed on a 10-minute test" (Feher et al., 1992, p. 91). Rigid reliance on specific cut-off scores can lead to errors of diagnosis, including diagnosing dementia with patients where there is no cognitive impairment and missing a diagnosis of dementia with patients who have cognitive impairment. MMSE results should be considered suspect for individuals who, by virtue of their academic or vocational histories, are assumed to have been very high-functioning premorbidly. Further suspect are results suggesting the absence of cognitive impairment in patients whose neurologic examinations or diagnostic evaluations suggest a lesion within the right hemisphere, patients who evidence memory impairment but fail only a few items on the MMSE, and those whose cognitive dysfunction has not yet resulted in a significant drop in verbal intellectual functions. In these cases, obtaining a valid assessment of cognitive function requires a more extensive and comprehensive norm-based neuropsychological evaluation.

These results support other researchers' (Nelson et al., 1986) findings that brief mental status tests do not necessarily add to the diagnostic accuracy achieved through clinical examination (i.e., incremental validity). Although the MMSE may be of clinical utility in training facilities, research on the instrument's sensitivity in detection of cognitive deficits that are not obvious clinically is inconclusive. Given these limitations, the question arises as to who should administer and interpret the MMSE. Although Folstein et al. (1975) indicate that the MMSE can be administered by virtually anyone, we caution that the instrument be administered and interpreted in conjunction with a thorough clinical interview conducted by a trained mental health professional who is attuned to the subtle nuances of test administration (e.g., anxiety, motivational factors, momentary lapses of attention, etc.) that can adversely affect performance. As with all clinical of attention, etc.) that can adversely affect performance. As with all clinical test data, clinical judgment must be used to weigh the possibilities for error in the individual test items and total score and the possible explanations of results substantially lower or higher than expected values. The items of the MMSE should be viewed solely as samples of the cognitive domains being assessed. If warranted, additional assessment should follow with more extensive, comprehensive, and norm-based neuropsychological examination.

In the neurorehabilitative setting, it should be noted that although the MMSE is useful in screening for neurocognitive dysfunction, findings are not particularly helpful for treatment planning or patient and family counseling. Part of the problem is that the MMSE yields only a single score of organic integrity and also is relatively insensitive to subtle cognitive loss. A comprehensive picture of the patient's neurocognitive strengths and weaknesses on which an individually tailored rehabilitative treatment plan can be based is lacking. Therefore, the MMSE is probably best reserved as an initial screening procedure that may suggest a need for more detailed mental status examination.

The Neurobehavioral Cognitive Status Examination

The Neurobehavioral Cognitive Status Examination (NCSE) represents a new approach to brief cognitive assessment (Kiernan, Mueller, Langston, & Van Dyke, 1987). This measure was designed to provide an independent assessment of multiple domains of cognitive functioning as opposed to a global estimate of cognitive functioning, as is the case with the MMSE and other screening measures. This is a theoretical departure from the MMSE, which assumes a unidimensional model of assessment of brain function.

The NCSE provides a differentiated profile of the patient's neurocognitive status and thereby highlights individual strengths and weaknesses in various domains of neurocognitive functioning. The NCSE assesses intellectual functioning in five areas of cognition: language (spontaneous speech, comprehension, repetition, and naming), construction, memory (immediate and 10-minute recall), calculations, and reasoning (abstraction and judgment). In addition, the NCSE independently assesses attention, level of consciousness, and orientation.

The NCSE has been used to screen for neurocognitive impairment in diverse patient populations, including patients with a neurosurgical diagnosis (Cammermeyer & Evans, 1988; Schwamm et al., 1987), patients who have had a cerebrovascular event (Mysiw, Beegan, & Gatens, 1989), older adult inpatients (Fields, Fulop, Sachs, Strain, and Fillit, 1993), and inpatients with substance abuse problems (Meek, Clark, & Solana, 1989). Research efforts also have included populations with varied presenting problems such as head injury, Parkinson's disease, multiple sclerosis, delirium after surgery, criminal behavior, and severe psychiatric problems (The Northern California Neurobehavioral Group, Inc., 1991).

Administration of the NCSE involves the use of a screen and metric format. This format reduces administration time significantly by allowing intact individuals to complete the examination in less than 5 minutes. Administration time for patients with neurocognitive impairment is roughly 10–20 minutes.

With the exception of the orientation and memory subtests, each subtest begins with a demanding screening item. The authors reported that 20% of the population with no cognitive impairment fail such screening items. When the subject is unable to pass a particular screening item, the procedure is to then begin with the easiest item and work up in difficulty. In this way, the metric items provide a relatively more exhaustive assessment of the area of concern and yield information about degree of impairment.

Scores for the NCSE are computed separately for each domain being assessed. Scores range from 0 (*severe impairment*) to 6 or 8 (*normal*). Scores on each area of the NCSE are then plotted on a graph to indicate level of functioning (e.g., average, below average, moderate impairment, or severe impairment). The profile obtained illustrates the overall pattern of abilities and deficits.

A unique feature of the NCSE is the establishment of cut-off scores for each area of cognition, rather than a composite cut-off score (e.g., as on the MMSE). The range of scores for different levels of impairment on the NCSE is relatively well defined, at least when compared with some of the other bedside screening measures.

Normative data for the NCSE (Kiernan et al., 1987) was obtained originally from 30 nondisabled younger adults (ages 20–39), 30 nondisabled adults (ages 40–66), and 59 nondisabled older adults (ages 70–92). This was in contrast with data from 30 individuals undergoing a neurosurgical procedure for documented brain lesions (age range 25–88). The accuracy of the original classifications (Kiernan et al., 1987) of cognitive impairment for the different areas assessed by the NCSE has yet to be systematically replicated. However, Logue, Tupler, D'Amico, and Schmitt's (1993) study of 866 psychiatric inpatients revealed that the performance of this group on the NCSE was consistently inferior compared with that of Kiernan et al.'s (1987) normative sample.

Psychometric Properties

Data on reliability of the NCSE are not currently available. The authors have argued that the usual reliability criteria do not apply well to this type of screening examination (The Northern California Neurobehavioral Group, Inc., 1991, p. 10).

Several studies have addressed the validity of the NCSE. Osmon, Smet, Winegarden, and Gandhavadi (1992) reported that the NCSE was sensitive to cognitive impairment in patients with a unilateral stroke but provided little discrimination between left- and right-hemispheric lesions. The NCSE is reported to demonstrate greater sensitivity than the MMSE (false positive rates of 7% and 43%, respectively) in detecting cognitive impairment in patients with documented brain lesions (Schwamm et al., 1987). The NCSE is also reported to have greater sensitivity than the MMSE in detecting cognitive impairment in an older adult inpatient population (Fields et al., 1993). Further, in the areas of orientation and memory, the NCSE was found to have greater sensitivity than the MMSE in early detection of cognitive dysfunction in patients who have had a stroke (Mysiw, Beegan, & Gatens, 1989). However, these findings have not been replicated.

There is limited research on the concurrent and construct validity of the NCSE. Performance on the NCSE has been found to be significantly associated with performance on Trails B (Spreen & Strauss, 1991) as well as with the Luria-Nebraska Neuropsychological Battery (Meek et al., 1989). Construct validity is also supported by the general theory of aging and changes in intellectual function. Logue et al. (1993) found a negative correlation between NCSE scores and age, with greater impairment in the NCSE scores as a function of age especially in areas assessing fluid abilities, such as memory, construction, and abstraction. Also as expected, the effect of age was least apparent in areas that assess crystallized functions, such as language and judgment.

Findings on the construct validity of the NCSE as assessed by subtest intercorrelations are inconsistent. Logue et al. (1993) reported low inter-correlations between subtests of the NCSE (ranging from .23 to .48). In contrast, Osmon et al. (1992) reported high intercorrelations between the NCSE subtests as evidence for an attention/concentration factor, a general language dimension, and a general memory dimension across a number of subtests of the NCSE. However, the reasoning subtests were not found to be correlated.

Indirect support for the construct validity of the NCSE comes from some evidence suggesting that NCSE scores are sensitive to improvement in cognitive abilities for individuals undergoing substance abuse treatment (Meek et al., 1989) and to early signs of intracranial pressure and complications in patients undergoing neurosurgical intervention (Cammermeyer & Evans, 1988). Conversely, NCSE performance has been reported to be affected by nonneurocognitive factors such as level of pain and psychological distress in adults with musculoskeletal pain (Kewman, Vaishampayan, Zald, & Han, 1991). Finally, the degree to which performance on the NCSE corresponds with radiographic information and brain function (assessed by CAT scans, magnetic resonance imaging [MRI], and single-photon emission computed tomography [SPECT] studies) is relatively unknown.

Special Considerations, Cautions, and Applications

A unique feature of the NCSE as a screening instrument is its use of a quantitative screen and metric structure to facilitate assessment of intact neurocognitive abilities as well as deficits. Proposed cut-off scores for different cognitive domains may provide some limited information that is potentially valuable for the planning of neurorehabilitative intervention. Finally, the NCSE's apparent sensitivity to cognitive impairment in diverse patient populations, such as patients with documented brain pathology, stroke patients, geriatric inpatients, and substance abusing inpatients, supports its use.

The NCSE, however, is limited in several ways. Like other measures, the NCSE is relatively insensitive to impairment in individuals with above-average levels of premorbid functioning and to frontal lobe pathology (The Northern California Neurobehavioral Group, Inc., 1991). The test does not assess language functions directly; hence, significant deficits in language will not be detected or quantified by the NCSE. Also, poor specificity is suggested for the NCSE by the finding that NCSE performance is affected by level of pain and psychological distress in adults with musculoskeletal pain (Kewman et al., 1991). Thus, limited research on specificity of the NCSE suggests caution in the use of this measure in a population in which neurocognitive impairment may be secondary to organic illness.

Reliability of the NCSE is unknown, and thus, systematic evaluation of reliability is needed for meaningful application of the NCSE (Yazdanfar, 1990). Another significant concern, especially with regard to neurorehabilitation planning, is that the factor structure of the NCSE has not been validated by replicated empirical research. Similarly, the accuracy of cut-off scores for determining levels of functioning on the NCSE has not been adequately validated. Hence, caution must be exercised when the goal is interpretation of factor scores. Further, the effects of education, gender, ethnic background, and socioeconomic class on NCSE performance have not been systematically evaluated.

Other criticisms of the NCSE relate to item difficulty and validity. Some authors have noted the screen items on the NCSE are too difficult even for the individual without impaired brain function and may result in high false positive rates. For instance, in contrast with the 20% failure rate reported by Kiernan et al. (1987), several authors (Logue et al., 1993; Meek et al., 1989) reported that over 50% of patients without impairment of brain function fail screen items, particularly in the areas of construction and reasoning. Finally, Logue et al. (1993) cited the correlation (.48) between the constructions and the memory subtests to support their observation that this particular construct is less valuable as a measure of constructional praxis due to its strong immediate visual memory component.

Conclusion

In view of the several limitations of the NCSE, possibly stemming from the relative lack of research on this new measure, it is reasonable to conclude that data generated by the NCSE regarding domains of neuro-cognitive dysfunction should be supplemented with a more in depth follow-up and convergent clinical data. For instance, with regard to possible constructional dyspraxia, the use of other screening measures for visual and spatial ability, such as the Clock Drawing test or the WAIS-R Block Design test, as well as analysis of the impact of the specific deficit in that patient's environment, may be advisable. Given the difficulty level of many screen items, it also may be prudent to consider the impact of education when interpreting results of the NCSE. The NCSE does seem to extend beyond simple screening of organic integrity and does provide some data useful for neurorehabilitative planning as well as family/patient counseling.

Dementia Rating Scale

Many of the brief screening devices, such as the Mini-Mental Status Examination, have been criticized as having a "floor effect" and being relatively insensitive to differences among patients with severe dementia. Standard neurocognitive measures, such as the WAIS-R and the Halstead-

Reitan neuropsychological battery (Reitan & Wolfson, 1993) also do not provide a sufficient lower-end range of simple items. Floor effects on these and other brief measures result in a limited description of the pattern of neurocognitive abilities for patients with moderate to severe dementia. As a consequence, the Dementia Rating Scale (DRS) was designed to differentiate levels of ability within groups of patients with dementia, particularly of the degenerative type, by providing a quick estimate of intact abilities in more severely affected patients (Mattis, 1976, 1988).

The most frequent application of this measure is in patients with dementia, most particularly with progressive dementias. Clinical and research applications have been primarily with patients ranging in age from 65 to 81 years. One recent exception was a study in which the DRS was found to reliably identify cognitive impairment for patients with a history of intravenous drug abuse diagnosed as HIV positive (Kovner et al., 1992).

The DRS consists of 36 tasks arranged in hierarchical order within five subscales. These subscales measure attention (8 items), initiation/perseveration (11 items), construction (6 items), conceptualization (6 items), and memory (5 items). The subscale designed to assess initiation/perseveration is a unique aspect of the DRS and may provide some information about frontal lobe involvement. However, sensitivity of the DRS to frontal impairment in patients with a diagnosis of dementia has not been systematically investigated. Administration time for the DRS is reported as approximately 10–15 minutes for older adult subjects without brain impairment and 30–45 minutes for patients with dementia (Mattis, 1976). The scoring system uses one point for each correct item and does not involve the use of partial credit. Subtotals for each of the five areas of assessment are added to yield a Total Dementia Rating Scale (TDRS) score. The maximum TDRS score possible on the DRS is 144, which represents a perfect score. Mattis (1976) initially recommended the use of a cut-off score of 139 as indicative of cognitive impairment and noted that a score of less than 100 implies doubtful survival. However, the small size of the sample ($n = 11$) from which these data were obtained limited generalizability of findings.

The establishment of norms for the DRS in the nondisabled elderly population has received substantial research attention (Butters, Wolfe, Martone, Granholm, & Cermak, 1985; Coblentz et al., 1973; Granholm & Wolfe, & Butters, 1985; Montgomery & Costa, 1983b; Moss, Albert, Butters, & Payne, 1986; Vitaliano, Breen, Albert, Russo, & Prinz, 1984b). Current norms for the DRS (Mattis, 1988) are based on a group of 85 community dwelling elderly subjects with normal neurocognitive function

(Montgomery & Costa, 1983b), ranging in age from 65 to 81 years (mean TDRS = 137.3 , SD = 6.9 , cut-off score = 123). Data from a longitudinal study of cognitive status in 30 patients with Alzheimer's disease (Coblentz et al., 1973) is reported in the manual (Mattis, 1988) as providing a comparison for purposes of cognitive decline assessment in patients with progressive dementia.

Psychometric Properties

One-week test–retest reliability of the DRS (total scores) for patients with a provisional diagnosis of Alzheimer's disease was reported to be above .90 (Mattis, 1976), as was the split-half reliability (Gardner, Oliver-Munoz, Fisher, & Empting, 1981). Gardner et al. reported reliabilities for the subtests as ranging from .61 on attention to .94 on conceptualization, with a mean subtest reliability coefficient of .84. Limited data are available on interrater reliability of the DRS.

The validity of the DRS is supported across several domains. Montgomery and Costa (1983a) assessed the accuracy of the total DRS cut-off score in discriminating between elderly subjects with normal and impaired brain function. They reported that 62% of patients with dementia, 36% of patients with focal brain damage, and 12% of subjects with psychiatric disorders scored in the impaired range on the DRS (total score < 136). All subjects who were depressed, but without a diagnosis of dementia, scored in the unimpaired range. All of the control subjects in their study obtained DRS total scores above 140.

There has been limited research on the validity of scores on the different subscales of the DRS. Some research suggests that the initiation/perseveration subscale does differentiate between controls and subjects with mild dementia, and that all the subscales differentiate mild from moderate dementia (Vitaliano et al., 1984a). However, mixed findings on the factor structure of the DRS suggest that caution must be exercised in the interpretation of "factor" scores on the DRS. For instance, Hersch (1979) was unable to replicate Mattis's factorial structure in a sample of patients in a long-term geriatric psychiatric facility. However, Colantonio, Becker, and Huff (1993) reported that a factor analysis of the DRS scores in patients with probable Alzheimer's disease suggests three underlying factors to performance on the DRS: Conceptual Organization, Visual-Spatial, and Memory and Orientation. Colantonio et al. (1993) noted that their results demonstrated a difference between this factor-analytic clustering and the clustering in the original scoring protocol of the DRS.

The DRS has been reported to have adequate concurrent validity.

Shay et al. (1991) noted an association between DRS performance and ratings on a scale of Instrumental Activities of Daily Living, both showing change as a function of the various stages of Alzheimer's dementia. Vitaliano et al. (1984a) reported that total DRS scores were significantly associated with functional competence in community residents diagnosed with Alzheimer's disease. Finally, total DRS scores have been found to correlate significantly ($r = .75$) with WAIS IQ scores (Mattis, 1976) and with a composite measure ($r = .67$) of the vocabulary subtest of the WAIS-R (Wechsler, 1981), the Boston Naming Test (Kaplan, Goodglass, & Weintraub, 1983), and the Benton Visual Retention Test (Montgomery & Costa, 1983a).

Criterion validity of the DRS has been demonstrated to be associated with physiological parameters. Gardner et al. (1981) reported a correlation of .86 between cerebral blood flow and DRS scores. Chase et al. (1984) demonstrated a positive association ($r = .69$) between DRS scores and left temporal metabolism as assessed by positron emission tomography in a group of 17 elderly patients diagnosed with Alzheimer's disease. Finally, Klauber, Butters, Parker, and Kripke (1991) found that sleep apnea in a sample of 235 nursing home patients was significantly correlated with all subscales on the DRS, particularly for patients with severe sleep apnea.

Special Considerations, Cautions, and Applications

The DRS has several limitations. Although criterion-related evidence of validity is valuable, there is little empirical data on the predictive utility of DRS scores for mortality, independence in activities of daily living, or prognosis for neurocognitive rehabilitation. Limited data are available addressing interrater reliability of the DRS. Imprecise administration procedures and unclear scoring criteria have also been noted (Spreen & Strauss, 1991). Spreen and Strauss (1991) have further pointed out that inasmuch as the DRS is sensitive to moderate and severe levels of cognitive impairment, its sensitivity to early stages of dementia remains undetermined. Further, the lack of a specific language scale (and specific naming) in the DRS contributes to insensitivity in the identification of aphasic disorders. Finally, the factor structure of the DRS subscales is unclear. In fact, Hersch (1979) was unable to replicate Mattis's factorial structure in a sample of geriatric patients in a long-term psychiatric facility, but Colantonio et al. (1993) reported three factors.

Conclusions

Despite these limitations, the DRS is perhaps the screening instrument of choice for assessment of neurocognitive ability in patients aged 65–81 years with known degenerative dementia. The greater sensitivity of the DRS to lower levels of neurocognitive functioning compared with other brief screening measures and comprehensive measures probably contributes to the popularity and usefulness of this measure. Hence, it may be useful for assessing neurocognitive functioning in the population of patients with dementias of various types. The DRS has the additional strength of being generally unaffected by gender or education (Vitaliano et al., 1984a). Finally, a unique feature of the DRS is the assessment of initiation/ perseveration and the potential frontal lobe involvement.

In view of the limitations outlined above, this measure seems a reasonable choice for neurorehabilitative applications in populations where moderate to severe neurocognitive impairment is found. Although the data are limited and there is a need for further research, this measure may prove useful for rehabilitative nursing home issues such as prognostication, establishing density of supervisory services needed, or establishing the capacity for independence in activities of daily living. Monitoring of mental status for changes in level of care and perhaps even response to treatment are other potential applications.

The Extended Scale for Dementia

The Extended Scale for Dementia (ESD) is a revised version of the Dementia Rating Scale. The ESD was developed by Hersch (1979) at the Psychogeriatric Unit of the London Psychiatric Hospital in Ontario, Canada, for use in studies of progressive intellectual decline. Questions regarding the variable difficulty level of the items, restricted scoring system, and relevance of use of Mattis's Dementia Rating Scale for older adults admitted to long-term psychiatric facilities prompted a revision of the DRS that resulted in the ESD (Hersch, 1979).

The Extended Scale for Dementia (ESD) includes 17 items from the DRS scale. Items added to the scale include counting backwards, counting by 3s, an information item ("How many weeks are there in a year?"), parts of the Paired Associate subtest from the Wechsler Memory Scale, simple arithmetic items, and three items of Block Design from the Wechsler Intelligence Scale for Children. The two writing and copying items of the DRS are combined into one "graphomotor" item on the ESD. Unlike the DRS, which treats orientation as a single area, the ESD handles orientation in three subsections: time, place, and age. Scoring criteria of the ESD also are expanded to allow for a greater range of points and for partial credit for less than perfect responses.

Helmes, Merskey, Hachinski, and Wands (1993) concluded that the ESD is useful for evaluating neurocognitive decline in geriatric patients in long-term psychiatric facilities. It is probably also useful in the same populations as the Dementia Rating Scale.

Psychometric Properties

Six-week test–retest reliability for the ESD was reported to be .94 (Hersch, 1979). Helmes et al. (1993) reported good internal consistency for the ESD, particularly for hospital samples (Cronbach's αs = .93, .95, and .64 for a mixed hospital sample, a sample of patients with Alzheimer's disease, and a sample of patients without cognitive impairment, respectively).

The ESD has reported sensitivity and specificity rates of 93% and 96%, respectively, in older adult controls and patients with dementia (Lau et al., 1988). Lau et al. warned against the use of this instrument with individuals younger than 65 years because the sensitivity rate for younger adults falls to around 75%. In terms of validity, Steingart et al. (1986) reported an association independent of age, education, and gender between lower scores on the ESD and white-matter lucencies on CAT scans of elderly volunteers from the community. Finally, ESD scores were reported to be unrelated to depression (Wands et al., 1990).

Special Considerations, Cautions, and Applications

The major criticisms of the ESD (Helmes et al., 1993) are of item difficulty and the ordering of items within subtests. Like the DRS, the ESD has significant ceiling effects and may not be useful with older individuals who have relatively intact cognitive abilities. With respect to particular items, the paired associate learning task added to the ESD has been found to be difficult and may result in some decreased specificity for the test (Helmes et al., 1993). Finally, the ordering of items within subtests of the ESD is not graded in difficulty level and may lead to underestimation of intact abilities.

The Blessed Scales: The Blessed Dementia Scale and The Blessed Information–Memory–Concentration Test

The original Blessed Scale (Blessed, Tomlinson, & Roth, 1968), designed as a quantitative measure of dementia, consists of two parts: (a) a rating scale of functional ability referred to as the Blessed Dementia Scale (BDS) or Blessed Dementia Rating Scale (BDRS) and (b) a brief mental status screen referred to as the Blessed Information–Memory–Concentration

Test (BIMC). These measures have often been treated separately in the literature. Here we review these two measures in combination.

The Blessed Dementia Scale (BDS) is a 22-item screening instrument that rates collateral information on changes in three areas of the patient's functional ability: (a) performance of everyday activities, (b) habits, and (c) personality, interests, and drives. The BDS often has been described as a behavioral scale (Huff & Growdon, 1986). Conversely, the Blessed Information–Memory–Concentration (BIMC) test is a 26-item measure of cognitive ability (Blessed et al., 1968). Areas assessed by the BIMC include orientation, concentration, recent memory (immediate and delayed verbal memory), and remote memory. A shortened version of the BIMC (Katzman et al., 1983) is available as a separate measure referred to as the six-item Short Blessed Test (sometimes called the Blessed Orientation Concentration Memory test). The BIMC contains two questions assessing concentration (months backwards, counting backwards from 20 to 1), three orientation questions, and one memory item (immediate and delayed verbal recall). We do not review the shortened measure because of its limited application in neurorehabilitation assessment.

A unique feature of the Blessed scales is their combined assessment of both functional ability and mental status, distinguishing them from other measures reviewed in this chapter. The most common use of the BDS and the BIMC is for clinical staging in patients with possible Alzheimer's disease. The BDS in particular has been recognized as a quantitative aid in the clinical examination for Alzheimer's Disease and Related Disorders Association Work Group (McDougall, 1990).

Both the BDS and the BIMC are most appropriate for use in the population of elderly patients with suspected or documented progressive dementia. They are probably equally as useful for other types of global dementias, such as mixed or vascular.

In scoring the Blessed scales, the evaluator uses collateral information from an informant to rate the functional capacity of the patient in three domains. Scores within each of the three areas of the BDS are then added to yield an overall score. The total score on the BDS can range from 0 (*normal*) to 28 (*severely demented*). Conversely, the BIMC is an objective measure of patient neurocognitive performance and requires use of collateral information only as a check of the accuracy of the patient's remote memory for personal information. The scoring system of the BIMC, based on number of errors, allows for partial credit. The maximum score on the BIMC is 33, with a score breakdown of 0–8 as *normal*, 9–19 as *moderately impaired*, and 20–33 as *severely impaired*. Thus, when combined, the BDS and BIMC provide data on neurocognitive ability and functional capacity.

Psychometric Properties

Test–retest reliability for both the BDS and the BIMC have been found to be adequate. Four-week test–retest reliability of the BDS has been found to be high (.88; Villardita & Lomeo, 1992). Reliability studies on the BIMC suggested that test–retest reliability for an interval of 1–6 weeks ranges from .82 to .90, which is similar to that for the MMSE (Fillenbaum, Heyman, Williams, Prosnitz, & Burchett, 1990; Thal et al., 1986). In addition, interrater reliability of the BDS has been reported as .59, intraclass correlations as .30, and limits of agreement for total scale scores as low (mean difference = −2.17, SD = 4.45; Cole, 1990).

Research suggests that the BDS correlates well with screening measures of cognitive impairment, such as the MMSE, the Blessed Information–Memory–Concentration Scale, the Sandoz Clinical Assessment Geriatric Scale, and the Gottfries-Breen-Steen scale (Stern et al., 1990; Villardita & Lomeo, 1992). BDS scores in Alzheimer's disease patients have also been found to be strongly associated with signs of aphasia, apraxia, and primitive reflexes (Huff & Growdon, 1986). Validity studies on the BIMC suggest that it correlates well (r = −.81) with the MMSE (Thal et al., 1987; Villardita & Lomeo, 1992). Equivalence of the BIMC and the MMSE is further supported by Thal et al.'s derivation of a formula through linear regression analysis to convert BIMC scores into MMSE scores (Thal et al., 1986).

Factor analysis of BDS items in 187 patients with clinically diagnosed Alzheimer's disease revealed that the BDS assesses four factors of functional capacity, including cognition, personality, apathy, and basic self-care (Stern et al., 1990). Construct validity of the BDS is also supported by several studies that document an association between BDS scores and various objective neuropathological indices, such as radiographic and histopathological findings in Alzheimer's disease patients (Halliday et al., 1992; Houck, Reynolds, Kopp, & Hanin, 1988; Bondareff et al., 1990; Richards et al., 1993).

BDS scores have demonstrated sensitivity to indices of disease severity and disease course in Alzheimer's disease—such as delusions (Richards et al., 1993), decreased REM sleep, and non-REM related sleep apnea (Blakemore, 1987; Hoch et al., 1986)—and to the effects of medication (cyclandelate) in patients with multi-infarct dementia (Blakemore, 1987). Finally, serial BDS scores showed deterioration in Alzheimer's disease patients' functional abilities over time (Rosen, Growdon, & Corkin, 1987). Results from a recent prospective study suggested that high baseline BDS scores are strong predictors of eventual dementia in groups of nondisabled community elderly (Aronson et al., 1990). However, the utility of the BDS scores in predicting progression of decline in functional ability of patients with possible Alzheimer's disease, particularly with regard to personality, is questionable (Berg, Edwards, Danzinger, & Berg 1987; Stern et al., 1990).

Results from various prospective studies on patients with Alzheimer's disease suggested that the BIMC has adequate predictive validity, particularly related to disease course. Data from a multicenter prospective study conducted in Italy (Lucca, Comelli, Tettamanti, Tiraboschi, & Spagnoli, 1993) suggested that BIMC scores may be helpful in predicting functional and behavioral deterioration. However, findings regarding the predictive validity of BIMC scores related to indices of disease severity, such as rate of deterioration and personality change, have been at best mixed (Stern et al., 1990, Jeste, Wragg, Salmon, Harris, & Thal, 1992). Research suggests that cognitive impairment as measured by the BIMC is not a good predictor of personality change in patients with Alzheimer's disease (Bozzola, Gorelick, & Freels, 1992).

Findings regarding the ability of the BIMC to discriminate between different levels of severity of dementia are also mixed. Certain BIMC items (such as those assessing memory) are reported to discriminate between patients with a diagnosis of no, questionable, or mild dementia (Katzman et al., 1988; Davis, Morris, & Grant, 1990). However, the BIMC has been found to be poor at distinguishing between moderate and severe dementia (Davis et al., 1990). Histopathologic findings have been more consistent. For example, BIMC scores have been shown to be correlated with neuropathological findings in Alzheimer's disease. Higher scores on the BIMC were associated with increasing numbers of cortical plaques (Blessed et al., 1968) and with synaptic density in the neocortex (Masliah et al., 1992).

Special Considerations, Cautions, and Applications

Both the BDS and the BIMC are limited in their ability to distinguish between different levels of severity of dementia. The BDS is also unable to distinguish between Alzheimer's disease and other types of dementias (McDougall, 1990), whereas the BIMC is unable to predict rate of deterioration in patients with progressive dementia. Davis et al. (1990) noted a limitation of the BDS related to the use of collateral information. Specifically, denial or misattribution may result in an underestimation of

functional deficits of patients. Finally, the relative lack of systematic in-
vestigations on the influence of age, gender, or education on BDS or BIMC
scores argues for the use of caution in interpreting scores. Although the
BDS has been adapted for use in Chinese (Zhang, 1991), Japanese (Fuld,
Muramoto, Blau, Westbrook, & Katzman, 1988) and Thai populations
(Phanthumchinda & Jitapunkul, 1991), little is known about the validity
of its use with different ethnic populations in the United States. Similarly,
Fillenbaum et al. (1990) found that specificity rates for Black patients and
community residents were lower (38.2%) as compared to those for Whites
(78.5%), suggesting a cultural bias in the BIMC.

Conclusion

The unique advantage of the Blessed scales is the combined assessment
of both functional abilities and objective measures of neurocognitive function. Specifically, these scales seem useful not only for quantifying the
severity of dementia, but also in assessing functional capacity in terms of
personality, apathy, and basic self-care skills. Thus, within a neurogeriatric
rehabilitation setting, the relevance of this measure is in terms of various
aspects of patient management. For example, this measure could be used
as a screen for neurogeriatric nursing home admission, as an aid in establishing type of placement needed, to monitor the disease course severity over time, or to develop a rehabilitative nursing plan of needed
supports and services.

Supplementary Bedside Mental Status Screening Measures

The next series of bedside screening measures is a compendium of assessment techniques that may have useful applications in special circumstances.
These methods might be included as adjuncts to either an abbreviated or
a comprehensive mental status examination. Administration and interpretation of this class of measures require keener behavioral observation and
greater experience with the qualitative aspects of various types of neurocognitive dysfunction. In general, these measures are best suited for process
observation and hypothesis generation. These methods can be quite useful
in extracting information for individualized neurorehabilitation planning.

Clock Drawing Test

The clock drawing test has a rich history in neurology (Critchley, 1953)
and has withstood the test of time as a neurocognitive screening proce-

dure. This bedside task is perhaps one of the easiest and most quickly administered, yet its interpretation is elusive and highly dependent on the observational skills of the examiner. The materials necessary for this procedure include a blank sheet of paper, a pencil, and a preprinted copy of a stimulus card if a "copy format" condition is going to be administered.

Numerous presentation formats exist for this test. They typically involve instructing the client to draw the face of a clock. Some administrations include instructions for spontaneous geometric drawing of a clock on a blank sheet of paper. Other instructions involve placing the hands of a clock at a particular setting within a predrawn circle, and yet other techniques involve copying a predrawn clock. There also are various permutations of these formats. Perhaps one of the better known methods, promoted by Kaplan and her colleagues, includes these instructions: "Draw the face of the clock showing the numbers and the two hands, set to ten after eleven." This is followed by a copy format (Goodglass & Kaplan, 1983, p. 58). These particular instructions, with the patient drawing on a blank sheet of paper, have been extensively analyzed and are particularly useful in eliciting a rich array of neurocognitive behaviors whereby qualitative cognitive strategies can be noted (Kaplan & Delis, 1994).

Some of the cognitive components necessary for the successful completion of the task, which can be observed or inferred, include intact auditory comprehension, abstraction of the semantic instructions, understanding the syntactic complexity of the verbal instructions, inhibition of the tendency to be pulled by certain perceptual features of the stimulus, visual memory, mental planning, visuoconstructional abilities, and motor programming. Thus, although the draw-a-clock procedure does seem to sample a wide range of neurocognitive functions, objective quantification of the qualitative aspects of patient performance has been a major challenge. To this end, we review here a number of published scoring strategies.

The draw-a-clock test has a potential application for any patient population requiring neurocognitive screening. It should be noted that most of the empirical data on this measure has been with the population of individuals with Alzheimer's disease, but the qualitative nature of the task lends itself well as a screening instrument in virtually any population. Normative data on this measure suggest that it is relatively free of age effects until the 7th decade and relatively free of educational confounds at or above the eighth-grade level (Goodglass & Kaplan, 1983). As an example, Ainslie and Murden (1993) advised caution when this measure is used as the sole neurocognitive screening test for dementia in older adults with little formal education: their results with this population had limited diagnostic value. Thus, if the individual or group to be tested has a limited educational background, the clock drawing test should be supplemented with other neurocognitive measures. Other clinical evidence and empirical data generally suggest that this instrument is relatively free of cultural bias and can be used in different ethnic populations (Shulman, Shedletsky, & Silveret, 1986; Cahn, Wiederholt, Salmon, & Butters, 1993).

Clinically, we have found this test useful with patients who have degenerative neurologic disorders, for patients with vascular disease, as an adjunct test used to aid in differentiating between neurologic and psychiatric disorders, and with populations with no dementia to severe dementia. We have found this test to be a very useful adjunct to the MMSE primarily because the MMSE is highly verbal. The draw-a-clock procedure supplements the verbal assessment with valuable visuoconstructional screening data.

Historically, there has been little in the way of standardized instructions or objective scoring procedures for the draw-a-clock test. Kaplan and her colleagues have had a significant impact on standardizing the qualitative process analysis of patient clock drawings by including this test as a part of the supplemental language test protocol of the Boston Diagnostic Aphasia Examination (Goodglass & Kaplan, 1983). Their copy form of the test factors out the visuospatial component of the task performance.

The original Goodglass and Kaplan scoring method was a scale of 0 to 3, but others have published more elaborate quantitative and qualitative scoring methods (Rouleau, Salmon, Butters, Kennedy, & McGuire, 1992). Perhaps the most complicated extension of the original Goodglass and Kaplan (1983) procedure involves presenting patients with a predrawn circle with instructions to draw a clock showing "ten past eleven" and then having them draw five predetermined clock settings and read five predetermined clock settings (Tuokko, Hadjistavropoulos, Miller, & Beattie, 1992). Scoring involves calculating error types according to seven categories for the drawings and a 3-point error system for the clock settings and readings.

Some of the popular instructions for the draw-a-clock procedure involve drawing to command. For example, Sunderland et al. (1989) provide the patient with a pencil and a blank sheet of paper. The patient is given the instructions: "First, draw a clock with all the numbers on it. Second, put hands on the clock to make it read 2:45." These instructions can be repeated as often as necessary, but no other directions can be given. Scoring of the finished drawing is on a 10-point scale from best to worst. An impairment cut-off score of 6 is used.

Mendez, Ala, and Underwood (1992) used a similar procedure to Sunderland et al. (1989) but included an extended scoring system. The patient is given a blank sheet of paper with instructions to draw a clock. This command is given both orally and in writing, and is repeated as necessary. After the clock drawing attempt, patients are asked both orally and in writing to indicate the time as ten after eleven. A 20-point scale is used to rate clock drawing, with a cut-off score of 18.

Libon, Swenson, Barnoski, and Sands (1993) incorporated both drawing to command and a copy condition using the original Goodglass and Kaplan (1983) "ten after eleven" instructions. To score patient drawings, they used the extended Sunderland et al. (1989) scoring procedure with a modification to accommodate for the differences associated with their particular procedure. They suggested a cut-off score of 7 for the drawing-to-command condition.

Other popular procedures involve a more structured task. For example, the Wolf-Klein, Silverstone, Levy, and Brod (1989) procedure includes providing the patient with a piece of paper and a preprinted circle 4 inches in diameter. The patient then is given the instruction "Draw a clock." The instruction can be repeated and there is no time limit on the task. Scoring involves matching the completed drawing with one of 10 clinical categories. The proposed cut-off scores are 1–6 as abnormal and 7–10 as normal. Similarly, the Shulman et al. (1986) instructions include giving the patient a predrawn circle. The patient then is instructed to draw a clock face showing the time as three o'clock. A rank ordering method of scoring severity of clock drawing errors along a 5-point scale is used to objectify impairment from mild to severe.

Psychometric Properties

Data on interrater reliability have been sparse, but when reported they have been acceptable. On the 10-point Sunderland et al. (1989) scoring system, an interrater reliability of .86 was reported. Mendez et al. (1992) reported an interrater reliability of .95 on their 20-point scoring system. They also reported test–retest reliability at 12 and 24 weeks as .78 and .76, respectively. Tuokko et al. (1992) reported reliability coefficients in the .90 to .95 range, with a test–retest reliability of .70 at 4 days, for their elaborate scoring method.

Validity data also are relatively sparse, but again, when reported, they have been acceptable. In a sample of patients with Alzheimer's disease versus older adult controls, Sunderland et al. (1989) reported highly significant differences between the groups, with relatively little overlap, indicating a sensitivity of 78% and a specificity of 96%. When individuals without cognitive impairment and patients with dementia were rated on a 5-point scale for their drawing of the face of a clock with the hands showing three o'clock on a predrawn circle, Shulman et al. (1986) reported a sensitivity of 86% and a specificity of 72%. Finally, Wolf-Klein et al. (1989) reported a sensitivity of 87% and a specificity of 93% in distinguishing between patients with Alzheimer's disease from older adult controls with and without depression.

Only one study directly compared the relative predictive validity of specific draw-a-clock procedures and suggested relative trade-offs for the various techniques (Ainslie & Murden, 1993). These authors reported on the use of three different draw-a-clock procedures as a screen to detect dementia across a broad educational continuum. The Wolf-Klein et al. (1989) scoring system yielded an overall sensitivity of 48% and a specificity of 93%. The Shulman et al. (1986) procedure had a sensitivity of 64% and a specificity of 78%. Finally, the Sunderland et al. (1989) procedure had a sensitivity of 75% and a specificity of 64%.

The draw-a-clock test has been found to be differentially sensitive to some types of disease processes. For example, Libon et al. (1993) found that a distinction could be made between Alzheimer's disease and vascular dementia. The major finding reported was a lack of improvement in the copy condition for vascular subjects. Rouleau et al. (1992) found significant differences in objective qualitative error analysis when comparing patients with Alzheimer's versus Huntington's disease equated for dementia severity. The types of errors included conceptual, "stimulus-bound," and perseverative responses in patients with Alzheimer's disease, whereas patients with Huntington's disease showed more graphic errors and no improvement in the copy condition. These findings, however, were not replicated in a study of patients with cortical versus subcortical vascular disease; albeit a different scoring system was used (Kirk & Kertesz, 1993).

A consistent finding of a significant hemispheric contribution to this drawing test has been replicated (Kirk & Kertesz, 1989, 1993). Right-hemispheric lesions result in visuospatial disturbance and neglect, and left-hemispheric lesions result in simplification and low-level errors of execution.

Concurrent validity has been reported by Sunderland et al. (1989), who found that the clock drawing scores correlated strongly with standard measures of dementia severity on the Dementia Rating Scale, Global Deterioration Scale, Blessed Dementia Rating Scale, and the Short Portable Mental Status Questionnaire (rs = .56, .59, .51, and .59, respectively). Libon et al.'s (1993) version of the Sunderland scoring system similarly revealed significant correlations in the .33 to .46 range with neurocognitive tests of executive and visuospatial function.

Special Considerations, Cautions, and Applications

The draw-a-clock test, like all other brief screening measures, has limitations in terms of specificity and sensitivity (and therefore, clinical application). Objective scoring methods add scientific rigor to clinical applications. Scoring methods such as the Sunderland et al. (1989) technique are useful if the goal is to detect a diffuse process. The Rouleau et al. (1992) procedure seems useful if the goal is to detect focal lesions. In general, the copy condition is a useful adjunct.

The draw-a-clock procedure in its various forms provides a rich sampling of neurocognitive behavior. Many of the published procedures can stand alone as a basic starting point for mental status screening or can be used as an adjunct test to a larger neurocognitive battery. The test is sufficiently robust in that it can be used in a patient population that ranges from neurologically intact to severely demented. Whether this additional information adds to the experienced clinician's hypotheses is unknown. Nevertheless, it is impressive that empirical data provide evidence that the draw-a-clock test, using a variety of administrative procedures and scoring systems, can distinguish between certain types of brain dysfunction. It is likewise impressive that the draw-a-clock procedure, using certain scoring systems, is sensitive not only to lateralization, but even brain dysfunction along the rostral–caudal continuum.

The chief limitation of the draw-a-clock test is its relatively high false negative and false positive rates. The more critical the need for accurate clinical diagnostic information, the more dangerous it is to rely on an abbreviated mental status screening score. In this light, it is important to recognize that it is not known if the draw-a-clock procedure actually adds sufficient data to the experienced clinician's diagnostic decision making process. Therefore, it is not prudent to use the draw-a-clock procedure (or any other abbreviated mental status exam) as the sole examination in making a diagnosis of dementia. This caution is especially true with older patients with limited formal education (Ainslie & Murden, 1993). Clearly, in these more difficult populations, this test should always be supplemented with other instruments.

A second limitation is that process analysis of error pattern is only in its infancy. To date, there are no sound empirical data strongly supporting an error analysis scoring system that has been adequately replicated for clinical application. Error analysis depends on the skill of the particular clinician. Therefore, in general, error analysis should serve as a basis for further hypothesis generation or teaching for both diagnostic and neurorehabilitative considerations.

Conclusion

Because of such empirically demonstrated qualities, this procedure is recommended as a solid starting point in the mental status examination, either individually or in combination with other neurocognitive screening techniques. When used individually, this test can serve as an objective initial neurobehavioral observation point. The advantage of the draw-a-clock test is that it is a very brief procedure with sensitivity and specificity comparable to other brief screening instruments. When used as an adjunct test, this procedure might even have greater predictive value. For example, if mental status screening begins with an instrument such as the Mini-Mental State Examination, the draw-a-clock test provides an excellent nonverbal, visuoperceptual adjunct. Finally, when included with a larger series of neurocognitive tests, this procedure adds further depth to the syndrome analysis. We have found that in case presentations to other professionals or treatment teams (especially the multidisciplinary team), a picture is worth a thousand words. This is particularly the case when this instrument is administered by the skilled practitioner who may use this and other test performances to develop hypotheses about the severity of impairment, lesion site, disease process, and so on.

Overall, when considering reliability, validity, ease of administration, and usefulness of data interpretation for the draw-a-clock neurocognitive screening procedure, we recommend a semistructured approach. The patient is given a blank sheet of white 8.5 × 11-inch paper and a pencil and provided with the instructions to set the hands of the clock at "ten after eleven." These instructions can be provided as often as necessary (although repeated instructions are noteworthy when interpreting the results). After the patient completes or attempts to complete the drawing, he or she is provided with a model and instructed to copy the figure. The Sunderland et al. (1989) and the Mendez et al. (1992) scoring systems are reasonable choices because of the ease of application and empirical support. Both systems seem to have equally acceptable properties of reliability and validity and they are straightforward to score and interpret.

The Rouleau et al. (1992) scoring method is particularly valuable if the goal is to objectify qualitative error analysis.

The real value of this procedure comes from careful observation of qualitative errors that occur during the process of clock construction, especially when comparing the draw-to-command with the copy format. In a very preliminary way, the process approach lends itself well to hypothesis generation of lesion localization and disease process. In terms of hypothesis generation for neurorehabilitation intervention, cognitive functions such as auditory comprehension, understanding the complexity instructions, self-regulation, memory, mental planning, visuoconstructional abilities, motor programming, as well as frustration tolerance to a demanding task, are all present. Thus, when administered by an experienced examiner, sophisticated neurocognitive brain/behavioral inferences and neurorehabilitative hypotheses can be generated. The resulting quantitative and qualitative information obtained seems invaluable in the generation of diagnostic and remedial hypotheses that can be validated with more detailed neurobehavioral observation or examination.

Behavioral Dyscontrol Scale

In recent years there has been a resurgence of interest in frontal release signs or reflexes as a quick, objective, and sensitive measure of neurocognitive dysfunction. The concept of a frontal release sign or simple primitive reflex that might distinguish normal from impaired cerebral function is based on an ontogenetic "release" phenomenon whereby perinatal reflexes again emerge during dementing conditions (Paulson, 1977). The adage "once a man, twice a child" describes the phenomenon. This reasoning is based on the Jacksonian concept of the "dissolution" of cerebral inhibition secondary to diffuse brain disease. Though theoretically interesting, the search for an easily elicited pathognomonic sign of dementia has been disappointing. In a review of the literature on "reflex dementia," Landau (1989) argued that although primitive reflexes have been shown to correlate with impaired performance on neurocognitive tests, the association is weak and these signs are of little diagnostic or localizing value. Such reflexes may be present in older adults without cognitive impairment and they may not even emerge until late in a dementing course. Landau further argued that even the various labels used to describe the phenomenon, such as *primitive reflex*, *frontal release sign*, *cortical disinhibition*, and so forth have not proved to be valid except as arbitrary classification terms.

Although the frontal release reflex has not proved to be clinically useful, the concept of loss of behavioral control secondary to brain damage (typically frontal regions) has been extensively described (Luria, 1980). There are a number of more extensive psychometric instruments (e.g., the Wisconsin Card Sorting Test, the Category Test, the Stroop Test) that may sample elusive qualities of higher cortical executive control. Aside from some of Luria's bedside techniques, however, screening instruments to elicit such signs are lacking.

Grigsby, Kaye, and Robbins (1992) have introduced a measure of "behavioral dyscontrol" that strikes a compromise between the quick but unreliable "frontal release sign" reflexes, the time-consuming psychometric procedures of "executive function," and some of the more highly qualitative bedside techniques used to elicit frontal signs (i.e., Lurian methods). The measure Grigsby et al. (1992) introduced is called the Behavioral Dyscontrol Scale and is based on Luria's theory of frontal lobe disinhibition. The rationale behind this scale is that patients sometimes demonstrate cognitive deficits in the everyday environment far in excess of what might be predicted based on mental status performance. Grigsby et al.'s main objective was to develop a measure that would predict a patient's capacity for independent regulation of his or her own behavior. A second objective was the hope that this scale might identify frontal lobe disorders. The authors reported that they were less concerned with the extent to which this instrument would localize a lesion (i.e., frontal lobe pathology) and, not surprisingly, the empirical support for the latter objective is still unknown. The main value of this instrument, then, is in assessing behavioral functioning with generalization to everyday life (i.e., independent behavioral regulation).

The Behavioral Dyscontrol Scale is a relatively short scale containing nine items that primarily evaluate motor functioning. It is probably best suited for use with older individuals where there is a diagnostic question of dementia (because these are the only norms available on this scale). It may be the instrument of choice when behavioral disruption is disproportional to a decline in mental status.

The specific rationale of this scale is the premise that inability to learn and perform simple motor tasks with the hands reflects a failure in the regulation of voluntary motor activity. Five of the items on this scale assess the capacity for inhibition and control of various aspects of simple movement (e.g., I tap once, you tap twice, and vice versa). Two of the items involve the learning of simple motoric behaviors (e.g., learn the sequence fist-edge-palm). One of the items samples the patient's capacity to shift the focus of attention while maintaining concentration on a task (e.g., alternate counting such as 1a2b3c). Finally, one item is an examiner's rating of the patient's insight into his or her own performance. Each item, in fact, is a clinician's rating of the observed behavior on a 3-point scale of *adequate performance, mildly to moderately deficient performance,* or *very impaired performance.* Scoring this scale involves a summation of points. The best possible score is 19 (Item 9 is rated on a 4-point scale). The authors reported that scores in the 0 to 6 range were indicative of severely impaired behavioral control; scores from 7 to 10 suggested moderately severe impairment, and scores of 11 to 15 reflected mild impairment. On the basis of their clinical experience, they suggested a cut-off score of 10 as predictive of those individuals who are likely to have difficulty regulating their own behavior. They also reported a table of percentile ranks for three normative samples.

Psychometric Properties

Grigsby et al. (1992) are the only authors to date to report on the reliability and validity of this scale. They report interrater reliability as .98. The authors caution that in their study, raters were experienced in the administration and scoring of this scale. Thus, inexperienced examiners would likely have lower interrater reliabilities. These authors also noted from their experience that naive examiners tend to inflate scores slightly. Other reliability indices indicate a test–retest stability in the .86 to .93 range up to a 6-month period. Finally, the Cronbach's alpha of internal consistency was .87.

In previous work with a very similar version of this scale, Kaye, Grigsby, Robbins, & Korzun (1990) found that this measure tended to predict autonomous functioning, impulsivity, and apathy. Although this measure does correlate with the MMSE, it seems to sample a different functional domain (motoric behavioral regulation) than measures that rely heavily on gross cognitive status and general orientation.

The validity of this measure was specifically tested by a principal components analysis, which yielded three factors. These factors have been interpreted in light of Luria's theory of frontal lobe regulation of behavior (Grigsby et al., 1992). Factor 1 was an ability to use intention to guide one's own behavior. Factor 2 was the inability to perceive one's own mistakes and use feedback to improve performance.Factor 3 was a capacity for inhibition.

Special Considerations, Cautions, and Applications

This measure is designed primarily for the population of older adults and seems to sample a different constellation of mental functions than do most abbreviated mental status examinations. Researchers have suggested that this measure is sensitive to frontal lobe dysfunction, but there are no empirical data as yet for this supposition. Instead, this measure clearly samples the regulation of complex motoric behavior and appears to predict autonomous functioning, impulsivity, and apathy. Limited empirical support suggests that there is no significant relationship between this measure and age (in the population of older adults), education, or depression. On the negative side, there appears to be a low ceiling effect on the measure, no significant predictive data presently available, and a need for initial familiarity and supervision by an experienced clinician to achieve reported interrater reliability.

Conclusion

This measure seems to offer an alternative to most abbreviated mental status examinations that capture a class of neurocognitive function heavily weighted with cognitive and general orientation items. This type of measure offers an alternative and seems of particular value in the neurorehabilitative setting. The major application would be in cases where the patient presents with disinhibition of behavior that is out of proportion to what their mental status score might predict. Although this technique is helpful in ruling out organic determinants, such cases should always initially include a differential diagnosis of psychologic versus organic determinants of the patient's behavior. This measure has been shown to assess autonomous functioning, impulsivity, and apathy. These are often the intangible aspects of behavior critical to neurorehabilitative success in terms of the patient's participation in therapies and generalization to the home environment.

This measure can easily be memorized, and therefore can be administered at the bedside at the examiner's discretion. Further research is needed to further validate predictive validity of this measure in the everyday environment and to determine whether this measure indeed samples frontal lobe behavior.

Unawareness Interview

Assessment of the construct of unawareness of neurocognitive deficit is another adjunct procedure that is a helpful addition to any mental status examination, whether abbreviated or extended. The goal is to understand the patient's perception of his or her own mental status. There is an abundance of literature which supports the contention that the extent to which a patient is unaware of his or her neurocognitive deficit is strongly tied to the extent to which he or she can be engaged in treatment (McGlynn & Schacter, 1989; Prigatano & Schacter, 1989). For example, the patient with a Wernicke's dysphasia has minimal awareness that his or her verbal output makes no sense. These patients are not only unmotivated to modify their language in speech therapy, but do not believe they have a problem in the first place. Lesions in other specific areas of the brain are associated with different types and degrees of unawareness. Examples include unawareness in the areas of attention to extrapersonal space, the hemiparetic limb, memory, or social impact. (For further discussion of measures of unawareness, see chapter 12.)

A modified version of Anderson and Tranel's (1989) unawareness interview schedule (Wagner & Cushman, 1994) has been used with patients in several different neurologic diagnostic populations. The measure is a clinical rating scale that samples awareness in the domains of reason for hospitalization (or outpatient visit), immediate and remote memory difficulty, disorientation, intellectual decline, dysphasia, visuoperceptual impairment, and emotional dyscontrol (i.e., pseudobulbar affect).

The interview is an 8-item questionnaire that samples seven neurocognitive domains. Administration of the interview usually takes about 5 to 10 minutes. The patient responds to the extent to which they believe that they have a problem in each cognitive domain. Their objective neurocognitive test performance in each particular domain is then compared with their perception of their ability. The discrepancy between patient perception of self-abilities and actual ability is then rated on a 3-point Likert scale as awareness versus unawareness of that particular domain. Summation of the 8-item subscales yields a total summary score of unawareness. As a clinical validity check, one can look for the unawareness pattern to make neurologic sense and fit with the lesion site or the type of disease process. For example, in Alzheimer's disease, there is an expected dissociation between unawareness of recent versus remote memory abilities.

Psychometric Properties

An unawareness interview schedule (Anderson & Tranel, 1989; Wagner & Cushman, 1994) can be used to detect unawareness of cognitive deficit in various neurodiagnostic categories. For example, researchers have demonstrated differences between patients who were neurologically unimpaired and patients with cerebrovascular disease (Wagner & Cushman, 1994). Similarly, a sensitivity has been shown to patients with dementia and closed-head injury (Anderson & Tranel, 1989). The brief questionnaire has been shown to have a high interrater reliability of .92. In our own unpublished interrater reliability studies on this instrument, we have likewise found coefficients in the .90 range.

Special Considerations, Cautions, and Applications

Instruments used to objectify unawareness of cognitive function are still experimental. Reliability and validity data are extremely limited. It is probably the case that an evaluator must have significant clinical skill to detect and understand the significance of the various components of organically mediated unawareness. In all cases, the phenomenon must be considered relative to the disease process in question.

Conclusion

The procedure of using the unawareness interview within the mental status examination is to first inquire as to the patient's perception of his or her symptoms and then to follow-up with objective measurement of his or her abilities. In part, the clinical value of incorporating such an unawareness interview within the neurobehavioral examination is that the mental status examination that follows often makes more sense to the patient. We have found patients to be more cooperative and motivated because the rationale of the mental status procedure is self-evident after they have been interviewed about their symptoms. More importantly, quantification of the neuropsychological symptom of unawareness of deficit has profound implications in the neurorehabilitative setting. In fact, the incorporation of such an interview before a brief or extended mental status examination seems applicable in most neuropsychological examination situations. The clinical value of the measure reviewed is that it is easily administered at bedside and has empirical support in objectifying the construct of unawareness of neurocognitive deficit.

At a minimum, the clinical use of such an objective rating system increases the clinician's awareness of the possibility of this syndrome. In terms of neurorehabilitative planning, the presence of unawareness can be a major barrier to successfully engaging the patient in therapy. For example, it is extremely unlikely that the patient will exert effort in therapy if he or she does not recognize that there is a problem to be addressed. Patients with fluent dysphasia are often the most difficult to successfully engage in speech therapy. Finally, unawareness is quite important in terms of general safety. It is most often the case that the patient who is unaware of his or her limitations is at increased risk for unsafe behavior. Such neuropsychological considerations need to be included in the neurorehabilitative plan. Assessment of unawareness becomes important not only for treatment planning, but also in accident prevention.

Applications of the Mental Status Examination

Each evaluation method reviewed here has its own particular strengths and weaknesses, depending on the intended application. Specific applications of mental status findings in neurorehabilitation is a separate and evolving topic beyond the scope of this chapter. However, we strongly believe that the incorporation of mental status screening is critical to all individually tailored neurorehabilitation plans. In fact, with the advances in the understanding of brain, behavior, and environment that have emerged out of neuropsychological, psychiatric, and behavioral neurologic research, to fail to include mental status screening in the treatment of all neurorehabilitation patients is to provide substandard care.

With reference to test selection, several words of caution and brief reference to some of the many potential clinical and research applications are in order. Health care practitioners have often come to neuropsychologists (either in person or by review of the literature) in search of that brief and simple mental status procedure that will definitively answer complex neurobehavioral patient care questions. Clinical experience and even the literature (Feher et al., 1992) suggest that practitioners often inappropriately rely on brief screening instruments to answer complex neurobehavioral questions. Overinterpretation of nonexistent neurocognitive factors such as memory, language, intellect, and the like arbitrarily derived from the face validity of an instrument and through rigid adherence to cut-off scores seems most problematic. The risk in the present environment of cost constraint in health care is that empirically validated methods of objective neurocognitive measurement will be neglected for the sake of brevity.

The current popularity of the neurosciences in clinical practice has propagated the conceptual simplicity of mental function. The brief bedside screening instrument, with its extreme ease of use and its single score of mental function has had a seductive appeal. These factors have combined to foster an artificial sense of neuropsychological confidence. Practitioners with limited experience may inadvertently engage in what can, at best, be described as marginal neurobehavioral patient care. We hope that this review and critique will promote a better understanding of the issues surrounding the strengths and limitations of these various bedside screening techniques.

Although we have focused here on brief mental status instruments, we must emphasize that both bedside and comprehensive neurocognitive measures are only an adjunct to the overall clinical examination. Other components of the neuropsychologic examination cannot be overemphasized. Some critical elements of the comprehensive neurobehavioral examination, which we did not review in detail, include obtaining a detailed history of the presenting illness from both patient and family; review of medical and neurologic risk factors of brain function; review of possible iatrogenic medication effects; review of possible contributory psychiatric history; review of the family history to determine genetic risk factors; careful behavioral observations; and completion of the formal mental status examination. Other important elements come from a clinician's professional experience. For example, clinical experience with the neurocognitive manifestations and prognoses of various neurologic diseases and the ability to recognize atypical presentations that do not make neurologic sense also contribute to the sound clinical neurobehavioral examination.

Clearly, the 5–10 minute screening examination falls short of providing anything except the most rudimentary snapshot of mental function. For this reason, a brief screening exam should never be considered a substitute for a comprehensive examination unless one is keenly aware of the associated restrictions with reference to diagnostic, prognostic, and treatment planning implications.

Theoretically, we believe that any mental status examination should conceptually follow a hierarchical framework (i.e., Luria, 1980). Behavioral observations and objective examination can then provide a rational framework for test selection and interpretation of the obtained results. Such an approach also provides a model for neurorehabilitative intervention (i.e., Christensen, 1986). Hierarchical components of neuropsychological function the evaluator should consider include, but are not limited to, level of consciousness, attention, orientation, psychomotor function, praxis, language functions, prosodic components of language, memory, perceptual abilities, intellect, mental flexibility and self-control, awareness of neurocognitive ability, personality, and emotional coping or reactions to neurologic disability. The clinician must also consider the actual neuroanatomic lesion sites; the nature of pathology (focal vs. diffuse); premorbid intellectual abilities; age; and the chronicity, severity, and nature of deficit relative to environmental demands. These factors are crucial to prognosis.

Brief structured bedside techniques are particularly valuable to guide practitioners who do not have extensive neurological or psychological training. Depending on the clinician's confidence, data from bedside screening can be used in determining the presence or absence of an organic disease process. Data from the bedside examination also may help determine the need for comprehensive evaluation. Indications might be equivocal findings or the need for more information in order to make a diagnosis. Other indications for further work-up might include brain dysfunction of known etiology and the need for further elaboration for treatment planning and patient and family education.

Finally, from a research perspective, brief, objective bedside neurocognitive measures provide an easily obtained and standardized method of data collection. Compilation of a single gross measure of neurocognitive function has the particular advantage of simplified statistical analysis. This fosters research in multiple areas of patient care, with the secondary effect of generating a more widespread recognition and understanding of the role of neurocognitive function in patient care.

Conclusion

We have tried to provide the reader with a review of potentially useful bedside measures and techniques with clinical and perhaps research applications. We conducted a review of the literature of the past decade in order to identify bedside mental status screening measures with supportive empirical data. From this list and other sources, we selected a representative sample of popular and seemingly useful measures for critical review.

We selected the Mini-Mental State Examination (MMSE) because of its outstanding popularity and recognition. This measure dwarfs all other measures in terms of number of references, and it is clearly the most widely recognized of all brief mental status measures. The major shortcoming of this measure is that the MMSE is based on a univariate model of organicity and yields only a single score. We selected the Neurobehavioral Cognitive Status Examination (NCSE) for review because it was developed in an attempt to overcome shortcomings of the MMSE. The NCSE appears to assess several components, or factors, of neurocognitive function, instead of providing a unitary score of mental function. The Dementia Rating Scale (DRS) and the Extended Scale for Dementia (ESD; which is an expansion of the former scale) appear to be useful for assessing patients with severe neurocognitive impairment as well as for rating change over time in the more severe, progressive syndromes.

The Blessed Dementia Scale (BSD) and the Blessed Information–Memory–Concentration Scale (BIMC) are popular in the geriatric patient population literature for assessment of degenerative conditions. These measures provide a functional correlate reported by the family and have good neuropathological validity data. These measures provide a sound alterative to the MMSE when assessing the older patient population.

We also reviewed measures that may provide an alternative to the standard psychometric approach of measuring neurocognitive function, and that may also provide useful qualitative data for neurorehabilitative treatment planning. The first of these was the draw-a-clock procedure. This technique of mental status assessment has a long tradition in the qualitative description of neurocognitive dysfunction. A second measure was a more recent and as yet relatively unknown instrument used to sample "frontal-like" neurocognitive behavior (the Behavioral Dyscontrol Scale). This measure differs from other bedside techniques in that it samples only complex motoric behaviors. The construct to be sampled is loss of behavioral control. Finally, we briefly reviewed a measure that samples awareness of neurocognitive function. The unawareness interview can be used as an adjunct to any brief or extended formal mental status examination and seems to provide data that are quite useful in neurorehabilitation planning.

Nelson et al. (1986) concluded a previous review of the literature with an observation that the chief advantage of brief, structured, routine bedside neurocognitive exams is that they provide standardized methods of data collection and may help practitioners who do not have extensive neurological or neuropsychological training. In the present review, we were unable to find any studies that directly compare the relative efficacy of multiple measures in the same patient populations. We conclude that there is little empirical support that one instrument are superior to any other. Rather, each of the measures we reviewed seems to have its own particular strengths and weaknesses.

An associated issue in selecting instruments is that we found no empirical data to support whether, and to what extent, any of the abbreviated bedside mental status screening tests add anything to clinical diagnostic accuracy that cannot be achieved by the unstructured interview by the experienced clinician. Based on the available literature, it would seem that all brief mental status screening instruments suffer from relatively high false-positive and false-negative results. We strongly believe that such measures should be used only as an adjunct to a sound clinical neurobehavioral examination.

Future development of instruments for mental status screening will have to address the problem that increasing brevity is associated with decreasing sensitivity and specificity. Perhaps greater understanding of brain–behavior functions and the application of technology may hold some promise. For example, further research aimed at the association of functional brain imaging (i.e., neuroSPECT, PET, and the combined MRI/SPECT technology) with mental status screening may provide greater understanding of brain–behavior correlates. Likewise, the use of computer technology in mental status screening is nearly nonexistent, but it seems to hold promise (Long & Wagner, 1986). Areas for the potential application of computer technology to neurocognitive assessment include test administration, scoring, and enhancement of human clinical decision making.

References

Ainslie, N. K., & Murden, R. A. (1993). Effect of education on the clock-drawing dementia screen in non-demented elderly persons. *Journal of the American Geriatric Society, 41*, 249–252.

American Psychiatric Association (1980). *Diagnostic and Statistical Manual of Mental Disorders* (3rd ed.). Washington, DC: Author.

Anderson, S. W., & Tranel, D. (1989). Awareness of disease states following cerebral infarction, dementia, and head trauma: Standardized assessment. *The Clinical Neuropsychologist, 3*, 327–339.

Anthony, J. C., LaResche, L., Niaz, U., Von Korff, M. R., & Folstein, M. F. (1982). Limits of the "Mini-Mental State" as a screening test for dementia and delirium among hospital patients. *Psychological Medicine, 12*, 397–408.

Aronson, M. K., Ooi, W. L., Morgenstern, H., Hafner, A., Masur, D., Crystal, H., Frishman, W. H., Fisher, D., & Katzman, R. (1990). Women, myocardial infarction, and dementia in the very old. *Neurology, 40*, 102–1106.

Ashford, J. W., Hsu, L. N., Becker, M., Kumar, V., & Bekian, C. (1986). Mini-mental status and activities of daily living: Cross validation by scalogram and item analysis techniques. *The Gerontologist, 26*, 143.

Ashford, J. W., Kolm, P., Colliver, J. A., Bekian, C., & Hsu, L. (1989). Alzheimer patient evaluation and the Mini-Mental State: Item characteristic curve analysis. *Journal of Gerontology, 44*, 139–146.

Balestreri, R., Fontana, L., & Astengo, F. (1987). A double-blind placebo controlled evaluation of the safety and efficacy of vinpocetine in the treatment of patients with chronic vascular senile cerebral dysfunction. *Journal of the American Geriatric Society, 35*, 425–430.

Beatty, W., & Goodkin, D. E. (1990). Screening for cognitive impairment in multiple sclerosis: An examination of the Mini-Mental State Examination. *Archives of Neurology, 47*, 297–301.

Berg, G., Edwards, D. F., Danzinger, W. L., & Berg, L. (1987). Longitudinal change in three brief assessments of SDAT. *Journal of the American Geriatric Society, 35*, 205–212.

Bird, H. R., Canino, G., Stipec, M. R., & Shrout, P. (1987). Use of the Mini-Mental State Examination in a probability sample of a Hispanic population. *Journal of Nervous and Mental Disease, 175*, 731–737.

Blakemore, C. B. (1987). Cyclandelate in the treatment of multi-infarct dementia. *Drugs, 33*(Suppl. 2), 110–113.

Bleecker, M. L., Bolla-Wilson, K., Kawas, C., & Agnew, J. (1988). Age-specific norms for the Mini-Mental State Exam. *Neurology, 33*, 1565–1568.

Blessed, G., Black, S. E., Butler, T., & Kay, D. W. (1991). The diagnosis of dementia in the elderly. *British Journal of Psychiatry, 159*, 193–198.

Blessed, G., Tomlinson, B. E., & Roth, M. (1968). Association between quantitative measures of dementia and of senile changes in cerebral grey matter of elderly subjects. *British Journal of Psychiatry, 114*, 797–811.

Bondareff, W., Raval, J., Woo, B., Hauser, D. L., & Colletti, P. M. (1990). Magnetic Resolution Imaging and severity of dementia in older adults. *Archives of General Psychiatry, 47*, 47–51.

Bozzola, F. G., Gorelick, P. B., & Freels, S. (1992). Personality changes in Alzheimer's disease. *Archives of Neurology, 49*, 297–300.

Brandt, J., Folstein, S. F., & Folstein, M. F. (1988). Differential cognitive impairment in Alzheimer's disease and Huntington's disease. *Annals of Neurology, 23*, 555–561.

Brayne, C., & Calloway, P. (1990). The association of education and socioeconomic status with the Mini-Mental State Examination and clinical diagnosis of dementia in elderly people. *Age and Ageing, 19*, 91–96.

Breen, A. R., Larson, E. B., Reifler, B. V., Vitaliano, P. P., & Lawrence, G. L. (1984). Cognitive performance and functional competence in coexisting dementia and depression. *Journal of the American Geriatric Society, 32*, 132–137.

Buckwalter, J. G., Sobel, E., Dunn, M. E., Diz, M. M., & Henderson, V. W. (1993). Gender differences on a brief measure of cognitive functioning in Alzheimer's disease. *Archives of Neurology, 50*, 757–760.

Burch, E. A., & Andrews, S. R. (1987). Cognitive dysfunction in psychiatric consultation subgroups: Use of two screening tests. *Southern Medical Journal, 80*, 1079–1082.

Butters, B., Wolfe, J., Martone, M., Granholm, E., & Cermak, L. S. (1985). Memory disorders associated with Huntington's disease: Verbal recall, verbal recognition, and procedural memory. *Neuropsychologia, 23*, 729–743.

Cahn, D. A., Wiederholt, W. C., Salmon, D. P., & Butters, N. (1993, November). *Detection of cognitive impairment in Spanish-speaking elderly with the clock drawing test.* Paper presented at the annual meeting of the National Academy of Neuropsychologists, Phoenix, AZ.

Cammermeyer, M., & Evans, J. E. (1988). A brief neurobehavioral exam useful for early detection of post-operative complications in neurosurgical patients. *Journal of Neuroscience Nursing, 20*, 314–323.

Cavanaugh, S., & Wettstein, R. M. (1983). The relationship between severity of depression, cognitive dysfunction, and age in medical inpatients. *American Journal of Psychiatry, 140*, 495–496.

Cavanaugh, S., & Wettstein, R. M. (1989). Emotional and cognitive dysfunction associated with medical disorders. *Journal of Psychosomatic Research, 33*, 505–514.

Chandler, J. D., & Gerndt, J. (1988). Cognitive screening tests for organic mental disorders in psychiatric inpatients. *Journal of Nervous and Mental Disease, 176*, 675–681.

Chase, T. N., Foster, N. L., Fedio, P., Brooks, R., Mansi, L., & Di Chiro, G. (1984). Regional cortical dysfunction in Alzheimer's disease as determined by positron emission tomography. *Annals of Neurology*, *15*, 170–174.

Coblentz, J. M., Mattis S., Zingesser, L., Kasoff, S. S., Wisniewski, H. M., & Katzman, R. (1973). Presenile dementia: Clinical aspects and evaluation of cerebrospinal dynamics. *Archives of Neurology*, *29*, 299–308.

Colantonio, A., Becker, J. T., & Huff, F. J. (1993). Factor structure of the Mattis Dementia Rating Scale among patients with probable Alzheimer's disease. *The Clinical Neuropsychologist*, *7*, 313–318.

Cole, M. G. (1990). Inter-rater reliability of the Blessed Dementia Scale. *Canadian Journal of Psychiatry*, *35*, 328–330.

Colohan, H., O'Callaghan, E., Larkin, C., & Waddington, J. L. (1989). An evaluation of cranial CT scanning in clinical psychiatry. *Irish Journal of Medical Science*, *158*, 178–181.

Critchley, M. (1953). *The parietal lobes*. New York: Hufner.

Crum, R. M., Anthony, J. C., Bassett, S. S., & Folstein, M. F. (1993). Population-based norms for the Mini-Mental State Examination by age and educational level. *Journal of the American Medical Association*, *269*, 2386–2391.

Cullum, C. M., Thompson, L. L., & Smernoff, E. N. (1993). Three-word recall as a measure of memory. *Journal of Clinical and Experimental Neuropsychology*, *15*, 321–329.

Davis, P. B., Morris, J. C., & Grant, E. (1990). Brief screening tests versus clinical staging in senile dementia of the Alzheimer's type. *Journal of the American Geriatric Society*, *38*, 129–135.

Davous, P., Lamour, Y., Debrand, E., & Rondot, P. (1987). A comparative evaluation of the short orientation memory concentration test of cognitive impairment. *Journal of Neurology, Neurosurgery and Psychiatry*, *50*, 312–317.

Department of Health and the Welsh Office. (1989). *General practice in the National Health Service: A new contract*. London: Author.

Devanand, D. P., Sackeim, H. A., Brown, R. P., & Mayeux, R. (1989). A pilot study of haloperidol treatment of psychosis and behavioral disturbance in Alzheimer's disease. *Archives of Neurology*, *46*, 854–857.

Escobar, J. I., Burnam, A., Karno, M., Forsythe, A., Landsverk, J., & Golding, J. M. (1986). Use of the Mini-Mental State Examination (MMSE) in a community population of mixed ethnicity: Cultural and linguistic artifacts. *Journal of Nervous and Mental Disease*, *174*, 607–614.

Fabrega, H., Jr., Mezzich, J., Cornelius, J., & Ahn, C. (1989). Variation in cognitive functioning in nonorganic psychiatric disorders. *Comprehensive Psychiatry*, *30*, 346–354.

Farber, J. F., Schmitt, F. A., & Logue, P. E. (1988). Predicting intellectual level from the Mini-Mental State Examination. *Journal of the American Geriatric Society*, *36*, 509–510.

Faustmen, W. O., Moses, J. A., Jr., & Csernansky, J. G. (1990). Limitations of the Mini-Mental State Examination in predicting neuropsychological functioning in a psychiatric sample. *Acta Psychiatrica Scandinavica*, *81*, 126–131.

Feher, E. P., Mahurin, R. K., Doody, R. S., Cooke, N., Sims, J., & Pirozzolo, F. J. (1992). Establishing the limits of the Mini-Mental State: Examination of "subtests." *Archives of Neurology*, *49*, 87–92.

Fields, S. D., Fulop, G., Sachs, C. J., Strain, J., & Fillit, H. (1993). Usefulness of the Neurobehavioral Cognitive Status Examination in the hospitalized elderly. *International Psychogeriatrics*, *4*, 93–102.

Fillenbaum, G. G., George, L. K., & Blazer, D. G. (1988). Scoring nonresponse on the Mini-Mental State Examination. *Psychological Medicine, 18*, 1021–1025.

Fillenbaum, G. G., Heyman, A., Wilkinson, W. E., & Haynes, C. S. (1987). Comparison of two screening tests in Alzheimer's disease. *Archives of Neurology, 44*, 924–927.

Fillenbaum, G., Heyman, A., Williams, K., Prosnitz, B., & Burchett, B. (1990). Sensitivity and specificity of standardized screens of cognitive impairment and dementia among elderly black and white community residents. *Journal of Clinical Epidemiology, 43*, 651–660.

Fillenbaum, G. G., Hughes, D. C., Heyman, A., George, L. K., & Blazer, D. G. (1988). Relationship of health and demographic characteristics to Mini-Mental State Examination score among community residents. *Psychological Medicine, 18*, 719–726.

Fisk, A. A., & Pannill, F. C. (1987). Assessment and care of the community-dwelling Alzheimer's disease patient. *Journal of the American Geriatric Society, 35*, 307–311.

Folstein, M. F., Anthony, J. C., Parhad, I., Duffy, B., & Gruenberg, E. M. (1985). The meaning of cognitive impairment in the elderly. *Journal of the American Geriatric Society, 33*, 228–235.

Folstein, M. F., Folstein, S. E., & McHugh, P. R. (1975). "Mini-mental State": A practical method for grading the cognitive state of patients for the clinician. *Journal of Psychiatric Research, 12*, 189–198.

Fratiglioni, L., Viitanen, M., Backman, L., Sandman, P. O., & Winblad, B. (1992). Occurrence of dementia in advanced age: The study design of the Kungsholmen Project. *Neuroepidemiology, 11*(Suppl. 1), 29–36.

Fuld, P. A., Muramoto, O., Blau, A., Westbrook, L., & Katzman, R. (1988). Cross-cultural and multiethnic dementia evaluation by mental status and memory test. *Cortex, 24*, 511–519.

Galasko, D., Klauber, M. R., Hofstetter, C. R., Salmon, D. P., Lasker, B., & Thal, L. J. (1990). The Mini-Mental State Examination in the early diagnosis of Alzheimer's dementia. *Archives of Neurology, 47*, 49–52.

Gardner, R., Oliver-Munoz, S., Fisher, L., Empting, L. (1981). Mattis Dementia Rating Scale: Internal reliability study using a diffusely impaired population. *Journal of Clinical Neuropsychology, 3*, 271–275.

George, L. K., Landerman, R., Blazer, D. G., & Anthony, J. C. (1991). Cognitive Impairment. In L. N. Robbins & D. A. Regier (Eds.), *Psychiatric disorders in America* (pp. 291–327). New York: Free Press.

Giordani, B., Boivin, M. J., Hal, A. L., Foster, N. L., Lehtinen, S. J., Bluemlein, L. A., & Berent, S. (1990). The utility and generality of Mini-Mental State Examination scores in Alzheimer's disease. *Neurology, 40*, 1894–1896.

Goodglass, H., & Kaplan, E. (1983). *The Assessment of Aphasia and Related Disorder*. Philadelphia: Lea & Febiger.

Granholm, E., Wolfe, J., & Butters, N. (1985). Affective arousal factors in the recall of thematic stories by amnesic and demented patients. *Developmental Neuropsychology, 1*, 317–333.

Grigsby, J., Kaye, K., & Robbins, L. J. (1992). Reliabilities, norms and factor structure of the Behavioral Dyscontrol Scale. *Perceptual and Motor Skills, 74*, 883–892.

Halliday, G. M., McCann, H. L., Pamphlett, R., Brooks, W. S., Creasey, H., McCusker, E., Cotton, R. G., Broe, G. A., & Harper, C. G. (1992). Brain stem serotonin-synthesizing in Alzheimer's disease: A clinicopathological correlation. *Acta Neuropathologica, 84*, 630–650.

Harrell, R. G., & Othmer, E. (1987). Postcardiotomy confusion and sleep loss. *Journal of Clinical Psychiatry, 48*, 445–446.

Helmes, E., Merskey, H., Hachinski, V. C., & Wands, K. (1993). An examination of psychometric properties of the Dementia Scale for dementia in three different populations. *Alzheimer's Disease and Associated Disorders, 6,* 236–246.

Hersch, E. L. (1979). Development and application of the Extended Scale for Dementia. *Journal of the American Geriatric Society, 27,* 348–354.

Hoch, C. C., Reynolds, C. F., Kupfer, D. J., Houck, P. R., Berman, S. R., & Stack, J. A. (1986). Sleep-disordered breathing in normal and pathologic aging. *Journal of Clinical Psychiatry, 47,* 499–503.

Holzer, C. E., Tischler, G. L., Leaf, P. J., & Myers, J. K. (1984). An epidemiologic assessment of cognitive impairment in a community population. *Research in Community and Mental Health, 4,* 3–32.

Horton, A. M., Slone, D. G., & Shapiro, S. (1987). Neuropsychometric correlates of the Mini-Mental State Examination: Preliminary data. *Perceptual and Motor Skills, 65,* 64–66.

Houck, P. R., Reynolds, C. F., Kopp, U., & Hanin, I. (1988). Red blood cell/plasma choline ratio in elderly depressed and demented patients. *Psychiatry Research, 24,* 109–116.

Huff, F. J., Becker, J. T., Belle, S. H., Nebes, R. D., Holland, A. L., & Boller, F. (1987). Cognitive deficits and clinical diagnosis of Alzheimer's disease. *Neurology, 37,* 1119–1124.

Huff, F. J., & Growdon, J. H. (1986). Neurological abnormalities associated with severity of dementia in Alzheimer's disease. *Canadian Journal of Neurological Sciences, 13,* 403–405.

Indaco, A., & Carrieri, P. B. (1988). Amitriptyline in the treatment of headache in patients with Parkinson's disease. A double-blind placebo-controlled study. *Neurology, 38,* 1720–1722.

Jagger, C., Clarke, M., Anderson, J., & Battock, T. (1992). Misclassification of dementia by the Mini-Mental State Examination—Are education and social class the only factors? *Age and Aging, 21,* 404–411.

Jeste, D. V., Wragg, R. E., Salmon, D. P., Harris, M. J., & Thal, L. J. (1992). Cognitive deficits of patients with Alzheimer's disease with and without delusions. *American Journal of Psychiatry, 149,* 184–189.

Jorm, A. F., Scott, R., Cullen, J. S., & MacKinnon, A. J. (1991). Performance of the Informant Questionnaire on Cognitive Decline in the Elderly (IQCODE) as a screening test for dementia. *Psychological Medicine, 21,* 785–790.

Jorm, A. F., Scott, R., Henderson, A. S., & Kay, D. W. (1988). Educational level differences on the Mini-Mental State: The role of test bias. *Psychological Medicine, 18,* 727–731.

Kafonek, S., Ettinger, W. H., Roca, R., Kittner, S., Taylor, N., & German, P. S. (1989). Instruments for screening for depression and dementia in a long-term care facility. *Journal of the American Geriatric Society, 37,* 29–34.

Kaplan, E., & Delis, D. C. (1994). *Clock drawing: A neuropsychological analysis.* New York: Oxford University Press.

Kaplan, E., Goodglass, H., & Weintraub, S. (1983). *Boston Naming Test.* Philadelphia: Lea & Febiger.

Katzman, R., Brown, T., & Fuld, P., Peck A., Schechter, R., & Schimmel, H. (1983). Validation of a short Orientation–Memory–Concentration test of cognitive impairment. *American Journal of Psychiatry, 140,* 734–739.

Katzman, R., Brown, T., Thal, T., Fuld, P. A., Aronson, M., Butters, N., Klauber, M. R., Wiederholt, W., Pay, M., & Xiong, R. B. (1988). Comparison of rate of annual change of mental status score in four independent studies of patients with Alzheimer's disease. *Archives of Neurology, 24,* 384–389.

Katzman, R., Zhang, M., Ya-Qu, O., Wang, Z. Y., Liu, W. T., Yu, E., Wong, S. C., Salmon, D. P., & Grant, I. (1988). A Chinese version of the Mini-Mental State Examination: Impact of illiteracy in a Shanghai dementia survey. *Journal of Clinical Epidemiology*, *41*, 971–978.

Kaye, K., Grigsby, J., Robbins, L. J., & Korzun, B. (1990). Prediction of independent functioning and behavior problems in geriatric patients. *Journal of the American Geriatric Society*, *38*, 1304–1310.

Keating, J. J. (1987). "Studying" for the Mini-Mental Status Exam. *Journal of the American Geriatric Society*, *35*, 594–597.

Kewman, D. G., Vaishampayan, N., Zald, D., Han, B. (1991). Cognitive impairment in musculoskeletal pain patients. *Journal of Psychiatry and Medicine*, *21*, 253–262.

Kiernan, R. J., Mueller, J., Langston, J. W., & Van Dyke, C. (1987). The Neurobehavioral Cognitive Status Examination: A brief but differentiated approach to cognitive assessment. *Annals of Internal Medicine*, *107*, 481–485.

Kirk, A., & Kertesz, A. (1989). Hemispheric contributions to drawings. *Neuropsychologia*, *27*, 881–886.

Kirk, A., & Kertesz, A. (1993). Subcortical contributions to drawings. *Brain and Cognition*, *21*, 57–70.

Kittner, S. J., White, L. R., Farmer, M. E., Wolz, M., Kaplan, E., Moes, E., Brody, J. A., & Feinleib, M. (1986). Methodological issues in screening for dementia: The problem of education adjustment. *Journal of Chronic Diseases*, *39*, 163–170.

Klauber, M. R., Butters, N., Parker, L., & Kripke, D. F. (1991). Dementia in the hospitalized elderly: Relation to sleep apnea. *Journal of the American Geriatric Society*, *39*, 258–263.

Kokmen, E., Smith, G. E., Petersen, R. C., Tangalos, E., & Ivnik, R. C. (1991). The Short Test of Mental Status: Correlations with standardized psychometric testing. *Archives of Neurology*, *48*, 725–728.

Kovner, R., Lazar, J. W., Lesser, M., Perecman, E., Kaplan, M. H., Hainline, B., & Napolitano, B. (1992). Use of the Dementia Rating Scale as a test for neuropsychological dysfunction in HIV-positive i.v. drug abusers. *Journal of Substance Abuse Treatment*, *9*, 133–137.

Landau, W. M. (1989). Reflex dementia: Disinhibited primitive thinking. *Neurology*, *39*, 133–137.

Lau, C., Wands, K., Merskey, H., Boniferro, M., Carriere, L., & Hachinski, V. C. (1988). Sensitivity and specificity of the Extended Scale for Dementia. *Archives of Neurology*, *45*, 849–852.

Li, G., Shen, Y. C., Zhao, W. Y., Li, S. R., & Lu, M. (1989). An epidemiological survey of age-related dementia in an urban area of Beijing. *Acta Psychiatrica Scandinavica*, *79*, 557–563.

Libon, D. J., Swenson, R. A., Barnoski, E. J., & Sands, L. P. (1993). Clock drawing as an assessment tool for dementia. *Archives of Clinical Neuropsychology*, *8*, 405–415.

Lindal, E., & Stefansson, J. G. (1993). Mini-Mental StateExamination scores: Gender and lifetime psychiatric disorders. *Psychological Reports*, *72*, 631–641.

Logue, P. E., Tupler, L. A., D'Amico, C., & Schmitt, F. A. (1993). The Neurobehavioral Cognitive Status Examination: Psychometric properties in use with psychiatric inpatients. *Journal of Clinical Psychology*, *49*, 80–89.

Long, C. J., & Wagner, M. T. (1986). Computer applications in neuropsychology. In D. Wedding, A. M. Horton, & J. Webster (Eds.), *The neuropsychology handbook: Behavioral and clinical perspectives* (pp. 548–569). New York: Springer.

Lucca, U., Comelli, M., Tettamanti, M., Tiraboschi, P., & Spagnoli, A. (1993). Rate of progression and prognostic factors in Alzheimer's disease: A prospective study. *Journal of the American Geriatric Society*, *41*, 45–49.

Luria, A. R. (1980). *Higher cortical functions in man* (2nd ed.). New York: Basic Books.

Magaziner, J., Bassett, S. S., & Hebel, J. R. (1987). Predicting performance on the Mini-Mental State Examination: Use of age- and educational-specific equations. *Journal of the American Geriatric Society*, *35*, 996–1000.

Martin, E. M., Wilson, R. S., Penn, R. D., Fox, J. H., Clasen, R. A., & Savoy, S. M. (1987). Cortical biopsy results in Alzheimer's disease: Correlation with cognitive deficits. *Neurology*, *37*, 1201–1204.

Masliah, E., Ellisman, M., Carragher, B., Mallory, M., Young, S., Hansen, L., De Teresa, R., & Terry, R. D. (1992). Three-dimensional analysis of the relationship between synaptic pathology and neuropil threads in Alzheimer's disease. *Journal of Neuropathology and Experimental Neurology*, *51*, 404–414.

Mattis, S. (1976). Mental Status Examination for organic mental syndrome in the elderly patient. In L. Bellak & B. Karasu (Eds.), *Geriatric psychiatry* (pp. 77–121). New York: Grune and Stratton.

Mattis, S. (1988). *Dementia Rating Scale: Professional Manual* Odessa, FL: Psychological Assessment Resources.

Mayeux, R., Stern, Y., Rosen, J., & Leventhal, J. (1981). Depression, intellectual impairment and Parkinson's disease. *Neurology*, *31*, 645–650.

McGlynn, S. M., & Schacter, D. L. (1989). Unawareness of deficits in neuropsychological syndromes. *Journal of Clinical and Experimental Neuropsychology*, *11*, 143–205.

McKhann, G., Drachman, D., Folstein, M., Katzman, R., Price, D., & Stadlan, E. M. (1984). Clinical diagnosis of Alzheimer's disease: Report of the NINCDS-ADRDA Work Group under auspices of the Department of Health and Human Services Task Force on Alzheimer's Disease. *Neurology*, *34*, 939–944.

Meek, P. S., Clark, I. I. W., & Solana, V. (1989). Neurocognitive impairment: The unrecognized component of dual diagnosis in substance abuse treatment. *Journal of Psychoactive Drugs*, *21*, 153–160.

Mendez, M. F., Ala, T., & Underwood, K. L. (1992). Development of scoring criteria for the clock drawing task in Alzheimer's disease. *Journal of the American Geriatric Society*, *40*, 1095–1099.

Mitrushina, M., & Satz, P. (1991). Reliability and validity of the Mini-Mental State Exam in neurologically intact elderly. *Journal of Clinical Psychology*, *47*, 537–543.

Molloy, D. W., Alemayehu, E., & Roberts, R. (1991). Reliability of a Standardized Mini-Mental State Examination compared with the traditional Mini-Mental State Examination. *American Journal of Psychiatry*, *148*, 102–105.

Montgomery, K. M., & Costa, L. (1983a). *Concurrent validity of the Mattis Dementia Rating Scale*. Paper presented at the International Neuropsychological Society Meeting, Lisbon.

Montgomery, K. M., & Costa, L. (1983b). *Neuropsychological test performance of a normal elderly sample*. Paper presented at the meeting of the International Neuropsychological Society, Mexico City.

Morris, J. C., Heyman, A., Mohs, R. C., Hughes, J. P., van Belle, G., Fillenbaum, G., Mellits, E. C., & Clark, C. (1989). The Consortium to Establish a Registry for Alzheimer's Disease (CERAD): Part I. Clinical and neuropsychological assessment of Alzheimer's disease. *Neurology*, *39*, 1159–1165.

Morris, J. C., Mohs, R. C., Rogers, H., Fillenbaum, G., & Heyman, A. (1988). Consortium to Establish a Registry for Alzheimer's Disease (CERAD) clinical and neurological assessment of Alzheimer's disease. *Psychopharmacological Bulletin*, *24*, 641–652.

Moss, M. B., Albert, M. S., Butters, N., Payne, N. (1986). Differential patterns of memory loss among patients with Alzheimer's disease, Huntington's disease, and Alcoholic Korsakoff syndrome. *Archives of Neurology, 43*, 239–246.

Murden, R. A., McRae, T. D., Kaner, S., & Bucknam, M. E. (1991). Mini-Mental State Exam scores vary with education in Blacks and Whites. *Journal of the American Geriatric Society, 39*, 149–155.

Myers, B. A. (1987). The Mini-Mental State in those with developmental disabilities. *Journal of Nervous and Mental Diseases, 175*, 85–89.

Mysiw, W. J., Beegan, J. G., & Gatens, P. F. (1989). Prospective cognitive assessment of stroke patients before inpatient rehabilitation. The relationship of Neurobehavioral Cognitive Status Examination to functional improvement. *American Journal of Physical Medicine Rehabilitation, 68*, 168–171.

National Institute of Mental Health. (1979). *The Diagnostic Interview Schedule*. Washington, DC: NIMH Center for Epidemiological Studies.

Naugle, R. I., Cullum, C. M., Bigler, E. D., & Massman, P. J. (1985). Neuropsychological and computerized axial tomography volume characteristics empirically derived dementia subgroups. *Journal of Nervous and Mental Disease, 173*, 596–604.

Naugle, R. I., & Kawczak, K. (1989). Limitations of the Mini-Mental State Examination. *Cleveland Clinical Journal of Medicine, 56*, 277–281.

Nelson, A., Fogel, B. S., & Faust, D. (1986). Bedside cognitive screening instruments: A critical review. *Journal of Nervous and Mental Disorders, 174*, 73–83.

Noser, A., Schonenberger, P. M., & Wettstein, A. (1988). Comparative study between the Folstein Mini-Mental State and the Zurich variant in demented and non-demented patients. *Schweizer Archiv für Neurologie und Psychiatrie, 139*, 69–77.

O'Connor, D. W., Pollitt, P. A., Hyde, J. B., Fellows, J. L., Miller, N. D., Brook, C. P., & Reiss, B. B. (1989). The reliability and validity of the Mini-Mental State in a British community survey. *Journal of Psychiatric Research, 23*, 87–96.

O'Connor, D. W., Pollitt, P. A., Treasure, F. P., Brook, C. P., & Reiss, B. B. (1989). The influence of education, social class and sex on Mini-Mental State scores. *Psychological Medicine, 19*, 771–776.

Osmon, D. C., Smet, I. C., Winegarden, B., & Gandhavadi, B. (1992). Neurobehavioral Cognitive Status Examination: Its use with unilateral stroke patients in a rehabilitative setting. *Archives of Physical Medicine and Rehabilitation. 73*, 414–418.

Ouvrier, R. A., Goldsmith, R. F., Ouvrier, S., & Williams, I. C. (1993). The value of the Mini-Mental State Examination in childhood: A preliminary study. *Journal of Child Neurology, 8*, 145–148.

Park, J. H., & Ha, J. C. (1988). Cognitive impairment among the elderly in a Korean rural community. *Acta Psychiatrica Scandinavica, 77*, 52–57.

Paulson, G. W. (1977). The neurological examination in dementia. In C. E. Wells (Ed.), *Dementia* (2nd ed., pp. 169–188). Philadelphia: F. A. Davis.

Pearlson, G. D., & Tune, L. E. (1986). Cerebral ventricular size and cerebrospinal fluid acetylcholinesterase levels in senile dementia of the Alzheimer type. *Psychiatry Research, 17*, 23–29.

Pearson, J. L., Cherrier, M., & Terri, L. (1989). The Mini-Mental State Exam and the Mental Status Questionnaire: Depression in Alzheimer's patients. *Clinical Gerontologist, 8*, 31–37.

Pfeffer, R. I., Kurosaki, T. T., Chance, J. M., Filos, S., & Bates, D. (1984). Use of the Mental Function Index in older adults: Reliability, validity and measurement of change over time. *American Journal of Epidemiology, 120*, 922–935.

Phanthumchinda, K., & Jitapunkul, S. (1991). Prevalence of dementia in an urban slum population in Thailand: Validity of screening methods. *International Journal of Geriatric Psychiatry, 6,* 639–646.

Prigatano, G. P., & Schacter, D. L. (Eds.), *Awareness of deficit after brain injury: Clinical and theoretical issues.* New York: Oxford University Press.

Reitan, R. M., & Wolfson, D. (1993). *The Halstead-Reitan Neuropsychological Test Battery: Theory and clinical interpretation.* Tucson, AZ: Neuropsychology Press.

Richards, M., Folstein, M., Albert, M., Miller, L., Bylsma, F., Lafleche, G., Marder, K., Bell, K., Sano, M., & Devanand, D. (1993). Multicenter study of predictors of disease course in Alzheimer disease (the "predictors study"): II. Neurological, psychiatric, and demographic influences on baseline measures of disease severity. *Alzheimer's Disease Association Disorders, 7,* 22–32.

Rizzolo, P. J., Wildman, D., & Bentz, E. J. (1991). Group screening for cognitive disorders in elderly persons. *Journal of the American Board of Family Practice, 4,* 131–137.

Rocca, W. A., Bonaiuto, S., Lippi, A., Lucian, P., Turtu, F., Cavarzeran, F., & Amaducci, L. (1990). Prevalence of clinically diagnosed Alzheimer's disease and other dementing disorders: A door-to-door survey in Appignano, Macerata Province, Italy. *Neurology, 40,* 626–631.

Rosen, T. J., Growdon, J. H., & Corkin, S. (1987). Comparison of rates of progression in Alzheimer's disease and Parkinson's disease. *Journal of Neural Transmission Supplementary, 24,* 105–107.

Roth, M., Tyme, E., Mountjoy, Q., Huppert, F. A., Hendrie, H., Verma, S., & Goddard, R. (1986). CAMDEX: A standardized instrument for the diagnosis of mental disorder in the elderly with special reference to the early detection of dementia. *British Journal of Psychiatry, 149,* 698–709.

Rouleau, I., Salmon, D. P., Butters, N., Kennedy, C., & McGuire, K. (1992). Quantitative and qualitative analysis of clock drawings in Alzheimer's and Huntington's disease. *Brain and Cognition, 18,* 70–89.

Rovner, B. W., Kafonek, S., Filipp, L., Lucas, M. J., & Folstein, M. F. (1986). Prevalence of mental illness in a community nursing home. *American Journal of Psychiatry, 143,* 1446–1449.

Salmon, D. P., Riekkinen, P. J., Katzman, R., Zhang, M. Y., Jin, H., & Yu, E. (1989). Cross-cultural studies of dementia: A comparison of mini-mental state examination performance in Finland and China. *Archives of Neurology, 46,* 769–772.

Salmon, D. P., Thal, L. J., Butters, N., & Heindel, W. C. (1990). Longitudinal evaluation of dementia of the Alzheimer's type: A comparison of 3 standardized mental status examinations. *Neurology, 40,* 1225–1230.

Schwamm, L. H., Van Dyke, C., Kiernan, R. J., Merrin, E. L., & Mueller, J. (1987). The Neurobehavioral Cognitive Status Examination: Comparison with the Cognitive Capacity Screening Examination and the Mini-Mental State Examination in a neurosurgical population. *Annals of Internal Medicine, 107,* 486–491.

Shay, K. A., Duke, L. W., Conboy, T., Harrell, L. E., Callaway, R., & Folks, D. G. (1991). The clinical validity of the Mattis Dementia Rating in staging Alzheimer's dementia. *Journal of Psychiatry and Neurology, 4,* 18–25.

Shulman, K., Shedletsky, R., & Silver, I. L. (1986). The challenge of time: Clock drawing and cognitive functioning in the elderly. *International Journal of Geriatric Psychiatry, 1,* 135–140.

Spreen, O., & Strauss, E. (1991). *A compendium of neuropsychological tests.* New York: Oxford University Press.

Steele, C., Lucas, M. J., & Tune, L. (1986). Haloperidol versus thioridazine in the treatment of behavioral symptoms in senile dementia of the Alzheimer's type: Preliminary findings. *Journal of Clinical Psychiatry, 47,* 310–312.

Steele, C., Rovner, B., Chase, G. A., & Folstein, M. (1990). Psychiatric symptoms and nursing home placement of patients with Alzheimer's disease. *American Journal of Psychiatry, 147*, 1049–1051.

Steingart, A., Lau, K., Fox, A., Diaz, F., Fisman, M., Hachinski, V., & Merskey, H. (1986). The significance of white matter lucencies on CT scan in relation to cognitive impairment. *Canadian Journal of Neurological Sciences, 13*, 383–384.

Stern, Y., Hesdorffer, D., Sano, M., & Mayeux, R. (1990). Measurement and prediction of functional capacity in Alzheimer's disease. *Neurology, 40*, 8–14.

Sunderland, T., Hill, J. L., Mellow, A. M., Lawlor, B. A., Gundersheimer, J., Newhouse, P. A., & Grafman, J. H. (1989). Clock drawing in Alzheimer's disease. *Journal of the American Geriatric Society, 37*, 725–729.

Swirsky-Sacchetti, T., Field, H. L., Mitchell, D. R., Seward, J., Lublin, F. D., Knobler, R. L., & Gonzalez, C. F. (1992). The sensitivity of the Mini-Mental State Exam in the white matter dementia of multiple sclerosis. *Journal of Clinical Psychology, 48*, 779–786.

Teng, E. L., & Chui, H. C. (1987). The Modified Mini-Mental State (3MS) examination. *Journal of Clinical Psychiatry, 48*, 314–318.

Teng. E. L., Chui, H. C., Schneider, L. S., & Metzger, L. E. (1987). Alzheimer's dementia: Performance on the Mini-Mental State Examination. *Journal of Consulting and Clinical Psychology, 55*, 96–100.

Teri, L., Larson, E. B., & Reifler, B. V. (1988). Behavioral disturbance in dementia of the Alzheimer's type. *Journal of the American Geriatric Society, 36*, 1–6.

Thal, L. J., Grundman, M., Golden, R. (1986). Alzheimer's disease: A correlational analysis of the Blessed Information Memory Concentration Test and the Mini-Mental State Exam. *Neurology, 36*, 262–264.

The Northern California Neurobehavioral Group, Inc. (1991). *Manual for the Neurobehavioral Cognitive Status Screening Examination*. Fairfax, CA: Author.

Tinklenberg, J., Brooks, J. O., Tanke, E. D., Khalid, K., Poulsen, S. L., Kraemer, H. C., Gallagher, D., Thornton, J. E., & Yesavage, J. A. (1990). Factor analysis and preliminary validation of the mini-mental state examination from a longitudinal perspective. *International Psychogeriatrics, 2*, 123–134.

Tombaugh, T. N., & McIntyre, N. J. (1992). The Mini-Mental State Examination: A comprehensive review. *Journal of the American Geriatric Society, 40*, 922–935.

Tsai, L., & Tsuang, M. T. (1979). The Mini-Mental State test and computerized tomography. *American Journal of Psychiatry, 136*, 436–439.

Tune, L., & Folstein, M. F. (1986). Post-operative delirium. *Advances in Psychosomatic Medicine, 15*, 51–68.

Tuokko, H., Hadjistavropoulos, T., Miller, J. A., & Beattie, B. L. (1992). The Clock Test: A sensitive measure to differentiate normal elderly from those with Alzheimer's disease. *Journal of the American Geriatric Society, 40*, 579–584.

Uhlmann, R. F., & Larson, E. B. (1991). Effect of education on the Mini-Mental State Examination as a screening test for dementia. *Journal of the American Geriatrics Society, 39*, 876–880.

Uhlmann, R. F., Larson, E. B., & Buchner, D. M. (1987). Correlations of Mini-Mental State and Modified Dementia Rating Scale to measures of transitional health status in dementia. *Journal of Gerontology, 42*, 33–36.

Uhlmann, R. F., Teri, L., Rees, T. S., Mozlowski, K. J., & Larson, E. B. (1989). Impact of mild to moderate hearing loss on mental status testing: Comparability of standard and written Mini-Mental State Examinations. *Journal of the American Geriatric Society, 37*, 223–228.

van der Cammen, T. J., van Harskamp, F., Stronks, D. L., Passchier, J., & Schudel, W. J. (1992). Value of the Mini-Mental State Examination and informants' data for the detection of dementia in geriatric outpatients. *Psychological Reports, 71*, 1003–1009.

Villardita, C., & Lomeo, C. (1992). Alzheimer's disease: Correlational analysis of three screening tests and three behavioral scales. *Acta Neurologica Scandinavica, 86*, 603–608.

Vitaliano, P. P., Breen, A. R., Russo, J., Albert, M., Vitiello, M. V., & Prinz, P. N. (1984a). The clinical utility of the dementia rating scale for assessing Alzheimer's patients. *Journal of Chronic Disease, 37*, 743–753.

Vitaliano, P. P., Breen, A. R., Albert, M. S., Russo, J., & Prinz, P. N. (1984b). Memory, attention, functional status in community-residing Alzheimer Type dementia patients and optimally healthy aged individuals. *Journal of Gerontology, 39*, 58–64.

Wagner, M. T., & Cushman, L. (1994). Neuroanatomic and neuropsychological predictors of unawareness of cognitive deficit in the vascular population. *Archives of Neuropsychology, 9*, 57–69.

Wands, K., Merskey, H., Hachinski, V. C., Fisman, M., Fox, H., & Boniferro, M. (1990). A questionnaire investigation of anxiety and depression in early dementia. *Journal of the American Geriatric Society, 38*, 535–538.

Warren, E. J., Grek, A., Conn, D., Herrmann, N., Icyk, E., Kohl, J., & Silberfeld, M. (1989). A correlation between cognitive performance and daily functioning in elderly people. *Journal of Geriatric Psychiatry and Neurology, 2*, 96–100.

Wechsler, D. (1955). *Manual for the Wechsler Intelligence Scale*. New York: The Psychological Corporation.

Wechsler, D. (1981). *Manual for the Wechsler Intelligence Scale–Revised*. New York: The Psychological Corporation.

Wolf-Klein, G. P, Silverstone, F. A., Levy, A. P., & Brod, M. S. (1989). Screening for Alzheimer's disease by clock drawing. *Journal of the American Geriatric Society, 37*, 730–734.

Yazdanfar, D. J. (1990). Assessing the mental status of the cognitively impaired elderly. *Journal of Gerontological Nursing, 16*, 32–36.

Zhang, M. (1991). Comparison of several screening instruments for dementia. *Chung Hua Shen Ching Ching Shen Ko Tsa Chih, 24*, 194–196.

Zillmer, E. A., Fowler, P. C., Gutnick, H. N., & Becker, E. (1990). Comparison of two cognitive bedside screening instruments in nursing home residents: A factor analytic study. *Journal of Gerontology, 45*, 69–74.

Behavioral Assessment in Medical Rehabilitation: Traditional and Consensual Approaches

James F. Malec and Carolyn Lemsky

Behavioral assessment is the initial phase in planning a behavioral intervention. The behavioral assessment determines whether an intervention is appropriate and, if so, the type of intervention that will be implemented. Consequently, the structure of behavioral intervention guides the process of the assessment. Most previous discussions of behavioral assessment (to which we will refer liberally later in this chapter) have focused on assessments of specific environmental or behavioral features relevant to intervention, such as stimulus control and contingency management. However, a behavioral assessment may also focus on other important factors, such as those relevant to developing a rationale for the intervention, to developing a working relationship with the patient and significant others, to addressing emotional reactions, and to developing expectations and attributions that support the intervention.

In a rehabilitation setting, a behavioral assessment must evaluate the complexities of the social and conceptual environment in order to pave the way for effective intervention. Ideally all parties involved with the patient will be involved in both the assessment and the intervention. We have called the model for this broadly based, integrative assessment a *consensual model*. The consensual model includes assessment of those elements specific to behavioral modification that are described by a more traditional model. In this chapter, we review assessment procedures relevant to both consensual and traditional models of behavioral assessment.

A Consensual Model

The consensual model finds an epistemological basis in postmodern social constructionism (Gergen, 1985). The basic premise underlying a consensual model of behavioral assessment is that people create social reality through their cognitive constructions. In a medical rehabilitation environment, behavioral assessment is rarely an operation that occurs between a solitary patient and a therapist. Almost always, behavioral assessment in rehabilitation settings includes interactions among many individuals (and their personal constructions) who are involved with the identified patient and his or her behavior. Jacobs (1993) has emphasized the desirability of including significant others with patients in behavioral assessments and interventions. He points out that without such involvement behavioral programming is often misdirected and behavioral changes may not be supported and maintained outside of the therapeutic environment. We agree with Jacobs and would only add that, in our experience, behavioral changes *will not* be maintained outside of the therapeutic context without intense involvement by both patients and significant others. Hence, behavioral assessment for effective intervention will involve assessment not only of the identified patient, but also of the significant others in her or his immediate and natural environment and the general structure of that natural environment (i.e., culture, subculture), as well as self-assessments by the primary behavior therapist and other involved providers.

Critical Elements of Psychological Interventions

As mentioned previously, the structure of behavioral intervention guides the process of the assessment. Consequently, a useful assessment must attend to key elements of intervention. From a behavioral perspective, Zeiss, Lewinsohn, and Munoz (1979) proposed four critical components of short-term cognitive-behavioral therapy for depression: (a) "Therapy should begin with an elaborated well-planned rationale"; (b) "therapy should provide training in skills that the patient can utilize to feel more effective in handling his or her daily life"; (c) "therapy should emphasize the independent use of these skills by the patient outside the therapy context"; (d) "therapy should encourage the patient's attribution that improvement in mood is caused by the patient's increased skillfulness, not by the therapist's skillfulness" (pp. 437–438). Meichenbaum's (1985) guidelines for developing behavioral stress management programs provide a similar list to that of Zeiss and associates and add another potentially critical factor: "establish a working relationship and enlist client and significant others as collaborators" (p. 20).

From a nonbehavioral perspective, Frank (1985), based on his review of the psychotherapeutic literature, identified four components to any psychotherapeutic process: (a) "an emotionally charged, confiding relationship with a helping person"; (b) "a healing setting . . . [that] heightens the therapist's prestige and strengthens the patient's expectations for help . . . [and] provides safety"; (c) "a rationale, conceptual scheme, or myth that provides a plausible explanation for the patient's symptoms and prescribes a ritual or procedure for resolving them"; (d) "a ritual that requires active participation of both patient and therapist and that is believed by both to be the means of restoring the patient's health" (pp. 59–60). Frank goes on to list five components of effective therapeutic rituals: (a) "strengthening the therapeutic relationship, thereby combatting the patient's sense of alienation"; (b) "inspiring and maintaining the patient's expectations of help"; (c) "providing new learning experiences"; (d) "arousing emotions"; (e) "enhancing the patient's sense of mastery or self-efficacy"; and (f) "providing opportunities for practice" (pp. 61–68). Thus, with the exception of the necessity of strong affect as a feature of a therapeutic process, behavioral and nonbehavioral therapists appear to agree on the critical elements of a successful intervention.

Key Elements of Behavioral Interventions in Rehabilitation

In medical rehabilitation settings, these key elements of effective behavioral change may be recapitulated as follows: (a) developing a rationale for behavioral problem identification and treatment to which therapist, client, and significant others, including other staff, can agree; (b) developing a collaborative, working relationship with all involved parties (e.g., identified patient, family and significant others, professional staff); (c) planning for episodic experiences of strong affect by all parties involved; (d) behavioral training; (e) behavioral practice for maintenance and generalization of new behavior outside of the therapeutic environment that is supported by significant others in that outside context (in some cases, this step may involve assisting the patient to develop an appropriate social support network); (f) developing attributions of an increased sense of mastery to the patient's skills or to elements of her or his natural environment. We believe these key elements describe the basic structure of any behavior change intervention that is directed at maintaining behavioral change in the long term outside of a highly regulated therapeutic environment.

Behavioral assessment includes assessment of elements relevant to each of these key components of intervention, rarely occurs sequentially, and is often iterative and recursive both before and during the process of treatment. Developing a therapeutic relationship and establishing a rationale are so closely linked, as are initial behavioral training and practice for generalization, that we discuss these components here concurrently. Thus, we elaborate behavioral assessment in rehabilitation settings under four major topic areas, beginning with the domain most familiar to behavioral clinicians: (a) assessment for behavioral training and practice, (b) assessment of factors relevant to developing a therapeutic rationale and a working relationship, (c) assessment in anticipation of strong affect, and (d) assessment of factors underlying the attribution of the source of change.

We discuss methods for developing a consensual assessment as well as ethical issues. For the purposes of this chapter, the terms *behavioral analysis* and *functional analysis* refer to the process described by Haynes and O'Brien (1990) as "the identification of important, controllable, causal functional relationships applicable to a specified set of target behaviors for an individual client" (p. 654). The term *behavioral assessment* is used to denote the more general use of cognitive–behavioral assessment methods from a culturally sensitive, integrative, consensual perspective.

Assessment for Behavioral Training and Practice

Basic Assumptions of Behavioral Analysis

Since the publication of the first behavioral analysis books and journals in the mid to late 1970s, the definition, technology, and applications of behavioral analysis have continuously evolved and expanded (Haynes, 1990; Kendall, 1990; O'Leary & Wilson, 1989). Initially, behavioral analysis developed in response to the particular needs of clinical behavior therapists (e.g., Barrios, 1988; Haynes, 1990). Early on, behavioral analysis was defined primarily by contrasting its goals, basic assumptions, and methods to nonbehavioral psychological assessment. Rather than aiming toward diagnosis and the delineation of intrapersonal traits, behavioral analysis assesses the functional relationships between an individual's behavior and her or his environment (Barrios, 1988). In contrast to non-behavioral psychological assessment, which focused on coming to a diagnosis, behavioral analysis intends to reveal situation-specific functional relationships (Haynes, 1990).

The methods of behavioral therapy are predicated on an empirical model of investigation (Barlow, Hayes, & Nelson, 1985; Barrios, 1988; Haynes, 1990; Kazdin, 1992). The process of behavioral analysis begins with the development of hypotheses about behavior that are then repeatedly modified according to the data collected and reassessed during the course of treatment. Behavioral assessment is conducted on an ongoing basis and is intended to influence the continued course of treatment and assessment. Another legacy of the empirical model is that every effort is made to reduce the degree of inference in assessment procedures. For example, behavioral observation is preferred over questionnaire measures. The ideal assessment procedure, then, is atheoretical and focuses on observable and verifiable behaviors (Haynes, 1990). Strict adherence to the ideals of atheoretical, observational assessment might prevent the development of heuristic models of behavior and make it impossible to evaluate certain aspects of human behavior. For this reason, behaviorists do use methods, such as tests and questionnaires, that require some inference.

According to Haynes (1990), several assumptions about the nature of behavioral disorders also affect behavioral analysis and treatment procedures: (a) behavioral disorders may be demonstrated through multiple response modes (e.g., verbal, overt behavioral, cognitive); (b) responses may covary with one another (belong to the same response class) or be independent of one another; (c) the amount of covariation across responses varies from individual to individual; (d) the frequency, duration, and intensity of behaviors vary from individual to individual; (e) when behaviors are demonstrated to covary, modification of one behavior may result in changes in other behaviors.

These basic assumptions lead to assessments that are idiographic (i.e., use procedures that vary from individual to individual). They also suggest that behavioral assessments are ideally multimodal, including assessment of a variety of response classes. Further, these assumptions imply that behavioral assessments should be designed to allow for the identification of classes of behaviors that share common controlling factors (functional response classes). Identification of functional response classes is useful when defining targets for further assessment and treatment, because modification of one member of a functional response class is likely to yield changes in other members of the functional response class. Finally, these basic assumptions are intended to lead the behaviorist to ferret out Person × Situation interactions, necessitating evaluation of the individual in her or his particular environment.

The Process of Behavioral Analysis

Although the methods and procedures of behavioral analysis have evolved considerably since their initial development, the main tasks of behavioral analysis have remained the same. They include (a) selection of a target behavior; (b) delineation of controlling variables in the environment; (c) planning of behavioral interventions; (d) the evaluation of interventions, and (e) the facilitation of client–therapist interactions (Barrios, 1988; Haynes, 1990). As described by Barrios (1988), the process of behavioral analysis begins with the assessment of a wide range of behavioral and environmental variables. Then, through an iterative process, behavioral analysis narrows its focus to the variables considered most critical in the case at hand in the following stages: screening, problem-identification, treatment selection, and treatment evaluation.

The familiar ABCs of behavioral analysis define the basic targets of assessment procedures: antecedents, behaviors, and consequences. Antecedents are the environmental conditions that exist prior to the performance of a given behavior. Behaviors are the individual's responses to environmental stimuli. Consequences are the results of a given behavior.

Originally, selection of target behaviors was confined to overt, observable behaviors. Recently, behaviorists have begun to include covert events (e.g., cognition) and diagnostic categories as legitimate targets of behavioral assessment (Barrios, 1988). In the broader context of this chapter, we suggest that targets of assessment in rehabilitation settings should include not only idiographic, but also contextual cognitive events—that is, the beliefs of all involved parties and of the social and cultural context in which the identified patient will eventually function.

Choosing the Target of Behavioral Analysis

Individuals with neurological disorders may present with multiple behavior problems, including behavioral excesses as well as behavioral or skill deficits (e.g., Lezak, 1989; Rosenthal & Bond, 1990; Wilson, 1991). Several authors have discussed parameters that may be used to determine which behaviors should become the focus of behavioral analysis and in-tervention (Barrios, 1988; Haynes, 1990; Kanfer, 1985). A complete dis-cussion of relevant issues may be found in these references.

Briefly, there is wide acknowledgement, even among traditional be-haviorists, that target behavior selection is a culture-bound process. As we stress throughout this chapter, care must be taken to consider the values, needs, desires, and safety of the client and his or her community (Haynes, 1990; Kanfer, 1985; Hawkins, 1986). In a rehabilitation context, the psychologist may use knowledge of behavioral assessment and treat-ment to improve participation in therapies (Wilson, 1991). The rehabil-itation team may be most willing to take the time and effort to complete an assessment and intervention for target behaviors that most interfere with the rehabilitation process. Given these factors, the specific behaviors selected for assessment and change should be those that most handicap the individual in attaining her or his goals; share the most variance with similar dysfunctional behavior (most representative of a response class); are most dangerous and therefore require immediate attention; or are most amenable to behavioral intervention. Note that most of these selec-tion criteria require subjective judgment.

For example, it is not uncommon for patients who complain of feel-ing anxious to refuse participation in therapies and bed-to-wheelchair transfers. A number of other anxiety-related complaints may also be present, such as difficulty sleeping, irritability, poor appetite, and demanding be-havior with caretakers. Transfers from bed to a wheelchair could become an initial target for assessment and treatment because refusal to leave the bed is likely to interfere significantly with meeting rehabilitation goals and creates the danger of physical deconditioning. Further, refusal to transfer probably shares variance with noncompliance with other activities that require physical mobility. Anxiety about transfers may be readily addressed using cognitive therapy and a desensitization paradigm. Finally, addressing bed-to-wheelchair transfers is likely to have the advantage of being an acceptable treatment goal for both the patient and the rehabil-itation team.

In addition to person-specific and situation-specific factors, knowl-edge of nomothetic data is essential to the efficient identification of target behaviors. The behavioral literature has been devoted to collecting data about the controlling variables related to a variety of behavioral disorders. For some diagnoses, there may be sufficient information available to indicate probable controlling variables (Haynes, 1990).

Over the past 5 years there has been much discussion about the drift of behavioral analysis methods away from the basic principles of idiographic analysis of situation-specific behavior and toward the inclusion of classic methods of psychological assessment (e.g., Barrios, 1988; Collins & Thompson, 1993; Haynes, 1990; Haynes & Uchigakiuchi, 1993). Prominent behaviorists have noted a decline in the use of behavior counts and direct observation (Kendall, 1990) and an increase in the number of self-report scales and inventories (Adams, 1989). A survey conducted in 1979 suggested that the use of behavioral instruments is often limited to questionnaire measures and interviews (Swan & MacDonald, 1978).

Follette and Hayes (1992) suggest that although they may have clinical utility, the methods and procedures of behavioral assessment are generally too broadly defined to be readily studied or replicated. On the other hand, Haynes (1990) and Hayes, Nelson, and Jarrett (1987) point out that there is remarkably little evidence that behavioral analysis actually improves treatment efficacy or is cost-effective. Behaviorally oriented treatments may be equally successful whether or not a thorough behavioral analysis was completed. Nonetheless, there is evidence that when properly applied, behavioral analysis provides information uniquely suited to behavioral interventions that is not supplied by other assessment methods and that may prevent treatment errors (see review in Hayes et al., 1987).

Although some behaviors have strong functional relationships with environmental factors, others do not. This is especially true in acute care settings serving people with neurologic impairments. For example, in the acute stages of recovery from traumatic brain injury, attention, memory, and the ability to accurately perceive environmental stimuli are often quite impaired. Agitated behavior at this stage of recovery is often not clearly associated with specific events or stimuli. Nevertheless, those experienced in working with individuals in this stage of recovery know that certain classes of staff responses may exacerbate agitation even though these behaviors appear to occur more or less randomly or are based on metabolic or other internal factors. Rather than completing an exhaustive behavior analysis, experienced rehabilitation staff develop patterns of responding to agitated patients that are designed to handle the general features of the behavior.

Methods for Behavioral Analysis in Medical Rehabilitation

Identifying and Addressing Barriers

On many inpatient rehabilitation units, patients with persistent and disruptive behavioral disturbances are the exception rather than the rule.

The team's practices have developed in order to provide quality care for the modal patient who is not verbally or physically abusive, demonstrates at least general compliance with therapies, and exhibits only mild behaviors associated with grief, minimization of disability, or dysphoria. Although behavioral programs might be helpful for many of these individuals, these patients generally negotiate their acute inpatient rehabilitation without undue difficulty.

As Jacobs (1988, 1993) indicates, behavior analysis procedures are gaining acceptance in rehabilitation treatment for individuals with traumatic brain injury as well as for individuals with dementia. An extensive literature supports the use of behavior analysis with individuals who have varied levels of intellectual and neurological impairment (c.f. Jacobs, 1993; Gianutsos & Gianutsos, 1984; Lezak, 1989; Malec, 1984; Wilson, 1991). However, Jacobs (1988) and Levenkron (1987) note that the procedures of behavior analysis are frequently misunderstood and misapplied in rehabilitation settings. Several authors have noted significant barriers to behavioral treatment in these settings (Jacobs, 1993; Levenkron, 1987; Zahara & Cuvo, 1984) that seem at least partly related to difficulties conducting complete behavioral analyses.

One reason that formal behavioral observation and formal behavior analysis procedures are infrequently used is that providers lack sufficient training. Jacobs (1988) states that the proper "implementation of behavioral programming requires extensive study and experience" (p. 342). In many clinical settings, time spent in assessment activities is not fully reimbursed or supported by the institution (Haynes, Lemsky, & Sexton-Radek, 1987a, 1987b). These contingencies may prevent clinicians from seeking training and developing skills in behavior assessment.

Many neurological disorders have behavioral and psychological sequelae that complicate the process of behavioral assessment (Lezak, 1989; Prigatano, 1986; Wilson, 1991). For example, both memory deficits and language impairment may interfere with self-report procedures. Frontal cerebral injuries may result in a lack of initiation, which is easily mistaken by staff, the family, and the patient himself or herself as depression. Frontal lobe damage may also result in indifference or lack of insight into disability, which may be mistaken for denial, or which staff and family members believe is unchangeable, given the patient's cognitive status (Schacter, 1991). Over time, these organic difficulties may actually come under the control of environmental contingencies. We have found that a tendency to attribute specific behavioral difficulties to either organic or environmental factors impedes the assessment and treatment process and prevents the team from devising compensatory strategies or aids. Nonetheless, assessment procedures and behavioral goals must be within the cognitive and physical capacities of the individual if the treatment procedure is to be effective (Wilson, 1991).

Recently, several authors have attempted to adapt the procedures of behavior analysis to the limited time and staff resources often found in acute care and outpatient settings (e.g., Derby et al., 1992; Durand & Crimmins, 1988). Derby and colleagues adapted behavior analysis procedures for use in 90-minute assessment sessions for self-abusive and aggressive behavior in developmentally delayed children. The literature related to self-abusive behaviors reveals several common antecedents (e.g., demanding tasks) and consequences (e.g., attention or escape) of this class of behaviors. Rather than completing a comprehensive behavior analysis, a team of professionals reviewed initial interview and other assessment data and decided on the most likely target behaviors, antecedents, and consequences. In the context of brief (10-minute) analog assessments, they determined whether or not the individual's behavior was responsive to contingencies as hypothesized.

Methods

Although the value of a detailed functional analysis is unproven in neurologic rehabilitation settings, our clinical experience suggests that formal behavioral analysis is beneficial in some circumstances. We agree with Follette and Hayes (1992) that a possible solution to increasing the use and empirical validation of functional analysis is to develop practical, systematic procedures on the basis of nomothetic information. We focus the remainder of our discussion of behavioral assessment techniques on techniques that we believe are not described in detail elsewhere and may prove to have clinical utility in medical rehabilitation settings.

Behavioral assessment strategies may be divided into four main categories: interviews, behavioral observation, reporting instruments, and psychophysiological assessment. We do not discuss psychophysiological measurement here because this is not a common clinical technique that is used in neurologic rehabilitation settings. Detailed discussions of each of these strategies can be found in a number of texts (e.g., Barlow, 1980; Bellack & Hersen, 1988).

The interview. In our practice, inpatient evaluations always begin with a review of the medical record and an initial interview. Behavioral interviews should cover the informants' understanding of the topography of the behavior in question as well as information on potential antecedents and consequences. The behavioral interview is described in detail in several recent works (e.g., Haynes, 1990; Morganstern, 1980). Additionally, several volumes detail the general procedures of behavioral interviewing for particular disorders, such as depression, anxiety-related disorders, sleep disturbance, and a variety of others (e.g., Bellack & Hersen, 1988). Rather than review this information here, we outline a few issues that are particular to the rehabilitation setting.

It is important to remember that the majority of patients admitted to a rehabilitation or medical unit do not expect to see a psychologist. Some would prefer not to talk to a psychologist, and most come to the interview with a variety of preconceived notions about the process of psychological evaluation. Additionally, patients may be disoriented and have difficulty understanding their current situation and the role of the psychologist. We have found it valuable to make the first priorities of the behavioral interview to briefly assess gross orientation, to clarify the purpose of psychological assessment in a rehabilitation context, and to obtain the patient's cooperation with the assessment process.

In most cases, global orientation can be assessed in a conversational manner. If there is any indication that the patient is having memory difficulties or is not aware of his or her current circumstance, formal mental status assessment should be undertaken. For the patient who is grossly oriented, we explain the role of the rehabilitation psychologist and state that all patients admitted to the rehabilitation unit are interviewed by a psychologist. We explain that (a) the rehabilitation psychologist is a member of the rehabilitation team and, as such, shares information with other team members; (b) a main function of the rehabilitation psychologist is to facilitate communication among team members—which includes the patient—and to try to minimize misunderstandings; (c) the rehabilitation psychologist is available to provide support for coping with illness or disability; (d) sensitive information that is not directly required by other members of the rehabilitation team will be confidential—just as in any other psychotherapeutic relationship—unless prior permission is obtained from the patient. The purpose of the interview can be described as an opportunity for the psychologist to get to know the patient and his or her particular concerns or difficulties and to be sure that members of the rehabilitation team and the patient are in agreement about the goals for rehabilitation.

For most rehabilitation and medical inpatients, the initial interview includes eight major topic areas: (a) the patient's understanding of his or her current situation and disability; (b) the patient's understanding of the philosophy and process of rehabilitation; (c) the patient's goals for rehabilitation; (d) the presence of premorbid psychological or substance abuse problems; (e) social, family, and work history; (f) current mood; (g) current and past coping styles; (h) formal or informal cognitive assessment. This list of topics is not exhaustive, but provides the basic framework from which potential psychological difficulties in rehabilitation may be detected. Information about culture and worldview relevant to establishing a therapeutic rationale is also frequently acquired in the process of such interviews with the identified patient, significant others, and involved staff.

When interviewing rehabilitation and neurologic patients, the interviewer should remember that it is not uncommon for such patients to experience some degree of learning impairment or memory loss. Disorganized thinking or language may impede the patient's ability to communicate effectively. Although open-ended questions may more accurately elicit the patient's personal understanding of the situation, increased structure may be necessary when patients are unable to structure their own communication effectively. As a rule of thumb, it is helpful to begin with less structure and increase the amount of structure as necessary. For example, one may begin with an open-ended question such as, "What happened that you came here, to the rehabilitation unit?" If the patient is unable to answer this type of question in a coherent way, then more focused questions are used, such as, "I understand that you had a fall, is that correct?" If the patient continues to have difficulty answering, one might ask, "In your medical record it says that you had a stroke and fell. Will you tell me about that?" Follow-up questions should include a full inventory of the abilities that the patient feels may have been affected by her or his illness or injury. It is often helpful to let the patient know that you have reviewed the medical record but are interested in how she or he sees the current situation. That way, the interview can be used to provide information and clarify misconceptions. When specific problems are identified, interviews may be used to collect information about the presenting complaint and to assist in the selection of a treatment target. Once a target behavior is selected, the interview may be used to collect information about the ABCs of the behavior.

Interviews may also be used to obtain information about the patient's and caregivers' attributions about the causes of the behavior in question and their attitudes toward assessment and treatment. Use of structured interviews ensures that topic areas will be adequately reviewed and that comparable information is collected from different informants. Interviewing of the patient and a family member independently enables assessment of the congruence of the perceptions of the patient and a significant other and may yield important information about family interactions.

Structured informant interviews designed to collect information about educational, occupational, interpersonal, and leisure functioning have been devised and published (Grant & Alves, 1987; Varney & Menefee, 1993). The Iowa Collateral Head Injury Interview (Varney & Menefee, 1993) covers 21 psychosocial sequelae of head injury; collateral informants indicate whether they are present or have become worse since the head injury. Interviewers provide standardized behavioral descriptions of each area and record responses on a standard form. Sample items include ratings of flat affect, absentmindedness, poor planning and anticipation, and stimulus-bound behavior. Although still in the process of development and validation, this interview provides a taxonomy that may help collateral informants recognize and define problem areas that may then become the subject of more thorough behavioral assessment.

Behavioral observation. For the purpose of this chapter, we define observation as the report of an observer, which is recorded at the time (or soon after) the behavior occurred. Behavioral observation may be either naturalistic (occurring in the natural environment) or analog (occurring as a part of a standardized protocol, e.g., Marsh & Knight, 1991). Observers may be trained researchers or participant-observers (members of the client's natural social network) who have been trained in data collection. In medical rehabilitation settings, the rehabilitation psychologist's position is much closer to that of a participant-observer than an objective researcher.

As described previously, the primary advantage of behavioral observation is that it allows assessment of behavior with a minimum of bias related to inferences by the assessors. A variety of observation strategies have been developed to assess behaviors that occur with varied intensity and frequency. In *time sampling*, periodic observations are scheduled either at random or at specific critical times. Behaviors may be coded according to their nature or frequency. *Critical event monitoring* is used with low-frequency behaviors. When a specific behavior occurs, the observer notes the presence of specific antecedents and consequences. *Analog observation* occurs in a specially created test situation that contains the critical elements of the natural setting in which the behavior occurs. *Naturalistic observation* occurs in the natural setting.

Behavioral observations are valid only if they are carefully conceived and subjected to formal psychometric evaluation. Potential sources of error in behavioral observation include inconsistency between raters, reactivity (i.e., the patient's performance is changed by the observation process itself), and lack of generalization beyond the assessment situation. Several surveys in the late 1970s indicated that behavior therapists often did not use behavioral observation because it was perceived to be impractical (Ford & Kendall, 1979; Wade, Baker, & Hartmann, 1979). This is particularly easy to understand in care environments in which increasingly fewer staff are available per patient and lengths of stay are declining.

Although organizing formal serial behavioral observations completed by staff may be daunting to most rehabilitation or medical psychologists, this approach does offer a specific advantage: objective information is obtained about the occurrence of behavior. Single or short series of behavioral observations can provide invaluable information to facilitate the rehabilitation process and to formulate treatment plans that generalize to the home environment. Several authors offer examples of situations in which simply watching a patient during therapy or a problem situation enables the therapist to behaviorally define the problem and therefore refine assessment and or treatment procedures (Levenkron, 1987; Lezak, 1989; Wilson, 1991).

Behavior reporting instruments. Behavior reporting instruments are a broad class of assessment tools that are used to systematically collect information about behavior. They may be completed by the client or caregivers. *Diaries* are brief forms that are completed by the client or the caregiver. The content of the diary depends on the target behavior and the particular goals of the assessment procedure. Like behavioral observation, diaries may be completed at regular intervals or only when a critical event occurs. Other reporting instruments ask clients or their caregivers to make retrospective reports about behavior.

As stated above, the use of self-report scales with people with brain damage may be limited by cognitive impairments and lack of insight. For this reason, observers—including family members, rehabilitation staff, and psychologists—may be called upon to complete ratings. There are measures that have been developed to assess the antecedents and consequences of behavior by caregivers. Durand and Crimmins (1988) developed the Motivation Assessment Scale (MAS) to assess the motivation for self-abusive behavior. Teachers' ratings of individuals with developmental disabilities on the MAS predicted how they would behave in analog settings ($r = .99$). Other research groups have developed questionnaires to assess the antecedents and consequences of headaches in children (Budd,

Workman, Lemsky, & Quick, in press), the consequences of alcohol use (Cooper, Russell, Skinner, & Windle, 1992), and the antecedents of anxiety (Taylor, Koch, McNally, & Crockett, 1992). We find approaches such as these promising. We would like to see similar caregiver scales for specific behavioral disturbances in individuals with neurologic impairments.

Another group of behavior rating scales has been specifically validated or used in empirical investigations with individuals who are brain-injured or otherwise neurologically impaired. Rather than provide information about the antecedents and consequences of classes of behaviors, these questionnaires are designed to detect the presence of specific difficulties. In the following sections, we very briefly review measures of global functioning as well as recently developed behavioral reporting instruments that may be used to assess psychiatric symptoms and social behavior in neurologically impaired individuals.

Global measures of behavioral impairment. Measures of functional impairment are covered in detail in chapter 4 and are reviewed only briefly here. In addition to the Mayo–Portland Adaptability Inventory, which will be described in some detail later, several outcome rating scales have been developed for use in rehabilitation settings. The Glasgow Outcome Scale (GOS; Jennett & Bond, 1975), the Disability Rating Scale (DRS; Rappaport, Hall, Hopkins, Belleza, & Cope, 1982), and the Functional Independence Measure (FIM; *Guide for the Uniform Data Set for Medical Rehabilitation*, 1993) are widely used to provide gross descriptions of functional levels in individuals with an acquired brain injury.

The GOS provides a description of 5 levels of recovery ranging from death to *good recovery*. Although originally the interrater reliability of the GOS was found to be high (.91 to .95; Jennett, Snoek, Bond, & Brooks, 1981), other investigators have achieved more modest results, particularly when individuals other than family members or staff who were very familiar with the patient's day-to-day functioning made the ratings (Anderson, Housley, Jones, Slattery, & Miller, 1993).

The DRS includes eight items falling in four categories: (a) arousability, awareness, and responsivity; (b) cognitive ability for self-care activities; (c) dependence on others; and (d) psychosocial adaptability. In each category, the rater selects the appropriate score on behaviorally anchored scales yielding a possible range of scores of 0 to 30. The DRS has been shown to be reliable when ratings are compared between rehabilitation professionals and family members (Hall, Hamilton, Gordon, & Zasler, 1993).

The FIM was developed by an American Congress of Rehabilitation Medicine and American Academy of Physical Medicine and Rehabilitation Task Force to rate the severity of patient disability and outcomes of medical rehabilitation (Hamilton, Granger, Sherwin, Zielezny, & Tashman, 1987). Ratings on a scale of 0 to 7 (0 = *needs total assist* to 7 = *completely independent*) are made by rehabilitation professionals on 18 items related to activities of daily living (e.g., eating and grooming), bowel and bladder control, mobility, communication, and social cognition. Rasch analysis revealed that the 13 items pertaining to motor functions and five items pertaining to cognitive functions can be summed into scales with good metric qualities (Linacre, Heinemann, Wright, Granger, & Hamilton, 1994). High interrater agreement on the FIM has been found for individual ratings as well as for total, cognitive, and motor scores (Hall et al., 1993). The FIM has been found to correlate with measures of physical impairment and to predict care demands in patients with multiple sclerosis (Granger, Cotter, Hamilton, Fiedler, & Hens, 1990) and stroke (Granger, Cotter, Hamilton, & Fiedler, 1993). The Functional Assessment Measure (FAM) was developed as a 13-item adjunct measure to the FIM to assess higher level community functioning in individuals with brain injuries. Preliminary work with the FAM suggests that interrater agreement is high (Hall et al., 1993).

Although the GOS has been shown to be reliable, it may not provide enough information to adequately track treatment-relevant changes beyond the acute stages of injury (Brooks, 1987). The DRS has been found to be more sensitive than the GOS in measuring change over time in individuals with brain injuries (Hall, Cope, & Rappaport, 1985), particularly in the postacute stage. However, the DRS may not include enough detail for the purpose of treatment planning. The DRS, the FIM, and the FAM have been shown to be highly intercorrelated in a sample of individuals with brain injuries (Hall et al., 1993). Of the three, Hall and colleagues (1993) suggested that the DRS provides the most practical and efficient measure of change from acute to postacute treatment phases, in part because it does not require observation by a rehabilitation professional and can be completed in a telephone interview. These authors also found that the FIM is well-suited to track outcomes in an inpatient setting because it is more sensitive to the kind of changes that occur during this stage.

Neurobehavioral scales. Several scales have been developed to measure psychiatric symptoms and adjustment to disability in individuals with neurologic disorders. The Neurobehavioral Rating Scale (NRS; Levin et al.,

1987) is a modification of the Brief Psychiatric Rating Scale designed specifically to assess cognitive and behavioral symptoms in individuals with neurobehavioral disorders. This instrument consists of 27 items on which a trained rater indicates the severity of specific symptoms on a 7-point scale from *not present* to *extremely severe*. Interrater reliability was good (.88 to .90) when independent ratings of a single interview with individuals with head injuries were made by well-trained raters (Levin et al., 1987). When administered by trained observers, items and scales of the NRS have been shown to correlate moderately with observer measures of depression and with caregiver ratings in patients with dementia (Sultzer, Levin, Mahler, High, & Cummings, 1992). It also has demonstrated adequate reliability when used in individuals with HIV infection (Hilton, Sisson, & Freeman, 1990). Although the NRS is based on a well-validated measure and has the potential for broad application, it has only been studied in a few populations to date. Further, rater training is necessary to insure interrater reliability in clinical or research applications.

The Neuropsychology Behavior and Affect Profile (NBAP; Nelson et al., 1989) was designed to measure personality change in individuals with brain damage. Items on this measure were created for five scales: indifference, inappropriateness, depression, mania, and pragnosia (a lack of the pragmatic aspects of language). Caregivers respond *yes* or *no* to a series of 106 statements describing behavior. Ratings are made both for behavior before illness or injury and for current behavioral status. In an initial reliability and validation study, this measure was shown to have moderate internal consistency across the 5 scales and high test–retest reliability (intraclass correlations were .92 to .99), and it distinguished 61 subjects with dementia from 88 elderly controls. Development of the NBAP followed appropriate test development procedures to arrive at a very well considered set of items. The NBAP has the advantage of providing change scores and has the potential for validation in populations other than dementia. Unfortunately, it has not yet been used in studies of varied populations.

The Katz Adjustment Scale (KAS; Katz & Lyerly, 1963) is another rating scale designed to assess adjustment and social behavior in the community (see also chapter 3). The full KAS has five scales and was originally developed for use with patients with psychiatric diagnoses. The first scale (KAS-R1), which contains 127 items related to emotional, behavioral, and psychological characteristics rated by patients' relatives, was investigated with individuals with brain injuries (Klonoff, Costa, & Snow, 1986). Each characteristic or behavior is rated on a 4-point scale of *almost never* to *almost always*. These authors found that severity of injury was moderately correlated with KAS-R1 ratings. Ten factors have been identified and refined in brain injury samples: Belligerence, Apathy/Amotivational Syndrome, Social Irresponsibility, Orientation, Antisocial Behavior, Speech/Cognitive Dysfunction, Bizarreness, Paranoid Ideation, Verbal Expansiveness, and Emotional Sensitivity (Fabiano & Goran, 1992; Goran & Fabiano, 1993). The resulting scale has 79 items that are both stable and independent and allow the clinician to identify particular areas in need of further assessment and treatment. Although Fabiano and Goran (1992) suggest that the revised KAS may be used in outcome research, its responsiveness to change with treatment has yet to be empirically validated.

The Sickness Impact Profile (SIP; Bergner, Bobbitt, Carter, & Gilson, 1981) was originally developed as a self-report measure of health-related dysfunction for medical populations (see discussion in chapter 7). The SIP has been found to be moderately correlated with neurocognitive measures and severity of injury scales, to separate individuals with brain injuries from controls without injuries, and to be a good measure of day-to-day functioning in this population based on correlations with an examiner rating of function (Temkin et al., 1988).

Over the past 10 years a great number of scales that include assessment of problematic behaviors and psychiatric symptoms in elderly individuals with dementia have been developed (Fisher & Carstensen, 1990). Those that have been subjected to empirical reliability and validity studies include the Blessed Dementia Scale (Blessed, Tomlinson, & Roth, 1968; see also chapter 3), the Cognitive Behavior Rating Scale (Williams, 1987), the Caretaker Obstreperous-Behavior Rating Assessment Scale (COBRA; Drachman, Swearer, O'Donnell, Mitchell, & Maloon, 1992), the Nurses' Observation Scale for Geriatric Patients (Spiegel et al., 1991), and the Revised Memory and Behavior Problems Checklist (RMBPC; Teri et al., 1992). We describe the RMBPC because it was conceived with a particular emphasis on the assessment of observable, potentially modifiable behaviors.

The RMBPC was developed from an original item pool consisting of the 30 items of the Memory and Behavior Problems Checklist (Zarit & Zarit, 1983) and 34 new items. Like the Memory and Behavior Problems Checklist, the RMBPC was designed to include ratings of the frequency with which each behavior occurs as well as the degree to which the behavior is disturbing to the caregiver on anchored 4-point Likert scales. Samples of items include: "crying," "suicidal threats," "arguing," "verbal aggression," "losing things," and "forgetting the day." The RMBPC yields a total score as well as three subscale scores: memory-related, depression, and disruptive behaviors. These scales were confirmed by factor analysis in 201 geriatric patients. The internal consistency of the full scale was good (α = .84 to .90), and individual subscale consistency ranged from .67 to .89. Construct validity was suggested by an expected pattern of correlations of both total RMBPC and RMBPC subscales with measures of cognitive functioning, mood, and caregiver burden. The RMBPC is unique in the manner in which it assesses caregiver burden concurrently with behavioral disturbance. Such information may be useful when attempting to select target behaviors for intervention.

Agitation and aggression scales. Among the most common, upsetting, and disruptive classes of behavioral disturbance in neurological patients are agitation and aggression. Brooke, Questad, Patterson, and Bashak (1992) conducted a prospective study of 100 consecutive admissions to a trauma unit presenting with moderate to severe closed head injury. They found that approximately 11% of their sample showed frank symptoms of agitation as defined by responses to the Overt Aggression Scale. However, in 35 patients, restlessness—defined as behavior requiring staff intervention but not meeting the criteria for overt aggression—was present. They found that although these behaviors were generally short-lived and usually lasted no more than a week, they could be quite upsetting to both staff members and caregivers.

Recently, scales have been developed specifically for the purpose of obtaining observer ratings of aggression and agitation. The Overt Aggression Scale (OAS; Yudofsky, Silver, Jackson, Endicott, & Williams, 1986) was designed to measure aggressive behaviors in adult and child patients with psychiatric diagnoses. The OAS provides for the description of the time of the incident as well as levels of verbal aggression, physical aggression against objects, physical aggression against self, and physical aggression against other people. Behaviors in each category are described in a behavioral fashion. For example, the first level of verbal aggression is described as "makes loud noises, shouts angrily." A section is also provided to record the nursing intervention. With trained nursing staff in an inpatient psychiatric setting, this scale demonstrated adequate interrater reliability for individual items and for the total scale score (intraclass correlation coefficients were .72 to 1.0). Although its reliability has not been tested in neurological samples, this rating scale has been used in samples of individuals with head injuries (Brooke et al., 1992).

The Agitated Behavior Scale (ABS; Corrigan, 1989) was developed in response to the need for a tool to assess agitation following traumatic brain injury. Corrigan followed detailed procedures in item generation and final selection as well as reliability and validity studies. An initial sample of 67 ratings made on 14 patients with traumatic brain injuries was used to select items. Only those items meeting rigorous reliability and validity criteria were retained, resulting in a scale for rating each of 14 behaviors on a 4-point scale from *absent* to *present to an extreme degree*.

Reliability and validity studies of the ABS were conducted with 191 observations by four raters of 35 patients with traumatic brain injuries. The ABS demonstrated good internal consistency (αs = .92 to .94) for each of the four raters. Because the ABS was the first attempt at validating an agitation scale, there was no available criterion measure for concurrent validity. The ABS demonstrated moderate correlations with global ratings of agitation by therapist raters. This scale is easily administered by rehabilitation staff and therefore may be useful in serial assessments.

Assessment of Factors Relevant to Developing a Therapeutic Rationale and a Working Relationship

Rehabilitation settings are complex social environments that include a number of powerful people—that is, people who have control of stimuli, rewards, and punishers that affect the patient. Establishing a rationale for treatment and a therapeutic relationship involves the initial assessment of the ways that these powerful people conceive of the problem situation that has become the suggested focus for behavioral assessment. The consensual model of behavioral assessment that we are proposing requires a genuine understanding of the models for behavior that the identified patient and significant others bring with them to the rehabilitation setting and an integration of these personal psychological models in establishing a therapeutic rationale.

In psychotherapy, the contract is often that the identified patient would like to alter beliefs and behaviors acquired previously in life that are presently interfering with comfort or success in life. The contract in the rehabilitation setting may be quite different. In the stress that surrounds an admission to a rehabilitation unit, patients and families are usually not interested in evaluating their beliefs. To the contrary, they tend to hold to their beliefs more strongly as a buffer against their currently extreme stress. Their beliefs serve as their connection to an extensive network of social support tied to shared religious or political values.

The consensual model does not view nonbehavioral, alternative models of behavior as unenlightened and their proponents as targets for education in the behavioral way of thinking. Nor does the consensual model support a prescriptive approach. Both the educational and the prescriptive approach fail to recognize that the alternative ways of conceptualizing appropriate and inappropriate behavior are usually deeply rooted in cultural, political, religious, or familial beliefs. Such beliefs are maintained by consistent prompts and social reinforcement that permeate every facet of the social experience of most rehabilitation patients and caregivers. Neither education nor the assertion of power will have much effect in the long term on these social constructs that operate against the introduction of behavioral principles. Consequently, behavioral interventions need to integrate the nonbehavioral constructs held by involved parties to provide a basis for establishing a therapeutic rationale and relationship and to result in long-term behavioral change.

This reality is demonstrated by the following common scenario. A rehabilitation patient is systematically reinforced by attention and praise from staff to dress herself independently, albeit at a slow speed and with the use of adaptive devices and clothing. After discharge from the hospital, however, her husband tends unintentionally to punish the patient by expressing frustration with the slowness of her dressing. Also because he "hates to see her struggle" with adaptive equipment, the husband differentially reinforces requests for help and does not prompt the use of the adaptive equipment. Within 2 weeks, the patient dresses each day with assistance from her husband. On rehabilitation recheck in 2 months, the husband complains to the rehabilitation physician that the patient is no longer able to dress herself.

In this case example, behavioral changes occurred on an inpatient rehabilitation unit through the application of behavioral principles by a well-trained staff. Following hospital discharge, these changes quickly dissipated, as the patient was reintegrated into a social milieu in which prompts and reinforcers follow principles other than those outlined in her behavioral plan. Besides being ultimately ineffective (and probably because they are predictably ineffective), behavioral interventions that are introduced into nonsupportive social environments eventually reduce the behavior therapist's credibility and power in the rehabilitation setting. A consensual approach, in contrast, is recommended to enhance both therapy and therapist effectiveness.

The Social Milieu in Medical Rehabilitation: Competing Worldviews

As mentioned previously, the basic premise underlying a consensual model of behavioral assessment is that people create social reality through their cognitive constructions. A system of socially subscribed beliefs has been termed "a worldview" (McLoughlin, 1991). Behaviorism may be such a worldview. Some would argue, as Jacobs (1993) has, that behaviorism is essentially an atheoretical technology that one may use without accepting the philosophy of behaviorism as described, for instance, by B. F. Skinner (1948) in *Walden Two*. However, our experience has been that most lay people and nonpsychology staff do not compartmentalize such concepts as readily as psychologists do. Most lay people and staff believe that the way one talks and behaves reflects one's beliefs. Thus, in rehabilitation settings in late twentieth-century American pluralistic society, when behaviorism is applied, the behavioral worldview will find itself in competition with other worldviews. We review here some of these nonbehavioral worldviews. Our review presents only examples, rather than a comprehensive listing, of common worldviews.

Political and Religious Worldviews

Several basic beliefs that are inherent in the democratic tradition as well as in most Western religious systems run contrary to the implicit epistemology of behaviorism. One of these is the belief in individual responsibility and motivation. A second is the belief in right and wrong. A third is the belief in a just universe.

The belief in individual responsibility and motivation is predicated on the concept that each person has a free will and is responsible for regulating his or her own behavior. Particularly in cases in which brain dysfunction precludes effective self-regulation as a goal for behavioral intervention, the application of behavioral principles runs contrary to this belief. A program of systematic prompts and contingency management may effectively change a patient's disturbed (or disturbing) behavior. However, this same program may leave caregivers who strongly believe in self-determination with a very uncomfortable feeling that they are violating a basic social precept by participating in controlling the patient's behavior externally.

People who have a strong conviction of right and wrong may experience a similar feeling of intense discomfort when an attempt is made to involve them in a behavioral management program. In their minds, a behavioral approach takes away not only the individual's responsibility to behave appropriately, but also the responsibility to know what is right. Within their ethical system, a limited degree of misbehavior, mistakes, or sins is more tolerable than taking away from an individual what they consider to be the definitively human capacity to know right from wrong.

Related to these beliefs is the idea of a just universe, which states that goodness is rewarded and that badness is punished. This belief can interfere with a behavioral approach in two ways. On the one hand, if a person ends up in rehabilitation through no fault of their own, then—in a just universe—they and their family should not have to expend additional effort to remedy the situation. From the viewpoint of the just universe, good things happen to good people, so things will work out in time. On the other hand, if a person has come to rehabilitation as a result of misbehavior on their part, then he or she deserves to suffer and is not worthy of heroic efforts such as behavioral assessment and treatment. From the just universe perspective, once such people "learn their lesson," their behavior will become more acceptable. A more contemporary secular version of the just universe principle is that only people with personality disorders become involved in severe traumatic and disabling injuries.

Cultural Worldviews

In American society, a variety of Western subcultures and non-Western cultures are represented. Each involves unique beliefs that must be understood, considered, respected, and integrated in an effective consensual behavioral assessment. Even a cursory review of some of these cultural differences is beyond the scope of this chapter. The excellent book *Multicultural Assessment Perspectives for Professional Psychology* (Dana, 1993) is recommended for a thorough review of cultural issues in psychology as practiced in the United States. Worthy of particular mention here is the way in which attributions of behavioral causation may vary among cultures, subcultures, and families. Various groups may emphasize the role of genetics, diet, spiritual influences, or individual moral development in their conceptualizations of unusual behavior. The job of the rehabilitation psychologist is the challenge of understanding how behavioral principles work within a given cultural system.

Beliefs about gender role behavior may also vary considerably among cultures, subcultures, families, and generations. In contemporary American society, the fluidity of gender role is explicitly recognized in professional settings. This concept, however, may be quite foreign to some individuals who represent the more conservative element of contemporary American culture, as well as to individuals within specific minority or foreign cultures. For instance, among some Americans, a husband may find much less discomfort managing the behavior of his wife than the wife has in assuming the dominant role in the relationship and managing the behavior of her husband. For some with an Hispanic background, the dominant role of the man may be more greatly underscored. For some foreign individuals from the Middle East, the idea of a woman regulating the behavior of a man may simply be inconceivable.

Worldviews Specific to Rehabilitation Culture

Rehabilitationists have traditionally embraced the Western cultural emphasis on individual responsibility and motivation. With the exception of psychology and social work staff, most members of rehabilitation teams in most rehabilitation centers reflect the lay culture in believing that motivation for improvement comes from within the person.

Another belief, common in rehabilitation settings, that frequently creates a barrier to establishing a consensual therapeutic rationale is the notion that behavioral disturbances should be addressed in rehabilitation settings primarily because these factors create barriers to physical rehabilitation. This belief implies that behavioral disorders that are associated with many disabling medical conditions are not in themselves appropriate foci for rehabilitation. This belief, based on the Cartesian notion of mind–body dualism, frequently leads to suboptimal patient treatment on the part of therapists who feel that the patient's behavior problems are "not their job." Such settings do not support a consensual approach that requires an interdisciplinary team effort, because behavioral assessment and intervention are considered to be only the psychologist's job.

In rehabilitation and medical settings, a medical, rather than a behavioral model, dominates the language and conceptualization of difficulties in living (Levenkron, 1987). In practical terms, this means that the majority of professionals on the treatment team, as well as many patients and families, are likely to use diagnostic terms such as *depression* and *anxiety* instead of discrete behavioral descriptions. Further, their ideas about treatment success may be tied to an expectation for the alleviation of the syndrome or disorder rather than to discrete behavioral changes.

Disciplinary languages may create barriers to discussion of behavior. Different disciplines may use the same terms, such as *short-term memory* or *functional*, to represent different concepts. Some disciplinary jargons may simply not include sufficient terminology to discuss behavioral issues in a sophisticated manner. Addressing barriers created by language and jargon requires careful attention to the way language is being used in discussion and frequent requests for clarification.

Idiosyncratic Worldviews

Brain dysfunction, stress and associated distress, and more severe mental illness may lead to misperceptions or misconstructions of reality that, in turn, create idiosyncratic worldviews. Contrary to the integrative approach that we are suggesting in general, it may not be constructive to attempt to integrate a worldview that has a pathological origin into a behavioral plan. However, in some cases, such integration may be the only viable approach. For instance, rather than futilely attempting to convince a patient with paranoid ideation that a certain therapist does not really have it in for him or her, it may be more efficient simply to switch therapists. Of greatest concern in identifying some beliefs as due to pathologic processes is the risk that these beliefs in actuality have their basis in the cultural, political, religious, or familial background of the patient.

Assessment in Anticipation of Strong Affect

Strong emotional arousal, usually negative in nature, is a common occurrence in medical rehabilitation settings (Malec & Neimeyer, 1983; Malec, Richardson, Sinaki, & O'Brien, 1990; Rohe, 1993). Such negative affect may occur among patients, family, and staff for a variety of reasons, including as a reaction to disability, disfigurement, and pain; because of interpersonal stress or loneliness created by hospitalization; as a direct consequence of organic brain damage; because of personality, family, or social issues that were present before the onset of disability; or because of stressors only peripherally related to rehabilitation issues. Distress itself may be the target for behavioral assessment and intervention. Distress may also interfere with learning in behavioral assessment and treatment paradigms. The most common barrier to effective education and training with patients and families in rehabilitation settings is the significant stress with which these individuals are often coping at times when educational interventions are attempted. Elsewhere in this chapter and this volume, examples of behavioral assessment techniques that may be used to assess and monitor distress are reviewed.

Strong affect also frequently occurs in response to significant behavioral change. Affective responses accompanying behavioral change are not necessarily positive in nature, even when the change is generally perceived as positive. We are not certain that the arousal of strong affect is essential to a successful behavioral change process, as Frank (1985) suggests. However, we suspect that this is the case. Our experience in a comprehensive postacute brain injury rehabilitation program (Malec, Schafer, & Jacket, 1992; Malec, Smigielski, DePompolo, & Thompson,

1993) has involved a number of cases in which very positive and long-standing behavioral changes have followed from apparently self-generated emotional crises.

The *extinction burst* is a well-known phenomenon in the animal behavioral literature that describes a dramatic increase in a behavior, accompanied by apparent emotional arousal, just prior to that behavior's extinction. In our experience, "extinction bursts" occur frequently when undesirable behavior extinguishes in medical rehabilitation settings. Such strong affect may occur for the identified patient as well as for other parties involved, including staff. Consequently, anticipation of emotional reactions from parties involved in the intervention is a prudent and critical element of the initial behavioral assessment process. Foreshadowing and interpretation of such affect as signifying—and perhaps necessary to— change rather than as a negative event will help the parties involved to support behavioral changes.

Assessment of Factors Underlying the Attribution of the Source of Change

The introduction to this chapter reviewed the opinions of both behavioral and nonbehavioral psychotherapists that an important factor in the generalization and maintenance of behavior change is the attribution of the source of change. The authors that we referenced agreed that maintenance and generalization of behavior change is enhanced if the source of the change is not perceived as inherent in the therapist or treatment setting. Consonant with the egocentric self "of western European origin" (Baumeister, 1986), these authors also suggest that the attribution of change agency will ideally reside within the individual who has changed.

We agree that attribution of change agency to the therapist or setting will negatively affect generalization of change. However, in contemporary medical rehabilitation settings, some cases present in which attribution of change to an egocentric self is not culturally supported. Dana (1993), as well as others (McLoughlin, 1991; Sampson, 1985, 1988), have described individuals—most often of non-European origin—whose self-concept is extended or sociocentric, and who are "responsible and obligated to a variety of other persons who are affected by the individual's actions and have to be considered in all decision-making and problem-solving situations" (Dana, 1993, p. 11). Following severe brain injury, particularly injury of the frontal lobes, patients may be bereft of a satisfactory sense of self. In such cases, responsibility for many aspects of their behavior must be assumed by care providers. In such cases as these, the attribution of change agency may more appropriately and effectively be to the individual's natural social environment rather than to the individual per se (as understood from the egocentric Western perspective). Thus, the degree to which attribution of the source of behavioral change is personal to the patient or is relegated to features of the patient's social environment will depend on the patient's cognitive competency as well as on her or his cultural beliefs about the degree to which behavior is determined by self as opposed to the environment.

Methods for Developing Consensus in Behavioral Assessment

Developing a therapeutic rationale and relationships typically begins with attempts to target a problematic behavior. These initial attempts at behavioral assessment bring the competing worldviews present in the rehabilitation social milieu into focus. The consensual behavioral model proposed here requires that a number of questions be answered: Who are the powerful people in the patient's social environment? How do these powerful people conceptualize the behavior in question and behavior in general (i.e., what are their worldviews)? To what degree can these worldviews be integrated? What aspects of the worldviews are flexible and which are so deeply seated that they are nonnegotiable?

In some cases, answering questions of this nature will lead to a dramatic change in the overall approach to the behavior in question. To offer an example: psychological consultation has been requested to address the disinhibited behavior of a patient with a brain injury who repeatedly tells his wife how sexy she is in the presence of staff. Discussion about this behavior with the patient and his wife reveals that he has always made such comments about her in the presence of friends as well as strangers and that she finds this flattering. Through this discussion and analysis, the behavioral plan changes from the requested effort to reduce "disinhibited" behavior to a simple request for the patient and his wife not to flirt in front of staff because it makes the staff uncomfortable.

A more poignant example is provided by the experience of one of the authors (JFM) many years ago as an intern working with a patient who was terminally ill and paraplegic as a result of incurable spinal cord cancer. The patient was attempting suicide by starvation in the hospital. He had been advised that he would die within 6 months, most of which time would be spent in pain. The clinical interview and discussion with this patient revealed that he was not severely depressed, psychotic, or cognitively impaired. His worldview included a deeply seated belief that a short life of disability and pain blurred by pain medications was not worth living. Consequently he wished to die immediately. We discussed— in more common parlance—how the worldview of hospital staff included a deeply seated belief that people should not die in the hospital and that, because of their convictions, medical staff were prepared to take heroic measures such as intravenous nutrition to sustain his life. The patient responded with some surprise, because he had initially assumed that hospital staff would understand his decision to die and would be supportive. After a few moments' thought, however, the patient recognized that the worldview of hospital staff could not be integrated with his own. This gentle man communicated a sincere respect for the worldview of the hospital staff that indicated a mission to sustain life at all costs, and agreed to start eating again. On follow-up in the hospital, the patient was found to be psychologically comfortable and eating regularly. He was dismissed from the hospital to home some distance away; so we do not know his ultimate decision regarding suicide.

One of our basic beliefs is that although behavioral principles have only been explicated as such during this century, such principles accurately describe most aspects of human interpersonal commerce. Consequently, behavioral principles must appear in most durable systems of human philosophy and government. The job of the rehabilitation psychologist, then, is (a) to discover how the systems of beliefs of patients, families, and staff use behavioral principles and (b) to present the behavioral assessment and treatment plan to them in their own terms.

For instance, although the Western religious and political tradition emphasizes personal responsibility, this same tradition also encourages the help and support of others for individuals who have fallen on misfortune. A behavioral assessment and treatment plan can be presented as a method by which family can assist a patient in regaining her or his self-control. Initially the family takes more responsibility for the behavior of the person who is debilitated, with a goal of this individual's ultimately resuming his or her normal degree of self-management. Similarly, behavioral management may be viewed as a method for relearning principles of right and wrong that have been shaken by the physical or psychological trauma of a severe injury or disease. Although most Western religions subscribe to the just universe principle, most also allow for exceptions. With support and discussion, families may be able to allow that sometimes bad things happen to good people, and that in such cases, heroic measures such as behavioral interventions are warranted to assist

Table 6.1

Areas Identified on the Mayo-Portland Adaptability Inventory as More Problematic By One Group Than By Another

Staff than patients	Staff than families	Patients than staff	Families than staff	Families than patients
Leisure	Social	Visuospatial	Visuospatial	Independent
Social	contact	abilities	abilities	living
contact		Fund of in-	Fund of in-	Paranoia
Independent		formation	formation	Initiation
living		Irritability	Irritability	Self-care
			Paranoia	
			Initiation	
			Anxiety	
			Depression	
			Delusions	

in dealing with the aftermath of such situations. The book entitled *When Bad Things Happen to Good People*, written by Rabbi H. S. Kushner (1981), may assist in such discussions.

Multirater Assessment

Differences are common among patients, staff, and families about what behaviors are problematic, how problematic these behaviors are, and which behaviors take greatest priority for change. One method that we have developed for assessing these various perspectives on behavior among outpatients with brain injuries involves alternative forms of the Mayo-Portland Adaptability Inventory (MPAI; Malec & Thompson, 1994). The MPAI is a revision of the Portland Adaptability Inventory (Lezak, 1987) that lists common areas of cognitive, emotional, physical, behavioral, and functional impairment and disability after brain injury. We have developed three alternative forms of the MPAI that are completed independently by patients, families or significant others, and staff.

Among the initial group of 20 patients and families completing the MPAI (Malec & Machulda, 1994), we found general agreement among patients, families, and staff that some problems are infrequent. Infrequent problems included hearing impairment, delusions and hallucinations, alcohol or drug abuse, and law violations. Conversely, all three groups agreed that problems with attention, memory, and in work or school were very common. In a number of other areas, patients, staff, and families disagreed about the severity of problems (see Table 6.1).

Some of the disagreements of patients or families with staff are probably explained by technical versus lay understanding of terms such as *anxiety, depression, visuospatial ability, fund of information*, and *delusions*. Other differences appear to reflect differing values attached to activities. For instance, patients who are eager to resume independent living usually feel they are more prepared for this step than staff and families, whose values often lead them to be protective of the patient. Other disagreements may reflect the specific experiences of parties involved. For example, families may tend to see more problems with initiation and self-care skills because patient failures in these areas usually create additional work for their families. Whatever the source of the disagreement, discussion of such differences in the individual case provides a starting place for identification of behaviors that have a high priority for change—that is, behaviors that all parties agree are problematic. Such discussion may also reveal the perceptions, attitudes, and values of one party that create barriers to the change desired by another party.

Education

Although we caution against the naive notion that education about behavioral methods will be highly effective in increasing the behavioral sophistication of patients, families, and staff, educational interventions help to establish an important background for behavioral assessment and treatment. Education in rehabilitation settings is appropriately directed at increasing understanding of the association between specific injuries and illnesses and physical, cognitive, emotional, and behavioral impairment. Educational efforts may also increase knowledge of basic behavioral principles. Such educational efforts may include lectures, seminars, and classes for patients, families, and rehabilitation team members about the complexity of motivation, the interaction of external and internal factors in determining behavior, and specific methods to increase desired behaviors. As in many other areas of life, people in rehabilitation settings often learn better and more quickly by doing than by seeing or hearing. Simply involving patients, families, and staff in behavioral assessment and treatment may teach them more about basic behavioral principles than hours of lectures and reading.

Negotiation, Program Evaluation, and Agreeing to Disagree

As a behavioral assessment and treatment plan is negotiated among involved parties, it is critical to the process that the plan and goals be ultimately explicit. It is just as important that some method for measuring the success of the plan must be defined. To assist everyone's memories, the plan, goals, and measures should be recorded in writing. In our experience, it is rare for all parties involved in a consensual behavioral assessment to completely agree about the plan and goals for the intervention. In the end, some parties—at best—will agree to disagree. Conversely, parties involved usually find it easier to agree on measures of success of the plan. Agreeing to disagree in this format usually means all parties agree to try some type of behavioral assessment and intervention to determine through the planned measurement process whether the plan accomplishes the stated goals, and most importantly, to discover whether the various parties like the changes in behavior that occur if the plan is effective.

Working With Staff Toward Consensual Behavioral Assessment

In our previous examples of consensual assessment, we have focused on integrating the perspective of patients and their significant others with the perspectives of staff. Severe agitation and aggressiveness from patients is a behavior that staff and significant others typically have no difficulty agreeing is problematic. Nonetheless, disagreements may arise in how to monitor and intervene with this behavior. In this section, we describe an approach for developing consensus among rehabilitation staff in order to provide a systematic approach to intervention with aggressive patients.

In acute rehabilitation settings, observational assessments are conducted primarily by therapy and nursing staff in consultation with the psychologist. A number of factors may interfere with optimal collaboration in behavioral assessment and subsequent treatment among staff, however. Previously we have mentioned some of these interfering factors generally. More specific examples include: (a) differing perceptions of the need for and focus of the proposed intervention; (b) inadequate understanding of the purpose of the techniques to be used; (c) failure to communicate the plan across shifts; (d) resentment about duties being added without the consent of staff members or without additional time or staff allocations; (e) lack of feedback to the staff and lack of reinforcement for collaborative participation. We have found that collaboration in behavioral procedures is optimal when staff members see a clear need for intervention in order to meet their goals with the patient, when the plan for assessment and treatment has been made in a team context, and when feedback regarding staff participation is available.

We were recently asked by other members of the rehabilitation team to help develop behavioral assessment and intervention procedures to manage aggressive patients. We wanted our assessment procedure to address the difficulties in obtaining staff participation noted above within the cost and time constraints of an inpatient acute care rehabilitation unit.

The process of assessment development began by eliciting the team's goals for behavioral assessment. Basic information on types of behavioral assessment procedures were reviewed by the psychologist member of the team (CL), who also generated recommendations about which procedures might be most useful in our treatment milieu. After discussion and several attempts at pilot assessments, the interdisciplinary team suggested that an assessment with some of the components of an event-monitoring form and some components of interval recording would probably be most useful.

Selection of target behaviors became an issue of concern to the committee. Committee members expressed the need to have a system for describing agitated, aggressive, and restless behavior. As a result of initial trial assessments, committee members admitted to some frustration with the use of global terms such as *confusion* and *agitation* that do not easily lend themselves to intervention. After reviewing the literature and available recording instruments, an initial taxonomy of behaviors was developed by the second author and presented to the committee for review. Through consensus, the committee reduced the list to behaviors they felt would be most reliably measured and clinically relevant.

Discussion of the practical implications of interval recording on our inpatient unit were reviewed. It was decided that interval recordings should occur each half hour during off-therapy hours and hourly during regular therapy hours. Staff members also favored simple behavioral ratings over narrative descriptions, but wanted a place to make notes of unusual occurrences. It was also suggested that staff—other than the psychologist— be able to initiate the behavioral assessment so that information could be collected as soon as a behavioral difficulty came to the staff member's attention.

It should be noted that all of these modifications came from the work of the interdisciplinary committee. When these modifications were made, active collaborative participation in the measurement process increased. As we continue to develop this assessment procedure, we hope to develop procedures based on staff's functional analysis of patients' behavior— much as Durand and Crimmins (1988) have done in working with children with developmental disabilities. It has been clear throughout the process of developing this assessment procedure that sensitivity to and integration of the perceptions and goals of involved staff with the behavioral perspective of psychology staff was essential to the successful development of the procedure. This integration of the rehabilitation worldviews of involved staff also appeared to be a necessary foundation for successful implementation of the project.

Ethical Considerations and Limitations of the Consensual Model

The consensual model for behavioral assessment described in this chapter requires a broad acceptance and respect for alternative worldviews. Understanding a worldview that is highly unfamiliar takes time. In some cases, the time required to understand very unfamiliar beliefs may realistically preclude consensual assessment and intervention. We also recognize that some alternative worldviews may be so contrary to the provider's own deep-seated beliefs that acceptance or even tolerance is not possible. Providers have the right not to provide service to individuals whose beliefs are morally offensive to them.

We would further suggest that individuals are best served by providers who share their worldviews. This idea is particularly relevant in working in multicultural settings. Providers who are familiar with or, ideally, have been raised in the culture of the people served in the rehabilitation setting will be in the best position to provide effective behavioral assessment and interventions. This principle is consistent with information on multicultural psychological treatment presented by Dana (1993). We believe that the consensual model presented here meshes well with Dana's more detailed recommendations for multicultural psychological assessment.

Recognizing that ethical perspectives also vary with worldview (Malec, 1993), the reader is referred to Feldman and Peay (1982) for a thorough review of ethical considerations in the use of behavioral analysis and other behavioral technologies from a humanistic perspective in Western society.

References

Adams, H. (1989). Has behavior therapy progressed? *Contemporary Psychology, 34*, 557–558.

Anderson, S. I., Housley, A. M., Jones, P. A., Slattery, J., & Miller, D. (1993). Glasgow Outcome Scale: An inter-rater reliability study. *Brain Injury, 7*, 309–317.

Barlow, D. H. (1980). *Behavioral assessment of adult disorders*. New York: Guilford Press.

Barlow, D. H., Hayes, S. C., & Nelson, R. O. (1985). *The Scientist Practitioner: Research and accountability in clinical and educational settings*. Elmsford, NY: Pergamon Press.

Barrios, B. A. (1988). On the changing nature of behavioral assessment. In A. S. Bellack,

& M. Hersen (Eds.), *Behavioral assessment: a practical handbook* (pp. 3–41). Elmsford, NY: Pergamon Press.

Baumeister, R. F. (1986). *Identity: Cultural change and the struggle for self*. New York: Oxford University.

Bellack, A. S., & Hersen, M. (Eds.). (1988). *Behavioral assessment: A practical handbook* (3rd ed.). Elmsford, NY: Pergamon Press.

Bergner, M., Bobbitt, R. A., Carter, W. B., & Gilson, B. S. (1981). The Sickness Impact Profile: Development and final revision of a health status measure. *Medical Care, 19*, 787–805.

Blessed, G., Tomlinson, B. E., & Roth, M. (1968). The association between quantiative measures of dementia and senile changes in the cerebral grey matter of elderly subjects. *British Journal of Psychiatry, 114*, 797–811.

Brooke, M. M., Questad, K. A., Patterson, D. R., & Bashak, K. J. (1992). Agitation and restlessness after closed head injury: A prospective study of 100 consecutive admissions. *Archives of Physical Medicine and Rehabilitation, 73*, 320–323.

Brooks, D. N (1987). Measuring neuropsychological and functional recovery. In H. S. Levin, J. Grafman, & H. M. Eisenberg (Eds.), *Neurobehavioral recovery from head injury* (pp. 57–72). New York: Oxford University Press.

Budd, K. S., Workman, D., Lemsky C. M., & Quick, D. (in press). Children's headache assessment scale (CHAS): Factor structure and psychometric properties. *Journal of Behavioral Medicine*.

Collins, F. L., & Thompson, J. K. (1993). The integration of empirically derived personality assesment data into a behavioral conceptualization and treatment plan. *Behavior Modification, 17*, 58–71.

Cooper, M. L., Russell, M., Skinner, J. B., & Windle, M. (1992). Development and validation of a three-dimensional measure for drinking motives. *Psychological Assessment, 4*, 123–132.

Corrigan, J. D. (1989). Development of a scale for assessment of agitation following traumatic brain injury. *Journal of Clinical and Experimental Neuropsychology, 11*, 261–277.

Dana, R. H. (1993). *Multicultural assessment perspectives for professional psychology*. Boston: Allyn and Bacon.

Derby, K. M., Wacker, D. P., Sasso, G., Steege, M., Northrup, J., Cigrand, K., & Asmus, J. (1992). Brief functional assessment techniques to evaluate aberrant behavior in an outpatient setting: A summary of 79 cases. *Journal of Applied Behavioral Analysis, 25*, 713–721.

Drachman, D. A., Swearer, J. M., O'Donnell, B. F., Mitchell, A. L., & Maloon, A. (1992). The Caretaker Obstreperous-Behavior Rating Assessment (COBRA) scale. *Journal of the American Geriatrics Society, 40*, 463–470.

Durand, V. M., & Crimmins, D. B. (1988). Identifying the variables maintaining self-injurious behavior. *Journal of Autism and Developmental Disorders, 18*, 99–117.

Fabiano, R. J., & Goran, D. A. (1992). A principal component analysis of the Katz Adjustment Scale in a traumatic brain injury rehabilitation sample. *Rehabilitation Psychology, 2*, 75–85.

Feldman, M. P., & Peay, J. (1982). Ethical and legal issues. In A. S. Bellack, M. Hersen, & A. E. Kazdin (Eds.), *International handbook of behavior modification and therapy* (pp. 231–261). New York: Plenum Press.

Fisher, J. E., & Carstensen, L. L. (1990). Behavior management of the dementias. *Clinical Psychology Review, 10*, 611–629.

Follette, W. C., & Hayes, S. C. (1992). Behavioral assessment in the DSM era. *Behavioral Assessment, 14*, 293–295.

Ford, J. D., & Kendall, P. C. (1979). Behavior therapists' professional behaviors: Converging evidence of a gap between theory and practice. *The Behavior Therapist*, *2*, 37–38.

Frank, J. D. (1985). Therapeutic components shared by all psychotherapies. In M. J. Mahoney & A. Freeman (Eds.), *Cognition and psychotherapy* (pp. 49–79). New York: Plenum Press.

Gergen, K. J. (1985). The social constructionist movement in modern psychology. *American Psychologist*, *40*, 266–275.

Gianutsos, R., & Gianutsos, J. (1984). Single-case experimental approaches to the assessment of interventions in rehabilitation. In B. Caplan (Ed.), *Rehabilitation Psychology Desk Reference* (pp. 443–470). Rockville, MD: Aspen.

Goran, D. A., & Fabiano, R. J. (1993). The scaling of the Katz Adjustment Scale in a traumatic brain injury rehabilitation sample. *Brain Injury*, *7*, 219–229.

Granger, C. V., Cotter, A. C., Hamilton, B. B., & Fiedler, R. C. (1993). Functional assessment scales: A study of persons after stroke. *Archives of Physical Medicine and Rehabilitation*, *74*, 133–138.

Granger, C. V., Cotter, A. C., Hamilton, B. B., Fiedler, R. C., & Hens (1990). Functional assessment scales: A study of persons with multiple sclerosis. *Archives of Physical Medicine and Rehabilitation*, *71*, 870–875.

Grant, I., & Alves, W. (1987). Psychiatric sequelae of head injury: Conceptual and methodological problems. In H. S. Levin, J. Grafman, & H. M. Eisenberg (Eds.), *Neurobehavioral recovery from head injury* (pp. 232–261). New York: Oxford University Press.

Guide for the Uniform Data Set for Medical Rehabilitation (Adult FIM), version 4.0. (1993). Buffalo, NY: State University of New York at Buffalo.

Hall, K., Cope, N., & Rappaport, M. (1985). Glasgow outcome scale and disability rating scale: Comparative usefulness in following recovery in traumatic head injury. *Archives of Physical Medicine and Rehabilitation*, *66*, 35–37.

Hall, K. M., Hamilton, B. B., Gordon, W. A., & Zasler, N. D. (1993). Characteristics and comparisons of functional assessment indicies: Disability Rating Scale, Functional Independence Measure, and Functional Assessment Measure. *Journal of Head Trauma Rehabilitation*, *8*, 60–74.

Hamilton, B. B., Granger, C. V., Sherwin, F. S., Zielezny, M., & Tashman, J. S. (1987). A uniform national data system for medical rehabilitation. In M. J. Fuhrer (Ed.), *Rehabilitation outcomes: Analysis and measurement* (pp. 137–150). Baltimore, MD: Paul H. Brookes.

Hawkins, R. P. (1986). Selection of target behaviors. In R. O. Nelson & S. C. Hays (Eds.), *Conceptual foundations of behavioral assessment* (pp. 331–383). New York: Guilford Press.

Hayes, S. C., Nelson, R. O., & Jarrett, R. B. (1987). The treatment utility of assessment. *American Psychologist*, *42*, 963–974.

Haynes, S. N. (1990). Behavioral assessment of adults. In G. Goldstein & M. Hersen (Eds.), *Handbook of Psychological Assessment* (pp. 423–452). Elmsford, NY: Pergamon Press.

Haynes, S. N., Lemsky, C., & Sexton-Radek, K. (1987a). The scientist–practitioner model in clinical psychology: Suggestions for implementing an alternative model. In J. R. McNamara & M. A. Appel (Eds.), *Critical issues, developments and trends in professional psychology* (Vol. 3, pp. 1–26). New York: Praeger.

Haynes, S. N., Lemsky, C., & Sexton-Radek, K. (1987b). Why clinicians infrequently do research. *Professional Psychology*, *18*, 1–5.

Haynes, S. N., & O'Brien, W. H. (1990). Functional analysis in behavior therapy. *Clinical Psychology Review*, *10*, 649–668.

Haynes, S. N., & Uchigakiuchi, P. (1993). Incorporating personality trait measures in behavioral assessment: Nuts in a fruitcake or raisins in a Mai Tai? *Behavior Modification*, *17*, 72–92.

Hilton, G., Sisson, R., & Freeman, E. (1990). The Neurobehavioral Rating Scale: An interrater reliability study in the HIV seropositive population. *Journal of Neuroscience Nursing*, *22*, 36–42.

Jacobs, H. E. (1988). Yes, behaviour analysis can help, but do you know how to harness it? *Brain Injury*, *2*, 339–346.

Jacobs, H. E. (1993). *Behavior analysis guidelines and brain injury rehabilitation*. Gaithersburg, MD: Aspen.

Jennett, B., & Bond, M. (1975). Assessment of outcome after severe brain damage. *Lancet*, *1*, 480–484.

Jennett, B., Snoek, M. R., Bond M., & Brooks, N. (1981). Disability after severe head injury: Observations on the use of the Glasgow Outcome Scale. *Journal of Neurology, Neurosurgery and Psychiatry*, *44*, 285–293.

Kanfer, F. H. (1985). Target selection for clinical change programs. *Behavioral Assessment*, *7*, 7–20.

Katz, M., & Lyerly, S. (1963). Methods for measuring adjustment and social behavior in the community. Rationale, description, discriminative validity and scale development. *Psychological Reports*, *13*, 503–535.

Kazdin, A. (1992). *Research design in clinical psychology*. New York: Macmillan.

Kendall, P. C. (1990). Behavioral assessment and methodology. In C. M. Franks, G. T. Wilson, P. C. Kendall, & J. P. Foreyt (Eds.), *Review of behavior therapy, theory and practice* (Vol. 12, pp. 44–71). New York: Guilford Press.

Klonoff, P. S., Costa, L. D., & Snow, W. G. (1986). Predictors and indicators of quality of life in patients with closed head injury. *Journal of Clinical and Experimental Neuropsychology*, *18*, 469–485.

Kushner, H. S. (1981). *When bad things happen to good people*. New York: Avon Books.

Levenkron, J. C. (1987). Behavior modification in rehabilitation: Principles and clinical strategies. In B. Caplan (Ed.), *Rehabilitatioin psychology desk reference* (pp. 183–146). Rockville: Aspen.

Levin, H. S., High, W. M., Goethe, K. E., Sisson, R. A., Overall, J. E., Rhoades, H. M., Eisenberg H. M., Kalisky, Z., & Gary, H. E. (1987). The Neurobehavioural Rating Scale: Assessment of the behavioural sequelae of head injury by the clinician. *Journal of Neurology, Neurosurgery and Psychiatry*, *50*, 183–193.

Lezak, M. D. (1987). Relationships between personality disorders, social disturbances, and physical disability following traumatic brain injury. *Journal of Head Trauma Rehabilitation*, *2*, 57–69.

Lezak, M. D. (1989). Assessment of psychosocial dysfunctions resulting from head trauma. In M. D. Lezak (Ed.), *Assessment of the behavioral consequences of head trauma* (pp. 113–141). New York: Alan R. Liss.

Lincare, J. M., Heinemann, A. W., Wright, B. D., Granger, C. V., & Hamilton, B. B. (1994). The structure and stability of the Functional Independence Measure. *Archives of Physical Medicine and Rehabilitation*, *75*, 127–132.

Malec, J. (1984). Training the brain-injured client in behavioral self-management skills. In B. A. Edelstein & E. T. Couture (Eds.), *Behavioral assessment and rehabilitation of the traumatically brain-damaged* (pp. 121–150). New York: Plenum Press.

Malec, J. F. (1993). Ethics in brain injury rehabilitation: Existential choices among Western cultural beliefs. *Brain Injury*, *7*, 383–400.

Malec, J. F., & Machulda, M. M. (1994). Differing perceptions of impairment after brain injury among staff, survivors, and families. *Archives of Physical Medicine, & Rehabilitation*, *75*, 727.

Malec, J., & Neimeyer, R. (1983). Psychologic prediction of inpatient spinal cord injury rehabilitation and performance of self-care. *Archives of Physical Medicine and Rehabilitation, 64*, 359–363.

Malec, J. F., Richardson, J. W., Sinaki, M., & O'Brien, M. W. (1990). Types of affective response to stroke. *Archives of Physical Medicine and Rehabilitation, 71*, 279–284.

Malec, J., Schafer, D., Jacket, M. (1992). Comprehensive–integrated postacute outpatient brain injury rehabilitation. *NeuroRehabilitation, 2*, 1–11.

Malec, J. F., Smigielski, J. S., DePompolo, R. W., & Thompson, J. M. (1993). Outcome evaluation and prediction in a comprehensive–integrated post-acute outpatient brain injury rehabilitation programme. *Brain Injury, 7*, 15–29.

Malec, J. F., & Thompson, J. S. (1994). Relationship of the Mayo-Portland Adaptability Inventory to functional outcome and cognitive performance measures. *Journal of Head Trauma Rehabilitation, 9*, 1–16.

Marsh, N. V., & Knight, R. G. (1991). Behavioral assessment of social competence following head injury. *Journal of Clinical and Experimental Neuropsychology, 13*, 729–740.

McLoughlin, Q. (1991). *Relativistic naturalism: A cross-cultural approach to human science.* New York: Praeger.

Meichenbaum, D. (1985). *Stress inoculation training.* Elmsford, NY: Pergamon Press.

Morganstern, K. P. (1980). Behavioral interviewing. In D. H. Barlow (Ed.), *Behavioral assessment of adult disorders* (pp. 129–179). New York: Guilford Press.

Nelson, L. D., Satz, P., Mitrushina, M., Van Gorp, W., Cicchetti, D., Lewis, R., & Van Lancker, D. (1989). Development and validation of the neuropsychology behavior and affect profile. *Psychological Assessment, 4*, 266–272.

O'Leary, K. D., & Wilson, T. G. (1989). *Behavior therapy, application and outcome.* Englewood Cliffs, NJ: Prentice-Hall.

Prigatano, G. P. (1986). *Neuropsychological rehabilitation after brain injury.* Baltimore: Johns Hopkins University Press.

Rappaport, M., Hall, H. M., Hopkins, K., Belleza, T., & Cope, D. N. (1982). Disability Rating Scale for severe head trauma: Coma to community. *Archives of Physical Medicine and Rehabilitation, 63*, 118–123.

Rohe, D. E. (1993). Psychological aspects of rehabilitation. In J. A. DeLisa & B. M. Gans (Eds.), *Rehabilitation medicine: Principles and practice* (pp. 66–82). Phildelphia: Lippincott.

Rosenthal, M., & Bond, M. R. (1990). Behavioral and psychiatric sequelae. In M. Rosenthal, E. R. Griffith, M. R. Bond, & J. D. Miller (Eds.), *Rehabilitation of the adult and child with traumatic brain injury* (pp. 179–192). Philadelphia: F. A. Davis.

Sampson, E. E. (1985). The decentralization of identity: Toward a revised concept of personal and social order. *American Psychologist, 40*, 1203–1211.

Sampson, E. E. (1988). The debate on individualism: Indigenous psychologies of the individual and their role in personal and societal functioning. *American Psychologist, 43*, 15–22.

Schacter, D. (1991). Unawareness of deficit and unawareness of knowledge in patients with memory disorders. In G. Prigatano & D. Schacter (Eds.) *Awareness of deficit after brain injury* (pp. 127–131). New York: Oxford University Press.

Skinner, B. F. (1948). *Walden two.* New York: MacMillan.

Spiegel, R., Brunner, C., Phil, L., Ermini-Funfschilling, D., Monsch, A., Notter, M., Math, D., Puxty, J., Tremmel, L., & Psych, D. (1991). A new behavioral assessment scale for geriatric out-and in-patients: The NOSGER (Nurses' Observations Scale for Geriatric Patients). *Journal of the American Geriatrics Society, 39*, 339–347.

Sultzer, D. L., Levin, H. S., Mahler, M. E., High, W. M., & Cummings, J. L. (1992). Assessment of cognitive, psychiatric and behavioral disturbances in patients with dementia: The Neurobehavioral Rating Scale. *Journal of the American Geriatrics Society, 40*, 549–555.

Swan, G. E., & MacDonald, M. L., (1978). Behavior therapy in practice: A national survey of behavior therapists. *Behavior Therapy*, *9*, 799–807.

Taylor, S., Koch, W. J., McNally, R. J., & Crockett, D. J. (1992). Conceptualizations of anxiety sensitivity. *Psychological Assessment*, *4*, 245–250.

Temkin, N., McLean, A., Dikmen, S., Gale, J., Bergner, M., & Almes, M. J. (1988). Development and evaluation of modifications to the sickness impact profile for head injury. *Journal of Clinical Epidemiology*, *41*, 47–57.

Teri, L., Traux, P., Logsdon, R., Uomoto, J., Zarit, S., & Vitaliano, P. P. (1992). Assessment of behavioral problems in dementia: The Revised Memory and Behavior Problems Checklist. *Psychology and Aging*, *7*, 622–631.

Varney, N., & Menefee, L. (1993). Psychosocial and executive deficits following closed head injury: Implications for orbital frontal cortex. *Journal of Head Trauma Rehabilitation*, *8*, 32–44.

Wade, T. C., Baker, T. B., & Hartmann, D. P. (1979). Behavior therapists' self-reported views and practices. *The Behavior Therapist*, *2*, 3–6.

Williams, J. M. (1987). *Cognitive behavior rating scales*. Odessa, FL: Psychological Assessment Resources.

Wilson, B. (1991). Behavior therapy in the treatment of neurologically impaired adults. In P. R. Martin (Ed.), *Handbook of behavior therapy and psychological science: An integrative approach* (pp. 227–252). Elmsford, NY: Pergamon Press.

Yudofsky, S. C., Silver, J. M., Jackson, W., Endicott, J., & Williams, D. (1986). The overt aggression scale for the objective rating of verbal and physical aggression. *American Journal of Psychiatry*, *143*, 35–39.

Zahara, D. J., & Cuvo, A. J. (1984). Behavioral applications to the rehabilitation of traumatically head injured individuals. *Clinical Psychology Review*, *4*, 477–491.

Zarit, S. H., & Zarit, J. M. (1983). Cognitive impairment. In P. M. Lewinsohn & L. Teri (Eds.), Clinical geropsychology (pp. 38–81). Elmsford, NY: Pergamon Press.

Zeiss, A. M., Lewinsohn, P. M., & Munoz, R. F. (1979). Nonspecific improvement effects in depression using interpersonal skills training, pleasant activities schedules, and cognitive training. *Journal of Clinical and Consulting Psychology*, *47*, 427–439.

7

Assessment of Pain and Pain Behavior

Richard W. Millard

Pain is a mental event that cannot be understood solely in terms of tissue damage. Psychometric approaches are important for measuring pain and associated behavior. Dichotomous definitions of pain as either functional or organic, have given way to explanations that accommodate mind, body, and environment. In 1965, Melzack and Wall, a psychologist and a physiologist, proposed the Gate Control Theory, which defined pain as a unitary biobehavioral "sensory and emotional experience." Using an applied behavioral orientation, Fordyce (1976) showed how pain behavior could be modified in clinical rehabilitation settings. Turk, Meichenbaum, and Genest (1983) further expanded awareness of pain as a mental event by demonstrating the utility of cognitive treatment approaches in pain management. Each of these developments had an impact on clinical practice, as psychologists began to fill increasingly important roles in management of pain. As clinical services expanded, many pain questionnaires, scales, and other assessment methods began to appear.

Evaluation is necessarily tailored to the kind of pain that is present. Pain may be classified by temporal variables (i.e., acute or chronic), by site or system (i.e., headache or low-back; muscular or neuropathic, etc.), by age of patient, by presence/absence of malignancy, and so forth. In primary care settings, where most patients with pain are seen, it is apt to be an intermittent but prevalent complaint that can be difficult to classify simply as acute or chronic (Von Korff, Deyo, Cherkin, & Barlow, 1993). This chapter reviews findings primarily from patients with chronic, non-malignant pain, because these individuals are commonly evaluated in medical rehabilitation settings. They probably constitute a biased sample. Such patients complain of symptoms that have become overly difficult to manage in primary care settings. They are unlike the general population. This is a potentially important threat to the validity of many pain assessment instruments (Turk & Rudy, 1990a), which have been devised in specialized pain clinics.

The first way to measure pain is by intensity. Beyond this, it is helpful to distinguish three broad measurement domains: physiological, behavioral, and cognitive–affective. This chapter is organized to review commonly available approaches in each of these areas. Comprehensive inventories (including the Minnesota Multiphasic Personality Inventory [MMPI] and the Millon Clinical Multiaxial Inventory) are described separately. Finally, the reader is directed to resources for specialized assessment of pediatric pain, cancer, headache, spinal cord injury, and other conditions.

Pain Intensity

Numeric Rating Scale

The easiest way to obtain a report of pain is by asking an individual to rate intensity on a Numeric Rating Scale (NRS). The range of numbers is usually 0 to 10 or 0 to 100, anchored with 0 indicating *no pain* and 10 or 100 denoting *the most intense pain imaginable* (Jensen & Karoly, 1992). The NRS can be administered verbally or on paper, and it lends itself to repeat administration, even over short intervals. It is practical to use and among the least intrusive ways of measuring pain intensity. It is also sensitive to treatment-related changes (e.g., Keefe, Schapira, Williams, Brown, & Surwit, 1981).

Visual Analogue Scale

A variation of the NRS is a Visual Analogue Scale (VAS), a 10-cm line with the ends anchored at *no pain* and *the most intense pain imaginable*. This scale does not contain marked intervals (like the NRS), and results are essentially handled like ratio data. Its reliability and validity, including sensitivity to treatment effects, has also been established in clinical settings (Price, McGrath, Rafii, & Buckingham, 1983; Scott & Huskisson, 1976). A companion VAS can be used to measure pain affect, or emotional qualities of pain that may be distinguishable from intensity (Price, Harkins, & Baker, 1987).

McGill Pain Questionnaire

Apart from simple numeric or visual analogue scales, the McGill Pain Questionnaire (MPQ) is the most widely used instrument for evaluating pain (Melzack, 1975; Melzack & Katz, 1992; Melzack & Torgerson, 1971; Turk, Rudy, & Salovey, 1985). Although intended to be given verbally, it is frequently administered as a paper-and-pencil questionnaire. The MPQ was derived from the assumption that pain comprises three critical dimensions: sensory–discriminative, motivational–affective, and cognitive–evaluative. It is designed to capture these subjective qualities through carefully chosen adjectives that are ranked in terms of severity (i.e., *tingling*, *itchy*, *smarting*, *stinging*). The full questionnaire also contains an outline of the human body for measuring pain location and a list of five adjectives to denote overall intensity (Present Pain Intensity, PPI; ranging from mild to excruciating). In addition to the PPI, the Pain Rating Index (PRI) is used to summarize the ordinal ratings of adjectives within each dimension (sensory, affective, cognitive). Turk et al. (1985) conducted a confirmatory factor analysis of PRI findings and found that there was little differentiation between these dimensions. They advised using only the total PRI score as an indicator of pain intensity.

Many investigations have provided data supporting the reliability and validity of the MPQ (e.g., Lowe, Walker, & McCallum, 1991; Pearce & Morley, 1989; Reading, Everitt, & Sledmere, 1982; Wilkie, Savedra, Holzemer, Tesler, & Paul, 1990), and it has been translated into several languages. Despite cultural adaptations, some of the adjectives in the MPQ can be unfamiliar to respondents. The distinction between adjectives denoting sensory versus affective qualities of pain appears to be most clear (Melzack & Katz, 1992). It is purported to be effective in differential diagnosis of pain syndromes because some conditions, such as neuropathic pain, are typically characterized by sensory descriptors. A short-form MPQ is available containing 15 of the most frequently endorsed sensory and affective descriptors, each rated on a 4-point scale from *none* to *severe*. Melzack (1987) reported that it correlates highly with the long form.

Descriptor Differential Scale

The Descriptor Differential Scale contains 12 descriptor items that are rated on a 21-point scale (Gracely & Kwilosz, 1988). These adjectives refer to the intensity of sensation (e.g., *faint, strong, slightly intense, extremely intense,* etc.). Beneath each adjective is a 21-point scale, anchored by (−) and (+). A cumulative pain intensity score is obtained by averaging the scale point value for each adjective. Like the MPQ, its multidimensionality is intended to prevent scaling biases that might result from using a single unitary pain intensity score. An alternative set of adjectives can be used to assess affective qualities of pain. Gracely and Kwilosz (1988) report excellent internal consistency and test–retest reliability using this scale with dental patients, although the format can be difficult for naive subjects to comprehend.

Summary

Pain is a covert process and there is no mechanical means to quantify it. Physiological changes or pathology (such as inflammation, muscular tension, or nerve damage) cannot be expected to correspond directly to pain. Self-report thus serves as the basis for reports of pain intensity, usually in terms of pain at its worst, least, current, and average intensity. Most measures of pain intensity show high intercorrelation (Jensen, Karoly, & Braver, 1986). The VAS and the NRS are highly practical in most clinical encounters, although the MPQ provides more qualitative information.

Physiological Assessment

Specialized physiological evaluations are sometimes conducted as part of the psychological evaluation of pain. Information about physiological parameters can be useful in examining the relationship between behavior (or cognition and affect) and the physical responses that may accompany pain. Portraying this relationship to the patient may serve as a continuing form of assessment. Treatment, in the form of biofeedback protocols, is usually structured to increase patient awareness of how to exert self-control over physiological responses. In this section I review the three most common forms of physiological assessment in chronic pain: myography, cardiovascular recordings, and measurements of skin conductance.

Myography

Myography, or assessment of the muscle, is particularly relevant in pain management because certain prevalent conditions (such as tension headache, temporomandibular dysfunction (TMD), and many cases of back pain) are accompanied by muscular tension or spasm. These physiological variables may respond to psychological interventions.

The surface electromyogram (EMG) is useful in representing electrical activity that accompanies muscular tension. Surface leads are usually placed on the frontalis muscle, although the site can be varied according to the kind of pain complaint (i.e., masseter for TMD, trapezius for pain in the cervical region, etc.). The EMG readings may be weak and are greatly influenced by placement of electrodes, which requires the clinician to possess specific technical knowledge in order to obtain accurate measurements. An assessment protocol might typically comprise measurement of muscular activity in response to postural and psychological stressors (Flor, Birbaumer, Schulte, & Roos, 1991; Flor, Turk, & Birbaumer, 1985). The relationship between pain intensity and EMG levels is not well understood, and new ambulatory monitoring schemes are helping to describe this connection (Flor, Miltner, & Birbaumer, 1992). As with other physiological measurements, EMG may be useful in portraying a visible method of self-regulation for patients. Wickramasekera (1989) describes protocols for obtaining frontalis EMG readings during initial evaluation of somatically focused patients. These are conducted as part of a "Trojan Horse Procedure" that is intended to illustrate mind–body connections for skeptical patients and facilitate entry into psychological treatment. This application is clinically appealing, although its validity is largely unexamined.

A dolorimeter (sometimes referred to as a pressure-point algometer) can be used to evaluate pain from *trigger-points*, or highly focal areas of local tenderness (Fischer, 1988). This device is similar to a dynamometer except that it is applied to the trigger point and pressure is exerted until a pain threshold is identified. Reeves, Jaeger, and Graff-Radford (1986) reported good interrater reliability with this device and found that the method could be sensitive to discrete muscular tenderness. Jensen, Andersen, Olesen, and Lindblom (1986) reported that the dolorimeter could portray changes in pain sensitivity following local anesthesia. Rather than using normative values, they recommended evaluating findings within subject trials. Although it is not widely used in clinical settings, this method is a potentially useful and valid means of recording changes in focal muscular tenderness as would be present in conditions such as fibromyalgia (Bradley, Anderson, Young, & Williams, 1989).

Cardiovascular Assessment

Cardiovascular measures include heart rate, blood pressure, and skin temperature. Skin temperature is the most prevalent cardiovascular measure for patients with pain, serving as an indicator of vasoconstriction that might accompany conditions such as Raynaud's disease, migraine headache, or reflex sympathetic dystrophy (Flor et al., 1992; Headley, 1987). Measurements are obtained by placing a thermistor on the skin. This equates surface temperature to electrical changes. Temperature feedback has been shown to be effective in reducing vasoconstriction associated with Raynaud's disease, which produces pain along with cold extremities (Freedman, 1991). It is also frequently used in management of migraine headache, although there is no evidence that it modifies vasoconstriction with this disorder. Instead, it may simply produce a non-specific perception of increased self-control. The utility of other cardio-vascular measures, such as blood pressure, blood volume, and heart rate, is less established in clinical settings (Flor et al., 1992). Thermography, or spectral photography of heat, has been a commercially appealing method of demonstrating temperature changes in association with pain, but un-fortunately lacks clinical value (McCulloch, 1989).

Skin Conductance

Skin conductance, or electrodermograpy (EDG), is the third most common form of physiological assessment performed for patients with chronic pain. There is much less evidence to support its application than for EMG or even cardiovascular measurements (Olton & Noonberg, 1980). It makes use of a physiologic sensor that is designed to measure changes in sweat gland activity. This technique is used as a general measure of arousal, or autonomic nervous system activity. It portrays mental changes more directly than other physiological measurements, so emotional concerns may appear to be represented by the the visual feedback display (Peek, 1987). This method possesses face validity in treatment for anxiety associated with pain, but there are mixed findings concerning its clinical utility. Some studies have reported that EDG can portray reactions to relevant stressors, but others have suggested that it merely reflects global physical changes (Flor et al., 1992; Peters & Schmidt, 1991).

Summary

Special caution is appropriate when conducting physiological assessment. First, it must be remembered that proper usage of these mechanical instruments requires specific technical skills (concerning instrumentation, placement of sensors, etc.) as well as knowledge of testing methods. This introduces new sources of error. Second, evaluations are typically conducted in the context of a single-subject design, so group or normative information is rare. Third, careless physiological monitoring may inadvertently abet patient beliefs that a mechanical instrument, rather than personal action, is serving as a basis for analgesia (Turner & Chapman, 1982).

Behavioral Assessment

Within a broad definition of behavior, there are many ways that pain behavior is assessed. These range from direct behavioral observation schemes (in controlled and natural environments) to pain behavior checklists and self-report questionnaires that evaluate functional interference. The behavioral assessment of pain overlaps with efforts to quantify disability. Disability refers to disruptions in the performance of routine abilities and behaviors. It may be defined as personal reactions to impairment, often pain (Harper et al., 1992; Susser, 1990). Such responses are largely reflected through pain behavior, providing the assessor with a rich field of inquiry. Disability questionnaires provide more subjective data than direct observation but require fewer resources to administer and may yield more practical information about routine daily activities (Millard, 1991). Behavioral measurements are ordinarily preferable to self-report questionnaires because they are less subject to bias. However, even objectively measured clinical signs (e.g., bending over, lifting) can be implicitly influenced by demand characteristics of the setting where the measurement occurs. Questionnaires thus provide a practical and inexpensive alternative. There are few head-to-head comparisons of these different assessment methods.

Direct Behavioral Observation

Keefe and Block (1982) devised a direct behavioral observational method for evaluating videotaped samples of pain behavior by patients with low back pain (e.g., guarding, bracing, sighing). This approach demonstrated strong interrater reliability (greater than .93) with evidence of concurrent (vs. total pain behavior) and discriminant (vs. healthy controls and depressed patients without pain) validity. It was also sensitive to treatment-related changes. This observational method was subsequently adapted for use with other pain samples (Romano et al., 1988) and diverse conditions.

Anderson et al. (1987) made modifications for patients with rheumatoid arthritis, adding coding categories to reflect behaviors such as rigidity and stiffness of affected joints. These measurements were sensitive in detecting treatment-related reductions in pain behavior (McDaniel et al., 1986) and have also been linked to disease variables (e.g., erythrocyte sedimentation rate, grip strength; Anderson et al., 1987). Keefe et al. (1987) adapted the direct behavioral observation method to evaluate pain behavior, positioning, and movement of patients with osteoarthritis of the knees. Observations were reliable and significantly associated with NRS reports of pain intensity ($r = .46$) as well as usage of coping strategies (Keefe, Caldwell et al., 1990). In one promising application, this method was used in observing spouse reactions to patient performance of physical tasks (Romano et al., 1991).

Follick, Ahern, and Aberger (1985) devised the Audiovisual Taxonomy of Pain Behavior for direct observation of patients with back pain. Patients are asked to perform specific activities, which are then recorded and coded. They found seven categories of pain behavior that could be frequently and reliably coded. Estimates of interrater reliability (over .83) were acceptable. These behaviors were useful in distinguishing patients with chronic pain from healthy controls. This observational method has not been as widely extended as the approach used by Keefe.

Functional Capacity Evaluation (FCE) is a specialized form of assessment that is usually performed with sophisticated biomechanical hardware to measure strength, range of motion, or cardiovascular endurance. Although the variables being assessed will vary according to pain site, specific protocols have been proposed (e.g., Mayer, Tencer, Kristoferson, & Mooney, 1984). The FCE is ostensibly performed to quantify functional limitations and guide decisions about legal disability status. These judgments must be based on normative data and evidence of optimal effort during testing (Polatin & Mayer, 1992). Some of the same issues that affect behavioral assessment are relevant during FCE, as discrete samples of behavior are examined in controlled settings. In addition, psychological factors, in terms of perceived failure or poor ability to interpret proprioceptive exhaustion signals, may influence demonstrated performance (Schmidt, 1985).

Behavioral and psychometric concerns affect physical examinations as well. Waddell, Somerville, Henderson, and Newton, (1992), in a study of 126 patients with chronic low back pain, found that only about 26% of variance in disability can be attributed to findings of physical impairment. This suggests the value of standardized or systematic protocols for quantifying behavioral responses to the physical examination. Pain behavior in the presence of the physician is a very important form of social communication, one that might legally sanction disability. Waddell, McCulloch, Kummel, and Venner (1980) offered one means of coding this information through a checklist of nonorganic signs of impairment. The behavioral responses that are measured include complaints of tenderness that follow nonanatomical patterns, complaints of pain in performing actions that do not affect the spine, or disproportionate pain behavior during examination. Five signs are coded in the system, and they were present most frequently among identified "problem patients" who had proven unresponsive to medical treatments. These signs were independent of age, sex, or type of employment and correlated moderately ($r = .36$, $n = 36$) with MMPI *Hs* scores. However, Greenough and Fraser (1991) reported that this approach may be less sensitive with patients who are minimally or mildly disabled.

Spratt, Lehmann, Weinstein, and Sayre (1990) describe a standard protocol for recording physical signs and pain behavior during the examination of patients with low back pain. The pain behaviors that are coded within this scheme are similar to those identified by Keefe and Block (1982). As with Waddell's method, the advantage of this approach is that it provides a systematic way of combining information about impairment with clinical observations of pain behavior. Spratt et al. (1990) report very high interrater and test–retest reliability. The validity of the protocol has yet to be established.

Ambulatory monitoring of patient activities has been attempted through the use of devices sensitive to motion. Sanders (1983) and Follick, Ahern, Laser-Wolston, Adams, and Molloy (1985) have developed electronic measurements of uptime (time not spent sitting or reclining), and Keefe and Hill (1985) have invented pressure sensitive insoles to evaluate abnormal gait patterns. Keefe reported that patients with gait abnormalities were more apt to be using narcotic medication or receiving pain-related financial compensation. These electromechanical approaches are potentially useful in the context of physical therapy but may be impractical or produce artifactual measurements if used within the natural environment.

Pain Behavior Checklists

The University of Alabama-Birmingham Pain Behavior Scale (PBS) is a checklist containing 10 pain behaviors (e.g., grimaces, downtime, medication use) rated on a 3-point scale (Richards, Nepomuceno, Riles, and Suer, 1982). It has shown impressive interrater reliability (.95; Richards et al., 1982), with results being logically associated to estimates of pain intensity (MPQ) and MMPI findings (Feuerstein, Greenwald, Gamache, Papciak, & Cook, 1985). Feuerstein et al. (1985) modified and validated the PBS for outpatient use. Although this scale appears to possess good psychometric qualities there is little information about its utility in relation to clinical outcomes.

Self-monitoring scales are used for continuing assessment within clinical programs for pain management (Fordyce, 1976). There is no widely used, standard format, although amounts of time spent sitting, standing, or reclining are usually tracked. This information might be augmented by self-reports of pain intensity, medication usage, or performance of specified exercises. The validity of patient diaries is naturally subject to question, and some studies have verified discrepancies between patient reports and observational data (Chapman & Brena, 1990; Kremer, Block, & Gaylor, 1981; Sanders, 1983). Some evidence suggests that this problem may be remedied if patients are given sufficient prior instruction about how to use diary methods (Follick, Ahern, & Laser-Wolston, 1984). The prospect of self-report bias argues against relying extensively on self-monitoring except in relation to other behavioral data.

Disability Questionnaires

The Functional Assessment Screening Questionnaire (FASQ) was initially developed to assess functioning among medical patients with moderate disability, although its value in evaluating pain-related disability has been demonstrated in a sample of 158 patients with chronic pain (Millard, 1989). It obtains an ordinal rating of how much difficulty is encountered when performing 15 signal activities (e.g., "doing grocery shopping," "cutting your toenails"). These activities are rated for level of difficulty on a 5-point scale for each item. Split-half estimates ($r = .84$) and interrater responses ($r = .71$, between 29 patients and their spouses) have indicated adequate reliability coefficients. Scores on the FASQ have differentiated individuals on the basis of employment status and type of pain complaint. Findings have been minimally related to psychological variables as indicated by MMPI scales, except for those containing numerous somatic items (Millard, 1989). It seems to possess a general factor structure that distinguishes obligatory from discretionary activities. In comparison with results for similar disability questionnaires, FASQ results seem to be minimally contaminated by cognitive–affective variables (Millard & Jones, 1991). It also offers the potential advantage of permitting communication across different rehabilitation populations, because the content is not limited to pain. Research is being conducted to examine the sensitivity of FASQ results to treatment-related changes and to examine how results correlate with direct behavioral observation methods.

The Sickness Impact Profile (SIP) is a behaviorally based checklist of 136 yes/no items grouped into 12 categories (e.g., Home Management, Mobility, Alertness Behavior). Scores are calculated for three dimensions of "impairment" (Physical, Psychosocial, and Other), reflecting the behavioral impact of sickness. The SIP has been used in large studies across multiple health complaints, including pain (Smith, Follick, Ahern, & Adams, 1986). Follick, Smith, and Ahern (1985) used the SIP to examine 107 patients with chronic low back pain and found that results on the physical dimension were significantly correlated with activity level, and psychosocial scores were significantly correlated with measures of distress. The total SIP score can be rather highly associated with depression ($r = .60$; Beck Depression Inventory; Watt-Watson & Graydon, 1989). Its sensitivity to treatment changes for clients with moderate disabilities has also been questioned (Turner, Clancy, McQuade, & Cardenas, 1990). In order to provide a more focused evaluation of disability from low back pain, 24 salient items have been culled from the SIP to create the Roland Disability Questionnaire (DQ; Roland & Morris, 1983). When studied for acute pain, these items correlated adequately with the full-scale SIP ($r = .85$), were sensitive to treatment changes, and correlated moderately ($r = .42$) to pain intensity and spinal flexion (Deyo, 1986). In a sample of patients with chronic pain complaints, this shorter scale also correlated favorably with the SIP Physical scale ($.82 < r < .91$; Jensen, Strom, Turner, & Romano, 1992). Findings on the DQ demonstrate concurrent validity with other disability questionnaires (Millard & Jones, 1991), although its clinical applications are limited to back pain.

The Chronic Disability Index (CDI) is a short (9-item) yes/no checklist that constitutes one part of a combined method for assessing disability and impairment. It contains inquiries about nine general activities (e.g., walking, sleeping, putting on footwear) that have been identified as common areas of difficulty due to back pain (Waddell, Main, Morris, Di Paola, & Gray, 1984). It assesses disability within an integrative model that links impairment, pain intensity, and psychological distress. Adequate inter-rater reliability was established in interviews of 30 patients ($.90 > r > .73$). Satisfactory intercorrelation among the constituent items also suggested that the CDI assesses disability as a single construct. Up to 480 patients were included in a comparison of results from the CDI and its associated impairment index. These findings indicated that information about physical impairment was able to explain 46% of variance in scores on the CDI. Findings have also overlapped with, but have been distinguishable from, reports of psychological distress. This is a brief and practical scale that can be easily repeated, although the content is limited to back pain.

The Chronic Illness Problem Inventory (CIPI) was developed to provide a problem-oriented record for chronic illnesses, using a format employed for a comparable inventory among patients with cancer (Kames, Naliboff, Heinrich, & Schag, 1984). It provides a broad-based estimate of disability: physical limitations, psychosocial functioning, health care behavior, and marital adjustment are all sampled. Evaluators who are primarily interested in self-reported physical limitations may be deterred by the inclusion of psychosocial variables. Although the CIPI was intended for various chronic illness groups, the original sample consisted of 115 respondents at a pain treatment facility. Items are grouped into 18 categories reflecting diverse areas of functioning (e.g., finances, appearance) with responses given on a 5-point scale. High internal consistency (for the 18 categories, mean $\alpha = .85$) and test–retest reliability over a 1-week interval ($r = .87$) were reported. Comparison to other chronic illness groups (38 obese patients and 15 chronic obstructive pulmonary disease patients) indicated the poorest functioning among patients with pain complaints (Kames et al., 1984). The ability to distinguish between these groups was construed as evidence of the measure's validity. Total scores on the CIPI and the SIP showed high intercorrelation in one prospective study of 95 patients with chronic back pain, and demonstrated similar associations to pain behaviors and MPQ-PRI scores (Romano, Turner, & Jensen, 1992).

The Oswestry Questionnaire (OQ) is a brief scale that provides a percentage score to reflect level of functioning among individuals receiving physical therapy. Items refer to activities of daily living that might be disrupted by low back pain (e.g., lifting, standing, sexual activity, sleeping), rated for difficulty on a 6-point scale. Pain intensity is also measured as one of the 10 items. The OQ has been shown to possess high test–retest reliability ($r = .99$) when comparing responses by 22 patients who completed the scale twice over a 24 hour interval. Items were found to be closely related to one another, suggesting good internal consistency. Scores are sensitive to changes following treatment as well (Fairbank,

Couper, Davies, & O'Brien, 1980). The OQ was initially developed for acute low back pain, yet it has been applied to evaluate chronic back pain as well. Some research has shown close correspondence between OQ scores and the degree of relaxation in back muscles during flexion (Triano & Schultz, 1987). Hazzard et al. (1989) used the scale to document clinical outcomes in an occupational rehabilitation program and found that it distinguished employed from unemployed patients at 1 year following treatment.

The Pain Disability Index (PDI) is an analog rating of function across seven content areas: family/home responsibilities, recreation, social activity, occupation, sexual behavior, self-care, and life-support activity (Tait, Pollard, Margolis, Duckro, & Krause, 1987). An alpha coefficient of .86 has been reported among a sample of 401 respondents (Tait, Chibnall, & Krause, 1990), reflecting high internal consistency. The seven items of the PDI have been found to constitute two factors (Tait et al., 1987) that reflect either obligatory activities (i.e., life support and self-care) or discretionary activities (e.g., occupation, sexual behavior). Good internal consistency has been demonstrated within these factors (.70 for the obligatory activities and .85 for the discretionary activities). Test–retest reliability has been reported for 46 patients who completed the PDI at a 2-month interval while awaiting inpatient pain treatment. Given that changes in disability were not anticipated, this revealed relatively poor consistency ($r = .44$). The validity of the PDI has been supported in various ways, including comparisons of patients with high versus low disabilities, patient versus nurse ratings, and age and sex differences. Gronblad et al. (1993) report that OQ findings were highly correlated ($r = .83$) with PDI results in patients with back pain. Its 11-point analog scaling is comparable to common methods for assessing pain intensity, and this may become confounded with similarly scaled reports of pain (Millard & Jones, 1991). Other potential drawbacks of this instrument are the lack of information concerning specific activities and its wording, which makes it difficult to portray disability that occurs with impairments other than pain.

Summary

Although all behavioral assessment of pain broadly evaluates activity patterns, there are very different ways to obtain this information, ranging from direct behavioral observation to self-monitoring and checklist methods. There has been little consideration of the relative merits of these different approaches, particularly in terms of their value for documenting treatment outcomes. Financial sponsors are typically interested in pain behavior (as opposed to mood or pain intensity), because it equates most closely to functional restoration. As the costs and benefits of rehabilitation programs for pain begin to be more closely examined, it seems likely that behavioral measurement methods will become increasingly refined, with particular emphasis on their sensitivity to enduring treatment-related changes.

Cognitive–Affective Assessment

Thoughts, beliefs, attitudes, self-statements, and expectancies are all examples of cognition that have been assessed in relation to pain. These areas overlap closely with mood variables (Turk & Rudy, 1992). There are pervasive difficulties in distinguishing topics of assessment, with considerable risk of confounded measurement. Models of stress and coping have served, often implicitly, as a basis of much research on pain-related cognition (Lazarus & Folkman, 1984). Coping, however, comprises cognition, behavior, and adaptational outcomes, so the assessor must take care not to mix these different dimensions (Jensen, Turner, Romano, & Karoly, 1991). Beliefs that serve as the basis of coping efforts may be considered as a second area of cognitive assessment, and clinical management of chronic pain frequently consists of efforts to change these interpretations and meanings. Many of these instruments emphasize beliefs of perceived threat and controllability of pain. Symptom perception and affect are two other areas that have been separately considered in evaluations of pain.

Coping

The Coping Strategies Questionnaire (CSQ Rosenstiel & Keefe, 1983) contains eight subscales of 6 items apiece, intended to measure diverse coping strategies such as "diverting attention," "catastrophizing," "pain behaviors," and "reinterpreting pain sensations." These rationally derived scales have proven difficult to identify when using factor analytic procedures (Lawson, Reesor, Keefe, & Turner, 1990; Spinhoven, Ter Kuile, Linssen, & Gazendam, 1989), and there are mixed findings concerning the validity of these factors in relation to clinical variables (such as pain intensity and psychological functioning; see Jensen et al., 1991). A Helplessness factor has been shown to explain large amounts of variance in global distress (50%) and depression (45%; Keefe, Crisson, Urban, & Williams, 1990) in one sample of 72 patients with chronic back pain.

Perhaps the most useful subscale is Catastrophizing, which might be more appropriately classified as a belief or an affective variable than a form of coping (Sullivan & D'Eon, 1990; Turk & Rudy, 1992). Its six items reflect negative outcome expectancies associated with the experience of pain. Catastrophizing is a coherent subscale of the CSQ (α = .78; Rosenstiel & Keefe 1983) and is negatively correlated with favorable treatment outcomes for chronic pain (Spinhoven & Linssen, 1991; Turner & Clancy, 1986).

The Vanderbilt Pain Management Inventory (Brown & Nicassio, 1987) contains 18 items reflecting either passive (e.g., "restricting activities," "depending on others") or active (e.g., "engaging in physical exercise," "distracting attention") coping efforts. Factor analysis was originally conducted on a sample of 259 patients with rheumatoid arthritis (RA) and confirmed with another sample of 101 patients with RA (Brown & Nicassio, 1987). Its validity is bolstered by prospective evidence of inverse relationships between active coping and functional status as portrayed by the Arthritis Impact Measurement Scales, as well as direct relationships between depression and passive coping (Brown, Nicassio, & Wallston, 1989).

A transactional model of stress and coping (Lazarus & Folkman, 1986) was used to develop the Ways of Coping Checklist (WCCL; Vitaliano, Russo, Carr, Maiuro, & Becker, 1985), which consists of 55 items that distinguish problem-focused from emotion-focused coping (for further discussion, see chapter 3). A number of studies conducted with patients with RA have indicated that various emotion-focused coping strategies (such as wishful thinking and self-blame) are positively associated with distress (Manne & Zautra, 1990; Parker, McCrae, Smarr, Beck, & Frank, 1988; Revenson & Felton, 1989). Buckelew et al. (1990) found that WCCL subscales were logically associated with pain beliefs. They identified some sex differences with this checklist in a sample of 160 patients with chronic pain. Turner, Clancy, and Vitaliano (1987) used the WCCL in examining responses to a nonpain stressor among 37 subjects with chronic low back pain. This is one of few studies that explicitly examined cognitive appraisal items from the WCCL.

Beliefs and Attitudes

Locus of control is the subject of a number of pain-specific instruments for measuring patient beliefs. Questionnaires such as the Multidimensional Health Locus of Control scale (MHLC; Wallston, Wallston, & DeVellis,

1978) are attempts to describe perceived control in terms of expectancies about sources of reinforcement. For example, Buckelew et al. (1990) used the MHLC to identify gender-related differences in locus of control beliefs among patients with chronic pain. The Pain Locus of Control scale (PLOC) was adapted from the multidimensional Health Locus of Control scale (Wallston et al., 1978) to provide a pain-specific measurement of patient beliefs. The word *pain* is substituted for *health* within questions. This 18-item questionnaire identifies beliefs about the locus of control of reinforcement. These are internal locus of control and external locus of control as portrayed by a belief in the influence of powerful others and a belief in the influence of chance. Toomey, Mann, Abashian, and Thompson-Pope (1991) have reported on its reliability and validity in relation to pain and disability and Crisson and Keefe (1988) have described how locus of control is logically associated with usage of coping strategies by patients with chronic pain. There is evidence that PLOC findings may be useful in predicting pain treatment outcomes (e.g., Lipchik, Milles, & Covington, 1993). Main and Waddell (1991) have also devised a pain locus of control scale that reportedly exhibits greater internal consistency and may be useful in predicting treatment response.

Lefebvre (1981) devised the Cognitive Errors Questionnaire (CEQ) to specify cognitive distortions akin to those described in Beck, Rush, Shaw, & Emery's (1979) cognitive therapy model of depression. It is composed of 24 vignettes from which respondents might demonstrate errors in the form of catastrophizing, overgeneralization, personalization, or selective abstraction. The situations that are depicted in the vignettes concern potentially upsetting events that involve pain or routine activities. Commonalities have been observed in the kinds of cognitive errors made both by depressed patients and patients with low back pain (Smith et al., 1986). Cognitive distortions measured by the CEQ, notably overgeneralization, were shown to be important predictors of disability (SIP) status even when controlling for pain and mood (Lefebvre, 1981; Smith et al., 1986). The CEQ has also been used to identify how cognitive distortions are related to both disability (Health Assessment Questionnaire) and distress among patients with RA (Smith, Peck, Milano, & Ward, 1988). Within regression models, CEQ findings accounted for significant amounts of variance in self-reported and interviewer-rated depression but not in disability, once disease severity was controlled in the analysis. While potentially useful in the context of treatment efforts that emphasize cognitive therapy, the CEQ has not been widely used and the vignette format may be cumbersome (DeGood & Shutty, 1992).

The Pain and Impairment Rating Scale (PAIRS) was specifically devised to evaluate patient beliefs that pain necessarily results in diminished functional status (Riley, Ahern, & Follick, 1988). Sample items include "Most people expect too much of me, given my chronic pain" and "I should have the same benefits as the handicapped because of my chronic pain problems." Riley reports good internal consistency (Cronbach's α = .82) and coherent association with SIP findings in the derivational sample of 56 patients with chronic pain. Findings on the PAIRS have been found to be distinguishable from affective variables and consistent over time (Slater, Hall, Atkinson, & Garfin, 1991). Rainville, Ahern, and Phalen (1993) prospectively examined the predictive utility of PAIRS scores among 72 patients with back pain who entered a rehabilitation program. Scores were not useful in identifying who would quit the program, but pain beliefs, as measured by the PAIRS, did change during treatment.

Flor and Turk (1988) developed the Pain Related Control Scale (PRCS) and the Pain Related Self-Statements Scale (PRSS) to examine how pain cognition mediated pain and disability in patients with chronic back pain and RA. The PRCS contains 15 items factor-derived into scales labeled Helplessness and Resourcefulness. These scales were negatively and weakly correlated, with good reliability. They are intended to portray global convictions about pain, whereas the PRSS reflects more situation-specific beliefs. The PRSS contains nine items factor-derived into scales labeled Catastrophizing and Coping. These two scales also demonstrated good reliability and were moderately negatively correlated. In the derivational study, Flor and Turk showed that these scales were more effective at predicting pain or disability than were disease variables (degenerative changes shown by radiologic studies). In a comparative study of cognitive measures, Main and Waddell (1991) reported somewhat poorer reliability for the PRCS/PRSS in comparison to locus of control scales or the CSQ (see discussion above) but were able to replicate the originally identified factor structure. They found a noteworthy overlap between the Catastrophizing factors of the CSQ and the PRSS (r = .69). Although the PRCS and the PRSS summarize recurrent instrumental beliefs in clinical management of chronic pain, there is relatively little information about their relationship to treatment outcome.

The Pain Beliefs and Perceptions Inventory (Williams & Thorn, 1989; PBAPI) distinguishes three factor-derived dimensions of pain beliefs: Self-Blame, Pain as Mysterious, and Beliefs About Duration. The PBAPI contains 16 items and was originally developed with 87 patients with chronic pain at an occupational rehabilitation center. Factor loadings were fairly low, mostly in the .50 to .65 range, with nine of the items loading on the temporal factor. Validity was supported by evidence of coherent associations with a range of salient clinical and outcome variables. Strong, Ashton, and Chant (1992) identified a fourth factor (Acceptance) in a cross-sectional study of 100 patients with back pain. They gave evidence to support the discriminant validity of PBAPI findings in relation to pain intensity and CSQ findings.

Models of self-efficacy (Bandura, 1977) have been extended to evaluate beliefs about performance of specific behaviors, often regarding physical exercise. For example, Dolce, Crocker, Moletteire, and Doleys (1986) followed 63 patients with chronic pain after completing a behavioral management program and found that self-efficacy beliefs were positively and significantly associated with reduced medication usage and improved work status. However these efficacy ratings did not account for meaningful variance in multiple regression analysis, which indicated that pain intensity and mood were potentially more relevant. It is difficult to locate standardized measures based on the self-efficacy construct, with the exception of the Arthritis Self-Efficacy Scale (ASE), a 20-item checklist that asks the patient to rate personal convictions about pain management and functional interference. Findings on this measure have been logically associated with disability and distress, as well as with treatment-related changes in these areas (Lorig, Chastain, Ung, Shoor, & Holman, 1989). Results do not necessarily correspond to treatment-related changes in pain intensity (O'Leary, Shoor, Lorig, & Holman, 1988). The ASE is limited by the fact that it refers specifically to arthritis, and much of its content resembles a disability checklist. The overall importance of evaluating self-efficacy (in comparison with other salient beliefs) is not well understood. It is logical to assume that individuals will engage in coping efforts that they believe they are capable of performing (Jensen et al., 1991).

The Pain Cognition Questionnaire contains 30 items that have been factor-analyzed to identify two positive scales, Distraction/Reassurance and Support/Trust, and two negative scales, Hopelessness and Helplessness (Boston, Pearce, & Richardson, 1990). Hopelessness and Helplessness were positively associated with poorer functioning (in terms of pain, disability, and distress), whereas the positive factors were predictive of better functioning. Factor loadings within scales were relatively low (i.e., .45–.74), and there is little information about the validity of this scale apart from the derivational study. It is unclear whether it affords any particular advantage over alternative questionnaires that evaluate pain beliefs or attitudes.

The Survey of Pain Attitudes is a broad list of statements (Jensen, Karoly, & Huger, 1987) that are endorsed to identify patient beliefs according to six factor-derived dimensions (Pain Control, Solicitude, Medical Cure, Disability, Medication, and Emotion). There are versions containing 35 items and 57 items, reflecting revisions (Jensen & Karoly, 1991). Results on this survey have been associated with health care utilization following pain treatment (Jensen et al., 1991). Strong et al. (1992) mostly replicated the factor structure of the 35-item version and provided evidence of its construct validity in relation to pain intensity and CSQ results.

The Pain Beliefs Questionnaire (PBQ) consists of 20 items that constitute two factors reflecting either Organic or Psychological Beliefs (Edwards, Pearce, Turner-Stokes, & Jones, 1992). Somewhat like the PAIRS, it serves to evaluate patient assumptions concerning the basis of pain-related disability. In a derivational study (Edwards et al., 1992), the PBQ clearly differentiated patients with chronic pain from healthy controls, with results from the Organic Scale being moderately and significantly correlated to MHLC evidence of external locus of control ($.40 < r < .43$). The PBQ is a newer scale and there is little information about its application within other studies.

Symptom Perception

One of the prominent explanations of chronic pain is that patients exhibit unusual vigilance for physiological cues (Barsky & Klerman 1983, Costa & McCrae, 1985a, Millard, Wells, & Thebarge, 1991). Apart from the Modified Somatic Perception Questionnaire (MSPQ), there are few questionnaire methods for measuring symptom perception that have been examined with clinical samples. The MSPQ is basically a symptom checklist with 13 items reflecting autonomic arousal (e.g., "sweating all over," "pain in stomach," "muscles twitching or jumping"). In a large derivational study (Main, 1983), the MSPQ showed noteworthy and significant correlations with MMPI Scale 1 (Hs; $r = .61$), Zung Depression Inventory scores ($r = .54$), and standing EMG readings from the erector spinae muscles ($r = .41$). Most research with the MSPQ has been conducted with back pain, although it is easily used with other clinical populations. It is useful as a general measure of symptom distress, following the assumption that chronic pain patients exhibit generalized, heightened awareness of physiologic cues (Watson & Pennebaker, 1989). Deyo, Walsh, Schoenfeld, and Ramamurthy (1989) covaried MMPI and Zung findings in analyzing MSPQ scores for patients with back pain and found that results were then only weakly correlated with functional or pain outcomes. It may be useful as much for its ability to portray distress over symptoms as for its description of physical symptoms themselves. Main, Wood, Hollis, Spanswick, and Waddell (1992) combined the MSPQ with a modified Zung and Waddell et al.'s (1980) nonorganic signs to produce a classification scheme that was useful in predicting the occurrence of chronic disability among patients with back pain.

Mood and Anxiety

Unless the affective dimension of pain is evaluated with an instrument such as the MPQ, mood is typically recorded using assessment tools that are not specific to pain and that are described elsewhere in this book (see chapters 6 and 10). The Beck Depression Inventory (BDI) is the questionnaire most frequently used for evaluating mood disturbance in relation to pain (e.g., RA: Smith et al., 1988; chronic back pain: Keefe, Crisson, et al., 1990; mixed pain complaints: McCracken, Zayfert, & Gross, 1992; Sullivan & D'Eon, 1990). Williams and Richardson (1993) conducted a principal components analysis of BDI findings among 207 patients with chronic pain and identified three factors, reflecting sadness, self-reproach, and somatic concerns. Not surprisingly, the most frequently endorsed items were those that loaded on the somatic factor. As with other diagnostic schemes for evaluating pain-related depression, the BDI poses risks of forming spurious conclusions about affective disturbance among patients with chronic pain. Scores might become inflated as patients endorse items reflecting difficulties with sleep or physical activities. This can produce the impression that a patient is more depressed than is actually true. Other commonly used instruments with pain samples include the Center for Epidemiologic Studies—Depression scale (e.g., back pain: Naliboff, Cohen, Swanson, Bonebakker, & McArthur, 1985; CES-D), the Zung Depression Inventory (e.g., back pain: Main, 1983; Main et al., 1992), the Profile of Mood States (e.g., RA: Affleck, Tennen, Pfeiffer, & Fifield, 1987) and the State-Trait Anxiety Inventory (e.g., mixed pain complaints: McCracken et al., 1992). The CES-D, for example, distinguishes somatic items from those that refer specifically to mood.

The Fear-Avoidance Beliefs Questionnaire (FABQ) consists of 16 questions that ask about the perceived relationship between pain and disability and the impact of work upon pain. The content is derived in part from the concept of disease conviction, as described by Pilowsky and Spence (1975) in the Illness Behavior Questionnaire. These two factors showed high internal consistency (αs = .88 and .77, respectively) (Waddell, Newton, Henderson, Somerville, & Main, 1993). Beliefs about the impact of work upon pain accounted for large portions of variance in disability (23%) and work loss (26%). An advantage of this questionnaire is that it is based on existing knowledge of disease conviction (Pilowsky & Spence, 1975), avoidance models (Philips, 1987), and Waddell's biopsychosocial descriptions of chronic low back pain (1987). The content, however, is geared exclusively to back pain, and to patients for whom occupational disability is a prominent concern.

The Pain Anxiety Symptoms Scale (PASS) consists of four scales (somatic anxiety, cognitive anxiety, fear, and escape/avoidance) with a total of 53 items that are rated on a 6-point scale of frequency. In a derivational study conducted with 104 heterogenous patients with chronic pain (McCracken et al., 1992), the PASS demonstrated good reliability, both for the total score and constituent scales; was logically associated to pain, distress, and anxiety symptoms; and made a significant and unique contribution in predicting functional status after controlling for pain and distress. There is little additional information about clinical applications for this scale, although it also has the advantage of being consistent with broader explanatory models of avoidant behavioral responses to chronic pain (Philips, 1987).

Summary

An unusual array of constructs have been identified to label pain-related cognition. These terms, including beliefs, attitudes, expectancies, and coping processes, are not well distinguished and may be only remotely or implicitly linked to broader explanatory models. This results in a situation where the evaluator may unwittingly obtain confounded measurements of similar phenomenon (Turk & Rudy, 1992). Catastrophic cognitions, perceived control, and mood states are recurring variables in a number of these questionnaires. Most knowledge of pain-related cognition is derived from correlational cross-sectional research. This offers a rich descriptive base but not much practical guidance for efficiently identifying and modifying salient cognitions within clinical settings.

Comprehensive Inventories

Pain Specific Inventories

The Multidimensional Pain Inventory is a comprehensive assessment protocol devised specifically for patients with chronic pain. It is divided into three parts, intended to evaluate pain intensity and its impact, how others are perceived as responding to the pain, and functional status. In this way it combines salient information about pain intensity, disability, cognition, affective status, and pain behavior or pain as social communication. It was initially developed with 120 patients with chronic pain (mostly male veterans), with factor-derived scales that were validated in relation to other established scales such as the MPQ, MHLC, and State–Trait Anxiety Inventory (Kerns, Turk, & Rudy, 1985). This resulted in 56 items with internal consistency coefficients ranging from .70 to .90. Turk and Rudy (1990b) have subsequently demonstrated how MPI findings can be used to identify three clinically useful kinds of response patterns: dysfunctional, interpersonally distressed, and adaptive copers. Either the entire MPI or portions of it have been used in a number of cross-sectional and outcome investigations (e.g., Flor & Turk, 1988; Romano et al., 1991). Like the CDI, the MPI is linked to a parallel system for measuring impairment. It is intended to serve as part of a multiaxial model (Turk, Rudy, & Stieg, 1988), measuring behavioral–functional and psychosocial domains that are complemented by quantifiable results from the medical or physical examination (Rudy, Turk, Brena, Steig, & Brody, 1990).

The Psychosocial Pain Inventory (PPI) is a structured interview comprising 25 questions that primarily elicit information about pain behavior and beliefs. It serves as a basis for further assessment with other inventories or scales. Items are variously scaled or categorized and weighted (Getto & Heaton, 1985) to produce a score between 0 and 68. Interrater reliability is excellent ($r = .98$). Wade, Dougherty, Hart, Rafii, and Price (1992) used 5 items from this inventory to demonstrate a meaningful relationship between illness behavior, suffering and personality factors (Neuroticism-Extraversion-Introversion; NEO-PI). The utility of the PPI in relation to treatment response has not been described and it seems mostly useful as a method to facilitate objective gathering of clinical information during the initial interview process.

Psychological Inventories

The Minnesota Multiphasic Personality Inventory (MMPI) is undoubtedly the most prevalent standardized inventory used for evaluating patients with pain. Many of the same constraints that are identified in chapter 10 are equally true in using the MMPI to evaluate pain. It is long and laden with confounding somatic content, and the content validity of its scales is open to question. These issues have been acknowledged by Love and

Peck (1987), Naliboff, Cohen, and Yellen (1982), Watson (1982), and others. The problem of somatic content is especially relevant for Scales 1 (*Hs*), 2 (*D*), and 3 (*Hy*), which are frequently elevated among chronic pain samples. Results may ultimately indicate generalized symptom distress, or even common symptoms of physical illness, rather than specific personality variables (Helmes & Reddon, 1993; Watson & Clark, 1984). Subgrouping of profile configurations has been recommended by some (i.e., Bradley & Van der Heide, 1984; Costello, Hulsey, Schoenfeld, & Ramamurthy, 1987; Moore, Armentrout, Parker, & Kivlahan, 1986; Rosen, Grubman, Bevins, & Frymoyer, 1987). Keller and Butcher (1991) advocate using the restandardized MMPI-2, although they also acknowledge that profile subtypes may have limited clinical utility. There have been a number of studies that investigate the relationship between MMPI scores and treatment outcomes (e.g., Guck, Meilman, Skultety, & Poloni, 1988), including surgery (e.g., Turner, Herron, & Weiner, 1986) and multidisciplinary treatment (Strassberg, Reimherr, Ward, Russell, & Cole, 1981), with Scales 1 and 3 being most frequently cited as possible predictors of poor outcomes. Content analysis of subscales is one alternative approach. Fordyce, Bigos, Batti'e, and Fisher (1992), for instance, found that two subscales of Scale 3 (Lassitude/Malaise and Denial of Social Anxiety) were useful in predicting occurrence of back pain complaints among 1,613 factory workers. Judging by its length alone, the MMPI is not among the most efficient means of collecting information. Despite possible psychometric shortcomings, the MMPI has continued to be a popular and familiar inventory in psychological evaluations of pain.

The Millon Behavioral Health Inventory (MBHI) and the Millon Clinical Multiaxial Inventory (MCMI) are also psychological inventories, but unlike the MMPI, they were standardized on a medical rather than mental health population. The MBHI contains 150 items and was specifically designed for evaluating individuals in medical settings. Gatchel, Mayer, Capra, Barnett, and Diamond (1986) used the MBHI within a battery of other questionnaires during a functional restoration program for back pain. They found that the Introversive Style and Emotional Vulnerability scales were predictive of biomechanical changes (i.e., biomechanical measurement of trunk strength using Cybex equipment). Gatchel, Deckel, Weinberg, and Smith (1985) have reported that the MBHI can be useful in predicting response to headache treatment as well. In a series of studies by Bradley and his colleagues (Bradley, Haile, & Jaworski, 1992), the MBHI Gastrointestinal Susceptibility and Somatic Anxiety scales have proven useful in distinguishing individuals with chronic pain from healthy controls and those with benign gastrointestinal diseases. Curiously, the Pain Treatment Responsivity scale has failed to indicate what its name implies (Gatchel et al., 1985, 1986; Sweet, Brewer, Hazlewood, Toye, & Paul, 1985). Uomoto, Turner, and Herron (1988) conducted a head-to-head comparison of the MCMI and MMPI in predicting surgical outcome among 129 patients receiving lumbar laminectomies. They used discriminant analysis and found that the two inventories yielded comparable classification rates (75.8% correctly classified using the MCMI vs. 78.6% using the MMPI). Uomoto et al. recommended that the MMPI may be preferable for these kinds of applications because there is more specific information about its constituent scales (e.g., *Hs, D, L, K*). For additional information on clinical uses of the MCMI, see Chapter 10.

The Symptom Checklist-90 (SCL-90) was developed with psychiatric populations to screen for nine types of disturbances (e.g., depression, interpersonal sensitivity, hostility). Derogatis (1983) provides extensive psychometric data describing this application although the response pattern may vary for chronic pain samples (Buckelew, DeGood, Schwartz, & Kerler, 1986; Shutty, DeGood, & Schwartz, 1986), who selectively endorse somatic aspects of anxiety or depression. Duckro, Margolis, and Tait (1985) compared the MPQ, the MMPI, the SCL-90 and the State–Trait Anxiety Scale in a study of 34 patients with chronic pain. They concluded that the SCL-90 appeared to reflect general distress rather than clearly differentiated disturbances. Jamison, Rock, and Parris (1988) and Butterworth and Deardorff (1987) consequently report separate classification strategies for patients with chronic pain. The scoring and interpretation of the SCL-90 may need to be modified among patients who report numerous physical symptoms.

The NEO Personality Inventory (NEO-PI) was developed by Costa and McCrae (1985b) to measure factors of normal personality functioning. Three of these factors are abbreviated in its title, namely Neuroticism, Extraversion, and Openness to Experience. The stability of these identified traits has been substantiated in large-scale prospective studies, with meaningful associations to the occurrence of health complaints (Costa & McCrae, 1985b; 1987). Wade, Dougherty, Hart, and Cook (1992) compared NEO-PI and MMPI scores among 59 patients with chronic pain and found that although most patients exhibited normal underlying personality structure, neuroticism scores were higher among those who reported on the MMPI that they were emotionally overwhelmed. Affleck, Urrows, Tennen, and Higgins (1992) reported that neuroticism, as measured by the NEO-PI, was among a number of variables that predicted usage of daily coping strategies in a prospective study of 75 individuals with RA. Neuroticism has been linked to pain unpleasantness, but not intensity (Wade, Dougherty, Hart, Rafii, et al., 1992). The neuroticism scale holds promise as an indicator of negative affectivity, a global disposition to experience negative affect that is accompanied by heightened vigilance for physiological sensations (Costa & McCrae, 1985a; Watson & Pennebaker, 1989). It could be a more useful and parsimonious way of evaluating the general distress that is captured by MMPI findings, but more information from clinical settings is necessary to understand how NEO findings are associated to treatment outcomes. For additional information about the NEO, see Chapter 10.

Special Applications

Many psychological assessment methods exist to evaluate other types of pain in addition to conditions that are chronic and nonmalignant. It is not possible to adequately summarize assessment methods for each of the groups. The following is a cursory review of resources that may be pursued for a few of these more specialized applications.

Most of the instruments that have been reviewed in this chapter are appropriate for evaluating patients with headache. Psychological assessment of patients with headache is less oriented toward standardized instruments than tracking symptoms (e.g., intensity, location, duration, frequency) and salient concomitant behaviors (e.g., pacing, medication usage, patterns of relaxation). Headache diaries are an integral component of treatment (Andrasik, 1992), primarily tracking intensity and medication usage. These are subject to the same difficulties that have already been mentioned for self-monitoring pain behavior.

Cancer pain is experienced much like nonmalignant pain (Turk & Fernandez, 1990), with marked psychological influences, yet concurrent disease processes can give rise to somatic complaints that alter assessment procedures (Millard, 1993). The Wisconsin Brief Pain Questionnaire (Daut, Cleeland, & Flanery, 1983) is one widely used screening instrument developed for cancer pain samples. The content is fairly comprehensive, covering pain intensity, beliefs, and disability. It can be supplemented by standardized assessment of mood or affect. In addition to disability, the impact of cancer pain may be considered in terms of quality of life. This represents a separate domain of assessment, reviewed elsewhere (e.g., see Cleeland & Syrjala, 1992).

Pediatric pain is a specialized area that calls for instruments that can accommodate developmental abilities of the child who is being assessed. If necessary, pain intensity may be evaluated using novel symbolic methods (McGrath & Brigham, 1992). Elliott and colleagues (Elliott, Jay, & Woody, 1987) have developed direct behavioral observation methods, suitable for use during painful procedures (i.e., bone marrow aspiration). The Varni-Thompson Pediatric Pain Questionnaire (Varni, Thompson, & Hanson, 1987) was devised to obtain comprehensive information about pain. Although developed for juvenile rheumatoid arthritis, it is acceptable for evaluating other pain complaints. There are three versions that can be completed by children, adolescents, or parents, and it is a potentially useful clinical screening tool.

Pain frequently follows spinal cord injury, and the psychometric utility of most pain instruments is poorly defined with this clinical population. Functional limitations need to be considered in conducting valid assessments (Wegener & Elliott, 1992). Chapters 4, 6, and 10 refer to other concerns with this group in more detail.

The social context of pain can be evaluated in terms of the home setting and work setting. As already reviewed, portions of the MPI inquire about family responses to pain. Bigos et al. (1991) used Work and Family Apgar scales, composed respectively of seven and six items, to consider general satisfaction with these settings in a very large prospective study of back pain complaints among factory workers. Job satisfaction, as portrayed by the Work Apgar, was highly predictive of eventual back injury report. Though considerably longer (90 items), the Work Environment Scale (WES) measures various dimensions of the work environment (relationships, personal growth, system maintenance and change; Moos, 1981b). Along with a companion Family Environment Scale (FES; Moos, 1981a), these scales have distinguished patients with low back pain from healthy controls and have been logically associated with MPQ findings (Feuerstein, Sult, & Houle, 1985). Tota-Faucette, Gil, Williams, Keefe, and Goli (1993) have also used FES scales to predict pain treatment outcome, in combination with cognitive variables, among a sample of 119 inpatients. There is a need to examine the validity of other standardized family assessment methods where a family member experiences chronic pain.

Conclusion and Summary

The evaluator may choose to develop a comprehensive protocol by combining assessment methods from each dimension (including pain intensity and physiological, behavioral, and cognitive−affective dimensions). The content and selection of instruments must necessarily be tailored to the type of pain complaint and the kind of patient with pain. Some assessment methods, such as for pain intensity, can be broadly applied across acute and chronic conditions. Others, notably many questionnaires that evaluate pain-related cognition, are specific for chronic nonmalignant pain. A number of checklists for evaluating pain-related disability are intended only for patients with back pain. The checklist format is frequently more practical to implement than direct physiological or behavioral observations. The evaluator is responsible for being certain that an instrument is appropriate for the temporal features of the pain being evaluated (acute, chronic) and the kind of condition (e.g., back pain, headache, cancer).

There is considerable variability in the quality of available information about reliability and validity for each of the instruments reviewed in this chapter. It is important to compare one's own clinical sample with those being examined in other studies. There may be important differences in terms of chronicity and the extent that the measures are based on patients with concurrent mental disorders. Normative values are often lacking, and more needs to be known about how these many instruments can actually be useful for understanding or enhancing clinical outcomes. The evaluator needs to remain mindful that most findings are derived from a highly selected group of patients, namely those with chronic, nonmalignant pain who have been referred away from primary care settings (Turk & Rudy, 1990a).

One useful way of organizing the assessment of patients with chronic pain is to separately seek information that will describe pain intensity, functional status, and distress. These variables account for three distinguishable and clinically relevant domains of what patients with pain will encounter (Millard, Wells, & Thebarge, 1991). The actual instruments that are selected will vary according to the disease and chronicity. For example, a patient with chronic low back pain might be evaluated using the MPQ (pain intensity), the FASQ (functional status), and the Catastrophizing scale of the CSQ (distress). This approach provides baseline data and can also be readminstered to document outcomes after treatment.

It is increasingly important to formulate psychological assessment protocols so that they will yield evidence that can serve as the basis of prospective comparisons. Purchasers of services (frequently financial sponsors such as workers' compensation agencies) rely on outcome data to make decisions about whether treatment will be made available. Without careful and understandable documentation of a patient's status, the rationale for using psychological methods of pain management may be obscured. As a result, patients gain access to more familiar, but frequently less effective, pharmacological or invasive treatments. Behavioral and cognitive behavioral approaches are effective in managing pain, but they may not be offered unless purchasers have access to information about the outcomes. Given that there is such a broad array of potential instruments for evaluating pain, one potentially beneficial line of research would be to describe what minimal set of scales can be constructed to both influence the selection of treatment methods and document outcomes.

Without careful selection of assessment tools, there is a significant risk of conducting redundant measurements. This is particularly true with the explosion of questionnaires that depict pain-related cognition (Jensen et al., 1991), where there is relatively little resolution between one construct and another, and where there may be only implicit linkages to broader explanatory models. As with other rehabilitation topics, one must take care not to confound aspects of chronic disease with psychopathology. There is strong evidence to suggest that this may occur with MMPI results (Naliboff et al., 1982; Watson, 1982), where somatic complaints that accompany chronic illness might be misconstrued as reflecting a personality disorder. In sum, the evaluator must be careful to avoid implementing assessment protocols that obtain unnecessary or biased information.

References

Affleck, G., Tennen, H., Pfeiffer, C., & Fifield, J. (1987). Appraisals of control and predictability in adapting to a chronic disease. *Journal of Personality and Social Psychology, 53*, 273–279.

Affleck, G., Urrows, H., Tennen, H., & Higgins, P. (1992). Daily coping with pain from rheumatoid arthritis: Patterns and correlates. *Pain, 51*, 221–230.

Anderson, K. O., Bradley, L. A., McDaniel, L. K., Young, L. D., Turner, R. A., Agudelo, C. A., Gaby, N. S., Keefe, F. J., Pisko, E. J., Snyder, R. M., & Semble, E. L. (1987). The assessment of pain in rheumatoid arthritis: Disease differentiation and temporal stability of a behavioral observation method. *The Journal of Rheumatology, 14*, 700–704.

Andrasik, F. (1992). Assessment of patients with headache. In D. C. Turk & R. Melzack (Eds.), *Handbook of Pain Assessment* (pp. 344–361). New York: Guilford Press.

Bandura, A. (1977). Self-efficacy: Toward a unifying theory of behavioral change. *Psychological Review, 87*, 191–215.

Barsky, A. J., & Klerman, G. L. (1983). Overview: Hypochondriasis, bodily complaints, and somatic styles. *American Journal of Psychiatry, 140*, 273–283.

Beck, A. T., Rush, A. J., Shaw, B. F., & Emery, G. (1979). *Cognitive therapy of depression*. New York: Guilford Press.

Bigos, S. J., Battie, M. C., Spengler, D. M., Fisher, L. D., Fordyce, W. E., Hansson, T. H., Nachemson, A. L., & Wortley, M. D. (1991). A prospective study of work perceptions and psychosocial factors affecting the report of back injury. *Spine, 16*, 1–6.

Boston, K., Pearce, S. A., & Richardson, P. H. (1990). The Pain Cognition Questionnaire. *Journal of Psychosomatic Research, 34*, 103–109.

Bradley, L. A., Anderson, K. O., Young, L. D., & Williams, T. (1989). Psychological testing. In C. D. Tollison (Ed.), *Handbook of chronic pain management* (pp. 570–591). Baltimore: Williams & Wilkins.

Bradley, L. A., Haile, J. M., & Jaworski, T. M. (1992). Assessment of psychological status using interviews and self-report instruments. In D. C. Turk & R. Melzack (Eds.), *Handbook of pain assessment* (pp. 193–213). New York: Guilford Press.

Bradley, L. A., & Van der Heide, L. H. (1984). Pain-related correlates of MMPI profile subgroups among back pain patients. *Health Psychology, 3*, 157–174.

Brown, G. K., & Nicassio, P. M. (1987). The development of a questionnaire for the assessment of active and passive coping strategies in chronic pain patients. *Pain, 31*, 53–65.

Brown, G. K., Nicassio, P. M., & Wallston, K. A. (1989). Pain, coping strategies, and depression in rheumatoid arthritis. *Journal of Consulting and Clinical Psychology, 57*, 652–657.

Buckelew, S. P., DeGood, D. E., Schwartz, D. P., & Kerler, R. M. (1986). Cognitive and somatic item response patterns of pain patients, psychiatric patients, and hospital employees. *Journal of Clinical Psychology, 42*, 852–860.

Buckelew, S. P., Shutty, M. S., Hewett, J., Landon, T., Morrow, K., & Frank, R. G. (1990). Health locus of control, gender differences and adjustment to persistent pain. *Pain, 42*, 287–294.

Butterworth, J. C., & Deardorff, W. W. (1987). Psychometric profiles of craniomandibular pain patients: Identifying specific subgroups. *Journal of Craniomandibular Practice, 5*, 225–232.

Chapman, S. L., & Brena, S. F. (1990). Patterns of conscious failure to provide accurate self-report data in patients with low back pain. *Clinical Journal of Pain, 6*, 178–190.

Cleeland, C. S., & Syrjala, K. L. (1992). How to assess cancer pain. In D. C. Turk & R. Melzack (Eds.), *Handbook of pain assessment* (pp. 362–387). New York: Guilford Press.

Costa, P. T., & McCrae, R. R. (1985a). Hypochondriasis, neuroticism, and aging. When are somatic complaints unfounded? *American Psychologist, 40*, 19–28.

Costa, P. T., & McCrae, R. R. (1985b). *The NEO Personality Inventory manual.* Odessa, FL: Psychological Assessment Resources.

Costa, P. T., & McCrae, R. R. (1987). Neuroticism, somatic complaints, and disease: Is the bark worse than the bite? *Journal of Personality, 55*, 299–316.

Costello, R. M., Hulsey, T. L., Schoenfeld, L. S., & Ramamurthy, S. (1987). P-A-I-N: A four cluster MMPI typology for chronic pain. *Pain, 30*, 199–210.

Crisson, J. E., & Keefe, F. J. (1988). The relationship of locus of control to pain coping strategies and psychological distress in chronic pain patients. *Pain, 35*, 147–154.

Daut, R. L., Cleeland, C. S., & Flanery, R. C. (1983). Development of the Wisconsin Brief Pain Questionnaire to assess pain in cancer and other diseases. *Pain, 17*, 197–210.

DeGood, D., & Shutty, M. S. (1992). Assessment of pain beliefs, coping, and self-efficacy. In D. C. Turk & R. Melzack (Eds.), *Handbook of pain assessment* (pp. 214–234). New York: Guilford Press.

Derogatis, L. (1983). *The SCL-90R Manual-II: Administration, scoring and procedures.* Baltimore: Clinical Psychometric Research.

Deyo, R. A. (1986). Comparative validity of the sickness impact profile and shorter scales for functional assessment in low-back pain. *Spine, 11*, 951–954.

Deyo, R. A., Walsh, N. E., Schoenfeld, L. S., & Ramamurthy, S. (1989). Studies of the Modified Somatic Perceptions Questionnaire (MSPQ) in patients with back pain: Psychometric and predictive properties. *Spine, 14*, 507–510.

Dolce, J. J., Crocker, M. F., Moletteire, C., & Doleys, D. M. (1986). Exercise quotas, anticipatory concern and self-efficacy expectancies in chronic pain: A preliminary report. *Pain, 24*, 365–372.

Duckro, P. N., Margolis, R. B., & Tait, R. C. (1985). Psychological assessment in chronic pain. *Journal of Clinical Psychology, 41*, 499–504.

Edwards, L. C., Pearce, S. A., Turner-Stokes, L., & Jones, A. (1992). The Pain Beliefs Questionnaire: An investigation of beliefs in the causes and consequences of pain. *Pain, 51*, 267–272.

Elliott, C. H., Jay, S. M., & Woody, P. (1987). An observational scale for measuring children's distress during medical procedures. *Journal of Pediatric Psychology, 12*, 543–551.

Fairbank, J. C., Couper, J., Davies, J. B., & O'Brien, J. P. (1980). The Oswestry low back pain disability questionnaire. *Physiotherapy, 66*, 271–273.

Feuerstein, M., Greenwald, M., Gamache, M. P., Papciak, A. S., & Cook, E. W. (1985). The pain behavior scale modification and validation for outpatient use. *Journal of Psychopathology and Behavioral Assessment, 7*, 301–315.

Feuerstein, M., Sult, S., & Houle, M. (1985). Environmental stressors and chronic low back pain: Life events, family, and work environment. *Pain, 22*, 295–307.

Fischer, A. A. (1988). Documentation of myofascial trigger points. *Archives of Physical Medicine and Rehabilitation, 69*, 286–291.

Flor, H., Birbaumer, N., Schulte, W., & Roos, R. (1991). Stress-related electromyographic response in patients with chronic temporomandibular pain. *Pain, 46*, 145–152.

Flor, H., Miltner, W., & Birbaumer, N. (1992). Psychophysical recording methods. In D. C. Turk & R. Melzack (Eds.), *Handbook of pain assessment* (pp. 169–192). New York: Guilford Press.

Flor, H., & Turk, D. C. (1988). Chronic back pain and rheumatoid arthritis: Predicting pain and disability from cognitive variables. *Journal of Behavioral Medicine, 11*, 251–265.

Flor, H., Turk, D. C., & Birbaumer, N. (1985). Assessment of stress-related psychophysiological reactions in chronic back pain patients. *Journal of Consulting and Clinical Psychology, 53*, 354–364.

Follick, M. J., Ahern, D. K., & Aberger E. W. (1985). Development of an audiovisual taxonomy of pain behavior: Reliability and discriminant validity. *Health Psychology, 4*, 555–568.

Follick, M. J., Ahern, D. K., & Laser-Wolston, N. (1984). Evaluation of a daily activity diary for chronic pain patients. *Pain, 19*, 373–382.

Follick, M. J., Ahern, D. K., Laser-Wolston, N., Adams, A. E., & Molloy, A. J. (1985). Chronic pain: Electromechanical recording device for measuring patients activity patterns. *Archives of Physical Medicine and Rehabilitation, 66*, 75–79.

Follick, M. J., Smith, T. W., & Ahern, D. K. (1985). The sickness impact profile: A global measure of disability in chronic low back pain. *Pain, 21*, 67–76.

Fordyce, W. E. (1976). *Behavioral methods for chronic pain and illness*. St. Louis: Mosby.

Fordyce, W. E., Bigos, S. J., Batti'e, M. C., & Fisher, L. D. (1992). MMPI scale 3 as a predictor of back injury report: What does it tell us? *Clinical Journal of Pain, 8*, 222–226.

Freedman, R. R. (1991). Physiological mechanisms of temperature biofeedback. *Biofeedback and Self-Regulation, 16*, 95–115.

Gatchel, R. J., Deckel, A. W., Weinberg, N., & Smith, J. E. (1985). Utility of the Millon Behavioral Health Inventory in study of chronic headaches. *Headache, 25,* 49–54.

Gatchel, R. J., Mayer, T. G., Capra, P., Barnett, J., & Diamond, P. (1986). Millon Behavioral Health Inventory: Its utility in predicting physical function in patients with low back pain. *Archives of Physical Medicine and Rehabilitation, 67,* 878–882.

Getto, C. J., & Heaton, R. K. (1985). *Psychosocial Pain Inventory: Manual.* Odessa, FL: Psychological Assessment Resources.

Gracely, R. H., & Kwilosz, D. M. (1988). The Descriptor Differential Scale: Applying psychophysical principles to clinical pain assessment. *Pain, 35,* 279–288.

Greenough, C. G., & Fraser, R. D. (1991). Comparison of eight psychometric instruments in unselected patients with back pain. *Spine, 16,* 1068–1074.

Gronblad, M., Hupli, M., Wennerstrand, P., Jarvinen, E., Lukinmaa, Kouri, J. P., & Karaharju, E. O. (1993). Intercorrelation and test–retest reliability of the Pain Disability Index (PDI) and the Oswestry Disability Questionnaire (ODQ) and their correlation with pain intensity in low back pain patients. *Clinical Journal of Pain, 9,* 189–195.

Guck, T. P., Meilman, P. W., Skultety, F. M., & Poloni, L. D. (1988). Pain–Minnesota Multiphasic Personality Inventory (MMPI) subgroups: Evaluation of long-term treatment outcome. *Journal of Behavioral Medicine, 11,* 159–169.

Harper, A. C., Harper, D. A., Lambert, L. J., Andrews, H. B., Lo, S. K., Ross, F. M., & Straker, L. M. (1992). Symptoms of impairment, disability and handicap in low back pain: A taxonomy. *Pain, 50,* 189–195.

Hazzard, R. G., Fenwick, J. W., Kalisch, S. M., Redmond, J., Reeves, V., Reid, S., & Frymoyer, J. W. (1989). Functional restoration with behavioral support. A one-year prospective study of patients with chronic low-back pain. *Spine, 14,* 147–161.

Headley, B. (1987). Historical perspective of causalgia. Management of sympathetically maintained pain. *Physical Therapy, 67,* 1370–1374.

Helmes, E., & Reddon, J. R. (1993). A perspective on developments in assessing psychopathology: A critical review of the MMPI and MMPI-2. *Psychological Bulletin, 113,* 453–471.

Jamison, R. N., Rock, D. L., & Parris, W. C. (1988). Empirically derived Symptom Checklist 90 subgroups of chronic pain patients: A cluster analysis. *Journal of Behavioral Medicine, 11,* 147–158.

Jensen, K., Anderson, H. O., Olesen, J., & Lindblom, U. (1986). Pressure-pain threshold in human temporal region: Evaluation of a new pressure algometer. *Pain, 25,* 313–323.

Jensen, M. P., & Karoly, P. (1991). Control beliefs, coping efforts, and adjustment to chronic pain. *Journal of Consulting and Clinical Psychology, 59,* 431–438.

Jensen, M. P., & Karoly, P. (1992). Self-report scales and procedures for assessing pain in adults. In D. C. Turk & R. Melzack (Eds.), *Handbook of pain assessment* (pp. 135–151). New York: Guilford Press.

Jensen, M. P., Karoly, P., & Braver, S. (1986). The measurement of clinical pain intensity: A comparison of six methods. *Pain, 27,* 117–126.

Jensen, M. P., Karoly, P., & Huger, R. (1987). The development and preliminary validation of an instrument to assess patients' attitudes toward pain. *Journal of Psychosomatic Research, 31,* 393–400.

Jensen, M. P., Strom, S. E., Turner, J. A., & Romano, J. M. (1992). Validity of the Sickness Impact Profile Roland scale as a measure of dysfunction in chronic pain patients. *Pain, 50,* 157–162.

Jensen, M. P., Turner, J. A., Romano, J. M., & Karoly, P. (1991). Coping with chronic pain: A critical review of the literature. *Pain*, *47*, 249–283.

Kames, L. D., Naliboff, B. D., Heinrich, R. L., & Schag, C. C. (1984). The Chronic Illness Problem Inventory: Problem-oriented psychosocial assessment of patients with chronic illness. *International Journal of Psychiatry in Medicine*, *14*, 65–75.

Keefe, F. J., & Block, A. (1982). Development of an observation method for assessing pain behavior in chronic low back pain patients. *Behavior Therapy*, *13*, 363–375.

Keefe, F. J., Caldwell, D. S., Queen, K. T., Gil, K. M., Martinez, S., Crisson, J. E., Ogden, W., & Nunley, J. (1987). Osteoarthritic knee pain: A behavioral analysis. *Pain*, *28*, 309–321.

Keefe, F. J., Caldwell, D. S., Williams, D. A., Gil, K. M., Mitchell, D., Robertson, C., Martinez, S., Nunley, J., Beckman, J. C., Crisson, J. E., & Helms, M. (1990). Pain coping skills training in the management of osteoarthritic knee pain: A comparative study. *Behavior Therapy*, *21*, 49–62.

Keefe, F. J., Crisson, J., Urban, B. J., & Williams, D. A. (1990). Analyzing chronic low back pain: The relative contribution of pain coping strategies. *Pain*, *40*, 293–301.

Keefe, F. J., & Hill, R. W. (1985). An objective approach to quantifying pain behavior and gait patterns in low back pain patients. *Pain*, *21*, 153–161.

Keefe, F. J., & Williams, D. A. (1992). Assessment of pain behaviors. In D. C. Turk & R. Melzack (Eds.), *Handbook of pain assessment* (pp. 277–292). New York: Guilford Press.

Keefe, F. J., Schapira, B., Williams, R. B., Brown, C., & Surwit, R. S. (1981). EMG-assisted relaxation training in the management of chronic low back pain. *American Journal of Clinical Biofeedback*, *4*, 93–103.

Keller, L. S., & Butcher, J. N. (1991). *Assessment of chronic pain patients with the MMPI-2*. Minneapolis: University of Minnesota Press.

Kerns, R. D., Turk, D. C., & Rudy, T. E. (1985). The West Haven–Yale multidimensional pain inventory. *Pain*, *23*, 345–356.

Kremer, E., Block, A., & Gaylor, M. (1981). Behavioral approaches to chronic pain: The inaccuracy of self-report measures. *Archives of Physical Medicine and Rehabilitation*, *62*, 188–191.

Lawson, K., Reesor, K. A., Keefe, F. J., & Turner, J. A. (1990). Dimensions of pain-related cognitive coping: Cross-validation of the factor structure of the Coping Strategy Questionnaire. *Pain*, *43*, 195–204.

Lazarus, R. S., & Folkman, S. (1984). *Stress, appraisal, and coping* (p. 25). New York: Springer.

Lefebvre, M. F. (1981). Cognitive distortion in depressed psychiatric and low back pain patients. *Journal of Consulting and Clinical Psychology*, *49*, 517–525.

Lipchik, G. L., Milles, K., & Covington, E. C. (1993). The effects of multidisciplinary pain management treatment on locus of control and pain beliefs in chronic non-terminal pain. *Clinical Journal of Pain*, *9*, 49–57.

Lorig, K., Chastain, R. L., Ung, E., Shoor, S., & Holman, H. R. (1989). Development and evaluation of a scale to measure perceived self-efficacy in people with arthritis. *Arthritis Rheum*, *32*, 37–44.

Love, A. W., & Peck, C. L. (1987). The MMPI and psychological factors in chronic low back pain: A review. *Pain*, *28*, 1–12.

Lowe, N. K., Walker, S. N., & McCallum, R. C. (1991). Confirming the theoretical structure of the McGill Pain Questionnaire in acute clinical pain. *Pain*, *46*, 53–60.

Main, C. (1983). The modified somatic perception questionnaire (MSPQ). *Journal of Psychosomatic Research*, *27*, 503–514.

Main, C. J., & Waddell, G. (1991). A comparison of cognitive measures in low back pain: Statistical structure and clinical validity at initial assessment. *Pain, 46*, 287–298.

Main, C. J., Wood, P. L. R., Hollis, S., Spanswick, C. C., & Waddell, G. (1992). The distress and risk assessment method: A simple patient classification to identify distress and evaluate the risk of poor outcome. *Spine, 17*, 42–52.

Manne, S. L., & Zautra, A. J. (1990). Couples coping with chronic illness: Women with rheumatoid arthritis and their healthy husbands. *Journal of Behavioral Medicine, 13*, 327–342.

Mayer, T. G., Tencer, A. F., Kristoferson, S., & Mooney, V. (1984). Use of noninvasive techniques for quantification of spinal range-of-motion in normal subjects and chronic low-back dysfunction patients. *Spine, 9*, 588–595.

McCracken, L. M., Zayfert, C., & Gross, R. T. (1992). The Pain Anxiety Symptoms Scale: Development and validation of a scale to measure fear of pain. *Pain, 50*, 67–74.

McCulloch, J. A. (1989). Differential diagnosis of low back pain. In C. D. Tollison (Ed.), *Handbook of pain management* (pp. 335–356). Baltimore: Williams & Wilkins.

McDaniel, L. K., Anderson, K. O., Bradley, L. A., Young, L. D., Turner, R. A., Agudelo, C. A., & Keefe, F. J. (1986). Development of an observation method for assessing pain behavior in rheumatoid arthritis patients. *Pain, 24*, 165–184.

McGrath, P. A., & Brigham, M. C. (1992). The assessment of pain in children and adolescents. In D. C. Turk & R. Melzack (Eds.), *Handbook of pain assessment* (pp. 295–314). New York: Guilford Press.

Melzack, R. (1975). The McGill Pain Questionnaire: Major properties and scoring methods. *Pain, 1*, 277–299.

Melzack, R. (1987). The short-form McGill Pain Questionnaire. *Pain, 30*, 191–197.

Melzack, R., & Katz, J. (1992). The McGill Pain Questionnaire: Appraisal and current status. In D. C. Turk & R. Melzack (Eds.), *Handbook of pain assessment* (pp. 152–168). New York: Guilford Press.

Melzack, R., & Torgerson, W. S., (1971). On the language of pain. *Anesthesiology, 34*, 50–59.

Melzack, R., & Wall, P. D. (1965). Pain mechanisms: A new theory. *Science, 150*, 971–979.

Millard, R. W. (1989). The Functional Assessment Screening Questionnaire: Application for evaluating pain-related disability. *Archives of Physical Medicine and Rehabilitation, 70*, 303–307.

Millard, R. W. (1991). A critical review of questionnaires for assessing pain-related disability. *Journal of Occupational Rehabilitation, 1*, 289–302.

Millard, R. W. (1993). Behavioral management of cancer pain. In R. B. Patt (Ed.), *Cancer pain* (pp. 85–97). New York: Lippincott.

Millard, R. W., & Jones, R. H. (1991). Construct validity of practical questionnaires for assessing disability of low back pain. *Spine, 16*, 835–838.

Millard, R. W., Wells, N., & Thebarge, R. W. (1991). A comparison of models describing reports of disability associated with chronic pain. *Clinical Journal of Pain, 7*, 283–291.

Moore, J. E., Armentrout, D. P., Parker, J. C., & Kivlahan, D. R. (1986). Empirically derived pain-patient MMPI subgroups: Prediction of treatment outcome. *Journal of Behavioral Medicine, 9*, 51–62.

Moos, R. H. (1981a). *Family Environment Scale: Manual*. Palo Alto, CA: Consulting Psychologists Press.

Moos, R. H. (1981b). *Work Environment Scale: Manual*. Palo Alto, CA: Consulting Psychologists Press.

Naliboff, B. D., Cohen, M. J., Swanson, G. A., Bonebakker, A. D., & McArthur, D. L. (1985). Comprehensive assessment of chronic low back pain patients and controls: Physical abilities, level of activity, psychological adjustment and pain perception. *Pain*, *23*, 121–134.

Naliboff, B. D., Cohen, M. J., & Yellen, A. N. (1982). Does the MMPI differentiate chronic illness from chronic pain? *Pain*, *13*, 333–341.

O'Leary, A., Shoor, S., Lorig, K., & Holman, H. R. (1988). A cognitive–behavioral treatment for rheumatoid arthritis. *Journal of Rheumatology*, *12*, 527–544.

Olton, D. S., & Noonberg, A. R. (1980). *Biofeedback: Clinical applications in behavioral medicine*. Englewood Cliffs, NJ: Prentice Hall.

Parker, J., McCrae, C., Smarr, K., Beck, N., & Frank, R. (1988). Coping strategies in rheumatoid arthritis. *Journal of Rheumatology*, *15*, 1376–1383.

Pearce, J., & Morley, S. (1989). An experimental investigation of the construct validity of the McGill Pain Questionnaire. *Pain*, *39*, 115–121.

Peek, C. J. (1987). A primer of biofeedback instrumentation. In M. Schwartz (Ed.), *Biofeedback: A practitioner's guide* (pp. 73–127). New York: Guilford Press.

Peters, M., & Schmidt, A. J. (1991). Psychophysiological responses to repeated acute pain stimulation in chronic low back pain patients. *Journal of Psychosomatic Research*, *35*, 59–74.

Philips, H. C. (1987). Avoidance behavior and its role in sustaining chronic pain. *Behaviour Research and Therapy*, *25*, 273–279.

Pilowsky, I., & Spence, N. D. (1975). Patterns of illness behaviour in patients with intractable pain. *Journal of Psychosomatic Research*, *19*, 279–287.

Polatin, P. B., & Mayer, T. G. (1992). Quantification of function in chronic low back pain. In D. C. Turk & R. Melzack (Eds.), *Handbook of pain assessment* (pp. 37–48). New York: Guilford Press.

Price, D. D., Harkins, S. W., & Baker, C. (1987). Sensory-affective relationships among different types of clinical and experimental pain. *Pain*, *28*, 297–307.

Price, D. D., McGrath, P. A., Rafii, R. A., & Buckingham, B. (1983). The validation of visual analogue scales as ratio scale measures for chronic and experimental pain. *Pain*, *17*, 45–56.

Rainville, J., Ahern, D. K., & Phalen, L. (1993). Altering beliefs about pain and impairment in a functionally oriented treatment program for chronic low back pain. *Clinical Journal of Pain*, *9*, 196–201.

Reading, A. E., Everitt, B. S., & Sledmere, C. M. (1982). The McGill Pain Questionnaire: A replication of its construction. *British Journal of Clinical Psychology*, *21*, 339–349.

Reeves, J. L., Jaeger, B., & Graff-Radford, S. B. (1986). Reliability of the pressure algometer as a measure of myofascial trigger point sensitivity. *Pain*, *24*, 313–321.

Revenson, T. A., & Felton, B. J. (1989). Disability and coping as predictors of psychological adjustment to rheumatoid arthritis. *Journal of Consulting and Clinical Psychology*, *57*, 344–348.

Richards, J. S., Nepomuceno, C., Riles, M., & Suer, Z. (1982). Assessing pain behavior: The UAB pain behavior scale. *Pain*, *14*, 393–398.

Riley, J. F., Ahern, D. K., & Follick, M. J. (1988). Chronic pain and functional impairment: Assessing beliefs about their relationship. *Archives of Physical Medicine and Rehabilitation*, *69*, 579–582.

Roland, M., & Morris, R. (1983). A study of the natural history of back pain: Part I. Development of a reliable and sensitive measure of disability in low-back pain. *Spine*, *8*, 141–144.

Romano, J. M., Syrjala, K. L., Levy, R. L., Turner, J. A., Evans, P., & Keefe, F. J. (1988).

Overt pain behaviors: Relationship to patient functioning and treatment outcome. *Behavior Therapy, 19,* 191–201.

Romano, J. M., Turner, J. A., Friedman, L. S., Bulcroft, R. A., Jensen, M. P., & Hops, H. (1991). Observational assessment of chronic pain patient–spouse behavioral interactions. *Behavior Therapy, 22,* 549–567.

Romano, J. M., Turner, J. A., & Jensen, M. P. (1992). The Chronic Illness Problem Inventory as a measure of dysfunction in chronic pain patients. *Pain, 49,* 65–70.

Rosen, J. C., Grubman, J. A., Bevins, T., & Frymoyer, J. W. (1987). Musculoskeletal status and disability of MMPI profile subgroups among patients with low back pain. *Health Psychology, 6,* 581–598.

Rosenstiel, A. K., & Keefe, F. J. (1983). The use of coping strategies in chronic low back pain patients: Relationship to patients characteristics and current adjustment. *Pain, 17,* 33–44.

Rudy, T. E., Turk, D. C., Brena, S. F., Steig, R. L., & Brody, M. C. (1990). Quantification of biomedical findings of chronic pain patients: Development of an index of pathology. *Pain, 42,* 167–182.

Sanders, S. H. (1983). Automated versus self-monitoring of up-time in chronic low-back pain patients: A comparative study. *Pain, 15,* 399–405.

Schmidt, A. J. (1985). Performance level of chronic low back pain patients in different treadmill test conditions. *Journal of Psychosomatic Research, 29,* 639–645.

Scott, J., & Huskisson, E. C. (1976). Graphic representation of pain. *Pain, 2,* 175–184.

Shutty, M. S., DeGood, D. E., & Schwartz, D. P. (1986). Psychological dimensions of distress in chronic pain patients: A factor analytic study of Symptom Checklist-90 responses. *Journal of Consulting and Clinical Psychology, 54,* 836–842.

Slater, M. A., Hall, H. F., Atkinson, J. H., & Garfin, S. R. (1991). Pain and impairment beliefs in chronic low back pain: Validation of the Pain and Impairment Relationship Scale (PAIRS). *Pain, 44,* 51–56.

Smith, T. W., Follick, M. J., Ahern, D. K., & Adams, A. (1986). Cognitive distortions and disability in chronic low back pain. *Cognitive Therapy and Research, 10,* 201–210.

Smith, T. W., Peck, J. R., Milano, R. A., & Ward, J. R. (1988). Cognitive distortion in rheumatoid arthritis: Relation to depression and disability. *Journal of Consulting and Clinical Psychology, 56,* 412–416.

Spinhoven, P., & Linssen, A. C. (1991). Behavioral treatment of chronic low back pain: I. Relation of coping strategy use to outcome. *Pain, 45,* 29–34.

Spinhoven, P., Ter Kuile, M. M., Linssen, A. C., & Gazendam, B. (1989). Pain coping strategies in a Dutch population of chronic low back pain patients. *Pain, 37,* 77–83.

Spratt, K. F., Lehmann, T. R., Weinstein, J. N., & Sayre, H. A. (1990). A new approach to the low back examination: Behavioral assessment of mechanical signs. *Spine, 15,* 96–102.

Strassberg, D. S., Reimherr, F., Ward, M., Russell, S., & Cole, A. (1981). The MMPI and chronic pain. *Journal of Consulting and Clinical Psychology, 49,* 220–226.

Strong, J., Ashton, R., & Chant, D. (1992). The measurement of attitudes towards and beliefs about pain. *Pain, 48,* 227–236.

Sullivan, M. J., & D'Eon, J. L., (1990). Relation between catastrophizing and depression in chronic pain patients. *Journal of Abnormal Psychology, 99,* 260–263.

Susser, M. (1990). Disease, illness, sickness: Impairment, disability and handicap. *Psychological Medicine, 20,* 471–473.

Sweet, J. J., Brewer, S. R., Hazlewood, L. A., Toye, R., & Paul, R. P. (1985). The Millon

Behavioral Health Inventory: Concurrent and predictive validity in a pain treatment center. *Journal of Behavioral Medicine, 8*, 215–226.

Tait, R. C., Chibnall, J. T., & Krause, S. (1990). The pain disability index: Psychometric properties. *Pain, 40*, 171–182.

Tait, R. C., Pollard, C. A., Margolis, R. B., Duckro, P. N., & Krause, S. J. (1987). The pain disability index: Psychometric and validity data. *Archives of Physical Medicine and Rehabilitation, 68*, 438–441.

Toomey, T. C., Mann, J. D., Abashian, S., & Thompson-Pope, S., (1991). Relationship between perceived self-control of pain, pain description and functioning, *Pain, 45*, 129–133.

Tota-Faucette, J. E., Gil, K. M., Williams, D. A., Keefe, F. J., & Goli, V. (1993). Predictors of response to pain management: The role of the family environment and changes in cognitive processes. *Clinical Journal of Pain, 9*, 115–123.

Triano, J. J., & Schultz A. B. (1987). Correlation of objective measure trunk motion and muscle function with low-back disability ratings. *Spine, 12*, 561–565.

Turk, D. C., & Fernandez, E. (1990). On the putative uniqueness of cancer pain: Do psychological principles apply? *Behaviour Research and Therapy, 28*, 1–13.

Turk, D. C., Meichenbaum, D., & Genest, M. (1983). *Pain and behavioral medicine: A cognitive–behavioral perspective.* New York: Guilford Press.

Turk, D. C., & Rudy, T. E. (1990a). Neglected factors in chronic pain treatment outcome studies—referral patterns, failure to enter treatment, and attrition. *Pain, 43*, 7–26.

Turk, D. C., & Rudy, T. E. (1990b). The robustness of an empirically derived taxonomy of chronic pain patients. *Pain, 43*, 27–35.

Turk, D. C., & Rudy, T. E. (1992). Cognitive factors and persistent pain: A glimpse into Pandora's box. *Cognitive Therapy and Research, 16*, 99–122.

Turk, D. C., Rudy, T. E., & Salovey, P. (1985). The McGill Pain Questionnaire reconsidered: Confirming the factor structure and examining appropriate uses. *Pain, 21*, 385–397.

Turk, D. C., Rudy, T. E., & Stieg, R. L. (1988). The disability determination dilemma: Toward a multiaxial solution. *Pain, 34*, 217–229.

Turner, J. A., & Chapman, C. R. (1982). Psychological interventions for chronic pain: A critical review: I. Relaxation training and biofeedback. *Pain, 12*, 1–21.

Turner, J. A., & Clancy, S., (1986). Strategies for coping with chronic low back pain: Relationships to pain and disability. *Pain, 24*, 355–364.

Turner, J. A., Clancy, S., McQuade, K. L., & Cardenas, D. D. (1990). Effectiveness of behavioral therapy for chronic low back pain: A component analysis. *Journal of Consulting and Clinical Psychology, 58*, 573–579.

Turner, J. A., Clancy, S., & Vitaliano, P. P. (1987). Relationships of stress, appraisal, and coping to chronic low back pain. *Behaviour Research and Therapy, 25*, 281–288.

Turner, J. A., Herron, L., & Weiner, P. (1986). Utility of the MMPI pain assessment index in predicting outcome after lumbar surgery. *Journal of Clinical Psychology, 42*, 764–769.

Uomoto, J. M., Turner, J. A., & Herron, L. D. (1988). Use of the MMPI and MCMI in predicting outcome of lumbar laminectomy. *Journal of Clinical Psychology, 44*, 191–197.

Varni, J. W., Thompson, K. L., & Hanson, V. (1987). The Varni/Thompson Pediatric Pain Questionnaire: I. Chronic musculoskeletal pain in juvenile rheumatoid arthritis. *Pain, 28*, 27–38.

Vitaliano, P., Russo, J., Carr, J., Maiuro, R., & Becker, J. (1985). The Ways of Coping

Checklist: Revision and psychometric properties. *Multivariate Behavioral Research*, *20*, 3–26.

Von Korff, M., Deyo, R. A., Cherkin, D., & Barlow, W. (1993). Back pain in primary care. *Spine*, *18*, 855–862.

Waddell, G. M. (1987). A new clinical model for the treatment of low-back pain. *Spine*, *12*, 632–644.

Waddell, G., Main, C. J., Morris, E. W., Di Paola, M., & Gray, I. C., (1984). Chronic low back pain, psychologic distress, and illness behavior. *Spine*, *9*, 209–213.

Waddell, G., McCulloch, J. A., Kummel, E., & Venner, R. M. (1980). Nonorganic physical signs in low-back pain. *Spine*, *5*, 117–125.

Waddell, G., Newton, M., Henderson, I., Somerville, D., & Main, C. J. (1993). A Fear-Avoidance Belief Questionnaire (FABQ) and the role of fear-avoidance beliefs in chronic low back pain and disability. *Pain*, *52*, 157–168.

Waddell, G., Somerville, D., Henderson, I., & Newton, M. (1992). Objective clinical evaluation of physical impairment in chronic low back pain. *Spine*, *17*, 617–628.

Wade, J. B., Dougherty, L. M., Hart, R. P., & Cook, D. B. (1992a). Patterns of normal personality structure among chronic pain patients. *Pain*, *48*, 37–43.

Wade, J. B., Dougherty, L. M., Hart, R. P., Rafii, A., & Price, D. D. (1992b). A canonical correlation analysis of the influence of neuroticism and extraversion on chronic pain, suffering, and pain behavior. *Pain*, *51*, 67–73.

Wallston, K. A., Wallston, B. S., & DeVellis, R. (1978). Development of the Multidimensional Health Locus of Control scale. *Health Education Monographs*, *6*, 160–170.

Watson, D. (1982). Neurotic tendencies among chronic pain patients: An MMPI item analysis. *Pain*, *14*, 365–385.

Watson, D., & Clark, L. A., (1984). Negative affectivity: The disposition to experience aversive emotional states. *Psychological Bulletin*, *96*, 465–490.

Watson, D., & Pennebaker, J. W. (1989). Health complaints, stress, and distress: Exploring the central role of negative affectivity. *Psychological Review*, *96*, 234–254.

Watt-Watson, J. H., & Graydon, J. E. (1989). Sickness impact profile: A measure of dysfunction with chronic pain patients. *Journal of Pain and Symptom Management*, *4*, 152–156.

Wegener, S. T., & Elliott, T. R. (1992). Pain assessment in spinal cord injury. *Clinical Journal of Pain*, *8*, 93–101.

Wickramasekera, I. (1989). Somatizers, the health care system, and collapsing the psychological distance that the somatizer has to travel for help. *Professional Psychology: Research and Practice*, *20*, 105–111.

Wilkie, D. J., Savedra, M. C., Holzemer, W. L., Tesler, M. D., & Paul, S. M. (1990). Use of the McGill Pain Questionnaire to measure pain: A meta-analysis. *Nursing Research*, *39*, 36–41.

Williams, A. D., & Richardson, P. H. (1993). What does the BDI measure in chronic pain? *Pain*, *55*, 259–266.

Williams, D. A., & Thorn, B. E. (1989). An empirical assessment of pain beliefs. *Pain*, *36*, 351–358.

8

Assessment of Family Functioning and Social Support

Thomas A. Novack and Randal J. Gage

To maximize generalization of skills from treatment to the community, family members of those receiving treatment must be involved in rehabilitation. Acknowledgment of the importance of the family in rehabilitation outcome has increased awareness that family members, particularly primary caregivers, are directly affected by the situation. There is ample evidence that family members of individuals with traumatic brain injury experience significant emotional distress and burden associated with the care of the person with injury (Lezak, 1988; Brooks, 1991; Camplair, Kreutzer, and Doherty, 1990). The burden of care may also be excessive for family members of persons with stroke (Tompkins, Schulz, and Rau, 1988; Williams, 1993). It is disconcerting that clinicians are depending on family members to maintain gains made in treatment, and even to promote further recovery, at a time when family members may be ill-equipped emotionally and behaviorally to cope with the situation. Fortunately, there is tentative information to suggest that participation in rehabilitation is beneficial to family members (Novack, Bergquist, Bennett, & Gouvier, 1991; Wells, 1974).

The focus on outcome after rehabilitation and family member distress is only part of the story, however. The characteristics of the family involved in the rehabilitation effort must also be considered. Each family brings to rehabilitation differing styles of communication, ways of dealing with stress, and means of resolving conflict. Although these styles may have a significant influence on the rehabilitation process and on events following hospital discharge, there are few studies examining these issues. Livingston (1987) found that caregiver premorbid psychiatric history was a significant predictor of family member distress after traumatic brain injury. This suggests that coping style, at least on an individual basis, may have a bearing on family response. Focusing on stroke, Evans, Bishop, Matlock, Stranahan, Smith, and Halar (1987) found that family functioning with respect to problem solving, communication, and affective involvement was associated with treatment adherence following discharge from a rehabilitation program. Families that exhibited better communication, problem-solving skills, and emotional responsivity were more likely to follow through with treatment at home. This area of study needs to be explored in much greater depth.

Unfortunately, many rehabilitation psychologists are unfamiliar or uncomfortable with evaluation of family issues and styles, which hampers research and clinical efforts. Many clinicians in a rehabilitation setting are not accustomed to providing formal evaluation of family members and may regard it as intrusive. However, there are several reasons to pursue a formal evaluation. First, a formal evaluation ensures that important areas of family functioning are not overlooked, which is always possible when proceeding solely on the basis of information obtained from interviews. Second, use of standardized evaluation allows comparison to other samples, such as normative data or clinical samples. Third, to the extent that objective evaluation can be used to group families based on particular characteristics, effective treatment can be established and generalized to other settings. This would prevent misapplication of treatment strategies; what works for one family may not work (or may even be detrimental) to another family. Finally, objective tests can be repeated to document change, which may be essential to justify treatment.

To fully understand the use of family assessment measures, we must place them within the context of a broader clinical evaluation. From a conceptual standpoint, family functioning and social support are among many factors (such as psychosocial stressors and intrapersonal factors) that can influence outcome after an illness or injury (Wallander, Varni, Babani, DeHaan, Wilcox, & Banis, 1989). Important issues need to be addressed, such as the family's understanding of the illness or injury leading to rehabilitation, the ability to recognize and use support mechanisms, and the availability of family resources. In many cases addressing these issues will have to be accomplished through interview and observation of the family, which should always supplement objective testing. Attention should also be directed to family functioning prior to the injury and to life cycle issues independent of rehabilitation issues (Rolland, 1994). For instance, trauma, such as in traumatic brain injury and spinal cord injury, often occurs to younger people in the process of developing independence from parents. How the person with injury and the parents react is partly a reflection of how well the family was coping with that stage of the life cycle prior to the injury. DePompei and Zarski (1991) provide an excellent review of how to incorporate such issues into the clinical evaluation of the family.

There are several ways of obtaining an objective evaluation of family functioning to supplement informal observation and interview data. As noted by Bishop and Miller (1988), self-report measures are likely the most widely recognized form of assessment, but interview measures, formal observation, and structured laboratory techniques have also been described in the literature. This chapter provides a review of the most widely used family assessment measures, with a special focus on rehabilitation applications. The need to focus on rehabilitation somewhat limits the discussion, because observation and laboratory measures are highly structured and potentially lengthy. Thus, we focus on self-report and interview measures, which are more likely to be used in a rehabilitation setting. The intention is to provide the reader with basic information about the scales and a brief review of how the scales have been used.

Self-Report Measures

The McMaster Family Assessment Device

The McMaster Family Assessment Device (FAD; Epstein, Baldwin, & Bishop, 1983) is intended to evaluate a broad range of intrafamilial relationship characteristics. The instrument is based on the McMaster Model of Family Functioning (Epstein, Bishop, & Levin, 1978) and provides comprehensive information regarding family problem solving, communication patterns, roles, affective responsiveness, affective involvement, and behavior control. A General Functioning Index indicates the overall level of family functioning. Families may demonstrate relative strengths and weaknesses relative to normative values in the dimensions measured.

The FAD was designed for evaluation of families presenting with a broad range of pathological interactional problems as well as families without such difficulties. The instrument currently includes 60 items that contribute to the six dimension scores and the General Functioning Index. Respondents evaluate each of the 60 statements on a 4-point scale ranging from *strongly agree* to *strongly disagree*. The FAD is administered in a self-report format and may be completed by family members beyond the age of 12 years.

Miller, Bishop, Epstein, and Keitner (1985) reported test—retest reliability coefficients ranging from .66 (Problem Solving) to .76 (Affective Responsiveness) for a 1-week interval derived from 45 people. In a previous study by the developers on the 53-item version of the FAD, Epstein et al. (1983) reported internal consistency coefficients ranging from .72 to .92 for the six dimension indices and the General Functioning Index. In a subsequent study involving a large sample of families with and without medical problems, Kabacoff, Miller, Bishop, Epstein, and Keitner (1990) reported internal consistency coefficients of the 60-item version ranging from .57 for the roles dimension to .86 for the General Functioning Index. Only the roles dimension was associated consistently with inadequate magnitudes of Cronbach's alpha (less than .70). Validity was evaluated by factor analysis, excluding the 12 General Functioning items from the scale, which were significantly correlated with many of the other items. Forty-four of the remaining 48 items loaded significantly on their respective hypothesized factors; however, 12 items loaded on multiple factors, making interpretation somewhat difficult. The model accounted for approximately 37% of the variance. Assessment of validity for the 53-item version (Miller et al., 1985) revealed low to moderate correlations with the Family Adaptability and Cohesion Scale—II and with the Family Unit Inventory in a sample of 45 individuals.

Clinical applications of the FAD in rehabilitation settings have been limited thus far. However, a series of studies have examined family characteristics as measured by the FAD and response to stroke. Bishop, Epstein, Keitner, Miller, and Srinivasan (1986) concluded that older couples in which one person had sustained a stroke at least 1 year earlier evidenced high levels of morale, general health, and family functioning as measured by the FAD. This conclusion must be tempered, however, by the fact that no measures of stroke severity or functional capacity were included in the study, and the sample of 22 people was quite small. A subsequent study (Evans, Bishop, Matlock, Stranahan, & Noonan, 1987) failed to detect significant correlations between variables often associated with stroke outcome (age, time since onset, self-care skills, perceptual neglect, emotional problems, and mental status) and the seven scores obtained from the FAD, as completed by a primary caregiver. Unfortunately, it was not clear if the information was collected at discharge from rehabilitation or at follow-up, which could have an impact on the degree of correlation.

Evans, Bishop, Matlock, Stranahan, Halar, and Noonan (1987) found that the FAD subscales Behavior Control and Affective Response, as evaluated by a primary caregiver for the 3 months preceding the stroke, were associated with rehospitalization during the first year after stroke. Although increased affective response in the family was associated with fewer rehospitalization days, better behavior control (reflecting fewer conflicts in the family) was unexpectedly correlated with increased hospitalization. The reasons for this were unclear. Family problem solving and communictaion were significant predictors of social adjustment for the person with stroke 6 months after onset. Cross-validation studies of this population will be necessary before these findings may be regarded as stable. Evans, Bishop, Matlock, Strahahan, Smith, and Halar (1987) found that problem solving, communication, affective involvement, and general functioning on the FAD were associated with primary caregiver adherence to medical recommendations following discharge from stroke rehabilitation. However, each of the correlations was weak, with no one individually accounting for more than 14.4% of the variance.

Use of the FAD with families (or at least primary caregivers) experiencing traumatic brain injury has been advocated by Zarski, DePompei, and Zook (1988). Poorer general functioning as assessed by the FAD was associated with greater discrepancy between ideal and actual family characteristics as measured by the Family Adaptability and Cohension Evaluation Scale—III (FACES-III). Communication and affective involvement subscales of the FAD significantly discriminated pathological from nonpathological families as defined by the FACES-III, but the specifics of this relationship were not discussed. The authors did not examine any parameters of everyday functioning in the study sample, which weakens any recommendation concerning the suitability of the FAD for a traumatically injured population.

Family Environment Scale

Moos (1974) constructed the Family Environment Scale (FES) to assess a respondent's perceptions of his or her nuclear family system. The FES is made up of 90 statements that are endorsed by the respondent as *true* or *false*. Like the McMaster FAD, the FES is completed by each available family member. Three primary family or systems dimensions are tested: interpersonal relationships among family members, the degree to which personal growth among members is promoted, and strength of systems maintenance. These three primary dimensions are subdivided into 10 subscales. The interpersonal relationships dimension consists of cohesion, expres-

siveness, and conflict. The components of personal growth are independence, achievement orientation, intellectual–cultural orientation, active–
recreational orientation, and the moral–religious emphasis of the family.
System maintenance is made up of family organization and the extent to
which rules and control are characteristic of the family. There are two
forms of the FES. Form R is indicative of the real or actual state of the
family as perceived by its individual members, and Form I reflects the
ideal state.

The total number of items endorsed in the positive direction constitutes the raw scores for each of the 10 subscales. Raw scores are converted to T scores, which may then be plotted on a profile sheet. Moos
and Moos (1981) suggest that examiners select any combination of four
separate scoring methods depending on the clinical questions. An "average family profile" is derived by dividing the total number of items
endorsed by all family members by the number of family members. The
authors also suggest comparing various dyads within the family, (e.g.,
sister–brother, mother–father). Third, T scores from each family member may be plotted on the same profile sheet to highlight areas of convergence and divergence. Last, an examiner may wish to consider the
Family Incongruence Score, which is calculated by dividing the total number of raw score deviations among every dyadic comparison by the total
number of family members. This score is believed to reflect the degree
of congruence among family members.

Moos (1974) published internal consistency estimates for the 10 subscales, which ranged from .61 to .78. Eight-week test–retest reliability
ranged from .68 to .86. A two-factor solution has been substantiated in
several factor analytic studies (Boake & Salmon, 1983; Fowler, 1981;
Fowler, 1982), essentially supporting the originally hypothesized factor
structure. The Cohesion factor focuses on interpersonal relationships
among family members, whereas the Control factor is hypothesized to
reflect the strength of family systems maintenance. However, a small but
consistent effect of response bias due to social desirability (Fowler, 1982)
and demographic characteristics (Boake & Salmon, 1983) may influence
responses to the FES. Specifically cited were number of children in the
family, which was positively correlated with control and negatively correlated with acceptance, and family socioeconomic status, which was positively correlated with the family's extent of involvement in cultural and
recreational activities.

Controversy about the psychometric properties of the FES has arisen
recently. Confirmatory factor analytic studies had been scarce until re-

cently, when Roosa and Beales (1990b) undertook a psychometric investigation of the instrument. Unfortunately, the investigators included only 5 of the 10 subscales in the analyses; the Personal Growth subscales were excluded. A variety of families experiencing stress as well as families without stress were administered the FES. Internal consistency estimates for the entire sample of 385 adults ranged from lows of .46 and .47 for the Expression and Control subscales, respectively, to a high of .71 for the Conflict subscale. Considerable variation of reliability estimates across family types was revealed for each of the 5 subscales examined. In most cases, the estimates were lower than those originally reported by Moos, although inclusion of all test items would have resulted in a more robust study. Also noteworthy is that a significant difference was found between the factor structure uncovered by Roosa and Beales and that originally posited by Moos. Loveland-Cherry, Youngblut, and Leidy (1989) also found low internal consistency, and they found that factor analysis results shifted based on the family members included. Thus, the stability of the FES factor structure has been called into question.

Moos (1990) responded with a legitimate appeal to adjust expectations for high internal consistency estimates in an instrument designed to evaluate a broad array of characteristics and issues. He also called for recognition of the trade-off between empirical and conceptual considerations when constructing and validating a family or systems instrument. Roosa and Beales (1990a) agreed, although they maintained that internal consistency estimates less than .70 indicate problems in scale construction. They also noted (Roosa & Beales, 1990a, 1990b) that including several members from each family in the original analyses probably artificially inflated the Cronbach's alpha coefficients.

Research with the FES has been extensive, with studies focusing on spouses of persons abusing alcohol (Moos, Finney, & Gamble, 1982), individuals with unipolar depression (Billings & Moos, 1985), and others (Billings, Cronkite, & Moos, 1983; Daniels, Moos, Billings, & Miller, 1987; Holahan & Moos, 1987; Moos, Finney, & Chan, 1981). Adequate validity of the FES with medical rehabilitation patients and their families remains to be determined. Scores obtained with this scale should be interpreted cautiously when used for clinical diagnostic purposes in a rehabilitation setting. Like the FAD, the FES is purported to be rooted in family systems theory. Consequently, adequate exposure to family systems theory and practice appears to be a prerequisite to selecting this instrument for administration and proper interpretation.

Family Adaptability and Cohesion Evaluation Scale—III

The three versions of the Family Adaptability and Cohesion Evaluation Scale are based on the Circumplex Model of Marital and Family Systems (Olson, Sprenkle, & Russell, 1979) and evaluate two characteristics of family functioning: cohesion and adaptability. Family cohesion reflects the extent of family member bonding and emotional investment in each other. Levels of cohesion range from disengaged to enmeshed, with two intermediate levels (separated and connected) being viewed as nonpathological. Family adaptability refers to the capacity of a family system to alter roles and exchange positions of authority, as well as the system's inherent body of rules, when either confronted with environmental stressors or traversing family developmental stages. Levels of adaptability, ranging from low to high, include rigid, structured, flexible, and chaotic. Again, the two intermediary levels of the factor are hypothesized to be associated with a heightened degree of family functioning.

In the progressive refinement of the FACES, the number of items has been reduced from the original 96 to the current 20 in the FACES-III. In effect, however, the FACES-III consists of 40 items, with the first 20 being readministered to assess the ideal state of the family. All versions of the FACES have a 5-point Likert scale format ranging from *almost never* to *almost always*. Scoring of cohesion is achieved by subtracting the total raw score for negative items (e.g., "it is hard to tell who does which household chores") from a specified constant. The resulting difference is then added to the sum of the positive items. The same scoring procedure is applied to the items measuring adaptability. Cut-off scores for the four levels of each factor are provided in the manual. The result is plotted on a 4 × 4 grid specifically identifying one of 16 possible combinations (flexibly connected, chaotically disengaged, etc.).

Internal consistency estimates for the items measuring cohesion and adaptability were .77 and .62 (Olson, 1986). Test–retest reliability coefficients for an interval of 4 to 5 weeks were .83 for cohesion and .80 for adaptability. Olson (1986) also indicated that there was "very good evidence" (p. 345) of validity and discriminative utility of the instrument, although specific information supporting these assertions was not reported. Refinement of the FACES has focused on minimizing the correlation between cohesion and adaptability, which stands at .03 for the FACES-III, suggesting that these are independent measures. Additional validation studies of the FACES-III and development of the FACES-IV are currently underway. The FACES-IV will incorporate a bipolar response format that will significantly alter the scoring criteria.

Parameters for use of the FACES-III and FACES-IV with a medical rehabilitation population have yet to be established. Until these instruments have been validated on a rehabilitation population, they should be used cautiously. One study (Zarski et al., 1988) involving families in which one member was head-injured found that dimensions of family satisfaction, which represents the discrepancy between the ideal and actual states of the family, were significantly discriminated by the general family functioning score on the FAD, supporting the validity of the FACES-III. However, the same study failed to support the anticipated curvilinear relationships of cohesion and adaptability, in which high and low scores are presumed to reflect pathology. Disengaged and rigid families obtained significantly lower scores on the FAD than enmeshed and chaotic families, even though these constructs are equated in pathology on the FACES-III. In the absence of evidence associating FACES-III results with everyday family functioning, it is difficult to strongly recommend use of the FACES-III with rehabilition populations based on the results of the Zarski et al. (1988) study. Additional studies examining the psychometric properties and the clinical utility of the FACES in a medical rehabilitation setting are warranted.

Interview Measures

Camberwell Family Interview

The Camberwell Family Interview (CFI) is a semi-structured interview (Brown & Rutter, 1966; Rutter & Brown, 1966; Vaughn & Leff, 1976) designed to unobtrusively elicit and evaluate potentially harmful emotional content and attitudes that a key relative may harbor toward a family member with psychiatric difficulties. It has been used largely to measure the construct of expressed emotion, as reflected by criticism, hostility, and emotional overinvolvement, that has been linked to diminished generalization of treatment gains among people with psychiatric disorders (Fischmann-Havstad & Marston, 1984; Hooley, Orley, & Teasdale, 1986; Hooley & Teasdale, 1989; Leff, 1988; Miklowitz, Goldstein, Nuechterlein, Snyder, & Mintz, 1988; Szmuckler, Berkowitz, Eisler, Leff, & Dare, 1987; Vaughn, 1989; Vaughn & Leff, 1976) as well as women diagnosed with rheumatoid arthritis (Manne & Zautra, 1989). Psychological interventions to reduce expressed emotion in key relatives have been associated with fewer incidents of recidivism among people experiencing schizophrenia (Anderson, Reiss, & Hogarty, 1986; Falloon, Boyd, & McGill, 1984; Hogarty, Anderson, Reiss, Kornblith, Greenwald, Javna, & Madonia, 1986; Leff, Kuipers, Berkowitz, Eberlein-Vries, & Sturgeon, 1982; Tarrier et al., 1988) and mood disorders (Falloon, Hole, Mulroy, Norris, & Pembleton, 1988). Although the utility of the CFI has not been determined in any medical rehabilitation settings, its potential for uncovering antagonistic family relationships that may be detrimental to the maintenance of treatment gains warrants further examination.

The CFI can be completed in about 90 minutes and is audiotaped to facilitate scoring. Key relatives provide information regarding the onset and course of symptoms during the 3-month period preceding hospitalization. Relatives are prompted to discuss the manner in which family functions have been affected by the behavioral changes of the person with psychiatric disorder. Critical remarks made by the relative in reference to the person with the disorder are tabulated by the interviewer. Over-protectiveness, perhaps indicative of enmeshment, is also assessed on a 6-point Likert scale which ranges from *absent* to *extremely high*. Various cut-off scores have been used in different studies, which creates problems for generalization to clinical settings.

Studies of the reliability and validity of the CFI have yielded largely favorable psychometric properties (Bishop & Miller, 1988; Kazarian, 1992), although no studies including a medical rehabilitation patient population have been published. An instrument such as the CFI, which affords the examiner the capacity to interpret in a standardized manner the verbal and nonverbal components of a key relative's attitude toward a person with illness or injury, may provide a valuable index of family functioning. Information gathered by the CFI may also inform the therapist of counterproductive family interaction patterns that may become the focus of therapy. However, the excessive time required to administer and score the CFI is a significant drawback, particularly in a clinical setting.

McMaster Structured Interview for Families

Like the CFI, the McMaster Structured Interview for Families (MCSIF) is a semistructured interview (Bishop & Miller, 1988). The MCSIF is dissimilar to the CFI in that it is a more general and comprehensive measure of family functioning, originally designed as an adjunctive measure to the FAD. The MCSIF provides detailed information regarding the six dimensions of the McMaster Model of Family Functioning (MMFF), which were listed in the discussion of the FAD. The MCSIF examines family functioning in more detail than the FAD. For example, the roles dimension is subdivided into role allocation and role accountability. Each family member's involvement in an assortment of household chores, such as shopping, cleaning, and yard work, is evaluated as to whether the task is done independently, with assistance, or not at all. After each member's level of participation in these chores is identified, follow-up inquiries are conducted. The family is asked if household jobs are flexible and if the family handles such jobs well. The instrument may enable the examiner to identify dysfunctional interaction patterns specific to a particular family, which may then be more readily addressed in therapy. Information derived from the instrument may also be used to generate ratings with the McMaster Clinical Rating Scale (MCCRS). The MCCRS is made up of a 7-point Likert scale that conveys the level of family functioning for each of the six MMFF dimensions. A score of 1 constitutes the lowest level, whereas scores of 5 through 7 are associated with increasingly nonpathological degrees of functioning. Unfortunately, the psychometric properties of the MCSIF and the MCCRS have yet to be adequately evaluated. The MCSIF also requires considerable time to administer and a training period before it can be reliably administered and interpreted. From a clinical standpoint, the MCSIF would be most suitable for evaluation of postrehabilitation functioning. Even then, interpretation of abnormality should be tentative unless supported by other measures or observations. Family functioning with regard to household chores can be imbalanced by illness or injury without the attribution of pathology MCSIF scores might imply.

Standardized Clinical Family Interview

The Standardized Clinical Family Interview (SCFI; Kinston & Loader, 1984) is a semistructured interview measure. The crux of the interview consists of gathering information from all family members on topics such as perceived extent of togetherness, systematic interactional patterns, similarities and dissimilarities among family members, and roles in the family. The entire interview lasts approximately 1 hour. The contents are largely atheoretical; no specific information is sought. The objective is to provide a semicontrolled environment in which family members may comfortably interact in their typical manner. Specific scoring criteria have not been published; however, a preliminary psychometric study (Kinston & Loader, 1986) supports the construct validity of the instrument. The establishment of sound psychometric properties and the validation of the SCFI on a variety of clinical and nonclinical populations remains to be done. Nevertheless, as with other interview formats, the advantage of the SCFI in relation to self-report measures is that it provides a means to unobtrusively observe and evaluate nonverbal as well as verbal components of communication among family members. In some cases, nonverbal communication may be more telling, and thereby heighten diagnostic precision. The SCFI has the flexibility in application to be used clinically, paticularly during the postrehabilitation phase, but its psychometric qualitites must be further defined before it is more than a thorough clinical interview.

In summary, self-report measures and, to a lesser extent, semistructured interview measures potentially provide the most efficient and expeditious identification of potential family problems in a rehabilitation setting. In vivo observation and laboratory assessment techniques have been reported in the literature as well, but they are more suitable for research purposes at this time. Three frequently cited self-report measures include the McMaster Family Assessment Device, the Family Environment Scales, and the Family Adaptability and Cohesion Evaluation Scales. Application of these measures to rehabilitation populations is appropriate, but caution is advised regarding interpretation of scores until the psychometric qualities of these scales are firmly established, particularly with respect to rehabilitation populations. The psychometric properties of the semistructured interview scales are equally uncertain. Use of interview scales should be limited to research or extreme clinical cases in which the time investment is warranted.

Social Support

Two competing hypotheses of social support have predominated in the literature. The buffering hypothesis posits that social support fortifies a person's coping abilities when confronted with an aversive situation (Cassel, 1974) but is otherwise of little consequence. Conversely, the relationship hypothesis holds that supportive relationships are associated with a diminished level of pathology and illness in both stressful and nonstressful situations (Cutrona, 1984). Questions have arisen, however, regarding the consistency of favorable outcomes associated with social support. Rook (1984) suggested that negative social interactions may impinge more intensely upon well-being than positive social interactions. Family members and friends, presumed to provide social support, may be bearers of unpleasant or unsupportive social interactions. As a result, skepticism exists regarding the characterization of the construct of social support as a useful explanatory variable. Coyne and DeLongis (1986) concluded that the construct is an oversimplification and insufficient to explain adaptation to stress.

The literature on social support is broad, but it is limited with reference to rehabilitation after illness or injury. Degree of social support is predictive of physical well-being, depression, and psychosocial functioning among people with spinal cord injury (Elliot, Herrick, Witty, Godshall, & Spruell, 1992; Rintala, Young, Hart, Clearman, & Fuhrer, 1992), although other factors, such as degree of assertiveness and perceived control, may play an interactive role (Elliot, Herrick, Patti, Witty, Godshall, & Spruell, 1991; Schulz & Decker, 1985). Similarly, Suls (1982) suggests that social support may enhance treatment compliance among people with disabilities. In contrast to positive results, there are indications that the beneficial impact of social support may diminish with time in chronic conditions (Brown, Wallston, & Nicassio, 1989; Fontana, Kerns, Rosenberg, & Colonese, 1989) and even that positive support, such as that derived in a marital relationship, may be detrimental to recovery (Turk, Kerns, & Rosenberg, 1992). The most reasonable interpretation of the effects of social support lies in viewing the construct as one of many factors influencing recovery from medical conditions, providing some unique predictive capacity but likely being mediated by other variables, such as depression (Elliott & Shewchuk, in press).

Interpersonal Support Evaluation List

The Interpersonal Support Evaluation List (ISEL; Cohen, Mermelstein, Kamarck, & Hoberman, 1985) is a derivation of social support theory (Cohen & McKay, 1984). It is purported to assess the domain of available social support resources that might be expected to bolster coping capacity when dealing with stressful circumstances. The ISEL is a 40-item inventory (general population form) or 48-item inventory (college student form) evaluating the perceived availability of four types of social support, with 10 items for each subscale. The Tangible Resources subscale focuses on available material support ("If I got stranded ten miles out of town, there is someone I could call to come get me"). The Appraisal subscale measures the perceived availability of a confidant with whom one may discuss problems ("There are very few people I trust to help solve my problems"). The Self-Esteem subscale indicates the perceived availability of companions who share similar capabilities and achievement status ("Most people

I know think highly of me"). Finally, the Belonging subscale evaluates the perceived availability of friends and affiliates, (e.g., "Most people I know don't enjoy the same things that I do"). Raw scores are derived by summing the number of items endorsed in the positive direction.

As part of an extensive series of psychometric evaluations, several studies examining the general population and college students were conducted (Cohen et al., 1985). The ISEL was administered on three separate occasions spanning 6 months. Internal consistency estimate ranges for each subscale were .73 to .81 (Tangible), .70 to .82 (Appraisal), .62 to .73 (Self-Esteem), and .73 to .78 (Belonging). Test–retest reliability coefficients for a 6-month interval were .74 (overall functional support index), .49 (Tangible), .60 (Appraisal), .54 (Self-Esteem), and .68 (Belonging). The low estimates of test–retest reliability were interpreted as evidence that social support changes over time and that the stability of particular types of support may differ across populations. Interscale correlations ranged from .31 to .81, with the modal distribution lying between .50 and .70, suggesting a moderate degree of independence between scales. Based on initial studies, ISEL scores appear to predict depression when the effects of anxiety are controlled, but only weak correlations were found between the ISEL and the Center for Epidemiological Studies Depression Scale. The authors believe that the most significant attribute of the ISEL is its capacity to highlight the types of support that are most beneficial to the preservation or improvement of health and well-being. Since the ISEL offers the potential for examination of a person's extended social network, the scale may provide crucial information about the impact that injury and illness have on that network, and conversely, how these changes affect the person with illness or injury and the nuclear family.

The ISEL is clearly in the early stage of development, but one study with a rehabilitation population has been published that highlights the potential use of the ISEL as well as its pitfalls. Friedland and McColl (1992) evaluated a social support program designed to maximize the quality and quantity of social support networks among individuals during the postacute phase of stroke recovery. A control group was included in the design. The program of 6 to 12 sessions was principally psychoeducational in format. The program focused on improving supportive interactions with members of each person's existing social network and developing novel support linkages when appropriate. The ISEL and the Social Support Inventory for Stroke Survivors (McColl & Friedland, 1989), as well as two scales that assess psychosocial adjustment, were administered at pretreatment, at posttreatment, and at 3-month follow-up. In the end, a significant treatment effect was not found. Perhaps the most compelling explanation for the lack of an effect centers on the questionable sensitivity of these instruments. The ISEL was not constructed for identifying and understanding potential differences between the premorbid social network and that which evolves following onset of illness or injury. Therefore, application of the ISEL in a rehabilitation setting must be veiwed tentatively.

The Inventory of Socially Supportive Behaviors

One of the more widely known measures of social support is the Inventory of Socially Supportive Behaviors (ISSB; Barrera, 1981; see Heitzmann and Kaplan, 1988, for a review). The ISSB is a 40-item inventory containing phrases describing specific supportive behaviors the respondent may have experienced during the preceeding month. The respondent rates the frequency of the occurrence of the supportive behaviors on a 5-point Likert scale ranging from *not at all* to *about every day*. The items include questions about whether someone is available to help in a stressful situation, acknowledges when something is done well, provides transportation when needed, or shares feelings experienced under similar circumstances. To score the ISSB, item totals are summed across six content domains: material aid, physical assistance, intimate interaction, guidance, feedback, and social participation. A total score may also be calculated. Based on a small sample ($n = 71$), internal consistency estimates were acceptable for two separate administrations (coefficient alphas were .93 and .94, respectively). Test–retest reliability for a 2-day interval ranged from .44 to .91 for each of the 40 items. Correlation of the ISSB with the Cohesion subscale of the Family Environment Scale ($r = .36$) was low. Additional validation studies would be beneficial.

Several unique applications of the ISSB to medical issues have been reported recently. Krause (1988) hypothesized that people aged 65 or older who participate in a strong social support system would demonstrate significantly less physician utilization during periods of substantial stress than would adults of a similar age in comparable circumstances who received less social support. It was determined that regardless of the stress experienced, as measured by a life-events checklist, individuals with less social support, particularly informational and tangible support as measured on the ISSB, sought significantly greater physician contact. Other results are not as supportive of the ISSB. Jacobson and Robins (1989) reported that bulimic and nonbulimic young adult females differed neither in self-reported levels of social support received nor with respect to an anticipated interaction between social dependency and lack of social support.

A modified version of the ISSB was administered on three separate occassions (Glass & Maddox, 1992) to 44 individuals during the postacute stage of stroke. The authors expected that ample social support would facilitate the recovery of physical functioning. People with either high or moderate degrees of social support demonstrated progressively improved recovery rates over a 6-month interval, whereas those with low support initially demonstrated spontaneous recovery but then remained stable or, in some cases, regressed. Emotional support strongly predicted recovery of function. Either excessive or insufficient levels of instrumental support were associated with suboptimal recovery rates. Finally, informational support was found to provide significantly greater benefit to persons who had incurred less severe strokes. The authors remained appropriately speculative about the cause of this significant interaction effect, noting that various types of social support may be mediated by different pathways (e.g., cognitive vs. emotional). The findings of the Glass and Maddox (1992) study and others focusing on medical populations provide justification for the continued development and adaptation of the ISSB for rehabilitation populations.

The Beaumont Lifestyle Inventory of Social Support

Recently, Tamler and Perrin (1992) reported on a newly developed social support screening instrument used with a variety of rehabilitation patients for the specific purpose of predicting discharge disposition at the time of hospital admission. Psychometric properties were not reported. The Beaumont Lifestyle Inventory of Social Support (BLISS) was administered by continuing care coordinators to an identified primary caregiver during standard intake interviews. The BLISS poses highly specific questions to determine the willingness and physical capacity of the caregiver and other available family members to provide the patient with assistance in activities of daily living. Willingness and ability to provide constant supervision or hire supplemental skilled assistants are also addressed. The BLISS accurately predicted destination for 87% of the cases, suggesting this instrument is a potentially expedient and valid predictive measure. As with other instruments, further attention to psychometric properties is warranted.

This study has heuristic value that could be beneficial to the design of future studies examining the construct of social support in a rehabilitation population. First, the inventory items were defined objectively, providing the clarity necessary to better understand and convey the type of social support under examination. The type of social support addressed by the BLISS is unique to the special needs of rehabilitation patients who have reached the discharge stage. Second, the authors established an objective and relevant criterion (discharge disposition) with which to evaluate the predictive value of the instrument. Consequently, the rationale for the use of the BLISS in a rehabilitation setting is readily obvious, although application of the scale may be limited by its specificity.

Evaluation of social support may be helpful prior to discharge from rehabilitation. Knowledge of the social network for a family is a necessary component of rehabilitation, but is usually evaluated in an informal manner. Objective measurement, particularly with an established scale such as the ISSB, provides the opportunity to confirm the relationship between social support and long-term rehabilitation outcome that is logically hypothesized by rehabilitiation professionals to exist. The BLISS provides a glimpse of a new generation of social support instruments, which will be very focused and thus more likely to be effective in predicting specific relationships.

Conclusion

A review of family and social support assessment instruments would be incomplete without consideration of potential problems associated with use of the scales. There are reasonable concerns about the validity of evaluating families during rehabilitation, considering this is an atypical and potentially very stressful experience for the family. Developers of family interview devices, for instance, suggest the evaluation take place in a relaxed, normal setting, which does not describe the circumstances of rehabilitation. In addition, the family's interest in evaluation and treatment may be limited during the rehabilitation program, because this may be perceived as diverting time and effort away from the person who is the primary recipient of treatment. A dilemma in providing treatment may also arise when family assessment is introduced into the rehabilitation setting. Conceptualizing the family as the treatment unit is the basis of family systems theory. Consequently, the interventions proposed by the rehabilitation psychologist may be at odds with the traditional role of providing service primarily to the person receiving rehabilitation. Ethical problems could conceivably develop if a rehabilitation therapist extends services beyond the patient to a marital couple or extended family. For example, enhancing family functioning might necessitate decreasing enmeshment or rigidity among family members, which could reduce supportive behaviors directed toward the patient and culminate in a suboptimal rate of recovery, particularly during early phases of recovery (Rolland, 1984). Therapists will need to clearly define who will be benefitted by potential interventions when drawing conclusions based on family assessment instruments.

All of the instruments presented in this chapter have shortcomings. First, with the exception of the BLISS, none of the tests were specifically designed for the purpose of evaluating the effects of rehabilitation, injury, or physical illness on the family. Second, some of the measures, such as the Camberwell Family Interview, require extended periods of time to administer and score. Third, it is unclear how impaired cognition, such as associated with traumatic brain injury or stroke, might affect the validity of the measures. For instance, might the discrepancy between survivors and family members in reporting of deficits following traumatic brain injury (Brooks, 1991) affect the results of a family evaluation? These issues can only be addressed with consistent application—and possible modification—of family assessment measures in rehabilitation settings.

Under present conditions it would be most logical to pursue limited clinical evaluation of family members during inpatient treatment, unless the focus is on alcohol or drug rehabilitation. Utilizing a measure of social support, such as the ISEL, and measures of emotional distress would be sufficient in most cases. If a family has a history of difficulties, a relatively brief measure of family functioning might be obtained during rehabilitation. Of the measures reviewed the strongest is the FAD, since it appears to be a stable instrument and has been utilized in a few rehabilitation studies. In contrast, the FES has not been as stable over time and the FACES-III is presently undergoing revision. Self-report measures of family functioning may be more informative for families with whom there will be continuing contact after discharge. The family interview measures, due to the time and expertise involved, would best be reserved for those situations in which extended family therapy is anticipated.

Existing scales assessing family and social support are strong on construct development, but weaker on construct validation. Concepts such as affectional response, systems maintenance, cohesion, and belonging, to name a few, are theoretically powerful, but the translation to successful everyday family functioning is often obscure. With the exception of the adaptability and cohesion of the FACES-III, the overlap between subscales of the same instrument raises questions about the independence of the measurements. The relationship between scales is inconsistent and may be contrary to theoretically based expectations, as noted in the Zarski et al. (1988) study. Anticipated changes in normal family functioning and social support undermine reliability and further complicate the interpretation of abnormality. More objective definition of constructs, with a focus on everyday family events and behaviors, is necessary if this situation is to be remedied.

Development of unique instruments for the rehabilitation setting, or at least obtaining normative values for existing tests using a rehabilitation population, should be strongly considered. Realistically, new instruments must have the benefit of brevity, allow for multiple administrations across time, and focus on primary caregivers of the person in treatment, who are more likely to be available and to affect the immediate recovery of the person. Of course, the person in treatment, if possible, should also participate in any evaluation examining the family unit. The traditonal focus on assessment of family and social support needs to be expanded to include internal and external factors that could affect rehabilitation and family outcome. Internal factors include level of emotional distress, knowledge base about recovery, locus of control, and past patterns of problem solving. External factors include availability of social support inside and outside the family, financial status, and presence of community programs. The purpose of evaluation is to direct treatment and measure outcome, which has to be monitored closely to justify rehabilitation efforts. It is imperative that those working in rehabilitation settings look to the quality and accuracy of assessment instruments, which will be achieved maximally if instruments are developed specifically for rehabilitation settings.

References

Anderson, C. M., Reiss, D. J., & Hogarty, G. E. (1986). *Schizophrenia in the family: A practitioner's guide to psychoeducation and management.* New York: The Guilford Press.

Barrera, M. (1981). Preliminary development of a scale of social support. *American Journal of Community Psychology, 9,* 435–447.

Billings, A., Cronkite, R., & Moos, R. (1983). Social environmental factors in unipolar depression: Comparisons of depressed patients and nondepressed controls. *Journal of Abnormal Psychology, 92,* 119–133.

Billings, A., & Moos, R. (1985). Psychosocial processes of remission in unipolar depression: Comparing depressed patients with matched community controls. *Journal of Consulting and Clinical Psychology, 53,* 314–325.

Bishop, D. S., Epstein, N. B., Keitner, G. I., Miller, I. W., & Srinivasan, S. V. (1986).

Stroke: Morale, family functioning, health status, and functional capacity. *Archives of Physical Medicine and Rehabilitation*, *67*, 84–87.

Bishop, D. S., & Miller, I. W. (1988). Traumatic brain injury: Empirical family assessment techniques. *Journal of Head Trauma and Rehabilitation*, *3*(4), 16–30.

Boake, C., & Salmon, P. G. (1983). Demographic correlates and factor structure of the Family Environment Scale. *Journal of Clinical Psychology*, *39*(1), 95–100.

Brooks, D. N. (1991). The head-injured family. *Journal of Clinical and Experimental Neuropsychology*, *13*(1), 155–188.

Brown, G. W., & Rutter, M. (1966). The measurement of family activities and relationships: A methodological study. *Human Relations*, *19*, 241–263.

Brown, G. W., Wallston, K., & Nicassio, P. (1989). Social support and depression in rheumatoid arthritis: A one-year prospective study. *Journal of Applied Social Psychology*, *19*, 1164–1181.

Camplair, P. S., Kreutzer, J. S., & Doherty, K. R. (1990). Family outcome following adult traumatic brain injury: A critical review of the literature. In J. S. Kreutzer & P. Wehman (Eds.), *Community integration following traumatic brain injury* (pp. 207–233). Baltimore MD: Brookes.

Cassel, J. (1974). Social science in epidemiology: Psychosocial processes and "stress," theoretical formulation. *International Journal of Health Services*, *4*, 537–549.

Cohen, S., & McKay, G. (1984). Social support, stress and the buffering hypothesis: A theoretical analysis. In A. Baum, S. E. Taylor, & J. E. Singer (Eds.), *Handbook of psychology and health: Social psychological aspects of health* (Vol. 4, pp. 253–267). Hillsdale, NJ: Erlbaum.

Cohen, S., Mermelstein, R., Kamarck, T., & Hoberman, H. M. (1985). Measuring the functional components of social support. In *Social support: Theory, research, and applications*. Boston: Dordrecht.

Coyne, J., & DeLongis, A. (1986). Going beyond social support: The role of relationships in adaptation. *Journal of Consulting and Clinical Psychology*, *54*, 454–460.

Cutrona, C. (1984). Social support and stress in the transition to parenthood. *Journal of Abnormal Psychology*, *93*, 378–390.

Daniels, D., Moos, R., Billings, A., & Miller, J. (1987). Psychosocial risk and resistance factors among children with chronic illness, healthy siblings, and healthy controls. *Journal of Abnormal Child Psychology*, *15*, 295–308.

DePompei, R., & Zarski, J. J. (1991). Assessment of the family. In J. M. Williams & T. Kay (Eds.), *Head injury: A family matter* (pp. 101–120). Baltimore, MD: Brookes.

Elliott, T. R., Herrick, S. M., Patti, A. M., Witty, T. E., Godshall, F. J., & Spruell, M. (1991). Assertiveness, social support, and psychological adjustment following spinal cord injury. *Behaviour Research and Therapy*, *29*, 485–493.

Elliott, T. R., Herrick, S. M., Witty, T. E., Godshall, & Spruell, M. (1992). Social support and depression following spinal cord injury. *Rehabilitation Psychology*, *37*(1), 37–47.

Elliott, T. R., & Shewchuk, R. M. (1995). Social support and leisure activities following severe physical disability: Testing the mediating effects of depression. *Basic and Applied Social Psychology*, *16*(4), 471–487.

Epstein, N. B., Baldwin, L. M., & Bishop, D. S. (1983). The McMaster Family Assessment Device. *Journal of Marriage and Family Therapy*, *9*, 171–180.

Epstein, N. B., Bishop, D. S., & Levin, S. (1978). The McMaster Model of Family Functioning. *Journal of Marriage and Family Counseling*, *4*, 19–31.

Evans, R. L., Bishop, D. S., Matlock, A. L., Stranahan, S., Halar, E. M., Noonan, W. C. (1987). Prestroke family interaction as a predictor of stroke outcome. *Archives of Physical Medicine and Rehabilitation*, *68*, 508–512.

Evans, R. L., Bishop, D. S., Matlock, A. L., Stranahan, S., & Noonan, C. (1987). Predicting poststroke family function: A continuing dilemma. *Psychological Reports*, *60*, 691–695.

Evans, R. L., Bishop, D. S., Matlock, A. L., Stranahan, S., Smith, G., Halar, E. M. (1987). Family interaction and treatment adherence after stroke. *Archives of Physical Medicine and Rehabilitation*, *68*, 513–517.

Falloon, I. R. H., Boyd, J. L., & McGill, C. W. (1984). *Family care of schizophrenia: A problem solving approach to the treatment of mental illness.* New York: Guilford Press.

Falloon, I. R. H., Hole, V., Mulroy, L., Norris, L. J., & Pembleton, T. (1988). Behavioral family therapy. In J. F. Clarkin, G. L. Haas, & I. D. Glick (Eds.), *Affective disorders and the family: Assessment and treatment* (pp. 117–133). New York: Guilford Press.

Fischmann-Havstad, L., & Marston, A. R. (1984). Weight loss maintenance as an aspect of family emotion and process. *British Journal of Clinical Psychology*, *23*, 265–271.

Fontana, A., Kerns, R., Rosenberg, R., & Colonese, K. (1989). Support, stress, and recovery from coronary heart disease: A longitudinal causal model. *Health Psychology*, *8*, 175–193.

Fowler, P. C. (1981). Maximum liklihood factor structure of the Family Environment Scale. *Journal of Clinical Psychology*, *37*, 160–164.

Fowler, P. C. (1982). Factor structure of the Family Environment Scale: Effects of social desirability. *Journal of Clinical Psychology*, *38*(2), 285–292.

Friedland, J. F., & McColl, M. A. (1992). Social support intervention after stroke: Results of a randomized trial. *Archives of Physical Medicine and Rehabilitation*, *73*, 573–581.

Glass, T. A., & Maddox, G. L. (1992). The quality and quantity of social support: Stroke recovery as psycho-social transition. *Social Science Medicine*, *34*, 1249–1261.

Heitzmann, C. A., & Kaplan, R. M. (1988). Assessment of methods for measuring social support. *Health Psychology*, *7*, 75–109.

Hogarty, G. E., Anderson, C. M., Reiss, D. J., Kornblith, S. J., Greenwald, D. P., Javna, C. D., & Madonia, M. J. (1986). Family psychoeducation, social skills training, and maintenance chemotherapy in the aftercare treatment of schizophrenia. *Archives of General Psychiatry*, *43*, 633–642.

Holahan, C. J., & Moos, R. (1987). Risk, resistance, and psychological distress: A longitudinal analysis with adults and children. *Journal of Abnormal Psychology*, *96*, 3–13.

Hooley, J. M., Orley, J., & Teasdale, J. D. (1986). Levels of expressed emotion and relapse in depressed patients. *British Journal of Psychiatry*, *148*, 642–647.

Hooley, J. M., & Teasdale, J. D. (1989). Predictors of relapse in unipolar depressives: Expressed emotion, marital distress, and perceived criticism. *Journal of Abnormal Psychology*, *98*, 229–235.

Jacobson, R., & Robins, C. J. (1989). Social dependency and social support in bulimic and nonbulimic women. *International Journal of Eating Disorders*, *8*, 665–670.

Kabacoff, R. I., Miller, I. W., Bishop, D. S., Epstein, N. B., Keitner, G. I. (1990). A psychometric study of the McMaster Family Assessment Device in psychiatric, medical, and nonclinical samples. *Journal of Family Psychology*, *3*, 431–439.

Kazarian, S. S. (1992). The measurement of expressed emotion: A review. *Canadian Journal of Psychiatry*, *37*, 51–56.

Kinston, W., & Loader, P. (1984). Eliciting whole-family interaction with a standardized clinical interview. *Journal of Family Therapy*, *6*, 347–363.

Kinston, W., & Loader, P. (1986). Preliminary psychometric evaluation of a standardized clinical family interview. *Journal of Family Therapy*, *8*, 351–369.

Krause, N. (1988). Stressful life events and physician utilization. *Journal of Gerontology*, *43*(2), S53–S61.

Leff, J. P. (1988). Expressed emotion in families. In F. Flach (Ed.), *The schizophrenias* (pp. 113–125). New York: Norton.

Leff, J. P., Kuipers, L., Berkowitz, R., Eberlein-Vries, R., & Sturgeon, D. (1982). A controlled trial of social intervention in the families of schizophrenic patients. *British Journal of Psychiatry, 141*, 121–134.

Lezak, M. D. (1988). Brain damage is a family affair. *Journal of Clinical and Experimental Neuropsychology, 10*(1), 111–123.

Livingston, M. G. (1987). Head injury: The relative's response. *Brain Injury, 1*(1), 8–14.

Loveland-Cherry, C. J., Youngblut, J. M., & Kline Leidy, N. W. (1989). A psychometric analysis of the Family Environment Scale. *Nursing Research, 38*(5), 262–266.

Manne, S. L., & Zautra, A. J. (1989). Spouse criticism and support: Their association with coping and psychological adjustment among women with rheumatoid arthritis. *Journal of Personality and Social Psychology, 56*, 608–617.

McColl, M. A., & Friedland, J. F. (1989). Development of a multidimensional index for assessing social support in rehabilitation. *Occupational Therapy Journal of Research, 9*, 218–234.

Miklowitz, D. J., Goldstein, M. J., Nuechterlein, K. H., Snyder, K. S., & Mintz, J. (1988). Family factors and the course of bipolar affective disorder. *Archives of General Psychiatry, 45*, 225–231.

Miller, I. W., Bishop, D. S., Epstein, N. B., & Keitner, G. I. (1985). The McMaster Family Assessment Device: Reliability and validity. *Journal of Marital and Family Therapy, 11*, 345–356.

Moos, R. (1974). *The Family Environment Scale.* Palo Alto, CA: Consulting Psychologists Press.

Moos, R. H. (1990). Conceptual and empirical approaches to developing family-based assessment procedures: Resolving the case of the Family Environment Scale. *Family Process, 29*, 199–208.

Moos, R., Finney, J., & Chan, D. (1981). The process of recovery from alcoholism: I. Comparing alcoholic patients with matched community controls. *Journal of Studies on Alcohol, 42*, 383–402.

Moos, R., & Finney, J., & Gamble, W. (1982). The process of recovery from alcoholism: II. Comparing spouses of alcoholic patients and spouses of matched community controls. *Journal of Studies on Alcohol, 43*, 888–909.

Moos, R., & Moos, B. (1981). *Family Environment Scale Manual.* Palo Alto, CA: Consulting Psychologists Press.

Novack, T. A., Bergquist, T. F., Bennett, G., & Gouvier, W. D. (1991). Primary caregiver distress following severe head injury. *Journal of Head Trauma and Rehabilitation, 6*(4), 69–77.

Olson, D. H. (1986). Circumplex Model VII: Validation studies and FACES III. *Family Process, 25*, 337–351.

Olson, D. H., Sprenkle, D. H., Russell, C. S. (1979). Circumplex model of marital and family systems: I. Cohesion and adaptability dimensions, family types, and clinical applications. *Family Process, 18*, 3–28.

Rintala, D. H., Young, M., Hart, K., Clearman, R., & Fuhrer, M. (1992). Social support and the well-being of persons with spinal cord injury living in the community. *Rehabilitation Psychology, 37*, 155–163.

Rolland, J. S. (1994). *Families, illness, & disability: An integrative treatment model.* New York: Basic Books.

Rook, K. (1984). The negative side of social interaction: Impact on psychological well-being. *Journal of Personality and Social Psychology, 46*, 1097–1108.

Roosa, M. W., & Beals, J. (1990a). A final comment on the case of the Family Environment Scale. *Family Process*, *29*, 209–211.

Roosa, M. W., & Beals, J. (1990b). Measurement issues in family assessment: The case of the Family Environment Scale. *Family Process*, *29*, 191–198.

Rutter, M., & Brown, G. W. (1966). The reliability and validity of measures of family life and relationships in families containing a psychiatric patient. *Social Psychiatry*, *1*(1), 38–53.

Schulz, R., & Decker, S. (1985). Long-term adjustment to physical disability: The role of social support, perceived control, and self-blame. *Journal of Personality and Social Psychology*, *48*, 1162–1172.

Suls, J. (1982). Social support, interpersonal relations, and health: Benefits and liabilities. In G. S. Sanders & J. Suls (Eds.), *Social psychology of health and illness* (pp. 255–277). Hillsdale, NJ: Erlbaum.

Szmuckler, G. I., Berkowitz, R., Eisler, I., Leff, J., & Dare, C. (1987). Expressed emotion in individual and family settings: A comparative study. *British Journal of Psychiatry*, *151*, 174–178.

Tamler, M. S., & Perrin, J. C. S. (1992). Beaumont Lifestyle Inventory of Social Support: Can it predict disposition prior to an inpatient rehabilitation admission? *American Journal of Physical Medicine and Rehabilitation*, *71*(3), 149–155.

Tarrier, N., Barrowclough, C., Vaughn, C. E., Bamrah, J. S., Porceddu, K., Watts, S., & Freeman, H. (1988). The community management of schizophrenia: A controlled trial of behavioral intervention with families to reduce relapse. *British Journal of Psychiatry*, *153*, 532–542.

Tompkins, C. A., Schulz, R., & Rau, M. T. (1988). Post-stroke depression in primary support persons: Predicting those at risk. *Journal of Consulting and Clinical Psychology*, *56*, 502–508.

Turk, D. C., Kerns, R. D., & Rosenberg, R. (1992). Effects of marital interaction on chronic pain and disability: Examining the down side of social support. *Rehabilitation Psychology*, *37*, 259–274.

Vaughn, C. E. (1989). Expressed emotion in family relationships. *Journal of Child Psychology and Psychiatry*, *30*, 13–22.

Vaughn, C. E., & Leff, J. P. (1976). The measurement of expressed emotion in the families of psychiatric patients. *British Journal of Social and Clinical Psychology*, *15*, 157–165.

Wallander, J. L., Varni, J. W., Babani, L., DeHaan, C. B., Wilcox, K. T., & Banis, H. T. (1989). The social environment and the adaptation of mothers of physically handicapped children. *Journal of Pediatric Psychology*, *14*, 371–387.

Wells, J. (1974). Family stroke education. *Stroke*, *5*, 393–396.

Williams, S. E. (1993). The impact of aphasia on marital satisfaction. *Archives of Physical Medicine and Rehabilitation*, *74*, 361–367.

Zarski, J. J., DePompei, R., & Zook II, A. (1988). Traumatic head injury: Dimensions of family responsivity. *Journal of Head Trauma and Rehabilitation*, *3*(4), 31–41.

Assessment of Vocational Interests and Aptitudes in Rehabilitation Settings

Michael J. Leahy

In preparing to enter or reenter the labor force following disability, individuals with disabilities may find that vocational assessment can play a fundamental role in the rehabilitation process. There are three general purposes for these types of assessment: (a) to assist the client in identifying vocational strengths, limitations, barriers, career interests, and aptitudes, (b) to provide this information to the client to facilitate self-understanding and to increase knowledge about the world of work and of available opportunities and resources, and (c) to identify career goals consistent with identified individual capacities and preferences, including a plan of services that identifies the type of training, interventions, or accommodations required by the client to achieve career aspirations.

The typical process and desired outcomes of vocational assessment are generally appropriate for addressing the initial informational needs of individuals following disability. The formal and informal approaches taken to gather this information, however, must be highly individualized to account for the heterogeneity present within this population and to appropriately address the specific vocational questions or hypotheses developed by the client and the rehabilitation professional. There has been a long-standing debate in rehabilitation regarding the appropriateness and value of using standardized assessment instruments with various disability populations. To address these concerns, I recommend a hierarchical arrangement or model of assessment procedures, with each level in the hierarchy contributing to greater efficiency of assessment at subsequent levels and permitting an individual to exit the assessment process whenever sufficient information has been obtained. In this regard, formal standardized interest and aptitude testing represents a first step in the hierarchy, serving the purpose of initial screening and contributing to the overall direction and cost-effectiveness of the entire vocational assessment process (Berven, 1980).

The purpose of this chapter is to review the contributions of interest and aptitude testing within the overall assessment process for individuals following disability. An introduction and overview to each of these assessment areas is provided, along with a discussion of issues regarding their development and application. This is followed by a series of specific reviews on selected interest inventories and aptitude test batteries. In addition, informal and nontraditional methods for assessing these areas are provided in order to acquaint the reader with alternative strategies to standardized testing in assessing the interests and aptitudes of individuals with disabilities.

Assessment of Vocational Interests

In rehabilitation settings, the exploration of the client's interests is the beginning phase of the vocational assessment process. The counseling interview, which can focus on the expressed and manifest interests of the client, is a valuable assessment strategy for both actively involving the client in exploring interests, preferences, and past activities and providing the counselor with important information regarding the client's general level of career maturity and knowledge of occupations. These initial observations are also helpful in selecting appropriate interest inventories for the more formal assessment of vocational interests, which typically follows.

Anastasi (1988) has indicated that the study of vocational interests has primarily been stimulated over the years by the educational and career counseling fields. Interest inventories, which are designed to ask clients to report their likes, dislikes, and preferences for various activities and occupations, have proven to be especially helpful in assisting clients to define their career interests (Hood & Johnson, 1991). Although interest inventories have been developed and used throughout this century, the more recently developed or revised inventories reflect the changes that career counseling has experienced over recent years, including an increasing emphasis on self-exploration, expanding the career options available to individuals, and concern regarding the sex fairness of interest inventories (Anastasi, 1988).

Although interest inventories have been classified in numerous ways, a particularly useful distinction is based on the type of scales used (Hood & Johnson, 1991). There are basically two different types of scales in use today that provide a distinguishing feature among available inventories. Some inventories, such as the Strong Interest Inventory (SII), use both types of scales. The first type of scale is homogeneous in nature and reflects the strength of an individual's interests in broad fields of activity. This type of scale is often described as a general or basic scale. The second type of scale is heterogeneous in nature, reflecting the similarity of an individual's interest patterns to those of individuals employed in a given occupation. These scales are referred to as occupational scales (Hood & Johnson, 1991).

In rehabilitation settings, although both types of scales may provide valuable information that can contribute to career decision making and planning, the choice of which scale to use should be well thought out. For example, for younger clients with limited work experience and knowledge of occupations, basic interest scales provide a useful counseling tool in exploring a broad range of occupational areas prior to the crystallization of specific occupational interests. For college age students and adults with disabilities, who have acquired more knowledge about the world of work through experience and exposure, occupational scales or inventories that identify scores related to specific occupations may be more efficient and appropriate.

Common Issues in Interest Assessment

Although objective and empirically based methods to assess interests are very commonly applied today, historically, this approach has tended to perpetuate group differences among occupations in relation to gender. In occupations that have been predominantly male or female dominated, differences related to gender have tended to influence the interpretation of results obtained by men and women on interest inventories (Anastasi, 1988). There has been considerable attention over the years devoted to the issue of gender bias and unfairness in interest assessment (Zunker, 1994). The National Institute of Education developed guidelines that identify gender bias as "any factor that might influence a person to limit— or might cause others to limit—his or her considerations of a career solely on the basis of gender" (Diamond, 1975, p. xxiii).

A variety of approaches have been recommended for dealing with issues of gender fairness, including the use of gender balanced scales

(Prediger & Johnson, 1979), separate norms (Johnasson, 1975), and special interpretive guidelines for women (Birk, 1975). Diamond (1975) has indicated that although changes in interest inventory approaches may appear slow, some progress has been made by calling for fairness in the construction of item pools, in the presentation of technical information, and in interpretive procedures. The issue of gender fairness may be of even greater concern for individuals with disabilities, because their disability may have already severely limited their career options.

Although there is a positive correlation between interest and aptitude (Anastasi, 1988), the presence of high interest in a particular career area does not mean that the individual has sufficient aptitudes and abilities for achievement and success in that area. Ability level may even affect the choice of which interest inventory to use. Academic achievement in the specific area of reading comprehension, for example, is an important consideration in the selection of the type of interest inventory one should use. Prior to the selection and administration of an inventory, both the reading comprehension and the career maturity level of the client should be assessed.

Another area of concern is the manner in which the client approaches the formal measurement of interests. For example, clients who are interested in the results of testing and have an understanding of the purpose of the inventory are most likely to respond in an honest fashion to the items presented. However, changes in interest scores can occur when clients alter the manner in which they approach the inventory. These could include cases where clients respond to items in terms of what they believe other people would like them to say regarding interests, rather than focusing on their own beliefs (Hood & Johnson, 1991).

When disability is present, there may be an even greater reason to spend time prior to testing to make sure that the client understands the purpose of the inventory and to assess his or her personal approach to the assessment of interests. For example, individuals with disabilities may exclude certain types of interests based on the belief that the functional limitations associated with their disability preclude them from participation in a type of activity or career area. This narrowing of options based on the perceived impact of the disability may unduly restrict or even eliminate areas of interest that the client could pursue.

This issue is particularly important in consideration of the Americans with Disabilities Act mandate for eliminating job discrimination by employers solely on the basis of disability and in light of advances made in recent years in accommodations and assistive technology that provide alternative ways of performing the essential functions of many jobs. At this stage in the assessment of interests, clients should be counseled to reduce any artificial self-restriction of interests on the basis of the perceived functional impact of disability. Time since injury and current adjustment issues the client is facing should also be explored prior to testing in order to assess potential impact on the client's approach to interest testing.

Another area of frequent concern for clients and rehabilitation personnel is the interpretation of highly elevated or flat profiles following interest assessment. Elevated profiles show a large number of scores considered to be high in interest level, whereas flat profiles consist of scores within the average range, with little differentiation among scores (Zunker, 1994). Although both of these situations cause some confusion in terms of identifying career direction, they provide valuable information to the counselor about the client's present situation. For example, as Hansen (1985) has suggested, flat or depressed profiles may indicate either that the individual has limited knowledge of the world of work or that the individual is highly indecisive about making choices at this time. Highly elevated scores may indicate either that the individual has a wide variety of interests or that the individual is reluctant to respond negatively (e.g., indicate dislike or indifference) to items. Further review of these profiles with the client will help provide reasons and causes for flat or elevated profiles that can be used in counseling to identify appropriate intervention and remediation strategies (Zunker, 1994).

Examples of Interest Inventories

In this section five different interest inventories are presented and briefly reviewed as examples of the types of inventories available for use with individuals with disabilities. The instruments presented include the Kuder General Interest Survey, Form E; the Kuder Occupational Interest Survey, Form DD; the Strong Interest Inventory; the Self-Directed Search; and the Wide Range Interest-Opinion Test. This list is certainly not exhaustive, but it is intended to provide a review of various different types of inventories counselors and clients can select from depending on the particular situation and the client's reading and career maturity level.

Kuder General Interest Survey, Form E
The Kuder General Interest Survey (KGIS) is designed to measure broad vocational interests for use in counseling during the initial occupational

exploration stages with clients. The 168-item survey is partially ipsative in character and is presented in forced-choice triads, consisting of three types of activities per item. Clients are required to identify their most preferred and least preferred activity within each item. The KGIS uses homogeneous scales to measure interests in 10 broad categories, including Outdoor, Mechanical, Computational, Scientific, Persuasive, Artistic, Literary, Musical, Social Service, and Clerical. An eleventh scale, designed as a verification scale, provides a measure of the sincerity of responses made.

The KGIS, Form E, was designed for use with students (from Grade 6 through college) and adults (all ages). The reading level was reduced from ninth grade to sixth grade to allow use with younger students and adults with limited reading comprehension skills (Hood & Johnson, 1991).

Administration of the KGIS on an individual basis typically takes 45–60 minutes. Form E is an untimed inventory and has both machine-scorable and hand-scorable versions available for use. The hand-scorable version requires individuals to record responses with a pin and corrugated paper by pushing the pin through the intended response on the combined survey and answer sheet. Although the hand-scoring version has the immediate advantage of self-scoring upon completion, it can present some difficulties for individuals with physical disabilities because of the level of manual and fine finger dexterity required. An alternative would be the use of an auxiliary aid to assist with this task or using the machine-scorable version, which uses the more routine paper-and-pencil format. Results are reported in relation to the 10 interest areas and the verification scale. Scores are reported as a profile of percentile ranks with categorization into high, average, and low interests. New norms were developed for the KGIS in 1987. Separate-gender norms are available for middle school and high school students.

The studies reported in the KGIS manual support the contention that the survey possesses adequate test–retest reliability for most situations. Test–retest reliabilities for the 10 subscales are generally equal to or greater than .70, with older students achieving somewhat higher reliabilities. Kuder-Richardson 20 (KR-20) internal consistency reliabilities for Grades 9–12 were between .80 and .90 for female and .86 and .92 for male students (Williams & Williams, 1988). Although there is no separate section on validity included in the KGIS manual, there is evidence reported to support the validity of the instrument. For example, as Hood and Johnson (1991) point out, a 25-year follow-up study by Zytowski in 1974 indicated that 53% of the students tested as 14-year-olds were employed in occupations consistent with their highest area of interest on the Kuder Preference Record, which is an earlier version of the KGIS. There remains the need for longitudinal research, particularly related to adults, to provide additional evidence of the validity of the KGIS with these populations.

In terms of special considerations and cautions, the KGIS is a fairly straightforward instrument that can be effectively used with individuals with disabilities given the appropriate circumstances. Care should be exercised in identifying which method of administration (hand-scoring, machine-scoring) should be selected on the basis of the client's physical capacities. As should be typical, counselors need to talk with their clients prior to administration to carefully explain the purpose of the survey and to check how the client is approaching the items in relation to disability factors. Because of its general nature, it should be used with clients who are very uncertain of their interests following disability, and it should be used primarily as a basic screening device to stimulate career exploration prior to further interest testing and occupational choice. The sixth-grade reading level of the KGIS also allows use by clients with disabilities who have limited reading comprehension skills but still need to broadly define potential vocational interests that can be pursued.

Kuder Occupational Interest Survey (KOIS), Form DD

The Kuder Occupational Interest Survey (KOIS) is related to the KGIS but uses heterogeneous scales to assess an individual's interest in specific occupations. It was designed to provide a measure of occupational and college major interests, for use in career counseling and specific occupational exploration. Individuals mark their most and least preferred activity among the 100 items, which are presented as a series of forced-choice triads. The KOIS consists of 104 occupational scales, 39 college major scales, 10 vocational interest estimates, and 8 experimental scales.

The KOIS, Form DD, is designed for use with students (from Grade 10 through college) and adults (all ages). Although it has a sixth-grade reading comprehension level, the interest survey should be used with individuals who are at a point in the career counseling process where specific scores related to occupations and college majors can be used to clarify and help crystallize specific interests for future planning.

Although the instrument is untimed, administration of the KOIS takes approximately 30 to 40 minutes to complete. Unlike the related KGIS, the KOIS is only machine-scorable, and users must pay for this nonlocal service. Both an interpretive guide to assist clients and counselors and an audiotape for individual client use have been made available by the publisher.

Results from the KOIS are reported in four separate sections: Dependability, Vocational Interest Estimates (VIES), the College Major scales, and the Occupational scales. The dependability measures for the KOIS are based on the verification scores, frequency of unreadable responses, and the magnitude of the highest College Major or Occupational scale score. Next the client's VIES are provided in relation to the 10 general interest scales originally constructed for use in the KGIS. These estimates are reported as percentiles and compared with both female and male groups. Finally, scores (lambda coefficients) on all the Occupational and College Major scales are reported in rank order for male and female norms.

Reliability data, reported in the manual, support the consistency of the VIES, the College Major and Occupational profiles, and the consistency of differences between scale pairs for the latter two profiles (Jepsen, 1988). Profile scores demonstrate high levels of reliability for both sexes at both high school and college levels (Hood & Johnson, 1991). For all studies described in the manual, median test–retest profile reliabilities for the Occupational scales were reported as equal to or greater than .90. Concurrent validity is reported based on a study that tested the validation of the Occupational and College Major scales in differentiating among the interests of a sample of 3,000 individuals drawn from 30 of the occupations and college majors included in the scales. The results indicated that two-thirds of the respondents obtained their highest score on their own Occupational or College Major scale (Hood & Johnson, 1991).

In terms of special considerations and cautions, the KOIS is a well-designed instrument for assisting clients with disabilities to differentiate among a limited group of occupations on the basis of similarity of interest patterns (Jepsen, 1988). Although only a sixth-grade reading level is required, caution should be exercised to ensure that the client is at a point where specific scores related to the types of occupations and college majors included in the instrument can be used to clarify interests for future planning. A review of the occupations included in the KOIS reveals that the survey represents a limited sample of occupations with no explanation provided in the manual regarding the rationale for selection. With this caution in mind, the survey can be very useful in appropriate situations with clients with disabilities.

Strong Interest Inventory

The Strong Interest Inventory (SII) is an updated version of a continuing series of inventories developed by E. K. Strong, Jr., that date back to 1927. In 1985, the SII replaced the well-known Strong-Campbell Interest

Inventory. The SII has developed a reputation as one of the most frequently used, well-researched, and highly respected instruments for measuring interests available today (Borgen, 1988; Hood & Johnson, 1991; Westbrook, 1985). As a fundamental basis to the measurement of interests, Strong postulated that individuals who have interests that are similar to those of persons working in a given occupation are more likely to find satisfaction in that specific occupation than are individuals without similar interests. The SII consists of 325 items, separated into seven sections, that measure a client's interest in a wide variety of occupations, occupational activities, hobbies, leisure activities, school subjects, and types of people (Zunker, 1994). The SII uses both homogeneous and heterogeneous scales and produces scores on several administrative indexes, three sets of interest scales, and two special scales (Hood & Johnson, 1991).

The SII was developed for use with individuals from age 13 through adulthood. The reading comprehension level was established at the sixth grade for the inventory. The SII is extensively used in high schools and by counselors in university counseling centers as well as by rehabilitation personnel working with individuals with disabilities. The strengths of the SII are its applicability to such a wide range of individuals and the variety of data generated on the interpretive report for use in counseling and career planning for these populations.

In terms of administration, the SII takes approximately 30 minutes to complete. Clients are required to indicate whether they *like*, are *indifferent* to or *dislike* each of the items that appear in the first five sections of the inventory (Occupations, School Subjects, Activities, Leisure Activities, and Types of People). In the sixth section, Preferences Between Two Activities, clients are asked to select which of the activities they prefer, and in the seventh section, clients have three response categories (*yes*, ?, or *no*) to select from in "Your Characteristics," which asks them to describe their personality by responding to various statements. After administration, the SII must be computer scored.

Results are reported in a well-organized and well-constructed profile format that provides easy access to information on the client's interests. The SII profiles are organized around Holland's (1985) occupational personality types: realistic, investigative, artistic, social, enterprising, and conventional. Two sets of homogeneous scales are included in the SII: General Occupational Themes (GOT) and Basic Interest Scales. The 23 Basic Interest Scales act as subscales to the six GOT scales, which are based on Holland's typology. The t scores obtained for these two scales are based on combined sex norms, but the authors provide bar graphs beside the scales on the profile report to indicate how the scores are distributed for each sex. Finally, there are 102 Occupational scales for men, and 105 Occupational scales for women. These scales are heterogeneous in nature and represent, with very few exceptions, the same occupations for men and women. The SII profile provides the client's scores for both the male and female Occupational scales, but plots only the same-sex scores (Hood & Johnson, 1991). As Zunker (1994) has indicated, the interpretation process typically involves an initial review of the general occupational theme scores, which provides a general overview of the client's interest patterns. It then moves to a review of the increasingly specific basic interest scores and finally to measures of interest for specific occupations.

In addition, there are a number of administrative indices provided as output to aid in the interpretation process. For example, there is an infrequent response index, which will indicate whether an individual has marked a significant number of rare or uncommon responses. Two other special scales are provided as part of the SII profile: the introversion–extroversion (IE) index and the Academic Comfort (AC) scale. The IE index provides an indicator of the client's preference for working with people or with things, and AC provides an indicator of the degree to which the client likes activities related to academic work.

There has been a significant amount of research performed over the years that provides compelling evidence regarding the reliability and validity of the SII. For example, the GOT and Basic Interest Scales are reportedly highly reliable in terms of both internal consistency and test–retest reliability over time (Hood & Johnson, 1991). Each of these scales reportedly possesses a high degree of content validity based on the manner in which it was constructed, and they have been shown through empirical validity studies to discriminate effectively among people employed in different occupations (Hansen & Campbell, 1985; Hood & Johnson, 1991). The Occupational scores are also reported to be highly reliable, especially for individuals over 20 years of age, and concurrent validation studies have demonstrated that the Occupational scales significantly discriminate between people within the occupation and people in general (Hansen & Campbell, 1985).

The SII represents a comprehensively designed and thoroughly researched interest inventory that can provide useful information on general career interest patterns and specific occupations for consideration by individuals with disabilities. Although the SII includes a variety of specific occupations, the emphasis is generally on higher level occupations. As a result of the variety of information provided and the potential value of such information in the interpretation process, counselors using the instrument should be very familiar with the inventory and interpretive guidelines. Although the sixth-grade reading level would require some clients to use a different inventory, adaptations and modifications made in the administration (e.g., readers, scribes, additional time) of the inventory in relation to the clients' physical capacities can provide access to the SII for individuals with severe disabilities.

The Self-Directed Search

The Self-Directed Search (SDS) was developed by Holland (1985) as a self-administered, self-scored, and self-interpreted vocational interest inventory and counseling tool for use in career exploration and choice. The instrument is based on Holland's widely used theory of personality types and work environments. The SDS is designed to provide a systematic study of the client's interests and abilities. This self-assessment of preferred activities and competencies is then related to over 1,300 occupations listed in the Occupational Finder, which accompanies the SDS. The inventory assesses clients' liking for various activities and occupations as well as their competencies and self-ratings of abilities.

The SDS was designed for use with junior and senior high school students, college and university students, and adults of all ages. A special form of the SDS (Form E) with a fourth-grade reading level is available for individuals with limited reading ability or educational levels below the ninth grade. Individuals usually take approximately 35 to 50 minutes to complete this self-assessment process.

Each section of the SDS includes items representing the six personality orientations and environmental models described by Holland: realistic (R), investigative (I), artistic (A), social (S), enterprising (E), and conventional (C). Holland's theory serves as the foundation for the SDS and postulates that client's are more likely to experience success, stability, and satisfaction in their selected occupation if the work environment they enter is consistent with their personality (Campbell, 1988). Raw scores are used to interpret the SDS. After completing the inventory, the client scores the SDS by summing responses (R,I,A,S,E,C) in order to arrive at a three-letter Holland summary code. This code is then used to locate specific occupations in the Occupational Finder.

In terms of reliability, the SDS was examined in relation to internal consistency using the KR-20, which yielded coefficients ranging from .67 to .94 for samples of 2,000 to 6,000 college freshman (Zunker, 1994). Internal consistency reliability (alpha) estimates of the summary scale reportedly range from .85 to .92 (Holland, 1985). Test–retest reliabilities examined at 3- to 4-week intervals revealed median coefficients of .81 for male and .83 for female students in a study of high school students (Zunker, 1994). Content validity appears to be supported through item content, and a series of studies (Holland, 1987) supporting the predictive validity of the SDS are found in the SDS manual.

The SDS provides interest assessment that is completely self-administered, scored, and interpreted. This advantage, along with the variety of occupational choices, provides the client with an opportunity to take a very straightforward but comprehensive instrument independently, which by itself could be of great value to the individual. Problems noted by previous reviewers (Campbell, 1988; Hood & Johnson, 1991) include self-scoring errors and issues related to sexual stereotypes, based on the use of raw scores in the interpretation process. As Zunker (1994) has indicated, additional research is needed and should be reported in the manual for use of the SDS with women, members of minority populations (including people with disabilities), and adults.

Wide Range Interest-Opinion Test

The Wide Range Interest-Opinion Test (WRIOT), developed by Jastak and Jastak (1978), is a nonverbal pictorial interest inventory developed for measuring interests and attitudes of individuals with limited reading skills or severe disabilities. The WRIOT consists of 450 pictures presented in groups of three per item (150 items). The client selects the most liked and least liked among the three pictures presented for each item in the test.

The WRIOT was developed specifically to provide a formal measure of interests and attitudes without requiring the individual to read and comprehend written items. The pictorial content comes from a wide range of unskilled, technical, professional, and managerial positions. The WRIOT can be individually or group administered, with no time limitations for completion. The authors report that the inventory takes approximately 40 minutes to complete.

The WRIOT can be either hand or computer scored. Results are presented in 18 separate general interest clusters and 8 attitudinal clusters. The results are reported by standard score ($M = 50$, $SD = 10$) for each cluster and attitude scale. A well-designed and easy to review profile is generated from the results and reports and plots scores in each of the 18 interest and 8 attitude clusters using five categories ranging from *very low* (20–31) to *very high* (69–80). Scores of 50 or more are considered positive interests and attitudes, and scores lower than 50 reflect negative interests and attitudes. The authors recommend that users consider the entire profile of scores in counseling and career exploration.

The manual provides a definition of each of the clusters and includes data regarding correlations with other clusters by gender and job title. Norms for all scales are available by age and gender. Means and standard deviations for each interest cluster and attitude scale are also provided by age and gender.

In terms of reliability, split-half coefficients by the Cureton formula for each scale in the 1979 edition ranged from .83 to .95 for male and from .82 to .95 for female respondents. Information available on validity is limited, but correlations with the Geist Picture Interest Inventory were conducted, with most correlations found to be high and within satisfactory ranges (Zunker, 1994). In total, the information available on the psychometric properties of the WRIOT is somewhat limited. Additional validity studies are warranted, particularly in relation to women, members of ethnic minority groups, and people with disabilities who have limited reading comprehension skills.

Although the nonreading format of this interest inventory is a compelling factor to consider for using the WRIOT with clients with disabilities that possess low reading levels, there are a number of cautions for potential users. First, while the nonreading format is an advantage in some situations, caution should be exercised in administering the WRIOT to ascertain whether the client understands the content of the pictures being presented. Although some of the pictures are unmistakably clear in depicting certain activities, others are more complex and could be misinterpreted. Second, information on the reliability and validity of this instrument is very limited when compared with those previously reviewed in this chapter. Finally, in terms of appropriate use, counselors should be aware of the general nature of this interest inventory and the limited range of occupations covered when considering it for use with clients with disabilities.

Summary

Typically the vocational assessment process begins with an exploration of the client's interests and preferences. Initial information provided by the client about interests provides a beginning point for the counselor and client to plan the exploration of interests and, if required, to identify appropriate assessment instruments to help in the process. The actual selection of an appropriate interest inventory is a critical step in this process. The inventories briefly reviewed in this chapter, though representing only a small subset of the available options, provide examples of the differences, strengths, and limitations of various formal approaches to the assessment of interests. In addition to considering the psychometric properties of these measures, counselors working with individuals with disabilities should carefully examine the reading level, types of scales employed, range of occupations covered, and administration concerns related to specific disability factors when selecting an inventory to ensure that it is appropriate for the intended use and consistent with the client's characteristics and needs.

Finally, information obtained from interest assessment provides a valuable counseling tool for further exploring potential interest areas with the client. This process may include the use of various forms of occupational information (e.g., *Dictionary of Occupational Titles, Guide for Occupational Exploration, Occupational Outlook Handbook*) to provide the client with additional information about potential career areas. Once tentative decisions have been reached regarding career options on the basis of the client's interests and preferences, the counselor and client can begin to address and explore the abilities, aptitudes, and functional capacities associated with these identified career areas in order to develop a match between the demands of the occupation and the functional capacities, skills, and aptitudes of the client.

Assessment of Aptitudes

Following the assessment of career interests, the client's and counselor's attention typically begins to focus on the identification of individual abilities, skills, and functional capacities related to the demands of preferred occupational areas. Although reference information is readily available regarding the general qualifications, required abilities, aptitudes, and physical demands of most occupations, similar data regarding the client's strengths and potential limitations in these areas need to be collected through informal and standardized assessment approaches.

Achievement and aptitude testing are two of the traditional standardized approaches to identifying the current level of skills and the capacity for further acquisition of skills (Power, 1991). Achievement testing, particularly in the verbal and numerical areas, is undertaken primarily to identify what the client has learned from previous formal education and individual experience. This information is not only useful in identifying a criterion level for further test selection (i.e., reading comprehension level) but also provides valuable information to compare against the basic academic skill demands of potential training programs and occupations of interest to the client. Aptitude testing, on the other hand, which measures the cumulative influence of a multitude of daily experiences, is designed to identify an ability or characteristic, which could be mental or physical, native or acquired, that indicates a client's capacity for learning a particular skill or competency (Anastasi, 1988; Power, 1991). Aptitude tests therefore measure relatively homogeneous and clearly defined segments of abilities (Anastasi, 1988).

Preliminary Activities

Before specific aptitude testing can be undertaken, a number of preliminary strategies for collecting and organizing other client assessment information should be used. All relevant information and previously collected assessment data regarding the client's work history, results of psychological testing (including intelligence testing), educational background, social and family history, interests and personality, medical and health status, and functional limitations imposed by the disability should be reviewed, organized, and integrated into a comprehensive case study of the client. This collection of existing information, along with the data collected from vocational interest testing, allows the counselor and client to develop an evaluation plan to guide the remaining portions of the assessment process. This plan, which is dynamic and changes as a result of new information, identifies key questions or hypotheses to be addressed in the remaining stages of the assessment process. The plan specifically identifies the methods, approaches, and strategies to be used to collect the assessment data needed to answer these questions or hypotheses.

At this point a thorough examination of the client's work history is particularly significant. A transferable skills analysis should be used to identify previously developed skills and abilities and their potential application to other occupations with similar demands. This process can be done through an informal review, through structured approaches such as the Vocational Diagnosis and Assessment of Residual Employability process (Sink & Field, 1981), or through the use of computer software such as OASYS and CAPCO (Brown, McDaniel, Couch, & McClanahan, 1994). These processes not only provide assistance in defining the client's current vocational capacities but also provide examples of occupations to further explore with the client.

If results from achievement testing are not available, the counselor should consider administering an achievement test to identify the client's verbal and numerical skills. Depending on the client's characteristics and educational background, there are a number of commonly used instruments to consider. These include the Wide Range Achievement Test—Revised (WRAT-R), the Adult Basic Learning Examination, and the Peabody Individual Achievement Test—Revised.

Finally, specific attention needs to be focused on the functional impact of the disability in relation to career choice. Comprehensive information from medical examinations and client self-report can be used to complete a functional capacities checklist that can be used to compare against the essential functional demands of preferred occupations and provide information helpful in conceptualizing potential accommodations.

Types of Instruments and Strategies

In the area of aptitude assessment there are a number of instruments and alternative strategies for the counselor to consider, depending on the client's characteristics and needs and the questions identified in the client's evaluation plan.

Standardized assessment approaches in multiple aptitude batteries, such as the Differential Aptitude Test and the General Aptitude Test Battery are particularly good for generating information on a wide variety of aptitudes and in comparing the client's aptitude profile with the demands of various occupational areas. Occupation-specific aptitude tests are also available and include such instruments as the Bennett Mechanical Comprehension Test and the Minnesota Clerical Test. Finally, aptitude measures such as the Crawford Small Parts Dexterity Test and the Purdue Pegboard are available for the assessment of highly specific aptitudes such as manual dexterity and eye–hand coordination.

Complementing these highly standardized approaches to the assessment of aptitudes are work samples, computerized test batteries, situational assessment strategies, and on-the-job evaluations. Although these latter approaches are less standardized, they provide a more realistic, experiential, and environmentally oriented assessment that could be a particular benefit to clients with severe disabilities that pose particular problems for standardized assessment.

Common Issues in Aptitude Assessment

Although most of the available multiple aptitude batteries provide differential measures of ability, Zunker (1994) believes that expectations regarding their predictive value may be excessively high. This issue is particularly important for clients to understand as they approach aptitude testing. Occupational success and predictions of job proficiency are complex issues involving many more factors than simply abilities. However, findings obtained from aptitude testing can provide valuable suggestions, insights, and clues to be considered along with other assessment information in the process of career decision making (Zunker, 1994).

One of the most significant issues in the area of aptitude testing for clients with disabilities relates to standardization (Berven, 1980; Power, 1991). When the functional limitations imposed by a disability require that the test administration be modified to accommodate the client with a disability, problems in standardization can occur. For example, scores obtained on aptitude tests derive meaning only through comparison with the available norm group. This comparison to a normative sample can only be made if the standardized testing conditions and procedures were explicitly followed. Deviations from standardized procedures can change the test, affect the score to some unknown extent, and generally invalidate comparison with the standardized norms (Berven, 1980). This problem is further compounded by the general lack of norms based on samples of individuals with disabilities (Power, 1991). When confronted with these issues, counselors should first seek out alternative tests or assessment strategies that will not require a modification in standardized administration. If there are no available options, care should be taken in the interpretation of results, which should be viewed very tenuously. The guidelines and suggestions for test modification procedures provided by Botterbusch and Michael (1985) should be consulted when the standard administration of an aptitude battery or test must be altered.

Finally, determining the impact of a disability during standardized testing may require careful observation. For example, medication effects or fatigue factors related to the impairment may negatively affect the client's ability to perform, particularly on a high-speed aptitude test. Berven described an example of such a situation: "To answer test items, spaces on an answer sheet are colored in with a pencil. Ordinarily, the test provides a relatively pure measure of verbal aptitude. However, an individual with limited function in the dominant hand may have difficulty coloring in the spaces on the answer sheet rapidly. Consequently, rather than representing a relatively pure measure of verbal aptitude, the score actually represents some combination of verbal and motor aptitudes, and it becomes difficult to assess the meaning of the score in terms of vocational and training potential" (Berven, 1980, p. 58).

To address these issues, the Standards for Educational and Psychological Testing (1985) provide standards for testing people with disabilities (Section 14), including a comprehensive discussion of the types of modifications made to various types of instruments to accommodate for disability factors. As indicated in the Standards, "despite the history of attempts to modify tests for handicapped people, significant problems remain . . . there have been very few empirical investigations of the effects of special accommodations on the resulting scores or on their reliability and validity" (Standards for Educational and Psychological Testing, 1985, p. 78). Clearly additional research is needed to address these concerns and to provide needed guidance and suggestions to counselors working with individuals with disabilities.

Examples of Aptitude Tests

In this section three different aptitude tests are presented and briefly reviewed as examples of the different types of tests available for use with individuals with disabilities. The instruments presented include the Differential Aptitude Test, the General Aptitude Test Battery, and APTICOM. In addition, a number of relevant occupation-specific and single aptitude tests are described.

Differential Aptitude Test (DAT), Fifth Edition, Form C

The Differential Aptitude Test (DAT) represents one of the most widely recognized and thoroughly researched aptitude tests available today (Zunker, 1994). The DAT was developed as an integrated battery of eight aptitude tests designed for educational and vocational guidance. The eight subtests are Verbal Reasoning, Numerical Ability, Abstract Reasoning, Clerical Speed and Accuracy, Mechanical Reasoning, Space Relations, Spelling, and Language Usage.

The DAT is designed for use with adults and with students in Grades 8 through 12. The test items, directions, and reports have been developed for the non-college-bound individual, and reading is required only when it is part of the ability being assessed (Power, 1991). In 1990, vocational technical school adult norms were made available. The DAT takes approximately 3 hours to complete and can be group or individually administered. Both hand- and machine-scored options are available.

The DAT generates nine scores: one for each test and an additional score that measures overall scholastic aptitude. Results are reported on either a computer-generated profile or a hand-plotted profile. The test has separate gender norms, with both percentiles and stanines reported. A considerable amount of evidence has been collected over the years supporting the reliability and validity of the DAT, including validity data that has correlated test scores with a variety of course grades and achievement tests. Although there is evidence that the test is a good predictor of high school and college grades, less evidence is available regarding the DAT's ability to predict occupational success (Zunker, 1994).

The DAT is a very technically sound, multiple aptitude battery. As Power (1991) has indicated, the DAT manual provides no information regarding the test battery's use with individuals with disabilities. However, for those clients with a 10th-grade education who are interested in technical occupations that involve math or science, the DAT may be particularly useful.

General Aptitude Test Battery

The General Aptitude Test Battery (GATB) was developed by the United States Employment Service as a group test for use in vocational and occupational counseling and is provided through local state employment services. These entities also provide GATB training to professionals to allow for the use of the GATB in other counseling and rehabilitation settings. Over the years the GATB has been frequently used in rehabilitation settings, particularly in the State–federal rehabilitation program. The GATB consists of 12 tests that measure nine occupational aptitude areas. These factors are General Learning Ability, Verbal, Numerical, Spatial, Form Perception, Clerical Perception, Motor Coordination, Finger Dexterity, and Manual Dexterity.

The GATB was designed for use with individuals from the ninth grade through adulthood. The group-administered instrument takes approximately 2½ hours to complete. The instructions for administration are very formal and standardized. Individuals taking the GATB need to have at least a sixth-grade reading level, the ability to stand, and use of upper extremities (Botterbusch & Michael, 1985). In 1971, a nonreading form called the NATB was introduced for individuals with limited reading scores.

Scores on the GATB are reported as standard scores with a mean of 100 and a standard deviation of 20 as related to the distribution of scores for persons working in occupational groups. Standard scores on all nine aptitude areas are calculated and can be related to Occupational Ability Patterns (OAPs). The validity studies conducted by the U.S. Employment Service provided the research to establish multiple cut-off scores that are important for success in various occupations. These cut-off scores were used to determine the OAPs for different work groups. The OAPs are cross-referenced with Dictionary of Occupational Titles codes for easy access to more detailed occupational information.

The U.S. Department of Labor has conducted continuous studies on the reliability and validity of the GATB over the years. The manual reports more than 450 studies involving some 25,000 individuals. Reliability, determined by equivalent form and test–retest, ranges from the .80s to the low .90s. The research that has established the evidence regarding the reliability and validity of the GATB is believed to be the strength of the battery (Zunker, 1994).

There are a number of significant concerns regarding the GATB's general use, particularly with individuals with disabilities. In recent years there have been charges of test bias, particularly in relation to racial and ethnic minority groups, for the use of the GATB in the placement process. As a result of these issues the Department of Labor commissioned a study by the National Research Council to establish the appropriateness of the GATB and abolished the use of separate test norms based on racial or ethnic background. Although these issues are very serious, Kates and Chan (1993) argue for the continued, yet cautious use of the GATB along with other assessment tools and strategies in the career counseling process for individuals with disabilities. Finally, one of the most significant barriers to the effective use of the GATB relates to the fact that all the tests are time limited. This is a particular concern for individuals with severe disabilities.

APTICOM

The APTICOM is a computer-based test battery designed to provide a quick vocational assessment of aptitudes, interests, and educational level. The aptitude portion of the APTICOM represents an alternative to the GATB and covers 10 of the aptitudes described by the Department of Labor. The aptitude portion contains 11 specific tests (color discrimination omitted), with much of the design and test item format resembling those of the GATB. The test battery is built into a slanted display console that contains a dedicated computer. Clients use an attached stylus to record answers in the computer for the multiple choice format (Brown et al., 1994).

The APTICOM was developed for use with English- or Spanish-speaking disadvantaged job applicants, high school or special education students, and rehabilitation clients. Administration for the entire battery takes approximately 2 hours, but the aptitude section is timed and limited to 28 minutes. The aptitude test battery provides raw scores and standard scores for each of the 11 tests. The Individual APTICOM Profile provides a chart that plots the 11 tests measuring the 10 aptitude areas. The computer-generated report lists all appropriate GOE codes that are recommended from the client's higher interest scores and aptitude scores in relation to OAPs.

The aptitude battery was developed on samples of young adults and was standardized on adults in the United States and Canada. Internal consistency and test–retest reliability coefficients are provided for all tests. Aptitude test–retest reliabilities range between .65 and .89, with most higher than .80. The aptitude tests were validated against the GATB aptitudes. Correlations were reported in the .80s for cognitive aptitudes, .60s for perceptual aptitudes, and .50s for dexterity (Botterbusch, 1988). The APTICOM represents a computerized alternative to the GATB in relation to aptitude testing. It also represents an example of the expanding computer-based test battery systems that have been used extensively in rehabilitation settings over the past 10 years or so.

Occupation-Specific and Single Aptitude Tests

Although multiple aptitude test batteries provide an advantage in assessing various aptitude areas and relating these findings to numerous occupations, there are times when aptitude information is required only in relation to a specific occupational area or particular skill. To address these needs there are a number of occupation-specific and single aptitude tests available for counselors to use. The following brief descriptions are provided as examples of these tests.

Bennett Mechanical Comprehension Test

Designed to measure the ability to perceive and understand the relationship of physical forces and mechanical elements in practical situations, the Bennett is a widely used test in rehabilitation settings. A final score in percentile form is provided for mechanical comprehension.

Minnesota Clerical Test

Designed for use as a screening tool for occupational selection and for career guidance decision making, this test, although identified as a clerical test, measures only one aspect of the occupation: the ability to notice the difference between two items within a specified period of time.

Crawford Small Parts Dexterity Test

This is a test frequently used in rehabilitation settings to measure fine eye hand coordination. The test requires the use of small pins, collars, screws, and tweezers and the use of both hands in assembly operations that are timed and compared with relevant norms.

Purdue Pegboard

This test is designed to measure both gross movements of hands, fingers, and arms and fingertip dexterity. Again, this is an assessment tool frequently found in rehabilitation settings. Scores for the five separate timed subtests are compared with relevant norms.

Summary

Aptitude assessment is a critical aspect of vocational assessment for individuals with disabilities. The selection of the type of aptitude test, as with interest testing, should be based on the client's characteristics and needs and in response to the questions about abilities that the counselor and client have identified on the evaluation plan. Information obtained from aptitude testing can then be combined with other relevant assessment information and career-related information to assist the client in developing occupational goals consistent with interests and abilities. In addition, during the rehabilitation planning stage, services, accommodations, and interventions should be identified that will assist the client in achieving identified career goals.

The most significant barrier to the appropriate use of aptitude tests in rehabilitation settings is problems in standardization when accommodations in test administration need to be made to accommodate the functional limitations imposed by various disabilities. Although these modifications are routinely made, there is very little empirical evidence to support the appropriateness of the resulting scores or the reliability and validity of the instrument when such alterations are made. In response to these problems, rehabilitation professionals over the years have developed an array of alternative strategies to assess individuals with disabilities. Work sample testing, job search software, situational assessment, and on-the-job evaluations are frequently relied on when standardized assessment procedures are inappropriate for the individual client.

Work samples have become a major component of most assessment programs in rehabilitation settings. These procedures, although structured, allow for more flexible use and provide a more realistic and less abstract experience for clients. Work samples have been defined as "a well defined work activity involving tasks, materials, and tools which are identical or similar to those in an actual job or cluster of jobs. It is used to assess and individual's vocational aptitude, worker characteristics, and vocational interests" (Task Force #7, Vocational Evaluation Project; Nadolsky, 1974, p. 2). In more recent years, job-search software programs have been added to the tools available for assessment in rehabilitation settings.

Finally, the more experientially focused assessment techniques—situational assessment and on-the-job evaluation—are critical strategies in the assessment process for individuals with severe disabilities. These procedures rely on simulated or real work environments as the medium for assessment and observation. Clients perform tasks associated with an occupation and are observed and appraised in relation to competitive performance expectations. This type of assessment is particularly useful in situations where accommodations are being used to enable individuals with severe disabilities to perform the essential functions of a particular job. These procedures have been described by Power (1991). Publications are available that critically review work sample systems, computerized test batteries, and job search software available for use with clients with disabilities (Brown et al., 1994).

Conclusion

The assessment of vocational interests and aptitudes is a critical component of the overall vocational assessment process for individuals with disabilities. Although there is an expanding array of instruments to use with these populations, evaluators need to know the strengths and limitations of these instruments and be keenly aware of issues related to assessment for individuals with disabilities in general. They must then take into account the individual client's characteristics and needs in order to make appropriate test selection decisions.

As Power (1991) has indicated, there are a number of specific disability effects that need to be assessed and considered in the selection of assessment procedures for the process to be a valuable experience for the client. These include (a) age at disability onset; (b) nature of physical and emotional limitations; (c) medication effects; (d) relationship of the client's life experiences to the content of the proposed assessment measures; (e) educational experiences; (f) physical tolerance; and (g) the extent to which accommodation technology has assisted the client in compensating for physical limitations. These factors interact not only in the selection of appropriate assessment strategies but also in the interpretation of results leading to the development of individualized vocational rehabilitation plans.

In interest assessment there are numerous well-developed, thoroughly researched, and technically sound inventories that are readily applicable for individuals with disabilities even though they were not constructed with this specific population in mind. There are, however, some important issues for counselors to be aware of, such as the gender fairness of the instrument, the required reading and career maturity level, and the range of occupations covered by the instrument.

The selection and use of appropriate aptitude measures, on the other hand, poses more problems and concerns when working with individuals with severe disabilities. Although there are numerous well-developed multiple aptitude batteries, the standardization requirements make test modification and the subsequent interpretation of results tenuous at best. There is no empirical support in terms of the effects that test modification may have on the scores themselves, and the validity and reliability of the instrument are also called into question in these cases. Clearly there is a need for research to address these issues, particularly in light of the increasing need for accommodations that has been supported through recent federal legislation (Americans with Disabilities Act, 1990). In part as a response to some of the problems encountered in the use of standardized testing procedures, numerous nontraditional approaches to the assessment of aptitudes have been developed and used in rehabilitation settings over the years. Although these strategies and approaches are intended to avoid some of the pitfalls associated with standardized testing, they have generally not been adequately supported by appropriate research methods and ongoing studies to evaluate their effectiveness.

As individuals with disabilities prepare to enter or reenter the labor force, vocational assessment, which includes the assessment of interests and aptitudes, can play a significant role in assisting the client in making critical decisions regarding career aspirations and specific plans to reach these goals. Given the significance of these issues, professionals working in this area must provide an assessment process that focuses on the informational needs of the client and that provides assessment tools appropriate for the situation given the particular characteristics of the client.

References

Anastasi, A. (1988). *Psychological testing* (5th ed.). New York: Macmillan.

Berven, N. L. (1980). Psychometric assessment in rehabilitation. In B. Bolton & D. Cook (Eds.), *Rehabilitation client assessment* (pp. 46–64). Baltimore: University Park Press.

Birk, J. M. (1975). Reducing sex bias: Factors affecting the client's view of the use of career inventories. In E. E. Diamond (Ed.), *Issues of sex bias and sex fairness in career interest measurement* (pp. 101–121). Washington, DC: National Institute of Education.

Borgen, F. H. (1988). Review of the Strong-Campbell Interest Inventory. In J. T. Kapes & M. M. Mastie (Eds.), *A counselor's guide to career assessment instruments* (2nd ed., pp. 121–126). Washington, DC: National Career Development Association.

Botterbusch, K. F. (1988). Review of the APTCOM. In J. T. Kapes & M. M. Mastie (Eds.), *A counselor's guide to career assessment instruments* (2nd ed., pp. 198–202). Washington, DC: National Career Development Association.

Botterbusch, K. F., & Michael, N. L. (1985). *Testing and test modification in vocational evaluation*. Menomonie, WI: Materials Development Center.

Brown, C. C., McDaniel, R. S., Couch, R. H., & McClanahan, M. C. (1994). *Vocational evaluation systems and software: A consumer's guide*. Menomonie, WI: Materials Development Center.

Campbell, N. J. (1988). Review of the Self-Directed Search. In J. T. Kapes & M. M. Mastie (Eds.), *A counselor's guide to career assessment instruments* (2nd ed., pp. 117–120). Washington, DC: National Career Development Association.

Diamond, E. E. (1975). Overview. In E. E. Diamond (Ed.), *Issues of sex bias and sex fairness in career interest measurement* (pp. xiii–xxix). Washington, DC: National Institute of Education.

Hansen, J. C. (1985). *User's guide for the SVIB-SII*. Palo Alto, CA: Consulting Psychologists Press.

Hansen, J. C., & Campbell, D. P. (1985). *Manual for the SVIB-SCII* (4th ed.). Stanford, CA: Stanford University Press.

Holland, J. L. (1985). *Making vocational choices: A theory of careers* (2nd ed.). Englewood Cliffs, NJ: Prentice-Hall.

Holland, J. L. (1987). *The Self-Directed Search: Professional manual*. Odessa, FL: Psychological Assessment Resources.

Hood, A. B., & Johnson, R. W. (1991). *Assessment in counseling: A guide to the use of psychological assessment procedures*. Alexandria, VA: American Association for Counseling and Development.

Jepsen, D. A. (1988). Review of the Kuder Occupational Interest Survey. In J. T. Kapes & M. M. Mastie (Eds.), *A counselor's guide to career assessment instruments* (2nd. ed., pp. 105–109). Washington, DC: National Career Development Association.

Johnasson, C. B. (1975). Technical aspects: Problems of scale development, norms, item differences by sex, and the rate of change in occupational group characteristics. In E. E. Diamond (Ed.), *Issues of sex bias and sex fairness in career interest measurement* (pp. 65–88). Washington, DC: National Institute of Education.

Kates, D. A., & Chan, F. (1993). The controversy over the GATB. In R. Frey & W. Garner

(Eds.), *The issues papers: Sixth national forum on issues in vocational assessment* (pp. 91–94). Menomonie, WI: Materials Development Center.

Nadolsky, J. M. (1974). The work sample in vocational evaluation: A consistent rationale. *Vocational Evaluation and Work Adjustment Bulletin, 7,* 2–5.

Power, P. W. (1991). *A guide to vocational assessment* (2nd ed). Austin, TX: Pro-ed.

Prediger, D. J., & Johnson, R. W. (1979). *Alternatives to sex-restrictive vocational interest assessment* (Research Rep. No. 79). Iowa City, IA: American College Testing Program.

Sink, J. M., & Field, T. F. (1981). *Vocational assessment planning and jobs*. Athens, GA: VSB.

Westbrook, B. W. (1985). Review of the Strong-Campbell Interest Inventory. In J. V. Mitchell, Jr., (Ed.), *The ninth mental measurements yearbook* (pp. 1481–1483). Lincoln, NE: Buros Institute of Mental Measurement.

Williams, J. A., & Williams, J. D. (1988). Review of the Kuder General Interest Survey. In J. T. Kapes & M. M. Mastie (Eds.), *A counselor's guide to career assessment instruments* (2nd ed., pp. 100–104). Washington, DC: National Career Development Association.

Zunker, V. G. (1994). *Using assessment results for career development* (4th ed.) Pacific Grove, CA: Brooks/Cole.

Measurement of Personality and Psychopathology Following Acquired Physical Disability

Timothy R. Elliott and Robert L. Umlauf

With the recent passage of the Americans with Disabilities Act, public awareness of the personal and social aspects of disability is increasing. In this chapter we attempt to provide some ideas, recommendations, and suggestions to psychologists who are interested in the use of psychological testing in their work with individuals who have sustained an acute-onset physical disability.

The psychological assessment of personality and behavioral disorders following acquisition of physical disability warrants the concern of any practicing psychologist. Although psychometric assessment is considered a hallmark of psychology, inappropriate and insensitive use of psychological instruments with clientele limited in physical capacity can produce erroneous and misleading results and imprecise observations about the respondent. This is a particular concern in rehabilitation, as test interpretations are usually translated into treatment recommendations, disability determinations, and eligibility for federal and state rehabilitation services. Thus, the need to provide expert psychological assessment in this realm is paramount. Unfortunately, the practice of psychological assessment of persons with physical disability has been marked by several misunderstandings and uncertainties. Myerson (1957) observed that psychologists often administer psychometric instruments to persons with disability but interpret the scores as if the respondents were nondisabled. Although this issue has been recently addressed in the standardized

The authors extend their gratitude to Jeffrey B. Brookings for his helpful suggestions concerning the 16PF and related resource materials.

administration of educational and aptitude tests (e.g., the Scholastic Aptitude Test, the General Aptitude Test Battery; Nester, 1993), few have questioned standardized administration of personality and psychopathology measures. Despite impairments with ambulation, vision, or sensory input, respondents are often bound to the same rules of administration applied to individuals without these limitations. Furthermore, the lack of appropriate norms and comparison groups, as well as the insensitivity of cookbook approaches to item content contaminated by the physical concomitants of acquired disability, limits test interpretation and application. Not surprisingly, then, a personality profile might reveal that a respondent with a physical disability was preoccupied with physical sensations or ailments. Critics have justifiably argued for the development of separate norms so that meaningful and appropriate comparisons can be made with peers who have similar physical limitations. Additionally, other established instruments might be administered, with caveats for considering the influence of the disability experience on responses to certain items.

Yet psychometric calibrations do not nullify the negative effects of prevailing uninformed professional views of persons with physical disability. Many clinical and counseling psychologists are trained to administer psychometric instruments with the explicit intention of detecting problematic areas for intervention (Wright & Fletcher, 1982). Ideally, the selection of any psychometric measure and assessment system should be intricately connected to a logical intervention program, generally (Kanfer & Saslow, 1967) and to rehabilitation, specifically (Glueckauf, 1993). Nevertheless, the impetus for psychological evaluation in the rehabilitation setting has been characterized by a preoccupation with the level of distress in reaction to acquired disability, the predisposing characteristics that might be related to the onset of disability, and the inevitable and deleterious impact of physical disability on personality functioning over time. For example, stage models—based primarily in Freudian psychodynamic conceptions—have consistently stipulated that the onset of a physical disability induces depression, which may or may not be preceded or followed by an array of other stagelike phenomena, including denial, compromise, and eventual acceptance (for a review of these models see Frank, Elliott, Corcoran, & Wonderlich, 1987). In part, these interpretations may be driven by the expectation that people with acquired disability are preoccupied with the limitations and concomitants imposed by the physical condition (Wright, 1983). Alternatively, these assumptions may reflect reckless generalizations from studies with small sample sizes

(Bourestrom & Howard, 1965) or from personal observations of some distressed patients of rehabilitation units (Elliott & Frank, 1990; Elliott, Yoder, & Umlauf, 1990). At any rate, the association between psychopathology of some sort and physical disability is rarely questioned in many psychological training programs.

When conducting psychological assessment within the inpatient rehabilitation setting, it is critical that the trained psychologist keep in mind the concerns regarding confidentiality and the sharing of sensitive clinical information. In a landmark book regarding ethics within the criminal justice system, Monahan has presented the concept of "who is the client?" (Monahan, 1980). This same question needs to be carefully considered prior to any psychometric assessment with individuals who have a newly acquired disability in the inpatient rehabilitation setting.

There are many clients for whom the psychologists may be performing the task of psychometric assessment. In some cases, the client may be the attending physician, who has requested assessment and assistance in determining how best to work with a given patient. However, there also may be other questions and concerns related to who this client may actually be. It is quite possible that the client may be the entire inpatient rehabilitation team, excluding the patient. It is critical that the clinician be sensitive to the reality that psychological test data must be carefully interpreted within the context of the particular setting. The patient should always be considered part of the rehabilitation team, and interpretation and disclosure of test data should always be in the best interest of the patient. There are published studies regarding the use of psychological test feedback to patients in assisting implementation of change (Lewak, Marks, & Nelson, 1990); yet this same process has not yet been evaluated within the inpatient rehabilitation setting.

In many cases, assessment instruments may be applied primarily for a client other than the patient. If this is the case, this needs to be openly discussed and presented to the patient prior to the completion of the assessment proceedings. It is quite possible that an individual with an acute onset disability may be involved in litigation or the criminal justice system. In this scenario, the clinician should consider which assessment tools are used and also how those tools are interpreted and included in the patient's medical record. In other cases, the psychologist may have a primary alliance with the team over and above the alliance with the patient. These concerns need to be carefully evaluated and examined in order to provide the most appropriate and honest appraisal of test selection and interpretation (Eyde, Robertson, & Kruge, 1993). In addition, another "client" may be embodied in a program evaluation project. There may be complications regarding how research data are presented or included within the clinical setting. Client confidentiality and the appropriate sharing of information require informed consent and careful consideration regarding the audience who will entertain interpretations of test data. The rehabilitation psychologist may be the only individual adequately trained to understand the impact of sharing clinically sensitive data obtained from psychometric assessment tools.

In this chapter, we review many of the major measures of behavioral disorders and personality and their utility in the evaluation of individuals with acquired physical disabilities. We provide basic psychometric information for each instrument and refer to sources that can provide appropriate normative data for use with people with disabling conditions (if these are available). Caveats regarding the use of each instrument are offered. Our comments are based primarily on empirical research and clinical experience with adults who have acquired physical disability; although the instrumentation may vary, the assessment issues we address are pertinent to the psychological assessment of children and adolescents who incur physical disability (Richards, Elliott, Cotliar, & Stevenson, in press). Measures of psychopathology, including broad measures of psychological functioning (the Minnesota Multiphasic Personality Inventory, the Millon Clinical Multi-Axial Inventory, the Symptom Checklist-90, and the Brief Symptom Index) are reviewed. Measures specific to the assessment of depression are then surveyed. Finally, we review contemporary measures of trait and social–cognitive measures of personality constructs.

Measures of Psychopathology and Maladjustment

Assessment of Psychological Adjustment

Minnesota Multiphasic Personality Inventory (MMPI)

Use of the MMPI and the MMPI-2 has been extremely broad, varied, and useful for psychologists in many different settings. The original instrument was developed in the 1940s at the University of Minnesota. It is important to recognize that this instrument was designed primarily for screening psychiatric patients, and there have been relatively few normative studies done with disabled populations. Yet the MMPI has become one of the most widely used psychological testing instruments in behavioral health (Piotrowsky & Lubin, 1990). Fordyce (1964) was one of the first to look at the use of the MMPI with individuals with spinal cord injuries (SCI). His initial work examined the different causes of injury and possible MMPI profiles that may be related to that type of injury. It is important to note that in this early study relatively low levels of pathology were found within the sample. Additionally, observed elevations were quite common when compared with other same age and same gender individuals (e.g., young college-aged males engaged in high-activity events). Thus, one of the early cautions in using the MMPI is that an appropriate comparison sample needs to be used in the clinical interpretation and decision-making process.

A more serious concern regarding the use of the MMPI relates to the physical concomitants of a specific disability rather than emotional or psychopathological concerns. In the first study of item-related confounds on the MMPI, 12 items were identified that significantly differentiate individuals with and without spinal cord injury (Taylor, 1970). This concept was expanded in a later study to look at empirical, factor-analytic evaluation of the MMPI correction factor for persons with SCI (Kendall, Edinger, & Eberly, 1978). This latter study corroborated Taylor's initial findings and also expanded our interpretive insights with the MMPI among people with SCI. Essentially, both studies found that five uncorrected scales produce higher elevations (Scales 1, 2, 3, 4, and 8) among those with SCI. It is typically useful, then, to score the MMPI twice: once with these items included and once with them deleted. This multiple scoring provides a range of response patterns, giving the clinician greater insight into the impact of physical descriptor items that can confound interpretation.

In the MMPI-2, significant efforts were taken to revise outdated and confounding items from the original instrument (Butcher, Dahlstrom, Graham, Tellegen, & Kaemer, 1989). The MMPI-2 provides newer normative data, the deletion of certain items, and alterations of outdated items. There are also additional content scales and supplemental scoring profiles that provide better assessment of validity and reliability. However, the Taylor correction (1970) was not replicated for use with the MMPI-2 and to date has not been reevaluated. Because the item order from the MMPI to the MMPI-2 has changed, it may be time-consuming to translate the item-order change; several of the items from the original MMPI were either significantly changed in wording or omitted. However, there may be several clinical situations in which it may be extremely useful to examine the variation in clinical profiles using the Taylor correction. Thus, it may be a wise investment to score the profile twice to examine the range and variability on the items in the Taylor correction. Future research could provide valuable information and enhance the use of the MMPI-2 in the clinical rehabilitation setting by examining the Taylor correction with this instrument.

Alternatively, many clinicians may find a recent study by Rodevich and Wanlass (in press) useful. These researchers clinically derived a T score correction procedure for MMPI-2 profiles from persons with SCI. Their correction procedure was developed in a different fashion than the original Taylor (1970) correction, and is therefore in need of replication. Nevertheless, Rodevich and Wanlass (in press) relied on expert raters to determine 28 items judged to be potentially confounded by the physical sequelae of SCI, and their sample size was larger than that in the Taylor (1970) study. The resulting procedure may be an efficient method for examining MMPI-2 profiles in the rehabilitation medicine setting.

Several authors have written about the difficulty in administering and developing computerized forms of the MMPI with individuals who have limited upper extremity capacity (Kewman & Lieverman, 1982; Richards, Fine, Wilson, & Rogers, 1983). The revised MMPI-2, as presented by National Computer Systems, allows for an interactive computer-based assessment that—with minor adaptations—allows someone with upper extremity impairment to complete the instrument with relatively few difficulties. However, the protocol has 567 questions and can be quite tiring for someone who has limited upper extremity capacity or for an individual who has retained physical capacity skills but is still in an acute-care status. Although no empirical data are available, there may be concerns regarding split-half reliability and consistency over time if this test is administered to someone who fatigues easily while sitting upright. There is a series of abbreviated MMPI scoring systems (Mini-Mult, MMPI-168, etc.), yet these have severe limits on validity and application regarding the prediction of specific personality factors. The incredible breadth, length, and variety of individual items is one of the primary reasons that MMPI is widely used.

Another issue stems from possible forensic or court-related testimony involving the patient (e.g., litigation, criminal proceedings). It is not uncommon for people injured in accidents (e.g., motor vehicle accident, faulty product, drinking and driving) to have an attorney assisting the patient in determining legal outcome. This might include a third-party lawsuit or criminal proceedings. In either case, it is not unrealistic for the psychologist to be subpoenaed to provide a professional opinion regarding the impact of the injury on the client. In these cases, the use of the

MMPI can provide a strong empirical basis for rendering an opinion (Kurleychek, 1983).

A more complicated issue with the MMPI concerns confidentiality and feedback. It is very common for the MMPI to be administered to inpatients in a hospital. Frequently, attending physicians request an evaluation of a patient's psychological status. It is important to keep in mind that the patient's mental set regarding who has access to this information can significantly influence the way in which the test is completed. If assessment results will be used as a part of a multidisciplinary team meeting, this needs to be carefully but honestly presented to the patient. It is clinically advisable to converse with the patient and provide direct, honest feedback about the test results (Lewak et al., 1990). To date, there have been no published studies regarding the ways in which psychological test data— such as the MMPI-2—affect the ways in which rehabilitation teams interact with a patient with a physical disability. Yet we have often observed psychology colleagues who present psychological interpretations from the MMPI in team rounds while neglecting to give such feedback to the client.

In summary, the MMPI-2 is a very powerful and useful instrument in assessing severe psychopathology, and it is a relatively valid and reliable tool in personality and psychopathological assessment. However, there are specific limits and concerns that the skilled clinician needs to take into consideration regarding interpretation and application of information garnered from the MMPI in the rehabilitation setting. Unfortunately, a thorough search of available computer databases (PsycLit, MEDLINE) reveals no contemporary research with the MMPI-2, physical disability, or medical rehabilitation. Clearly, further research regarding the physical descriptor factors within the MMPI-2 and subsequent normative data could prove very useful.

Millon Inventories

Millon has developed a very extensive and theoretically based set of assessment tools for use in clinical settings. The Millon Clinical Multiaxial Inventories (MCMI) provide a rapid assessment of both Axis I and Axis II diagnostic information. The MCMI-2 is one of the few psychological tests that can provide diagnostic information congruent with the criteria of the Diagnostic and Statistical Manual of Mental Disorders, third edition, revised (DSM-III-R); the recent MCMI-III presumably coincides with DSM-IV criteria. The Millon Behavioral Health Inventory (MBHI) can also provide information that allows the clinician to obtain a broader assessment of the patient's attitudes toward health and health professionals. The primary strength of the Millon scales is the theoretical linkage to the diagnostic nomenclature. This strength can also be considered one of its weaknesses, as it is strongly oriented toward the detection of pathology. One of the caveats within the MCMI-2 manual stipulates the need for careful consideration of the patient population and why the test is being administered. The same concerns addressed in the introduction and the previous section on the MMPI should be taken into account when presenting information to the rehabilitation team as well as the patient.

A patient with a personality disorder on an inpatient unit can generate significant concerns for a rehabilitation staff. Any clinician who has worked with a patient with a severe borderline personality disorder on an inpatient unit knows the major turmoil that ensues when this patient becomes distressed, "splits" staff, or inappropriately discharges strong emotion. Thus, it can be helpful when a skilled clinician uses an instrument such as the MCMI-2 to assist in differentiating severe personality disorder from an individual who may be experiencing significant frustration and emotional distress that may accompany the inpatient experience in rehabilitation medicine.

Unfortunately, there are no available empirical studies to provide normative data for the use of the Millon scales in the rehabilitation setting. Because this is an unstudied area, the clinician needs to be very careful regarding inferences made based on these types of tests. Several items on the MCMI and MCMI-2 describe physical sensations that can reflect actual experiences following traumatic injury (e.g., "Lately, I've been sweating a great deal and feel very tense," "I very often lose my ability to feel any sensations in parts of my body," "I have a hard time keeping my balance when walking"). The confounding effects of these items on profiles gleaned from patients in the rehabilitation setting is unknown.

One study in progress is examining the use of the MBHI on the inpatient SCI unit (Moverman, 1993). Essentially, the MBHI can provide useful screening data to the rehabilitation team regarding an individual patient's health attitudes and personality factors that may influence the patient's compliance and cooperation with the rehabilitation program. This ongoing study concerns the utility of this tool as a primary screening instrument, rather than psychodiagnostic tool per se.

In summary, the Millon scales may be useful in determining DSM-III-R diagnostic data in a rapid and easily administered format. However, there are significant clinical concerns regarding how these data will be shared within the medical setting. Patients may be pathologized by the rehabilitation team on the basis of Millon results. Further research should provide more updated normative data regarding the incidence, preva-lence, and scale elevations for people in the inpatient and outpatient rehabilitation setting.

Derogatis Scales of Psychological Functioning

The Symptom Checklist-90-R (SCL-90-R; Derogatis, 1977) and the Brief Symptom Inventory (BSI; Derogatis & Spencer, 1982) were designed to assess the intensity of several psychological complaints. The SCL-90-R con-tains 90 items that are rated on a scale from 0 (*not at all*) to 4 (*extremely*). There are nine clinical scales measuring Somatization, Obsessive–Com-pulsive, Interpersonal Sensitivity, Depression, Anxiety, Hostility, Phobic Anxiety, Paranoid Ideation, and Psychoticism. Three global distress in-dices are generated from the overall item responses: The Global Severity Index, Positive Symptom Distress Index, and Positive Symptom Total. Test–retest reliability coefficients for the duration of 1 week range from .78 to .90; internal consistency coefficients have ranged from .77 to .90 (Derogatis, 1977). The Global Severity Index (GSI) has been considered by the author as the best overall measure of global psychological distress: It is an index of the depth of the problems reported by the respondent. The Positive Symptom Distress (PSD) measure is purported to reflect the intensity of the problems reported. Finally, the Positive Symptom Total (PST) provides a count of the number of positive symptoms endorsed by the respondent. The SCL-90-R is a pencil-and-paper questionnaire, re-quiring respondents to read each item and respond directly onto the questionnaire. Raw scores are transposed into clinical scores with the use of the normative data provided in the manual. Validity coefficients for each scale are provided in the manual.

The BSI is a 53-item self-report measure of psychological distress derived from the SCL-90-R. The authors maintain that the BSI is appro-priate for medical populations (Derogatis & Melisaratos, 1983). Each item on the BSI is rated on a 5-point scale (ranging from 0 = *not at all* to 4 = *extremely*). Respondents are required to indicate the degree to which they have experienced a particular symptom in the previous week. The authors report adequate internal consistency coefficients for the 9 subscales rang-ing from .71 to .85 (Derogatis & Spencer, 1982), and similar coefficients have been found in other research (.75 to .89; Boulet & Boss, 1991). The authors report adequate test–retest reliabilities (.68 to .91 over a 2-week period), and correlates with other psychological measures (e.g., the MMPI) support the convergent, discriminant, predictive, and construct validity of the BSI (Derogatis & Melisaratos, 1983). As in the case of the SCL-90-

R, the BSI provides three global indices of distress (the GSI, the PSD, and the PST). The BSI has evidenced relatively high scale-by-scale correlations with the SCL-90-R.

The SCL-90-R has been used in a variety of methods in the rehabilitation setting. For example, the SCL-90-R subscales were used as dependent variables in a study of persons with limb amputations and distress as a function of age and time since amputation (Frank et al., 1984). Means and standard deviations for this sample are available in that report. Generally, the large majority of patients with spinal cord injury report adequate adjustment on the basis of SCL-90-R scores (Buckelew, Frank, Elliott, Chaney, & Hewett, 1991). If a score of .65 is considered to be an elevation of clinical concern, it is notable that Buckelew et al. (1991) found no single subscale score to warrant the interpretation of significant distress, based on their sample of 106 persons with SCI. In a fine-grain analysis of the reliability and validity of the SCL-90-R in a rehabilitation setting, Buckelew and colleagues found the internal consistency coefficients varied considerably between items that measured cognitive–affective status and other items that assessed more somatic complaints (Buckelew, Burk, Brownlee-Dufeck, Frank, & DeGood, 1988). Furthermore, the interitem correlations displayed some variation between the different samples (people with SCI, those with chronic pain, and a control group of college students).

In one important preliminary study of psychological aspects and rehabilitation outcome, Malec and Neimeyer (1983) found the SCL-90-R depression scale to be significantly predictive of length of hospitalization among persons with spinal cord injury, and GSI scores were significantly predictive of patient self-care skills. Additionally, the SCL-90-R depression scale and the GSI evidenced significant correlations with the Beck Depression Inventory (.89 and .86, respectively). Another study has found GSI scores to be lower among patients with internal expectancies for health outcomes (Frank, Umlauf, et al., 1987). People with SCI and who are experiencing higher levels of life stress have evidenced significantly higher SCL-90-R profiles than those individuals with lower levels of life stress, regardless of the time since the onset of SCI (Frank & Elliott, 1987). Cross-sectional and longitudinal research have found that patients with SCI who have elevated profiles on the SCL-90-R demonstrate less adaptive coping strategies in response to their injury, including wish-fulfilling fantasy, emotional expression, self-blame, and threatenization (Buckelew, Baumstark, Frank, & Hewett, 1990; Hanson, Buckelew, Hewett, & O'Neal, 1993).

Applications of the Brief Symptom Inventory have determined that this measure does not provide a parallel profile of the SCL-90-R when used with individuals with SCI (Tate, Kewman, & Maynard, 1990). Tate et al. (1990) found that BSI profiles for 79 people with SCI were significantly higher on all scales than the normative sample provided by the test developers, and scores from the Obsessive–Compulsive, Interpersonal Sensitivity, Depression, Psychoticism, and GSI scales from the BSI were significantly lower than scores on the SCL-90-R among persons with SCI. Many of the items endorsed on the BSI might reflect somatic symptoms that are common physical concomitants of SCI. In an extension of this work, Tate, Forchheimer, Maynard, Davidoff, and Dijkers (1993) determined that the BSI depression scale is a sensitive index of depression among those with SCI (Tate et al., 1993). This study also found the reliability coefficients of the BSI ranged from .74 to .87 for the sample, and the BSI depression scale was significantly correlated (.53) with the Zung self-rating depression scale (Zung, 1965). However, these authors could not replicate the nine factor solution reported by the developers of the BSI with the sample of people with SCI. The BSI depression scale had a high degree of specificity toward the prediction of depression (87%) for this sample. More recently, BSI norms for people with spinal cord injury have been developed (Heinrich, Tate, & Buckelew, 1994), and a correction factor is currently being developed for BSI profiles from patients with spinal cord injury (Tate, personal communication, February, 1994).

Summary

Although many clinicians have acclimated to the routine use of broad-based measures of psychopathology and maladjustment, time constraints and physical limitations of patients in the rehabilitation setting dictate a judicious application of these instruments in medical rehabilitation. The MMPI-2, for example, may not be an appropriate device for assessing inpatients with a newly acquired disability. Other disciplines and therapists will vie for time to conduct thorough evaluations for comprehensive rehabilitation, and the patient may be physically unable to leave the hospital room or maintain a sitting position to complete the questionnaire. Furthermore, a psychologist may find more specific, refined instruments more compatible with a bedside interview. Individuals with relatively uneventful behavioral patterns may produce flat profiles, giving a clinician very little to say regarding personality functioning and treatment recommendations. Other devices—such as the BSI and SCL-90-R—may provide no more than a calibration of a patient's current level of distress. Finally, many patients may simply find the content of some items to be intrusive, offensive, or irrelevant, and the worth of psychological service may be held suspect. Judicious use of these tools is urged, with careful regard to the preinjury history of the patient and the needs of the particular clinical setting. The MMPI may be best suited for outpatient services in which the psychologist has limited opportunity to observe patient behavior. Similarly, the Millon scales may be ideal in elucidating medical and psychosocial adjustment issues when evidence of maladjustment has been documented, particularly when neglect and noncompliance with therapeutic regimens is suspected.

Assessment of Depression

Given the long history of clinical preoccupation with depressive symptomatology in the rehabilitation literature, this behavioral phenomenon has received extensive clinical and empirical attention. Unfortunately, many of the clinical studies have relied on anecdotal observations and are thus highly biased (for critical review see Frank, Elliot, et al., 1987). Notable studies that have used standardized, reliable diagnostic systems have repeatedly found that depression—as a clinical syndrome with clearly defined parameters—is not an inevitable reaction to the onset of acquired physical disability (Frank, Kashani, Wonderlich, Lising, & Visot, 1985; Fullerton, Harvey, Klein, & Howell, 1981; Howell, Fullerton, Harvey, & Klein, 1981; Kashani, Frank, Kashani, Wonderlich, & Reid, 1983). These studies indicate, however, that a significant minority of persons with physical disability display depressive behaviors at some time following the onset of injury. Furthermore, interview systems may sometimes be clinically cumbersome and time consuming. Therefore, the use of self-report instruments as screening devices in the rehabilitation setting is highly desirable. Several popular measures of depression have been scrutinized in this regard.

The Center for Epidemiological Studies—Depression Scale (CES-D)

The CES-D was designed to measure depressive symptomatology in the general population (Radloff, 1977). This questionnaire contains 20 items designed to assess current levels of depressive behavior, with a particular emphasis on the impact of depressed mood. Items are keyed on a 4-point scale, ranging from *rarely or none of the time* to *most or all of the time*. Respondents indicate how often they experienced each symptom in the preceding week. Scores on the instrument range between zero and 60, and a score greater than 16 has been found to differentiate depressed from nondepressed adults in community samples (Craig & Van Natta, 1978). Radloff (1977) has reported internal consistency coefficients ranging from .84 to .90 in several field applications. Turner and McLean (1989) reported an alpha coefficient of .88 for a sample of individuals with physical disabilities ($N = 731$; Turner & McLean, 1989).

Studies utilizing the CES-D in the investigation of depression following spinal cord injury have yielded interesting yet disparate results. For example, Schulz and Decker (1985) found the mean score on the CES-D (9.7) was very similar to the average score reported by the general population (9.2). However, a study of a larger sample of community residing adults with SCI found the mean score for this group to be higher than that of the general population, and the average score of the female respondents was significantly higher than that of the male respondents (14.7 and 11.1, respectively; Fuhrer, Rintala, Hart, Clearman, & Young, 1993). The CES-D scores of persons with amputations has been found to be slightly higher than those of the general population (11.31; Rybarczyk et al., 1992). In the most thorough study of the CES-D among people with acquired physical disabilities to date, Turner and McLean (1989) found that individuals with severe physical disabilities had a higher mean score than those with less severe disabling conditions (16.65 and 11.05, respectively). Additionally, these researchers noted a variation in scores as a function of age, but gender differences were minimal. Finally, these scores were higher than those of a community sample, and the authors concluded that individuals with physical disability should be considered at risk for the development of depressive symptomatology.

Empirical research has also revealed meaningful correlates of CES-D scores. For example, decreased levels of social support have been associated with higher CES-D scores among community residing persons with SCI (Rintala, Young, Hart, Clearman, & Fuhrer, 1992; Schulz & Decker, 1985). Schulz and Decker (1985) found that higher CES-D scores were associated with poor self-assessed health status and decreased perceptions of control over one's life. Fuhrer et al. (1993) found CES-D scores were significantly predictive of social integration, occupation, and mobility as measured by the Craig Handicap Assessment and Reporting Technique (Whiteneck, Charlifue, Gerhart, Overholser, & Richardson, 1992) after controlling for the variance attributable to self-reported functional independence and functional level of disability. Finally, systematic research by Rybarczyk and colleagues (Rybarczyk et al., 1992; Rybarczyk, Nyenhuis, Nicholas, Cash, & Kaiser, in press) has found that those who experienced greater social discomfort following leg amputation evidenced higher CES-D scores. Thus, the CES-D appears to have considerable clinical and theoretical value for use in the rehabilitation setting.

Beck Depression Inventory (BDI)

The BDI is a 21-item self-report measure of depressive symptoms and their severity (Beck, Ward, Mendelson, Mock, & Erbaugh, 1961). Each item has a 4-point response option to note the degree of severity. Research has displayed relatively high correlations between the BDI and other self-report measures of depression (e.g., Tanaka-Matsumi & Kameoka, 1986). Respondents are to describe their experience on each item for the preceding week. Items are rated on a 0 (*not at all*) to 3 (*extreme form of each symptom*) scale. The BDI has adequate internal consistency (.84) and correlations with other depression measures among college students range from .54 to .68 (Tanaka-Matsumi & Kameoka, 1986). A total score is derived by summing the responses to each particular item.

The BDI has been used in several clinical and theoretical investigations of adjustment to acquired physical disability. Malec and Neimeyer (1983) found the BDI total score to be significantly predictive of length of inpatient stay among 28 patients. The average score for their sample was 11.04. The BDI was also correlated highly with the SCL-90-R GSI score (.86), the SCL-90-R depression scale (.96), the MMPI-168 factor score (.83), and the *D* scale from the MMPI (.77). Frank and Elliott (1987) found that patients experiencing high levels of life stress had significantly higher depression scores than patients with SCI with lower levels of life stress (11.81 and 5.2, respectively). Similarly, Frank et al. (1984) found that younger individuals had higher BDI scores than older individuals as time progressed following amputations. Umlauf and Frank (1983) found that patients with higher BDI scores expected to be hospitalized longer and had lower levels of functional independence and mobility than those with lower scores. In a second study, patients with spinal cord injury who had the highest expectations of recovery of functional abilities reported the lowest BDI scores of three patient subgroups, and they displayed a greater change in activities of daily living following rehabilitation (Umlauf & Frank, 1987). Longitudinal research has demonstrated that differences between people with SCI and community-residing adults without disability are pronounced immediately following discharge from inpatient rehabilitation, but these differences can dissipate within the course of a year (Richards, 1986).

The BDI has been criticized for having items that may be confounded by the physical sequelae of acquired physical disability. These items relate to physical appearance, ability to work, weight loss, and the report of physical problems such as constipation. Many of these symptoms commonly occur following the onset of physical disability (Peck, Smith, Ward, & Milano, 1989). Other evidence suggests that although somatic items on depression scales such as the CES-D and the BDI may bias prevalence estimates of depression on patients with chronic physical conditions, correlations between depression scores and other psychological variables are not likely to be adversely inflated (Blalock, Devellis, Brown, & Wallston, 1989).

Inventory to Diagnose Depression (IDD)

The IDD is a 22-item self-report instrument developed to measure depressive behavior (Zimmerman, Coryell, Corenthal, & Wilson, 1986). This instrument contains an attractive feature unknown in other self-report depression inventories. It is designed to provide (a) categorical diagnoses of major depressive disorder (MDD) according to DSM-III criteria and DSM-III-R criteria, (b) binary decisions about the presence or absence of individual symptoms, and (c) severity estimates of depressive symptomatology. Test–retest reliabilities and internal consistency markers have been impressive in comparison with interview systems and other self-report measures of depression. For example, test–retest reliabilities have ranged from .91 to .93 (Zimmerman et al., 1986; Zimmerman & Coryell, 1987). These studies also report internal consistency coefficients of .92. Comparisons with interview systems and other self-report measures of depression have revealed correlations ranging from .80 to .87 (Zimmerman, Coryell, Wilson, & Corenthal, 1986; Zimmerman & Coryell, 1987). The IDD requires a respondent to indicate the severity of each symptom of depression on a 5-point Likert scale. The sum of these responses provides a total severity score that serves as a single index of depressive behavior. The IDD items are designed so that a binary decision can be made regarding the presence or absence of a symptom, according to clinical severity. For example, an item score of zero represents an absence of disturbance, a score of 1 represents some clinical severity, and a score of 2 or more is considered to be a positive symptom endorsement (Zimmerman et al., 1986).

Several studies have related the IDD total scores to psychological and demographic variables of interest. Elliott and Harkins (1991) found that individuals with spinal cord injury complaining of persistent pain had elevated IDD scores in comparison with those patients without pain. Goal-directed, problem-focused orientations have been found to be important characteristics of persons with SCI who report fewer problems as measured by the IDD (Elliott, Godshall, Herrick, Witty, & Spruell, 1991; Elliott, Witty, Herrick, & Hoffman, 1991). Higher IDD scores have also been associated with decreased leisure activities (Elliott & Shewchuk, 1995), lower assertiveness (Elliott, Herrick, et al., 1991), lower levels of social support (Elliott, Herrick, Witty, Godshall, & Spruell, 1992), and an increased likelihood to develop secondary complications among persons with SCI (e.g., decubiti, urinary tract infections; Herrick, Elliott, & Crow, 1994).

Frank et al. (1992) found the endorsement of dysphoria—represented by symptoms of negative self-evaluations, depressed affect, and suicidal ideation—constituted a core element of depression common to persons with SCI, individuals with rheumatoid arthritis, college students, and community-residing adults. This study also indicated that 11% of a sample with SCI met clinical criteria for major depressive disorder, in comparison with 4% of the community-residing adults and 14% of patients with rheumatoid arthritis. In a Bayesian analysis of individual symptoms to assess diagnostic value to predict depression among persons with SCI, endorsement of lack of interest or pleasure was the best diagnostic indicator of depression for persons with paraplegia. Symptoms efficiently predicting major depressive disorder for persons with paraplegia and those with quadriplegia included psychomotor disturbance, appetite change, and sleep disturbance (Clay, Hagglund, Frank, Elliott, & Chaney, in press). However, inability to concentrate best predicted the presence of major depressive disorder among persons with quadriplegia. These studies suggest that the contribution of somatic items on the IDD may be less important to the identification of depression among persons with acquired physical disability than originally assumed.

Zung Self-Rating Depression Scale (Zung)

The Zung scale (Zung, 1965) has 20 items that are rated on a 1 (*some of the time*) to 4 (*all of the time*) Likert scale. The Zung scale was developed to assess the severity of psychological and physiological manifestations of depression. Acceptable alpha coefficients have been documented (e.g., .81; Tanaka-Matsumi & Kameoka, 1986). Validity coefficients with other measures of depression have ranged from .61 to .81 (Schaefer et al., 1985). Evidence indicates that the Zung scale has better validity coefficients with DSM-III criteria for depression than other popular self-report measures (Schaefer et al., 1985). A Zung score greater than 55 is considered indicative of a diagnosis of major depression (Schaefer et al., 1985; Zung, 1965).

In the most comprehensive study to date of the Zung scale in a rehabilitation setting, Davidoff et al. (1990) found the mean score for a sample of people with SCI was significantly higher than the average score from a community sample (49 vs. 37.1). A somatic subscale score from the Zung was calculated, and the score for those with spinal cord injury was predictably higher than the average score for the control group (16.6 vs. 11.6). However, the affective subscale score was also higher for those with spinal cord injury (22.6 vs. 18.1). Demographic variables and characteristics related to type of injury and injury onset were unrelated to Zung scores among people with SCI. Further study revealed no significant differences between mean scores on a battery of neuropsychological tests between patients with SCI categorized as either depressed or nondepressed on the basis of the Zung scale (Davidoff, Roth, Thomas, & Doljanak, 1990). Finally, a recent study has concluded that the Zung may be a very effective tool for identifying individuals with SCI who are at risk for developing clinical levels of depression during or following hospitalization (Tate et al., 1993).

Summary

The heightened clinical and research focus on depression enables us to make several observations regarding the utility of these measures. The CES-D has an established value as a research instrument, but clinicians preferring a thorough screening device may prefer administering the Zung. This instrument contains fewer items potentially confounded by physical disabilities and has a higher correlation with interview methods for diagnosing depression. Other clinicians, who have the time and investment in face-to-face interviews with persons with newly acquired disabilities, may use the Inventory to Diagnose Depression as a semistructured interview. The IDD covers criteria necessary for determining clinical diagnoses for major depression; in an initial interview a clinician may inquire further about the history and course of each symptom. Such information may be pivotal in selecting appropriate medical and psychosocial interventions. In comparison, the Beck Depression Inventory may be too confounded by somatic-based items; nevertheless, it is relatively easy to administer and may be used repeatedly to monitor adjustment over time (e.g., Richards, 1986).

It may be particularly important to scrutinize reported problems in separate domains of cognitive (low self-worth, lack of pleasure, hopelessness, etc.), affective (sad, mood, irritability, etc.), and somatic (sleep disturbance, appetite disruption) complaints to determine effective intervention in the rehabilitation setting. Sleep disturbance—a common complaint among persons with recent onset SCI—can induce mood disturbance and decreased energy that can potentially impair motivation and performance in therapies. These may be addressed with psychopharmacological interventions. Cognitive aspects of depression may warrant psychological interventions. Thus, discarding somatic items on depression scales can potentially eliminate valuable information for the rehabilitation team effort. It is recommended that the psychologist carefully review symptom patterns on any depression measure and rely less on any total score.

Measures of Personality

Measures of nonpathological, "normal" personality in the rehabilitation setting have not been covered in the clinical and the theoretical literature as much as the instruments surveyed earlier in this chapter. Clinical preoccupation with aberrant behaviors culminating in or subsequent to the onset of acquired disability have dominated the attention of clinicians and theorists alike. Therefore, very few comments can be made based on prior empirical studies with nonpathological personality instruments in rehabilitation, despite the attractive qualities of these measures and the obvious appropriateness of these devices for use with this clientele. We briefly review several trait and social–cognitive measures of individual differences.

Trait Measures of Personality

Neuroticism, Extroversion, and Openness Personality Inventory (NEO-PI)
The NEO-PI (Costa & McCrae, 1985) is a measure of trait aspects of personality. The NEO-PI is based on the five-factor model of personality that has recently stimulated considerable research (Digman, 1990). As defined by the developers, the five-factor model of personality consists of Extroversion, Neuroticism, Openness to Experience, Conscientiousness, and Agreeableness. Neuroticism refers to a general disposition toward the experience of negative affectivity, a sense of vulnerability, emotional instability, maladaptive coping, unrealistic ideas, and excessive cravings. Extroversion is defined as the propensity for interpersonal interaction,

stimulation, and positive affectivity. Openness to Experience encompasses the appreciation of experience, intellectual curiosity, and aesthetic sensitivity. Agreeableness refers to the individual's interpersonal orientation in terms of thoughts, feelings, and actions, including trust, altruism, and sympathy. The Conscientiousness scale assesses preferences for structure, organization, self-discipline, and motivation in goal-directed behavior.

The NEO-PI consists of 181 items that are rated on a 5-point scale (ranging from *strongly disagree* to *strongly agree*). Internal consistency coefficients range from .85 to .93 for the Neuroticism, Extroversion, and Openness to Experience scales; coefficients range from .76 to .86 for the Agreeableness and Conscientiousness scales, respectively (Leong & Dollinger, 1990). Test–retest coefficients acquired from an adult sample at 3- and 6-year intervals indicate temporal stability for the five scales, with coefficients ranging from .64 to .85 (McCrae & Costa, 1991). Substantial study has correlated the five studies with a variety of similar and dissimilar measures to establish convergent and divergent validity (Costa & McCrae, 1985).

Although the NEO-PI has been well-received, it has yet to be systematically studied in the rehabilitation environment. In the one application to date, Rohe and Krause (1993) found that individuals with SCI scored higher on the fantasy subscale and the Openness to Experience factor than a normative sample; those with SCI also scored higher on the excitement-seeking facet of the Extroversion factor. However, those with SCI scored lower on two other facets of Extroversion (assertiveness, activity) and on the Conscientiousness factor than the normative sample. The clinical implications of these data have yet to be explored, and results may certainly be specific to the population sampled by the researchers. It is notable that no significant differences occurred on the Neuroticism scale, which contains several items that could have been potentially confounded by their reference to physical sensations and complaints. According to the developers of the NEO-PI, Neuroticism should predict emotional distress among persons with acquired disability, and Conscientiousness scores may be associated with adherence to therapeutic regimens. Nevertheless, these possibilities require empirical scrutiny.

Sixteen Personality Factor Questionnaire—Form E (16PF)

The 16PF-Form E is a personality inventory based on the factor analytic description of personality promoted by Cattell (Cattell, Eber, & Tatsuoka, 1970). Form E has 128 items with a fixed, forced-choice response format. It measures 16 primary normal personality characteristics and five second-order dimensions. The second-order dimensions—Extroverted, Adjusted, Tough-Minded, Independent, and Disciplined—are thought to parallel the "big five" factors assessed by the NEO-PI (McCrae & John, 1992). The Form E manual has extensive normative data for individuals with a wide array of physical impairments (Eber, Cattell, & IPAT Staff, 1985).

The use of the 16PF and its psychometric properties among persons with various disabilities has been discussed in some detail elsewhere (Brookings, Bolton, & Young, 1994; Bolton & Brookings, 1993a). The 16PF is often favorably considered for several reasons. The personality dimensions assessed by the 16PF appear to be relatively independent of psychopathology (Bolton & Dana, 1988) and self-concept (Bolton, 1979) among persons with physical disabilities, sensory impairments, behavioral disorders, and mental retardation. The purported primary and secondary factors have been replicated among these clients (Bolton, 1977), and the profile scores have been meaningfully related to vocational interest patterns (Bolton, 1986). A computerized scoring package has been developed for use with similar clientele (Bolton, 1987).

Several observations can be made regarding the use of the 16PF with people who incur physical disabilities. Prior research supports the basic structure and psychometric adequacy of the instrument with this population, and thus it can provide a cogent description of personality that can be potentially useful to the person, the psychologist, and the rehabilitation team. The utility of these dimensions in light of the broad research on personality, generally, and the relation to indices of adjustment and performance criteria germane to rehabilitation medicine settings is less clear. There are many unresolved issues concerning the theoretical properties of the 16 factors in the extant literature. Consequently, clinicians employing the 16PF rely primarily on research conducted by Cattell and his colleagues to draw meaningful inferences about presumed behaviors and characteristics of respondents. When the 16PF has been studied in other arenas (e.g., substance abuse rehabilitation), it is often used in an atheoretical fashion. Perhaps contemporary research will examine correlates of the secondary factors as proxies of the "big five" personality dimensions with behavioral health and rehabilitation populations.

Finally, the 16PF scores may not be sensitive predictors of environment-specific behaviors (e.g., work satisfactoriness; Bolton & Brookings, 1993b) among those with disabilities. Despite this shortcoming, Brookings et al. (1994) advise that the 16PF can be a useful component of an overall assessment package with vocational rehabilitation clients. Research examining the relation of 16PF scores to rehabilitation outcomes among those with acquired physical disabilities is certainty warranted.

Personal Styles Inventory

The Personal Styles Inventory is designed to measure normal-range characteristics according to a circumplex model. The characteristics assessed by this inventory are considered commonplace, everyday behaviors that are easily recognized and interpreted by clients (Kunce, Cope, & Newton, 1993). Personal styles are measured in three key subsystems including styles of expressing emotions, behaving, and thinking. Each style is explained in terms of its relationship to two major personality dimensions, including extroversion (vs. introversion) and stability (vs. change). Furthermore, scores are presented in terms of a client's "natural" proclivity (termed *basic behavior*), and present manifestations of these styles (termed *current behavior*). Thus, the model defines eight global personality traits and demarcates an individual's current preference on each dimension in contrast to fundamental characteristics.

All scores on this instrument are described in terms of everyday behaviors. High and low scores on each scale indicate only the strength of the style, and no single item is uniquely sensitive to any form of psychopathology. Additionally, none of the items refer to physical problems or health-related complaints.

The instrument has been subjected to considerable psychometric investigation, and adequate reliability and validity coefficients are presented in the manual (Kunce et al., 1993) and in introductory overviews (Kunce, Cope, & Newton, 1991). Of striking importance is the emphasis on the nonpathological assessment of personality characteristics in three broad domains (thinking, emotional expression, and behavior) on the dimensions of extroversion and preference for change.

The instrument may be particularly sensitive to the environmental press that individuals with stigmatizing conditions encounter following the onset of physical disability. For example, an individual may have a rather basic style in the three domains that is subsequently challenged by physical and psychological barriers that often accompany physical disability, or by the demands of the inpatient rehabilitation setting. This instrument may prove sensitive to the different reactions individuals have to the rehabilitation environment, value changes that can occur following the onset of disability, and the wide range of reactions to therapeutic regimens typically prescribed to persons with severe and permanent injuries. The manual provides case examples and insightful comments for applying the instrument in career assessment, counseling interventions (e.g., self-insight, reframing, interpersonal skills, defining personal goals), team building, and medical staff consultation (Kunce et al., 1993). Particular attention is given to rehabilitation issues in personal adjustment and vocational counseling (Kunce et al., 1993; pp. 51–56). The manual also contains normative data for comparative purposes. This instrument may have great potential for use with staff and patients in a rehabilitation setting.

Social-Cognitive Measures

Locus of Control (LOC)

The perceived degree of control over behavior reinforcement has been applied in several studies of reaction to acquired disability. Unfortunately, the nature of measurement has often varied, ranging from the use of unidentified locus of control (LOC) measures (e.g., Shadish, Hickman, & Arrick, 1981) to the use of domain-specific scales (e.g., a sex-related LOC measure; Linton, 1990). Although the use of domain-specific LOC measures is theoretically consistent with social learning models, it weakens the generalizability and clinical relevance of the research. Studies have found that an internal orientation has been related to lower depression scores (Shadish et al., 1981) and to shorter length of stay in rehabilitation hospital (Swenson, 1976). One program of research has used the Multidimensional Health Locus of Control Scale (MHLOC; Wallston, Wallston, & DeVellis, 1978). The MHLOC is an 18-item questionnaire to assess health-related expectancies for reinforcement. Individuals rate each item on a 6-point scale. Three subscales are provided: Internal, Chance, and Powerful Others. Ratings for items loading on each respective factor are summed to make up the three subscale scores. Internal consistency coefficients for the subscales have ranged from .67 to .77, and correlations with similar measures of generalized expectancies have ranged from .28 to .80 (Wallston et al., 1978). Relevant research indicates the test–retest coefficients for this scale over a 7-month period indicate that the Internal and Powerful Other subscales are relatively stable over time (.58 and .76, respectively), but the Chance subscale may lack temporal stability (.10; Winefield, 1982). Preliminary data indicated that the Chance and Internal subscales correlated significantly with health status in theoretically consistent directions (Wallston et al., 1978). The Internal and Chance subscales have been shown to be salient predictors of distress and adjustment among persons with a variety of health concerns (Wallston, 1989).

Higher scores on the Internal subscale have been related to lower depression scores (Frank, Umlauf, et al., 1987), and external expectancies have been related to decreased mobility and activities of daily living (Umlauf & Frank, 1983, 1987) for rehabilitation patients. However, factor analytic work with a sample of patients in a rehabilitation medicine setting did not replicate the three-factor solution reported by the developers (Umlauf & Frank, 1986). These researchers found considerable overlap between the Chance and Powerful Others subscale items, indicating a general external factor. Notably, the Internal factor was replicated. Therefore, the Internal construct appears to be of particular merit in the assessment of persons with acquired disabilities.

Problem Solving Inventory (PSI)

The PSI is a measure of self-appraised problem-solving ability (Heppner, 1988). The PSI assesses the degree to which individuals perceive a high degree of confidence in their ability to solve everyday problems (the Problem Solving Confidence factor), their ability to regulate emotional reactions to problems (the Personal Control factor), and their general tendency to approach rather than avoid problems (the Approach–Avoidance factor).

The PSI contains 32 items that are rated on a 6-point Likert scale (1 = *strongly agree* to 6 = *strongly disagree*). Separate scores are derived for these factors and a total score is computed by summing the factor scores. Reliability estimates reveal that these constructs are internally consistent (alpha coefficients range from .72 to .90; $N = 150$) and stable over a 2-week period (test–retest correlations range from .83 to .89; $N = 31$; Heppner, 1988). Validity estimates have accumulated over several studies, revealing that the PSI total score and subscales are significantly related in predicted directions with a variety of self-report and observational measures (Heppner, 1988). Lower PSI scores denote a more positive appraisal of personal problem solving skills.

The PSI has been correlated in meaningful directions with several variables pertinent to rehabilitation. In one study, self-appraised effective problem solving was associated with lower depression scores and less psychosocial impairment secondary to disability among 90 individuals with SCI (Elliott, Godshall, et al., 1991). Effective problem solving was also associated with a greater willingness to behave assertively in tense situations among the sample. Other research has found self-appraised problem-solving skills can moderate the effects of social support to psychosocial functioning of individuals with SCI (Elliott, Herrick, & Witty, 1992). Herrick, Elliot, and Crow (in press) found that the tendency to approach and define problems was associated with a lower incidence of secondary complications among 53 people with SCI. The models of problem solving have particular clinical importance, as this perspective leans heavily on a cognitive–behavioral tradition that emphasizes the role of social learning in the acquisition of particular problem skills. Thus, individuals who score lower on problem-solving skills may benefit from cognitive–behavioral interventions designed to enhance their problem-solving repertoire (Nezu & Perri, 1989).

Summary of Nonpathological Scales

Many psychologists shy away from nonpathological personality measures for a variety of reasons. Some scales provide a relatively circumscribed, unidimensional assessment of personality functioning, thus limiting clinical utility. Other clinicians prefer to screen for evidence of psychopathology or emotional maladjustment. Yet many of these devices are geared toward intervention techniques that can be applied in the rehabilitation setting, and others yield information that may prove most useful in enhancing patient self-awareness and growth. These measures may be most helpful in exploring relative strengths and concerns for each respondent that could be addressed in rehabilitation programs. Ideally, informed psychologists will be attuned to the assessment of personal resources and capabilities in the psychological evaluation of persons with acquired disability, and nonpathological personality instruments will then be incorporated into assessment batteries.

Clinical Applications

When considering the utility of different instruments, the psychologist should carefully consider the needs of each client in the treatment setting. In the inpatient rehabilitation setting, for example, patients may be limited by their level of injury, endurance, and attention span. The psychologist may be compelled to conduct an in-depth bedside assessment with occasional disruptions and a lack of privacy. Nevertheless, it is imperative that the psychologist ascertain basic behavioral styles and current psychosocial status. Thus, a clinical interview may be significantly augmented by the use of a broad-based measure of nonpathological personality predispositions and a more specific measure of psychological adjustment. For these reasons, the first author routinely administers the Personal Styles Inventory to patients admitted for initial rehabilitation, as this device has nonthreatening items and results can be easily communicated to staff and patient. The Inventory to Diagnose Depression is used as a semistructured interview, offering several opportunities to inquire about other relevant behavioral patterns and reactions (e.g., leisure interests, anxiety-related symptoms, sleep-related problems, concerns about sexuality) in the initial interview.

In contrast, the second author has conducted many psychological evaluations of outpatients involved in litigation surrounding the onset and course of the disability (e.g., tetraplegia acquired in a motor vehicle accident). These patients have typically been seen 1 year postinjury, and the representing attorney is very interested in testing results. In these situations, the MMPI (or MMPI-2), scored with and without the Taylor correction, is an extremely useful tool. With the multiple validity scales, the extensive research base, and the rich forensic literature, this tool is an excellent choice when the potential exists for expert witness testimony. Combined with a thorough clinical interview and review of medical records from hospitalization, the multiple "clients"—the patient, the attorney, the court, and the expert witness—can all be served.

Other situations may dictate domain-specific measures. Some patients return to the inpatient setting years after injury onset with debilitating complications from neglect and poor adherence to self-care regimens. Individuals with spinal cord injuries, for example, are susceptible to decubitus ulcers (i.e., pressure sores) if they do not adhere to regimens for periodic pressure reliefs and daily skin checks. Patients who develop these conditions may have deficiencies in systematically defining and solving problems generally (Herrick, 1991). Others may feel little control over health outcomes and may harbor fatalistic attributions about their health. Thus, an evaluation may be enriched with the inclusion of the Problem Solving Inventory and one of the Health Locus of Control scales. However, other patients with these conditions may be too preoccupied with outstanding characterological issues. A recent case seen by the first author involved a 26-year-old man with three diagnosed pressure ulcers in a period of 7 years, each requiring expensive surgical repair and postoperative care. Responses to the Millon Clinical Multiaxial Inventory revealed significant elevation (over a base rate of 75) on the histrionic–gregarious and the dependent–submissive scales. Other evaluations of patients with decubiti and suspected neglect have revealed significant elevation on scales pertaining to narcissistic, passive–aggressive, sociopathic, and schizoidal tendencies. Presumably, these characterological problems contribute to inabilities to engage in routine, daily health maintenance behaviors. Profiles on the MCMI (and MCMI-2) may lend insight into patient dynamics that impede adherence and provide staff direction for meaningful psychosocial interventions.

Concluding Remarks and Unresolved Issues

Many issues remain elusive in the assessment of individuals with physical disabilities at this point. Some of these issues pertain to issues specific to those with mobility impairment; others reflect problems encountered by practicing psychologists in our diverse society. Most of them have yet to be illuminated with programmatic, insightful research.

To a great extent, we have glossed over possible confounds that might exist in the lack of standardized administration of instruments with persons with mobility deficits. Several instruments have been adapted for computer applications with persons who have mobility impairments (e.g., the MMPI), and some questionnaires may be administered in an interview format (e.g., the IDD). The degree to which the means of administration confounds response patterns is basically unknown. Although there has been some literature on the possible differences between self-report and interviewer-administered versions of the MMPI, this has not been replicated with our population of interest. This is a potential confound in any assessment practice, and we do not know if different administration procedures radically affect the results of the instruments we have covered in our discussion.

Physical disability may exert an influence as well on other aspects of psychological assessment. Profiles on the MMPI can be artificially elevated by reasonable concerns about physical functioning, and correcting for these response patterns can restore a sense of normalcy to the profile in comparison to normative data. However, honest attention and frank openness about physical functioning and certain sensations may in fact be adaptive among those with severe physical disabilities. The lack of attention and openness about such matters may indicate an unwillingness to attend to such matters, or a careless disregard for one's physical health. This type of surveillance may be critical in maintaining health and staving off secondary complications (e.g., decubitus ulcers, infections) that often result from personal neglect and poor adherence to behavioral regimens. It may be that we may err in our attempt to normalize profiles without taking into consideration the unique demands that might accompany a severe physical disability.

Furthermore, our lack of sensitivity to the environmental press imposed on individuals with disability may alter response patterns. We simply do not know the degree to which personality is affected by the acquisition of a physical disability and resulting environmental press that follows in its wake. Ultimately, this is an issue that can never be completely resolved: Longitudinal research would provide limited insight into possible changes on response patterns from the time of onset to some point in time after injury. There is evidence, however, that indicates measurable behaviors persist after the onset of physical disability. For example, recent programmatic work has found that individuals with significant blood alcohol levels at time of injury report more significant substance abuse problems preinjury (Heineman, Mamott, & Schnoll, 1990) and many resume their patterns of substance use within the first postinjury year (Heineman, Keen, Donohue, & Schnoll, 1988). Additionally, vocational interest patterns have demonstrated remarkable stability over several years among a sample of persons with SCI (Rohe & Athelstan, 1982). It is possible that certain behavioral patterns, then, persist following the onset of physical disability and over time.

Unresolved issues concerning predictive validity may circumscribe our ability to make meaningful predictions about these instruments and the occurrence of future behaviors. Several global social–cognitive variables have been associated with self-reported levels of distress and adjustment, but we have yet to understand the relation of these constructs to secondary complications indicative of behavioral adherence to therapeutic regimens (e.g., decubitus ulcers). Commonplace personality constructs may provide a general description about an individual but very little insight about future behaviors in a specific context. Bolton and Brookings (1993b) found that behaviorally based observational ratings were better prospective predictors of work satisfaction than 16PF scores. Observational ratings tied to clearly defined behavioral criteria may be better indicators of later performance in specific environments than self-report personality variables.

An unexplored issue germane to our diverse society pertains to cultural sensitivity. Much has been written about the impact of ethnicity on the assessment process, generally; research has yet to examine these issues in the rehabilitation setting. National trends indicate that more people of African American and Hispanic heritage are acquiring severe physical disability, and these persons are more likely than Caucasians to incur disability from acts of violence (Elliott, Richards, DeVivo, Jackson, & Stover, 1994). Preliminary evidence indicates that people of African American descent are less likely to be employed following disability than Caucasians with similar conditions (James, DeVivo, & Richards, 1993), and rehabilitation outcomes may be meaningfully related to an array of environmental and personality characteristics (e.g., ethnicity of the service provider, self-esteem; Asbury, Walker, Belgrave, Maholmes, & Green, 1994). It is imperative that future researchers closely examine cultural factors in assessment and outcomes for rehabilitation efforts to be delivered efficiently to these clients.

Finally, the selective attention to certain presumed tendencies and affective reactions has needlessly limited our sensitivity to other problems among people with acquired physical disabilities. Anecdotal research, in particular, has focused on depressive behaviors; empirical research has often sought to identify the "imprudent, impulsive, and excitement seeking" tendencies of those who might jeopardize their health by risk-taking activities prior to injury (e.g., Fordyce, 1964; Rohe & Krause, 1993). Thorough research that uses more objective and specific measures of "imprudence" and sensation-seeking have failed to support this latter hypothesis (Ditunno, McCauley, & Marquette, 1985) and it is likely that all of these studies are quite sensitive to sampling and the vagaries of catchment areas for separate clinics.

More important, clinicians suspect that anxiety disorders are common in the rehabilitation medicine setting. There are several plausible reasons for this. Many persons sustain physical disability in acts of violence (e.g., assaults) and trauma (e.g., falls, motor vehicle accidents). Symptoms of posttraumatic stress disorder and other anxiety syndromes are observed among persons victimized by violence, crime, and naturally occurring traumatic events (Norris & Kaniasty, 1994; Resnick, Kilpatrick, Dansky, Saunders, & Best, 1993). Many of the social anxieties reported by individuals with severe physical disability parallel specific diagnostic criteria for generalized social phobia (e.g., fear of being watched, fear of embarrassing accidents; Dunn, 1977; Dunn & Herman, 1982). No systematic research has examined the incidence, prevalence, and correlates of anxiety disorders among persons with acquired physical disability, and the possible detrimental effects on quality of life, community integration, and social mobility.

References

Asbury, C. A., Walker, S., Belgrave, F. Z., Maholmes, V., & Green, L. (1994). Psychosocial, cultural, and accessibility factors associated with participation of African-Americans in rehabilitation. *Rehabilitation Psychology, 39*, 113–121.

Beck, A. T., Ward, C. H., Mendelson, M., Mock, J., & Erbaugh, J. (1961). An inventory for measuring depression. *Archives of General Psychiatry, 4*, 53–63.

Blalock, S. J., DeVellis, R., Brown, G., & Wallston, K. A. (1989). Validity of the center for epidemiological studies depression scale and arthritis population. *Arthritis and Rheumatism, 32*, 991–997.

Bolton, B. (1977). Evidence for the 16PF primary and secondary factors. *Multivariate Experimental Clinical Research, 3*, 1–15.

Bolton, B. (1979). The Tennessee self-concept scale and the normal personality sphere (16PF). *Journal of Personality Assessment, 43*, 608–613.

Bolton, B. (1986). Canonical relationships between vocational interests and personality of adult handicapped persons. *Rehabilitation Psychology, 31*, 169–182.

Bolton, B. (1987). A computer generated vocational personality report. *Vocational Evaluation and Work Adjustment Bulletin, 20*(4), 155–158.

Bolton, B., & Brookings, J. B. (1993a). Appraising the psychometric adequacy of rehabilitation assessment instruments. In R. Glueckauf, L. B. Sechrest, G. Bond, & McDonel (Eds.), *Improving assessment in rehabilitation and health* (pp. 109–132). Newbury Park, CA: Sage.

Bolton, B., & Brookings, J. B. (1993b). Prediction of job satisfactoriness for workers with severe handicaps from aptitudes, personality, and training ratings. *Journal of Business and Psychology, 7*, 359–366.

Bolton, B., & Dana, R. (1988). Multivariate relationships betwen normal personality functioning and objectively measured psychopathology. *Journal of Social and Clinical Psychology, 6*, 11–19.

Boulet, J., & Boss, M. W. (1991). Reliability and validity of the brief symptom inventory. *Psychological Assessment, 3*, 433–437.

Bourestrom, N., & Howard, M. (1965). Personality characteristics of three disability groups. *Archives of Physical Medicine and Rehabilitation, 46*, 626–632.

Brookings, J. B., Bolton, B., & Young, G. (1994). Employability assessment of persons with disabilities: Research, instruments, and applications. *Assessment in Rehabilitation and Exceptionality, 1*, 259–275.

Buckelew, S. P., Baumstark, K., Frank, R. G., & Hewett, J. (1990). Adjustment following spinal cord injury. *Rehabilitation Psychology, 35*, 101–109.

Buckelew, S. P., Burk, J., Brownlee-Duffeck, M., Frank, R. G., & DeGood, D. (1988). Cognitive and somatic aspects of depression among a rehabilitation sample: Reliability and validity of SCL-90-R research subscales. *Rehabilitation Psychology, 33*, 67–75.

Buckelew, S. P., Frank, R. G., Elliott, T. R., Chaney, J., & Hewett, J. (1991). Adjustment to spinal cord injury: Stage theory revisited. *Paraplegia, 29*, 125–130.

Butcher, J. N., Dahlstrom, W. G., Graham, J. R., Tellegen, A., & Kaemmer, B. (1989). *MMPI-2 (Minnesota Multiphasic Personality Inventory—2): Manual for administration and scoring.* Minneapolis: University of Minnesota Press.

Butcher, J. N., & Hostetler, K. (1990). Abbreviating MMPI item administration: Past problems and prospects for MMPI-2. *Psychological Assessment, 2*, 12–21.

Cattell, R. B., Eber, H. W., & Tatsuoka, M. N. (1970). *Handbook for the 16PF.* Champaign, IL: Institute for Personality and Ability Testing.

Clay, D. L., Hagglund, K. J., Frank, R. G., Elliott, T. R., & Chaney, J. (in press). Enhancing the accuracy of depression diagnosis in patients with spinal cord injury using Bayesian analysis. *Rehabilitation Psychology*.

Costa, P. T., & McCrae, R. (1985). *The NEO Personality Inventory: Manual*. Odessa, FL: Psychological Assessment Resources.

Craig, T., & Van Natta, P. A. (1978). Current medication use in symptoms of depression in a general population. *American Journal of Psychiatry, 135*, 1036–1039.

Davidoff, G., Roth, E., Thomas, P., & Doljanac, R. (1990). Depression and neuropsychological test performance in acute spinal cord injury patients: Lack of correlation. *Archives of Clinical Neuropsychology, 5*, 77–88.

Davidoff, G., Roth, E., Thomas, P., Doljanac, R., Dijkers, M., Berent, S., Wolf, L., Morris, J., & Yarkoney, G. (1990). Depression among acute spinal cord injury patients: A study utilizing the Zung self-rating depression scale. *Rehabilitation Psychology, 35*, 171–179.

Derogatis, L. R. (1977). *Symptom checklist-90R administration, scoring, and procedures manual*. Towson, MD: Clinical and Psychometric Research.

Derogatis, L. R., & Melisaratos, N. (1983). The brief symptom inventory: An introductory report. *Psychological Medicine, 13*, 595–605.

Derogatis, L. R., & Spencer, P. N. (1982). *The brief symptom inventory (BSI): Administration, scoring, and procedures manual*. Baltimore, MD: Division of Medical Psychology, Johns Hopkins University School of Medicine.

Digman, J. M. (1990). Personality structure: Emergence of the five factor model. *Annual Review of Psychology, 41*, 417–440.

Ditunno, P. L., McCauley, C., & Marquette, C. (1985). Sensation-seeking behavior and the incidence of spinal cord injury. *Archives of Physical Medicine and Rehabilitation, 66*, 152–155.

Dunn, M. (1977). Social discomfort in the patient with SCI. *Archives of Physical Medicine and Rehabilitation, 58*, 257–260.

Dunn, M., & Herman, S. (1982). Social skills and physical disability. In D. M. Doleys, R. Meredity, & A. R. Diminero (Eds.), *Behavioral medicine: Assessment and treatment strategies* (pp. 117–144). New York: Plenum Press.

Eber, H. W., Cattell, R. B., & IPAT Staff. (1985). *Manual for Form E of the 16PF*. Champaign, IL: Institute for Personality and Ability Testing.

Elliott, T. R., & Frank, R. G. (1990). Social and interpersonal reactions to depression and disability. *Rehabilitation Psychology, 35*, 135–147.

Elliott, T. R., Godshall, F., Herrick, S., Witty, T., & Spruell, M. (1991). Problem-solving appraisal and psychological adjustment following spinal cord injury. *Cognitive Therapy and Research, 15*, 387–398.

Elliott, T. R., & Harkins, S. W. (1991). Psychosocial concomitants of persistent pain among persons with spinal cord injuries. *NeuroRehabilitation, 1*(4), 9–18.

Elliott, T. R., Herrick, S., Patti, A., Witty, T., Godshall, F., & Spruell, M. (1991). Assertiveness, social support, and psychological adjustment following spinal cord injury. *Behaviour Research and Therapy, 29*, 485–493.

Elliott, T. R., Herrick, S., & Witty, T. (1992). Problem solving appraisal and the effects of social support among college students and persons with physical disabilities. *Journal of Counseling Psychology, 39*, 219–226.

Elliott, T. R., Herrick, S., Witty, T., Godshall, F., & Spruell, M. (1992). Social support and depression following spinal cord injury. *Rehabilitation Psychology, 37*, 37–48.

Elliott, T., Richards, J. S., DeVivo, M., Jackson, A., & Stover, S. (1994). Spinal cord injury model systems of care: The legacy and the promise. *NeuroRehabilitation, 4*, 84–90.

Elliott, T. R., & Shewchuk, R. (1995). Social support and leisure activities following severe physical disability: Testing the mediating effects of depression. *Basic and Applied Social Psychology*, *16*, 471–487.

Elliott, T. R., Witty, T., Herrick, S., & Hoffman, J. (1991). Negotiating reality after physical loss: Hope, depression, and disability. *Journal of Personality and Social Psychology*, *61*, 608–613.

Elliott, T. R., Yoder, B., & Umlauf, R. (1990). Nurse and patient reactions to social displays of depression. *Rehabilitation Psychology*, *35*, 195–204.

Eyde, L. D., Robertson, G. J., & Kruge, S. E. (1993). *Responsible test use: Case studies for assessing human behavior*. Washington, DC: American Psychological Association Press.

Fordyce, W. E. (1965). Personality characteristics in men with spinal cord injury as related to manner of onset of disability. *Archives of Physical Medicine and Rehabilitation*, *45*, 321–325.

Frank, R. G., Chaney, J., Clay, D. L., Shutty, M., Beck, N., Kay, D., Elliott, T., & Grambling, S. (1992). Dysphoria: A major symptom factor in persons with disability or chronic illness. *Psychiatry Research*, *43*, 231–241.

Frank, R. G., & Elliott, T. R. (1987). Life stress and psychologic adjustment following spinal cord injury. *Archives of Physical Medicine and Rehabilitation*, *68*, 344–347.

Frank, R. G., Elliott, T. R., Corcoran, J., & Wonderlich, S. (1987). Depression after spinal cord injury: Is it necessary? *Clinical Psychology Review*, *7*, 611–630.

Frank, R. G., Kashani, J., Kashani, S., Wonderlich, S., Umlauf, R., & Ashkanazi, G. (1984). Psychological response to amputation as a function of age and time since amputation. *British Journal of Psychiatry*, *144*, 493–497.

Frank, R. G., Kashani, J. H., Wonderlich, S., Lising, A., & Visot, L. (1985). Depression and adrenal function in spinal cord injury. *American Journal of Psychiatry*, *142*, 252–253.

Frank, R. G., Umlauf, R. L., Wonderlich, S., Ashkanazi, G., Buckelew, S., & Elliott, T. (1987). Differences in coping styles among persons with spinal cord injury: A cluster-analytic approach. *Journal of Consulting and Clinical Psychology*, *55*, 727–731.

Fuhrer, M. J., Rintala, D. H., Hart, K. A., Clearman, R., & Young, N. E. (1993). Depressive symptomatology in persons with spinal cord injury who reside in a community. *Archives of Physical Medicine and Rehabilitation*, *74*, 255–260.

Fullerton, D. T., Harvey, R., Klein, M., & Howell, T. (1981). Psychiatric disorders in patients with spinal cord injury. *Archives of General Psychiatry*, *32*, 1369–1371.

Glueckauf, R. L. (1993). Use and misuse of assessment in rehabilitation: Getting back to the basics. In R. L. Glueckauf, L. B. Sechrest, G. R. Bond, & E. McDonel (Eds.), *Improving assessment in rehabilitation and health* (pp. 135–155). Newbury Park, CA: Sage.

Hanson, S., Buckelew, S. P., Hewett, J., & O'Neal, G. (1993). The relationship between coping and adjustment after spinal cord injury: A five-year follow-up study. *Rehabilitation Psychology*, *38*, 41–51.

Heineman, A. W., Keen, M., Donohue, R., & Schnoll, S. (1988). Alcohol use by persons with recent spinal cord injury. *Archives of Physical Medicine and Rehabilitation*, *69*, 619–624.

Heineman, A. W., Mamott, B., & Schnoll, S. (1990). Substance abuse by persons with recent spinal cord injury. *Rehabilitation Psychology*, *35*, 217–228.

Heinrich, R. K., Tate, D. G., & Buckelew, S. P. (1994). Brief symptom inventory norms for spinal cord injury. *Rehabilitation Psychology*, *39*, 49–56.

Heppner, P. P. (1988). *The Problem-Solving Inventory: Manual*. Palo Alto, CA: Consulting Psychologists Press.

Herrick, S., Elliott, T. R., & Crow, F. (in press). Self-appraised problem solving ability and secondary complications among persons with spinal cord injury. *Journal of Clinical Psychology in Medical Settings*.

Herrick, S., Elliott, T. R., & Crow, F. (1994). Social support and the prediction of health complications among persons with spinal cord injuries. *Rehabilitation Psychology, 39*, 231–250.

Howell, T., Fullerton, D. T., Harvey, R., & Klein, M. (1981). Depression in spinal cord injured patients. *Paraplegia, 19*, 284–288.

James, M., DeVivo, M., & Richards, J. S. (1993). Postinjury employment outcomes among African-Americans and white persons with spinal cord injury. *Rehabilitation Psychology, 38*, 151–164.

Kanfer, F. H., & Saslow, G. (1967). Behavioral diagnosis. In C. M. Frank (Ed.), *Behavior therapy: Appraisal and status*. New York: McGraw-Hill.

Kashani, J. H., Frank, R. G., Kashani, S. R., Wonderlich, S., & Reid, J. (1983). Depression among amputees. *Journal of Clinical Psychiatry, 44*, 256–258.

Kendall, P. C., Edinger, J., & Eberly, C. (1978). Taylor's MMPI correction factor for spinal cord injury: Empirical endorsement. *Journal of Consulting and Clinical Psychology, 46*, 370 371.

Kewman, D. G., & Lieverman, H. J. (1982). MMPI: Two automated forms. *Archives of Physical Medicine and Rehabilitation, 63*, 329–331.

Kunce, J. T., Cope, C. S., & Newton, R. M. (1991). Personal styles inventory. *Journal of Counseling and Development, 70*, 334–341.

Kunce, J. T., Cope, C. S., & Newton, R. M. (1993). *PSI-120 manual: A Personal Styles Inventory*. Columbia, MO: Educational and Psychological Consultants.

Kurleychek, R. T. (1983). Defending the MMPI as an expert witness. *American Journal of Forensic Psychology, 4*, 23–33.

Leong, F. T. L., & Dollinger, S. J. (1990). NEO personality inventory. In D. J. Keyser & R. C. Sweetland (Eds.), *Test critiques* (Vol. III, pp. 527–539). Austin, TX: PRO-ED.

Lewak, R. W., Marks, P. A., & Nelson, G. E. (1990). *Therapist's guide to the MMPI and MMPI-2: Providing feedback & treatment*. Muncie, IN: Accelerated Development.

Linton, S. (1990). Sexual satisfaction in males following spinal cord injury as a function of locus of control. *Rehabilitation Psychology, 35*, 19–27.

Malec, J., & Neimeyer, R. (1983). Psychological prediction of duration of inpatient spinal cord injury rehabilitation and performance of self-care. *Archives of Physical Medicine and Rehabilitation, 64*, 359–363.

McCrae, R. R., & Costa, P. T. (1991). The NEO personality inventory: Using the five factor model in counseling. *Journal of Counseling and Development, 69*, 367–374.

McCrae, R. R., & John, O. P. (1992). An introduction to the five-factor model and its applications. *Journal of Personality, 60*, 175–215.

Monahan, J. (1980). *Who is the client? The ethics of psychological intervention in the criminal justice system*. Washington, DC: American Psychological Association Press.

Moverman, R. (1993, September). *Use of the Millon Behavioral Health Inventory with the spinal cord injury inpatient population*. Paper presented at the American Association of Spinal Cord Injury Psychologists and Social Workers, Las Vegas, NV.

Myerson, L. (1957). Special disabilities. *Annual Review of Psychology, 8*, 437–457.

Nester, M. A. (1993). Psychometric testing and reasonable accommodation for persons with disabilities. *Rehabilitation Psychology, 38*, 75–85.

Nezu, A., & Perri, M. (1989). Social problem solving therapy for unipolar depression: An initial dismantling investigation. *Journal of Consulting and Clinical Psychology, 57*, 408–413.

Norris, F. H., & Kaniasty, K. (1994). Psychological distress following criminal victimization in the general population: Cross-sectional, longitudinal, and prospective analyses. *Journal of Consulting and Clinical Psychology, 62,* 111–123.

Peck, J., Smith, T. W., Ward, J., & Milano, R. (1989). Disability and depresion in rheumatoid arthritis. *Arthritis and Rheumatism, 32,* 1100–1106.

Piotrowski, C., & Lubin, B. (1990). Assessment practices of health psychologists: Survey of APA Division 38 clinicians. *Professional Psychology: Research, and Practice, 21,* 99–106.

Radloff, L. S. (1977). The CES-D scale: A self-report depression scale for research in the general population. *Applied Psychological Measurement, 1,* 385–401.

Resnick, H. S., Kilpatrick, D. S., Dansky, B., Saunders, B., & Best, C. (1993). Prevalence of civilian trauma and post-traumatic stress disorder in a representative national sample of women. *Journal of Consulting and Clinical Psychology, 61,* 984–991.

Richards, J. S. (1986). Psychologic adjustment to spinal cord injury during first post-discharge year. *Archives of Physical Medicine and Rehabilitation, 67,* 362–365.

Richards, J. S., Elliott, T. R., Cotliar, R., & Stevenson, V. (in press). Pediatric medical rehabilitation. In M. C. Roberts (Ed.), *Handbook of Pediatric Psychology* (2nd ed.) New York: Guilford Press.

Richards, J. S., Fine, P. R., Wilson, T., & Rogers, J. (1983). A voice operated method for administering the MMPI. *Journal of Personality Assessment, 47,* 167–170.

Rintala, D. H., Young, N. E., Hart, K. A., Clearman, R., & Fuhrer, M. J. (1992). Social support and the well-being of persons with spinal cord injury living in the community. *Rehabilitation Psychology, 37,* 155–163.

Rodevich, M. A., & Wanlass, R. L. (in press). The moderating effect of spinal cord injury on MMPI-2 profiles: A clinically derived I score correction procedure. *Rehabilitation Psychology.*

Rohe, D. E., & Athelstan, G. (1982). Vocational interests of persons with spinal cord injury. *Journal of Counseling Psychology, 29,* 283–291.

Rohe, D. E., & Krause, J. S. (1993, August). *The five factor model of personality: Findings among males with spinal cord injury.* Paper presented at the convention of the American Psychological Association, Toronto, Ontario, Canada.

Rybarczyk, B. D., Nyenhuis, D., Nicholas, J., Cash, S., & Kaiser, J. (in press). Body image, perceived social stigma and the prediction of psychosocial adjustment to leg amputation. *Rehabilitation Psychology.*

Rybarczyk, B. D., Nyenhuis, D., Nicholas, J., Schulz, R., Alioto, R., & Blair, C. (1992). Social discomfort and depression in a sample of adults with leg amputations. *Archives of Physical Medicine and Rehabilitation, 73,* 1169–1173.

Schaefer, A., Brown, J., Watson, C., Plemel, D., DeMotts, J., Howard, M., Petrik, N., & Balleweg, B. (1985). Comparison of the validities of the Beck, Zung, and MMPI depression scales. *Journal of Consulting and Clinical Psychology, 53,* 415–418.

Schulz, R., & Decker, S. (1985). Long-term adjustment to physical disability: The role of social support, perceived control, and self-blame. *Journal of Personality and Social Psychology, 48,* 1162–1172.

Shadish, W. R., Hickman, D., & Arrick, M. (1981). Psychological problems of spinal cord injury patients: Emotional distress as a function of time and locus of control. *Journal of Consulting and Clinical Psychology, 49,* 297.

Swenson, E. (1976). *The relationship between local of control expectancy and successful rehabilitation of the spinal cord injured.* Unpublished doctoral dissertation, Arizona State University.

Tanaka-Matsumi, J., & Kameoka, V. A. (1986). Reliabilities and concurrent validities of popular self-report measures of depression, anxiety, and social desirability. *Journal of Consulting and Clinical Psychology, 54*, 328–333.

Tate, D. G., Forchheimer, M., Maynard, F., Davidoff, G., & Dijkers, M. (1993). Comparing two measures of depression in spinal cord injury. *Rehabilitation Psychology, 38*, 53–61.

Tate, D. G., Kewman, D. G., & Maynard, F. (1990). The brief symptom inventory: Measuring psychological distress in spinal cord injury. *Rehabilitation Psychology, 35*, 211–216.

Taylor, G. P. (1970). Moderator-variable effect on personality-test-item endorsements of physically disabled patients. *Journal of Consulting and Clinical Psychology, 35*, 183–188.

Turner, R. J., & McLean, P. D. (1989). Physical disability and psychological distress. *Rehabilitation Psychology, 34*, 225–242.

Umlauf, R. L., & Frank, R. G. (1983). A cluster-analytic description of patient subgroups in the rehabilitation setting. *Rehabilitation Psychology, 28*, 157–167.

Umlauf, R. L., & Frank, R. G. (1986). Multidimensional health locus of control in a rehabilitation setting. *Journal of Clinical Psychology, 42*, 126–128.

Umlauf, R. L., & Frank, R. G. (1987). Cluster analysis, depression, and ADL status. *Rehabilitation Psychology, 32*, 39–44.

Wallston, K. A. (1989). Assessment of control and health-care settings. In A. Steptoe & A. Appels (Eds.), *Stress, personal control, and health* (pp. 85–105). Chichester, UK: Wiley.

Wallston, B. S., Wallston, K. A., & DeVellis, R. (1978). Development of the multidimensional health locus of control scales. *Health Education Monographs, 6*, 160–170.

Whiteneck, G. G., Charlifue, S., Gerhart, K., Overholser, J., & Richardson, G. (1992). Quantifying handicap: A new measure of long-term rehabilitation outcomes. *Archives of Physical Medicine & Rehabilitation, 73*, 519–526.

Winefield, H. (1982). Reliability and validity of the Health Locus of Control Scales. *Journal of Personality Assessment, 46*, 614–619.

Wright, B. A. (1983). *Physical disability: A psychosocial approach*. New York: Harper & Row.

Wright, B., & Fletcher, B. (1982). Uncovering hidden resources: A challenge in assessment. *Professional Psychology, 13*, 229–235.

Zimmerman, M., & Coryell, W. (1987). The inventory to diagnose depression (IDD): A self-report scale to diagnose major depressive disorder. *Journal of Consulting and Clinical Psychology, 55*, 55–59.

Zimmerman, M., & Coryell, W. (1988). The validity of a self-report questionnaire for diagnosing major depressive disorder. *Archives of General Psychiatry, 45*, 738–740.

Zimmerman, M., Coryell, W., Corenthal, C., & Wilson, S. (1986). A self-report scale to diagnose major depressive disorder. *Archives of General Psychiatry, 43*, 1076–1081.

Zimmerman, M., Coryell, W., Wilson, S., & Corenthal, C. (1986). Evaluation of symptoms in major depressive disorder. Self-report vs. clinician ratings. *Journal of Nervous and Mental Disease, 174*, 150–153.

Zung, W. (1965). A self-rating depression scale. *Archives of General Psychiatry, 12*, 63–70.

11

The Role of Nonstandard Neuropsychological Assessment in Rehabilitation: History, Rationale, and Examples

Bruce Caplan and Judith Shechter

One hallmark of the development of contemporary clinical psychology and neuropsychology has been the refinement of well-standardized test instruments to obtain quantitative measurements of various cognitive, emotional, and behavioral factors (Goldstein, 1987; Russell, 1986). Clinicians point with pride to tests of proven reliability and validity (Franzen, 1989) that constitute their professional armamentarium. Psychology students are taught that tests must be administered in strict adherence to the guidelines laid down in test manuals; those who deviate from standard procedures risk sabotaging the validity of those measures, incurring the wrath of their teachers and supervisors, and serving a spell in "psychological purgatory." Admittedly, some authors make provision for (or even encourage) testing the limits of the individual patient's abilities by, for example, allowing them to work beyond designated time limits or offering cues or additional structure. However, these tactics are generally permitted only after completion of standard administration (Freeman, 1962; Thorpe & Mahrer, 1959).

The eminent psychometric theorist Cronbach wrote: "Any departure from standard administrative practice changes the meaning of scores" (1960, p. 185). However, we believe that it is necessary to re-think what that meaning is and what it should be, especially in the evaluation of individuals with disabilities. Our theoretical position is that a critical difference exists between *testing* and *evaluation*. We view the former as a largely mechanical enterprise that, because of its rigidity, lends itself well to group or computer-based applications. Evaluation is, by contrast, an art applied on an individual basis that involves not only testing skills, but also professional creativity, observational expertise, flexibility, and ingenuity in the service of developing a multidimensional understanding of patients—their abilities and deficits, their emotional state, self-regulatory functions, the impact of environmental variables on test performance, and so forth.

Thus, Although the merits of unvarying standardized procedures are unarguable for some purposes, we contend that clinical assessment of cognitively compromised or emotionally distressed patients frequently demands a more flexible approach. In this, we concur with the statement of two experienced neuropsychologists who wrote:

> In evaluating clinical patients, however, the neuropsychological examiner encounters a wide range of emotional and physical problems that can interfere with testing and sometimes cause the results to be invalid. Through sensitive handling of the patient *and appropriate minor adjustments in testing procedures* (emphasis added), such problems can usually be overcome, while still adhering to the essential standardized aspects of the test. (Heaton & Heaton, 1981, p. 526)

Other authors have made similar points. In setting forth guidelines for the evaluation of stroke patients, Hibbard and Gordon (1992) explicitly stated, "Testing procedures should be modified to test maximal functioning and learning abilities" (p. 14). Barbara Wilson, a pediatric neuropsychologist, wrote

> There are situations in which the test administration procedures must be modified in order to obtain meaningful information . . . the whole issue of goals of an assessment enters here. For some, adherence to standardized procedures is important and a "cannot do" score is felt to be sufficient information. For others—and we generally find ourselves in this group—the goal of the assessment is to obtain all information possible about the functioning capacities of the child and to facilitate the production of maximum performance (pp. 157–158).

A focal concept of this chapter is that cognitive, emotional, or physical limitations, though certainly worthy of assessment in their own right, may undercut the validity of certain tests, thereby forcing examiners to choose between (a) by-the-book administration that yields data of questionable meaning and (b) procedural modification in an attempt to derive some useful information from the measures. A major objective of this chapter is to suggest ways that clinicians may avoid this kind of psychometric showdown by viewing the evaluation process in a less constrained manner.

By way of illustration, consider the hazards of attempting to assess verbal memory in a patient with expressive aphasia. The typical format for testing this function requires the individual to repeat material (e.g., story content, word lists, digit strings) that is read by the examiner. That expressive aphasic patients perform poorly under such conditions does not necessarily mean that they have not heard, understood, and retained the material, but perhaps merely that, as a consequence of their language disorder, they are unable to report it. Lezak (1984, p. 46) describes a number of difficulties (e.g., short-term memory impairment, cognitive slowing, aphasia, impulsivity) that can hamper performance of mental arithmetic problems, even if basic mathematical skills remain intact. In this chapter, we provide a number of illustrations of similar clinical conundra and offer solutions ranging from modification of an existing test or alteration of administration procedure to development of a new measure. We endorse Lezak's (1987) philosophy of psychological assessment, which views tests as tools by which we sharpen and expand our clinical observations. We concur with her assertion that "when the patient's situation or the circumstances do not allow for a standardized application of a test that might still provide needed information about the patient, the examiner should feel free to use the test anyhow" (1987, p. 46), because the results may illuminate certain aspects of the patient's abilities or deficits.

In certain instances, judicious test selection may obviate the need to modify standardized tests. For example, Lalonde, Botez, and Botez (1992) used measures of visual spatial functions (e.g., Raven Matrices, Hooper Visual Organization Test) with no motor component in their study of patients with olivopontocerebellar atrophy (OPCA) who, virtually by definition, are motor-impaired. Clearly, the performance of OPCA patients on such measures as Block Design (Wechsler, 1981) or the Trail Making Test (Reitan & Tarshes, 1959) would be diminished by this factor alone and would complicate inferences about the extent to which other relevant abilities were compromised or preserved. Several studies of cognitive functioning in spinal-cord-injured patients with possible concurrent concussion have employed extensive collections of motor free measures (e.g., Richards, Brown, Hagglund, Bua, & Reeder, 1988; Roth, et al., 1989; Wilmot, Cope, Hall, & Acker, 1985). Wilson and McMillan (1986) discuss the advantages of computerized testing of individuals with disabilities, especially the availability of a variety of response media that can capitalize on even very limited controlled movements. They describe a battery of tests that they have developed, covering an impressive range of intellectual functions, and state that they have tested over 150 severely disabled individuals who would have otherwise been "not testable." Ebener, Burkhead, and Merydith (1994) and Golden and Robbins (1985) discuss the particular usefulness of certain tests for given groups of individuals with disabilities—for example, the Peabody Picture Vocabulary Test (Dunn & Dunn, 1981) and Peabody Individual Achievement Test (Markwardt, 1989) for those with expressive impairment, the Haptic Intelligence Scale (Jordan, 1978) for persons with impaired vision, and the Hiskey-Nebraska Test of Learning Aptitude (Hiskey, 1966) and the Leiter International Performance Scale (Leiter, 1948) for individuals with diminished hearing. Ebener et al. caution, however, that examiners may find some of these measures either invalid or out of date, and they suggest considering the use of portions of other standardized tests, "if reasonable accommodations are made during the administration" (p. 93).

Historical Perspective

We assume that most readers are quite familiar with the historical development of and rationale for standardized assessment, but many may be unaware that nonstandard techniques have an honorable pedigree as well, especially in the fields of rehabilitation and neuropsychology. The relevant literature is scattered, residing in publications targeting clinical psychologists, neuropsychologists, vocational counselors, educational specialists, and others. Nonetheless, it is clear that clinicians have long wrestled with the question of whether the risks and losses entailed by jettisoning standard procedures are offset by the value of modifications that may restore construct or ecological validity. Before describing some specific modifications of test materials and process that contemporary clinicians might use, we first consider some of the antecedent writings on nonstandard approaches.

For a half century it has been understood that evaluation of individuals with disabilities might require alteration of certain aspects of testing. Sattler and Theye (1967) reviewed the variety of deviations from standardized procedures in individual intelligence testing that had been reported up to that time. The ambivalence of their own position is reflected in their carefully hedged statement that, although the studies they reviewed "do not appear to strongly confirm the assumption that modifying standard procedures seriously affects the overall test results," nonetheless "the experimenter should follow standard procedures" (pp. 349–350). This contradicts their statement earlier in the paper that "a more accurate estimate of intellectual ability can be obtained, on some occasions, by 'violation' of standard procedures" (p. 347). Moreover, they quoted Schonell (1956), who referred to the evaluation of "some badly handicapped children when a pedantic adherence to the instructions will produce a result not only unfair to the individual but quite incorrect and misleading" (p. 137).

A subsequent review article by Sattler and Tozier (1970) concerning test modifications used with children with cerebral palsy and "other handicapped groups" clearly recognized the need for nonstandard procedures, as well as the attendant risks. They noted a number of modifications that had already been used by others, including multiple choice formats, pantomiming instructions, helping to steady the patient's hand while performing motor tasks, enlarging stimulus materials, and use of pointing or eye-movement response modes. Although Sattler and Tozier stated that such strategies may be necessary in order to make standardized tests applicable to these populations, they acknowledged the unknown and variable impact of clinical judgment: "In effect, each examiner may be creating his own test. Generally, little is known about the effects of modifications on the obtained test results" (p. 392). Nonetheless, they concluded, "The majority of the findings suggest, however, that modifying test procedures has not necessarily produced significant changes in performance" (pp. 394–395). They called for both further research comparing performance elicited under standard and nonstandard conditions and standardization of particular procedural modifications in order to understand their impact or lack thereof.

In the same year that the Sattler and Tozier article appeared, several contributors (e.g., Mittler, 1970; Reed, 1970; Reynell, 1970) to a British volume concerning assessment of individuals with mental and physical disabilities described comparable sorts of modifications of materials and administration procedures. These included giving instructions by demonstration rather than verbally and administering subsets of items from particular tests as the patient's abilities, cooperation, and so on would permit.

In the second edition of his widely used textbook on assessment of children, Sattler (1982) stated unequivocally that some items of the Stanford-Binet cannot legitimately be administered to children with sensory or motor impairments. "Whenever children's physical handicaps impede their ability to respond to the test questions, the test should not be administered *unless appropriate modifications are possible*" (emphasis added; p. 117). He listed several modifications that examiners could employ when administering the Standford-Binet to children with disabilities; these tactics included the use of pantomime, multiple choice formats (with the examiner pointing to response alternatives one by one and the subject indicating *yes* by whatever means available when the examiner arrives at the desired response), enlarging materials, permitting written or pointing responses, and allowing hearing-impaired individuals to read written test questions. He also devoted an entire appendix to detailed descriptions of two nonstandard methods for administering the Wechsler Intelligence Scale for Children-Revised Performance subtests to individuals who are hearing-impaired. He warned clinicians to view with caution scores obtained with nonstandard formats, stating that they should be viewed "only as an approximate estimate of the child's level of intellectual functioning, since there is no way of determining to what extent standard norms apply" (p. 177). Interestingly, elsewhere in the book (p. 159), Sattler asserted (in contrast to his earlier claim) that nonstandard administration is "likely to result in scores that differ from those obtained under standard administrative procedures" (although he did maintain that enlarging test materials probably has little impact), implying that the nonstandard scores will be higher. We agree with this claim and maintain that it is desirable, as construct validity is enhanced thereby. Equally important (perhaps more so in the current climate of increased accountability) is that the test's *utility*—that is, the uses to which clinical inferences are put in the service of the patient—may well be greater.

In her landmark textbook on neuropsychological assessment, Lezak (1983) noted that two particular patient populations, the elderly and "the severely handicapped patient," might require special testing procedures. Recognizing that the availability of age-corrected norms is not a panacea, Lezak argued that normal consequences of aging such as sensory loss, inflexibility, and diminished strength and speed should not be allowed to produce spurious decrements of test performance. In that spirit, Popkin, Schaie, and Krauss (1983) developed a parallel form of the Primary Mental Abilities Test (PMA; Thurstone & Thurstone, 1949) to be used with older adults. This modification (called the Adult Mental Abilities Test) eliminated several extraneous factors that were felt to compromise the performance of elderly subjects on the PMA. Printed materials were photoenlarged, the computer-scored response sheet was eliminated and subjects were allowed to give their answers directly on the test materials, and readability of test materials was improved "via better spatial blocking of the stimulus items themselves" (p. 48). These modifications produced significant improvements on the Verbal and Number subtests, with less substantial impact noted on the Space and Reasoning measures. In 1985, the Schaie-Thurstone Test of Adult Mental Abilities (STAMAT) was published (Schaie, 1985).

Lezak's discussion of testing procedures to be used with individuals with severe disabilities emphasizes (a) establishing that the patient has adequate verbal comprehension and (b) establishing a reliable response modality. Lezak draws a distinction between *optimal* and *standard* testing conditions, asserting that these are generally identical, but noting that some brain-damaged patients "will be unable to perform well within the confines of the standard instructions" (p. 120). She then addresses a variety of deviations from standard procedures that may be necessary or desirable with such individuals, including rephrasing of test questions, elaborating on the standard instructions, locating visually presented materials in the intact visual field, and providing encouragement and positive feedback for effort. In her discussion of the Wechsler Adult Intelligence Scale—Revised (WAIS-R), Lezak recommends some nonstandard procedures that anticipate the development of the WAIS-R-NI (Kaplan, Fein, Morris, & Delis, 1991), which is discussed below.

Heinrichs (1990) recently discussed the paradigm shift in neuropsychology from a neurodiagnostic emphasis to a functional one. He noted that neuropsychological assessment has shown substantial validity when used to draw inferences about disease states ("medical neuropsychology"), but he argues that this validity cannot be directly transferred to situations where assessment results are to be used to draw conclusions about daily life competence ("ecological neuropsychology") or to develop intervention programs ("rehabilitation neuropsychology"), although it is in the latter two spheres that practitioners are increasingly active. Heinrichs argues that test validation must "become more multidimensional" and "include ecological and rehabilitative aspects" (p. 175). He challenged neuropsychologists "to play a more active role in the development of utilities for assessment data" (p. 175), including the creation of instruments with some predictive validity for both rehabilitation outcome and ecological competence. Although we support efforts to develop entirely new instruments in the service of these goals, we believe that in some instances, less dramatic approaches may suffice, among which we include minor modifications of existing procedures.

At this point, it is perhaps advisable to consider the argument that standardized procedures should be preserved, even if this places the individual with a disability at a disadvantage, because of the predictive value of the tests for "real world" purposes: school placement, vocational counseling, and so forth. The argument here is that the real world (despite the provisions of the Americans with Disabilities Act) does not typically make accommodation for the disabled, and it is therefore important to know how well the (unassisted) individual can measure up. However, we agree with Heaton and Heaton (1981) that "the goal of testing is to obtain the best performance the patient is capable of producing" (p. 528); to do so occasionally requires "partialing out" of the process those factors that cause spurious depression of test scores. In this way, examiners may be able to identify the range and magnitude of environmental modifications that would allow the individual to function in a more independent and fulfilling capacity.

As a real world analogue, consider the person with expressive aphasia described above whose verbal memory may be intact, but cannot be tested via the usual channels. Adequate verbal memory would certainly be considered an essential skill for many job-related activities. If the specific job requirements (either existing or susceptible to modification) permit verbal memory demands to be satisfied by writing rather than by speaking, then the individual may well be able to perform satisfactorily. Such a modification would seem to fall under the heading of "reasonable accommodation" mandated under the Americans with Disabilities Act of 1990 (ADA) as discussed by Ebener et al. (1994). Evaluation of vocational potential must take into account the complexity of cognitive functions, recognizing that several different skills may be subsumed under a single domain name. In a series of elegant studies, Schacter and his colleagues (Schacter & Glisky, 1986; Glisky & Schacter, 1987) have demonstrated the fractionation of memory systems, showing that severely amnestic patients may have sufficiently preserved capacity to acquire "domain-specific knowledge" to be able to learn relatively complex computer programming tasks. Certainly, as suggested by Leung (1984), it is the responsibility of rehabilitation psychologists to endeavor to identify person and environment factors that hinder functional achievement of individuals with disabilities and work to diminish the impact of these factors.

In addition to issues of validity and relevance, there are legal considerations that may actually mandate modification of certain test procedures in the assessment of individuals with disabilities. Nester (1993) has reviewed the relevant legislation and accompanying regulations. For example, section 504 of the Rehabilitation Act of 1973 included provision for "reasonable accommodation" in testing including "appropriate adjustment or modification of examinations"; these regulations applied to agencies of the federal government and to recipients of federal grant monies. The Americans with Disabilities Act of 1990 broadened the applicability of these provisions to the entire private sector. As Nester points out, the ADA forbids employers from using hiring criteria that eliminate from consideration individuals with disabilities, unless the skill in question is demonstrably job-related for the particular position. The elaborative regulations clearly state:

> It is unlawful for a covered entity to fail to select and administer tests concerning employment in the most effective manner to ensure that, when a test is administered to a job applicant or employee who has a disability that impairs sensory, manual, or speaking skills, the test results accurately reflect the skills, aptitude, or whatever other factor of the applicant or employee that the test purports to measure, rather than the impaired sensory, manual, or speaking skills of such employee or applicant (except where such skills are the factors that the test purports to measure). (Equal Employment Opportunity Commission, paragraph 1630.11)

As noted above, Ebener et al. (1994) argue that modification of standard measures should be considered a primary method of satisfying the ADA's mandate to provide reasonable accommodations.

Several sections of the *Standards for Educational and Psychological Testing* (1985) pertain directly to the use of test modifications with individuals with disabilities. This document notes that *validity*

> refers to the appropriateness, meaningfulness, and usefulness of the specific inferences made from test scores. . . . The inferences regarding specific uses of a test are validated, not the test itself. . . . Professional judgment should guide the decisions regarding the forms of evidence that are most necessary and feasible in light of the intended uses of the test and any likely alternatives to testing (p. 9).

This supports the notion of "differential validity," according to which performance on a test may produce dissimilar predictions for different groups (Baron, 1990). We expect that research would demonstrate differential validity of many standardized tests for disabled and nondisabled populations.

The Standards place upon test developers the onus of investigating "probable sources of variance that would confound the construct or domain definitions underlying the test," further stating that "evidence from research should be provided to justify the use of novel item or test formats" (Standard 3.12). We agree with this aim, but contend that, in the absence of the desired data, clinicians can and should use well-reasoned modifications, assuming these are described and discussed in written reports or oral communications. Each procedural alternation should be described and justified, both standard and nonstandard scores should be given (if both were obtained), and the examiner should offer an explanation for any difference in the two scores. We believe that this practice at least partially satisfies Standard 6.2:

> When a test user makes a substantial change in test format, mode of administration, instruction, language, or content, the user should revalidate the use of the test for the changed conditions or have a rationale supporting the claim that additional validation is not necessary or possible.

Standard 6.11 cautions clinicians to entertain "rival hypotheses" as explanations for a test taker's poor performance on a given test at a particular time. A number of potential influences are listed including "clinically relevant history," as well as "ethnicity . . . language, age . . . medication, visual impairments, or other handicapping conditions . . . such alternate explanations for a test taker's level of performance should be considered before intepreting the test taker's score as reflecting ability level with respect to the skills being tested."

In a brief chapter titled "Testing People Who Have Handicapping Conditions," the Standards encourage the development and application of tests and procedures specifically for assessment of individuals with disabilities, although the tone is an ambivalent one. The relevant Standards are summarized as follows: clinicians who use modified tests in the assessment of individual disabilities must have the requisite psychometric expertise, as well as the necessary knowledge of the effects on test performance of different disabilities; the latter may be gained either from training and experience or consultation with knowledgable individuals (Standard 14.1). Pilot testing of modified tests is desirable, and reliability and validity data should be collected (Standards 14.3 and 14.6). In general, standardized procedures "should be strictly observed. Exceptions should be made only on the basis of carefully considered professional judgment, primarily in clinical applications" (Standard 15.1).

Thus, we believe that considerations of validity, utility, fairness, professional ethics, and law support the use of nonstandard modified test procedures in the evaluation of individuals with disabilities.

We now turn our attention to specific examples of such modifications and to tests developed specifically for subgroups of persons with disabilities. In general, individuals with expressive language problems (e.g., from stroke or brain injury) may benefit from the provision of multiple choice alternatives for responding and permission to answer by pointing. Tasks requiring manual responses can be given to individuals with upper extremity motor impairments (e.g., quadriplegia) if the test permits the subject to instruct the examiner in the manipulation of stimulus materials (e.g., describing the correct order for the scrambled picture sequences on the WAIS-R Picture Arrangement). Patients with diminished visual acuity might be offered photoenlarged materials, and those with unilateral neglect may require spatial rearrangement of stimuli (e.g., see discussion of Raven Matrices below). Elimination of time limits may be indicated for individuals with several types of disabilities affecting psychomotor skill (e.g., cerebral palsy, multiple sclerosis) or necessitating use of the non-dominant hand (e.g., stroke). The following discussion is illustrative, not exhaustive. We describe the content of each test and its administration, note the conditions that could artifactually depress performance, and suggest some "reasonable accommodations." Empirical findings are described where these exist.

Examples of Modified Tests

Wechsler Adult Intelligence Scale—Revised

The Wechsler Adult Intelligence Scale—Revised (WAIS-R; Wechsler, 1981) is certainly the most widely used adult intelligence test. It consists of 11 subtests tapping such major cognitive functions as verbal abstraction ability, expressive vocabulary, arithmetic skills, constructional functions, and visual–perceptual and analytic abilities. Six subtests constitute the Verbal portion and five make up the Performance segment. All Verbal subtests and one Performance measure (Picture Completion) typically require overt verbal responses, and the remaining four Performance tasks demand motor responses. Thus, individuals with limitations of speech or manual function are placed at a pronounced disadvantage. We discuss below two independent efforts to modify or expand the WAIS-R to make it more suitable for use with individuals with disabilities.

In 1988, Berninger, Gans, St. James, and Connors reported on their modification of 9 of the 11 WAIS-R subtests to foster their administration to individuals with speech or upper extremity motor dysfunction. Because the Digit Span and Digit Symbol subtests were not felt to lend themselves to modification, they were eliminated and the IQ indices were prorated. Multiple choice responses were created for all subtests of the Verbal portion and for the Picture Completion subtest. The response alternatives were printed on laminated cards, which were shown to the subject while the examiner read them aloud. Subjects made their selection by one of several response modalities (naming the letter of their choice, pointing, or via a series of binary *yes* or *no* answers as the examiner read each alternative). Furthermore, the stimulus materials for Picture Completion and Picture Arrangement were photoenlarged; for the latter, speech-impaired subjects could answer yes/no questions from the examiner regarding placement of individual picture cards. A similar examiner-manipulated process was followed for the two constructional measures—Block Design and Object Assembly—for which stimulus materials were displayed on a magnetic board. Berninger et al. chose to calculate scores without regard to the usual time limits, largely because of the motor impairments of the target population. Furthermore, they elected to disregard the standard discontinuation criteria in view of the "fragmented educational histories reported by many of the experimental subjects," (p. 251) which likely contributed to a certain unevenness of achievement within given cognitive domains. Thirty-two control subjects (hospital employees or students) and 16 individuals with severe disabilities were given both the standard and modified versions, although only the Verbal portion was administered in standard format to the group with disabilities; these individuals responded via electronic communication devices. For the control subjects, significant correlations (range, .52 to .84) were obtained between modified and standard raw scores for all subscales (with the exception of Similarities) and for the summary IQ indices. For the individuals with disabilities, all correlations between raw scores on the two versions were significant (range, .77 to .91). Regrettably, no further investigations have been conducted with this modified WAIS-R.

In 1991, Kaplan, Fein, Morris, and Delis published WAIS-R *as a Neuropsychological Instrument*, which systematized the application to the WAIS-R of Kaplan's "process approach" to neuropsychological assessment. In the preface to the manual, the authors state the impetus for their work: "To understand more fully the diverse ways in which examinees with different types of brain dysfunction perform on such standardized tests as the WAIS, we found it necessary to modify the administration and scoring of such instruments" (p. iii). The authors urge that examiners be flexible in selecting which modifications to employ in a given case. They also note that they attempted to preserve standard administration in order to permit scaled scores to be derived in the usual fashion. Subjects are unaware of certain innovations (such as the examiner noting the progress of performance on Digit Symbol at 30, 60, and 90 s); other modifications are used only after standard procedures are completed (i.e., "testing the limits"). Kaplan et al. devote an entire chapter to the potential impact of an examinee's disabilities (including visual problems, motor impairment, aphasia, difficulty with set maintenance, diminished motivation) and offer suggestions about ways of minimizing their impact.

Among the modifications included in the WAIS-R-NI are the use of multiple choice response plates for Information, Vocabulary, Comprehension, and Similarities; the provision of extra (superfluous) blocks on Block Design as well as a second administration of failed items with a superimposed grid to guide placement of the blocks; and additional presentation of failed Arithmetic problems with printed versions of the questions that the examinee may read aloud, followed by provision of paper and pencil, and ultimately presentation of the actual numerical problem. Time limits are generally disregarded. Furthermore, three new puzzles have been added to Object Assembly, and two new subtests have been developed. On Spatial Span (a visual analogue of Digit Span), the subject is presented with a board containing 10 randomly arrayed blocks that are numbered only on the side facing the examiner. After the examiner taps a certain sequence of blocks, the subject must reproduce the series. Two trials are given at each length from 2 to 8 blocks. Both forward and backward spans are obtained. The other new subtest is Sentence Arrangement, a verbal analogue of Picture Arrangement. Subjects are given sets of cards (from 3 to 8 cards per set), each with a word printed on it. The cards are presented with the words in scrambled order, and the subject must place them in a sequence that makes an acceptable sentence. Kaplan et al. also provide a number of tables containing cumulative percentages for various levels of intrasubtest and intersubtest scatter.

As of this writing, we are unaware of any published studies of the WAIS-R-NI with any particular patient population. Indeed, given the authors' above-noted position that different sets of modifications will be applicable in different cases, it is difficult to imagine a systematic study of the WAIS-R-NI that does not undercut the conceptual thrust of the test — that is, providing a set of possible expansions and modifications of the WAIS-R to be selected on an as-needed basis in order to provide the most informative assessment of a particular individual. However, the usefulness of the WAIS-R-NI would be enhanced by focused studies examining the impact of individual modifications (e.g., the addition of extraneous blocks) and providing normative data on the newly developed measures. Furthermore, it would be useful to know the average degree of improvement that should be expected under the multiple choice conditions for the four relevant Verbal subtests (and whether this varies as a function of age, education, or other demographic variables). A similar point applies to the

Arithmetic subtest; what degree of improvement under "written arithmetic" conditions should be considered clinically meaningful, reflecting attention or memory difficulty rather than mathematical disability? Despite the need for further clarification and development, the WAIS-R-NI remains a valuable tool for the rehabilitation neuropsychologist.

Achievement Tests

In general, few adaptations exist of standard achievement tests. One commercially available modification is the large-type edition of the Wide Range Achievement Test—Revised (Jastak & Wilkinson, 1984). This is a widely used measure consisting of three subtests evaluating oral reading, spelling, and written arithmetic in individuals aged 5–75 years. Although no empirical research exists regarding the comparability of the standard and large-type versions, it seems reasonable to recommend use of the latter with individuals demonstrating impaired visual acuity.

In the Manual for the Peabody Individual Achievement Test—Revised (Markwardt, 1989), users are cautioned about the necessity of verbatim administration of test items. However, in a brief section, examiners are urged to make certain allowances for individuals with those disabilities that preclude pointing or oral responses. In such instances, it is permissible for the examiner to point to the various response alternatives, allowing the subject to respond by whatever means possible (e.g., head nod, eye blink). Also, on the General Information subtest, subjects who cannot provide oral responses are allowed to answer in writing.

Interested readers are referred to the volume by Willingham et al. (1988) that describes an extensive series of studies comparing standard and nonstandard administrations of the Scholastic Aptitude Test and the Graduate Record Examination in individuals with four disabling conditions: hearing impairment, visual impairment, physical limitations, and learning disability. Their general conclusion was that, "With the exception of test timing, these results indicate that the nonstandard versions of the SAT and GRE administered to handicapped examinees are generally comparable to the standard tests in most important respects" (Willingham, et al., 1988, p. xiii).

Raven Matrices

The Raven Matrices are a set of three (Colored, Standard, Advanced) visually administered tests requiring pattern matching and completion skills as well as analogical reasoning (Raven, 1960, 1965). The various forms of the Raven have often been considered to be good measures of nonverbal general intelligence, although success on those items requiring reasoning is fostered by the use of verbal mediation strategies. For each Raven item, a major design or set of designs is positioned at the top of the page, below which are six or eight response alternatives arrayed in two rows of three or four items each. The individual must select the response alternative that correctly completes a gap in the major design or pattern series.

As observed by Costa, Vaughan, Horowitz, and Ritter (1969), patients with unilateral neglect tend to make their selections from the column ipsilateral to the lesioned hemisphere. Because the position of the correct response is balanced across locations, this position preference artifactually limits the neglecting patient's performance, thereby undercutting the validity of the Raven as a measure of visual–perceptual and reasoning skills. Therefore, Gainotti, D'Erme, Villa, and Caltagirone (1986) described two new versions of the Colored Matrices (originally reported by Caltagirone, Gainotti, & Miceli, 1977) in which the six response alternatives are shown in a single column located just beneath the major figure. Furthermore, in the version of the test designed for use with right-brain-damaged individuals, the major figure (i.e., the portion with the gap) was rotated 180° so that the missing portion appeared on the left side of the sheet (the side more likely to be neglected by right-hemisphere patients), thereby drawing their attention to that side and fostering better examination of the overall design. Gainotti et al. reported similar levels of performance on the modified Raven in left- and right-brain-damaged subject groups, but within the left-brain-damaged group, aphasics scored worse than nonaphasics. Gainotti et al. also administered the standard version of the Colored Matrices to 65 control subjects, the "right hemisphere version" to 40 other controls and the "left hemisphere version" to an additional 36 normal subjects. Statistical analysis showed that the new forms of the test were of comparable difficulty to each other and to the unaltered format.

Expanding on the work of Gainotti et al., Caplan (1988) used a modified Colored Matrices using only the midline vertical alignment of response alternatives; the 180° rotation for right-hemisphere patients was not used. In order to examine the magnitude of improvement achieved by individual patients with the modified format, Caplan administered half of the items in nonstandard form and the other half in standard format. The two half-tests were as closely matched for difficulty level as was feasible. For each half-test, six items were selected from each of the three sets; items were chosen from each set so that the correct response occurred once in each of the six locations. Using a "position preference index" (adapted from Costa et al., 1969) calculated from performance on the standard portion to define neglect, Caplan found that the neglecting group scored significantly higher ($p < .005$) on the midline version than on the standard. Test format, however, did not affect the scores of subjects without neglect.

Thus, it appears that modifying the test format to eliminate the lateral scanning component restores the validity of the Colored Matrices as a measure of visual–perceptual and visual–verbal reasoning abilities for patients with unilateral neglect who might otherwise obtain spuriously low scores. Clinicians who use the midline version in the assessment of patients with known or suspected neglect avoid the inefficiency of administering the entire Raven test merely to document the presence of neglect. We advise administering a short measure such as visual cancellation (Caplan, 1985; Weinberg et al., 1977; Weintraub & Mesulam, 1985) or reading (Caplan, 1987) to detect neglect. If evidence of clinically significant neglect is obtained, examiners may wish to consider using midline modifications of this and other visual–perceptual measures, where feasible.

Visual Form Discrimination and Visual Memory

Impaired memory function is probably the most common problem among patients seen by neuropsychologists. Furthermore, rehabilitation patients with poor memory are at a pronounced disadvantage, as much of rehabilitation therapy involves learning new skills or relearning old ones. Comprehensive testing of various components memory is therefore an indispensable component of rehabilitation neuropsychological assessment, but problems demonstrated by particular diagnostic groups may pose challenges to the examiner who wishes to obtain useful test data.

The difficulties involved in evaluating verbal memory in persons with aphasia were noted above. A comparable problem is encountered in the assessment of visual memory in individuals with impairment of the dominant upper extremity (e.g., spinal cord injury, cerebral palsy, dominant hemiparesis), as most measures of visual recall require a drawing response. Among the most common measures of visual memory is the Benton Visual Retention Test (Benton, 1974, Sivan, 1992), which requires the individual to draw sets of geometric figures following 10 seconds of exposure. Benton (1950, 1965) and his colleagues (Benton, Hamsher, & Stone, 1977) developed multiple choice motor-free versions of the Visual Retention Test with 14, 15, and 16 items, respectively. Although some adult normative data were provided in the 1950 publication and in the 1965 typewritten manual, the 1977 manual gives adult norms for only 20 "hospital control patients." In the early 1980s, the stimulus materials (which had previously been unpublished) began to be marketed by Oxford University Press, although the test (now called Visual Form Discrimination) was then offered as one of visual matching (in which the target shapes and the response alternatives were exposed simultaneously), instead of visual memory (Benton, Hamsher, Varney, & Spreen, 1983).

Because we are frequently asked to evaluate the memory functioning of individuals with limited use of the dominant upper extremity (e.g., due to hemaplegia or quadriplegia), we decided to resurrect the original purpose of the multiple choice format and began to develop a normative data base against which the performance of clinical populations can be compared. Using the 16-item Visual Form Discrimination plates, we expose each target plate (which contains two large geometric shapes and a smaller peripheral one) for 10 s, followed by presentation of the plate containing the four response alternatives; subjects must select the set of shapes that is identical to that on the target plate. All 16 items are administered in this memory format. Following completion of this procedure, the examiner returns to those items that were failed under memory conditions and simultaneously presents both the target plate and the response alternatives, allowing the subject to select the correct response (match format). This permits separate assessment of visual memory and visual matching skills, thereby allowing identification of patients whose poor performance in the memory condition may have been caused by deficits in visual perception per se. This parallels the contrast available with the standard Visual Retention Test, in which one set of items is administered in a memory format and another in a copy condition; comparison of performance levels on the two sets allows identification of individuals whose apparently poor visual memory may be substantially attributable to visual–perceptual or graphomotor deficit. It must be noted that, in our procedure, the reliability of assessment of visual–perceptual skill varies across subjects, as the number of match items administered depends on the number of memory errors committed.

Results to date (Caplan & Caffery, in press) reveal an average control group performance of 12.9 correct (*SD* = 1.85) of the 16 items (80.6%) under the memory administration and 15.8 (*SD* = .41) correct (98.8%)

when match items are added. A heterogeneous group of 51 rehabilitation inpatients scored significantly lower on both memory (10.7 correct; *SD* = 2.72, *p* < .0001) and memory plus match (14.7 correct, *SD* = 1.96; *p* < .001) administrations. Using a cut-off point of two standard deviations below the control group average memory score (i.e., 9.2 correct), 35% of the patients were found to have impaired visual memory. A similar procedure for the memory plus match score (cut-off point, 15 correct) identified 54% of patients as impaired. All patients with CT-documented evidence of right hemisphere involvement showed visual memory deficit; four of these, however, exhibited marginal improvement at best under the match administration, suggesting that poor visual–perceptual skill may explain much of their difficulty on the memory version.

Ricker, Axelrod, and Konarzewski-Nassau (1993) administered the Visual Form Discrmination Test (VFD) in both standard (i.e., match) and 10-s delayed recognition memory formats to small samples of young (mean age, 23.7 years) and elderly (mean age, 80.1 years) neurologically normal adults. They used the standard VFD scoring system, according to which a correct answer is awarded 2 points, an error involving the small peripheral figure earns 1 point, and other responses are given 0 points. The groups achieved comparable performance on both administrations. The younger group obtained an average score of 13.0 correct under the memory administration, whereas the older subject group mean was 12.0. For clinical purposes, it seems superfluous to administer both memory and match versions in their entirety, as did Ricker et al.

Thus, this modification of standard administration of Visual Form Discrimination allows assessment of visual memory function in individuals with upper extremity impairment. Furthermore, using the procedure specified above, the clinician can identify the relative contributions of visual–perceptual impairment and memory deficit to poor performance on this multiple choice visual memory test.

Maze Learning

Lincoln and Staples (1987) adopted another approach to evaluation of visual memory in individuals with limited upper extremity function. They developed an apparatus consisting of two toggle switches, one operated by the examiner and the other by the patient. The latter is to imagine that the switch controls the movement of his or her wheelchair through a series of imaginary mazes and learn the sequence of right and left turns that would be required to navigate the mazes. The examiner's switch is hidden from the patient's view. The examiner moves the switch to trace the correct path through a maze, and the patient must learn the route on a trial-and-error basis. As long as the direction of the patient's switch conforms to that of the examiner, a light remains illuminated. If the light goes off, the patient must correct the error, turning the light back on, before proceeding to the next choice point in the maze. Three different maze sequences were created, with 3, 5, and 7 choice points, respectively. The first maze is used to familiarize patient with the task; a combined error score is derived for the second and third mazes.

Lincoln and Staples tested 50 orthopedic inpatient controls and 20 patients with a diagnosis of head injury or stroke who had demonstrated impairment on the Benton Visual Retention Test. For the control group, significant correlations were obtained between performance on the maze test and most scores on both the Benton and the Visual Reproduction subtest of the Wechsler Memory Scale; this provided some support for the assertion that the maze test does indeed assess some aspect of memory. Next, Lincoln and Staples determined a 2-week test–retest reliability coefficient of .73 in a new sample of 34 control subjects. Further analyses of the data from the first group of controls demonstrated significant correlations between error score on the maze learning test and both WAIS-R Vocabulary ($r = -.38$) and Raven Progressive Matrices ($r = -.69$). Lincoln and Staples provided preliminary norms for the maze learning test for three levels of intelligence as determined by performance on the Raven Matrices. They note that the maze learning test cannot be considered a pure measure of visual memory, as some individuals may adopt a verbal mediation strategy, learning the series of turns by applying *left* and *right* labels. It does not appear that the necessary apparatus is commercially available, but Lincoln and Staples provide a schematic diagram of the circuitry.

Block Design

On the Block Design subtest of the Wechsler Adult Intelligence Scale—Revised (Wechsler, 1981), the individual must use red and white blocks to construct two samples made by the examiner and seven printed designs. As with most neuropsychological tests, performance of Block Design requires several subskills including psychomotor speed and visual–perceptual and spatial reasoning abilities as well as self-monitoring and self-correcting skills. Because standard administration of Block Design requires manual manipulation of the blocks themselves, the test (which has been called the best WAIS-R index of spatial organization and a good index of general ability; Lezak, 1983) cannot be administered to quadriplegic patients. Two studies, however, investigated variants of Block Design that permitted evaluation of certain component skills.

Bolla-Wilson, Robinson, Price, and Squires (1984) developed multiple choice matching versions of both the Block Design and Object Assembly subtests of the WAIS-R. For the former, subjects viewed the target stimulus and four alternative choices: a "negative image" in which the red and white portions were reversed, a 180° rotation, a spatially displaced pattern, and an identical match of the target. This approach permitted Bolla-Wilson et al. to evaluate the visual–perceptual and analytic components of Block Design performance.

More recently, Caplan and Caffery (1992) described the Block Pattern Analysis Test (BPAT), which they developed "to allow evaluation of the nonmotor cognitive skills required by the Block Design task" (p. 338). Items on the BPAT consist of three squares (see Figure 11.1). In the upper middle portion of the page is a 2×2 or 3×3 square containing numbers that designate the four or nine segments, respectively. At the bottom of the page are two designs that can be constructed from the WAIS-R blocks. The designs are near-replicas, as they differ on only one portion. Subjects must compare the two designs and, using the numbered grid, report the number of the section that produces the distinction between the two patterns. Both accuracy and speed of response are measured. Caplan and Caffery reported that control subjects generally found the test to be quite easy, obtaining high accuracy scores ($M = 11.6$), with average response latencies of around 4 s per item. By contrast, 69% of a small group of rehabilitation inpatients referred for neuropsychological assessment demonstrated diminished accuracy, long response latencies, or both. Interestingly, certain dissociations were noted for particular patients between performance on the BPAT and on the WAIS-R Block Design, suggesting that the two tests engage partially disparate sets of abilities.

The development of the BPAT is a good example of how a new measure can emerge from modest clinical flexibility in testing the limits. Initially, we probed the performance of patients who failed easy Block Design items by testing the accuracy of their "same-different" judgments about pairs of block faces. We then would ask them to compare one two-block design with another, again stating whether they were identical or different in some way; if the latter, they might be asked to specify the part of each two-block pattern that was not the same and then to rearrange one to make it match the other. This informal procedure eventually led

Figure 11.1

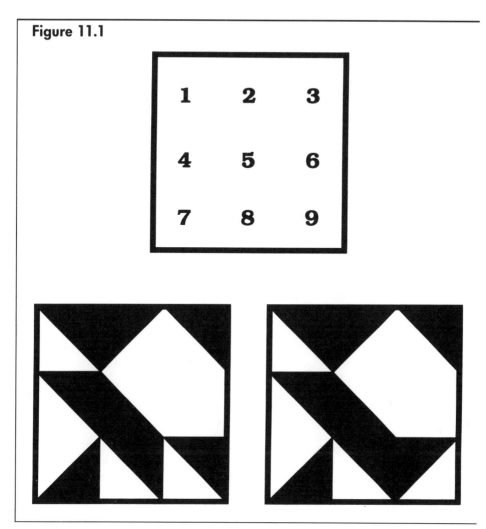

Sample 9-block item from the Block Pattern Analysis Test (Caplan & Cafferty, 1992b).

to the notion of creating a series of marginally dissimilar pairs of patterns as described above in order to gain a better understanding of certain subskills that contribute to performance on the more complex Block Design task. This led to the establishment of written instructions, a consistent set of stimulus plates, a normative data base, and thus, a (partially) standardized test.

Hooper Visual Organization Test

Seidel (1994) used a "fractionation" approach with the Hooper Visual Organization Test (Hooper, 1958) that resembles the process underlying development of the BPAT. Under standard administration conditions for the Hooper test, subjects are presented with cards depicting fragmented object drawings and must identify the object by mentally assembling the pieces. Clearly, individuals with limited naming ability—either young children or patients with acquired anomia—are at a disadvantage on this test. For a study of Hooper test performance in young children, Seidel showed individual items with the parts correctly assembled and asked the children to name the items. In this way, he was able to update and enlarge the number of acceptable responses for certain items. An alternative use for the modified materials, however, would be to contrast subjects' "mental synthesis" abilities with their constructional skills by allowing them to assemble those items that were failed under standard administration conditions.

Indented Paragraph Reading Test

Evaluation of oral reading ability is typically straightforward. Subjects are presented with written text (single words, sentences, paragraphs) and read the material aloud while the examiner monitors and records the accuracy of their performance. In virtually all types of aphasia except pure word deafness, reading ability is disrupted, but the form of the reading disturbance is less predictably related to intrahemispheric locus of lesion than is true for expressive speech disorders. Although aphasic reading disturbances are quite common and therefore generally undergo some evaluative scrutiny, disturbances of reading from nondominant hemisphere lesions may be more subtle and elusive. Probably the most common type of right-hemispheric reading problem is *neglect dyslexia*, in which patients omit or misperceive the initial letters of a given word, or else they omit the first word of a line because of diminished capacity to refixate their gaze from the right-side margin of one line to the left side of the next. Interestingly, patients with neglect generally do not spontaneously complain of difficulty with reading (Kinsbourne & Warrington, 1962), and they will often become evasive if asked to demonstrate their reading ability, maintaining that their prescription glasses are out of date, that they are not interested in the proffered reading material, and so forth. It is also important to point out that the degree of manifest neglect may vary as a function of such factors as the extent of the patient's awareness of the problem, fatigue, and stimulus density. Clinical observation suggests that the capacity to compensate for neglect may develop progressively and that some individuals may demonstrate adequate scanning on one occasion or test but not another.

To provide a brief screening tool for the assessment of neglect dyslexia, Caplan (1987) developed the Indented Paragraph Reading Test (IPRT), which consisted of a 30-line passage with a variable left-side margin (see Figure 11.2). The first word in each line was indented between 0 and 25 spaces, and the magnitude of indentation for each line was chosen in a quasirandom fashion. This format was created so that each leftward refixation required an independent scan under the control of the patient. Formation of a spatial set based on knowledge of the width of the sheet would therefore be of limited help. The test was constructed in this way because left-side neglect following right-hemisphere lesions is far more common than right-side neglect following left-hemisphere damage. However, it would seem an easy task to develop a similar form with a variably indented right-side margin.

Caplan administered the IPRT to 43 patients with documented right-hemisphere damage and 23 with left-hemisphere involvement. Subjects read the paragraph aloud, and the examiner recorded all misreadings and omissions as well as time to completion. Elapsed time proved difficult to interpret, as some patients completed the task quickly and accurately while others finished rapidly, but by virtue of leaving out substantial portions of the text. Only 5 left-hemisphere patients (21.7%) made omissions, the majority of which were right-side omissions. By contrast, 46.5% of the right-hemisphere patients omitted at least one word. One-third of the right-hemisphere patients omitted more than 5 words, and nearly 1 out of 7 made more than 25 omissions. Of particular note is the fact that all 5 subjects with left-hemisphere involvement who made omissions had shown no evidence of neglect on two other visual–perceptual tests that require some degree of scanning (Raven Matrices, Matching Familiar Figures Test). Similarly, 5 right-hemisphere patients who had shown normal scanning on the other tests gave evidence of neglect on the IPRT.

Two subsequent studies reported somewhat disparate results regarding the utility of the Indented Paragraph Reading Test. Towle and Lincoln (1991) studied two groups of right-hemisphere-involved stroke patients using three paragraphs: one with straight margins, one with variable indentation on either the right or left side, and the IPRT. Performances on the three paragraphs were very highly intercorrelated, and all were found to be sensitive to mild degrees of neglect. Towle and Lincoln also contrasted the IPRT with two subtests from the Behavioral Inattention Test (BIT; Wilson, Cockbrun, & Halligan, 1987) requiring

Figure 11.2

Trees brighten the countryside and soften the harsh lines of city
streets. Among them are our oldest and largest living
things. Trees are the best-known plants in man's experience. They are
graceful and a joy to see. So it is no wonder that people want
to know how to identify them. A tree is a woody
plant with a single stem growing to a height of ten
feet or more. Shrubs are also woody, but they are usually
smaller than trees and tend to have many stems growing
in a clump. Trees are easiest to recognize by their leaves. By
studying the leaves of trees it is possible to
learn to identify them at a distance. One group of trees has simple leaves
while others have compound leaves in which the blade is
divided into a number of leaflets. The leaf blade may have a
smooth uncut edge or it may be toothed. Not
only the leaves but also the flowers, fruit, seeds, bark,
buds, and wood are worth studying. When you look at a tree, see it as a
whole; see all its many parts; see it as a living
being in a community of plants and animals. The oldest trees live
for as long as three or four thousand years. Some grow almost
as tall as a forty story sky-scraper. The largest
trees contain enough wood to build dozens of average size
houses. Trees will always be one of the most important natural
resources of our country. Their timber, other
wood products, turpentine and resins are of great value. They also are
valuable because they hold the soil, preventing floods. In
addition, the beauty of trees, the majesty of forests,
and the quiet of woodlands are everyone's to
enjoy. Trees can be studied at every season, and they should be. Each
season will show features that cannot be seen at other times.
Watch the buds open in spring and the leaves unfold.

Indented Paragraph Reading Test (Caplan, 1987).

cancellation and oral reading; the Vocabulary subtest of the Wechsler Adult Intelligence Scale was administered to control for level of intelligence. Although performance on the IPRT correlated significantly with both BIT subtests, Towle and Lincoln reported unsatisfactory measures of agreement (kappa coefficients) between the tests in their sensitivity to neglect.

A more recent study by Bachman, Fein, Davenport, and Price (1993) employed the IPRT together with several other measures of neglect in a longitudinal study of recovery following right-hemisphere stroke. Using as their criterion evidence of neglect on at least two of the four paper-and-pencil measures, they found 69.6% of their subjects demonstrated neglect, the same percentages as detected by the IPRT, although some subjects were identified as neglecters by one criterion but not the other. Bachman et al. conclude, "In summary, the IPRT was equally sensitive to neglect as the composite of the four paper-and-pencil tests, with agreement on 74% of subjects and conflicting classification on the remaining 26%" (p. 491). Other important findings from this study include the following: (a) IPRT performance was not correlated with educational level, indicating that the test may be used with individuals who have received little formal education. (b) The original criterion for identification of neglecters was confirmed as valid. (c) The IPRT was found to reflect diminished neglect in recovering right-hemisphere stroke patients.

Measures of Affect, Personality, and Psychosocial Status

Whereas the preceding discussion has dealt with the evaluation of cognitive functions, this section addresses the problems that attend assessment of emotional and social functioning in certain groups of individuals with disabilities. Here again, the literature is somewhat sparse and scattered, but a consistent theme can be discerned: Individuals with disabilities may obtain spuriously pathological scores on these types of intrustruments (if they complete them honestly and thoughtfully) because natural consequences of their conditions may force them to respond to certain questions in ways that suggest, for example, depression, anxiety, or hysteria in the nondisabled population. For instance, Ebener et al. (1994) point out that the response to an inventory item such as "Would you rather read a book or climb a mountain?" may be entirely determined by the individual's disability rather than by avocational interest or character. Therefore, clinicians who uncritically apply to disabled individuals normative standards derived from physically healthy groups run the risk of misdiagnosis.

An early example of this type of problem can be found in the study by Taylor (1970) that identified 12 Minnesota Multiphasic Personality Inventory (MMPI) items that describe typical sequelae of spinal cord injury (e.g., "I have difficulty starting and holding my urine"). Individuals with spinal cord injury who honestly answer these questions, therefore, tend to obtain certain scale elevations (1, 2, 3, 8) suggesting emotional distress. Eliminating these items alters the obtained profile, partially "normalizing" it (Kendall, Edinger, & Eberly, 1978; see also chapter 10 in this volume).

Artifactual elevation of MMPI scales has been found in several other groups of individuals with disabilities. Meyerink, Reitan, and Selz (1988) observed elevations on scales 1, 2, 3, and 8 in a sample of individuals with multiple sclerosis who were accurately reporting their symptoms. Individuals with brain injury have been reported to show inflated MMPI profiles (combinations of scales 1, 2, 3, 7, and 8) by a number of investigators (e.g., Cripe & Dodrill, 1988; Dikmen & Reitan, 1977; Gass, 1991; Gass & Russell, 1991; Novack, Daniel, & Long, 1984).

Two groups of researchers have studied the effect of removing certain MMPI items that are felt to relate to common correlates of head trauma; in both instances, previously pathological elevations were reduced. The "neurocorrective approach" used by Alfano, Paniak, and Finlayson (1993) eliminated 24 items that had been endorsed in the pathological direction by at least 30% of their sample of 102 patients with closed head injury. A principle components analysis revealed two factors: one consisting largely of problems with attention or concentration, sensory motor dysfunction, or problems with significant life activities (Neurobehavioral factor) and another dealing with emotional and somatic complaints (Emotional/Somatic factor). When the Neurobehavioral factor items were eliminated and the protocols rescored, a "general flattening" (i.e., normalizing) of the average profile was observed.

Gass has studied patients with closed head injury (1991) and with stroke (1992) to identify potentially confounding items on the MMPI-2 (Butcher, Dahlstrom, Graham, Tellegen, & Kaemmer, 1989). For the head trauma group, a 14-item Neurologic Complaints factor was identified, which concerned a number of common neurobehavioral consequences of head trauma such as impaired concentration and memory, weakness, and problems with reading comprehension. This factor was found to be the major source of variance that discriminated between normal adults and the head-injured sample. Gass recommends that clinicians score MMPI-2 profiles of head trauma patients in both the standard fashion and the neurocorrected manner—that is, after eliminating the confounding items. He also notes that content scales exist for the MMPI-2 that may be used with neurologically impaired patients, as some of these (e.g., Depression, Bizarre Mentation, Social Discomfort, Family Problems) are free of the neurologic-complaints items. In his 1992 study, Gass determined that a set of 21 neurologic-complaints items accounted for the largest portion of variance that discriminated between 110 poststroke individuals and the MMPI-2 normative sample. Gass concluded that genuine neurologic symptoms caused spurious elevations on Scales 1, 2, 3, and 8. Once again, he recommended use of the content scales as well as double scoring of the protocols, once in standard fashion and a second time following elimination of the identified stroke-related items that the patient has endorsed. In both articles, Gass provides correction tables to assist clinicians in calculating adjusted raw scores.

In view of the widespread clinical use of the MMPI and MMPI-2, it is not surprising that most studies have used this measure. Some investigations examined the phenomenon of spurious elevations on the Symptom Checklist-90—Revised (SCL-90-R; Derogatis, 1983). The SCL-90-R is a 90-item self-report inventory of psychopathology. Studies by several investigators (DiCesare, Parente, & Anderson-Parente, 1990; Lezak, 1989; Lezak, Whitham, & Bourdette, 1990; Marsh, Knight, & Godfrey, 1990; O'Donnell, DeSoto, & Reynolds, 1984) described elevations in neurologic groups (multiple sclerosis, traumatic brain injury). The Obsessive–Compulsive scale was reported by two studies (O'Donnell et al., 1984; Lezak, 1989) to be elevated among head trauma patients, but O'Donnell et al. noted that 5 of the 8 items on their cognitive-deficit subscale were found on the Obsessive–Compulsive dimension. This prompted us to examine the SCL-90-R in some detail for other items that could cause artifactual inflation of this and other dimensions as well as the summary indices in the head trauma population (Woessner & Caplan, 1995). Ten experts on the neurobehavioral consequences of traumatic brain injury reviewed the SCL-90-R items and indicated those that they believed to reflect "usual consequences" of this condition. Fourteen items were judged by at least 80% of the experts as constituting "brain injury symptoms." These items loaded on 5 of the 9 individual dimensions, most heavily so on the Obsessive–Compulsive, Depression, and Hostility scales. A sample of 23 mildly to moderately brain-injured subjects demonstrated pervasive elevations, scoring at very high levels (82nd percentile and above, relative to the normative sample) on all dimensions including the supposedly uncontaminated ones. The patient sample endorsed 88 of the 90 SCL-90-R symptoms significantly more frequently than did the normative group.

Clinicians must be especially cautious in interpreting SCL-90-R profiles of brain-injured patients, as a single bona fide response may cause a given scale to reach a pathological elevation. For instance, reporting a high level of distress about "feeling easily annoyed or irritated" would produce a clinically significant elevation on the Hostility scale. Note that the patients' responses indicate that they were extremely bothered by feeling annoyed and irritated, not that they actually were extremely irritable. Thus, a self-conscious individual might be considerably upset by a small change in actual behavior. It remains to be seen whether a neurocorrective approach can be taken with the SCL-90-R, although the fact that it contains many fewer items per scale than does the MMPI does not inspire optimism.

Summary

We have tried to review in this chapter the theoretical and practical rationales supporting the use of nonstandard assessment techniques in the rehabilitation setting. Few would contest the assertion that neuropsychological assessment of many rehabilitation patients is complicated by the presence of certain sensory, motor, cognitive, and perceptual impairments. Although these may, in fact, represent the reason for the patient's presence on the rehabilitation unit, they often limit the scope of the evaluation that can be conducted; for example, psychomotor tasks cannot be administered in a valid fashion to individuals with quadriplegia. Furthermore, the effect of a particular disability may diminish test validity; for instance, tests requiring visual–perceptual analysis given to patients with unilateral neglect may merely reveal the presence of neglect, failing to identify other perceptual deficits. Especially in an era characterized by increasingly cost-conscious consumers and payors, we believe that psychologists cannot justify rigid insistence on the use of standardized procedures that may yield much in the way of a numerical profile, but less in the way of genuine insight and understanding of the patient's skills, weaknesses, and needs.

Some may argue that all good clinicians adopt a flexible posture, even those who use set batteries of standardized tests. However, the proliferation of practice parameters (with their attendant economic and legal implications) raises concern that clinicians will be increasingly loathe to venture outside of predetermined assessment guidelines. Others may fear that our position invites anarchy, subverting the psychometric foundations of sound clinical practice. However, we believe that the professional literature—including empirical research, conceptual formulations, and ethical standards—provides sufficient grounds for arguing that in the matter of nonstandard assessment, clinicians should "experiment boldly, interpret cautiously," collect data in a systematic fashion (if feasible), and publish their findings.

Skeptics should remember that every test that we currently accept as standardized was once an unstandardized test in development and before that perhaps a pilot study to test a notion that was serendipitously generated during a boring administrative meeting.

We contend that evaluation is best conducted by individuals who blend solid technical skills with judicious creativity (and perhaps a bit of daring) in an effort to obtain findings that will truly be of use to the patient. Rational use of nonstandard methods can best enable clinicians to ensure that they obtain meaningful results that will ultimately improve the lives of their patients.

References

Alfano, D. P., Paniak, C. E., & Finlayson, M. A. (1993). The MMPI and closed head injury: A neurocorrective approach. *Neuropsychiatry, Neuropsychology, and Behavioral Neurology, 6,* 111–116.

Bachman, L., Fein, G., Davenport, L., & Price, L. (1993). The indented paragraph reading test in the assessment of left hemi-neglect. *Archives of Clinical Neuropsychology, 8,* 485–496.

Baron, H. (1990). When is testing fair? *The Occupational Psychologist, 11,* 19–23.

Benton, A. L. (1950). A multiple choice type of the visual retention test. *Archives of Neurology and Psychiatry, 59,* 699–707.

Benton, A. L. (1965). *Manuel du Test de Retention Visuelle: Applications cliniques et experimentales* [Manual for the Visual Retention Test: Clinical and experimental applications] (2nd ed.). Paris: Centre de Psychologie Appliquee.

Benton, A. L. (1974). *The Revised Visual Retention Test* (4th ed.). New York: The Psychological Corporation.

Benton, A., Hamsher, K., Varney, N., & Spreen, O. (1983). *Contributions to neuropsychological assessment: A clinical manual.* New York: Oxford University Press.

Benton, A., Hamsher, K., & Stone, F. (1977). *Visual Retention Test: Multiple Choice Form I.* Iowa City: Department of Neurology, University Hospitals, University of Iowa.

Berninger, V., Gans, B. M., St. James, P., & Connors, T. (1988). Modified WAIS-R for patients with speech and/or hand dysfunction. *Archives of Physical Medicine and Rehabilitation, 69,* 250–255.

Bolla-Wilson, K., Robinson, R., Price, T., & Squires, N. (1984, February). *Visuoconstructional assemby difficulty: Influence of site of lesion and task.* Paper presented at the 12th annual meeting of the International Neuropsychological Society, Houston, Texas.

Butcher, J. N., Dahlstrom, W. G., Graham, J. R., Tellegen, A., & Kaemmer, B. (1989). *Manual for the Restandardized Minnesota Multiphasic Personality Inventory*: MMPI-2. Minneapolis: University of Minnesota Press.

Caltagirone, C., Gainotti, G., & Miceli, G. (1977). Una nuova versone delle matrici colorate elaborata specificamente per i pazienti con lesioni emesferiche focali. [A new version of the Colored Matrices developed specifically for patients with focal hemispheric lesions]. *Minerva Psichiatrica, 18*, 9–16.

Caplan, B. (1985). Task factors in unilateral neglect. *Cortex, 21*, 69–80.

Caplan, B. (1987). Assessment of unilateral neglect: A new reading test. *Journal of Clinical and Experimental Neuropsychology, 9*, 359–364.

Caplan, B. (1988). Nonstandard neuropsychological assessment: An illustration. *Neuropsychology, 2*, 13–17.

Caplan, B., & Caffery, D. (in press). Visual form discrimination as a multiple-choice memory test: Preliminary normative data. *Clinical Neuropsychologist*.

Caplan, B., & Caffery, D. (1992). Fractionating block design: Development of a test of visuospatial analysis. *Neuropsychology, 6*, 385–394.

Costa, L. D., Vaughan, H. G., Horowitz, M., & Ritter, W. (1969). Patterns of behavioral deficit associated with visual spatial neglect. *Cortex, 5*, 242–263.

Cripe, L. I., & Dodrill, C. B. (1988). Neuropsychological test performances with chronic low-level formaldehyde exposure. *Clinical Neuropsychologist, 2*, 41–48.

Cronbach, L. J. (1960). *Essentials of psychological testing* (2nd ed.). New York: Harper.

Derogatis, L. R. (1983). *SCL-90–R: Administration, scoring, & procedural manual—II for the r(evised) version*. Towson, MD: Clinical Psychometric Research.

DiCesare, A., Parente, R., & Anderson-Parente, J. K. (1990). Personality changes after traumatic brain injury: Problems and solutions. *Cognitive Rehabilitation, 8*, 14–18.

Dikmen, S., & Reitan, R. M. (1977). Emotional sequelae of head injury. *Annals of Neurology, 2*, 492–494.

Dunn, L. M., & Dunn, L. M. (1981). *Peabody Picture Vocabulary Test—Revised*. Circle Pines, MN: American Guidance Service.

Ebener, D. J., Burkhead, E. J., & Merydith, S. P. (1994). The Americans with Disabilities Act: Implications for vocational assessment. *Assessment in Rehabilitation and Exceptionality, 1*, 91–97.

Equal Employment Opportunity Commission. (1991). Equal employment opportunity for individuals with disabilities. *Federal Register, 56*, 35725–35753.

Franzen, M. D. (1989). *Reliability and validity in neuropsychological assessment*. New York: Plenum Press.

Freeman, F. S. (1962). *Theory and Practice of Psychological Testing* (3rd ed.). New York: Holt, Rinehart & Winston.

Gainotti, G., D'Erme, P., Villa, G., & Caltagirone, C. (1986). Focal brain lesions and intelligence: A study with a new version of Raven's colored matrices. *Journal of Clinical and Experimental Neuropsychology, 8*, 37–50.

Gass, C. S. (1991). MMPI-2 interpretation and closed head injury: A correction factor. *Psychological Assessment, 3*, 27–31.

Gass, C. S., & Russell, E. W. (1991). MMPI profiles of closed head trauma patients: Impact of neurologic complaints. *Journal of Clinical Psychology, 47*, 253, 260.

Gass, C. S. (1992). MMPI-2 interpretation of patients with cerebrovascular disease: A correction factor. *Archives of Clinical Neuropsychology, 7*, 17–27.

Glisky, E. L., & Schacter, D. L. (1987). Acquisition of domain-specific knowledge in organic amnesia: Training for computer-related work. *Neuropsychologia, 25*, 893–906.

Golden, C. J., & Robbins, D. E. (1985). Considerations in cases of visual, auditory, or motor impairment. In D. P. Swiercinsky (Ed.), *Testing adults: A reference guide for special psychodiagnostic assessments* (pp. 89–100). Kansas City, MO: Test Corporation of America.

Goldstein, G. (1987). Neuropsychological assessment for rehabilitation: Fixed batteries, automated systems, and non-psychometric methods. In M. Meier, A. Benton, & L. Diller (Eds.), *Neuropsychological rehabilitation* (pp. 18–40). New York: Guilford Press.

Heaton, S. R., & Heaton, R. K. (1981). Testing the impaired patient. In S. B. Filskov & T. J. Boll (Eds.), *Handbook of clinical neuropsychology* (pp. 526–544). New York: Wiley.

Heinrichs, R. W. (1990). Current and emergent applications of neuropsychological assessment: Problems of validity and utility. *Professional Psychology: Research and Practice*, *21*, 171–176.

Hibbard, M. R., & Gordon, W. A. (1992). The comprehensive psychological assessment of individuals with stroke. *NeuroRehabilitation*, *2*, 9–20.

Hiskey, M. S. (1966). *Manual for the Hiskey-Nebraska Test of Learning Aptitude*. Lincoln, NE: Union College Press.

Hooper, H. E. (1958). *The Hooper Visual Organization Test Manual*. Los Angeles: Western Psychological Services.

Jastak, S., & Wilkinson, G. S. (1984). *Wide Range Achievement Test administration manual*. Wilmington, DE: Jastak Associates.

Jordan, S. (1978). Haptic Intelligence Scale for adult blind. *Perceptual and Motor Skills*, *47*(1), 203–222.

Kaplan, E., Fein, D., Morris, R., & Delis, D. C. (1991). *WAIS-R as a neuropsychological instrument: WAIS-R-NI Manual*. New York: The Psychological Corporation.

Kendall, P., Edinger, J, & Eberly, C. (1978). Taylor's MMPI correction factor for spinal cord injury: Empirical endorsement. *Journal of Consulting and Clinical Psychology*, *46*, 370–371.

Kinsbourne, M., & Warrington, E. K. (1962). A variety of reading disability associated with right hemisphere lesions. *Journal of Neurology, Neurosurgery, & Psychiatry*, *25*, 339–344.

Lalonde, R., Botez, T., & Botez, M. I. (1992). Methodologic considerations in neuropsychological testing of ataxic patients. *Archives of Neurology*, *49*, 218.

Leiter, L. G. (1948). *Leiter International Performance Scale*. Chicago: Stoelting.

Leung, P. (1984). Training in rehabilitation. In C. J. Golden (Ed.), *Current topics in rehabilitation psychology* (pp. 17–27). Orlando: Grune & Stratton.

Lezak, M. D. (1983). *Neuropsychological assessment* (2nd ed.). New York: Oxford University Press.

Lezak, M. D. (1984). An individualized approach to neuropsychological assessment. In P. E. Logue & J. M. Schear (Eds.), *Clinical neuropsychology: A multidisciplinary approach* (pp. 29–49). Springfield, IL: Charles C Thomas.

Lezak, M. D. (1987). Assessment for rehabilitation planning. In M. Meier, A. Benton, & L. Diller (Eds.), *Neuropsychological rehabilitation* (pp. 41–58). New York: Guilford Press.

Lezak, M. D. (1989). Assessment of psychosocial dysfunctions following head trauma. In M. D. Lezak (Ed.), *Assessment of the behavioral consequences of head trauma* (pp. 113–143). New York: Alan R. Liss.

Lezak, M. D., Whitham, R., & Bourdette, D. (1990). Emotional impact of cognitive inefficiencies in multiple sclerosis. *Journal of Clinical and Experimental Neuropsychology*, *12*, 50(A).

Lincoln, N. B., & Staples, D. (1987). A maze learning test for the assessment of memory with physically disabled patients. *Clinical Rehabilitation*, *1*, 197–201.

Markwardt, F. C. (1989). Peabody Individual Achievement Test—Revised: Manual. Circle Pines, MN: American Guidance Service.

Marsh, N. V., Knight, R. G., & Godfrey, H. P. D. (1990). Long-term psychosocial adjustment following very severe closed head injury. *Neuropsychology*, *4*, 13–27.

Meyerink, L. H., Reitan, R. M., & Selz, M. (1988). The validity of the MMPI with multiple sclerosis patients. *Journal of Clinical Psychology*, *44*, 764–768.

Mittler, P. F. (1970). Assessment of handicapped children: Some common factors. In P. Mittler (Ed.), *The psychological assessment of mental and physical handicaps* (pp. 343–373). London: Tavistock.

Nester, M. A. (1993). Psychometric testing and reasonable accommodation of persons with disabilities. *Rehabilitation Psychology*, *38*, 75–85.

Novack, T. A, Daniel, M. S., & Long, C. J. (1984). Factors related to emotional adjustment following head injury. *International Journal of Clinical Neuropsychology*, *6*, 139–142.

O'Donnell, W. E., DeSoto, C. B., & Reynolds, D. McQ. (1984). A cognitive deficit subscale of the SCL-90–R. *Journal of Clinical Psychology*, *40*, 241–246.

Popkin, S., Schaie, K., & Krauss, I. (1983). Age-fair assessment of psychometric intelligence. *Educational Gerontology*, *9*, 47–55.

Raven, J. C. (1960). *Guide to using the Standard Progressive Matrices*. London: H. K. Lewis

Raven, J. C. (1965). *Guide to using the Coloured Progressive Matrices*. London: H. K. Lewis.

Reed, M. (1970). Deaf and partially hearing children. In P. Mittler (Ed.), *The psychological assessment of mental and physical handicaps* (pp. 403–441). London: Tavistock.

Reynell, J. (1970). Children with physical handicaps. In P. Mittler (Ed.), *The psychological assessment of mental and physical handicaps* (pp. 443–469). London: Tavistock.

Richards, J. S., Brown, L., Hagglund, K., Bua, G., & Reeder, K. (1988). Spinal cord injury and concomitant traumatic brain injury: Results of a longitudinal investigation. *American Journal of Physical Medicine*, *67*, 211–216.

Ricker, J. H., Axelrod, B. N., & Konarzewski-Nassu, S. (1993, August). *Visual form discrimination and recognition in elderly and young adults*. Paper presented at the 101st annual convention of the American Psychological Association, Toronto, Ontario, Canada.

Reitan, R. M., & Tarshes, E. L. (1959) Differential effects of the lateralized brain lesions on the Trail Making Test. *Journal of Nervous and Mental Disease*, *129*, 257–262.

Roth, E., Davidoff, G., Thomas, P., Doljanac, R., Dijkers, M., Berent, S., Morris, J., & Yarkony, G. (1989). A controlled study of neuropsychological deficits in acute spinal cord injury patients. *Paraplegia*, *27*, 480–489.

Russell, E. W. (1986). The psychometric foundation of clinical neuropsychology. In S. B. Filskov & T. J. Boll (Eds.), *Handbook of clinical neuropsychology*, (Vol. 2, pp. 45–80). New York: Wiley.

Sattler J. M., & Theye, F. (1967). Procedural, situational, and interpersonal variables in individual intelligence testing. *Psychological Bulletin*, *68*, 347–360.

Sattler, J., & Tozier, L. (1970). A review of intelligence test modifications used with cerebral palsied and other handicapped groups. *The Journal of Special Education*, *4*, 391–398.

Sattler, J. (1982). *Assessment of Children's Intelligence and Special Abilities* (2nd ed.). Boston, MA: Allyn & Bacon.

Schacter, D. L., & Glisky, E. L. (1986). Memory remediation: Restoration, alleviation, and the acquisition of domain-specific knowledge. In B. P. Uzzell & Y. Gross (Eds.), *Clinical neuropsychology of intervention* (pp. 257–282). Boston, MA: Martinus Nijhoff.

Schaie, K. W. (1985). *Manual for the Schaie-Thurstone Test of Adult Mental Abilities* (STAMAT). Palo Alto, CA: Consulting Psychologists Press.

Schonell, F. E. (1956). *Educating spastic children*. London: Oliver & Boyd.

Seidal, W. T. (1994). Applicability of the Hooper Visual Organization Test to pediatric populations: Preliminary findings. *The Clinical Neuropsychologist, 8*, 59–68.

Sivan, A. B. (1992). *The Benton Visual Retention Test Manual* (5th ed.). New York: The Psychological Corporation.

Standards for education and psychological testing. (1985). Washington, DC: American Psychological Association.

Taylor, G. (1970). Moderator-variable effect on personality test item endorsements of physically disabled patients. *Journal of Consulting and Clinical Psychology, 35*, 183–188.

Thorpe, T. R., & Mahrer, A. R. (1959). Predicting potential intelligence. *Journal of Clinical Psychology, 15*, 286–288.

Thurstone, L. L., & Thurstone, T. G. (1949). *Examiner manual for the SRA Primary Mental Abilities Test.* Chicago: Science Research Associates.

Towle, D., & Lincoln, N. B. (1991). Use of the indented paragraph reading test with right hemisphere-damaged stroke patients. *British Journal of Clinical Psychology, 30*, 37–45.

Wechsler, D. (1981). *Wechsler Adult Intelligence Scale-Revised.* New York: The Psychological Corporation.

Weintraub, S., & Mesulam, M. M. (1985). Mental state assessment of young and elderly adults in behavioral neurology. In M. M. Mesulam (Ed.), *Principles of behavioral neurology* (pp. 71–123). Philadelphia, PA: Davis.

Weinberg, J., Diller, L., Gordon, W. A., Gerstman, L. J., Lieberman, A., Lakin, P., Hodges, G., & Ezrachi, O. (1977). Visual scanning training effect on reading-related tasks in acquired right brain damage. *Archives of Physical Medicine and Rehabilitation, 58*, 479–486.

Willingham, W. W., Ragosta, M., Bennett, R. E., Braun, H., Rock, D. A., & Powers, D. E. (1988). *Testing handicapped people.* Boston, MA: Allyn & Bacon.

Wilmot, C. B., Cope, D. N., Hall, K. M., & Acker, M. (1985). Occult head injury: Its incidence in spinal cord injury. *Archives of Physical Medicine and Rehabilitation, 66*, 227–231.

Wilson, B. C. (1986). An approach to neuropsychological assessment of the preschool child with developmental deficits. In S. B. Filskov & T. J. Boll (Eds.), *Handbook of clinical neuropsychology* (Vol. 2, pp. 121–171). New York: Wiley.

Wilson, B., Cockburn, J., & Halligan, P. (1987). *Behavioural Inattention Test.* Titchfield, Fareham, Hants, England: Thames Valley Test Co; Gaylord, MI: National Rehabilitation Services.

Wilson, S. L., & McMillan, T. M. (1986). Finding able minds in disabled bodies. *Lancet, 2*, 1444–1446.

Woessner, R., & Caplan, B. (1995). Affective disorders following mild to moderate brain injury: Interpretive hazards of the SCL-90–R. *Journal of Head Trauma Rehabilitation, 10*, 78–89.

Assessing Awareness of Deficits: Recent Research and Applications

Jeffrey R. Campodonico and Susan M. McGlynn

I t has been known for many years that brain damage can produce profound changes in behavior, cognition, and physical functioning that can persist well beyond the acute phase of recovery. Patients are often unaware of these changes and minimize the impact of their limitations on everyday activity. Although some patients steadfastly deny any suggestion that they are impaired, others simply do not appreciate their deficits and exhibit unconcern, disbelief, or triviality when confronted by them. It then comes as no surprise that altered self-awareness creates a major obstacle in rehabilitation and psychosocial adjustment (Ben-Yishay et al., 1985; Bond, 1984; Bond & Brooks, 1976; Ford, 1976; Prigatano & Fordyce, 1986). Moreover, unawareness may create serious problems for family members who have trouble managing patients (Lezak, 1978, 1988). Given these problems, routine assessment of awareness disturbances appears critical for effective treatment and aftercare planning.

Unawareness of deficit generally refers to patients' lack of insight or appreciation of a particular deficit or cluster of impairments. The term *unawareness* is often used interchangeably with *anosognosia* and *denial of illness*, despite differences in the original meanings of these designations (for review, see McGlynn & Schacter, 1989; Prigatano & Schacter, 1991). Impaired awareness can manifest in different forms, be produced in various kinds of brain damage, and differ with respect to the type of assessment procedure used. Research in awareness of deficit has dealt

Preparation of this manuscript was supported by National Institute on Aging Grant R01 AGO 8441.

primarily with patients who have sustained direct neurological and neuropsychological impairment. Awareness disturbances are commonly observed in different forms of brain damage. Some of these conditions include degenerative dementia (e.g., Alzheimer's disease, Parkinson's disease, Huntington's disease, Pick's disease), cerebral vascular disease (e.g., stroke, multi-infarct dementia, anterior communicating artery aneurysms), and traumatic brain injury.

Different theories about impaired awareness of deficits have emerged over the years. Early investigators of anosognosia posited a direct relationship between the locus of brain damage and anosognosia. Notably, Babinski (1914) postulated an association between unawareness of left hemiparesis and damage to right posterior brain regions (cited in Redlich & Dorsey, 1945). A different group of researchers contended that unawareness results from general intellectual decline following diffuse brain impairment (Sandifer, 1946). More recently, scientists have focused on the role of the frontal lobes in altered self-awareness (Prigatano, 1992; for review, see Stuss & Benson, 1984, 1986).

Some investigators have postulated that patients' lack of insight into the severity of their deficits is, in part, a product of psychological defensiveness or denial (Guthrie & Grossman, 1952; Perry & Cooper, 1986; Rosenthal, 1983; Taland, 1965; Weinstein, 1991; Weinstein & Kahn, 1955). According to this theory, some individuals following brain damage are unable to cope with the reality of their disabilities and, as a result, present themselves in a favorable light to avoid severe anxiety. Similarly, impaired awareness can be conceptualized as a consequence of one's premorbid personality structure. Thus, individuals with a lifelong pattern of denial attempt to maintain a sense of well-being and perfectionism to protect against feelings of inadequacy. Theoretically, after brain damage these persons manifest a more accentuated pattern of psychological defensiveness in reaction to the grave, life-threatening situation. Patients also may deliberately deny their deficits in order to maintain their independence or avoid unfavorable consequences (e.g., loss of job, inability to drive, or residential placement).

The purpose of this chapter is to review the contemporary methods of assessing patients' awareness of their deficits and to discuss some of the important methodological and conceptual issues. Recent advances in this field have stimulated the development of new objective instruments for awareness assessment. Although many of these tools are in the early stages of validation and refinement, some have shown preliminary psychometric and theoretical merit and are worthy of consideration.

Objective assessment of awareness may (a) assist in the early diagnosis and implementation of effective rehabilitative interventions, (b) be useful in gauging patients' progress in rehabilitation, (c) aid in predicting patients' safety in functional areas, (d) foster the development of awareness-enhancing interventions, and (e) help refine our current understanding of brain–behavior relationships in the study of conscious experience.

Assessing Awareness of Deficits: Systematic Approaches

Assessing awareness of deficits has been approached in several ways. Perhaps the most common method involves observation and direct questioning about a patient's neurological or neuropsychological deficits. For example, one might ask an individual with hemiparesis whether they have noticed any changes in their physical ability, or if they intend to resume their premorbid physical activity. This approach typically relies on the clinician's ability to elicit information from the patient via interview or direct observation and puts the burden of proof on clinical judgment and subjectivity. Early studies of anosognosia used subjective methods in studying patients with obvious neurological defects. Current knowledge of anosognosia, however, has extended beyond physical defects to include awareness of neuropsychological deficits (e.g., memory, language, visual–perceptual) and emotional–personality sequelae of brain damage (McGlynn & Schacter, 1989). Given this broader and more complex conceptualization of anosognosia, inferences about patients' awareness based solely on clinical impressions may be inadequate and lead to erroneous conclusions. Ideally, assessment of awareness would be based on systematic, objective criteria derived from a theoretical framework.

In recent years, there has been a sharp increase in the number of objective methods used in assessing awareness of deficits. Although some instruments have been developed to measure specific areas of patients' awareness, others capture a broader range of psychosocial and behavioral indices. In either case, questions range from open-ended inquiries such as "Why are you in the hospital?" to more direct questions like "How much difficulty do you have reading the newspaper in the morning?" Some instruments vary with respect to the kind of content sampled, and others differ strictly in format. Generally, each of the procedures that we discuss has the goal of identifying individuals who lack awareness of deficits by comparing their subjective perceptions to a measure of reality.

Our review of the literature suggests that there are generally three systematic approaches that can be used to quantify awareness of deficits: (a) contrasting patients' and informants' perceptions of patients' abilities or questionnaires; (b) comparing patients' perceptions of their abilities with empirical data; or (c) having patients predict their performance on a series of tasks, and comparing their predictions with actual test performance.

Patients' Versus Informants' Perceptions

A number of questionnaires have been developed that ask patients to rate (on a Likert scale) the degree to which they perceive changes or difficulties across a spectrum of physical, cognitive, emotional, and psychosocial abilities. For example, participants rate each item on a 5-point scale (0 to 4, where 0 = *no difficulty*, 2 = *some difficulty*, and 4 = *a great deal of difficulty*) indicating the degree to which they experience difficulty with various aspects of memory now, as compared with before their illness. Informants who are familiar with the patients' premorbid and current status are asked to rate patients on the same questions. In theory, informants' ratings provide a source of objectivity that is then contrasted with patients' subjective ratings to obtain an index of awareness of deficit. Such discrepancies not only emphasize areas of particular concern for different people in contact with patients but also indicate the degree to which patients are aware of their own deficits (Brooks & Lincoln, 1984).

A number of investigations have examined awareness of memory impairment in persons with brain damage (Boake, Freeland, Ringholz, Nance, & Edwards, 1987; Jarho, 1973; Luria, 1976; McGlynn, Schacter, & Glisky, 1989; Rimel et al., 1981; Schacter, Glisky, & McGlynn, 1990; Shimamura & Squire, 1986; Vilkki, 1985). Impaired awareness of memory deficit is commonly observed in various forms of cerebral damage. Some researchers have utilized self-reports of memory change to assess the degree of awareness of deficit. Many of these questionnaires were adopted from metamemory research assessing persons with brain-damage, and results revealed that a significant proportion of patients overestimated their everyday memory functioning.

The Memory Assessment Clinic Self-Report Scale (MAC-S; Crook & Larrabee, 1990) is a 49-item questionnaire that asks patients to rate, on a 5-point scale, the degree to which they experience memory difficulties in everyday life (e.g., "How often do you forget where you have put objects [such as keys] in the home or office?" 1 = *Very Often*, 3 = *Occa-*

sionally, and 5 = *Very Rarely*). A low score on each question indicates poor memory and a high score reflects good memory. An analogous version of the questionnaire (MAC-F) was designed for family members to complete. Awareness of memory difficulties is derived by subtracting the mean MAC-S score from the mean MAC-F score.

Feher, Mahurin, Inbody, Crook, and Pirozzolo, (1991) found that patients with Alzheimer's disease (AD) significantly overestimated their memory functioning on the MAC-S. These researchers also found satisfactory test–retest reliability (4 weeks; r = .73) for this instrument, as well as significant correlations between family members' scores and objective memory scores. Moreover, Crook and Larrabee (1990) reported mean scores on the MAC-S for a large sample of healthy individuals that can be used as an anchor point for studying awareness in neurological groups. A factor analytic study of this instrument was reported as well (for more information, see Crook & Larrabee, 1992).

McGlynn and Kazniak (1991a) devised the Daily Difficulties Questionnaire to assess awareness of deficits in patients with Huntington's disease (HD). The questionnaire consists of 24 items asking patients to rate, on a 7-point scale, the degree to which they currently experience difficulties in everyday life compared with 5 years ago. One-half of the items are related to motor abilities (e.g., walking up a flight of stairs), and the remaining items tap into cognitive functions (e.g., recalling the order of things that you did yesterday). Ratings of the questionnaire can be obtained verbally or administered in a paper-and-pencil format. Discrepancies between patients' and caregivers' ratings concerning the patients' difficulties constitute an index of patients' awareness of their difficulties. In addition, patients and relatives provide ratings of the relative's ability in order to establish whether unawareness is specific to a patient's degree of functioning or associated with a global decline of judgment capacity.

These investigators found that individuals with HD overestimated their everyday memory on the questionnaire. McGlynn and Kazniak (1991b) adapted the questionnaire for use in individuals with AD and also found significant differences between these patients' perceptions of their everyday memory ability and caregivers' perceptions, providing additional validity to the instrument. Additionally, it was noted that patients' diminished awareness of their deficits was not a result of global deterioration of judgment capacity, but rather a specific breakdown in their capacity for self-evaluation.

To measure a broader set of questions related to patients' awareness of memory disturbance, McGlynn, Schacter, and Glisky (1989) developed a battery of instruments, which included the Everyday Memory Questionnaire, the General Self-Assessment Questionnaire, and the Item Recall Questionnaire. Each inventory was designed to assess qualitative differences in unawareness and to provide converging evidence of this disorder.

The Everyday Memory Questionnaire consists of 10 specific everyday situations that require remembering different types of information. Patients are presented with hypothetical situations (e.g., "How likely would you be able to remember a telephone conversation with a friend [10 minutes, 1 hour, 1 day, 1 week] after it occurred?") and are asked to rate, on a 7-point scale, the likelihood that they would remember the target information. A unique feature of this instrument requires patients to rate (on the same scale) the likelihood of remembering each item before their illness, as well as rating the probability that their spouse would remember the same information. Spouses are required as well to rate their own performance and the patients' performance on the same items; this allows a richer set of comparisons and enhances the internal validity of the instrument.

The General Self-Assessment Questionnaire is made up of 18-items and requires patients to rate the degree to which they experience difficulties with various aspects of memory on a scale of zero to 6 (0 = *a great deal of difficulty* and 6 = *no difficulty at all*). Significant others are provided with analogous versions of the questionnaire. A supplementary section of the questionnaire was developed by others (Campodonico, Templer, Mulder, Goka, & Schuyler, 1993), which asks patients and relatives to rate, in a similar fashion, the degree to which they perceive changes in various aspects of their personality and emotional functioning.

Finally, the Item Recall Questionnaire has patients predict how many items they would be able to remember from a larger list of words (both now and prior to illness) after four delay intervals (e.g., 10 minutes, 1 hour, 1 day, and 1 week). One-half of the items consist of easy words (e.g., names of familiar people), and the remainder are considered to be difficult (e.g., unfamiliar names). It is assumed that if patients are aware of their own memory functioning and memory processing in general, they should report better recall of the easy items. Not only are patients asked to predict their own performance on this task, but they are also required to predict their spouses' performance. Conversely, spouses are required to predict their own performance and the patient's performance.

Although the internal validity of these instruments is preliminary, in a well-controlled study of two amnesic patients McGlynn, Schacter, and Glisky (1989) found significant differences between the two patients' awareness of their memory impairment. As predicted, the patient with circumscribed frontal lobe damage over-rated his memory capacity on each of the questionnaires, whereas the patient with only temporal lobe involvement could accurately indicate the extent of her memory problems, relative to her spouse. Thus, administration of these questionnaires provided converging evidence of awareness of memory deficit. Campodonico, Templer, Mulder, Goka, and Schuyler (1992) additionally found significant differences between a heterogeneous group of individuals with traumatic brain injury and their significant others' ratings on the General Self-Assessment Questionnaire. In their study, patients generally underestimated their physical, cognitive, and personality changes; thus providing additional support of the instrument's validity.

The foregoing results are important for two reasons. First, they underscore the need to utilize multiple sampling procedures in assessing awareness. McGlynn and Schacter (1989) contend that awareness of deficit may not be an "all or none" disorder, but can vary in quality and severity across neurological groups and assessment techniques. Controlling for possible qualitative differences in awareness may be best addressed through a multiple sampling approach. In their battery, questions ranged from concrete, contextually based material to more abstract inquiries of performance, allowing for a richer set of analyses. As we will discuss later, there have been studies that illustrate important discrepancies between self-awareness assessment procedures.

Second, multiple tools in assessing awareness may have important implications in rehabilitative settings. This approach may be useful for gauging patients' awareness over time. It would allow one to examine whether an intervention was effective and determine whether the result generalized across other techniques. For example, one could train an unaware patient to increase the accuracy of his or her predictions on the Item Recall Questionnaire and then observe whether a similar effect was noted on the Self-Assessment and Everyday Memory Questionnaires (or vice versa). Schacter, Glisky, and McGlynn (1990) reported that they were able to enhance awareness in their amnesic patient during extensive feedback training, though the long-term effects of their treatment have not been determined.

The Patient Competency Rating Scale (PCRS; Prigatano et al., 1986; Roueche & Fordyce, 1983) is a 30-item, 5-point behavioral rating scale that asks patients and families to make judgments concerning the perceived degree of competency the patient currently demonstrates in carrying out a wide variety of daily tasks (e.g., "How much of a problem do you have in scheduling daily activities?"). Ten of the 30 items were identified a priori as being items for which patients with head injuries would likely underestimate their degree of impairment, based on previous research (e.g., acting appropriately when around friends, adjusting to unexpected changes). Eight additional items were included that strictly involve physical activities (e.g., preparing meals, doing laundry). It is expected that the latter items will produce little or no disagreement between patients and relatives. Thus, if these different items are rated in the expected directions, the internal validity of the instrument is enhanced.

Normative studies of the PCRS in patients with traumatic brain injuries provide preliminary support for its psychometric properties. Notably, Prigatano, Altman, and O'Brien (1990) found that patients consistently underestimated their behavioral limitations on the questions that they predicted would produce disagreement (e.g., items related to perceived abilities in handling emotional and social interactions), while showing little disagreement on the other questions that involved one's ability to carry out basic activities of daily living. These investigators also reported adequate reliability for PCRS total scores (patients, $r = .97$; relatives, $r = .92$). Concurrent validity of the PCRS with other indices of injury severity has shown mixed results. Although Prigatano and Altman (1990) observed a larger number of brain lesions (reported by head CT and magnetic resonance imaging findings) in those patients with reduced awareness on this instrument, no consistent pattern of cognitive deficits emerged.

Functional Scales Adapted for Use in Awareness Assessment

Several instruments have been used to assess patients' capacity to perform everyday functional activities. Some of these scales have been modified for the purpose of assessing awareness of deficits and include the Physical Self-Maintenance Scale (PSMS; Lowenthal, 1964) and the Instrumental Activities of Daily Living Scale (IADL; Lawton & Brody, 1969). As is similar to the results derived from metamemory questionnaires, patients have shown diminished awareness of their functional limitations when given these instruments.

The PSMS consists of six self-report activities that are associated with basic physical self-care (e.g., feeding, dressing, toileting, grooming, ambulating, and bathing), whereas the IADL is made up of eight items that measure a more complex set of everyday activities (e.g., shopping, taking medication, handling finances). DeBettignies, Mahurin, and Pirozzolo

(1990) found that patients with AD exhibited diminished insight, relative to informants, into their independent living skills as compared with both healthy individuals and individuals with multi-infarct dementia. Although impaired awareness was not associated with patients' severity of dementia or depression, it was related to level of caregiver burden. In a different study, however, Mangone et al. (1991) found that the discrepancies between persons with AD and their caregivers on these scales correlated significantly with overall dementia severity, depression, and neuropsychological test data (notably, tasks that are sensitive to frontal lobe damage). These discrepant findings may be due to differences in the samples of patients studied, variations in the stage and course of disease, or dissimilarities of cognitive tests.

The major criticisms of this approach in assessing awareness of deficit, as with some other approaches that we will discuss later, are the following: (a) the question of external validity, (b) the assumption that caregivers provide accurate ratings, (c) the limited scope of content, and (d) variability in the construction of items.

First, it is difficult to know whether patients' awareness disturbance on questionnaires actually generalizes to real-life situations or is a product of the artificial testing condition. Because many questionnaires rely solely on patients' verbalized responses, observational data is needed to support whether these questionnaires tap into real-life behaviors. Second, it is not uncommon for caregivers to minimize or deny the severity of patients' deficits, given their own psychological distress around this issue (McKinlay & Brooks, 1984; Prigatano, 1991). It is possible that many patients who are otherwise unaware of their deficits may not differ with their caregiver on a particular questionnaire and are judged to be aware. Although greater objectivity may be gained with staff members' ratings, these individuals often do not have access to patients' premorbid capacities and are thus unable to make comparisons.

Another potential criticism relates to the content of several questionnaires. Instruments that do not sample a wide range of abilities may inadvertently overlook some problem areas. Conversely, scales that sample a broad range of abilities without focusing on certain aspects of behavior may be insufficient in isolating potentially critical areas. Finally, questionnaires may tap into different levels of awareness, depending on the nature of the content, the format of the test questions, and the assessment procedure employed. Therefore, careful consideration regarding the choice of instruments used to assess awareness of deficit is important.

Self-Report Versus Empirical Data

Unlike self-informant discrepancy ratings, this method allows one to measure the relationship between patients' perceptions of their deficits and their actual cognitive abilities. Although this procedure exerts more control over variables through verification of cognitive test scores, the ecological validity is less certain. This technique also requires greater knowledge of neuropsychological tests and awareness interviewing skills.

Anderson and Tranel (1989) developed a standardized instrument, the Awareness Interview, to evaluate patients' awareness of cognitive and motor impairments. This technique was designed to provide a quantitative measure of awareness related to a broad range of cognitive and motor impairments. Patients' subjective responses to several questions (ranging from motor abilities to memory and language functions) are scored by the examiner on a 3-point scale (e.g., 3 = *denies deficit*; 1 = *acknowledges deficit*). To obtain an index of awareness, these scores are then compared with their actual neuropsychological test performance coded on a comparable 3-point scale (for more information about the statistical analysis in obtaining an awareness index, see Anderson & Tranel, 1989). These investigators reported good interexaminer reliability data ($r = .92$) for their assessment tool. In addition, patients' level of unawareness was strongly associated with degree of intellectual impairment, temporal disorientation, and right-hemispheric laterality. Using the same scale, Wagner and Cushman (1994) found that impaired awareness occurred more frequently in patients with cortical lesions than in those with subcortical damage, and it appeared to be a function of both degree of general cognitive impairment and lesion site. Further, there was evidence for distinct subtypes of impaired awareness.

Using a similar approach, Hibbard (1990; cited in Hibbard, Godon, Stein, Grober, & Sliwinski, 1992) developed an Awareness Questionnaire specifically for patients with stroke, which consists of a series of standardized questions probing patients' understanding of their physical, cognitive, and affective changes. Patients' subjective descriptions of post-stroke changes are scored on a 3-point rating scale and are subsequently contrasted with empirical data within the same domain of functioning; for example, patients' ratings of their mood are directly compared with scores on the Beck Depression Inventory. Hibbard et al. (1992) reported high interobserver reliability on the questionnaire ($r = .95$) and found that as a group, unilateral stroke patients ($N = 82$) minimized the degree to which they experienced cognitive or affective changes despite exhibiting intact awareness of their physical defects. Unlike Anderson and Tranel's (1989) study, these investigators found that both left hemisphere and right hemisphere groups were equally impaired in terms of acknowledging their cognitive deficits. These discrepant findings may be attributable to differences in the samples of patients studied, time since stroke at the time of assessment, or differences in assessment techniques used to examine cognition and awareness.

In general, many of the same criticisms of the previous procedure apply to this approach, particularly the issue of ecological validity. Additional criticisms include (a) the questionable accuracy of examiners' ratings of patients' subjective descriptions, (b) lack of consistency in the selection of cognitive tasks, and (c) possible confound in applying broad cut-off scores.

First, although the foregoing studies have demonstrated good interexaminer reliability, such observations appear to require a sufficient amount of training and expertise on behalf of the examiner, as well as considerable knowledge of cognition and anosognosia. This is particularly problematic if further probing is required beyond the established criteria. Second, it is not entirely clear what tests should be used in conjunction with self-report data. Given our knowledge of qualitative differences in cognitive processes, greater in-depth analysis of cognitive task performance may be necessary. To illustrate this point, if a patient states that he has trouble with his memory (e.g., remembering a conversation after 20 minutes), his delayed recall performance on verbal tasks would likely constitute the ideal source for comparison, rather than a global index of memory functioning. Finally, statistical cut-off scores should not be routinely applied to all patients, given that individuals vary in premorbid intellectual capacity and, presumably, metacognitive abilities. Using such stringent methods would cast doubt on the validity of the procedure. In general, more research is needed to examine the internal and external validity of this technique in assessing awareness.

Self-Prediction of Cognitive Task Performance

Another way to directly assess awareness of deficits is by examining how accurately patients predict their performance on standard neuropsychological tests. This approach is perhaps the most concrete and contextually based method of measuring awareness of deficit. For example, patients may be presented with a list of words and asked to estimate how many of these words they could remember after 1 minute, 10 minutes, or 24 hours. Patients' self-predictions are later compared with their actual test performance, constituting a direct measure of awareness. In general, this procedure allows for greater in-depth analysis of self-awareness variables, relative to their other approaches. However, given the emphasis on internal validity and manipulation of experimental variables, generalization to everyday activities is equivocal. Although this approach does not employ standard questionnaires or a uniform set of cognitive task criteria, its theoretical merit is worthy of discussion.

McGlynn and Kazniak (1991b) evaluated awareness of memory disorder in patients with AD by asking them to predict their performance on 12 memory tasks. Spouses of the patients were asked to predict patients' performance as well. As part of their investigation, patients and spouses also predicted spouses' performance on these tasks so the experimenters could examine whether unawareness involves a global breakdown in making accurate judgments or a selective deficit in self-evaluation. Results of the investigation are in keeping with previous research. Patients with AD tended to overestimate their actual performance on memory tasks. However, these researchers discovered that patients could accurately predict their spouses' performance on memory tasks, suggesting that their impaired awareness was attributable to a selective breakdown in self-evaluative ability, rather than a global estimation deficit.

In a similar investigation, McGlynn and Kazniak (1991a) studied whether HD patients could make accurate predictions of their performance on a series of motor and cognitive tasks. Interestingly, these patients made accurate predictions of their cognitive task performance, despite overestimating their abilities on the Daily Difficulties Questionnaire. This discrepancy may have important implications with respect to conceptualizing the qualitative differences in assessing anosognosia. These investigators contended that the questionnaire placed greater weight on patients' ability to evaluate change over time (e.g., "Compared to five years ago, how much difficulty do you have remembering someone's name after 5 minutes?"), whereas predictions of cognitive task performance stress one's ability to monitor current functioning (e.g., "How many words from this list could you recall after 5 minutes?"). Thus, patients with HD may be accurate in predicting the likelihood of performing a given task in the present sense, but have difficulty estimating their current abilities when compared with the past. Patients with AD, on the other hand, were shown to overestimate their performance on both measures, suggesting they have trouble in both areas. It is also possible that task performance predictions provided the HD group with sufficient contextual information to produce accurate self-predictions, whereas the content of the Daily Difficulties Questionnaire may have been more ambiguous. The AD patients' inability to benefit from the imposition of contextual information suggests that their awareness disturbance stems from a loss of knowledge about their current functioning (retention deficit), rather than a retrieval deficit. This contention is generally consistent with previous research that has examined differential patterns of memory disturbance between subcortical and cortically based dementias (for a review see Cummings, 1990).

In a recent study, Gasquoine (1992) examined awareness of deficit in patients with head-injury using a multiple sampling procedure. Patients were first asked via indirect questions to spontaneously recall their current problems ("What problems are you currently experiencing from the accident?"); they were then administered a structured questionnaire that required them to rate their current cognitive abilities (e.g., "How is your concentration now?"). In the final procedure, patients completed a similar rating scale that reworded previous questions in more concrete, behavioral terminology (e.g., the word *concentration* was replaced with the phrase, "ability to stick to a task such as listening to a conversation or reading a newspaper."). Interestingly, patients reported greater sensory and cognitive deficits on the structured questionnaires in contrast to free report, with the greatest perceived difficulties on the more concrete, behavioral questionnaire. Thus, patients performed most poorly when assessing their abilities using a more abstract, open-ended approach, and acknowledged deficits more accurately with the imposition of concrete, contextual information. Ideally, future studies should examine patients' self-report using qualitatively different procedures in other forms of brain damage (notably AD).

Interestingly, in an earlier investigation by Schacter, McLachlan, Moscovitch, and Tulving (1986; cited in Schacter, 1991), only patients with AD overpredicted their free recall performance when compared with individuals with head injuries and anterior communicating artery aneurysms. All groups were impaired when given the free recall task. Further studies in this area may help delineate qualitative differences in impaired awareness that can guide clinical assessment strategies.

The use of cognitive task performance predictions may not only have value in identifying those who are unaware of deficits but also have important applications in treatment. In a performance-based group-treatment approach, Youngjohn and Altman (1989) examined the effectiveness of having patients learn to identify their cognitive deficits. They presented a broad range of cognitive tasks to a sample of head-injured and stroke patients and then asked these individuals to predict their level of performance. After each task was completed, participants received immediate feedback related to the accuracy of their predictions, in the context of an "awareness group" training session. These researchers found a positive treatment effect within a simple training session. However, the major drawback of this study, and with most studies that use cognitive task performance predictions, is a lack of knowledge as to whether assessing and treating patients' impaired awareness in the laboratory can be maintained and generalized to everyday situations.

Another major shortcoming of this procedure relates to the artificiality of the testing condition. Specifically, how accurately could patients estimate their performance on such an unfamiliar task, independent of the nature and degree of their unawareness? It would appear that making such predictions is rather technical and requires inferential skills related to what is normal for them as well as for others. Finally, as alluded to earlier, the external validity of this approach is perhaps the least understood given the emphasis on experimental variables. Future research should attempt to correlate laboratory self-predictions with actuarial data to examine the issue of generalizability and clinical utility.

Ancillary Procedures in Assessing Altered Self-Awareness

Although assessing patients' awareness of deficits can be approached with the procedures described in the foregoing sections, there are tests that have addressed different aspects of impaired self-awareness; notably psychological denial and repression. Although impaired awareness of deficits has been discussed thus far in patients with neurological dysfunction, several studies have shown that patients with no known neurological deficit may deny or minimize their illness (Dougherty, Templer, & Brown, 1986; Havick & Maeland, 1986; for review see Lewis, 1991). These observations have led some researchers to associate impaired awareness with psychological denial (or *defensive denial*). Research into denial has generally emerged from psychodynamic writings. In Anna Freud's (1948) book *The Ego and the Mechanisms of Defense*, she refers to denial as a common defense mechanism that operates to reduce a threatening portion of reality in order to allow the individual to function under less psychic stress. In an early investigation of patients with brain damage, Weinstein and Kahn (1955) concluded that patients' awareness disturbance was attributed to lifelong patterns of defensiveness and an unconscious motivation "to be well" in the face of crisis. Other researchers have noted similar findings (Guthrie & Grossman, 1952; Levine & Zigler, 1975; Rosenthal, 1983; Taland, 1965).

Some theorists have underscored the interaction between organic and psychological factors in unawareness of deficits (Bond, 1984; Fordyce, 1983; Prigatano, 1985; Prigatano et al., 1986). The ability to distinguish these two factors in practice, however, is generally difficult. Perhaps one of the reasons for this is the lack of criteria used in studying the construct of denial. This shortcoming is generally reflected in the paucity of scales developed to assess denial of illness. In fact, our review of the literature indicates that there are no objective instruments specifically geared for assessing denial of illness after brain damage. Some of the more common instruments that have shown validity as indices of psychological denial, however, may have adjunctive value in understanding the nature of impaired awareness.

The Minnesota Multiphasic Personality Inventory (MMPI; Hathaway & McKinley, 1943) is a widely respected and commonly used test of emotional functioning. Studies of the MMPI with neurological patients have dealt primarily with the association between lesion site or cognitive status and degree of emotional distress (Dikmen & Reitan, 1974; Gasparrini, Salz, Heilman, & Coolidge, 1978; Gass & Russell, 1986, 1987). It has often been inferred that the absence of clinical scale elevations in individuals with brain damage indicates unawareness of deficits. However, such an interpretation of scores provides, at best, a rough estimate of denial and is generally insufficient.

A number of MMPI scales were developed between 1956 and 1965 specifically to identify persons who use repression and denial in their everyday lives. The K scale consists of 30 items that measure psychological defensiveness (Heilbrun, 1961). Individuals who obtain moderate to marked scores on the K scale have been found to lack personal insight and understanding into their behaviors and are defensive about some kind of perceived inadequacy. This scale is the only validity scale on the MMPI that was derived in a standardized manner. Dahlstrom, Welsh, and Dahlstrom (1975) reported good test–retest reliability coefficients for this scale (ranging from .78 to .92, for an interval up to 2 weeks, and .52 to .67 for intervals from 8 months to 3 years). However, there is no reported normative data on the K scale for brain-damaged individuals or other rehabilitation populations.

The Repression–Sensitization Scale (R-S scale; Byrne, Barry, & Nelson, 1963) is composed of 127 items from the MMPI. Low scores on this scale are felt to represent psychological denial, whereas high scores reflect sensitization or intellectualization. An R-S scale score is determined by calculating the difference between the sums of the raw scores on three defensive scales (Lie [L], K, and Little-Fisher Denial) and three measures of discomfort (Depression [D], Psychasthenia [Pt], and the Welsh, 1956, Anxiety Scale). Bryne et al. (1963) found a split-half reliability coefficient of .94 for the R-S scale. This scale has shown adequate reliability and validity across instruments designed to measure a similar behavioral dimension. The R-S scale has been studied in patients with neuropsychiatric disorders (Ullmann, 1962) and traumatic brain injuries (Campodonico et al., 1992). In the latter study, it was found that awareness of emotional–behavioral changes was associated with level of repression. Specifically, patients who displayed high levels of repression during the early stages of recovery tended to exhibit impaired awareness of deficits at follow-up. This finding seems to indicate a dual component to impaired awareness that involves a combination of deficient self-monitoring and psychological denial.

Most of the procedures used to assess defensive denial and unawareness of deficits have relied exclusively on patients' verbalizations of their perceived difficulties. It may be that other important clinical manifestations and behaviors (e.g., reaction to therapy) would provide additional and perhaps more cogent evidence of denial of deficit. Sometimes patients behave in ways significantly different than what they report about themselves. For example, in our clinical experience we have noted some patients who invariably deny or minimize the vocational impact of their neurological impairments but knowingly engage in rehabilitative efforts aimed to increase their occupational competence. Other patients will openly acknowledge these sorts of limitations but resist therapeutic interventions. Therefore, using techniques that assess both verbal and behavioral aspects of denial may enhance diagnostic acumen in clinical settings.

With this distinction in mind, Hackett and Cassem (1974) devised a quantitative rating scale, the Hackett-Cassem Denial Scale, to assess denial in critically ill coronary medical patients. This instrument is made up of 33 items that encompass both nonverbal and verbal objective criteria of psychological denial. Questions were derived primarily from clinical experience and from empirically noted behavioral traits of patients who display denial (Hackett & Cassem, 1974). Items include information such as "How long did it take the patient to seek help after the symptoms began?" and "Did the patient need reassurance?" or "Did he/she avoid direct questions about their illness?" Each item is rated on a scale ranging from 0–3, with high scores indicating greater denial behavior. In general, this rating scale has shown good interrater reliability and discriminant validity with coronary patients. Rating scale scores were also highly correlated with clinical judgments (Froese, Cassem, Hackett, & Vasquez, 1974). Normative data is not available, however, in persons with brain-damage or those in rehabilitation.

Denial can also be viewed from a somewhat different perspective. Several of the tools discussed thus far are sensitive to patients' need to obtain approval by responding in culturally appropriate and acceptable ways (for a review, see Paulhus, 1991). It may be that patients who deny or minimize deficits may feel that it is undesirable to admit to deficits, and they consequently cast themselves in a favorable light. This may be especially true if their independence or competence are in question. Crowne and Marlowe (1960) developed the Social Desirability Scale (SDS). This scale is made up of 33 questions and asks individuals to rate (*true* or *false*) whether certain statements reflect perceptions that they have about themselves. Each question taps into culturally sanctioned behaviors that are unlikely to occur (e.g., "I never resent being asked to return a favor"). In theory, an individual's endorsement of these items reflects some aspect of social desirability and psychological defensiveness. A major objective in the development of the SDS was the elimination of pathological item content, because it is often difficult to determine whether these kinds of responses are attributable to social desirability or to a genuine absence of pathological symptoms. This instrument has shown good psychometric stability across normal and psychiatric populations (for a review see Crowne, 1979; Crowne & Marlowe, 1964). Much like the other defensiveness scales, the SDS has not been studied in patients with brain damage.

The Balanced Inventory of Desirable Responding (BIDR; Paulhus, 1984, 1988; cited in Paulhus, 1991) consists of 40 items and requires respondents to rate their agreement with each statement on a 7-point scale. This scale is composed of two subscales, Self-Deceptive Enhancement and Impression Management, which are balanced in scoring and do not have psychopathological item content. Self-deceptive enhancement content (20 items) emphasizes exaggerated claims of positive cognitive attributes (i.e., overconfidence in one's judgments and rationality) and is generally less subject to purposeful manipulation, whereas the Impression Management scale systematically examines a wide variety of desirable behaviors that are presumably more conscious (e.g., "I always pick-up my litter"). Preliminary reliability and validity data for this scale are promising in normal subjects.

There are many questions and criticisms of these procedures in assessing awareness of deficit. Aside from the issue of poor operationalization of denial, a major criticism concerns the questionable applicability of these tools to people with documented or suspected brain damage. It may prove erroneous to make inferences about one's premorbid denial patterns in the context of brain damage. Not infrequently, behavioral and personality changes that occur after brain damage bear little resemblance to premorbid demeanor (Blumer & Benson, 1975). Given this observation, it would not be surprising to see uncharacteristic coping and reaction patterns in patients following cerebral dysfunction. If the goal of these tools is to tap into longstanding, pervasive aspects of personality, changes in behavior secondary to neurological insult may confound the theoretical basis of these instruments. Perhaps one way to obviate this problem is to develop systematic, family-based interviews or questionnaires aimed to measure enduring personality patterns in patients. It should be borne in mind that measures of denial are not intended to supersede direct measures of awareness of deficit, but should be used only in conjunction with these procedures.

Correlates of Impaired Awareness: Some Possible Implications

Thus far, we have outlined several ways to measure awareness of deficit and psychological denial. In recent years, several studies have shown significant correlations between anosognosia and psychological adjustment following brain damage. A brief discussion of these correlates may have important implications with regard to subsequent diagnosis and treatment of anosognosia. Some researchers have shown intact awareness in patients who display depressive symptoms following brain damage (Nockleby & Deaton, 1987; Ranseen, Bohaska, & Schmitt, 1990). Also, it is not uncommon for patients to exaggerate their disabilities and view themselves as grossly impaired despite contradictory evidence. This has been referred to as the "catastrophic reaction" (Goldstein, 1948). Other studies have demonstrated an association between the absence of emotional distress and impaired awareness (Burke, Rubin, Morris, & Berg, 1988; Teri & Wagner, 1991). Some patients may appear unconcerned about their deficits and may be less inclined to recognize any changes or initiate appropriate responses (Bear, 1983). In extreme cases, patients may present with *anosodiaphoria* or total unconcern related to their deficits. On the basis of these studies, routine assessment of patients' depression and emotional adjustment may serve as a valuable adjunct to studying awareness of deficits.

The preponderance of research to date suggests that the severity of emotional, behavioral, and cognitive deficits, secondary to frontal system damage, closely relates to the degree of decreased insight. This contention is based on cumulative studies of patients who show poor awareness of their deficits after sustaining prefrontal lobe injury (for a review see Stuss & Benson, 1984, 1986).

In recent years, scientists have discovered that the frontal system plays an important role in receiving, monitoring, and guiding output of other brain regions. This area is important in forming the basis of the *executive system*, which has been implicated in goal formulation, planning, and self-awareness (Lezak, 1983). Not surprisingly, studies have shown that damage to this brain region can result in a breakdown in one's ability to regulate and monitor cognitive, behavioral, and emotional states (Stuss & Benson, 1986). Therefore, careful attention to the underlying neuropathology and changes in executive functioning may help signal the need for assessing awareness in these at-risk patients.

Future Directions

There are several important theoretical and empirical issues that need to be further explored to advance our understanding of awareness of deficits. As mentioned in an earlier section, impaired awareness is not an "all or none" phenomenon, but varies along a qualitative and quantitative spectrum. Some people may exhibit domain-specific forms of altered awareness, and others may have generalized manifestations. In addition, there may be differences in whether patients require only prompting to facilitate awareness or whether their reduced awareness reflects a loss of knowledge. To identify additional qualitative variables, further research is warranted. Continued exploration and synthesis of existing models of consciousness may also give rise to a more precise taxonomy of impaired awareness.

Research in metamemory with normal persons can provide useful conceptual models to examine possible differential patterns of impaired awareness in brain-damaged individuals. Cavanaugh (1989) postulated three different categories of awareness of memory functioning: (a) "systemic" awareness; (b) "epistemic" awareness; and (c) "on-line" awareness. *Systemic awareness* relates to knowledge about how the memory system works. *Epistemic awareness* concerns one's ability to know the extent and accuracy of one's general knowledge base. *On-line awareness* relates to one's ability to monitor ongoing memory processes. Each category differs not only in terms of its focus but also with respect to the type of information used to complete its directive. For example, systemic awareness focuses primarily on stored content knowledge and is essentially a static phenomenon (e.g., "I know that, in general, rehearsing the names of people after being introduced will enhance subsequent recall"), whereas epistemic and on-line awareness requires a specific context for activation ("I feel that I know that person from somewhere"). Future investigators should attempt to explore differential patterns of impaired awareness using this type of model. It is possible that altered awareness in some patients stems from a breakdown in on-line memory monitoring, whereas others may experience a loss of knowledge about the accuracy and extent of their own memory capacity.

Neuropsychological data may be an important vehicle for examining possible relationships between other cognitive processes and awareness of deficit. Although much of the work to date is preliminary and has yielded mixed results, some studies have shown that a breakdown in certain neuropsychological operations (such as frontal–executive system functioning) may have important implications with regard to certain forms of impaired awareness (Campodonico et al., 1992; Campodonico, Templer, & Mulder, 1995; McGlynn & Schacter, 1989; Stuss, 1991). As mentioned in an earlier section, impaired awareness may parallel memory system dysfunction by manifesting as either a retrieval or a knowledge deficit, depending on the nature and severity of cerebral involvement. Thus, careful analysis of patterns of neuropsychological impairment may contribute significantly to an understanding of awareness. Multiple regression procedures that are theoretically motivated and use large sample sizes may be one effective way to explore which cognitive variables contribute to impaired awareness. The use of single subject designs may also generate hypotheses to test in a more systematic manner. Multiple assessments could be advantageous in terms of examining the effects of awareness training and treatment over time. However, other methodologies can be equally advantageous, particularly those that emphasize greater control of subject and experimental variables to allow for in-depth analysis.

In addition to these theoretical implications, neuropsychological test data used in conjunction with awareness assessment procedures appear to have two major clinical advantages. First, it can provide objective information about patients' cognitive strengths and deficits, which can be retrospectively contrasted with patients' self-reports. Second, it can be used as a prospective technique to guide the type of awareness instrument indicated for subsequent administration and analysis. If, on the other hand, the issue of response bias, confabulation, or defensive denial is in question, administration of one of the ancillary procedures listed may be considered. This is especially befitting in persons who tend to make exaggerated claims about their overall functioning.

Although several research and clinical tools specifically designed to assess awareness of deficits have been described, additional procedures and validation studies are clearly needed. Ideally, future investigations should explore the concurrent and construct validity of several established instruments. Another major goal is to correlate awareness of deficit with observation–behavioral data. For example, some investigators have shown higher rates of motor vehicle accidents in patients with dementia (Drachman, 1988; Friedland et al., 1988; cited in Feher et al. 1991), which may presumably be due to their inability to appreciate the functional impact of their cognitive and physical limitations. More data is also needed to examine the test–retest reliability, validity, and other psychometric properties of the promising instruments described here.

From a rehabilitative standpoint, assessing awareness of deficits requires a comprehensive and flexible approach. Employing multiple tools in assessment to examine whether there is convergence or variation among procedures may have important diagnostic implications. A clinician might begin assessing awareness with a general screening questionnaire, ranging from questions related to basic physical activities to inquiries concerning perceived cognitive and emotional change. If an area of impaired awareness is identified with appropriate screening, a more extensive questionnaire specific to that area could then be administered for better quantification and closer inspection. For example, if memory was identified initially as a primary source of difficulty, one of the more extensive memory awareness questionnaires (such as the MAC-S) could be administered to analyze the nature and severity of the patient's impaired awareness. If, on the other hand, a patient had trouble appreciating a wide range of deficits, a comprehensive follow-up instrument (such as the PCRS) might be most appropriate.

To summarize, increased knowledge about the underlying mechanisms of impaired awareness could have major consequences for treatment. Patients who do not appreciate the impact of their deficits on functional activities are far less likely to implement otherwise successful compensatory aids (e.g., calendars, notebooks, daily reminders). Early identification and treatment of altered awareness in rehabilitation settings can maximize patients' use of compensatory strategies, minimize the risk for impaired safety, and enhance overall psychosocial adjustment. To achieve these objectives, however, assessment techniques need to be developed further in rehabilitation settings.

References

Anderson, S. W., & Tranel, D. (1989). Awareness of disease states following cerebral infarction, dementia, and head trauma: Standardized assessment. *The Clinical Neuropsychologist, 3*(4), 227–339.

Babinski, J. (1914). Contribution a l'etude des troubles mentaux dans l'hemiplegic organique cerebrale (Anosognosia) [Contribution to the study of mental troubles in organic cerebral hemiplegia (anosognosia)]. *Revue Neurologique* (Paris), *12*, 845–848.

Bear, D. M. (1983). Hemispheric specialization and the neurology of emotion. *Archives of Neurology, 40*, 195–202.

Ben-Yishay, Y., Rattok, J., Lakin, P., Piasetsky, E., Ross, B., Silver, S., Zide, E., & Ezrachi, O. (1985). Neuropsychologic rehabilitation: Quest for a holistic approach. *Seminars in Neurology, 5*, 252–258.

Blumer, D., & Benson, D. F. (1975). Personality changes with frontal and temporal lobe lesions. In D. F. Benson & D. Blumer (Eds.), *Psychiatric aspects of neurologic disease* (Vol. 1, pp. 151–170). New York: Grune & Stratton.

Boake, C., Freeland, J., Ringholz, G. M., Nance, M., & Edwards, K. E. (1987). Awareness of memory loss after severe head injury [Abstract]. *Journal of Clinical and Experimental Neuropsychology, 9*, 53.

Bond, M. (1984). The psychiatry of closed head injury. In N. Brooks (Ed.), *Closed head injury* (pp. 148–178). New York: Oxford University Press.

Bond, M. R., & Brooks, D. N. (1976). Understanding the process of recovery as a basis for the brain-injured. *Scandanavian Journal of Rehabilitation Medicine, 8*, 127–133.

Brooks, N., & Lincoln, N. B. (1984). Assessment for rehabilitation. In B. A. Wilson & N. Moffat (Eds.), *Clinical management of memory problems* (pp. 28–45). London: Aspen.

Burke, W. J., Rubin, E. H., Morris, J. C., & Berg, L. (1988). Symptoms of "depression" in dementia of the Alzheimer's type. *Alzheimer's Disease and Associated Disorders, 2*, 356–362.

Byrne, D., Barry, J., & Nelson, D. (1963). Relation of the revised repression–sensitization scale to measures of self-description. *Psychological Reports, 13*, 323–334.

Campodonico, J. R., Templer, D. I., & Mulder, P. (1995). Predictors of impaired awareness of deficit in post-acute brain injured patients. Manuscript in preparation.

Campodonico, J. R., Templer, D. I., Mulder, P., Goka, R., & Schuyler, B. (1992). Impaired awareness for complex deficits following traumatic brain injury [Abstract]. *Journal of Clinical and Experimental Neuropsychology, 14*, 74.

Campodonico, J. R., Templer, D. I., Mulder, P., Goka, R., & Schuyler, B. (1993). Impaired awareness for complex deficits following traumatic brain injury. *Dissertation Abstracts International, 54*(2), Section B. University Microfilms No. 9310564.

Cavanaugh, J. C. (1989). The importance of awareness in memory aging. In L. W. Poon, D. C. Rubin, & B. A. Wilson (Eds.), *Everyday cognition in adulthood and late life*. New York: Cambridge University Press.

Crook, T. H., & Larrabee, G. J. (1990). A self-rating scale for evaluating memory in everyday life. *Psychology and Aging, 5*(1), 48–57.

Crook, T. H., & Larrabee, G. J. (1992). Normative data on a self-rating scale for evaluating memory in everyday life. *Archives of Clinical Neuropsychology, 7,* 41–51.

Crowne, D. P. (1979). *The experimental study of personality*. Hillsdale, NJ: Erlbaum.

Crowne, D. P., & Marlowe, D. (1960). A new scale of social desirability independent of psychopathology. *Journal of Consulting Psychology, 24,* 349–354.

Crowne, D. P., & Marlowe, D. (1964). *The approval motive*. New York: Wiley.

Cummings, J. L. (1990). *Subcortical dementia*. New York: Oxford University Press.

Dahlstrom, W. G., Welsh, G. S., & Dahlstrom, L. E. (1975). *An MMPI handbook*: II. Research applications (rev. ed.). Minneapolis: University of Minnesota Press.

DeBettignies, B. H., Mahurin, R. K., & Pirozzolo, F. J. (1990). Insight for impairment in independent living skills in Alzheimer's disease and multi-infarct dementia. *Journal of Clinical and Experimental Neuropsychology, 12*(2), 355–363.

Dikmen, S., & Reitan, R. M. (1974). MMPI correlates of localized structural lesions. *Perceptual and Motor Skills, 39,* 831–840.

Dougherty, K., Templer, D. I., & Brown, R. (1986). Psychological states in terminal cancer as measured over time. *Journal of Counseling Psychology, 33,* 357–359.

Drachman, D. A. (1988). Who may drive? Who may not? Who shall decide? *Annals in Neurology, 24,* 787–788.

Feher, E. P., Mahurin, R. K., Inbody, S. B., Crook, T. H., & Pirozzolo, F. J. (1991). Anosognosia in Alzheimer's disease. *Neuropsychiatry, Neuropsychology, and Behavioral Neurology, 4*(2), 136–146.

Ford, B. (1976). Head injuries—What happens to survivors. *The Medical Journal of Australia, 1,* 603–605.

Fordyce, W. E. (1983, August). *Denial of disability in spinal cord injury: A behavioral perspective*. Paper presented at the 91st annual convention of the American Psychological Association, Anaheim, California.

Freud, A. (1948). *The ego and the mechanisms of defense*. (C. Baines, trans.), London: Hogarth Press.

Frieland, R. P., Koss, E., Kumar, A., Gaine, S., Metzler, D., Haxby, J. V., & Moore, A. (1988). Motor vehicle crashes in dementia of the Alzheimer's type. *Annals in Neurology, 24,* 782–786.

Froese, A., Cassem, N. H., Hackett, T. P., & Vasquez, E. (1974). Validation of anxiety, depression, and denial scales in a coronary care unit. *Journal of Psychosomatic Research, 18,* 137–142.

Gasparrini, W. G., Satz, P., Heilman, K. M., & Coolidge, F. L. (1978). Hemispheric asymmetries of affective processing as determined by the MMPI. *Journal of Neurology, Neurosurgery, and Psychiatry, 41,* 470–473.

Gasquoine, P. G. (1992). Affective state and awareness of sensory and cognitive effects after closed head injury. *Neuropsychology, 6,* 187–196.

Gass, C. S., & Russell, E. W. (1986). MMPI correlates of lateralized cerebral lesions and aphasic deficits. *Journal of Consulting and Clinical Psychology, 54,* 359–363.

Gass, C. S., & Russell, E. W. (1987). MMPI correlates of performance intellectual deficits in patients with right hemisphere lesions. *Journal of Clinical Psychology, 43,* 484–489.

Goldstein, K. (1948). *Language and language disturbances*. Orlando, FL: Grune & Stratton.

Guthrie, T. C., & Grossman, E. M. (1952). A study of the syndromes of denial. *Archives of Neurology and Psychiatry, 69,* 362–371.

Hackett, T. P., & Cassem, N. H. (1974). Development of a quantitative rating scale to assess denial. *Journal of Psychosomatic Research, 18,* 93–100.

Hathaway, S. R., & McKinley, J. C. (1943). *Booklet for the Minnesota Multiphasic Personality Inventory.* New York: The Psychological Corporation.

Havick, O. E., & Maeland, J. G. (1986). Dimensions of verbal denial in myocardial infarction. *Scandanavian Journal of Psychology, 27,* 326–339.

Heilbrun, A. B. (1961). The psychological significance of the MMPI *K* scale in a normal population. *Journal of Consulting Psychology, 25,* 486–491.

Hibbard, M. R. (1990, May). Unawareness in stroke patients: A problem of the mind, not the body. Paper presented at the American Congress of Rehabilitation Medicine, Phoenix, Arizona.

Hibbard, M. R., Gordon, W. A., Stein, P. N., Grober, S., & Sliwinski, M. (1992). Awareness of disability in patients following stroke. *Rehabilitation Psychology, 37*(2), 103–120.

Jarho, L. (1973). Korsakoff-like amnesia syndrome in penetrating brain injury. *Acta Neurologica Scandanavia, 49,* 44–137.

Lawton, M. P., & Brody, E. M. (1969). Assessment of older people: Self-maintaining and instrumental activities of daily living. *The Gerontologist, 9,* 179–186.

Levine, J., & Zigler, E. (1975). Denial and self-image in stroke, lung cancer, and heart disease patients. *Journal of Consulting and Clinical Psychology, 43,* 751–757.

Lewis, L. (1991). Role of psychological factors in disordered awareness. In G. P. Prigatano & D. L. Schacter (Eds.), *Awareness of deficit after brain injury: Clinical and theoretical issues* (pp. 223–239). New York: Oxford University Press.

Lezak, M. D. (1978). Living with the characterologically altered brain injured patient. *Journal of Clinical Psychiatry, 39,* 592–598.

Lezak, M. D. (1983). *Neuropsychological assessment* (2nd ed.). New York: Oxford University Press.

Lezak, M. D. (1988). Brain damage is a family affair. *Journal of Clinical and Experimental Neuropsychology, 10*(1), 111–123.

Lowenthal, M. F. (1964). *Lives in distress.* New York: Basic Books.

Luria, A. R. (1976). *Neuropsychology of memory.* Washington, DC: Winston.

Mangone, C. A., Hier, D. B., Gorelick, P. B., Ganellen, R. J., Langenberg, P., Boarman, R. B., & Dollear, W. C. (1991). Impaired insight in Alzheimer's disease. *Journal of Geriatric Psychiatry and Neurology, 4,* 189–193.

McGlynn, S. M., & Kazniak, A. W. (1991a). Unawareness of deficits in dementia and schizophrenia. In G. P. Prigatano & D. L. Schacter (Eds.), *Awareness of deficit after brain injury: Clinical and theoretical issues* (pp. 84–110). New York: Oxford University Press.

McGlynn, S. M., & Kazniak, A. W. (1991b). When metacognition fails: Impaired awareness of deficit in Alzheimer's disease. *Journal of Cognitive Neuroscience, 3*(2), 183–189.

McGlynn, S. M., & Schacter, D. L. (1989). Unawareness of deficits in neuropsychological syndromes. *Journal of Clinical and Experimental Neuropsychology, 11,* 143–205.

McGlynn, S. M., Schacter, D. L., & Glisky, E. L. (1989, February). *Unawareness of deficit in organic amnesia.* Paper presented at the 17th annual meeting of the International Neuropsychological Society, Vancouver, British Columbia, Canada.

McKinlay, W. W., & Brooks, D. N. (1984). Methodological problems in assessing psychosocial recovery following severe head injury. *Journal of Clinical Neuropsychology, 6,* 87–99.

Nockleby, D. M., & Deaton, A. V. (1987). Denial versus distress: Coping patterns in post head trauma patients. *International Journal of Clinical Neuropsychology, 9*(4), 145–148.

Paulhus, D. L. (1984). Two component models of social desirable responding. *Journal of Personality and Social Psychology, 46*, 598–609.

Paulhus, D. L. (1988). *Assessing self-deception and impression management in self-reports: The Balanced Inventory of Desirable Responding.* Unpublished manual, University of British Columbia, Vancouver, Canada.

Paulhus, D. L. (1991). Measurement and control of response bias. In J. P. Robinson, P. R. Shaver, & L. S. Wrightsman (Eds.), Measures of Social Psychological Attitudes: Vol. I. *Measures of personality and social psychological attitudes.* San Diego: Academic Press.

Perry, J. C., & Cooper, S. H. (1986). What do cross sectional measures of defense mechanisms predict? In G. E. Valliant (Ed.), *Emperical studies of ego mechanisms of defense* (pp. 116–138). Washington, DC: American Psychiatric Press.

Prigatano, G. P. (1985, February). *The problem of self-awareness after brain injury: Methodological and clinical considerations.* Paper presented at the 13th annual meeting of the International Neuropsychological Society, San Diego, California.

Prigatano, G. P. (1991). Disturbances of self-awareness of deficit after traumatic brain injury. In G. P. Prigatano & D. L. Schacter (Eds.), *Awareness of deficit after brain injury: Clinical and theoretical issues* (pp. 111–126). New York: Oxford University Press.

Prigatano, G. P. (1992). The relationship of frontal lobe damage to diminished awareness: Studies in rehabilitation. In H. S. Levin, H. M. Eisenberg, & A. L. Benton (Eds.), *Frontal lobe function and dysfunction* (pp. 381–397). New York: Oxford University Press.

Prigatano, G. P., & Altman, I. M. (1990). Impaired awareness of behavioral limitations after traumatic brain injury. *Archives of Physical Medicine and Rehabilitation, 71*, 1058–1064.

Prigatano, G. P., Altman, I. M., & O'Brien, K. P. (1990). Behavioral limitations that traumatic-brain-injured patients tend to underestimate. *The Clinical Neuropsychologist, 4*(2), 163–176.

Prigatano, G. P., & Fordyce, D. J. (1986). Cognitive dysfunction and psychosocial adjustment after brain injury. In G. P. Prigatano, J. Fordyce, H. Zeiner, J. Roueche, M. Pepping, & B. Woods (Eds.), *Neuropsychological rehabilitation after brain injury* (pp. 1–17). Baltimore: Johns Hopkins University Press.

Prigatano, G. P., Fordyce, P. J., Zeiner, H. K., Roueche, J. R., Pepping, M., & Casewood, B. (1986). *Neuropsychological rehabilitation after brain injury.* Baltimore: The Johns Hopkins University Press.

Prigatano, G. P., & Schacter, D. L. (Eds.). (1991). *Awareness of deficit after brain injury: Clinical and theoretical issues.* New York: Oxford University Press.

Ranseen, J. D., Bohaska, L. A., & Schmitt, F. A. (1990). An investigation of anosognosia following traumatic head injury. *International Journal of Clinical Neuropsychology, 12*(1), 29–36.

Redlich, F. C., & Dorsey, J. F. (1945). Denial of blindness by patients with cerebral disease. *Archives of Neurology and Psychiatry, 53*, 407–417.

Rimel, R. W., Giordani, B., Barth, J. T., Boll, T. J., & Jane, J. A. (1981). Disability caused by minor head injury. *Neurosurgery, 9*, 221–228.

Rosenthal, M. (1983). Behavioral sequelae. In M. Rosenthal, E. R. Griffith, M. R. Bond, & J. D. Miller (Eds.), *Rehabilitation of the head injured adult* (pp. 197–208). Philadelphia: Davis.

Roueche, J. R., & Fordyce, D. J. (1983). Perception of deficits following brain injury and their impact on psychosocial adjustments. *Cognitive Rehabilitation, 6,* 4–7.

Sandifer, P. H. (1946). Anosognosia and disorders of body scheme. *Brain, 69,* 122–137.

Schacter, D. L. (1991). Unawareness of deficit and unawareness of knowledge in patients with memory disorders. In G. P. Prigatano & D. L. Schacter (Eds.), *Awareness of deficit after brain injury: Clinical and theoretical issues* (pp. 127–151). New York: Oxford University Press.

Schacter, D. L., Glisky, E. L., & McGlynn, S. M. (1990). Impact of memory disorder on everyday life: Awareness of deficits and return to work. In D. Tupper & K. Cicerone (Eds.), *The neuropsychology of everyday life. Vol. I: Theories and basic competencies* (pp. 231–298). Boston: Kluwer.

Schacter, D. L., McLachlan, D. R., Moscovitch, M., & Tulving, E. (1986). Monitoring of recall performance by memory-disordered patients [Abstract]. *Journal of Clinical and Experimental Neuropsychology, 8,* 103.

Shimamura, A. P., & Squire, L. R. (1986). Memory and metamemory: A study of the feeling of knowing phenomenon in amnesic patients. *Journal of Experimental Psychology: Learning, Memory, and Cognition, 12,* 452–460.

Stuss, D. T. (1991). Disturbance of self-awareness after frontal system damage. In G. P. Prigatano & D. L. Schacter (Eds.), *Awareness of deficit after brain injury: Clinical and theoretical issues* (pp. 63–83). New York: Oxford University Press.

Stuss, D. T., & Benson, D. F. (1984). Neuropsychological studies of the frontal lobes. *Psychological Bulletin, 95,* 3–28.

Stuss, D. T., & Benson, D. F. (1986). *The frontal lobes.* New York: Raven Press.

Taland, G. A. (1965). *Deranged memory. A psychonomic study of the amnesia syndrome.* New York: Academic Press.

Teri, L., & Wagner, A. W. (1991). Assessment of depression in patients with Alzheimer's disease: Concordance among informants. *Psychology and Aging, 6,* 280–285.

Ullmann, L. P. (1962). An empirically derived MMPI scale which measures facilitation-inhibition of recognition of threatening stimuli. *Journal of Clinical Psychology, 18,* 127–132.

Vilkki, J. (1985). Amnesic syndromes after surgery of anterior communicating artery aneurysms. *Cortex, 21,* 431–444.

Wagner, M. T., & Cushman, L. A. (1994). Neuroanatomic and neuropsychological predictors of unawareness of cognitive deficit in a vascular population. *Archives of Clinical Neuropsychology, 9*(1), 57–70.

Weinstein, E. A. (1991). Anosognosia and denial of illness. In G. P. Prigatano & D. L. Schacter (Eds.), *Awareness of deficit after brain injury: Clinical and theoretical issues* (pp. 240–257). New York: Oxford University Press.

Weinstein, E. A., & Kahn, R. L. (1955). Denial of illness: Symbolic and physiological aspects. Springfield, IL: Charles C Thomas.

Welsh, G. S. (1956). Factor dimensions A and R. In G. S. Welsh & W. G. Dahlstrom (Eds.), *Basic readings on the MMPI in psychology and medicine* (pp. 264–281). Minneapolis: University of Minnesota Press.

Youngjohn, J. R., & Altman, I. M. (1989). A performance-based group approach to the treatment of anosognosia and denial. *Rehabilitation Psychology, 34,* 217–222.

Appendix
Testing Resources

Ellen L. Cronk

A number of print and electronic sources can be used to identify assessment instruments for a specific purpose. Some include reviews; others have brief descriptions but may provide more recent publication information. Reference librarians and other researchers may be able to suggest additional sources for specialized areas. To learn more about guidelines for developing and selecting instruments, consult the Joint Committee on Testing Practices' *Standards for Educational and Psychological Testing* (1985). This manual was developed by three professional organizations: the American Educational Research Association, the American Psychological Association, and the National Council on Measurement in Education and is currently being revised and updated.

To identify instruments, one source that is easy to use is *Tests: A Comprehensive Reference for Assessments in Psychology, Education and Business*, edited by Richard C. Sweetland and Daniel J. Keyser (1991, Austin, TX: Pro-Ed). Arranged by topic within three broad discipline areas, this source gives purpose, age range, and publication information, but not reliability, validity, or reviews. Author, title, and publisher indexes are supplemented by indexes to those instruments that can be used with hearing impaired, visually impaired, and physically impaired clients. The editors recommend contacting test publishers for more detailed information on use with these special populations.

The Educational Testing Service has published a multivolume index to the thousands of tests and research measures in its collection, the *ETS Test Collection Catalog* (1986–1993. Princeton, NJ: ETS). Individual volumes cover achievement tests; vocational tests; measures for special populations; cognitive, aptitude, and intelligence tests; attitude tests; and affective and personality measures. Indexed by title, author, and subject descriptors, entries indicate availability from author or publisher. Some measures included are available as ERIC documents or ETS Tests in Microfiche and may be available at research libraries.

Through a cooperative agreement between ETS and the ERIC Clearinghouse on Assessment and Evaluation, the ETS indexes can now be searched over the Internet by researchers with gopher capability through the gopher site at Catholic University of America. Keyword searching with Boolean operators allows you to narrow the focus of your search but also allows you to search the equivalent of all the print volumes at one time. Because some words are not searchable, read the "Basic Info on ERIC/ETS Test File" section first. If you are not familiar with gopher software, check with your librarians or computing center staff. You can access this database by connecting to *gopher.cua.edu*, then select *special resources*, then *eric clearinghouse on assessment and evaluation*, and then *test locator*. Many other resources are provided by this gopher, including full-text information digests on assessment topics, bibliographies, and links to testing information at other Internet locations.[1]

The *Mental Measurements Yearbooks* (1938 to date. Lincoln, NE: Buros Institute for Mental Measurements, University of Nebraska; earlier editions published by Gryphon Press), are sometimes referred to simply as "Buros" after founding editor Oscar K. Buros. They contain in-depth reviews of standardized tests with information on reliability, validity, and norming. In spite of the title, earlier editions appeared at irregular intervals but now are published every two years with one supplement between volumes. Each edition covers new measures and only major revisions of older titles, so be sure to check earlier editions for listings and reviews of older tests. Entries are arranged alphabetically by test title; the Classified Subject Index lists titles under broad headings; the Score Index identifies measures with subscores for particular topics.

Test Critiques, edited by Daniel J. Keyser and Richard C. Sweetland (1984 to date. Austin, TX: Pro-Ed; earlier editions by Test Corporation of America but now available from Pro-Ed), is an ongoing series of volumes with detailed descriptions and reviews of many well-known tests. The indexes in the latest volume will include listings for earlier volumes. Entries within each volume are arranged alphabetically by test title.

---

1. Resources on the Internet tend to develop over time, so the headings suggested may change somewhat. For more information on this database, contact the ERIC Clearinghouse at the Department of Education, 209 O'Boyle Hall, The Catholic University of America, Washington DC 20064, 202-319-5120, or send an electronic mail message to eric_ae@cua.edu.

Both of these review sources include citations to journal articles examining the reliability and validity of the measures or their use in specific testing situations. For additional reviews or applications, and for critiques of instruments not included in these sets, search journal indexes or abstracts in your field by combining terms such as *test reliability, test reviews,* or *test validity* with terms for your interest area or with titles of instruments. Electronic versions of *Psychological Abstracts* (PsycLit on CD-ROM, PsycInfo online) and ERIC are useful resources for tests in many areas. Again, reference librarians may have suggestions for other databases or particular terms and strategies to meet your needs.

Commercial test publishers and some researchers provide catalogs describing forms, manuals, scoring services, and related materials. Specimen sets (usually a manual and one test form) are often available even when indexes do not mention them, and some publishers offer discounts for certain categories of customers.

Many scales and questionnaires are developed for research purposes and may only appear or be referred to in journal literature. The *Directory of Unpublished Experimental Mental Measures*, edited by Bert Goldman et al. (1974 to date. Washington, DC: American Psychological Association; formerly published by Behavioral Publications/Human Sciences Press), indexes such measures in education, psychology, and sociology. All volumes are indexed by subject; since volume 3, a cumulative author index is included. *Tests in Microfiche* (1975 to date. Princeton, NJ: Educational Testing Service) provide a number of otherwise unpublished scales on individual microfiche. The author's address will be included and some supporting documentation may appear. (Note: This set has individual indexes and a cumulative index covering 1975–1987, available from ETS; items are also included among the entries in the *ETS Test Collection Catalog* and the ERIC Clearinghouse gopher described above.)

Many more specialized guides to assessments are available. Those listed here have been useful to our students, but check with librarians, other researchers, and publishers to identify others.

Dictionary of Behavioral Assessment Techniques, edited by Michel Hersen and Alan S. Bellack (1988, New York: Pergamon Press), describes and indexes behavioral scales and observation techniques.

Handbook of Family Measurement Techniques, edited by John Touliatos, Barry F. Perlmutter, and Murray Arnold Straus (1990. Newbury Park, CA: Sage), covers measures of interaction, intimacy, family values, parenthood, roles and power, and adjustment.

Gender Roles: A Handbook of Tests and Measures, by Carole A. Beere (1990, Westport, CT: Greenwood Press), describes gender, marital, and employment roles and ability to balance multiple roles. Development and validity information is included.

Sex and Gender Issues: a Handbook of Tests and Measures, also by Carole A. Beere (1990. Westport, CT: Greenwood Press), provides similar information for measures of sexuality, family and sexual violence, contraception, maternity, eating disorders, body image, etc.

Research Instruments in Social Gerontology, edited by David A. Mangen and Warren A. Peterson (1982–84. Minneapolis: University of Minnesota Press, three volumes) provides descriptions, psychometric information, and either sample questions or the complete scale for measures of clinical and social psychology, social roles and social participation, and health, program evaluation, and demographics of the elderly.

Psychware Sourcebook, edited by Samuel Krug (1988. Kansas City, MO: Test Corporation of America) describes tests administered by computer as well as computerized scoring services and related products. It is indexed by software compatibility and includes sample output pages for about half the products.

Test Index

Author Index

Numbers in italics refer to listings in reference sections.

Subject Index

About the Editors

Laura A. Cushman received her PhD from Wayne State University; her dissertation focused on a neuropsychological model of memory processing. She is currently an Associate Professor in the Department of Orthopedics, Division of Rehabilitation Medicine at the University of Rochester School of Medicine and Dentistry. She practices clinically and conducts research in the areas of neuropsychology and rehabilitation psychology and has been published widely in these areas. She has a particular interest in applied neuropsychology and cognitive factors affecting the rehabilitation process.

Dr. Marcia Scherer has been on the faculty of the National Technical Institute for the Deaf, Rochester Institute of Technology, since 1986. She is also a member of the psychology faculty at the University of Rochester, where she received her PhD and MPH degrees. Dr. Scherer's 1993 book, *Living in the State of Stuck*, discusses how the lives of people with disabilities have been affected by technological advances and is based on her National Science Foundation-supported dissertation research. Dr. Scherer has written book chapters and many research articles on technology use, quality of life, and psychosocial influences on rehabilitation outcome and has presented her research findings in conferences and symposia throughout the U.S. and Europe. Her Matching Person and Technology (MPT) Model is being used internationally.